CIVIL PROCEDURE 2016

THIRD SUPPLEMENT TO THE 2016 EDITION

Up-to-date generally to 3 October* 2016.

* Please see Publisher's Note

TO ACCESS THE WHITE BOOK UPDATING SERVICE VIA
HTTP://WWW.SWEETANDMAXWELL.CO.UK/WHITEBOOK YOU NEED TO ENTER THE
FOLLOWING PASSWORD:
WB2016

SWEET & MAXWELL

THOMSON REUTERS

Published in 2016 by Thomson Reuters (Professional) UK Limited (Registered in England &
Wales, Company No 1679046.
Registered Office and address for service: 2nd Floor, 1 Mark Square, Leonard Street, London
EC2A 4EG) trading as Sweet & Maxwell.
Typesetting by Sweet & Maxwell electronic publishing system.
Printed and bound in the UK by CPI Group (UK) Ltd, Croydon, CR0 4YY.
For further information on our products and services, visit
http://www.sweetandmaxwell.co.uk.

No natural forests were destroyed to make this product; only farmed timber was used and
replanted.

British Library Cataloguing in Publication Data
A catalogue record for this book is available from the British Library

ISBN–978–0–41405–681–7

Civil Procedure 2016 published on 29 March 2016. The Third Supplement contains updating material for both Volumes of *Civil Procedure 2016* and brings the work up-to-date to 3 October 2016, with the exception of the Practice Direction amendments introduced by the 86th CPR Update. These were not published by the Ministry of Justice by the time this Supplement went to press, so a Fourth Supplement will include them to publish later in the Autumn.

This Supplement covers the following updates:

- Amendments to Practice Directions 2A, 51K and 51L made by the 84th CPR Update to come into force on 3 October and 29 September respectively.
- The Civil Procedure (Amendment No.3) Rules 2016 (SI 2016/788) and the 86th CPR Update bring into force the substitution of Part 52 on Appeals, which has amended the way in which the Court of Appeal determines applications for permission to appeal in the Court of Appeal. Parts 45, 47, 76, 80 and 88 are consequentially amended.
- Commentary is included with the new Part 52, including a mini-destination table of the new and old Rules. The new Part is paragraphed '52n' and headed [After 3 October 2016] to differentiate it from the 'old' Part 52 which will still appear on the CD and White Book on Westlaw. The commentary to the 'old' Part 52 has been suitably amended and updated.
- The Access to Justice (Destination of Appeals) Order 2016 simplifies the Appeals process by diverting to the High Court appeals which would otherwise lie within the jurisdiction of the Court of Appeal, in particular appeals from the County Court [note: the version included in this Supplement is draft. The final version had not been laid by the time this Supplement went to press and will be included in the Fourth Supplement but we have taken the opportunity to add commentary to the draft version]. Part 40 (Judgments, Orders, Sale of Land) and Part 63 (Intellectual Property Claims) are subsequently amended.
- A new Rule 26.2A(5A) is introduced to formalise the Multi-Track Pilot Scheme where multi-track cases in London should be automatically transferred to the County Court in Central London rather than local hearing centres.
- The introduction of a new Administrative Court Guide.
- The inclusion of the Senior Master's Note on the change of practice regarding the Practice Master.
- Amendments to the commentary to the Practice Direction on Civil Recovery Proceedings following the issue of the Senior Master's Practice Note from April 2016 regarding claims made under the Proceeds of Crime Act 2002.
- A host of commentary, legislation and case law updates.

The Fourth Cumulative Supplement will publish as soon as possible, later in the Autumn, once the Practice Direction-making document has been received from the Ministry of Justice. *Civil Procedure News* will continue to keep you abreast of developments for the remainder of the subscription year.

We welcome feedback from subscribers—please email *whitebook@sweetandmaxwell.co.uk* with any comments or suggestions.

The White Book Team
September 2016

PREFACE

On p.xiii of the 2016 edition of the *White Book*, in the preliminary pages, the date of Lord Justice Jackson's preface is printed as "January 12, 2015". This is incorrect and should state "11 December 2015".

The publishers apologise for the error.

List of Editors

EDITOR-IN-CHIEF

THE RIGHT HONOURABLE LORD JUSTICE JACKSON
Lord Justice of Appeal; Honorary Fellow of Jesus College, Cambridge

GENERAL EDITORS

SENIOR MASTER B. FONTAINE
Senior Master of the Senior Courts in the Queen's Bench Division and Queen's Remembrancer; Central Authority for the Hague Conventions on Service and Taking of Evidence; Central Body under the EC Service and Evidence Regulations; Former Member of the Civil Procedure Rule Committee
PROFESSOR I. R. SCOTT Q.C. (Hon)
Emeritus Professor, University of Birmingham; Honorary Bencher of Gray's Inn

EDITOR OF CIVIL PROCEDURE NEWS

DR J. SORABJI
Barrister; Principal Legal Adviser to the Lord Chief Justice and the Master of the Rolls; UCL Judicial Institute

SENIOR EDITORIAL BOARD

SENIOR COSTS JUDGE A. GORDON-SAKER
Senior Courts Costs Office
THE RIGHT HONOURABLE LORD JUSTICE HAMBLEN
Lord Justice of Appeal
ROBERT N. HILL
Recorder, Deputy District Judge and Regional Costs Judge, North Eastern Circuit; Former District Judge and Former Member of the Civil Procedure Rule Committee
HIS HONOUR JUDGE NIC MADGE
Inner London Crown Court and Central London Civil Justice Centre

EDITORS

JONATHAN AUBURN
Barrister, 11 King's Bench Walk
DR SIMON AUERBACH
Recorder and Employment Judge, Central London Employment Tribunal
MR REGISTRAR BAISTER
Chief Bankruptcy Registrar of the High Court
DR STUART BARAN
Barrister, Three New Square
V. C. BELL
Barrister, High Court Chancery Chambers
HIS HONOUR JUDGE NIGEL BIRD
Manchester Civil Justice Centre
DISTRICT JUDGE SUZANNE BURN
A District Judge on the South Eastern Circuit; Former Member of the Civil Procedure Rule Committee
MARTIN CHAMBERLAIN Q.C.
One of Her Majesty's Counsel
SARA COCKERILL Q.C.
One of Her Majesty's Counsel
MASTER DAVID COOK
A Master of the Senior Courts, Queen's Bench Division
THE HONOURABLE MR JUSTICE COULSON
Judge of the Queen's Bench Division of the High Court; Presiding Judge of the North Eastern Circuit; Member of the Civil Procedure Rule Committee
REGISTRAR DERRETT
A Bankruptcy Registrar of the High Court

MASTER R. EASTMAN
A Master of the Senior Courts, Queen's Bench Division
LAURA FELDMAN
Senior Associate (Barrister), Eversheds
M. GIBBON Q.C.
One of Her Majesty's Counsel, Maitland Chambers
JOAN GOULBOURN
Of the Public Guardianship Office
DISTRICT JUDGE MICHAEL HOVINGTON
Manchester County Court; Member of the Civil Procedure Rule Committee
R. JAY
Solicitor
E. JEARY
Of the Court Funds Office
MASTER JERVIS KAY Q.C.
Admiralty Registrar and a Master of the Senior Courts, Queen's Bench Division; One of Her Majesty's Counsel
CHRISTOPHER KNIGHT
Barrister, 11 King's Bench Walk
DISTRICT JUDGE M. LANGLEY
A District Judge of the Central London County Court
THE HONOURABLE MR JUSTICE LEWIS
Judge of the Queen's Bench Division of the High Court; Presiding Judge, Wales
SARA MASTERS Q.C.
One of Her Majesty's Counsel
MASTER VICTORIA MCCLOUD
A Master of the Senior Courts, Queen's Bench Division
DISTRICT JUDGE SIMON MIDDLETON
Truro Courts of Justice and Bodmin County Court
KARON MONAGHAN Q.C.
One of Her Majesty's Counsel
HELEN MOUNTFIELD Q.C.
One of Her Majesty's Counsel
JOHN O'HARE
Deputy Costs Judge; formerly a Master of the Senior Courts Costs Office
HIS HONOUR JUDGE RICHARD PARKES Q.C.
A Circuit Judge on the South Eastern Circuit
EDWARD PEPPERALL Q.C.
One of Her Majesty's Counsel, St Philips Chambers; Member of the Civil Procedure Rule Committee
MASTER N. PRICE
A Master of the Senior Courts, Chancery Division
MASTER ROBERTS
A Master of the Senior Courts, Queen's Bench Division; Member of the Civil Procedure Rule Committee
DISTRICT JUDGE RICHARD ROBINSON
Principal Registry of the Family Division
DISTRICT JUDGE PHILIP ROGERS
A District Judge on the South Eastern Circuit
C. SANDERS
Solicitor
IAN SEWELL
Costs Clerk, Supreme Court of the United Kingdom
DR J. SORABJI
Barrister; Principal Legal Adviser to the Lord Chief Justice and the Master of the Rolls; UCL Judicial Institute

CONTENTS

CONTENTS

TABLE OF CASES

TABLE OF STATUTES

References in bold type are to the paragraph at which that article is set out in full.

TABLE OF INTERNATIONAL AND EUROPEAN LEGISLATION, TREATIES AND CONVENTIONS

VOLUME 1

SECTION A   CIVIL PROCEDURE RULES 1998

PART 1

OVERRIDING OBJECTIVE

Encouraging co-operation between parties

Replace the second paragraph with:

Various provisions in the CPR encourage party co-operation once proceedings have been **1.4.4** commenced. A good illustration is provided by r.29.4 which states that the court may approve without a hearing proposals agreed by the parties for the management of proceedings on the multi-track and give directions in the terms proposed. Other illustrations include r.15.5 (agreement extending period for filing defence) and r.26.4 (agreement to request stay to allow for settlement of case), and r.35.7 (agreement on single joint expert). The efforts made by the parties to resolve their dispute is a factor to which the court should have regard in deciding the amount of costs (r.44.4(3)(a)). In *Hertsmere Primary Care Trust v Rabindra-Anandh* [2005] EWHC 320 (Ch); *The Times,* April 25, 2005, Lightman J. disapproved of a party's failure to cooperate with his opponents by his declining to respond to their request for him to explain to them the basis upon which he asserted that their offer did not comply with the provisions of Pt 36. See further Vol.2 Section 11 (Duty of the Parties), subs.E (para.11-15) and *OOO Abbott v Econowall UK Ltd* [2016] EWHC 660 (IPEC), 23 March 2016, unrep. (HHJ Hacon).

PART 2

APPLICATION AND INTERPRETATION OF THE RULES

Words and expressions defined in r.2.3(1)

"preferred hearing centre"

After "Salford. As", add:

the CCMCC is not a hearing centre and as   **2.3.8.2**

"filing"

After "meant lodging in a court once a document having those effects (see) now r.9.2).", replace "Practice Direction 4 (Court Forms" with:

5A (Court Documents)   **2.3.9**

Replace r.2.4 with:

Power of judge, Master or District Judge to perform functions of the court[1]

2.4   Where these Rules provide for the court to perform any act then, 2.4 except where an enactment, rule or practice direction provides otherwise, that act may be performed—

    (a)   in relation to proceedings in the High Court, by any judge, Master, Registrar in Bankruptcy or District Judge of that Court; and

    (b)   in relation to proceedings in the County Court, by any judge of the County Court.

---

[1] Amended by the Civil Procedure (Amendment) Rules 2014 (SI 2014/407), and the Civil Procedure (Amendment No.3) Rules 2016 (SI 2016/788).

Effect of rule

Replace the second paragraph with:

2.4.1   Persons who are not judges of the High Court may exercise the jurisdiction of the High Court. The Senior Courts Act 1981 s.9(1) states that at the request of the appropriate authority "a person" who is not a High Court judge may exercise the jurisdiction of the High Court. Such a "person" may be a circuit judge, a recorder or a tribunals judge (see Vol.2, para.9A-30). The result is that judges who, by virtue of their office, have authority to exercise the jurisdiction of the (inferior) County Court may, where requested, have authority to exercise the jurisdiction of the (superior) High Court (colloquially, such judges are said to be "ticketed"). Section 68(1) of the 1981 Act states that provision may be made by rules of court as to cases in which jurisdiction of the High Court may be exercised by such circuit judges or recorders as the Lord Chief Justice may (with the concurrence of the Lord Chancellor) nominate "to deal with official referees, business", that is to say, with Technology and Construction Court business. Rules of court dealing with TCC claims are now found in CPR Pt 60. A TCC judge means any judge authorised to hear TCC claims (see paras 2E-1 and 9A-253). TCC claims may be begun and dealt with in the High Court or in certain County Court hearing centres. Where a claim is dealt with in the High Court, and by a circuit judge duly nominated, the result is that High Court jurisdiction is being exercised by a person other than a High Court judge. Formerly, para.(c) of s.68(1) of the 1981 Act also stated that provision could be made by rules of court as to cases in which jurisdiction of the High Court could be exercised by masters, registrars, district registrars (i.e. district judges) or other officers of the court. Paragraph (c) was omitted by the Civil Procedure Act 1997, and Sch.1 para.2 of that Act now states that Civil Procedure Rules may provide for the exercise of the jurisdiction of any court within the scope of the rules (which includes the High Court and the County Court) "by officers or other court staff" (Vol.2, para.9A-766). Rule 2.4(a), which states that where the CPR provide for the High Court to perform any act in relation to proceedings, that act may be performed by any Master, Registrar in Bankruptcy or District Judge of that Court (except where an enactment, rule or practice direction provides otherwise), was made in exercise of that particular rule-making power. (Registrars in Bankruptcy were added to the officers included in this provision by SI 2016/788, it having been recognised that such officers hear and determine company matters falling within the remit of the CPR.)

Masters

Replace the first paragraph with:

2.4.3   For appointment of Masters of the Queen's Bench and Chancery Divisions of the High Court, see the Senior Courts Act 1981 s.89 (Vol.2, para.9A-303+). Under r.2.4, except where otherwise provided, Masters may perform any act which may be performed by the court "in relation to proceedings in the High Court"; no distinction is drawn between High Court cases proceeding at the Royal Courts of Justice or in a district registry. In terms of the doctrine of precedent, there is no distinction as between Masters, as officers of the High Court, and judges of the High Court; precedent operates as between courts and not within courts as between the different types of judicial officer or judge exercising judicial functions: *Coral Reef Ltd v Silverbond Enterprises Ltd* [2016] EWHC 874 (Ch), 20 April 2016, unrep. (Master Matthews). The jurisdiction of Masters in relation to proceedings in the County Court granted by former RSC Ord.107 is now dealt with under Pt 30 (Transfer) of the CPR. As to special powers of Queen's Bench Masters on certain applications returnable in the month of August, see Practice Direction 39B (Court Sittings), para.2.5 (39BPD.4). Although Masters may now also sit in the County Court as judges of the County Court (see County Courts Act 1984 s.5 (as amended)).

Delete paragraph 2.4.5 "The County Court Legal Advisers Pilot"

The County Court Legal Advisers Pilot

Replace with:

2.5.4   Practice Direction 51K provides for a pilot scheme whereby certain types of order may be made by legal advisers in relation to money claims commenced in the County Court Money Claims Centre or County Court Business Centre under authority from the Designated Civil Judges for Northampton & Leicester Trial Centre and Greater Manchester Civil Justice Centre and Manchester Outer. The scope of the jurisdiction is set out in the schedule to the Practice Direction and the pilot runs from 1 October 2015 to 31 March 2017: see 84th PD-updating Instrument.

PRACTICE DIRECTION 2A—COURT OFFICES

2APD.2.1 *Add new paragraph 2APD.2.1:*
    Paragraph 2.2 of the Practice Direction will be omitted with effect from 3 October 2016 (84th amendment to the Civil Procedure Rules 1998). There will no longer be a requirement for a Practice Master to be present in the Central Office. [See notice issued by the Senior Master dated

18 July 2016 which provides information about the Urgent Applications List before the QB Masters, which will come into effect from 3 October 2016.]

Add new Practice Note after Practice Direction 2A:

SENIOR MASTER PRACTICE NOTE 3 OCTOBER 2016

1. As a result of amendments to the relevant Practice Direction there will **2APN.1** not be a Practice Master sitting in the Queen's Bench Division from 3 October 2016.

2. The Chambers List will be replaced by an Urgent Applications List which will be listed every day from 10.30am to 1.00pm and from 2.00pm to 4.30pm. The Room number and the name of the Master hearing each list will be on the Notice Board in the Queen's Bench Masters corridor.

3. The first 15 minutes of each list (morning and afternoon) will be the "Solicitors' Clerks' List" and reserved for clerks from solicitors' firms to see Masters.

4. Applications up to a maximum of 45 minutes' duration will be listed at 10.45am and 2.15pm to be heard so soon thereafter as time permits. No more than a total of 2hrs and 15 minutes of applications will be listed in any one morning or afternoon Urgent Applications List.

5. Any person who wishes an application to be heard in the Urgent Applications List who has not previously issued and listed an application (a 'very urgent application') may have the application heard in the Urgent Applications List on the day of attendance if time permits, as long as the application is first issued and listed by QB Masters' Listing. If there is insufficient time to hear the application on the day of issue the Master sitting will give any appropriate direction including for re-listing. Applicants seeking to be heard on a very urgent basis shall attend QB Masters' Listing in Room E102 before reporting to the Usher with their listed and issued application.

6. There will be an usher present outside the Master's room to take a note of parties' details and bring in the Court Record Forms to the Master. The Master and the applicants will also be assisted by a member of the Case Progression team.

7. All parties attending shall provide their full details to the Usher and shall produce their issued and listed application notice. Members of the Public wishing to observe the court (but not to address the court) should ask the usher to be admitted to the Masters' room and will be permitted to do so unless directed otherwise by the court.

Barbara Fontaine
The Senior Master
18 July 2016

PART 3

THE COURT'S CASE AND COSTS MANAGEMENT POWERS

Forms

Replace with:

The number of court forms is vast. A selection of forms concerned with case management is **3.0.3** listed below. A number of forms have been revised or introduced by The Civil Procedure (Amendment) Rules 2016 with effect from 6th April 2016.

- **N19** Limited Civil Restraint Order
- **N19A** Extended Civil Restraint Order
- **N19B** General Civil Restraint Order

- **N244** Application Notice
- **PF52** Order in the Queen's Bench Division for case management and costs management directions in the Multi-Track
- **PF52A** Shortened **PF52** in the Queen's Bench Division for multi-track case and costs management directions in Mesothelioma and Asbestosis claims
- **CH1** Case Management Directions for normal use in Chancery Division (replaces Proc01A)
- **CH2** Full Draft Case Management directions (replaces Proc01)
- **PF84A** Request for Judgment on failure to comply with an order made under r.3.5(1) (previously **PF85A**)
- **PF84C** Application for entry of judgment on failure to comply with an order made under r.3.5(1) (r.3.5(5))
- **PF85A** Application for order arising on failure to comply with a condition imposed under r.3.1(3)

I. Case Management

Extending or shortening time limits

Replace the sixth paragraph with:

3.1.2   As to extending time limits in consent orders, see *Siebe Gorman & Co Ltd v Pneupac Ltd* [1982] 1 W.L.R. 185; [1982] 1 All E.R. 377, CA; *Ropac Ltd v Inntrepreneur Pub Co* [2001] C.P. Rep 31; [2001] L. & T.R. 10; *Zappia Middle East Construction Co Ltd v Clifford Chance (Extension of Time)* [2001] EWCA Civ 1387; and *Placito v Slater* [2003] EWCA Civ 1863; [2004] 1 W.L.R. 1605, CA and *Safin (Fursecroft) Ltd v Badrig* [2015] EWCA Civ 739; [2016] L & TR 11. In *Siebe Gorman* the Court of Appeal made the point that when an order is expressed to be made "by consent" it is ambiguous. One meaning is that the words evidence a real contract between the parties (i.e. a contract excluding the jurisdiction of the court to extend time) in which case the court would only interfere with such an order on the same grounds as it would with any other contract. The other meaning is that the words mean "the parties hereto not objecting". In the latter case there is no real contract and the order can be varied by the court in the same circumstances as any other order. In *Ropac*, Neuberger J. held that given the overriding objective under r.1.1, the court had jurisdiction under r.3.1(2)(a) and r.3.9 to extend a time limit even where this was contrary to an agreement between the parties. This was a wider jurisdiction than under the RSC. However, he added that the court should place very great weight on what the parties have agreed and should be slow, save in unusual circumstances, to depart from what the parties have agreed. In *Safin (Fursecroft) Ltd v Badrig's Estate* [2015] EWCA Civ 739, the Court of Appeal reviewed the many cases cited above and held that, not only is there jurisdiction under the CPR to extend any time limits in a consent order, including an order which resolved the substantive dispute between the parties and even where the parties have stated expressly that time is of the essence, but also that the discretion is not limited to the existence of "unusual circumstances". Rather, the weight to be given to the fact of the parties' agreement will depend on all the circumstances, of which the fact that the agreement was one disposing of the substantive dispute rather than a case management decision will always be highly important and often decisive.

After the sixth paragraph, add new paragraph:

     In *Safin* the Court of Appeal neither approved nor disapproved the case law on the power of the court to discharge or vary undertakings given to the court. *Di Placito v Slater* [2003] EWCA Civ 1863; [2004] 1 W.L.R. 1605, in which the Court of Appeal considered *Eronat v Tabbah* [2002] EWCA Civ 950 and especially the observations of Mance LJ at paragraphs [20] and [21] of that case, is authority that the discretion of the court to discharge or modify a time limit contained in a voluntary undertaking can only be exercised if there are "special circumstances".

After the eighth paragraph (beginning with "Rule 3.1(2)(a) does not"), add new paragraph:

     The court has no jurisdiction under r.3.1(2)(a) to extend time for payment under a Part 36 offer as Part 36 is a self-contained code; Titmus v General Motors UK Ltd [2016] EWHC 2021 QB (Elizabeth Laing J); 7th July 2016, unrep. *Titmus v General Motors UK Ltd* [2016] EWHC 2021 QB (Elizabeth Laing J); 7th July 2016, unrep.

Making orders subject to conditions

After the fourth paragraph (beginning with "In Huscroft v P&O Ferries (above)"), add new paragraph:

3.1.4   In *Deutsche Bank AG v Unitech Global Ltd* [2016] EWCA Civ 119, 3 March 2016, CA, unrep., the Court of Appeal (1) noted that the *Huscroft v P&O Ferries* case (above) provides authority for the proposition that, where there is a specific rule in the CPR which deals with a particular type of application, r.3.1(3) cannot be relied upon as a means of circumventing the requirements of that specific rule, (2) explained that, where on an application for summary judgment under Part 24 the court makes a conditional order requiring a party to pay money into court and providing that "that party's claim will be dismissed or his statement of case struck out if he does not comply", the court's power to make such an order is not derived from any specific rule in Part 24 but is derived from r.3.1(3), and (3) held, accordingly, that the court below erred in considering the claimant's application for a conditional order, first in reliance on Part 24 and then, separately, under r.3.1(3). (See further para.24.6.6 below.)

Varying or revoking final orders

Add new paragraph at end:

3.1.12 The court's power under r.3.1(7) to vary or revoke an order could not be used to support a second application to set aside a default judgment under r.13.3; see: *Samara v MBI & Partners UK Ltd* [2016] EWHC 441 (QB), applying *Roult*.

Early neutral evaluation

Replace the second paragraph with:

3.1.20 ENE is a form of dispute resolution which has been developed by judges seeking to further the overriding objective by actively managing cases, such that they help the parties settle the whole or part of the case (see in particular the decision of HH Judge Birss as he then was in *Fayus Inc v Flying Trade Group Plc* [2012] EWPCC 43; and see *Frey v Labrouche* [2012] EWCA Civ 881 at [41] in which Lord Neuberger made it clear that judges are permitted to express preliminary views as to points at issue). The court's decision whether or not to conduct ENE is not dependent in any way on the consent of the parties. It is simply part of the court's inherent jurisdiction to control proceedings. However, if all parties seek ENE, the court will usually give directions for it unless it decides that ENE would not be appropriate in that case (see, for instance the guidance given in The Chancery Guide 2016 para.18.7, see Vol.2, para.1A-139).

After the second paragraph (beginning with "ENE" is a form) add new paragraph:

If ENE takes place, the decision whether to accept the evaluation given by the court is entirely dependent upon the consent of the parties. The provisional views expressed by the court are not by themselves binding upon the parties unless they consent to the making of an order giving effect to them (see *Seals v Williams* [2015] EWHC 1829 (Ch); [2015] 4 Costs L.O. 423, Norris J).

Effect of rule

Add new paragraph at end:

3.1A.1 Given that on an application for relief from sanction under r.3.9, the fact that a person is unrepresented is most unlikely to amount to a good reason for breach (see para.3.9.6.9), it is all the more important that the court sets a realistic directions timetable under r.3.1A (2) or (3).

Collateral attacks upon earlier decisions

After the third paragraph (beginning with "The claimant's appeal in Amin"), add new paragraph:

3.4.3.3 In *Kamoka v The Security Service* [2016] EWHC 769 (QB), Irwin J, it was held that abuse of process in the sense of the Hunter case was capable of applying in closed material proceedings.

Pointless and wasteful litigation

Add new paragraph at end:

3.4.3.4 In *Sobrinho v Impresa Publishing SA* [2016] EWHC 66 (QB); [2016] E.M.L.R. 12, Dingemans J, it was held that although the meaning of the words complained of in a newspaper article, which was the subject of libel proceedings brought by an international banker against a Portuguese publishing company, implied illegality on the part of the banker, publication of the article had not caused serious harm to the banker's reputation in England and Wales. The claimant's reputation had been so effectively restored by the reporting of his and other evidence to a Parliamentary inquiry in Portugal that the pursuit of the instant proceedings was "not worth the candle" and was an abuse of process, *Jameel* applied.

Other forms of abuse

Add new paragraph at end:

3.4.3.6 In *Lewis v Ward Hadaway (A Firm)* [2015] EWHC 3503 (Ch); [2016] 4 W.L.R. 6, it was held that the issuing of claim forms deliberately understating the value of claims in order to defer paying higher court fees was an abuse of process. However, in the circumstances, and having regard to the overriding objective, it was held that it would be disproportionate to strike out the claims which were arguable and very substantial. To strike out the claims would be to enable the defendant to avoid claims entirely without a trial on the merits. The full fees had been paid before the claims forms were served.

Claim "totally without merit"

Replace the third paragraph with:

3.4.10 In *R. (Grace) v Secretary of State for the Home Department* [2014] EWCA Civ 1091; [2014] 1 W.L.R.

342, the Court of Appeal stated that the proper meaning of "totally without merit" is simply "bound to fail". The court made the point that no judge would certify an application as totally without merit unless he was confident that the case was truly bound to fail. *Grace* was followed in *R. (Wasif) v Secretary of State for the Home Department* [2016] EWCA Civ 82. However, in *Wasif*, the court warned that an application should not be labelled as being totally without merit merely because it was unsuccessful. The court should distinguish between an unsuccessful application in respect of which some rational argument could be raised and an unsuccessful application in support of which no rational argument could be raised. Whilst it might be said that both types of claim were "bound to fail", the making of a "totally without merit" certificate was appropriate only in the latter case (see [15] to [17]).

Effect of rule

Replace the second paragraph with:

3.5.1   In the cases falling within r.3.5(2) the judgment can be obtained by filing a request stating that the right to enter judgment has arisen because the court's order has not been complied with. The request may be in Form **PF84A** (as renumbered in April 2016). In other cases the party entitled to judgment under this rule must make an application in accordance with Pt 23 (General rules about applications for court orders).

Effect of rule in general terms

Replace the last paragraph with:

3.9.1   It should be noted that r.3.9 comes into play, not merely where a party has failed to comply with any rule, etc., but only where a sanction is imposed as a result of that failure. The rule in its current form was first implemented in April 2013 (see further, paras 3.9.2 and 3.9.3, below). The new wording gave rise to an avalanche of new cases in respect of which the Court of Appeal has now clearly re-stated how the courts should deal with applications under r.3.9 (the *Mitchell/Denton* principles, as to which see paras 3.9.3 to 3.9.4.4, below). These principles now underscore the court's approach to rule-compliance in all circumstances whether or not r.3.9 itself is engaged (see further on this, paras 3.9.5 ("Effect of *Mitchell/Denton* principles on applications to set aside default judgments") and 3.9.7 ("Effect of *Mitchell/Denton* principles in all cases of non-compliance").

The first stage: assess seriousness and significance of breach

Add new paragraph at end:

3.9.4.1   *British Gas Trading Ltd v Oak Cash and Carry Ltd* [2016] EWCA Civ 153; [2016] 2 Costs LO 289; [2016] CP Rep 27, involved an unless order following a failure to file a pre-trial checklist. The Court of Appeal held that in assessing the seriousness or significance of the breach of an unless order it was also necessary to look at the underlying breach. It was not possible to look at an unless order in isolation. The reference in the first sentence of paragraph 27 in *Denton* to "unrelated failures" is a reference to earlier breaches of rules or orders which the applicant has committed during the course of the litigation. The phrase "the very breach" in para.27 of *Denton*, when applied to an unless order, means: the failure to carry out the obligation which was (a) imposed by the original order or rule and (b) extended by the unless order. Jackson LJ, giving the leading judgment, added that the very fact that a party has failed to comply with an unless order (as opposed to an 'ordinary' order) is undoubtedly a pointer towards seriousness and significance. However, it was acknowledged that not every breach of an unless order is serious or significant. See 3.9.4.3 for the court's consideration of the third stage.

Where applications for relief from sanctions are made in respect of two separate sanctions the court should consider each breach separately at the first stage but should consider both of them together at third stage (*McTear v Englehard* [2016] EWCA Civ 487; [2016] 4 W.L.R 108; especially at [33], [34], [41] and [42]).

The Third Stage: all the circumstances of the case, including r.3.9 (1)(a) and (b)

Add new paragraph at end:

3.9.4.3   In *British Gas Trading Ltd v Oak Cash and Carry Ltd* [2016] EWCA Civ 153; [2016] 2 Costs LO 289; [2016] CP Rep 27 (noted in para.3.9.4.1, above and 3.9.6.10, below), the Court of Appeal regarded the defendant's lack of promptness in applying for relief from sanction as the critical factor for consideration at the third stage. Had the application been made promptly, it would have been granted. However, when the delay in applying for relief was added to all the other factors, it could be seen that the defendant's default had substantially disrupted the progress of the action. The application for relief was refused.

The importance of discouraging opportunism by the non-defaulting party

In the 3rd paragraph, replace "R.(Idira) v The Secretary of State for the Home Department [2015] EWCA Civ 1187" with:

3.9.4.4   *R. (Idira) v The Secretary of State for the Home Department* [2015] EWCA Civ 1187; [2016] 1 W.L.R. 1694

Effect of Mitchell/Denton principles on applications to set aside default judgments

Add new paragraphs at end:

In *Gentry v Miller* [2016] EWCA Civ 141; [2016] 1 W.L.R. 2696, a road accident claim was noti- **3.9.5**
fied to the defendant's insurer in April 2013. On 8 August 2013 the claimant obtained judgment in
default of an acknowledgment of service and later, on 17 October 2013, at an unopposed hearing,
the damages payable were assessed at £75,089. The insurer was informed as to that assessment in
late October 2013. On 25 November 2013 the defendant's insurer made a set aside application
under r.13.3 in respect of the default judgment. On 10 February 2014 the solicitors nominated by
the insurer made a further application to cease acting for the defendant and for an order joining
the insurer as a second defendant in order to allege that the claim was fraudulent. After some
further proceedings, including an application made under r.39.3, the orders sought in the February application were made, the default judgment was set aside on an application under r.13.3 and
the judgment for £75,089 was set aside under r.39.3 (judgment at trial obtained in the absence of a
party). The claimant's first appeal as to these set asides were heard and dismissed. On the claimant's
second appeal, the Court of Appeal reinstated both the default judgment and the judgment for
£75,089. It was held that the *Mitchell/Denton* principles were relevant to the application to set aside
a default judgment and also to the application under CPR r.39.3 once the express requirements of
those rules had been considered (see [23] and [24]).

As to r.13.3 the insurer had shown real prospects of success but could not show that it had acted
promptly once it knew or ought to have known of the default judgment. It had inexcusably
delayed action for more than 2 months. The defendant's insurer first knew of the possibility of a
claim in April 2013 and of the commencement of proceedings in July 2013 and knew or ought to
have known of the default judgment on 19 September 2013 if not earlier, but did not make a set
aside application until 25 November 2013 (see [31]). As to r.39.3 the court must first consider the
three mandatory requirements of CPR r.39.3(5), before considering the question of whether relief
from sanctions is appropriate, applying the *Mitchell/Denton* principles. The promptness of the application is a pre-condition under CPR r.39.3(5)(a). In this case the insurer had not applied
promptly but had delayed for approximately 4 months, from October to February (see [40]).

Had the court had to apply the *Mitchell/Denton* principles, questions of delay would also have
been considered at the outset but not in respect of the failure to apply promptly. The sanction
from which relief was sought in respect of the default judgment would have been the failure to file
an acknowledgment of service. The sanction from which relief was sought in respect of the judgment for £75,089 would have been the failure to attend the trial. The promptness of the application would have been considered only at stage three (as part of all the circumstances). On the facts,
the insurer's allegations of fraud would not have been a determinative factor under the *Mitchell/
Denton* principles. Thus, as to the fraud allegation, the insurer would have to pursue what remedies
it could by way of a new fraud action (see [41]).

Change title of paragraph: **3.9.6.4**

**Breach which does not imperil future hearing dates or otherwise disrupt the case in hand or
litigation generally**

Add new paragraph at the beginning:

In *Denton* the Court of Appeal accepted that, in many cases, a court might conclude that a
breach is not serious or significant if it does not imperil future hearing dates and does not otherwise
disrupt this case or litigation generally. Nevertheless it declined to adopt this as a test of seriousness
and significance, holding that some breaches are serious even though they are incapable of affecting the efficient progress of litigation, e.g. a failure to pay court fees (see judgment at [26] and see
Joshi and Welch Ltd v Taj Foods Ltd [2015] EWHC 3905 (QB), Green J).

No good reason for breach

Replace the first paragraph with:

Case examples of reasons held not to be good reasons explaining a failure to comply with a rule, **3.9.6.9**
practice direction or order include the following: "...overlooking a deadline will rarely be a good
reason" ([41]); "...well-intentioned incompetence, for which there is no good reason, should not
usually attract relief from a sanction unless the default is trivial" ([48]). See also *Newland Shipping &
Forwarding Ltd v Toba Trading FZC* [2014] EWHC 210 (Comm); [2014] 2 Costs L.R 279; Hamblen J
(the loss of legal representation as a result of a dispute over fees payable in respect of it); *British Gas
Trading Ltd v Oak Cash & Carry* [2014] EWHC 4058 (QB) (upheld on appeal; [2016] EWCA Civ
153; [2016] 2 Costs LO 289; [2016] CP Rep 27 (noted in para.3.9.4.1, above and 3.9.6.10, below),
McGowan J (personal difficulties suffered by the applicant's solicitor whose wife was subject to
ongoing medical problems, where the solicitor was a member of a firm large enough to enable
work to be delegated to other fee earners with sufficient experience and skill to ensure that tasks
were properly completed).

Replace the third and fourth paragraphs with:

The fact that a litigant was awaiting a funding decision by the Legal Aid Agency does not, by itself, amount to a good reason for missing a deadline; it is no more than a factor which may be taken into account (*R. (Kigen) v Secretary of State for the Home Department* [2015] EWCA Civ 1286; [2016] 1 W.L.R. 723). To hold otherwise would place those who apply for and obtain legal aid in a better position than those who, through no fault of their own, are forced to represent themselves (Moore-Bick LJ at [18]).In *Nata Lee Ltd v Abid* [2014] EWCA Civ 1652; [2015] 2 P & CR 3, Briggs LJ stated that the fact that a party is not professionally represented is not of itself a reason for the disapplication of rules and orders. There may be cases in which the fact that a party is a litigant in person has some consequence in the determination of applications for relief from sanctions, but this is likely to operate at the margins; see [53].

In *Chadwick v Burling* [2015] EWHC 1610 (Ch); [2015] 3 Costs L.R. 589, Warren J, citing Lee, stated that the court was not obliged to enquire into the state of knowledge and intellectual capacity of every litigant in person who said that he did not understand the process or realise that he had certain rights. The fact that the court was dealing with a litigant in person could only be relevant at the margins, where, for example, there was some extremely complex factor or complicated order which a lay person might find it difficult to understand; see [42].

Note that *Lee* and *Chadwick* were decided before the implementation of r.3.1A which requires the court, when exercising any powers of case management, to have regard to the fact that a party is unrepresented. Thus, for example, in cases involving litigant in persons, the courts may allow longer time limits in their procedural directions than they would if all parties were represented (see further, r.3.1A.1). However, the new rule does not expressly assist litigants in person to obtain relief from sanctions in respect of a breach of a time limit.

Delay in applying for relief

Add new paragraph at end:

3.9.6.10   In *British Gas Trading Ltd v. Oak Cash and Carry Ltd* [2016] EWCA Civ 153; [2016] 2 Costs LO 289; [2016] CP Rep 27 the defendants failed to comply with an unless order concerning the filing of a pre-trial checklist (see further on this case, para.3.9.4.1, above) and subsequently their defence was struck out and judgment was entered against them. Their application for relief was delayed for 31 days in circumstances such that, had the court granted the relief requested it would have had to fix a new trial date some time after the original trial window. The Court of Appeal upheld the lower court's decision to refuse relief from sanctions.

Relevance of "all the circumstances"

In the second paragraph, replace "Abdulle v Commissioner of Police of the Metropolis [2015] EWCA Civ 1260" with:

3.9.6.11   *Abdulle v Commissioner of Police of the Metropolis* [2015] EWCA Civ 1260; 2016 1 W.L.R. 898

Replace the fourth paragraph with:

The fact that the non-compliance has caused the loss or adjournment of a trial date is often fatal to the grant of relief (see for example *British Gas Trading Ltd v Oak Cash & Carry Ltd* [2016] EWCA Civ 153; [2016] 2 Costs LO 289; [2016] CP Rep 27, trial date lost because a trainee solicitor filed a directions questionnaire in mistake for a listing questionnaire, thereby breaching an unless order; the loss of the trial date was regarded as a matter of grave concern bearing in mind the impact that it would have not only on the conduct of this case but also on other cases awaiting dates for hearings).

Add new paragraph at end:

Allegations of fraud do not give rise to any exemption from of disapplication of the *Mitchell/Denton* principles even where those allegations have real prospects of success (*Gentry v Miller* [2016] EWCA Civ 141; [2016] 1 W.L.R. 2696, noted in para.3.9.5, above).

Delete paragraph 3.9.6.13 "Other non-compliance cases governed by Mitchell/Denton principles".

Delete paragraph 3.9.6.14 "Non-compliance cases not governed by Mitchell/Denton principles".

Replace title and paragraph with:

Effect of Mitchell/Denton principles in all cases of non-compliance

3.9.7   The *Mitchell/Denton* principles now underscore the court's approach to rule-compliance generally whether or not a particular failure to comply with a rule, practice direction or court order has resulted in the imposition of an express sanction. As to applications to strike out a statement of case under r.3.4(2)(c) see *Walsham Chalet Park Ltd v Tallington Lakes Ltd* [2014] EWCA Civ 1607; [2015] C.P.Rep 16, noted in para.3.4.1, above. As to applications to set aside default judgments, see para.3.9.5, above. As to out-of-time applications for extensions of time (implied sanction cases) see *Elliott v Stobart Group Ltd* [2015] EWCA Civ 449 and *R. (Hysaj) v Secretary of State for the Home Depart-*

ment [2014] EWCA Civ 1633; [2015] 1 W.L.R. 2472 noted in para.3.9.6.7. As to applications under r.39.3 to set aside a judgment at trial made in the applicant's absence, see *Gentry v Miller* [2016] EWCA Civ 141; [2016] 1 W.L.R. 2696 noted in para.3.9.5.The *Mitchell/Denton* principles do not apply to every application to the court for an indulgence of one kind or another. They do not apply to applications to amend pleadings, even where such an amendment is sought at a very late stage (*Ahmed v Ahmed* [2016] EWCA Civ 686 at [16] as to which, see further, para.17.3.7, below). The *Mitchell/Denton* principles do not apply to in-time applications for extensions of time (see para.3.9.6.2), there being no non-compliance in such cases. As yet there is no caselaw stating whether or not the *Mitchell/Denton* principles affect the court's approach to cases falling within r.3.10 (General power of the court to rectify matters where there has been an error of procedure) as to which, see paras 3.10.1 to 3.10.3, below.

Civil restraint orders

Add new paragraph at end:

The jurisdiction of the High Court under CPR r.3.11 to make a civil restraint order only applies **3.11.1** to High Court and County Court proceedings: "the court" could not be interpreted as meaning a tribunal such as the employment tribunal. However, where the inferior court had no jurisdiction to make a restraint order, the High Court had the power to assist the inferior court by making a general civil restraint order under its inherent jurisdiction; *Law Society v Otobo* [2011] EWHC 2264 (Ch), April 20, 2011, unrep. (Proudman J.). *Otobo* was followed in *Nursing & Midwifery Council v Harrold* [2015] EWHC 2254 (QB); [2006] I.R.L.R 30 (Hamblen J).

II. Costs Management

Costs management to be prospective not retrospective

Add new paragraph at end:

In *Sarpd Oil International Ltd v Addax Energy SA* [2016] EWCA Civ 120; [2016] BLR 301; [2016] 2 **3.12.2** Costs LO 227, the Court of Appeal was concerned with the role of costs budgets in determining the scope of an order for security for costs. The court described how the costs budgeting regime operates and stated that although a costs budget set out the incurred costs element and the estimated costs element, under CPR PD3E para.7.4 the court did not formally approve the incurred costs element but only the estimated costs element; and it was only in relation to that approved estimated costs element that the court would not depart from the approved budget "unless satisfied that there is good reason to do so" r.3.18(b). However, the court could still comment on the incurred costs element of costs budgets, as well as take them into account when considering the reasonableness and proportionality of items in the estimated costs element. Those comments will carry significant weight when exercising its general discretion as to costs at the end of a trial. Therefore, depending on the court's comments, the practical effect of a comment on already incurred costs might be similar to the effect of formal approval of the estimated costs element in a cost budget. Significantly, Sales LJ, giving the judgment of the court, stated that parties coming to the first CMC to debate their respective costs budgets therefore know that that is the appropriate occasion on which to contest the costs items in those budgets, both in relation to the incurred costs elements in their respective budgets and in relation to the estimated costs elements.

Effect of rule

Replace with:

This rule is explicit and the consequences of failure to comply Draconian; the defaulting party is **3.14.1** deemed to have filed a budget comprising only the applicable court fees. Rule 3.18 provides that, when assessing costs on the standard basis where a costs management order has been made, the court will not depart from an approved or agreed budget unless satisfied that there is "a good reason to do so". It would seem that, when assessing costs, the court may also depart from a deemed budget if satisfied that there is "a good reason to do so". In one respect r.3.14 is narrower than it appears: it is not engaged if a party merely fails to exchange a budget with another party. The sanction of a deemed budget is applied only if a party fails to file a budget with the court. However, in another respect, the rule is much wider than it appears: in *Mitchell v News Group Newspapers Ltd* [2013] EWCA Civ 1537; [2014] 1 W.L.R. 795; [2013] 6 Costs L.R. 1008, CA, the Court of Appeal confirmed that r.3.14 applies not only to parties who fail to file a budget at all, but also to parties who fail to file a budget within the time prescribed by r.3.13 (see judgment at [30]). In *Mitchell* the Court of Appeal stated that the merit of this rule is that it sets out a stark and simple default sanction which applies unless relief from sanctions is appropriate (as to which see para.3.9.3, above). In that case, the failure to file a costs budget in time had caused the cancellation of a hearing in another case and the Master's decision to refuse to grant relief from sanctions was upheld. In other cases, where the consequences of breach were not so material, the late service of a costs budget was held to be neither serious nor significant and relief from sanctions was granted (see for example *Utilise TDS Ltd v Cranstoun Davies* [2014 EWHC 834 (Ch) (45 minutes delay), *Azure East Midlands Ltd v Manchester Airport Group Property Developments Ltd* [2014] EWHC 1644 (TCC) (2 days delay) and *Murray v BAE Systems Plc*, 22 December 2015, unrep., HH Judge Peter Gregory, (7 days delay)).The penalty imposed by an order under r.3.14 may subsequently be reduced if the party upon whom it was imposed later becomes entitled to costs under r.36.13 (acceptance of a claimant's offer) or r.36.17 ("Costs consequences following judgment"); see r.36.23, below, and the commentary thereto.

Approving budgets and withholding approval

To the end of the first paragraph, add:

3.15.2   In *Group Seven Ltd v Nasir* [2016] EWHC 620 (Ch); [2016] 2 Costs LO 303, Morgan J directed the parties to review their budgets having regard to a miscellany of points set out in his written judgment.

III.   Costs Capping

Replace r.3.19 with:

Costs capping orders—General[1]

3.19   3.19—(1)   For the purposes of this Section—

(a)   "costs capping order" means an order limiting the amount of future costs (including disbursements) which a party may recover pursuant to an order for costs subsequently made; and

(b)   "future costs" means costs incurred in respect of work done after the date of the costs capping order but excluding the amount of any additional liability.

(2)   This Section does not apply to judicial review costs capping orders under Part 4 of the Criminal Justice and Courts Act 2015 or to protective costs orders.

(Rules 46.16 to 46.19 make provision for judicial review costs capping orders under Part 4 of the Criminal Justice and Courts Act 2015.)

(3)   [Omitted]

(4)   A costs capping order may be in respect of—

(a)   the whole litigation; or

(b)   any issues which are ordered to be tried separately.

(5)   The court may at any stage of proceedings make a costs capping order against all or any of the parties, if—

(a)   it is in the interests of justice to do so;

(b)   there is a substantial risk that without such an order costs will be disproportionately incurred; and

(c)   it is not satisfied that the risk in subparagraph (b) can be adequately controlled by—

(i)   case management directions or orders made under this Part; and

(ii)   detailed assessment of costs.

(6)   In considering whether to exercise its discretion under this rule, the court will consider all the circumstances of the case, including—

(a)   whether there is a substantial imbalance between the financial position of the parties;

(b)   whether the costs of determining the amount of the cap are likely to be proportionate to the overall costs of the litigation;

(c)   the stage which the proceedings have reached; and

(d)   the costs which have been incurred to date and the future costs.

(7)   A costs capping order, once made, will limit the costs recoverable by the party subject to the order unless a party successfully applies to vary the order. No such variation will be made unless—

---

[1] Introduced by the Civil Procedure (Amendment) Rules 2013 (SI 2013/262) and amended by the Civil Procedure (Amendment No.2) Rules 2016 (SI 2016/707).

(a) there has been a material and substantial change of circumstances since the date when the order was made; or

(b) there is some other compelling reason why a variation should be made.

Effect of Section III

After the first paragraph, add as a new paragraph:

By the Civil Procedure (Amendment No.2) Rules 2016 (SI 2016/707), paras (1) and (2) of r.3.19 **3.19.1** were substituted, and para.(3) omitted, as a consequence of amendments made to Pt 46 (Costs— Special Cases) by that statutory instrument and brought into effect on 8 August 2016, in particular the insertion in that Part of Section VI (rr.46.16 to 46.19) (Judicial Review Costs Capping Orders under Pt 4 of the Criminal Justice and Courts Act 2015), following upon the bringing into force of ss.88 to 90 of the 2015 Act (see Vol.2 paras 9A-1312 to 9A-1314). In effect, by ss.88 to 90 and rr.46.16 to 46.19 a separate regime is provided for the granting of costs capping orders in judicial review proceedings. The provisions of Section VI of Pt 46 do not apply to a costs capping order under r.3.19 (r.46.16(2)). See further para.46.16.1below.

PRACTICE DIRECTION 3D—MESOTHELIOMA CLAIMS

"Mesothelioma"

Replace the fourth paragraph with:

In May 2002 a special list for asbestos related illness claims was set up at the Royal Courts of **3DPD.1.1** Justice (RCJ), which is now conducted by Master Eastman, Master Fontaine, Master Davison, Master Gidden and some deputy masters of the Queen's Bench Division, and administered by staff there (contact: qb.asbestos@hmcts.gsi.gov.uk). Over the years, an efficient practice has been developed in that list to resolve claims for damages for mesothelioma (most of which are made against former employers) quickly and wherever possible, to provide compensation during the lifetime of the victim of exposure either by interim payment or full assessment of damages. Experience in that list has shown that in over 95 per cent of claims, there is no real prospect of success of any defence and that if liability can be eliminated as an issue at an early stage, by pro-active use of the court's case management powers, then almost all claims can be quickly timetabled and managed to settlement of the issue of quantum. Experience has also shown that in many claims in which life expectancy is short and which need to be dealt with expeditiously, where there is some probability of a real prospect of a defence being shown which relates to exposure and breach of duty, the alleged victim'sevidence should be taken on deposition and recorded on a DVD and a transcript made available, in case death occurs before any sort of trial can be arranged and the victim's evidence is lost.

"At the first case management conference the court will ..."

Replace with:

It is the practice in all mesothelioma claims for the court not only to order an early CMC but **3DPD.6.5** also at that first CMC wherever possible to set the date for (and timetable to) an assessment of damages, on the supposition that the defendant will not be, or has not been, able to show cause. If the defendant does show cause that date or one as near to it as possible can be used for a trial. Directions will be issued based upon **PF 52A** (April 2016 edition) and no other standard form.

PART 6

SERVICE OF DOCUMENTS

I. Scope of this Part and Interpretation

"claim" "claim form"

Replace the third paragraph with:

For date of service of a claim form see r.6.14. Where the particulars of claim are contained in a **6.2.3** separate document and are not served with the claim form, the particulars of claim are not "a claim form" for the purposes of Pt 6 and the deemed service provisions in r.6.26 will apply to the particulars of claim when served in the United Kingdom. The combined effect of rr.6.3, 6.14, 7.5(1) and 6.26 is that where the Claim Form and Particulars of Claim are separate, but delivered together, the only method of service that would give the same date of deemed service for both Claim Form and Particulars of Claim is service by first class post, or by document exchange or other service that provides delivery on the next business day. See table in Note 6APD.10. Unless the context of the method of service, "of necessity" means that the claim form served will be a copy of the original sealed by the court, as for example service by fax or other electronic means, for service to be valid, an original claim form sealed by the court must be served: *Hills Contractors and Construction Ltd v Struth* [2013] EWHC 1693 (TCC), [2014] 1 W.L.R.1 (Ramsey J.). (Though see the earlier first instance decision in *Weston v Bates* [2012] EWHC 590 Q.B., March 15, 2012, unrep.).

II.   Service of the Claim Form in the Jurisdiction or in specified circumstances within the EEA

Effect of rule (r.6.5)

Replace the second paragraph with:

6.5.1   Personal service is one of the "methods of service" for the service of claim forms listed in r.6.3(1). In the CPR the most important of the provisions stating that service of documents (whether documents in the form of originating process or some other form) should be by the method of personal service are those found in Part 81 relating to applications and proceedings in relation to contempt of court and the service of certain documents (including court orders) in such applications and proceedings. The appropriate form of originating process for proceedings falling within Section III of Part 81 (Committal for interference with the due administration of justice) is Part 8 claim form. Rule 81.14(1) states that the claim form must be served personally on the respondent "unless the court otherwise directs".

Practice and supporting evidence

Add new paragraph at end:

6.15.2   There is a warning for practitioners in the drafting of an order under r.6.15 in *Dubai Financial Group LLC v National Private Air Transport Services* [2016] EWCA Civ 71 where the CA held, Longmore J dissenting, that the requirement in r.6.15(4)(c) that an order "must" specify the period for filing an acknowledgement of service, behoved the judge to specify a date for that, and if a defendant was never under a valid obligation to acknowledge service, either as specified by the Rules or by an order of court, then judgment in default could not be entered against it because it was not in default at all.

"good reason to authorise"

Before the last paragraph (beginning with "In Brown v Innovatorone Plc"), add new paragraph:

6.15.3   In *Bill Kenwright Ltd v Flash Entertainment FZ LLC* [2016] EWHC 1951 (QB), 28 July 2016, unrep. (Haddon-Cave J), where the court upheld an order for service of a claim form out of the jurisdiction by an alternative method (registered mail to a foreign address), the judge explained that, although it is clear that the existence of a Service Treaty is relevant to the court's discretion as a matter of comity and must be taken into account when considering whether there is a good reason to make an alternative service order, the matter is not immutable. In that case a combination of factors constituted "good reason" for authorising service by an alternative method, including lengthy delay if the relevant Service Treaty method was used.

Retrospective operation—"steps already taken"

Add new paragraphs at end:

6.15.5   But note that in *OOO Abbott v Econowall UK Ltd* [2016] EWHC 660 (IPEC) it was held that applications under r.6.15 were to be considered in the light of *Abela v Baadarani* [2013] UKSC 44; 1 W.L.R. 2043, and the court rejected the defendants' contention that the case of *Bethel Construction Ltd* (see above) meant that the requirements of CPR r.7.6(3) were to be imported into r.6.15 in cases concerning failure to serve a claim form in time. The case involved conduct falling short of the overriding objective, which, together with the fact that the defendants knew the content of the claim form by delivery of a photocopy of the unsigned claim form, amounted to sufficient collectively to authorise service retrospectively, deemed by delivery of the unsigned photocopy claim form.

In *Barton v Wright Hassall LLP* [2016] EWCA Civ 177 the CA considered the correct approach when considering for the purposes of r.6.15(2) whether steps taken by a claimant to bring a claim form to defendant's attention, but falling short of compliance should be deemed to count as 'good service'. The CA dismissed an application by a litigant in person for an order for alternative service where the claim form had been attempted to be served by email, the claimant mistakenly thought that service by email was permitted, where the defendant's solicitors conduct could not be criticised, they had done nothing to encourage the claimant to believe that he had effected good service and the claimant had received correspondence with the correct address for service. At para.19 the court summarises the authorities and current state of the law regarding validation of service.

In *Gee 7 Group Ltd v Personal Management Solutions Ltd* [2016] EWHC 891 (Ch); 6 April 2016, unrep. (Arnold J, Ch. D.) the court held that, even looked at cumulatively, the factors relied upon for seeking a retrospective order for alternative service, namely (a) the claim form being brought to the defendants' attention; (b) the limitation period not expiring and therefore the ability to issue another claim form; (c) the absence of prejudice if service was treated as effective; (d) the assertion that the claimants thought they were entitled to serve the defendants' solicitors; and (e) no denial of authority by the defendants' solicitors, were not good enough reasons for authorising service by an alternative method.

Change title of paragraph: **6.15.7**

Service out of jurisdiction by an alternative method

Replace the third paragraph (where the citation for Abela v Baardarani has changed) with:
In *Bacon v Automatic Inc* [2011] EWHC 1072; [2012] 1 W.L.R. 753 (Tugendhat J.), the judge stated that on an application for permission for service by an alternative method there should be evidence as to whether the proposed method of service is permitted by the law of the country in which the claim form is to be served. However, given the fact that in *Abela v Baadarani* [2013] UKSC 44 the Supreme Court has held that rr.6.15(1) and (2) only come into effect where the method used is not one permitted by Pt 6, which would include service under r.6.40(3)(c), the evidence required would now seem to be that the proposed method of service (or in retrospective cases the method that has been used): (1) is not permitted under Pt 6; and (2) will not be or was not contrary to the law of the country where the claim form or other document is to be served pursuant to r.6.40(4).

Add new paragraphs at end:
In *Maughan v Wilmot* [2016] EWHC 29 (Fam) involving the equivalent provision to r.6.15 in the FPR, permission had been granted to serve by email on the applicant husband because he had been travelling between a number of countries when service was attempted. The husband applied to set aside default judgment on the grounds that the Hague Convention on Service applied and the court should be reluctant to order service by alternative means where the convention or a bilateral treaty applied. The application was refused, holding that a good reason not to serve under the Convention and grant an order for alternative service would be, as here, delay and inability to pin down the defendant's location.
In *Asefa Yesuf Import and Export v A.P. Moller-Maersk A/S t/a Maersk Line* [2016] EWHC 1437 (Admlty), although primarily a case on challenging jurisdiction under r.11, provided guidance on the application of Article 15 of the Service Regulation, holding that the principle in *Alder v Orlowska (C-325/11) [2012] EUECJ*, that national rules deeming or declaring steps taken to serve a judicial document outside the methods in the Regulation to be valid service are inconsistent with the Regulation, along with Regulation's direct effect, meant that rr. 3.10, 6.15 and 6.16 were not applicable.

Effect of rule (r.6.18)

Add new paragraph at end:
In *Tanir v Tanir* [2015] EWHC 3363 (QB) the operation of the deeming provision in r.6.18(2) **6.18.1** was considered. Because in the instant case it was far from certain on the evidence that the court ever had served the claim form by post, it was held that the claimant could not rely on the rule and a default judgment was set aside.

III.   *Service of Documents other than the Claim Form in the United Kingdom or in specified circumstances within the EEA*

Effect of rule (r.6.22)

Replace the third paragraph with:
Personal service is one of the "methods of service" for the service of documents (other than **6.22.1** claim forms) listed in r.6.20(1). An example of provisions in the CPR requiring service by the method of personal service of such documents is r.71.3 (expressed as subject to the court's power to dispense with service); note also r.65.3 (service of applications for housing injunctions), Practice Direction (Interim Injunctions) para.7.4 (service of search orders) (see para.25APD.7 below). In Part 81 (Applications and proceedings in relation to contempt of court) numerous rules provide for personal service of documents; see rr.81.6, 81.7(1) and (2), 81.15(5), 81.22, 81.23(1), 81.26(4), 81.34(2) and 81.35. Where those provisions take effect it is commonly further provided that, by rule or by court order, either that service may be dispensed with or that it may effected by an alternative method; see rr.81.8, 81.15(6), 81.24 and 81.26(5).

In the fourth paragraph, after "other stipulated method.", replace "Examples are" with:
An example is

IV.   Service of the Claim Form and other Documents out of the Jurisdiction

Service of claim form out of the UK—permission not required where court has power to determine claim under particular legislation (rr.6.33(3))

Replace the first paragraph (where the citation for Fern Computing Consultancy Ltd v Intergraph Cadworx & Analysis Solutions Inc s changed) with:

6.30.6   Rule 6.33(3) states that a claim form may be served out of the United Kingdom on a defendant without the permission of the court provided that each claim against the defendant is a claim which the court is empowered to hear by any other enactment (as to which see paras (1), (2) and (2B) of r.6.33) notwithstanding that the defendant is abroad and the relevant conduct occurred overseas. In the case of *In re Harrods (Buenos Aires) Ltd* [1992] Ch. 72, CA, the background to this rule (then RSC Ord.11 r.1(2)(b)) was explained and it was said (at p.116 per Dillon L.J.) that, to be within it an enactment must, if it does not use the precise wording of the rule, at least indicate on its face that it is expressly contemplating proceedings against persons who are not within the jurisdiction of the court or where the wrongful act, neglect or default giving rise to the claim did not take place within the jurisdiction. In the *Harrods* case it was held, applying that test, that rule did not permit the service out of the jurisdiction without leave, of a petition under the Companies Act 1985 s.459. See also: *Fern Computing Consultancy Ltd v Intergraph Cadworx & Analysis Solutions Inc* [2014] EWHC 2908 (Ch); [2014] Bus L.R. 1397 (Mann J.), where held that the Commercial Agents (Council Directive) Regulations 1992 (SI 1993/3053) did not use the wording of the rule, or anything like it, to confer jurisdiction on the English court; *In re Banco Nacional de Cuba* [2001] 1 W.L.R. 2039 (Lightman J.), where held that the wording of the Insolvency Act 1986 s.423 did not bring that section within the rule.

Service of claim form in Scotland or Northern Ireland—permission not required where court has power to determine claim under the 1982 Act (r.6.32(1))

Replace the third paragraph (where the citation for Cook v Virgin Media Ltd has changed) with:

6.30.7   In *Cook v Virgin Media Ltd* [2015] EWCA Civ 1287; [2016] I.L.Pr. 6, the Court of Appeal explained that the several rules in Sch.4 do not mirror the Judgments Regulation, but reproduce provisions of the Regulation with modifications, tailored to make them appropriate to UK domestic law (para.30). The rules set out in Sch.4 apply in relation to the international jurisdiction of the UK courts, as well as where there is no international question of jurisdiction (e.g. in cases where there is simply a question of whether the English courts or the Scottish courts have jurisdiction) (ibid).

Add new paragraph 6.30.11.1:

6.30.11.1   For examples of the various grounds on which applications have been made see: the following cases. *Erdenet Mining Corp v Kazakhstan* [2016] EWHC 299 (Comm): held that, in deciding, on an interlocutory basis, whether there was a good arguable case where a contract had a clause to the effect that the English courts had jurisdiction the court was bound to apply the ratio in *Canada Trust Co v Stolzenberg (No.2) (Mareva Injunction) Times,* 10 November 1997 i.e. one side had to have a much better argument on the available material, as to whether an oral agreement in relation to jurisdiction had been reached. *Apollo Ventures Co Ltd v Surinder Singh Manchanda* [2016] EWHC 1416 (Comm): the defendants unsuccessfully argued that there was no serious issue to be tried and that none of the jurisdictional gateways were satisfied. *Heraeus Medical GmbH v Biomet UK Healthcare Ltd* [2016] EWHC 1369 (Ch): Defendant failed to set aside an order for service out of the jurisdiction on the grounds of alleged non disclosure.

"statement of the grounds" (r.6.34(1)(a))

Add new paragraph at end:

6.34.2   In *Heraeus Medical GmbH v Biomet UK Healthcare Ltd* [2016] EWHC 1369 (Ch) Mann J concluded that, although the claimant's solicitor had stated in **Form N510** that there were no proceedings concerning the same claim in another member state, whereas there were proceedings in Germany, the claimants could rely on an element of conditionality and say that England was the appropriate forum if they were wrong on the territorial effect of the German proceedings.

"after service"

Replace with:

6.35.2   In this rule, and in para.6 of Practice Direction 6B, the response periods are fixed as a certain number of days "after service".

Principles upon which permission to serve outside the jurisdiction is granted

Rule 6.36 and para.3.1 of 6BPD

Replace the fourth paragraph (where the citation for Brownlie v Four Seasons Holdings Inc has changed) with:

6.37.15.1   In *CH Offshore Ltd v PDV Marina SA* [2015] EWHC 595 (Comm) the court rejected a defendant's argument that a third party was a necessary and property party under CPR PD 6B para.3.1(4). There was no single investigation to be carried out in respect of the main claim and the third party claim, and they were not bound by a common thread. They arose under very different contracts which gave rise to different and separate issues and were not back-to-back. In *Brownlie v Four Seasons Holdings Inc* [2015] EWCA Civ 665; [2015] C.P. Rep. 40 the CA held that consequential loss suffered in England as a result of an accident abroad is insufficient to found English jurisdiction. Such loss does not constitute "damage ... sustained within the jurisdiction" for the purposes of the tort jurisdiction gateway in CPR PD 6B para.3.1(9)(a). This gateway has to be interpreted consistently with the European regime on jurisdiction and applicable law. The judgment also contains clarification on the standard of proof: see *Canada Trust Co v Stolzenberg* above. It follows *Erste Group Bank AG (London) v JSC (VMZ Red October)* [2015] EWCA Civ 379, where a differently constituted CA doubted whether it was correct to interpret "damage" for the purposes of the tort jurisdictional gateway as extending to consequential loss, and expressly stated that it had "serious reservations as to whether those first instance cases were right" in relation to the first instance decisions of *Booth v Phillips* [2004] EWHC 1437 (Comm); [2004] 1 W.L.R. 3292, *Cooley v Ramsey* [2008] EWHC 129 (QB) (see para.6.37.43 below). The effect of those decisions is to reverse the trend of those first instance decisions in widening the test for the jurisdictional gateway under CPR PD 6B para.3.1(9)(a).

Jurisdiction clauses

Replace the ninth paragraph (beginning with "A non-exclusive jurisdiction") with:

    A non-exclusive jurisdiction clause raises a strong prima facie case that such jurisdiction is forum conveniens (*E.D. & F. Man Ship Ltd v Kvaerner Gibraltar Ltd (The Rothnie)* [1996] 2 Lloyd's Rep. 206 (Creswell J.)); *Highland Crusader Offshore Partners LP v Deutsche Bank AG* [2009] EWCA Civ 725. For a review of the relevant principles, see *Standard Chartered Bank (Hong Kong) Ltd v Independent Power Tanzania Ltd* [2016] EWCA Civ 411, 28 April 2016, unrep.   **6.37.19**

Paragraph 3.1(1) to (5) of 6BPD: General grounds and interim remedies

Paragraph 3.1(3) of 6BPD: "necessary or proper party" where a claim is made against someone on whom the claim form has been or will be served

"necessary or proper party"

Add new paragraph at end:

    In *Lungowe v Vedanta Resources Plc and Konkola Copper Mines (KCM)* [2016] EWHC 975 (TCC), 27 May 2016 (Coulson J), the Judge held that notwithstanding the fact that the appropriate forum for the determination of the Claimant's claim against KCM was Zambia (to which almost every relevant connecting factor pointed), the claim against KCM would nevertheless proceed before the English Court it being the determinative factor that the claim against Vedanta would be heard in England in any event.   **6.37.29**

Service on a defendant out of the United Kingdom (r.6.40(3) and (4))

Replace the second paragraph with:

    There is no express provision in Section IV of Pt 6 permitting service of a claim form out of the jurisdiction by an alternative method, but it is now settled that the court has such jurisdiction and that it is derived from the court's power to give directions as to service under r.6.37(5)(b)(i) (*Cecil v Bayat* [2011] EWCA Civ 135; [2011] 1 W.L.R. 3086, CA and *Abela v Baadarani* [2013] UKSC 44 (judgment of Lord Clarke, para.20)). This authorises the court to make an order for alternative service (i.e. by a method or at a place not otherwise permitted by Pt 6) pursuant to r.6.15(1), and also to make such an order with retrospective effect pursuant to r.6.15(2). Where the court grants an application made by a claimant under r.6.15 for service of a claim form out of the jurisdiction by an alternative method, the order must specify the matters referred to in r.6.15(4), including the date on which the claim form is deemed served, otherwise the order would be defective (*Bill Kenwright Ltd v Flash Entertainment FZ LLC* [2016] EWHC 1951 (QB), 28 July 2016, unrep. (Haddon-Cave J), para.61). A method of service "not otherwise permitted by this Part" has been held by the Supreme Court in *Abela v Baadarani* [2013] UKSC 44 in the context of service out of the jurisdiction as occurring in cases (and only in cases) where none of the methods provided in r.6.40(3) has been adopted, including of course service by a method permitted by the law of the country in which the claim form or document is to be served. The starting point is that the defendant has not or will not be served by such a method and the question to be asked by the court is whether there is good reason in prospective cases to declare that service by the proposed method or at the proposed place shall be regarded as good service and in retrospective cases that it should be regarded as having amounted to good service. Speed is a relevant consideration but, in general, the desire of a claimant to avoid the delay inherent in service by the methods permitted by r.6.40 cannot of itself justify an order for service by an alternative method (*Cecil v Bayat* op cit). In *Abela v Baadarani* [2013] UKSC 44 Lord Clarke made clear that he was saying nothing about the position   **6.40.5** where a Convention or Treaty applied and Burnton L.J.'s dicta in Cecil that while the fact that proceedings will come to the attention of the defendant more speedily by an alternative method than by service under the Hague Convention is a relevant consideration under r.6.15 it is in general not a sufficient reason for an order for service by an alternative method. In such cases it is of course open to the claimant to use a method permitted by the law of the country in which service is to be effected subject to r.6.40(4). See further para.6.15.7 (Service abroad of domestic process) above.

Effect of rule

Replace the first paragraph with:

6.47.1   Rule 6.47 (unless disapplied in certain circumstances which otherwise might apply) prevents a claimant from taking further steps against a defendant served with a claim form out of the jurisdiction, until the claimant files written evidence showing that such service has been duly effected. When served under the Service Regulation procedure the certificate of service from the authority that served the documents is required. The written evidence must show that the claim form has been duly served out of the jurisdiction "in accordance with this Part". Where, by an order obtained under r.6.15, the claimant has effected service by an alternative method, r.6.47 requires that the claimant should file written evidence that the claim form has been duly served by that method, a requirement that will be satisfied if written evidence is produced which shows that such steps as the court may have specified in the order made under r.6.15 have been complied with (*Bill Kenwright Ltd v Flash Entertainment FZ LLC* [2016] EWHC 1951 (QB), 28 July 2016, unrep. (Haddon-Cave J) at para.62).

In the second paragraph, after "largely possession claims).", delete "The principle is that when service takes place out of the United Kingdom there is no deemed service, so written evidence of service must always be filed in such cases whether there is a fixed date or not.".

PRACTICE DIRECTION 6A—SERVICE WITHIN THE UNITED KINGDOM

Add new paragraph 6APD.10.1:

Editorial note

6APD.10.1   Comparison of deemed dates of service for Claim Form and Particulars of Claim when Particulars of Claim are served separately from Claim Form.

METHOD OF SERVICE CPR 6.3 and 6.26	DEEMED DATE OF SERVICE OF CLAIM FORM CPR 6.14 and 7.5(1); 6.5(3)	DEEMED DATE OF SERVICE OF PARTICULARS OF CLAIM CPR 6.26
First Class Post, document exchange or other service that provides delivery on the next business day	The second business day after completion of the step. e.g. posted, left with, delivered to or collected by the relevant document delivery service on Monday, deemed served on Wednesday (unless Monday is a Bank Holiday, then deemed service on Thursday); or posted, left with, delivered to or collected by the relevant document delivery service on Friday, deemed served on the following Tuesday (unless Monday is a Bank Holiday, then deemed service on Wednesday).	The second day after it was posted, or left with, delivered to or collected by the relevant service provider, provided that day is a business day, if not the next business day after that day. e.g. posted, left with, delivered to or collected by the relevant document delivery service on Monday, deemed served on Wednesday posted, left with, delivered to or collected by the relevant document delivery service on Friday, deemed served on the followingMonday (unless Monday is a Bank Holiday, then deemed service on Tuesday).
Delivery of the document or leaving it at the relevant place	Second business day after delivering to or leaving at the relevant place. e.g. delivered /left on Monday, served on Wednesday; (unless Monday is a Bank Holiday, then deemed service on Thursday) delivered/left on Friday, deemed served on Tuesday (unless Monday is a Bank Holiday, then deemed service	If delivered/left at permitted address on a business day before 4.30pm, on that day, or in any other case, the next business day. e.g. delivered/left 4pm Monday, deemed served Monday (unless Monday is a Bank Holiday, then deemed service on Tuesday); delivered/ left 5pm Monday, deemed served Tuesday delivered/left

	on Wednesday).	4pm Friday, deemed served Friday; delivered/left 5pm Friday, deemed served the following Monday (unless Monday is a Bank Holiday, then deemed service on Tuesday).
Personal Service	Second business day after leaving claim form in accordance with r.6.5 (3). e.g. left on Monday, deemed served on Wednesday (unless Monday is a Bank Holiday, then deemed service on Tuesday); left on Friday, deemed served on the following Tuesday (unless Monday is a Bank Holiday, then deemed service on Wednesday).	If served personally before 4.30pm, on a business day, on that day, or in any other case, the next business day. e.g. personally delivered 4pm Monday, deemed served Monday (unless Monday is a Bank Holiday, then deemed service on Tuesday); personally delivered 5pm Monday, deemed served Tuesday personally delivered 4pm Friday, deemed served Friday; personally delivered 5pm Friday, deemed served the following Monday (unless Monday is a Bank Holiday, then deemed service on Tuesday).
Fax	Second Business day after transmission of the fax is completed. e.g. transmission of fax completed on Monday, deemed served on Wednesday (unless Monday is a Bank Holiday, then deemed service on Thursday); transmission of fax completed on Friday, deemed served on the following Tuesday (unless Monday is a Bank Holiday, then deemed service on Wednesday).	If transmission of the fax is before 4.30pm on a business day, on that day, or in any other case, the next business day. e.g. transmitted 4pm Monday, deemed served Monday (unless Monday is a Bank Holiday, then deemed service on Tuesday); transmitted 5pm Monday, deemed served Tuesday; transmitted 4pm Friday, deemed served Friday; transmitted 5pm Friday, deemed served the following Monday (unless Monday is a Bank Holiday, then deemed service on Tuesday).
Email or other Electronic Method	Second Business day after sending the email or other electronic transmission. e.g. transmission on Monday, deemed served on Wednesday (unless Monday is a Bank Holiday, then deemed service on Thursday); transmission on Friday, deemed served on the following Tuesday (unless Monday is a Bank Holiday, then deemed service on Wednesday).	If electronic transmission is before 4.30pm on a business day, on that day, or in any other case, the next business day. e.g. transmitted 4pm Monday, deemed served Monday (unless Monday is a Bank Holiday, then deemed service on Tuesday); transmitted 5pm Monday, deemed served Tuesday; transmitted 4pm Friday, deemed served Friday; transmitted 5pm Friday, deemed served the following Monday (unless Monday is a Bank Holiday, then deemed service on Tuesday).

NOTES ON RULES OF JURISDICTION IN JUDGMENTS REGULATION (RECAST)

A.   INTRODUCTION

2.   Scope and exclusions

Replace the last paragraph (where the citation for Cook v Virgin has changed) with:

6JR.5   In *Cook v Virgin Media Ltd* [2015] EWCA Civ 1287; [2016] 1 W.L.R. 1672, a case in which a claimant domiciled in Scotland brought a claim in an English court against a company situated in England for damages for personal injuries arising from an accident in Scotland, the Court of Appeal explained (referring to a leading text) that the Regulation does not have any role where (as in the instant case) the matter "is demonstrably wholly internal to the United Kingdom", so that the only jurisdictional question which may arise is as to the part of or a place within the United Kingdom which has jurisdiction (para.25).

(b)   Exclusion of arbitration (art.1.2(d))

Replace the seventh paragraph (where the citation for Gazprom OAO has changed) with:

6JR.7   In *Claxton Engineering Services Ltd v TXM Olaj-Es Gazkutato Kft* [2011] EWHC 345 (Comm); [2011] 1 Lloyd's Rep. 510 (Hamblen J), it was explained that the anti-suit injunction granted in the Front Comor case was found by the ECJ to be incompatible with the Judgments Regulation because it interfered with the court of another Member State's deciding on its own jurisdiction under the Regulation. The judge held that an injunction restraining an arbitration in another Member State (Hungary) was not incompatible because it did not interfere with the court of a Member State deciding on its own jurisdiction; it interfered with an arbitration (albeit foreign arbitration), and arbitration is outside the scope of the Judgments Regulation. The Judgments Regulation governs conflicts of jurisdiction between courts of Member States. Arbitral tribunals are not courts of a State. In the case of *Gazprom OAO* (C-536/13) EU:C:2015:316; [2015] 1 W.L.R. 4937; [2015] 1 Lloyd's Rep. 610, the ECJ ruled that where an arbitral tribunal in one Member State (State A) makes an award prohibiting a party from bringing certain claims before the courts of Member State (State B), the Judgments Regulation does not preclude the courts of State B from recognising and enforcing, or refusing to recognise or enforce, such injunctive arbitral award.

B.   GENERAL JURISDICTION: PERSON TO BE SUED IN MEMBER STATE WHERE DOMICILED

3.   Domicile

Add to the end of the last paragraph:

6JR.12   For guidance as to the factors to be considered in determining domicile under the recast Judgments Regulation, see *Eng King Ltd v Petrillo*, 4 May 2016, unrep (Judge Waksman Q.C.)

C.   SPECIAL JURISDICTION: PERSON MAY BE SUED IN ANOTHER MEMBER STATE

1.   Special jurisdiction—general (arts 7 and 8)

(a)   Special jurisdiction—particular matters (art.7)

(i)   Matters relating to contract (art.7(1))

Replace the eleventh paragraph with:

6JR.15   "Obligation in question" does not include a quasi-contractual obligation to make restitution (*Kleinwort Benson Ltd v Glasgow City Council* [1999] 1 A.C. 153, HL). Nor does it include a claim of a co-insurer for contribution against a co-insurer in a case of double insurance: *XL Insurance Co SE (formerly XL Insurance Co Ltd) v AXA Corporate Solutions Assurance* [2015] EWHC 3431 (Comm) (Judge Waksman QC). On the other hand, the obligation in question could be the obligation to make full disclosure on placement of reinsurance in London (*Agnew v Lansforsakringsbolagens AB* [2001] 1 A.C. 223; [2000] Lloyd's Rep 317; [2000] 1 All E.R. 737, HL).

(ii)   Matters relating to tort, delict or quasi-delict (art.7(2))

To the end of the fifth paragraph (beginning with "In a case of negligent mis-statement"), add:

In *Kolassa v Barclays Bank Plc* (C-375/13) [2015] C.E.C. 753; [2015] I.L.Pr. 14 a claim was **6JR.16** brought against the bank on the basis of alleged mistakes and wrongful information in a prospectus issued by it. The CJEU ruled that under Art.5(3) (now Art.7(2)) the court where the investor was domiciled and had its bank account had jurisdiction as this was the place where the loss occurred.

2.   Special Jurisdiction—Insurance, Consumer and Individual Employee Contracts (arts 10 to 23)

(a)   Jurisdiction in matters relating to insurance (arts 10 to 16)

Replace the fourth paragraph with:

Article 11(1)(b) states that an insurer domiciled in a Member State may be sued, not only in the **6JR.26** courts of the Member State where he is domiciled, but also in another Member State, in the case of actions brought by the policyholder, the insured or a beneficiary, in the courts for the place where the plaintiff is domiciled. Article 13(2) states that art.11 shall apply to actions brought "by the injured party directly against the insurer, where such direct actions are permitted". Article 13(3) adds that, if the law governing such direct actions provides that the policy holder or the insured may be joined as a party, then "the same court shall have jurisdiction over them". These provisions acknowledge that the national laws of Member States may differ as to whether or not actions by injured parties directly against the insurers of the persons who injured them are permitted, and that, if such actions are permitted, that the detailed substantive and procedural provisions governing such direct actions may differ. In *Hoteles Pinero Canarias SL v Keefe* [2015] EWCA Civ 598; [2016] 1 W.L.R. 904, the Court of Appeal held that under Art.11(3) (now Art.13(3)) a claimant could bring a claim in tort against the owner of a hotel in circumstances where the claimant also had a direct claim against the company's insurer as there was no requirement that the claim against the hotel's owner concerned the underlying policy or some other insurance dispute.

After the fourth paragraph (beginning with "Article 11(1)(b) states") add new paragraph:

A direct right of action against insurers in road traffic cases was required to be introduced into the laws of all Member States (insofar as it did not already exist) by Directive 2000/26/EC of the European Parliament and Council of 16 May 2000. In the United Kingdom, the direct claim for these purposes was first provided for by the European Communities (Rights against Insurers) Regulations 2002 (SI 2002/3061). A simple question arises: if a person (C) domiciled in Member State A is injured in a car accident in Member State B, where the other driver and that driver's insurers (D) are domiciled in Member State B, can C bring an action against D in the courts of Member State A? In *Odenbreit v FBTO Schadeverzekeringen NV* (C-463/06) [2007] E.C.R. I-11321; [2008] 2 All E.R. (Comm) 763; [2008] I.L.Pr. 12, the European Court of Justice ruled that the answer to this question was "yes", provided, as art.11(2) (now art.13(2)) states, such a direct action is "permitted". That settles the question of jurisdiction. (The question as to what law the court of Member State A should apply to the determination of the action is, of course, a different matter.) In a given case, the question whether or not a direct action is "permitted" is to be determined in accordance with the lex causae (not the lex fori) (*Maher v Groupma Grand Est* [2009] EWCA Civ 1191; [2010] 1 W.L.R. 1564; *Jones v Assurances Generales de France (AGF) SA* [2010] I.L.Pr. 4 (Judge Birtles)).

(b)   Jurisdiction over consumer contracts (arts 17 to 19)

Add new paragraph at end:

In *Hobohm v Benedikt Kampik Ltd & Co KG* (C-297/14) EU:C:2015:844; [2016] 2 W.L.R. 940 a **6JR.27** consumer, domiciled in Germany, entered into a brokerage contract with an intermediary in Spain to buy a holiday apartment in Spain being built by a German developer and marketed in Germany via a prospectus written in German. The developer encountered financial difficulties and the intermediary proposed to the consumer to finish the work in the apartment and for that purpose a transaction management contract was concluded in Spain between the consumer and the intermediary. The consumer brought a claim for sums paid under the transaction management contact before the German courts on the basis of the special provisions relating to consumer contracts. Jurisdiction was challenged on the basis that although the brokerage contract was a consumer contract, the transaction management contract was not. The CJEU held that where a contract which was not a consumer contract was closely linked to a previous contract that was a consumer contract, the consumer could rely upon art.16(1) (now art.18(1)), and that a sufficient link was established where (i) the parties to both contracts were the same in law and fact, (ii) the economic objective of the contracts was identical and (iii) the second contract complemented the first in that it made it possible to achieve the objectives of the first contract.

(c)   Jurisdiction over individual contracts of employment (arts 20 to 23)

Replace the ninth paragraph (where the citation for Petter v EMC Europe Ltd has changed) with:

A member of a group of companies that does not directly employ the relevant employee may be **6JR.28** treated as an employer for the purposes of arts 20 to 23 the Judgments Regulation (*Samengo-Turner v J & H Marsh & McLennon (Services) Ltd* [2007] EWCA Civ 723; [2007] 2 All E.R. (Comm) 813; [2007] I.L.Pr. 52; *Petter v EMC Europe Ltd* [2015] EWCA Civ 828; [2016] I.L.Pr. 3 (where held that, as a stock award agreement between an American company and their employee (employed through a UK subsidiary) fell within the Regulation, the court was bound to disregard the agreement's foreign exclusive jurisdiction clause, assume jurisdiction, and grant an anti-suit injunction).

D.   EXCLUSIVE JURISDICTION: JURISDICTION REGARDLESS OF THE DOMICILE OF THE PARTIES (ART. 24)

2.   *Rights in immovable property*

Add new paragraph at end:

6JR.30   In *Komu v Komu* (C-605/14) EU:C:2015:833; [2016] 4 W.L.R. 26, the CJEU held that an action concerning a number of Finnish domiciled parties for the termination of the co-ownership of properties in Spain fell within the exclusive jurisdiction of the Spanish Court under (what is now) Art.24(1).

E.   PROROGATION OF JURISDICTION (ARTS 25 AND 26)

2.   *Jurisdiction by agreement (choice of court agreement) (art.25.1)*

To the end of the penultimate paragraph (beginning with "Article 25.1 states"), add:

6JR.35   In *Perella Weinberg Partners UK LLP v Codere SA* [2016] EWHC 1182 (Comm), 17 May 2016, unrep. (Walker J), it was held that a clause expressed to confer non-exclusive jurisdiction on the English Courts "for the benefit of" the Claimants did not in fact confer exclusive jurisdiction on those Courts."

4.   *Stay of proceedings where court seised on basis of exclusive jurisdiction agreement*

Jurisdiction derived where defendant enters appearance (art.26)

Replace the second paragraph with:

6JR.39   Article 26 states that, apart from jurisdiction derived from other provisions of the Regulation, a court of a Member State before which a defendant enters an appearance "shall have jurisdiction". (By entering an appearance the defendant is deemed to have submitted to the jurisdiction.) The article adds that this rule shall not apply where another court has exclusive jurisdiction under art.24 (Exclusive jurisdiction) (see para.6JR.29 above). (Jurisdiction based on submission to one court does not trump, as it were, jurisdiction based on a rule of jurisdiction conferring exclusive jurisdiction on another court.) And it shall not apply where the defendant entered appearance "to contest the jurisdiction". Jurisdiction is not conferred on a court under art.26 where a defendant enters an appearance, not only for the purpose of making submissions contesting the court's jurisdiction, but additionally for the purpose of making other submissions (including submissions as to the merits of the claim). For a period uncertainty on this latter point was caused by the fact that the comparable article in the 1968 Convention, as amended (art.18), contained the phrase "solely to contest the jurisdiction". Whether or not a Defendant "enters an appearance" is a question of national procedural law provided that does not undermine the effective operation of the Regulation, see *Deutsche Bank AG London Branch v Petromena ASA* [2015] EWCA Civ 226; [2015] 1 W.L.R. 4225. For what might or might not constitute submission to the jurisdiction, see *Winkler v Shamoon* [2016] EWHC 217 (Ch), 18 February 2016, unrep.

F.   *Priority of Jurisdiction—Lis Pendens and Related Actions*

Same cause of action

Replace the third paragraph (where the citation for Barclays Bank plc v Ente Nazionale di Previdenza ed Assistenza dei Medici e Degli Odontoiatri has changed) with:

6JR.45   The principles underlying the concept of "same cause of action" were explained, and the reasoning in the *Starlight Shipping Company* case was applied, at first instance in *Barclays Bank plc v Ente Nazionale di Previdenza ed Assistenza dei Medici e Degli Odontoiatri* [2015] EWHC 2857 (Comm)[2015] 2 Lloyd's Rep. 527 (Blair J.), at paras 63 to 72.

Degree to which proceedings must be "related"

Replace the last paragraph (where the citation for Maxter Catheters SAS v Medicina Ltd has changed) with:

In *Maxter Catheters SAS v Medicina Ltd* [2015] EWHC 3076 (Comm), [2016] 1 W.L.R. 349 it was **6JR.46** explained (1) that an *action en référé* brought in a French court is to be distinguished from an *action au fond*, and that the former action is a summary procedure most often used to prevent imminent harm, danger or unlawful activity, (2) that for the purposes of art.30 the *action en référé* does not appear to be relevant because it is not designed to produce a judgment on the merits, and (3) that in the instant case because the former action was not designed to resolve the substantive dispute between the parties it did not constitute proceedings parallel to proceedings in English court which gave rise to a risk of inconsistent judgments. However, the judge further explained (para.37) that under the Judgments Regulation the mere fact that the court in country A granted provisional relief will not mean that the court in country B where substantive proceedings were later commenced will be the court first seised, because, if the proceedings before the court in country A can, although they commenced with the grant of provisional relief, proceed to a determination of the substantive issue between the parties (as in an English action), then the court of country A can be regarded as the court first seised.

PART 8

ALTERNATIVE PROCEDURE FOR CLAIMS

Add new paragraph 8.1.3:

In *Phillips v Willis* [2016] EWCA Civ 401 it was held that Stage 3 proceedings issued under **8.1.3** PD8B cannot be converted to Pt 7 proceedings under r.8.1(3) as that would incur grossly disproportionate costs to the damages at stake.

PRACTICE DIRECTION 8A—ALTERNATIVE PROCEDURE FOR CLAIMS

This Practice Direction supplements CPR Part 8 and Schedule 1 and Schedule 2 to the CPR

Section C Special Provisions

Application for detailed assessment of a returning officer's account

Replace paragraph 17.1 with:

17.1

(1) An application by— **8APD.17**

    (a) by the Secretary of State under section 30 of the Representation of the People Act 1983 or paragraph 4 of Schedule 1 to the Recall of MPs Act 2015;

    (b) the Welsh Ministers under article 24 of the National Assembly for Wales (Representation of the People) Order 2007; or

    (c) the Electoral Commission under paragraph 17 of Schedule 3 to the European Union Referendum Act 2015,

for the detailed assessment of a returning officer's account must be made by claim form.

(2) In this paragraph and paragraphs 17.3 to 17.5 and 17.8, references to the returning officer are to be read—

    (a) for applications under the Recall of MPs Act 2015, as references to the petition officer;

    (b) for applications under the National Assembly for Wales (Representation of the People) Order 2007, as references to—

        (i) the constituency returning officer, in relation to a constituency election; and

        (ii) the constituency and regional returning officer, in relation to a regional election; and

    (c) for applications under the European Union Referendum Act 2015, as references to the counting officer or Regional Counting Officer.

Other proceedings under the Representation of the People Acts

8APD.17   *Replace paragraph 17A.1 with:*

17A.1(1)   This paragraph applies to proceedings under the Representation of the People Acts (other than proceedings under section 30 of the Representation of the People Act 1983) and the European Union Referendum (Conduct) Regulations 2016 ("the 2016 Regulations").

   (2)   The jurisdiction of the High Court under those Acts in matters relating to Parliamentary and local government elections, or under the 2016 Regulations, will be exercised by a Divisional Court except that—

   (a)   any jurisdiction, under a provision of any of those Acts, or under the 2016 Regulations, exercisable by a single judge will be exercised by a single judge;

   (b)   any jurisdiction, under any such provision, exercisable by a Master will be exercised by a Master; and

   (c)   where the court's jurisdiction in matters relating to Parliamentary elections is exercisable by a single judge, that jurisdiction in matters relating to local government elections is also exercisable by a single judge.

PRACTICE DIRECTION 8B—THE PRE-ACTION PROTOCOLS FOR LOW VALUE PERSONAL INJURY CLAIMS IN ROAD TRAFFIC ACCIDENTS AND LOW VALUE PERSONAL INJURY (EMPLOYERS' LIABILITY AND PUBLIC LIABILITY) CLAIMS—STAGE 3 PROCEDURE

Note

Replace with:

8BPD.7.1   Paragraphs 7.1 to 7.3 demonstrate that, under the Stage 3 procedure, the material that the court will consider in determining the amount of damages is restricted. The procedure builds on the Stage 2 process. It is not designed to give the parties the opportunity to put forward new material that was not exchanged during that process. Where the defendant opposes the claim because the claimant has filed and served additional or new evidence with the claim form that had not been provided under the Protocol, the court will dismiss the claim (para.9.1). The power of the court to order that the claim is not suitable to continue under the Stage 3 process is a power the court may exercise on its own initiative. However, in *Phillips v Willis* [2016] EWCA Civ 401 the court set aside an order of the District Judge, made on his own initiative, to transfer a credit hire claim (all other claims having been settled) from the Stage 3 procedure to Pt 7 proceedings allocated to the small claims track. No further evidence was necessary and the directions given would have required parties to incur costs grossly disproportionate to the damages at stake. The case illustrates that transfer out of the Protocol Stage 3 procedure to Pt 7 will be rare and for exceptional cases only.

PART 11

DISPUTING THE COURT'S JURISDICTION

Effect of Part 11

After the third paragraph (beginning with "Rule 11(2)"), add new paragraph:

11.1.1   Rule 11(5) only has substance in a case where the jurisdiction of the English court was or might be in issue. It does not apply to a case where the English court has jurisdiction, but is being asked to stay the proceedings on non conveniens grounds. However, r.11(4) is mandatory and if a party seeks to make an application out of time for a stay of proceedings on non conveniens grounds it must apply for an extension of time. In that event, the normal relief from sanctions principles apply because, in dealing with an application for an extension of time, even where (as in r.11(4)) there is no express sanction for default, there is a potential implicit sanction which is brought into play by the court refusing to extend time, with the effect that the party in default is prevented from taking some procedural step that it would or may have been open to him to make had he been in time (*Le Guevel-Mouly v AIG Europe Ltd* [2016] EWHC 1794 (QB), 19 July 2016, unrep. (Hickinbottom J)).

Replace the fourth paragraph (where the citation for Cook v Virgin Media Ltd has changed) with:

In *Cook v Virgin Media Ltd* [2015] EWCA Civ 1287; [2016] I.L.Pr. 6, a claimant (C) domiciled in Scotland brought a claim in the English County Court against a company (D) situated in England for damages for personal injuries arising from an accident in Scotland. D filed an acknowledgment of service but made no application to stay or strike out the proceedings on forum non conveniens grounds, and made no application under r.11(1) for a declaration as to jurisdiction. On its own initiative, the court stayed the proceedings on the ground that Scotland was the most convenient forum for the claim, and after hearing submissions, in exercise of case management powers, struck out the claim on that ground. The Court of Appeal dismissed C's appeal, holding that the lower court had power, under r.3.1(2)(f), to stay or, under r.3.1(2)(m), to strike out C's claim, and expressed the opinion that the better course would be to stay rather than to strike out (especially where the defendant has admitted liability). In reaching its decision the Court rejected C's submission (made in reliance on the decision of the Court in *Hoddinott v Persimmon Homes (Wessex) Ltd* [2007] EWCA Civ 1203; [2008] 1 W.L.R. 806, CA), to the effect that (1) because D had not applied for a declaration under r.11(1), they were to be treated as having accepted the English court's jurisdiction, and (2) in those circumstances the English court should exercise that jurisdiction. The Court explained (distinguishing Hoddinott) that in the instant case the County Court was not considering whether it should decline jurisdiction under r.11, but was acting of its own initiative and exercising its case management powers in accordance with the overriding objective. The court was not prevented by D's failure to make an application under r.11(1) from exercising those powers or from exercising them in the way it did.

Replace the ninth paragraph with:

However it is inconsistent with an intention to challenge the jurisdiction that a defendant should seek an extension of time for their defence, advance a defence on the merits in reliance of a purported settlement and threaten to strike out the claim if the claimant refuses to discontinue it, *Global Multimedia International Ltd v ARA Media Services* [2006] EWHC 3612 (Ch); [2007] 1 All E.R. (Comm) 1160. The rule is strict: the application must be promptly made and be supported by evidence (r.11(4)). There is, however, power to extend time for compliance: see *Sawyer v Atari Interactive Inc* [2005] EWHC 2351 (Ch); [2006] I.L.Pr. 8, paras 42–48; *Polymer Vision R & D Ltd v Van Dooren* [2011] EWHC 2951 (Comm), [2012] I.L.Pr. 14, para 74 (Beatson J.) (where the authorities are examined). A request by a defendant for an extension of time for service of a defence cannot be construed as also being a request for an extension of time for making an application to contest the jurisdiction. A request for an extension of time for service of a defence is capable of amounting to a submission to the jurisdiction. Where waiver by conduct is asserted the question is whether a reasonable person in the shoes of the claimant would have understood the defendant's conduct as waiving any irregularity as to service. Furthermore, r.11(5) carries with it a presumption of waiver; *Hoddinott v Persimmon Homes (Wessex) Ltd* [2007] EWCA Civ 1203; [2008] 1 W.I.R. 806. A defendant cannot rely upon r.3.4 to avoid the Part 11 regime: *Burns-Anderson Independent Network Plc v Wheeler* [2005] EWHC 575. If the application is successful the court will grant a declaration (see r.11(6)); if the application is not successful the acknowledgment of service ceases to have effect but the defendant may file a further acknowledgment which does then amount to a submission to the jurisdiction (see r.11(7) and (8)). If a defendant wishes to appeal against a decision rejecting its jurisdiction challenge, it should ask for an extension of time for filing a second acknowledgement of service sufficient for an application for permission to appeal or an appeal to be determined, and should not file a second acknowledgement of service as the latter will be treated as a submission to the jurisdiction, see *Deutsche Bank AG London Branch v Petromena ASA* [2015] EWCA Civ 226; [2015] 1 W.L.R. 4225. For what might or might not constitute submission to the jurisdiction, see *Winkler v Shamoon* [2016] EWHC 217 (Ch), 18 February 2016, unrep.

After the ninth paragraph (beginning with "However it is inconsistent") add new paragraph:

The periods set out in r.6.35 for the service of a defence run during the time provided for a defendant to make an application under Pt 11 with the consequence that, where a challenge is not pursued, the time for service of the defence may have expired unless extended by agreement or order; see *Flame SA v Primera Maritime (Hellas) Ltd* [2009] EWHC 1973 (Comm). Not every issue of jurisdiction has to be disposed of at this stage and the court may postpone a question of jurisdiction to a later stage where it is convenient to do so; as for instance, where the justiciability of an issue may be disputed (*Kuwait Airways Corp v Iraqi Airways Co* [1995] 1 W.L.R. 1147; [1995] 3 All E.R. 694, HL). Although not expressly stated in Pt 11, the relief granted by the court may relate to only part of the case (*Kuwait Airways Corp* above).

PART 12

DEFAULT JUDGMENT

"judgment in default of an acknowledgment of service"

Replace the second paragraph with:

12.3.1   Where a claimant has issued an application for default judgment (being unable simply to file a request) and the defendant has filed an acknowledgment of service, but did so after the period for doing so fixed by r.10.3 had expired and after the application for default judgment had been issued, the claimant is not prevented from obtaining default judgment by the defendant's late filing of an acknowledgment of service, because the question whether the conditions in r.12.3(1) are satisfied has to be judged at the time when the claimant's application is made (*Taylor v Giovani Developers Ltd* [2015] EWHC 328 (Comm), February 6, 2015, unrep. (Popplewell J.), where the defendant's application for an extension of the period for filing of its acknowledgment of service was refused). In *Almond v Medgolf Properties Ltd* [2015] EWHC 3280 (Comm); 19 May 2015, unrep. Phillips J agreed with Popplewell J in *Taylor v Giovanni Developers* that on an application for default judgment, the question as to whether the conditions in r.12.3(1) are satisfied must be considered at the date of the issue of the application. Where the acknowledgment of service is filed after the period for doing so fixed by r.10.3 had expired but before after the claimant's application for default judgment had been issued, it seems the same position obtains. That is, the defendant's late filing of the acknowledgment is ineffective to prevent the entry of default judgment unless the defendant applies for and obtains an extension of the relevant period (*Taylor v Giovani Developers Ltd*, op cit, a point doubted but not resolved in *ESR Insurance Services Ltd v Clemons* [2008] EWHC 2023 (Comm), 11 August 2008, unrep. (Blair J). Phillips J in *Almond v Medgolf Properties Ltd* said that he has some doubt as to whether default judgment could be entered where an acknowledgment of service had been filed late but before the application for default judgment had been issued. See further paras 10.2.1 and 11.1.1 above.

"judgment in default of defence"

Add new paragraph at end:

12.3.3   The effect of the late filing of a defence on an application for default judgment was considered by Deputy Master Pickering in *Billington v Davies* [2016] EWHC 1919 (Ch) where it was held that the reference to "a defence" in r.12.3(2)(a) must be a reference to a defence which has either been served within the time permitted by the rules or in respect of which an extension of time has been granted.

"an amount of money to be decided by the court"

To the end of the last paragraph, add:

12.4.4   Where the claim was issued in the CCMCC, and has not already been sent to a County Court hearing centre, upon judgment being entered under this rule for an amount to be decided by the court, the claim will be transferred to the preferred court (see r.12.5A).

Add new paragraphs at the beginning:

12.11.2   In *Football Dataco Ltd v Smoot Enterprises Ltd* [2011] 1 W.L.R. 1978 Briggs J considered an application made under Pt 23 for judgment in default against the defendants in the form of a final injunction where they had been served with the claim outside the jurisdiction in circumstances where permission of the court was not required. He held that the requirement under r.12.11(1) that it must appear to the court that the claimant is entitled to judgment needs to be interpreted in the light of the aggregation of the prescribed circumstances in which an application under Pt 23 is required. He held that the purpose of the requirement for an application is either to enable the court to tailor the precise relief so that it is appropriate to the cause of action asserted, or otherwise to scrutinise the application in particular circumstances calling for more than a purely administrative response. He also held that the fact that there was an outstanding appeal to the Court of Appeal in a related case and that court had made a reference to the European Court of Justice did not prevent the court granting a final injunction in circumstances where the particulars of claim disclose a cause of action which is not obviously bad and the defendants have not taken the basic steps to challenge it.In *S v Beach* [2015] 1 W.L.R. 2701 the court was concerned with an application for a final injunction made on notice where the defendants had not filed an acknowledgment of service but the second defendant had written a letter setting out his defence, which the court had considered when considering the merits and before granting judgment in default of acknowledgment of service and a final injunction. The second defendant later applied to set that order aside and Warby J considered r.12.11 and how it was linked to r.13.3 and held that they provided a self-contained regime governing the procedure for the grant, variation or setting aside of judgment in default and all such orders as the court considered the Claimant was entitled to where the conditions prescribed by those rules had been, or were alleged to have been, satisfied. He held that the procedure in r.12.11 is efficient and proportionate, that the judgment is final and, to the extent that it involves consideration of what relief is justified on the basis of the facts alleged in the statements of case, it does have an element of merits assessment.

PART 13

SETTING ASIDE OR VARYING DEFAULT JUDGMENT

Effect of rule

Add new paragraph at end:

13.3.1 In *Samara v MBI & Partners UK Ltd* [2016] EWHC 441 (QB), 4 March 2016, unrep. Cox J held that a decision made by a judge under r.13.3 was a final decision and could not be the subject of a second application to set aside judgment or a further challenge by reference to r.3.1(7). The only way forward for a dissatisfied party is to appeal.

PART 14

ADMISSIONS

Judgment

Replace with:

14.6.5 As provided by r.14.6(7), judgment is for "an amount to be decided by the court". Where the judgment is entered in a claim issued in the CCMCC, then unless the claim has already been sent to a hearing centre, it will be sent to the preferred court (see r.14.7A). The court will give case-management directions including allocating the case to the relevant track if it is necessary.

PART 16

STATEMENTS OF CASE

Editorial introduction

To the end of the last paragraph, add.

16.0.1 In *Sobrany v UAB Transtira* [2016] EWCA Civ 28, [2016] RTR 18, [2016] Lloyd's Rep IR 266, issues arose as to insurance taken out in support of credit hire agreements. In its Defence the defendant referred to the issue of only one insurance policy. However, when being cross-examined, the claimant stated that two policies had been issued. The Court of Appeal upheld the trial judge's decision to allow the defendant to advance arguments on the basis of this evidence. Although, generally speaking a defendant should not be permitted to advance a positive case inconsistent with its pleading, different considerations applied where a defendant sought to rely on evidence the claimant had in effect volunteered.

Defence of tender before claim

Replace with:

16.5.6 The expression "defence of tender before claim" is defined in the Glossary. The defence may be raised in response to any money claim, whether or not a specified amount is claimed. Where the defendant wishes to rely on this defence they must make a payment into court of the amount they say was tendered (r.37.3). Reliance upon this defence will often reap substantial advantages in costs for the defendant if the claimant cannot later prove an entitlement to a sum larger than was tendered. In all cases, whether claims for debts or damages, the court may treat this defence as akin to a pre-action offer to settle and therefore may make an order that the claimant should pay rather than receive costs incurred in the period after the date the tender was made. However, in damages actions, the claimant may still be entitled to an order for his costs incurred before the date of tender (contrast the common law defence of "tender before action", available in debt cases only, which, if successful, leads to an order dismissing the claim with costs against the claimant: see *RSM Bentley Jennison (A Firm) v Ayton* [2015] EWCA Civ 1120; [2016] 1 W.L.R. 1281, CA and the cases cited therein).

PART 17

AMENDMENTS TO STATEMENTS OF CASE

Late amendments

Replace the first paragraph (where the citation for Su-Ling v Goldman Sachs International has changed) with:

17.3.7   An important factor for the court to consider when permission to amend is sought close to the trial date is whether the amendment will put the parties on an unequal footing or will place or add an excessive burden to the respondent's task of preparing for trial so as to jeopardise the trial date or so as to inevitably cause a postponement of the trial. A very late amendment is one made when the trial date has been fixed and where the grant of permission to amend would cause the trial date to be lost. Parties and the court have a legitimate expectation that trial fixtures will be kept. A heavy burden lies upon a party seeking a very late amendment. He must provide a good explanation as to why he did not apply earlier and must show the strength of the new case and why justice to him, his opponent and other court users requires him to be able to pursue it (*Quah v Goldman Sachs International* [2015] EWHC 759 (Comm)). In the following cases permission to amend at or just before trial was granted: *Cobbold v Greenwich LBC* [1999] EWCA Civ 2074; August 9, 1999, unrep., CA; *Willis v Quality Heating Services* [2000] L.T.L., March 24, CA; *Electronic Data Systems Ltd v National Air Traffic Services* [2002] EWCA Civ 13, CA.

Replace the fifth paragraph with:

The relevant authorities on late amendment were examined and applied in *Brown v Innovatorone Plc* [2011] EWHC 3221 (Comm), November 28, 2011, unrep. (Hamblen J.): relevant factors include the history as regards the amendment and the explanation as to why it was being made late; the prejudice which would be caused to the applicant if the amendment was refused; the prejudice which would be caused to the resisting party if the amendment was allowed; whether the text of the amendment was satisfactory in terms of clarity and particularity (see [5]–[14] of judgment). In *Hawksworth v Chief Constable of Staffordshire* [2012] EWCA Civ 293, CA, unrep., the Court of Appeal stated, obiter, that it might appropriate to permit an amendment at trial in respect of a matter which, although not raised in the pleadings, had nevertheless been raised in some of the witness statements and experts' reports served pre-trial (and see further on this case, and *Sobrany v UAB Transtira* [2016] EWCA Civ 28, [2016] RTR 18, [2016] Lloyd's Rep IR 266, both noted in para.16.0.1, above). In *Dany Lions Ltd v Bristol Cars Ltd* [2014] EWHC 928 (QB) (amendment sought two days before trial) Andrews J refused to allow amendments prompted by a reappraisal of the merits of the case by newly instructed counsel and stated that the practice on late amendments should also take account of the stricter views as to defaults in compliance with rules which were indicated by the Court of Appeal in *Mitchell v News Group Newspapers Ltd* [2013] EWCA Civ 1537; [2014] 1 WLR 795; [2014] 2 All ER 430.

Add new paragraph after the fifth paragraph (beginning with "The relevant authorities"):

The principle arising from *Swain Mason v Mills & Reeve* (see above) applies only where a new point of substance is raised. In *Ahmed v Ahmed* [2016] EWCA Civ 686, the claimants applied to have letters of administration revoked on the basis that the will annexed to them had not been duly executed or witnessed. At the start of the trial the claimants obtained permission to amend their particulars of claim so as to allege that the will had been forged. The Court of Appeal dismissed an appeal against that grant of permission; the amendment was no more than a formality bringing the claimants' case into line with what had been argued for at least six months. The appellants had not been taken by surprise by the amendment and, indeed, had themselves sought at the pre-trial review, permission to call a handwriting expert.

Replace the sixth paragraph with:

The principles relevant to the determination of late applications for permission to amend were summarised by Carr J. in *Quah v Goldman Sachs International* [2015] EWHC 759 (Comm), March 23, 2015, unrep. (at para.38), and that summary has been relied on by other judges sitting at first instance subsequently (e.g. *Skelwith (Leisure) Ltd v Armstrong* [2015] EWHC 3487 (Ch), November 27, 2015, unrep. (Newey J.) at para.10; *Poulton Plaiz Ltd v Barclays Bank plc* [2015] EWHC 3667 (QB), December 4, 2015, unrep. (Picken J.) at para.9; *Davidson v Seelig* [2016] EWHC 549 (Ch), 15 March 2016, unrep. (Henderson J) at para.43).

Correcting name of party (r.17.4(3))

Replace the last paragraph with:

Rules 17.4(3) and 19.5(3)(a) both deal with mistakes as to the name of a party intending to sue **17.4.5** or be sued. Both are to be construed as the CPR equivalent to RSC Ord 20 r.5 and so should be read together. The statutory authority for them, so far as they involve issues of limitation, is s.35 of the Limitation Act 1980. In *Adelson v Associated Newspapers Ltd* [2007] EWCA Civ 701; [2007] 4 All E.R. 330 the Court of Appeal provided a definitive account of the principles to be applied. Mistakes as to the name of a party divide into two categories: errors of identification (e.g. in a road accident claim, the claimant erroneously identifies as the proper defendant "X", the owner of a vehicle involved in the accident, rather than "Y", the driver of that vehicle at the relevant time); and errors of nomenclature, i.e. errors as to the name of the intended party (e.g. in a claim to enforce easements the claimant wishes to sue the current owner of the servient land but the claim form erroneously names as defendant a previous owner of that land). The mistake envisaged by both rr.17.4(3) and 19.5(3)(a) is one of nomenclature, not of identification (see *Adelson* at [33]). The simplest cases are those in which the name given in the claim form is merely incomplete or is just a misspelling. The problem cases are those in which the claimant knows only the attributes of the person they wish to sue (e.g. their neighbour, their landlord, their employer or the manufacturer of an object) but has no personal knowledge of the name of that person. The guidance given in *Adelson* is that, where such a claimant has made enquiries, has been incorrectly informed that a named person has those attributes and has commenced a claim naming that person as the defendant, but describing in the claim form or statement of case the attributes of the person intended to be sued, their mistake is likely to be classified as an error of nomenclature: the name used for the defendant is not the appropriate name to describe the person that the claimant intended to sue. Such a mistake is therefore remediable (if the court thinks it just to allow the amendment) even where the relevant limitation period has expired; see *Adelson* at [30] and [56] in which the *Sardinis Sulcis* test (see above) was cited with approval (for further information about *Adelson*, see para.19.5.7, below).

Although r.17.4(3) and r.19.5(3)(a) are alike in the principles to be applied they differ as to the type of cases they cover. Most of the cases in which r.17.4(3) is appropriate are cases in which the mistake relates to a defendant upon whom the claim form has been served even though that defendant is misnamed therein. The simplest examples are cases in which the name given for the defendant is incomplete or incorrect and the defendant files an acknowledgment of service giving their full or correct name (see further, Practice Direction 10, para.5.2, set out in para.10PD.5, above; an acknowledgment of service making such a correction does not relieve the claimant from the necessity of amending his claim form but such an amendment is unlikely to be opposed). Cases in which r.19.5(3)(a) is appropriate are those in which, if an amendment is allowed, a new person will be joined to the proceedings. If that person is joined as a defendant the claim form must subsequently be served upon him and he will then be required to acknowledge service or file a defence; a defendant for whom he is to be substituted will cease to be a party to the proceedings.

Rule 17.4(3) specifies that the mistake as to name "must not be such as to cause any reasonable doubt as to the identity of the party in question" (i.e., the person in respect of whom a mistake as to name has been made). There is no such "reasonable doubt" rider in r.19.5(3)(a). However, it is now established that this is a distinction without a difference; in cases in which r.19.5(3)(a) is addressed, doubts as to the identity of the party in question are relevant to the court's underlying discretion as to whether to allow the amendment. Indeed, permission to amend is likely to be refused if the court considers that the mistake of name has caused reasonable doubt as to the identity of the party in question; see, for example, *Horne-Roberts v SmithKline Beecham plc* [2001] EWCA Civ 2006; [2002] 1 W.L.R. 1662 at [44]; *Adelson* (above) at [57]); *Lockheed Martin Corporation v Willis Group Ltd* [2010] EWCA Civ 927; [2010] P.N.L.R. 34, CA at [47].

PART 19

PARTIES AND GROUP LITIGATION

Add new paragraph 19.1.2:

Parties must be persons

Rule 2.3(1) defines "claimant" as a person who makes a claim, and "defendant" as a person **19.1.2** against whom a claim is made. The term "person" is also used in the rules describing who can become a litigation friend (rr.21.4 and 21.6) or a party to an additional claim (rr.20.5, 20.6 and 20.8). The word "person" itself is not defined in the CPR but can be taken to mean a human being or other entity which is recognised by the law as the subject of rights and duties. "Person" includes a body of persons corporate or unincorporate" (Interpretation Act 1978 s.5 and Sch.1). Other entities, such as animals or trees, cannot be made parties to proceedings. Claims which purport to be made by them are liable to be struck out (see, for example, *Moosun v HSBC Bank Plc* [2015] EWHC 3308 (Ch)).

Special provisions are made in respect of persons who are children or protected parties (as to which, see generally Pt 21, below). A child or protected party must have a litigation friend to conduct proceedings on their behalf except where (in the case of a child) the court otherwise orders (r.21.2). Save where the court otherwise orders, any step taken in proceedings by or against a child or protected party has no effect unless the child or protected party has a litigation friend (r.21.3(4)).

Other special provisions are made for the bringing of proceedings by or against persons who, at the time the relevant cause of action accrued, were partners carrying on that partnership business within the jurisdiction (Practice Direction 7A, paras 5A and 5B (see above, paras 7APD.5A and 7APD.5B). Where that partnership has a name, unless it is inappropriate to do so, claims must be brought in or against the name under which that partnership carried on business at the time the cause of action accrued (PD para.5A.3).

In the case of partnerships and other unincorporated bodies of persons which fall outside PD7A para 5A, a representative action may be brought by or against them under r.19.6 (summarised in para.19.1.1, above). Alternatively, members of the partnership or body of persons must sue or be sued as individuals and the full names of each person by or against whom the proceedings are taken should appear in the title of those proceedings (Practice Direction 7A, para.4.1(3), see para.7APD.4, above). Proceedings brought in the name of a partnership or body of persons without compliance with Practice Direction 7A, para.5A or r.19.6 are not a nullity and, even at a late stage, the court may make orders regularising them (see, for example, *Williams v Devon County Council* [2016] EWCA Civ 419 at [28] to [31] noted in para.19.6.2, below).

As to proceedings intended to bind the estates of deceased persons, see below, r.19.8 and the commentary thereto.

I. Addition and Substitution of Parties

"evidence" (r.19.4.(3))

Replace with:

19.4.3   See Practice Direction, para.1.3 (see para.19APD.1), Pt 32 and the Practice Direction to Pt 32 (see para.32PD.1). In *Allergan Inc v Sauflon Pharmaceuticals Ltd* [2000] All E.R. (D.) 106, Ch D, Pumfrey J. refused an application to join a party as a second defendant where the claimant failed to plead a good arguable case. In *Pece Beheer BV v Alevere Ltd* [2016] EWHC 434 (IPEC) HH Judge Hacon stated that, in most cases, in order to show a good arguable case for this purpose, the correct test to be applied is that which would be applied in an application to strike out a claim against a defendant pursuant to CPR r.3.4(2)(a) or (b) (as to which, see further paras 3.4.2 and 3.4.3, above).

"party ... named in mistake for the new party" (r.19.5(3)(a) and s.35(6)(a))

Replace the second paragraph with:

19.5.5   Neither r.19.5(3)(a) nor s.35(6)(a) elaborate upon what is meant by "mistake" in this context. It is now well established that the mistake must be as to the name of the new party rather than as to the identity of that party, applying the generous test of this type of mistake laid down in *Sardinia Sulcis* [1991] 1 Lloyd's Rep.201, CA (as to which, see further, para.19.5.7, below). The person who made the mistake must be the person responsible, directly or through an agent, for the issue of the claim form and it must be demonstrated that, had the mistake not been made, the new party would have been named in the pleading (*Adelson v Associated Newspapers Ltd* [2007] EWCA Civ 701, [2008] 1 W.L.R. 585 at [55]. In other words the mistake has to be causally relevant: but for the mistake, the new party would have been named. In *Adelson* the claimants failed to obtain permission to amend because they had failed to prove that the mistake they had made had caused the omission of the new parties' names from the claim form (see further, para 19.5.7, below).

Rule 19.5(3) (unlike r.17.4(3)) does not expressly state that the mistake as to name relied on as "must not be such as to cause any reasonable doubt as to the identity of the party in question" (i.e. the new party; the words in quotation marks are taken from r.17.4(3)). However, it is now firmly established that in cases in which r.19.5(3)(a) is addressed, doubts as to the identity of the new party are relevant to the court's underlying discretion as to whether to allow the amendment. Indeed, permission to amend is likely to be refused if the court considers that the mistake of name has in fact caused reasonable doubt as to the identity of the new party; see, for example, *Horne-Roberts v SmithKline Beecham plc* [2001] EWCA Civ 2006; [2002] 1 W.L.R. 1662 at [44]; *Adelson* (above) at [57]); *Lockheed Martin Corporation v Willis Group Ltd* [2010] EWCA Civ 927; [2010] P.N.L.R. 34,CA at [47].

Relationship between r.19.5(3)(a) and r.17.4(3) mistakes

Replace the last paragraph with:

19.5.6   See further on this topic, para.17.4.5, above.

Cases on mistake (r.19.5(3)(a))

Replace from the second paragraph (beginning with "Wherever issues of mistake") to the end of the eighth paragraph (beginning with "In Adelson, the court") with:

In *Adelson v Associated Newspapers Ltd* [2007] EWCA Civ 701; [2008] 1 W.L.R. 585 the Court of **19.5.7** Appeal reviewed the, somewhat chaotic case law on r.19.5(3)(a) and applied the approach adopted in *The Sardinia Sulcis* [1991] 1 Lloyd's Rep 201. Their lordships also ruled that the contrary approach stated in *Morgan Est (Scotland) Ltd v Hanson Concrete Productions Ltd* [2005] EWCA Civ 134; [2005] 1 W.L.R. 2557 was not correct and should not be followed, and ruled that the "working test" proposed by the court in *Weston v Gribben* [2006] EWCA Civ 1425 should not be relied on.

Replace the tenth paragraph (beginning with "In the latter case") with:

The Court of Appeal applied this test in *Parsons v George* [2004] EWCA Civ 912; [2004] 1 W.L.R. 3264, CA (where the pre- and post-CPR authorities are extensively reviewed and explained by Dyson L.J. at paras 8 to 20) and in *Kesslar v Moore & Tibbits (A Firm)* [2004] EWCA Civ 1551, (where it was noted that a striking feature of the test is that it permits, subject to the court's discretion, the substitution of a completely new defendant who had no connection with the party originally impleaded). In *Kesslar* (at [25]) it was said that the test, which is now known as the *Sardinia Sulcis* test, involved no infringement of ECHR, art. 6.

Replace the twelfth paragraph (beginning with "Cases in which") with:

Cases in which, though a party was mis-named, their identity was made clear by reference to a description which is specific to the particular case, and which therefore may be regarded as examples of the application of the *Sardinia Sulcis* test are:

- *Mitchell v Harris Engineering Co* [1967] 2 Q.B. 703, CA (claimant's employers);
- *Rodriguez v Parker* [1967] 1 Q.B. 116 (driver of a particular car);
- *Evans Construction Co Ltd v Charrington & Co Ltd* [1983] Q.B. 810, CA (competent landlord);
- *Thistle Hotels Ltd v Sir Robert McAlpine & Sons Ltd*, The Times, April 11, 1989, CA (proprietor of an hotel);
- *The Sardinia Sulcis* [1991] 1 Lloyd's Rep. 201 (merger of companies);
- *Crook v Aaron Dale Construction and Roofing Ltd* [1997] P.I.Q.R. P36, CA (claimant's employer);
- *Horne-Roberts v Smithkline Beecham Plc* [2001] EWCA Civ 2006; [2002] 1 W.L.R. 1662, CA (manufacturers of a specifically identified batch of vaccine);
- *Parsons v George* [2004] EWCA Civ 912; [2004] 1 W.L.R. 3264, CA (competent landlord);
- *Kesslar v Moore & Tibbits (A Firm)* [2004] EWCA Civ 1551 (professional advisers).

Replace the last paragraph with:

For an example of a case in which an application under r.19.5(3) was refused on the basis that it had not been shown that the mistake alleged had caused the issue of the claim form without the names of the new parties now sought to be joined, see *Adelson v Associated Newspapers Ltd* [2007] EWCA Civ 701; [2008] 1 W.L.R. 585. In that case a defamation claim was commenced in the name of a parent company which was described in the particulars of claim as a trading company; an application was made to substitute, for the name of the parent company, the names of itself and two of its subsidiary companies (which were trading companies). The application was refused: although a mistake had been made as to as to the structure of the group of companies or the roles played by the members of the group, it had not been shown that, but for that mistake, the subsidiary companies would have been named in the claim form.

II. Representative Parties

Effect of rule

Add new paragraph at end:

Representative proceedings which are commenced without complying with r.19.6 are not **19.6.2** thereby rendered a nullity. In *Williams v Devon County Council* [2016] EWCA Civ 419 a group of persons calling themselves "Sustainable Totnes Action Group" wished to dispute certain orders made by a local authority. The proceedings were commenced in the name of the group without naming any of its members as parties and without complying with r.19.6. At the trial, in order to regularise the proceedings, the trial judge ordered that one member of the group, Ms Williams, be substituted as claimant. The defendants' appeal against that order was dismissed (see [28] to [31]).

The death of a potential claimant is not covered by r.19.8

Add to the end of the first paragraph:

Milburn-Snell was followed by a differently constituted Court of Appeal in *Bank of Scotland v Hussain* [2012] EWCA Civ 264 (noted in para.19.8.3, below). **19.8.2**

Claims by or against a company which has been dissolved or struck off

Replace (where the citation for Steans Fashions Ltd v Legal & General Assuraqnce Society Ltd has changed) with:

19.8.4   If it is discovered, after proceedings have been commenced, that a company named as a party has been dissolved or struck off the Companies Register, the court has a discretion to stay the proceedings pending an application to the Companies Court for the restoration of the company to the Register under (what is now) s.1029 of the Companies Act 2006 (*Steans Fashions Ltd v Legal & General Assurance Society Ltd* [1995] 1 B.C.L.C. 332). Section 1032 of the Act provides that an order of restoration may (according to its terms) retrospectively validate any claim which was purportedly commenced by the company after it had been dissolved or struck off (*Joddrell v Peaktone Ltd* [2012] EWCA Civ 1035; [2013] 1 All E.R.13).

Claim form and application for permission to continue

Replace the third paragraph (where the citation for Hook v Sumner has been changed) with:

19.9A.1   An applicant for permission under s.261 has to establish a prima facie case for the giving of permission to bring the claim in respect of a cause of action which arises from some negligence, default, breach of duty or breach of trust by a director of the company in whom that cause of action is vested. As to the meaning of the term "prima facie" in this context, see *Bhullar v Bhullar* [2015] EWHC 1943 (Ch). In deciding whether to grant permission the court must consider a range of factors including the strength of the claim and the amounts or value at stake (*Stainer v Lee* [2010] EWHC 1539 (Ch); [2011] B.C.C. 134). Normally a company should be the only party entitled to enforce a cause of action belonging to it, and that a member should only be able to maintain proceedings in relation to alleged wrongs done to the company only in exceptional circumstances (*Bamford v Harvey* [2012] EWHC 2858 (Ch); [2013] Bus. L.R. 589; *Cinematic Finance Ltd v Ryder* [2010] EWHC 3387 (Ch); [2012] B.C.C. 797). The availability of an alternative remedy is an important factor for the court to consider, but it was not an absolute bar to a grant of permission; the possibility of an alternative remedy did not mean that it was inevitable that a person seeking a derivative action would be denied permission (*Hughes v Weiss* op cit; *Parry v Bartlett* [2011] EWHC 3146 (Ch); [2012] B.C.C. 700 (bringing an "unfair prejudice" petition under Companies Act 2006, s.994 was inappropriate where the company was not trading and its shares had no value); *Cullen Investments Ltd v Brown* [2015] EWHC 473 (Ch) (Mark Anderson QC) (derivative action sought as a precautionary response to the defendant's defence in a personal action which denied that he owed relevant duties to anyone other than the company); *Hook v Sumner* [2015] EWHC 3820 (Ch), 27 November 2015, QB, HH Judge David Cooke (the claimant was entitled not to proceed by way of an unfair prejudice petition because he did not want his shares to be bought out by the majority).

III.   Group Litigation

Note

Add new paragraph at end:

19.10.1   In *Schmidt v Depuy International Ltd* [2016] EWHC 638 (QB) the court declined to make a GLO in a number of product liability claims against the same manufacturer, even though it accepted that there were common or related issues of fact and law and a large enough group of claimants, because it concluded that the claims within the group, when subjected to scrutiny, were atypical, would not benefit from a GLO, and were not likely to be informative to the court in respect of other GLOs made in respect of other manufacturers of similar products.

Editorial note

Replace the fifth paragraph (where the citation for T (formerly H) v Nugent Care Society (formerly Catholic Social Services) has changed) with:

19.13.1   Subsection (e): cut-off dates only limit entry to the group litigation. They have no bearing on limitation and do not preclude an individual from seeking the court's permission to join the group at a later date or to issue separate proceedings (subject to the overriding objective and proportionality). See *T (formerly H) v Nugent Care Society (formerly Catholic Social Services)* [2004] EWCA Civ 51; [2004] 1 W.L.R. 1129.

Add new paragraph at end:

In *Pearce v Secretary of State for Energy and Climate Change* [2015] EWHC 3775 (QB) Turner J extended a cut off date but observed that cut off dates were essential in GLOs to secure the good case management of the claims within its scope. The parties depend upon some level of certainty as to the cut off date in order to decide how to deploy their resources and when. Accordingly extensions to the cut off date should not be regarded as the norm. However if a mechanistic approach were taken whereby the cut off date were to regarded as sacrosanct, there is a risk that unexpected developments may give rise to a situation such as in the instant case, an accumulation of residual applications by claimants who had not met the cut off date, which would have the potential to further disrupt the progress of the GLO. Those competing matters had to be balanced.

PRACTICE DIRECTION 19B—GROUP LITIGATION

Add new paragraph 19BPD.24.2:
For a decision in relation to costs budgeting in multiple party cases which is relevant to GLO **19BPD.24.2**
Litigation see *Various Claimants v Ministry of Defence (Iraqi Civilian Litigation)* [2016] EWHC 1221 (QB).

PART 20

COUNTERCLAIMS AND OTHER ADDITIONAL CLAIMS

Add new paragraph 20.6.1:

Claim by defendant against co-defendant
It would not be right to permit a defendant (D1) to commence a claim for contribution against **20.6.1**
co-defendant (D2) when neither D1 nor the claimant is currently making a factual case against D2 which, if proved, would potentially entitle D1 to recover contribution from him. For D1 to commence proceedings under Part 20 in these circumstances would be an improper use of the court's process, in the same way as it is an abuse of process for a claimant to commence or continue proceedings which the claimant has no present intention of pursuing (*Kazakhstan Kagazy Plc v Zhunus* [2016] EWHC 1048 (Comm); [2016] 4 W.L.R. 86 (Leggatt J) at para. 40).

PART 21

CHILDREN AND PROTECTED PARTIES

Effect of rule

Add new paragraph at end:
In *R. (C) v Secretary of State for Justice* [2016] UKSC 2; [2016] 1 W.L.R. 444, the Supreme Court **21.10.2**
stated that it is necessary to draw a distinction between ordinary civil proceedings in which a mental patient may be involved (not always as a protected party), and proceedings relating to a patient detained in a psychiatric hospital, or otherwise subject to compulsory powers, under the Mental Health Act 1983. The Supreme Court held that there should be no presumption of anonymity in every case in proceedings concerning powers under the 1983 Act. The question in all these cases is that set out in r.39.2(4): is anonymity necessary in the interests of the mental patient? A balance has to be struck to be struck between the public's right to know and who the principal actors are. An anonymity order should be made if in the absence of such an order the therapeutic enterprise involving the patient might be put in jeopardy.

PART 22

STATEMENTS OF TRUTH

Form of statement of truth

To the end of the last paragraph, add:
The definition of "budget" in the CPR Glossary was added by the Civil Procedure (Amendment) **22.1.16**
Rules 2013 (SI 2013/262) r.21(a) with effect from 1 April 2013, and para.2.2A was inserted in Practice Direction 22 by Update 60, with effect from the same date. The form of words in para.2.2A was substituted by Update 69 with effect from 22 April 2014, but the definition of "budget" in the Glossary was not amended in the light of this substitution. The result is that the Glossary definition is misleading.

PART 23

GENERAL RULES ABOUT APPLICATIONS FOR COURT ORDERS

Application "totally without merit"

Replace the third paragraph with:

23.12.2   Under r.23.12, consideration by the court of the question whether it is appropriate to make a civil restraint order (CRO) is triggered by a finding that the application was totally without merit (TWM). The least severe of the several forms of CRO may not be made unless at least two applications made by the party have been found to be TWM. The questions (1) whether the court should record a finding of TWM and (2) whether it is appropriate to make a CRO are distinct and raise different considerations. In *R. (Grace) v Secretary of State for the Home Department* [2014] EWCA Civ 1091, [2014] 1 W.L.R. 3432, CA, a High Court judge on paper dealt with and dismissed an application under r.54.4 for permission to proceed with a judicial review claim and, in accordance with r.23.12(a), recorded the fact that the application was totally without merit with the result that, by operation of r.54.12(7), the applicant was barred from requesting that the dismissal of the application be re-considered at a hearing. (No question of whether it was appropriate to make a CRO arose.) The Court of Appeal held that, in these circumstances, the proper test for determining whether an application is totally without merit was whether it was "bound to fail"; it was not necessary for it to be shown that the application was abusive or vexatious. Subsequently, in *R. (Wasif) v Secretary of State for the Home Department* [2016] EWCA Civ 82, 9 February 2016, CA, unrep., the Court recognised the continuing difficulty about the proper approach to be taken by the High Court or the Upper Tribunal in considering whether to certify an application for permission to apply for judicial review as TWM and gave further guidance (see further para.3.4.10 above and para.54.12.1 below).

PART 24

SUMMARY JUDGMENT

Forms

24.0.3 *Replace list with:*
- **N244** Application notice
- **No.44** Judgment under Pt 24
- **No.48** Judgment after decision of preliminary issue
- **PF11** Application for Pt 24 judgment (whole claim)
- **PF12** Application for Pt 24 judgment (one or some of several claims)
- **PF13** Order under Pt 24 (No.1)
- **PF14** Order under Pt 24 (No.2)
- **PF15** Order under Pt 24 (for assessment of solicitor's bill of costs) (Pt 48)

A conditional order

After "so (see para.4.", replace "3" with:

24.6.6   4

Add new paragraph at end:

The court's power to make a conditional order on a summary judgment application is not limited to cases in which the respondent raises a case (claim or defence) as to which success, although possible, is improbable. In *Deutsche Bank AG v Unitech Global Ltd* [2016] EWCA Civ 119, 3 March 2016, CA, unrep., summary judgment had been sought in respect of a loan agreement; the defendants, challenging the validity of that agreement, sought an order for rescission which, if granted, would inevitably be on terms that they must refund to the claimants the original sums borrowed. In those circumstances the Court of Appeal held that the lower court could have made a conditional order even though the defendant's case for rescission could not be said to have been improbable. The Court of Appeal held that paragraphs 4 and 5 of Practice Direction 24 are not exhaustive of the court's options as to the orders it may make on an application for summary judgment; the relevant power to impose conditions, as to payments into court or otherwise, is not found in Part 24, but is contained in r.3.1(3) (referred to in the parenthesis following r.24.6). See further para.3.1.4 above.

Setting aside order for summary judgment

Replace the first paragraph with:

24.6.8 The orders the court may make on an application for summary judgment include: (1) judgment on the claim, (2) the striking out or dismissal of the claim, (3) the dismissal of the application, (4) a conditional order (Practice Direction (The Summary Disposal of Claims), para.5.1; see para.24PD.5 below). Where the applicant or any respondent to an application for summary judgment fails to attend the hearing of the application, the court may proceed in their absence. Where, in the absence of the applicant or any respondent, an order is made at the hearing, r.23.11 would appear to have the effect of enabling the court on the application of the absent party (or of its own initiative) to re-list the application for further consideration. However if, at the hearing of the application, the court gives summary judgment against the absent party, the question which then arises is whether that party may apply to the court to have the judgment set aside or varied. Under the former summary judgment rules contained in the RSC (and applied in county courts by operation of CCR Ord.9 r.14(5)), it was expressly provided that any judgment given against a party who did not appear at the hearing of an application for summary judgment could be set aside or varied by the court on such terms as it thought just (RSC Ord.14 r.11, see also RSC Ord.86 r.7). The purpose of this rule was to reverse the effect of the decision of the Court of Appeal in *Spira v Spira* [1939] 3 All E.R. 924, CA, and to remove the anomaly that, although every other judgment (including a judgment at trial) given in the absence of a defendant could be set aside (at least in certain circumstances), a summary judgment could not, though it could be made the subject of an appeal. CPR Pt 24 contains no such express provision and the omission is not made good by CPR r.39.3(3), as it is confined to the setting aside of a judgment given at trial in the absence of a party (see further para.39.3.8 below). Further, the matter is not dealt with by r.23.11, which is confined to orders made on applications (including, as suggested above, orders made on summary judgment applications other than summary judgment, e.g. conditional orders.) However, it seems to be readily assumed that the position is retrieved by Practice Direction (Summary Disposal of Claims), para.8.1 which states that, if an order for summary judgment under Pt 24 is made against a respondent who does not appear at the hearing of the application, the respondent may apply "for the order to be set aside or varied" (see para.24PD.8 below). In this context "order" includes judgment on the claim (ibid., para.5.1(1)). On the hearing of an application the court "may make such order as it thinks just" (ibid., para.8.2). It is not always easy to tell whether particular paragraphs in practice directions supplementing CPR rules are attempting (1) merely to narrate what the rules they are supplementing say, or (2) to put an authoritative gloss on those rules. In *Tubelike Ltd v Visitjourneys.com Ltd* [2016] EWHC 43 (Ch), 22 January 2016, unrep. (Chief Master Marsh), it was stated that, although the matter is not entirely free from doubt, para.8.1 of Practice Direction 24 is intended to supplement the rules in Part 24 and to give the court a power it would not otherwise have if an order is made in the absence of a party (para.20).

After the first paragraph (beginning with "The orders the") add:

Other CPR provisions permitting applications to set aside or vary judgments given in the applicant's absence set out the criteria which the court must apply (e.g., r.3.6(2) (application must be made promptly) and r.39.3(5) (application must be made promptly, good reason shown for absence and reasonable prospects of success) and see also the *Mitchell/Denton* criteria in applications under r.3.9 and r.13.3). PD 24 does not provide any guidance about the criteria the court should apply in applications under para 8.1. In *Tubelike Ltd v Visitjourneys.com Ltd* (see above), Chief Master Marsh considered that an application under para.8.1 was analogous to an application under r.39.3 (failure to attend the trial) and so had regard to the r.39.3(5) factors (summarised above) "without being a slave to the requirements of that rule" and to the provisions of the overriding objective (r.1.1, above).

Replace "See further paras 39.3.8 and 40.9.2." with:

See further paras 3.1.9.2 (above) and 39.3.8 and 40.9.2 (below).

PART 25

INTERIM REMEDIES AND SECURITY FOR COSTS

I. Interim Remedies

Interim injunction (r.25.1(1)(a))

Add new paragraph 25.1.12.6.1:

25.1.12.6.1 *Notification injunctions*—The High Court has power under the Senior Courts Act 1981 s.37(1) to make an order for, what may be called a "notification injunction", that is to say a free-standing order not ancillary to another order (such as a freezing injunction) requiring the defendant to notify the claimant prior to (or shortly after) entering into a transaction by which property is disposed of (*Holyoake v Candy* [2016] EWHC 970 (Ch); [2016] 3 W.L.R. 357 (Nugee J)). The purpose is that, if such a transaction may seriously damage the claimant's position, a freezing order can be applied for. This is a less invasive interference with the defendant's rights than a freezing order (presumably with a less onerous potential liability under the cross-undertaking in damages). The claimant needs to establish a "good arguable case" (the test being the same as for a freezing order), and to assert some substantive right to prevent the defendant disposing of an asset, or some credible evidence of a threatened dissipation such as would justify a freezing injunction (ibid).

The return date and subsequent consideration by the court

After the first paragraph, add new paragraph:

25.1.12.8   Good practice requires that, at a return date hearing, the applicant should draw to the attention of the court and the respondent the respects (if any) in which the draft order prepared by them differs from the original order made without notice (*JSC BTA Bank v Ablyazov* [2009] EWHC 3267 (Comm); [2010] 1 All E.R. (Comm) 1040 (Teare J)).

Undertaking by defendant in lieu of injunction

Add new paragraph at end:

25.1.14.1   In *Montvale Invest Ltd v Terra Raf Trans Traiding Ltd* [2015] EWHC 3710 (Ch), 21 December 2015, unrep. (Chief Master Marsh), upon the claimant (C) proposing before proceedings were commenced to apply for a freezing order, the defendant (D) gave an undertaking. The undertaking did not contain any express provision which permitted review or variation and there was no lesser formulation such as that the undertaking was given "until further order". After proceedings had been commenced D applied to the court for a variation of the undertaking. The Chief Master noted that none of the authorities concerning the circumstances in which the court could vary an undertaking given in lieu of a freezing order dealt with an undertaking which had been given before the issue of proceedings, but held that the court had jurisdiction to entertain D's application as it would be surprising if the court is unable, whatever the circumstances, to modify or discharge a purely contractual undertaking given in connection with proposed proceedings merely because the undertaking was given prior to the commencement of the claim, or the issuing of the application which the undertaking was intended to obviate. The jurisdiction arises where there is "good cause" which makes the continuation of the undertaking unnecessary, oppressive or unjust, and will be exercised sparingly.

Orders in relation to relevant property (r.25.1(1)(c))

Inspection of relevant property (r.25.1(1)(c)(ii))

Add new paragraph at end:

25.1.18   The powers of the court under sub-para.(ii) of r.25.1(1)(c), and also under sub-paras (i) and (iv), were exercised in *Orb arl v Ruhan* [2015] EWHC 3638 (Comm), December 14, 2015, unrep. (Walker J). The circumstances were unusual. It was alleged that a computer hacker, having been employed to "drop" child pornography onto the computer system of the claimants for the purpose of causing injury to them, and to prejudice the fair trial of ongoing proceedings, was now offering the same materials to the claimants in return for a cash payment. The claimants wished to inspect the materials, but were concerned that to have or to access such materials would of itself be a criminal offence. The Court authorised the claimants, their lawyers and their computer experts to take custody of, preserve, inspect and experiment upon the specified materials including by inter-rogating the data, making appropriate reports to the police and prosecuting authorities.

Freezing injunction (formerly Mareva injunction) (r.25.1(1)(f))

Applicant's duties

25.1.25.4   *Delete the penultimate paragraph (beginning with "Good practice requires").*

Evidence

In the seventh paragraph (beginning "Where the respondent"), after "[2012] I.L.Pr. 15 (at paras 163 to 167).", add:

25.1.25.5   If the defendant's assets are held in a complex, opaque and offshore structure, that is not of itself sufficient to infer a risk of dissipation, but it is capable of being regarded as contributing to the risk if there is other material on which to infer such a risk (*Holyoake v Candy* [2016] EWHC 970 (Ch); [2016] 3 W.L.R. 357 (Nugee J), at para.27).

Example of order to restrain disposal of assets

Replace the first paragraph with:
The example of an order for a freezing injunction annexed to Practice Direction 25A (Interim **25.1.25.6**
Injunctions) (see para.25APD.10 below) may be adapted for either worldwide or domestic relief.
The content of the example may be modified as appropriate in any case. Any departure from the
standard wording must be drawn to the attention of the judge hearing the without notice
application. It is expressly provided that the court may, if it considers it appropriate, require the
applicant's solicitors, as well as the applicant, to give undertakings (ibid. paras 6.1 and 6.2). The
examples, modified in certain respects, are also contained in App.5 to the Admiralty and Commercial Courts Guide (see Vol.2, para.2A-162).

Varying, clarifying or revoking order

In the first paragraph, replace "para.25PFD.10" with:
see para.25APD.10. **25.1.25.9**

Order to provide information about property or assets (r.25.1(1)(g))

To the end of the penultimate paragraph, before the fullstop, add:
, and in *Orb A.R.L. v Fiddler* [2016] EWHC 361 (Comm), 26 February 2016, unrep. (Popplewell **25.1.26**
J) at paras 82 to 90 (where held that applicant was seeking order for illegitimate purpose)

Search order (formerly Anton Piller order) (r.25.1(1)(h))

Jurisdiction—county courts

After "High Court judge", add:
or a judge of the Court of Appeal **25.1.27.2**

Applicant's disclosure duties where application made without notice

To the end of the second paragraph (beginning with "It is well-established"), add:
The duty to make full and frank disclosure, and the principles which apply, on a without notice **25.3.5**
application were explained in detail in *Orb A.R.L. v Fiddler* [2016] EWHC 361 (Comm), 26 February 2016, unrep. (Popplewell J) at para.36, where a Norwich Pharmacal order was discharged for
serious failures of the duty of sufficient gravity to require that it should not be re-granted, even
were there otherwise merit in making the order.

Discharge of injunction for material non-disclosure

Replace the third paragraph with:
In deciding what should be the consequences of any breach of duty it is necessary for the court **25.3.6**
to take account of all the relevant circumstances, including the gravity of the breach, the excuse or
explanation offered, and the severity and duration of the prejudice occasioned to the defendant,
including whether the consequences of the breach were remediable and had been remedied; above
all, the court has to bear in mind the overriding objective and the need for proportionality (see
r.1.1) (*Memory Corporation Plc v Sidhu (No.2)* [2000] 1 W.L.R. 1443, CA). Although discharge of the
order is not automatic on any non-disclosure being established of any fact known to the applicant
which is found by the court to have been material, it would only be in exceptional circumstances
that a court would not discharge an order where there had been deliberate non-disclosure or
misrepresentation (*Congentra AG v Sixteen Thirteen Marine S.A.* [2008] EWHC 1615 (Comm); [2008]
2 Lloyd's Rep. 602 (Flaux J), at para.62). Further, whilst it is no answer to a complaint of non-
disclosure to say that even if the relevant matters had been placed before the court, the result
would have been the same, that is a relevant consideration in the exercise of the court's discretion
(ibid). For summary of the authorities on the exercise of the court's discretion to continue or re-
grant the order, notwithstanding serious non-disclosure, see *Alphasteel Ltd v Shirkhani* [2009]
EWHC 2153 (Ch), July 30, 2009, unrep (Teare J.) (where the freezing order was limited to assets
within the jurisdiction). The principles about how the court should respond to a breach of the duties of an ex parte applicant were examined in *Dar Al Arkan Real Estate Development Co v Al Refai*
[2012] EWHC 3539 (Comm), 12 December 2012, unrep. (Andrew Smith J) at paras 148 & 149. See
also *Metropolitan Housing Trust v Taylor* [2015] EWHC 2897 (Ch), 19 October 2015, unrep. (Warren
J) at paras 36 & 37.

Effect of rule

Replace the first paragraph with:
For extended commentary on interim payments, see Vol.2, Section 15 Interim Remedies, **25.6.1**
subs.E, paras 15-99 to 15-132.

Replace the fourth paragraph with:
Contrary to what is said in this rule, "interim payment" is not defined by r.25.1(1)(k). That paragraph merely repeats part of the definition of interim payment given by the Senior Courts Act 1981 s.32(5) and leaves out the final phrase "to or for the benefit of another party to the proceedings" (cf. RSC Ord.29 r.9), a part of the definition that was crucial to the decision in *Securities and Investments Board v Scandex Capital Management A/S* [1998] 1 W.L.R. 712; [1998] 1 All E.R. 514, CA. In *Deutsche Bank AG v Unitech Global Ltd* [2016] EWCA Civ 119, 3 March 2016, CA, unrep., the Court of Appeal explained that section 32 only sets out a rule-making power in respect of orders for interim payments, and that it is r.25.1(1)(k) which provides the jurisdiction for the court to make such an order.

Evidence

Add new paragraph at end:

25.6.4   An application for an interim payment order must be decided by the court on the basis of the evidence before it; see further Vol.2 para.15-101.

Effect of rule

In the second paragraph, after "for further information", add:

25.7.1   as to the test to be applied

II.   Security for costs

Amount of security

Replace the first paragraph with:

25.12.7   The amount of security awarded is in the discretion of the court, which will fix such sums as it thinks just, having regard to all the circumstances of the case (r.25.13(1)(a)). The court's exercise of that discretion is quintessentially a matter of case management with which an appeal court should be slow to interfere (*Stokors SA v IG Markets Ltd* [2012] EWCA Civ 1706). In some cases the amount of security may be limited to the extra burden or risk involved in seeking to enforce orders for costs subsequently obtained (see further, para.25.13.5). In other cases the amount of security may relate to the total costs likely to be incurred in opposing the claim or appeal. In cases in which a costs management order has been made (as to which, see para.3.12.1, above) the defendant's approved or agreed costs budget will be a strong guide as to the likely costs order to be made after trial, if the claim fails; this budget should be used as the relevant reference point (in relation to the incurred costs elements and also the estimated costs elements) for considering the amount which should be ordered for security for costs (*Sarpd Oil International Ltd v Addax Energy SA* [2016] EWCA Civ 120; [2016] C.P.Rep 24). Security is not always awarded on a full indemnity basis. If the application is made late, security may be limited to future costs only or refused altogether (and see further, para.25.12.6 "Ideal time for applying", above). In other cases one of the factors for the court to consider is the possibility that the proceedings may soon settle. In such a situation it may be sensible to make an arbitrary discount of the costs estimated as likely future costs, but there is no hard and fast rule. Each case has to be decided on its own circumstances, and it may not always be appropriate to make such a discount. For a pre-CPR authority on this point, see *Procon (Great Britain) Ltd v Provincial Building Co Ltd* [1984] 1 W.L.R. 557, [1984] 2 All E.R. 368, CA. However, today, a frequently preferred alternative to discounting is for the court to order security for the whole costs, to be paid in instalments as the action progresses.

Replace the second paragraph with:
The amount of security allowed often takes into account costs incurred in complying with a pre-action protocol. However, as to the costs of a failed mediation incurred pre-action, see *Lobster Group Ltd v Heidelberg Graphic Equipment Ltd* [2008] EWHC 413 (TCC); [2008] 2 All E.R. 1173. If as a result of the claim the defendant commences third party proceedings (an "additional claim" as to which, see para.20.7, above) and it is likely that, if the claim fails, the claimant will also be required to pay all the costs of the third party proceedings, the amount of security to be awarded may also take into account all such costs incurred or to be incurred by the defendant and by the third party (*Sarpd Oil International Ltd v Addax Energy SA* [2016] EWCA Civ 120; [2016] C.P.Rep 24).

Subsequent applications concerning security for costs

After the fourth paragraph (beginning with "Once an order"), add new paragraph:

25.12.11   An order providing for additional security may be made even after judgment at trial has been given (*Excalibur Ventures LLC v Gulf Keystone Inc* [2013] EWHC 4278 (Comm); *Republic of Djibouti v Boreh* [2016] EWHC 1035 (Comm); in each case the significant and relevant change justifying such an order was a decision to award costs against the claimant on the indemnity basis). In calculating the amount of a post-judgment increase, the court may take into account any interest on costs awarded and also the likely costs of detailed assessment proceedings (*Excalibur*). A post-judgment order for security may lack an appropriate sanction if it is not complied with. This led the court in

Dar International FEF Co v Aon Ltd [2003] EWCA Civ 1833; [2004] 1 W.L.R. 1395 (noted below) to exercise its discretion to refuse to make the order sought in that case. In other cases, there may be some indirect method of enforcement which is appropriate; for example, sanctions in respect of further proceedings in the action (*Republic of Djibouti*) or an order giving the defendants leave to join persons funding the claimant for the purpose of seeking a non-party costs order against them (*Excalibur*). Another possibility is that, instead of ordering further security, the court may order the claimant to pay the appropriate increase as an interim payment of costs, such payment to be made in addition to the sums already paid or secured in the proceedings. If the court also grants an extension of time for the commencement of detailed assessment proceedings, the defendants may seek to enforce the interim payment order before they have incurred significant expense in the detailed assessment proceedings.

Discretionary power to order security for costs

After the third paragraph (beginning with "In considering an"), add new paragraph:

An order for security for costs is intended to give a measure of protection to defendants who are **25.13.1** put to the cost of defending themselves against claims made by persons to whom one or more of the conditions set out in r.25.13(2) applies. Although the making of such an order is discretionary, it is unlikely to be refused on the basis that the defendants in question are wealthy enough to survive without such protection, or are protected by some other means, such as a right of indemnity against a third person (*LIC Telecommunications Sarl v VTB Capital Plc, (QB)* HH Judge Waksman QC 14 July 2016, unrep.).

PART 26

CASE MANAGEMENT—PRELIMINARY STAGE

Replace r.26.2A with:

Transfer of money claims within the County Court[1]

26.2A—(1)   This rule applies where the claim is for an amount of money 26.2A in the County Court, specified or unspecified.

(2)   If at any time a court officer considers that the claim should be referred to a judge for directions, the court officer may send the proceedings to the defendant's home court or the preferred hearing centre or other County Court hearing centre as may be appropriate.

(3)   Subject to paragraphs (5) and (5A), if the defendant is an individual and the claim is for a specified sum of money, at the relevant time the claim must be sent to the defendant's home court (save that where there are two or more defendants, one or more of whom are individuals, the claim must be sent to the home court of the defendant who first files their defence).

(4)   Subject to paragraphs (5) and (5A), in any other claim to which this rule applies, the court must, at the relevant time, send the claim to the preferred hearing centre.

(5)   Subject to paragraph (5A), if, on their directions questionnaire—

(a)   a defendant under paragraph (3) has specified a hearing centre other than the defendant's home court; or

(b)   a claimant under paragraph (4) has specified a hearing centre other than the preferred hearing centre,

the claim must be sent to that other hearing centre.

(5A)   At the relevant time, the claim must be sent to the County Court at Central London if—

---

[1] Amended by the Civil Procedure (Amendment) Rules 2013 (SI 2013/262), the Civil Procedure (Amendment) Rules 2014 (SI 2014/407), the Civil Procedure (Amendment No.4) Rules 2014 (SI 2014/867), the Civil Procedure (Amendment No.5) Rules 2015 (SI 2015/1881), the Civil Procedure (Amendment No.3) Rules 2016 (SI 2016/788), and the Civil Procedure (Amendment No.3) Rules 2016 (SI 2016/788).

(a)   the claim is started at the County Court Business Centre or the County Court Money Claims Centre;

(b)   a court officer provisionally decides, pursuant to rule 26.3, that the track which appears to be most suitable for the claim is the multi-track; and

(c)   either—

(i)   in respect of a defendant under paragraphs (3) and (5)(a), the home court (or the home court of the defendant who first files their defence) or the hearing centre specified on the directions questionnaire; or

(ii)   in respect of a claimant under paragraphs (4) and (5)(b), the preferred hearing centre or the hearing centre specified on the directions questionnaire,

is one of the hearing centres listed in Practice Direction 26 at paragraph 10.4.".

(6)   The relevant time for the purposes of this rule is when—

(a)   all parties have filed their directions questionnaires;

(b)   any stay ordered by the court or period to attempt settlement through mediation has expired; or

(c)   if the claim falls within Practice Direction 7D—

(i)   the defence is filed; or

(ii)   enforcement of a default judgment other than by a warrant of control is requested,

whichever occurs first.

Effect of rule

After the second paragraph (beginning with "The "relevant time" for claims"), add new paragraph:

26.2A.3   Para.(6) was added to this rule (and consequential amendments made to paras (3), (4) and (5)) by r.6 of the Civil Procedure (Amendment No.3) Rules 2016 (SI 2016/788) and took effect on 3 October 2016. Para.(6) provides that multi-track cases issued or sent to the "London Group" of County Court hearing centres should be automatically transferred directly to the County Court at Central London (which is the Civil Trial Centre for all such cases). This puts on a formal basis a transfer procedure tested in a pilot scheme, that is Practice Direction 51I (The County Court at Central London Multi-Track Pilot Scheme) (see para.51.2.11). By operation of other paragraphs in r.26.2A, a case issued in the County Court Money Claims Centre or by the online process at the County Court Business Centre is transferred to a local hearing centre when, and if, a case is defended and a trial for determination of the claim is required. At the end of the case management process and once the matter is ready for trial the case will either remain at the local hearing centre or be transferred to the appropriate hearing centre for trial. The procedure stated in para.(6) is designed to reduce delays between transfer to the local hearing centre and resolution of the matter at a trial centre for higher value claims initially sent to London hearing centres.

Delete paragraph 26.2A.4 "County Court at Central London Multi-Track Pilot Scheme".

26.11.1   *Change title of paragraph:*

Effect of rule

Replace with:

By the Civil Procedure (Amendment No.8) Rules 2013 (SI 2013/3112), r.26.11 was substituted with effect from 1 January 2014. The former rule required an application for a claim to be tried by a jury to be made within 28 days of service of the defence. That rule is preserved by para.(1) of the rule as replaced for a claim other than a claim for libel and slander, for which different provision is made in para.(2); see further Vol.2 para.9A-258.

26.11.2   *Change title of paragraph:*

Senior Courts Act 1981 s.69 and County Courts Act 1984 s.66

PART 29

The Multi-track

Fixing the trial date

In the fourth paragraph (beginning with "The Queen's Bench Guide"), replace "once affixed date" with:
once a fixed date

29.2.6

PART 31

Disclosure and Inspection of Documents

(c)   Legal Professional Privilege generally

Use of an independent lawyer to review seized material

Replace with:
Where a search is undertaken pursuant to a search warrant, an independent lawyer should be **31.3.30.2**
present to assess claims made for legal professional privilege: *R. v Customs and Excise Commissioners Ex p. Popely* [1999] S.T.C. 1016; *R. v Middlesex Guildhall Crown Court ex p. Tamosius* [2000] 1 W.L.R. 453. There is a range of guidance covering the process of determining the status of potentially privileged documents, including the Attorney General's Guidelines on Disclosure (2013), Attorney General's Supplementary Guidelines on Digitally Stored Material (2011), and the Serious Fraud Office's Operational Handbook. An independent lawyer should be used to determine whether seized material is protected by legal professional privilege, as this involves close consideration of the content and context of a document or communication. However that does not mean that an independent lawyer must, as a matter of law, be used for the preliminary sift of paper or electronic material, identifying documents, files or communications as potentially attracting legal professional privilege, but without close consideration of the content and context: *R. (McKenzie) v Director of the Serious Fraud Office* [2016] EWHC 102 (Admin); [2016] 1 W.L.R. 1308, D.C. para.40. The latter case also upheld the legality of the guidance in the Serious Fraud Office's Operational Handbook.

Limiting standard disclosure

Add new paragraphs at end:
In *Illumina Inc v Premaitha Health Plc* [2016] EWHC 1516 (Pat) standard disclosure going back a **31.5.4**
further 14 years was not ordered, where disclosure going back four years had previously been ordered, and had led to costs of £200,000 being incurred, to no benefit. It was necessary in patent cases to conduct a proper cost-benefit analysis before ordering disclosure.
In *Positec Power Tools (Europe) Ltd v Husqvarna AB* [2016] EWHC 1061 (Pat) standard disclosure was not ordered relating to an issue where the likely probative value of what would be produced from that exercise would not be worth the cost.

Disclosure of electronic data

Add new paragraph at end:
In *Pyrrho Investments Ltd v MWB Property Ltd* [2016] EWHC 256 (Ch) it was held that predictive **31.6.5**
coding may be ordered in an electronic disclosure process. Nothing in the CPR or Practice Directions prohibited use of such software. There were cases where a full manual review would be "unreasonable" within CPR PD 31B para.25. The use of predictive coding promoted the overriding objective and was appropriate in the instant case.

Supplemental list

Add new paragraph at end:
In *McTear v Engelhard* [2016] EWCA Civ 487; [2016] 4 W.L.R. 108 the ongoing duty to disclose **31.11.1**
r.31.11 was relevant in considering the extent to which documents found after the expiry of the disclosure order could be used, albeit that the ongoing duty did not excuse a breach of the order. When considering the use of documents discovered after the expiry of a disclosure order, the court should consider subsequent applications for an extension of time and relief from sanctions separately.

"... under any Act for disclosure before proceedings have started"

Replace the sixth paragraph with:

31.16.1   Applications for pre-action disclosure pursuant to s.33(2) of the Senior Courts Act 1981 and CPR r.31.16 must be made prior to the commencement of proceedings, as the court does not have jurisdiction to make such an order once proceedings have been issued: *Personal Management Solutions Ltd v Gee 7 Group Wealth Limited* [2015] EWHC 3859 (Ch), paras 14-18. However pre-action disclosure under CPR r.31.16 may be ordered even where there already are other extant proceedings covering related issues, where the pre-action disclosure relates to some different causes of action not raised in the extant proceedings: *Anglia Research Services Ltd v Finders Genealogists Ltd* [2016] EWHC 297 (QB).

Rule 31.16(3)(a), (b) and (d)

After the sixth paragraph (beginning with "In Black v Sumimoto"), add as a new paragraph:

31.16.4   In *Ittihadleh v Metcalfe* [2016] EWHC 376 (Ch) the Court exercised its discretion to refuse pre-action disclosure as the parties had entrenched such positions of hostility towards each other that the prospects of any disclosure, whatever it might reveal, enabling the dispute to be resolved without proceedings, was negligible and probably non-existent, and thus even though the disclosure sought was not unduly onerous, the remaining factors all weighed heavily and determinatively against making such an order.

Note

Replace the last paragraph with:

31.20.1   Permission of the court is still required even where an inadvertently disclosed document indicates that there might have been serious non-disclosure of relevant documents by a party: *Property Alliance Group Ltd v The Royal Bank of Scotland Plc* [2015] EWHC 3341 (Ch); [2016] 4 W.L.R. 3 (Birss J).

Subsequent use of disclosed documents

Add new paragraph at end:

31.22.1   In *Chodiev v Stein* [2016] EWHC 1210 (Comm) an order under r.31.22(2) restricting the use of documents obtained through disclosure was not made where those documents had been referred to at a public hearing. The presumption in favour of open justice was not displaced by the generally private and confidential nature of the documents. Any restrictions on the use of documents obtained through disclosure could only be made in the public interest and not in the interests of the litigants. The wording of r.31.22 did not limit the range of applicants for an order restricting the use of a disclosed document. There was no reason why such an application should not be made where the disclosing party had obtained the document from a third party. The court retained an inherent jurisdiction to make an order where it was in the interests of justice to do so.

PART 32

EVIDENCE

Video evidence

Replace with:

32.1.4.1   A party wishing to adduce film or video evidence to attack an opponent's case is subject to all the rules as to disclosure and inspection of documents contained in Pt 31. In the interests of case management, and in discharge of the duty arising under r.1.3, the party should raise the matter with the procedural judge at the first practicable opportunity (see also para.2.7). In exercise of their powers to control evidence at trial (r.32.1) it may be appropriate for a judge to give directions requiring a party to give notice in advance of those parts of the video footage relied on (*Rall v Hume* [2001] EWCA Civ 146; [2001] 3 All E.R. 248, CA). In a personal injuries case, where video evidence is available which, according to the defendant, undermines the case of the claimant to an extent that it would substantially reduce the award of damages, it will usually be in the overall interests of justice to require that the proponent should be permitted to cross-examine the claimant and their expert advisers upon it (ibid.). See also *Jones v University of Warwick* [2003] EWCA Civ 151; [2003] 1 W.L.R. 954, CA. For examples of the application of the relevant principles in personal injury cases, see *O'Leary v Tunnelcraft Ltd* [2009] EWHC 3438 (QB), November 10, 2011, unrep. (Swift J.) (defendant's application for permission to adduce surveillance film and photograph evidence refused where made month before trial and amounted to an "ambush"); *Douglas v O'Neill* [2011] EWHC 601 (QB); Unreported 9 February 2011. (Judge Andrew Collender QC) (defendant's application for permission to adduce DVD surveillance evidence allowed where, though made shortly before trial, disclosed at first reasonable opportunity after claimant had produced signed witness statement); *Hayden v Maidstone and Tunbridge Wells NHS Trust* [2016] EWHC 1121 (QB), 12 May 2016, unrep. (Foskett J) (observations on fair practice where late deployment of surveillance evidence by defendant in personal injury claim).

Exclusion of witnesses from the court

Replace with:

CPR r.32.2(1) states that the general rule is that any fact which needs to be proved by the evidence of witnesses is to be proved at trial by their oral evidence given in public. In civil trials the witnesses as to fact of both parties are normally allowed to remain in court throughout the hearing. But, for the purpose of preventing the evidence of such witnesses from being influenced by what they have heard and seen of witnesses called to testify before them, the judge has power on his or her own initiative or on the application of a party to exclude them from the hearing until they are called, and also to require them to remain in court after they have testified. No rule of law requires that in a trial witnesses must remain out of court until their turn to give testimony arises; it is purely a matter within the discretion of the court (*Moore v Lambeth County Court Registrar* [1969] 1 W.L.R. 141, CA; *In re Nightingale, Green v Nightingale* [1975] 1 W.L.R. 80, and *R (Elvington Park Ltd) v York Crown Court* [2011] EWHC 2213 (Admin), August 26, 2011 unrep., and authorities referred to there). In *Luckwell v Limata* [2014] EWHC 536 (Fam), February 13, 2014, unrep. (Holman J.), it was stated that a judge should only exclude witnesses if satisfied, on the facts and in the circumstances of the particular situation, that it would, for good reasons, be an appropriate step to take.In *Tomlinson v Tomlinson* [1980] 1 W.L.R. 322, DC, it was stated that the power to exclude witnesses does not extend to parties themselves, who have a right to remain in court throughout, or to their solicitors, or to the parties' expert witnesses, and that dictum has been much cited since. The question whether a claimant who proposed to testify (as distinct from a non-party witness) may or should be excluded from the court room whilst other witnesses were testifying was considered by the Court of Appeal in *Da Costa v Sargaco* [2016] EWCA Civ 764, 13 July 2016, CA, unrep., where two claimants made claims for damages arising from a road traffic accident, and where the defendant alleged that the claims were fraudulent and put the credibility of the two claimants in issue. On the defendant's application, which the claimants resisted, the trial judge directed that each claimant should be excluded from the court room while the other gave evidence. Following the dismissal of their claims, the claimants appealed to the Court of Appeal, principally on the ground that the judge had erred in her findings that the claims were fraudulent, but also contending that the judge's exclusion direction was made without jurisdiction and was wrong. The Court of Appeal reviewed the authorities arguably relevant to the question whether the judge's direction infringed the claimants' right to a fair and public hearing at common law and under art.6 of the ECHR. The Court explained (1) that there is no absolute requirement that, in order to ensure his or her fair trial, a party should have the opportunity to be present throughout the entirety of the hearing, and (2) that situations may arise in which it might possibly be necessary and permissible to proceed without a hearing without a party being present in court. The Court noted that this was not a case of a claimant being excluded from court whilst an opposing party or an opposing party's witnesses gave evidence. Both claimants were represented by the same counsel "and were telling essentially the same story", the elements of which they knew from the witness statements each had filed. Without expressly saying so the Court conceded that the judge had power to give a direction of the type challenged by the claimants, but concluded that in the instant case it was "extremely difficult to contemplate" that there was any sufficient reason for that direction. The fundamental problem was that the judge did not take as her starting point that the claimants were entitled to be present throughout the trial or, indeed, give any weight to this at all in the reasons given for her decision. However, reviewing the trial as a whole, it was not rendered unfair by the judge's direction.

32.1.4.3

PRACTICE DIRECTION 32—EVIDENCE

Annex 3

Video conferencing generally

Replace the fourth paragraph (beginning with "It should not be presumed") with:

4. It should not be presumed that all foreign governments are willing to allow their nationals or others within their jurisdiction to be examined before a court in England or Wales by means of VCF. If there is any doubt about this, enquiries should be directed to the Foreign and Commonwealth Office (Legalisation Office) sopenquiries@fco.gov.uk with a view to ensuring that the country from

32PD.33

which the evidence is to be taken raises no objection to it at diplomatic level. The party who is directed to be responsible for arranging the VCF (see paragraph 8 below) will be required to make all necessary inquiries about this well in advance of the VCF and must be able to inform the court what those inquiries were and of their outcome.

PART 34

WITNESSES, DEPOSITIONS AND EVIDENCE FOR FOREIGN COURTS

Forms

Replace with:

34.0.5   A number of forms have been revised and introduced by The Civil Procedure (Amendment) Rules 2016 with effect from 6th April 2016.
*   **N20** Witness summons
*   **N21** Order for examination of deponent (before the hearing)
*   **N93** Order under the Evidence (Proceedings in Other Jurisdictions) Act 1975
*   **No.32** Order for examination within jurisdiction of witness before trial or hearing (r.34.8)
*   **No.33** Application for an order for the issue of a letter of request to judicial authorities out of the jurisdiction (r.34.13 and PD34A para.5)
*   **No.34** Order for the issue of a letter of request to judicial authorities out of the jurisdiction (r.34.13)
*   **No.35** Draft Letter of request for examination of witness out of jurisdiction (to be filed by a party under r.34.13(6))
*   **No.37** Order for appointment of special examiner to take evidence of witness out of jurisdiction (r.34.13(4) and PD34A para.5.8)
*   **PF152** Evidence in support of application for Examination of a Witness and production of documents under the Evidence (Proceedings in other Jurisdictions) Act 1975 (r.34.17 and PD34A para.6.3)
*   **PF153** Certificate following examination under the Evidence (Proceedings in Other Jurisdictions) Act 1975 (r.34.19(2))
*   A to J under the Taking of Evidence Regulations
*   Annex A to the Practice Direction: draft Letter of Request (where the Taking of Evidence Regulation does not apply).

PART 35

EXPERTS AND ASSESSORS

Expert evidence at trial

Add new paragraph at end:

35.0.5   *Kennedy v Cordia (Services) LLP* [2016] UKSC 6; [2016] 1 W.L.R. 597, S.C. was a personal injury claim by a home carer who slipped on snow over ice on an ungritted sloping path to a client's home. An engineer with expertise in health and safety prepared a report for the Claimant, criticised the risk assessment carried out by the Defendant, which omitted falls in bad weather, and for not offering the Claimant anti-slip footwear attachments. The first instance court found for the Claimant but the appeal court concluded that permission should not have been given for the expert as health and safety was not a recognized area of scientific expertise, and that the Defendant had taken adequate steps to protect the Claimant. The Supreme Court thoroughly reviewed the law on the admissibility of expert evidence in civil claims, and how courts should police performance of expert's duties, and concluded that this expert's report did assist the court because the expert had direct experience of carrying out risk assessments and had conducted helpful research into how this particular risk could have been avoided. The appeal was allowed.

Contrast this with the decision in *Robshaw v United Lincolnshire Hospital NHS Trust* [2015] EWHC 923 QB, a clinical negligence case, in which the defendant applied to adjourn the trial on the basis that they would be prejudiced by their inability to cross examine the claimant's paediatric neurologist expert who was had a stress related illness and it might not be possible for him to attend trial for the foreseeable future. Foskett J decided that the claimant would have possibly greater forensic and logistical difficulties because of the absence of their expert at trial and as the neurologists had met and prepared a joint statement it would be fair for the trial to proceed rather than adopt the defendant's proposal that the claimant instruct a new expert.

Effect of rule

Add new paragraph at end:

35.1.1   *HK v Secretary of State for the Home Department* 2016 EWHC 857 (Admin) concerned the need for expert evidence in asylum seeker judicial review claims. In group litigation involving Bulgarian migrants the Claimants had obtained and served late and without permission of the court, a report from Amnesty International about reception conditions and operation of the Bulgarian asylum system. The judge, with some reluctance, allowed the report into evidence because this was a test case and the report was from a respected Non-Governmental Agency. But the weight it would attract would reflect the circumstances—it was the work of more than one individual and the signatory would not agree to be cross. Part 35 did apply to J.R. and the fact that Tribunals allowed into evidence without permission or disclosure to the other party, expert reports did not mean the courts should do the same. All the Bulgarian appeals were dismissed.

Personal injury and clinical negligence cases

Add new paragraph at end:

35.1.2   *Kennedy v Cordia (Services) LLP* [2016] UKSC 6; [2016] 1 W.L.R. 597, S.C. provided a helpful summary of the role of liability expert evidence in personal injury claims and concluded health and safety experts could assist the court in slipping accident at work claims.

Effect of rule

After the tenth paragraph (beginning with "Carruthers v MP Fireworks"), add new paragraph:

35.5.1   *Coyne v Morgan and Harrison*, Birmingham County Court concerned a building dispute in which the Defendant had instructed a structural engineer who wished not to continue to be instructed after preparing a draft report, meeting the Claimant's expert at a joint inspection and expressing some views in favour of the Claimant, although the Defendant wanted to retain him. The court gave permission for the Defendant to instruct another expert, provided the first expert's report was disclosed although this was not a case of "expert shopping".

Effect of rule

After the sixth paragraph (beginning with "In Mwamda v East London Bus"), add new paragraph:

35.7.1   In *Yearsley v Mid Cheshire Hospitals NHS Trust* [2016] EWHC 1841 (QB) it was held that the instruction of a single joint expert was inappropriate to assess whether the claimant's significant and longstanding dementia had been contributed to by the defendant's negligence and whether the claimant had capacity.

PART 36

OFFERS TO SETTLE

I. Part 36 Offers to Settle

Scope of Pt 36

Replace the second paragraph (where the citation for Van Oord UK Ltd v Allseas UK Ltd has changed) with:

36.2.3   *Counterclaims and other additional claims*—Rule 36.2(3)(a) now clarifies that Part 36 offers can be made in respect of counterclaims and other additional claims. This was always the case (see *AF v BG* [2009] EWCA Civ 757; [2009] All E.R. (D) 249; [2010] 2 Costs L.R. 164, CA) but the clarification is welcome in view of the difficulty perceived in the old rules in *F&C Alternative Investments (Holdings) Ltd v Barthelemy (Costs)* [2011] EWHC 2807 (Ch); [2012] Bus. L.R. 891, Ch D (Sales J); overturned on appeal: [2012] EWCA Civ 843; [2013] 1 W.L.R. 548; [2012] 4 All E.R. 1096, CA. The matter is put beyond doubt by the signpost at the end of this rule to rr.20.2 to 20.3 and by the wording of the new form **N242A**. When making an offer in a case concerning a counterclaim or other additional claim, it is important to make clear whether it is intended to be a claimant's or a defendant's offer. By way of example, a counterclaiming defendant may wish to make a claimant's offer (where the offer is to accept some payment on the counterclaim) or a defendant's offer (where the offer is to pay some money on the claim). Such offer may be limited to the counterclaim or claim; alternatively it may take the other adverse claim into account: see rr.36.5(1)(d) to (e). See also the guidance notes on form **N242A** and *Van Oord UK Ltd v Allseas UK Ltd* [2015] EWHC 3385 (TCC); [2016] 1 Costs L.O. 1, 30 November 2015 (Coulson J).

Costs to be determined by the court—paras (4) to (6)

Replace the second paragraph (where the citation for Dutton v Minards has changed) with:

36.13.3   In one case (that of late acceptance of an offer relating to the whole claim under r.36.13(4)(b)) express provision is made. First, in the absence of agreement, the court must, "unless it considers it unjust", make the costs orders specified by r.36.13(5). Secondly, r.36.13(6) provides that in deciding whether it would be unjust to make such orders the court will consider the matters listed in r.36.17(5). These rules are rather more elaborate than the comparable provisions that applied before 6 April 2015, which simply provided that the default orders would be made "unless the court orders otherwise". There is, however, no change to the proper approach since paras (5)–(6) codify the decisions in *PGF II SA v OMFS Co 1 Ltd* [2013] EWCA Civ 1288; [2014] 1 W.L.R. 1386; [2014] 1 All E.R. 970, CA; *SG (A Child) v Hewitt (Costs)* [2012] EWCA Civ 1053; [2013] 1 All E.R. 1118; [2012] Costs L.R. 937, CA; *Lumb v Hampsey* [2011] EWHC 2808 (QB), 11 October 2011, unrep. (Lang J); *Dutton v Minards* [2015] EWCA Civ 984; [2015] 6 Costs L.R. 1047, 16 July 2015. See also *Purser v Hibbs* [2015] EWHC 1792 (QB), 19 May 2015, unrep. (HHJ Maloney QC) for confirmation that the new rules codify *Lumb*.

"more advantageous" (r.36.17(2))

Replace the last paragraph with:

36.17.2   Where the defendant makes a payment to the claimant after the date of the Part 36 offer (not being an interim payment made generally on account of the claim) such that the value of the claim is reduced, the Part 36 offer becomes more attractive: *LG Blower Specialist Bricklayer Ltd v Reeves* [2010] EWCA Civ 726; [2010] 1 W.L.R. 2081; [2011] 2 All E.R. 258, CA. See, contra, *Littlestone v MacLeish* [2016] EWCA Civ 127; [2016] 2 Costs L.O. 275; *Times*, 15 April 2016, in which Briggs LJ doubted Blower, holding that a later payment was made on account of both the claim generally and the Part 36 offer.

Claimant's offer (rr.36.17(1)(b) and 36.17(4))

Replace with:

36.17.4   Where, upon judgment being entered, judgment against the defendant is "at least as advantageous" to the claimant as the proposals in the claimant's Part 36 offer (r.36.17(1)(b)), then the court must, "unless it considers it unjust to do so", make the orders provided for by r.36.17(4). The jurisdiction arises upon judgment being entered, irrespective of the particular steps or process that led to judgment (e.g. trial, summary judgment, breach of order or rule). In *McPhilemy v The Times Newspapers Ltd (No.2)* [2001] EWCA Civ 933; [2002] 1 W.L.R. 934; [2001] 4 All E.R. 861, CA, Simon Brown LJ observed, at para.28:

> "[These provisions are] not designed to punish unreasonable conduct but as an incentive to encourage claimants to make, and defendants to accept, appropriate offers of settlement. That incentive cannot work unless the non-acceptance of what ultimately proves to have been a sufficient offer ordinarily advantages the claimant in the respects set out in the rule."

The provisions of r.36.17(4) apply equally in the case of an effective Part 36 Offer made in a provisional costs assessment notwithstanding r.47.15(5): *Lowin v W Portsmouth & Co Ltd,* 20 June 2016, unrep., QB.

Indemnity costs (r.36.17(4)(b))

Replace the first paragraph with:

36.17.4.2   Rule 36.17(4)(b) requires the court to award the claimant costs on an indemnity basis. Such order is likely to be more favourable to the claimant than would otherwise be the case. The costs to which the claimant is entitled under r.36.17(4)(b) are those which would, on the application of the principles set out in r.44.2, be awarded, disregarding the effect of the Part 36 offer (*Kastor Navigation Co Ltd v AGF MAT (Costs)* [2003] EWHC 472 (Comm); *The Times*, 29 March 2003, affirmed on this point by the Court of Appeal [2004] EWCA Civ 277; [2004] Lloyd's Rep. 199; [2005] 2 All E.R. (Comm) 720, CA. See, however, *Greenwich Millennium Village Ltd v Essex Services Group Plc* [2014] EWHC 1099 (TCC); [2014] T.C.L.R. 4 (Coulson J), at para.29). See, contra, *Webb v Liverpool Women's NHS Foundation Trust* [2016] EWCA Civ 365; [2016] C.P. Rep. 30; [2016] Costs L.R. 411; 14 April 2016, unrep.: (1) the successful claimant is entitled to all of his costs on an indemnity basis, unless it would be unjust to do so, (2) the court should not first consider the costs that would have been awarded under Pt 44, (3) Kastor distinguished. Where the offeror is treated as having filed a costs budget limited to court fees, or is otherwise limited in his recovery of costs to such fees, "costs" in r.36.17(4)(b) has the meaning given in r.36.23.

"considers it unjust to do so" (r.36.17(5))

Replace the fifth paragraph (where the citation for Yentob v MGN Ltd has changed) with:

36.17.5   In *Yentob v MGN Ltd* [2015] EWCA Civ 1292; [2015] 6 Costs L.R. 1103, the Court of Appeal upheld a decision of Mann J to depart from the usual order in a phone-hacking case upon the claimant failing to obtain a judgment more advantageous than the newspaper's Part 36 offer on the grounds that only limited admissions had been made and it was unlikely that the defendant would have agreed to make a statement in open court pursuant to para.6.1 of the Practice Direction to Pt 53. In a passage that was approved on appeal, Mann J. cautioned, at para.43,

> "In what I might call a more normal case, it seems to me that the desire to have a trial in order to have a finding of a judge in public as to what happened is unlikely to be a legitimate objective in Part 36 terms so as to justify a claimant refusing to accept a Part 36 offer and insisting on going to trial."

Rule 36.17(5)(e)—a genuine attempt to settle proceedings

To the end of the last paragraph, add:

In *Jockey Club Racecourse Ltd v Willmott Dixon Construction Ltd* [2016] EWHC 167 (TCC); [2016] 4 **36.17.5.1** W.L.R. 43; [2016] 1 Costs L.R. 123, a 95% offer was effective in an open-and-shut case.

Add new paragraph 36.17.7:

"… upon judgment being entered" (r.36.17(1))

These words should not be interpreted narrowly. Where, for example, an offer is made "net of **36.17.7** CRU benefits", it may not be possible to determine whether the offer has been effective immediately on entering judgment: *Crooks v Hendricks Lovell Ltd* [2016] EWCA Civ 8; [2016] Costs 1 L.O. 103.

Add new paragraph 36.21.2:

Editorial note

The provisions of Pt 36 trump those of Pt 45, accordingly indemnity costs are recoverable under **36.21.2** r.36.17(4) in Section IIIA cases: *Broadhurst v Tan* [2016] EWCA Civ 94; [2016] 1 W.L.R. 1928; [2016] 2 Costs L.O. 155.

Add new paragraph 36.22.1.1:

"… without regard to any liability for recoverable amounts" (r.36.22(3))

Where the offer is made "net of CRU benefits" see *Crooks v Hendricks Lovell Ltd* [2016] EWCA Civ **36.22.1.1** 8; [2016] Costs 1 L.O. 103.

PART 37

MISCELLANEOUS PROVISIONS ABOUT PAYMENTS INTO COURT

Defence of tender before claim

Replace the last paragraph (where the citation for RSM Bentley Jennison (A Firm) v Ayton has changed) with:

Ever since the CPR were introduced, the Glossary has defined "a defence of tender before **37.2.1** claim" as "a defence that, before the claimant started proceedings, the defendant unconditionally offered to the claimant the amount due or, if no specified amount is claimed, an amount sufficient to satisfy the claim" (see Glossary at Section E). Such definition purports to extend the defence of tender before claim to unliquidated claims. However, r.2.2 provides that the Glossary is "a guide to the meaning of certain legal expressions ... but is not to be taken as giving those expressions any meaning in the Rules which they do not have in the law generally." In *RSM Bentley Jennison (A Firm) v Ayton* [2015] EWCA Civ 1120; [2016] 1 W.L.R. 1281; [2016] P.N.L.R. 10, the Court of Appeal confirmed that the defence remains limited to debt actions, notwithstanding the definition offered in the Glossary.

PART 39

MISCELLANEOUS PROVISIONS RELATING TO HEARINGS

"hearing to be in public" (r.39.2)

Add new paragraph at end:

In *Ewing v The Crown Court sitting at Cardiff and Newport* [2016] EWHC 183 (Admin) the Divisional **39.2.1** Court (dealing with a criminal case) concluded that those who attend public court hearings should be free to take notes and no prior permission to do so is required. The court may prohibit the taking of notes but only where the taking of notes would interfere with the administration of justice (see paras 23 and 24).

Anonymity of party or witness (r.39.2(4))

Replace with:

39.2.11   The power of the court to order that the identity of any party or witnesses must not be disclosed is a broad power and the "interests" involved may include, although they are not limited to, privacy and confidentiality. The question whether a court should grant anonymity to a party or witness is separate from the question whether the court should sit in private. Obviously, the two questions may arise in the same practical context. Where a court sits in private but gives judgment in public, and there is a continuing need to protect the interests which justified the hearing being held in private in the first place, the court may "anonymise" the judgment by identifying parties or witness by letter only (e.g AB v CD; witness X). This may be done, for example, where a court considers that, by naming the parties or witnesses, the court itself would infringe their art.8 Convention rights as to privacy and family life and therefore act unlawfully under the Human Rights Act s.6 (*Re Guardian News and Media Ltd* [2010] UKSC 1; [2010] 2 W.L.R. 325, SC, at [28] per Lord Rodger). The question of whether a court should grant an order under r.39.2(4), or any other anonymity order, is not a matter of the judge's discretion, but is a matter of obligation under the Human Rights Act 1998 s.6 and ECHR art.8. The test to be applied is whether there is sufficient general public interest in publishing a report of proceedings that identifies the party to justify any resulting curtailment of that party's art.8 rights. (*AMM v HXW* [2010] EWHC 2457 (QB), October 7, 2010 unrep. (Tugendhat J.) (where anonymity order made together with interim injunction in proceedings for injunction restraining publication of information which claimant claimed to be private)). In *Secretary of State for the Home Department v AP (No.2)* [2010] UKSC 26; [2010] 1 W.L.R. 1652, S.C., an individual (D) subject to a control order appealed successfully to the Supreme Court against conditions as to place of residence imposed by the order which had been upheld by the Court of Appeal. An anonymity order, protecting D from being identified, had been in force throughout the proceedings. By the time the Court's judgment was handed down, D was no longer subject to a control order, but was on bail pending deportation with a residence condition imposed. The Supreme Court ordered that the anonymity order should be continued after judgment and that the judgment and any reports of it should not reveal the identity of D. In the circumstances, the public interest in publishing a full report of the proceedings and judgment had to give way to the need to protect D from violence and did not justify curtailing his right to respect for his private and family life. In *R. (C) v Secretary of State for Justice* [2016] UKSC 2; [2016] 1 W.L.R. 444, SC, the Supreme Court held that there is no presumption of anonymity of the identity of a mental patient detained or otherwise subject to compulsory powers in every case of proceedings under the Mental Health Act 1983. The question in all these proceedings is (as r.39.2(4) provides): is anonymity necessary in the interests of the mental patient? Cases have arisen where the court has anonymised its written judgment even after a public hearing. See further *Revenue and Customs Commissioners v Banerjee (No.2) (Note)* [2009] EWHC 1229 (Ch); [2009] 3 All E.R. 930 (Henderson J.) (where party's application for anonymity in judgment following public hearing refused), and authorities referred to there. The power of the court referred to in r.39.2(4) goes beyond the "anonymising" of judgments and includes apower to make orders restraining others (including the press) from disclosing the identities of parties and witnesses (see *Re Guardian News and Media Ltd.*, op cit, at [30] per Lord Rodger).

The exclusion of witnesses until called

Add new paragraph at end:

39.2.12   The power to exclude a party from a part of a trial was dealt with by the Court of Appeal in *Da Costa v Sargaco* [2016] EWCA Civ 764. In a case where fraud was alleged the trial Judge had ordered that each of the two claimants should be excluded from the court whilst the other gave evidence. Black LJ (with whom other members of the court agreed) found that the Judge's order was wrong. The starting point must always be that that the Claimants were each entitled to be present throughout the trial (see para.61). The Court of Appeal went on to consider if the hearing had been rendered unfair by the exclusion and concluded that it had not. The appeal based on the wrongful exclusion was therefore dismissed. Applications to exclude a party in similar circumstances are by no means uncommon. *Da Costa* suggests that such exclusion may be permissible provided that no prejudice arises. See para.32.1.4.3 above.

"the court may grant the application only if ..." (r.39.3(5))

Before the fourth paragraph (beginning with "Note that if"), add new paragraph:

39.3.7   In *Mohun-Smith v TBO Investments Ltd* [2016] EWCA Civ 403; [2016] 1 W.L.R. 2919, CA, the Court of Appeal held that, in the circumstances, a judge had adopted too rigorous approach in refusing a defendant's application to set aside judgment pursuant to r.39.3, particularly to the question of promptness, and had erred in holding that the defendant did not have a good reason for attending trial. The Court gave guidance on the approach judges should adopt to the assessment of the evidence adduced in support of an application under r.39.3(3).

Add new paragraph at end:

In *Mohun-Smith v TBO Investments Ltd* [2016] EWCA Civ 403; [2016] 1 W.L.R. 2919, CA, the Court of Appeal stated that if the court is satisfied that the conditions r.39.3(5) are met, and that it is right to exercise its discretion to grant the application, it will often be appropriate to do so on the condition that the applicant pay the other side's costs and pay a sum on account of those costs within a short period.

PART 40

JUDGMENTS, ORDERS, SALE OF LAND ETC.

I. Judgments and Orders

Replace r.40.2 with:

Standard requirements[1]

40.2—**(1)** Every judgment or order must state the name and judicial title **40.2** of the person who made it, unless it is—

    (a) default judgment entered under rule 12.4(1) (entry of default judgment where judgment is entered by a court officer) or a default costs certificate obtained under rule 47.11;

    (b) judgment entered under rules 14.4, 14.5, 14.6, 14.7 and 14.9 (entry of judgment on admission where judgment is entered by a court officer);

    (c) a consent order under rule 40.6(2) (consent orders made by court officers);

    (d) an order made by a court officer under rule 70.5 (orders to enforce awards as if payable under a court order); or

    (e) an order made by a court officer under rule 71.2 (orders to obtain information from judgment debtors).

(2) Every judgment or order must—

    (a) bear the date on which it is given or made; and

    (b) be sealed(GL) by the court.

(3) Paragraph (4) applies where a party applies for permission to appeal against a judgment or order at the hearing at which the judgment or order was made.

(4) Where this paragraph applies, the judgment or order shall state—

    [omit]

    (b) whether an appeal lies from the judgment or order and, if so, to which appeal court, with an indication of the division of the High Court where the High Court is the appeal court;

    (c) whether the court gives permission to appeal; and

    (d) if not, the appropriate appeal court, including the appropriate division where relevant, to which any further application for permission may be made.

---

[1] Amended by the Civil Procedure (Amendment) Rules 2000 (SI 2000/221), the Civil Procedure (Amendment No. 4) Rules 2001 (SI 2001/2792), the Civil Procedure (Amendment No. 4) Rules 2005 (SI 2005/3515), the Civil Procedure (Amendment No.2) Rules 2009 (SI 2009/3390), the Civil Procedure (Amendment No.2) Rules 2012 (SI 2012/2208), and the Civil Procedure (Amendment No.3) Rules 2016 (SI 2016/788).

Effect of judgment before entry—altering judgment

Add new paragraph at end:

40.2.1   Where a party shows that consent to an order has been obtained by fraud the order should not be perfected but set aside and the hearing or case reopened: *Sharland v Sharland* [2015] UKSC 60; [2015] 3 W.L.R. 1070, SC, and see Setting aside consent judgments and orders, below at para.40.6.3.

Altering draft judgment

To the end of the sixth paragraph, add:

40.2.1.0.2   In *Quan v Bray* [2015] EWCA Civ 1401, 14 December 2015, CA, unrep., the Court of Appeal, after handing down a judgment giving a wife permission to appeal to the Court from a decision of a Family Division judge made in proceedings involving her and her husband, dismissed an application by the husband to reconsider that judgment in which he alleged there were factual errors. The Court stressed that in giving permission an appeal court is neither confirming nor rejecting any of the findings within the judgment at first instance.

Setting aside consent judgments and orders

Add new paragraph at end:

40.6.3   Where before an order is perfected a party shows that her consent has been obtained by fraud, then the order should not be perfected, but the case should be reopened unless the fraud would not have influenced a reasonable person and the court should not in reopening the case deal with it on the basis only of the material then before it, but the case should be reheard: *Sharland v Sharland* [2015] UKSC 60; [2015] 3 W.L.R. 1070, SC.

Effect of rule

Replace with:

40.14A.1   The provenance of this rule is CCR Ord.22 (Judgments and Orders) r.8 (Certificate of judgment) (see 2013 edition of the *White Book* Vol.1, para.cc22.8). For further explanation see para.40.9A.1 above. Rule 83.19 (Creditor's request for transfer to the High Court for enforcement) applies where the creditor makes a request for a certificate of judgment under r.40.14A(1) in the circumstances provided for in that rule. As to transfer to High Court from County Court of possession orders for purposes of enforcement, see commentary in 83.13.1 and 83.19.2, and on County Courts Act 1984 ss.41 and 42 (Vol.2 para.9A-481.1).

PRACTICE NOTE—(CHANCERY DIVISION—PRODUCTION OF ORDERS FOR MASTERS AND JUDGES)

Add new paragraph at beginning:

Editorial note

40PN.0.1   See now Chancery Guide, Ch.22, Vol.2 paras 1A–192-202.

PART 44

GENERAL RULES ABOUT COSTS

I.   General

Reasons

To the end of the paragraph, add:

44.2.4   The reasons for a judge's costs order made at the end of a trial may be largely discernible from the transcript of the judgment, but where counsel are not sure they should seek from the judge a note of the reasons for the order (*Darougar v Belcher* [2002] EWCA Civ 1262, 25 July 2002, CA, unrep., at para.7 per Keene LJ).

Offers to settle (r.44.2(4)(c))

Add new paragraph at end:

44.2.13   In a case where r.36.14 applies (claimant fails to obtain a judgment more advantageous than a defendant's Part 36 offer or judgment against the defendant is at least as advantageous to the claimant as the proposals contained in a claimant's Part 36 offer), an issue-based or proportionate costs order may only be made if it would be unjust to make the order provided by the rule. In such a case the court does not exercise its discretion under r.44.2: *Webb v Liverpool Women's NHS Foundation Trust* [2016] EWCA Civ 365.

Protective costs orders

Replace with:

44.2.16

Normally, orders made by the court in the exercise of the discretion to award costs, stated in the Senior Courts Act 1981 s.51(1) and re-iterated in r.44.2(1), are made at the end of the proceedings to which they relate (whether interlocutory, final or appeal). However, the discretion is wide enough to enable the court to make an order for costs in advance, based on assumptions as to the possible outcomes (and, therefore, the possible costs liabilities) of the proceedings. Such orders are described as "protective" (or "pre-emptive", "prospective" or "anticipatory") costs orders. For general circumstances in which such orders may be made, see commentary on s.51(1) in Vol.2 para.9A-202; for particular circumstances, see Vol.1 para.48GP.76 (Protective Costs Orders) and para.48GP.79 (Trustees, personal representatives). The power of the court to make protective costs orders and judicial review costs capping orders must be distinguished from the powers to make "costs management" orders (see Section II of CPR Part 3 at para.3.12 et seq above), and to make "costs capping" orders (limiting the amount of future costs which a party may recover pursuant to an order for costs subsequently made) (see Section III of CPR Part 3 at para.3.19 et seq above). With effect from August 8, 2016, ss.88 to 90 of the Criminal Justice and Courts Act 2015 removed the ability of the High Court and the Court of Appeal to make costs capping orders in judicial review proceedings unless specified criteria are met (for texts of these sections, see Vol.2 paras 9A-1312 to 9A-1314). The rules of court supporting this regime are contained in Section VI of Part 46. This dedicated form of costs order is defined as a "judicial review costs capping order" (r.46.16(1)(a)). See further paras 46.16.1and 54.6.3below.

II. Qualified One-Way Costs Shifting

Proceedings which include a claim for damages for personal injuries, etc

Add new paragraphs at end:

44.13.1

An appeal by a claimant against the dismissal of his claim for personal injuries is part of proceedings which include a claim for personal injuries and the claimant was entitled to the protection of qualified one-way costs shifting in respect of the costs of the appeal: *Parker v Butler* [2016] EWHC 1251 (QB).

Qualified one-way costs shifting does not apply to a claim against the Motor Insurers' Bureau under reg.13(1) of The Motor Vehicles (Compulsory Insurance) (Information Centre and Compensation Board) Regulations 2003, which provides for compensation following a road accident in an EEA or subscribing State, other than the United Kingdom, where the vehicle of the driver responsible cannot be identified: *Howe v Motor Insurers' Bureau* [2016] EWHC 884 (QB). Such a claim is not for damages for personal injuries, but rather a claim for statutory compensation.

PART 45

FIXED COSTS

IIIA. Claims Which No Longer Continue Under the RTA or EL/PL Pre-Action Protocols—Fixed Recoverable Costs

Add new paragraph 45.29B.1:

Part 36 offers

45.29B.1

Where a claim no longer continues under the protocol pursuant to r.45.29A(1), r.36.14 applies with the modifications set out in r.36.14A. If judgment is entered against the defendant on terms at least as advantageous to the claimant as the proposals contained in the claimant's Part 36 offer, r.36.14(3) will apply. The claimant will be awarded fixed costs to the last staging point provided by r.45.29C and Table 6B and, unless the court considers it unjust, costs assessed on the indemnity basis from the date on which the relevant period expired: *Broadhurst v Tan* [2016] EWCA Civ 94.

Add new paragraph 45.29C.1:

Where a claim settled at court on the day listed for trial, the claim was "disposed of at trial" and

45.29C.1

the trial advocacy fee under Table 6B was payable: *Mendes v Hochtief (UK) Construction Ltd* [2016] EWHC 976 (QB).

IV. Scale Costs For Claims in the Intellectual Property Enterprise Court

Effect of Section

Add new paragraph at end:

45.30.1 Where the claimant's conduct did not amount to abuse and the circumstances were not truly exceptional, but the claimant had failed to formulate its case properly leading to a striking-out application which was withdrawn by consent, the court awarded an extra £5,000 over the IPEC application cap. The overall cap for the claim could not be disturbed: *Skyscape Cloud Services Ltd v Sky Plc (IPEC, June 8, 2016, unrep., Judge Hacon).*

Effect of rule

To the end of the sixth paragraph (beginning with "Rule 45.31(1) imposes"), add:

45.31.1 Where a defendant had succeeded on its counterclaim but part of the claim had been adjourned, the defendant asked for its costs of the counterclaim to be assessed. The court held that it could not assess the costs until all of the issues, including the adjourned claim, had been resolved: *Global Flood Defence Systems v Johan Van Den Noort Beheer BV* [2016] EWHC 189 (IPEC).

VII. Costs Limits in Aarhus Convention Claims

Replace r.45.41 with:

Scope and interpretation[1]

45.41 **45.41—(1) This Section provides for the costs which are to be recoverable between the parties in Aarhus Convention claims.**

(2) In this Section, "Aarhus Convention claim" means a claim for judicial review of a decision, act or omission all or part of which is subject to the provisions of the UNECE Convention on Access to Information, Public Participation in Decision-Making and Access to Justice in Environmental Matters done at Aarhus, Denmark on 25 June 1998, including a claim which proceeds on the basis that the decision, act or omission, or part of it, is so subject.

(Rule 52.19 makes provision in relation to costs of an appeal.)

PART 46

COSTS—SPECIAL CASES

Editorial introduction

Replace with:

46.0.1 This Part was enacted by the Civil Procedure (Amendment) Rules 2013 (SI 2013/262) and came into effect on April 1, 2013. It is divided into four Sections. Rules which before that date were found in CPR Part 48 (Costs—Special Cases) are contained in this Part, together with five rules (r.46.7 and rr.46.11 to 46.14) which were formerly in Pt 44 and which are more conveniently placed in this Part. The exact derivation of the several rules is explained in commentary following the first rule of each Section. As enacted by SI 2013/262, this Part consisted of Sections I to IV. Section V was added by the Civil Procedure (Amendment No.2) Rules 2015 (SI 2015/670) with effect from 13 April 2015 (see further para.46.15.1 below), and Section VI by the Civil Procedure (Amendment No.2) Rules 2016 (SI 2016/707) with effect from 8 August 2016 (see further para.46.16.1 below).

---

[1] Amended by the Civil Procedure (Amendment No.3) Rules 2016 (SI 2016/788).

I. Costs Payable by or to Particular Persons

Insurers

After the third paragraph, add new paragraph:

In a case where insurers were conducting the defence of their impecunious insured but withdrew **46.2.6** shortly before judgment in default was entered, in the belief that they would not in fact be liable to indemnify their insured, it was nevertheless appropriate to make a costs order against the insurers. The insurers had been acting exclusively or predominantly in their own interests in defending the claim and that part of the claim which the insurers would have been liable to indemnify had not been abandoned: *Legg v Sterte Garage Ltd* [2016] EWCA Civ 97.

Solicitors acting on own account

To the end of the last paragraph, add:

On appeal, the decision was affirmed save that the Administrative Court should have remitted **46.5.6** the assessment to the tribunal rather than substitute its own figures: [2016] EWCA Civ 478.

II. Costs Relating to Legal Representatives

Editorial note

Replace the last paragraph (where the citation for Eurasian Natural Resources Corp Ltd v Dechert LLP has changed) with:

On a detailed assessment under s.70 of the Solicitors Act 1974 the implied waiver of privilege **46.10.2** necessary to enable the solicitor to contest the challenge is limited and the material remains protected by privilege as regards third parties: *Eurasian Natural Resources Corp Ltd v Dechert LLP* [2016] EWCA Civ 375.

Add new section VI: **46.16**

VI. Judicial Review Costs Capping Orders under Part 4 of the Criminal Justice and Courts Act 2015

Judicial review costs capping orders—general[1]

46.16—(1) For the purposes of this Section—

    (a) "judicial review costs capping order" means a costs capping order made by the High Court or the Court of Appeal in accordance with sections 88, 89 and 90 of the 2015 Act; and

    (b) "the 2015 Act" means the Criminal Justice and Courts Act 2015.

(2) This Section does not apply to a costs capping order under rule 3.19. (Rule 3.19 makes provision for orders limiting the amount of future costs (including disbursements) which a party may recover pursuant to an order for costs subsequently made.)

Editorial note

Sections 88 to 90 of the Criminal Justice and Courts Act 2015 remove the ability of the High **46.16.1** Court and the Court of Appeal to make costs capping orders in judicial review proceedings unless specified criteria are met. In effect those sections provide a separate and quite detailed regime regulating the making of what are described in r.46.16(1)(a) as "judicial review costs capping orders". For texts of ss.88 to 90 of the 2015 Act, see Vol.2 paras 9A-1312 to 9A-1314, and for explanation of underlying policy para.9A-1312.2. Section VI of Pt 46 contains the rules of court necessary to support this regime. That Section was inserted in Pt 46 by the Civil Procedure (Amendment No.2) Rules 2016 (SI 2016/707). The provisions of the Section (rr.46.16 to 46.19) came into force on 8 August 2016, and the relevant transitional provision in the statutory instrument states that they do not apply to an application for judicial review made before that date. These rules are supplemented by paras 10.1 and 10.2 of Practice Direction 46; see para.46PD.10 below. As the parenthesis following r.46.16 indicates, rules supporting the court's general jurisdiction to grant costs capping orders are found in Section III (rr.3.19 to 3.21) of CPR Pt 3. Rule 46.16(2) states that the provisions of Section VI of Pt 46 do not apply to a costs capping order under r.3.19.

---

[1] Introduced by the Civil Procedure (Amendment No.2) Rules 2016 (SI 2016/707).

Applications for judicial review costs capping orders[1]

46.17   46.17—(1)   An application for a judicial review costs capping order must—

    (a)   be made on notice and, subject to paragraphs (2) and (3), in accordance with Part 23; and

    (b)   be supported by evidence setting out—

        (i)   why a judicial review costs capping order should be made, having regard, in particular, to the matters at sub-sections (6) to (8) of section 88 of the 2015 Act and sub-section (1) of section 89 of that Act;

        (ii)   a summary of the applicant's financial resources;

        (iii)   the costs (and disbursements) which the applicant considers the parties are likely to incur in the future conduct of the proceedings; and

        (iv)   if the applicant is a body corporate, whether it is able to demonstrate that it is likely to have financial resources available to meet liabilities arising in connection with the proceedings.

(2)   Subject to paragraph (3), the applicant must serve a copy of the application notice and copies of the supporting documents on every other party.

(3)   On application by the applicant, the court may dispense with the need for the applicant to serve the evidence setting out a summary of the applicant's financial resources on one or more of the parties.

(4)   The court may direct the applicant to provide additional information or evidence to support its application.

Court to consider making directions[2]

46.18   46.18   If the applicant is a body corporate, and the evidence supporting its application in accordance with rule 46.17(1)(b)(iv) sets out that it is unable to demonstrate that it is likely to have financial resources available to meet liabilities arising in connection with the proceedings, the court must consider giving directions for the provision of information about the applicant's members and their ability to provide financial support for the purposes of the proceedings.

Applications to vary judicial review costs capping orders[3]

46.19   46.19—(1)   An application to vary a judicial review costs capping order must be made on notice and, subject to paragraphs (2) and (3), in accordance with Part 23.

(2)   Subject to paragraph (3), the applicant must serve a copy of the application notice and copies of any supporting documents on every other party.

(3)   If the application is supported by evidence setting out a summary of the applicant's financial resources, the court may, on application by the applicant, dispense with the need for the applicant to serve such evidence on one or more of the parties.

---

[1] Introduced by the Civil Procedure (Amendment No.2) Rules 2016 (SI 2016/707).
[2] Introduced by the Civil Procedure (Amendment No.2) Rules 2016 (SI 2016/707).
[3] Introduced by the Civil Procedure (Amendment No.2) Rules 2016 (SI 2016/707).

This Practice Direction supplements Part 46

Add new paragraph 46PD.10:

Judicial review costs capping orders under Part 4 of the Criminal Justice and Courts Act 2015: rules 46.16 to 46.19

10.1 Unless the court directs otherwise, a summary of an applicant's **46PD.10** financial resources under rule 46.17(1)(b)(ii) must provide details of—

(a) the applicant's significant assets, liabilities, income and expenditure; and

(b) in relation to any financial support which any person has provided or is likely to provide to the applicant, the aggregate amount—

  (i) which has been provided; and

  (ii) which is likely to be provided.

10.2 An application to the High Court for a judicial review costs capping order must normally be contained in, or accompany, the claim form.

PART 47

PROCEDURE FOR DETAILED ASSESSMENT OF COSTS AND DEFAULT PROVISIONS

III. *Costs Payable by One Party to Another—Default Provisions*

Effect of rule

After the first paragraph, add new paragraph:

Where a party has obtained a default costs certificate after costs-only proceedings under r.46.14, **47.11.1** that party will be entitled to the costs of the costs-only proceedings in addition to the fixed costs for the commencement of detailed assessment proceedings: *Tasleem v Beverley* [2013] EWCA Civ 1805.

IV. *Costs Payable by One Party to Another—Procedure where Points of Dispute are Served*

Replace r.47.14 with:

Detailed assessment hearing[1]

47.14—**(1)** **Where points of dispute are served in accordance with this** **47.14** **Part, the receiving party must file a request for a detailed assessment hearing within 3 months of the expiry of the period for commencing detailed assessment proceedings as specified—**

  (a) **in rule 47.7; or**

  (b) **by any direction of the court.**

(2) **Where the receiving party fails to file a request in accordance with paragraph (1), the paying party may apply for an order requiring the receiving party to file the request within such time as the court may specify.**

(3) **On an application under paragraph (2), the court may direct that, unless the receiving party requests a detailed assessment hearing within the time specified by the court, all or part of the costs to which the receiving party would otherwise be entitled will be disallowed.**

(4) **If—**

  (a) **the paying party has not made an application in accordance with paragraph (2); and**

---

[1] Amended by the Civil Procedure (No.3) Rules 2016 (SI 2016/788).

> > (b)   the receiving party files a request for a detailed assessment hearing later than the period specified in paragraph (1),

the court may disallow all or part of the interest otherwise payable to the receiving party under—

> > (i)   section 17 of the Judgments Act 1838; or
> > (ii)   section 74 of the County Courts Act 1984,

but will not impose any other sanction except in accordance with rule 44.11 (powers in relation to misconduct).

> (5)   No party other than—
> > (a)   the receiving party;
> > (b)   the paying party; and
> > (c)   any party who has served points of dispute under rule 47.9,

may be heard at the detailed assessment hearing unless the court gives permission.

> (6)   Only items specified in the points of dispute may be raised at the hearing, unless the court gives permission.

> (7)   If an assessment is carried out at more than one hearing, then for the purposes of rule 52.12 time for appealing shall not start to run until the conclusion of the final hearing, unless the court orders otherwise.

(Practice Direction 47 specifies other documents which must be filed with the request for hearing and the length of notice which the court will give when it fixes a hearing date.)

Add new title and paragraph 47.15.2:

Costs of provisional assessment

47.15.2   Where the receiving party's costs were assessed at a higher figure than her Part 36 offer and she was entitled to her costs of the assessment on the indemnity basis under r.36.17(4), the cap on the costs of assessment provided by r.47.15(5) did not apply: *Lowin v W Portsmouth & Co Ltd* (QBD, Elisabeth Laing J., unrep., 20 June 2016)

PART 48

PART 2 OF THE LEGAL AID, SENTENCING AND PUNISHMENT OF OFFENDERS ACT 2012 RELATING TO CIVIL LITIGATION FUNDING AND COSTS: TRANSITIONAL PROVISION IN RELATION TO PRE-COMMENCEMENT FUNDING ARRANGEMENTS

2.   Savings provisions in the 2012 Act and commencement order

After the third paragraph (beginning with "Article 3 of SI 2013/77"), add as a new paragraph:

48.0.2.4   Article 2 of the Legal Aid, Sentencing and Punishment of Offenders Act 2012 (Commencement No.12) Order 2016 (SI 2016/345) brought into force, on 6 April 2016, s.44 and s.46 in relation to insolvency proceedings, thereby removing the exclusion of those proceedings from the commencement of those sections effected by art.4 of SI 2013/77. (The transitional provisions in s.44(6) and s.46(3) of the 2012 Act have effect in respect of the provisions commenced by this Order.)

Replace the first sentence of the last paragraph with:

It is expected that, in due course, s.44 and s.46 will be brought into force in relation to proceedings of the types which remain covered by the saving provisions.

Effect of CPR Pt 48

Replace the second paragraph with:

48.0.3   As indicated above, the significant amendments made by s.44 and s.46 of the 2012 Act relate to what are defined in r.43.2(1)(k), as it stood before April 1, 2013, as a "funding arrangement", specifically, a CFA providing for the payment of a success fee, an insurance policy taken out against the risk of costs liability, and an agreement with a membership organisation to meet legal costs. The draftsman has met the considerable challenges posed in the drafting of Part 48 by distinguishing between a funding arrangement as defined by r.43.2(1)(k), made in relation to insolvency-related proceedings, publication or privacy proceedings, or a mesothelioma claim, and a funding arrangement so defined but entered into in relation to other proceedings. Both forms of funding arrangement are defined as a "pre-commencement funding arrangement". In relation to proceedings other than insolvency-related proceedings, publication or privacy proceedings, or a mesothelioma claim, "pre-commencement" means a funding arrangement made before April 1, 2013. In relation to insolvency-related proceedings, publication or privacy proceedings, or a mesothelioma claim, "pre-commencement" means a funding arrangement made at any time before s.44 and s.46 of the 2012 Act come into force; that is to say, at any time before April 1, 2013, or during the subsequent period in which the savings provisions in the 2012 Act and the commencement order explained above may continue to have effect. As noted above (para.48.0.2.4), in relation to insolvency-related proceedings, those saving provisions ceased to have effect on 6 April 2016. In respect of insolvency-related proceedings, s.44 and s.46 came into force on 6 April 2016.

Add new paragraph 48.2.2:

The relevant date for insolvency-related proceedings

In respect of insolvency-related proceedings, s.44 and s.46 came into force on 6 April 2016: **48.2.2**
Legal Aid, Sentencing and Punishment of Offenders Act 2012 (Commencement No.12) Order 2016 (SI 2016/345) art.2.

PART 44

[BEFORE APRIL 1, 2013] GENERAL RULES ABOUT COSTS

Rule 44.3(4)(c)—offers to settle

Add new paragraph at end:

Where a case had settled on terms offered by the defendants 6 months earlier but which offer **44x.3.20**
was withdrawn after 21 days for no good reason, the appropriate order was that the claimant should have his costs to the date of the offer with no order as to costs thereafter: *Patience v Tanner* [2016] EWCA Civ 158.

Rule 44.3(6)—types of order

Add to the end of the third last paragraph (beginning with "In respect of the question"):

In *Involnert Management Ltd v Aprilgrange Ltd* [2015] EWHC 2834 (Comm) the court ordered that **44x.3.22**
interest should run at the Judgments Act rate from three months after the orders for costs were made and at 2% over base rate during those three months.

GENERAL PRINCIPLES AND CASE LAW RELATING TO COSTS AND THEIR ASSESSMENT

Liquidation

Add new paragraph at end:

In misfeasance proceedings brought by liquidators against the directors, the **48GP.74**
court concluded that a disputed entry in the company's accounts was genuine. The directors sought their costs of that issue. The court decided that overall the liquidators had won the proceedings and the validity of the entry was not a freestanding allegation which it had been unreasonable for them to pursue. The directors had failed to engage with the litigation and had failed to explain the entry. Accordingly they should pay the costs of that issue: *Bishop v Fox*, 9 February 2016, unrep., Proudman J.

Trustees, personal representatives

Powers of the court as to costs

(iv) *Special factors*

Replace paragraph (where the citation for Exchange Securities & Commodities Ltd (No.2) has changed) with:

Examples of other special factors which might make a pre-trial order ap- **48GP.79** propriate include the following: Where it is essential for the due administration of justice for a liquidator or administrator to obtain the court's decision because there are large classes of persons, e.g creditors, who might be affected by the decision (*Exchange Securities & Commodities Ltd (No.2), Re* (1986) 2 B.C.C. 98932 at 395). Again the application might be a test case in which a decision is necessary on a point in order to resolve a number of pending cases (*Re Wedstock* [1988] B.C.L.C. 354 (above) at 360–361).

PART 51

TRANSITIONAL ARRANGEMENTS AND PILOT SCHEMES

County Court at Central London Multi-Track Pilot Scheme

Replace with:

51.2.11   By CPR Update 75 (July 2014) Practice Direction 51I (The County Court at Central London Multi-Track Pilot Scheme), made under Pt 51 and supplementing Pt 26, was introduced. It provides for a pilot scheme in respect of money claims issued at the County Court Business Centre and the County Court Money Claims Centre for a period of 12 months from October 1, 2014 to September 30, 2015. By CPR Update (August 2015) para.1.1 of this Practice Direction was amended for the purpose of extending the operation of this scheme for a further period of twelve months to September 30, 2016. (See para.51IPD.1 below.) In the light of experience gained by this pilot scheme, with effect from 3 October 2016, para.(6) was inserted in r.26.2A (Transfer of money claims within the County Court), putting on a formal basis a procedure for transferring to the County Court at Central London higher value claims initially sent to London hearing centres for determination. See para.26.2A.3.

The County Court Legal Advisers Pilot Scheme

Replace with:

51.2.13   By Update 79 (April 2015) Practice Direction 51K (The County Court Legal Advisers Pilot Scheme) was made under r.51.2 (see para.51KPD.1 and following below). It provides for a pilot scheme in respect of, and applies to, claims started in the County Court Business Centre and the County Court Money Claims Centre, initially for a period of 12 months from 1 October 2015 to 30 September 2016. By Update 84 (July 2016) the period was extended to 18 months from 1 October 2015 to 31 March 2017. By Update 84 (July 2016), with effect from 29 September 2016, the Schedule to PD 51K (Jurisdiction of County Court that may be exercised by a legal adviser) (see para.51KPD.4 below) was amended by the insertion of paras 2A and 9A, adding two further "work types".

New Bill of Costs Pilot Scheme

After "Costs Pilot Scheme")", replace "to operate for six months beginning on October 1, 2015" with:

51.2.14   which initially operated from October 1, 2015, to April 1, 2016. By Update 83 the period was extended to September 30, 2016, and by Update 84 (July 2016) was further extended to September 30, 2017.

Shorter and Flexible Trials Pilot Schemes

To the end of this paragraph, add:

51.2.16   As to the court's discretion to transfer an existing case into or out of the Shorter Trials Scheme, see *Family Mosaic Home Ownership Ltd v Peer Real Estate Ltd* [2016] EWHC 257 (Ch); [2016] 4 W.L.R. 37 (Birss J)).

Pilot for Insolvency Express Trials

Replace "para.51OPD.1 below" with:

51.2.17   para.51PPD.1 below).

Add new paragraphs at end:

The aim of the Insolvency Express Trials (IET) pilot scheme is to provide litigants in the Bankruptcy and Companies Court with a speedy, streamlined procedure, and an early date for the trial or disposal of simple applications by the bankruptcy registrars with consequential costs savings for the parties. Use of the IET pilot scheme is voluntary: applicants can decide which of their cases (if any) should proceed under the scheme, but there is provision for the respondent to object and for the court to remove an application from the IET list if it thinks fit. The scheme applies to simple applications which require limited directions and disclosure (only one directions hearing is envisaged) and can be disposed of finally in no more than two days. The trial date given will be a fixture and will not be capable of being be vacated by consent; and an adjournment will only be granted in exceptional circumstances. If sufficient time has been allowed in the time estimate judgment will generally be given at the trial. If judgment is reserved it will generally be handed down within four weeks of the trial. Costs will either be assessed summarily or detailed assessment may be ordered.

The costs management provisions of the CPR do not apply, but there is a costs cap, at present fixed at £75,000. This was fixed before the abolition of the insolvency exemption from the Legal Aid, Sentencing and Punishment of Offenders Act 2012 (see para.48.0.2.4 above) which otherwise removed the ability to recover CFA uplifts and after-the-event insurance premiums. It is hoped that the present figure can be reduced as a result.

Practitioners should note that the IET list operates alongside and in addition to the regimes created by Practice Direction 51N—Shorter and Flexible Trials Pilot Schemes (see para.51.2.16 above).

Comments and suggestions from users of the IET scheme should be sent to the chief registrar or may be made via the Bankruptcy and Companies Court Users' Committee.

PRACTICE DIRECTION 51K—THE COUNTY COURT LEGAL ADVISERS PILOT SCHEME

1. Scope and interpretation

Replace paragraph 1.1 with:

1.1 This Practice Direction is made under rule 51.2. It provides for a pilot **51KPD.1** scheme ("the County Court Legal Advisers Pilot Scheme") in respect of, and applies to, claims started at the County Court Business Centre ("CCBC") and the County Court Money Claims Centre ("CCMCC") for a period of 18 months from 1 October 2015 to 31 March 2017.

Schedule

Jurisdiction of the County Court that may be exercised by a legal adviser

Replace with:

Work type	Restrictions on the exercise of jurisdiction and modifications of the Civil Procedure Rules	
1. Order to rectify a procedural error pursuant to rule 3.10	Limited to those instances where the court serves a claim contrary to the claimant's instructions.	**51KPD.4**
2. Application to extend time for service of the claim form pursuant to rule 7.6	Limited to the first application, unless the claim would normally be allocated to the small claims track, and further limited to applications made within the period specified in rule 7.5 for service of the claim form.	
2A. Applications for an extension of time in which to serve the particulars of claim	Limited to the first application, unless the claim would normally be allocated to the small claims track, and further limited to applications made within the period specified in rule 7.4 for service of the particulars of claim.	

Work type	Restrictions on the exercise of jurisdiction and modifications of the Civil Procedure Rules
3. Applications to amend a claimant's or defendant's address or details after service, pursuant to rule 17.1(2)	Limited to applications prior to the expiration of the relevant limitation period and claims which have been, or would normally be, allocated to the small claims track.
4. Application to amend the particulars of claim or the amount of the claim pursuant to rule 17.1(2)	Limited to— (a) applications received before a defence is filed; or (b) if an application is received after a defence is filed, claims which have been, or would normally be, allocated to the small claims track.
5. Application to add or substitute a party to the proceedings pursuant to rule 19.4	Limited to applications where all existing parties, upon whom the claim has been served and who have acknowledged service, and the proposed new party agree to the addition or substitution and are in agreement that the application may be dealt with without a hearing.
6. Application or request to set aside default judgment, pursuant to rule 13.2	
7. Application to set aside default judgment, pursuant to rule 13.3	Limited to applications where— (a) all parties consent; and (b) the judgment is not satisfied.
8. Application to vary default judgment entered under Part 12, pursuant to rule 13.3	Limited to applications where— (a) the application relates to the time and rate of payment; and (b) all relevant parties consent.
9. Application to make a counterclaim after a defence has been filed, pursuant to rule 20.4(2)(b)	Limited to applications where all parties consent.
9A. Application to appoint a new litigation friend in substitution for an existing one pursuant to rule 21.7(1)(c).	
10. Application to extend time for complying with a notice of proposed allocation in accordance with rule 26.3(1)	Limited to one application per party, unless the claim has been provisionally allocated to the small claims track, and

Work type	Restrictions on the exercise of jurisdiction and modifications of the Civil Procedure Rules
	subject to the further limitation that time can be extended for a period not exceeding 28 days.
11. Application to stay proceedings pursuant to rule 26.4(2A) or to extend the period of a stay pursuant to rule 26.4(3)	Limited to one application and where all parties consent.
12. Application to remove a stay of proceedings made pursuant to rule 26.4(2Λ) or (3)	Limited to applications where all parties consent.
13. Applications for interim payments pursuant to rule 25.6	Limited to applications where all parties consent to the payment.
14. Entering and sealing an agreed judgment pursuant to rule 40.6(2) in any case where the requirements in Form EX224 are not met	
15. Applications for judgments or orders in terms agreed pursuant to rule 40.6(5)	
16. Application for an Order that a solicitor has ceased to act pursuant to rule 42.3	

PRACTICE DIRECTION 51L—NEW BILL OF COSTS PILOT SCHEME

This Practice Direction supplements CPR rule 47.6 and paragraph 5.1 of Practice Direction 47.

General

Replace paragraph 1.1 with:

1.1 This Practice Direction is made under rules 47.6 and 51.2. It provides for **51LPD.1** a pilot scheme ("New Bill of Costs Pilot Scheme") to operate, from 1 October 2015 to 30 September 2017.

Before the existing Part 52, add new Part 52 [After 3 October 2016]:

PART 52

[AFTER 3 OCTOBER 2016] APPEALS

Contents

Introductory Note

52n.0.1   Rule 10 of, and the Schedule to, the Civil Procedure (Amendment No.3) Rules 2016 (SI 2016/788) substituted for Part 52 a new Part 52. The rules in the new Part came into effect on 3 October 2016.

The principal amendments made to Part 52 as re-enacted concern the procedure for appeals to the Court of Appeal and relate to the determination of applications for permission to appeal to that Court and the exercise of functions of the Court by court officers. The objective is to reduce waiting times by ensuring that applications for permission to appeal are dealt with quickly and, where an oral hearing is required, promptly. The making of these and other amendments presented an opportunity to re-enact the whole of Part 52, setting out the rules in a more logical order. The Practice Directions supplementing Part 52 have been revised and amended and all are expected to be re-issued in CPR Update 86.

By a separate legislative initiative, that is the enactment of the Access to Justice Act 1999 (Destination of Appeals) Order 2016, replacing the Access to Justice Act 1999 (Destination of Appeals) Order 2000 (SI 2000/1071), also coming into force on 3 October 2016, new arrangements are made for the destination (or routes) of appeals, principally for the purpose of husbanding the resources of the Court of Appeal. These arrangements enlarge the circumstances in which appeals which would otherwise lie to that Court should lie instead to the High Court and abolish the distinction between interim and final decisions in this context. As and where necessary rules in the new Part 52 reflect the changes so made to routes of appeals. The effects of the legislation relating to routes of appeal are set out in provisions in Practice Directions supplementing Part 52.

Rule 16(1) of the statutory instrument states that, where an appellant's notice has been issued before 3 October 2016, the provisions of Part 52 in force immediately before that date continue to apply in relation to that case. In the new Part 52, r.52.24 (Who may exercise the powers of the Court of Appeal) re-enacts, but in a significantly amended form, r.52.16 as it stood in the old Part 52. Rule 16(2) of SI 2016/788 provides that, where a request was made under r.52.16 before 3 October 2016, for (a) review of a decision of a court officer; or (b) reconsideration of a decision of a single judge or a court officer made without a hearing, the provisions of r.52.16 in force immediately before that date continue to apply for the purposes of that review or reconsideration.

The new Part 52 is divided into seven Sections, whereas the old Part 52 had four. In the new

Part 52, Sections V, VI and VII accord with Sections II, III and IV in the old. What was Section I is exploded into four Sections, they are Sections I to IV. The principal objective of the new Part is revealed by the fact that two of those Sections, Section II (rr.52.3 to 52.7) and Section III (rr.52.8 to 52.11), contain rules dealing with applications for, and the granting or refusal of, permission to appeal (some of which were previously found in Section II).

In the new Part 52, 18 of the 30 rules are in the same terms as rules in the old Part 52, apart from minor changes in a few instances (correcting grammatical errors or rendering provisions gender neutral etc). Those 18 rules and their counterparts in the old Part 52 are as follows:

New	Old
52.1	52.1
52.2	52.2
52.14	52.5A
52.15	52.6
52.16	52.7
52.17	52.8
52.18	52.9
52.19	52.9A
52.20	52.10
52.21	52.11
52.22	52.12
52.23	52.14
52.25	52.12A
52.26	52.18
52.27	52.19
52.28	52.20
52.29	52.21
52.30	52.17

The whole of, or a part of, a further nine of the 30 rules in new Part 52 replicate with amendments (of varying degrees of importance), the whole of, or part of, rules in the old Part 52. Those rules are:

New	Old
52.3	52.3(1) to (3)
52.4(3) to (6)	52.3(4A) to (5)
52.6	52.3(6) & (7)
52.7	52.13
52.8	52.15
52.9	52.15A
52.10	52.15B
52.12	52.4
52.13	52.5
52.24	52.16

Rules in the new Part 52 not appearing in either of the above lists include paras (1) and (2) of r.52.4 (Determination of applications for permission to appeal to the County Court and High Court), and r.52.5 (Determination of applications for permission to appeal to the Court of Appeal). Those rules make significant changes to the law relating to the handling of applications for permission to appeal and for the granting or refusal of permission; see further para.52.4.1and para.52.5.1. Also not included in either of the above lists is r.52.11 (Appeals from the Employment Appeal Tribunal) which is a new provision in Part 52 (see para.52.11.1).

I. Scope and interpretation

Scope and interpretation

52n.1   52n.1—(1)   The rules in this Part apply to appeals to—
  (a)   the civil division of the Court of Appeal;
  (b)   the High Court; and
  (c)   the County Court.

(2)   This Part does not apply to an appeal in detailed assessment proceedings against a decision of an authorised court officer.

(3)   In this Part—
  (a)   "appeal" includes an appeal by way of case stated;
  (b)   "appeal court" means the court to which an appeal is made;
  (c)   "lower court" means the court, tribunal or other person or body from whose decision an appeal is brought;
  (d)   "appellant" means a person who brings or seeks to bring an appeal;
  (e)   "respondent" means—
      (i)   a person other than the appellant who was a party to the proceedings in the lower court and who is affected by the appeal; and
      (ii)   a person who is permitted by the appeal court to be a party to the appeal; and
  (f)   "appeal notice" means an appellant's or respondent's notice.

(4)   This Part is subject to any rule, enactment or practice direction which sets out special provisions with regard to any particular category of appeal.

Effect of rule

52n.1.1   This rule replaces former r.52.1, and is in the same terms. For relevant commentary, see para. 52.1.1 et seq.

Parties to comply with Practice Directions 52A to 52E

52n.2 **All parties to an appeal must comply with Practice Directions 52A to 52E.**

Effect of rule

52n.2.1   Practice Directions 52A to 52E supplementing Part 52 are expected to be re-issued in CPR Update 86. These Directions largely replicate those published in CPR Update 59 (September 2012), as subsequently amended, but include new directions to the extent necessary to supplement those rules in the new Part 52 which differ significantly from, or which had no counterpart among, rules in the old Part 52.

II. Permission to appeal – General

Permission to appeal

52n.3   52n.3—(1)   An appellant or respondent requires permission to appeal—
  (a)   where the appeal is from a decision of a judge in the County Court or the High Court, or to the Court of Appeal from a decision of a judge in the family court, except where the appeal is against—
      (i)   a committal order;
      (ii)   a refusal to grant habeas corpus; or
      (iii)   a secure accommodation order made under section 25 of the Children Act 1989; or
  (b)   as provided by Practice Directions 52A to 52E.
(Other enactments may provide that permission is required for particular appeals.)

(2)   An application for permission to appeal may be made—
  (a)   to the lower court at the hearing at which the decision to be appealed was made; or
  (b)   to the appeal court in an appeal notice.
(Rule 52.12 sets out the time limits for filing an appellant's notice at the ap-

peal court. Rule 52.13 sets out the time limits for filing a respondent's notice at the appeal court. Any application for permission to appeal to the appeal court must be made in the appeal notice (see rules 52.12(1) and 52.13(3)).)

(3) Where the lower court refuses an application for permission to appeal—

    (a) a further application for permission may be made to the appeal court; and

    (b) the order refusing permission must specify—

        (i) the court to which any further application for permission should be made; and

        (ii) the level of judge who should hear the application.

Effect of rule

    Previously there were two rules in Part 52 dealing with permission to appeal, they were r.52.3 **52n.3.1** (Permission) and r.52.13 (Second appeals to the Court). In the new Part 52 there are five, this rule and rr.52.4 to 52.7. Rule 52.3 accords with former r.52.3(1) to (3), but in para.(1) "or to the Court of Appeal from a judge in the family court," is added before "except". For commentary on former r.52.3(1) to (3), see para.52.3.1 et seq.

Determination of applications for permission to appeal to the County Court and High Court

    52n.4—(1) Where an application for permission to appeal is made to an **52n.4** appeal court other than the Court of Appeal, the appeal court will determine the application on paper without an oral hearing, except as provided for under paragraph (2).

    (2) Subject to paragraph (3) and except where a rule or practice direction provides otherwise, where the appeal court, without a hearing, refuses permission to appeal, the person seeking permission may request the decision to be reconsidered at an oral hearing.

    (3) Where in the appeal court a judge of the High Court, a Designated Civil Judge or a Specialist Circuit Judge refuses permission to appeal without an oral hearing and considers that the application is totally without merit, the judge may make an order that the person seeking permission may not request the decision to be reconsidered at an oral hearing.

    (4) For the purposes of paragraph (3), "Specialist Circuit Judge" means any Circuit Judge in the County Court nominated to hear cases in the Mercantile, Chancery or Technology and Construction Court lists.

    (5) Rule 3.3(5) (party able to apply to set aside, etc., a decision made of court's own initiative) does not apply to an order made under paragraph (3) that the person seeking permission may not request the decision to be reconsidered at an oral hearing.

    (6) A request under paragraph (2) must be filed within 7 days after service of the notice that permission has been refused.

Effect of rule

    Rule 52.4 is concerned with the determination of applications for permission to appeal to the **52n.4.1** County Court and the High Court. Rule r.52.5 is concerned with the determination of applications for permission to appeal to the Court of Appeal.

    In r.52.4, paras (1) and (2) are new provisions. Paragraph (1) establishes the new general rule that, where an application for permission to appeal is made to an appeal court other than the Court of Appeal, the appeal court will determine the application "on paper without an oral hearing". Paragraph (2) provides for exceptions to this rule. Paragraphs (3) to (6) replicate para.(4A)(a), para.(4A)(b), para.(4B), and para.(5) in former r.52.3. For commentary on those paragraphs in former r.52.3, see para.52.3.1 et seq.

Determination of applications for permission to appeal to the Court of Appeal

    52n.5—(1) Where an application for permission to appeal is made to the **52n.5** Court of Appeal, the Court of Appeal will determine the application on paper without an oral hearing, except as provided for under paragraph (2).

(2)   The judge considering the application on paper may direct that the application be determined at an oral hearing, and must so direct if the judge is of the opinion that the application cannot be fairly determined on paper without an oral hearing.

(3)   An oral hearing directed under paragraph (2) must be listed—

(a)   no later than 14 days from the date of the direction under that paragraph; and

(b)   before the judge who made that direction,

unless the court directs otherwise.

(4)   The Court of Appeal may, in any direction under paragraph (2)—

(a)   identify any issue or issues on which the party seeking permission should specifically focus its submissions at the oral hearing in order to assist the court to determine the application; and

(b)   direct the respondent to serve and file written submissions and to attend the oral hearing.

Effect of rule

52n.5.1   Previously, Part 52 contained no dedicated rule dealing exclusively with applications to the Court of Appeal for permission to appeal to that Court. However, in Practice Direction 52C (Appeals to the Court of Appeal) it was provided in para.15 (Determination of applications for permission to appeal) that an application would generally be considered by the Court without a hearing in the first instance, but if an application was refused the applicant would be entitled to have the decision reconsidered at a hearing, except where the rules provided otherwise (e.g. where the application had been determined as totally without merit). Rule 52.5(1) provides that an application will be determined on paper without an oral hearing. By r.52.5(2) the Court retains a discretion to direct that an application should be considered at an oral hearing, and must so direct in the circumstances stated in that sub-rule. Rule 52.5 applies to the determination of applications for permission to appeal however arising, including arising under the rules in Section III of Part 52. The changes mean that there is no longer an entitlement to have an oral renewal hearing in the Court of Appeal.

Permission to appeal test – first appeals

52n.6   52n.6—(1)   Except where rule 52.7 applies, permission to appeal may be given only where—

(a)   the court considers that the appeal would have a real prospect of success; or

(b)   there is some other compelling reason for the appeal to be heard.

(2)   An order giving permission under this rule or under rule 52.7 may—

(a)   limit the issues to be heard; and

(b)   be made subject to conditions.

(Rule 3.1(3) also provides that the court may make an order subject to conditions.)

(Rule 25.15 provides for the court to order security for costs of an appeal.)

Effect of rule

52n.6.1   Paras (1) and (2) of this rule respectively replicate paras (6) and (7) of former r.52.3. But in para.(1) the words "Except where rule 52.7 applies," and in para.(2) the words "under this rule or under rule 52.7," are new. For commentary on paras (6) and (7) of former r.52.3, see para.52.3 et seq.

Permission to appeal test – second appeals

52.7n   52n.7—(1)   Permission is required from the Court of Appeal for any appeal to that court from a decision of the County Court, the family court or the High Court which was itself made on appeal, or a decision of the Upper Tribunal which was made on appeal from a decision of the First-tier Tribunal on a point of law where the Upper Tribunal has refused permission to appeal to the Court of Appeal.

(2)   The Court of Appeal will not give permission unless it considers that—

(a) the appeal would—
      (i) **have a real prospect of success; and**
      (ii) **raise an important point of principle or practice; or**
(b) **there is some other compelling reason for the Court of Appeal to hear it.**

Effect of rule

In contrast to the rule it replaces (that is, r.52.13) this rule amplifies the second appeal test by **52n.7.1** providing, not only that the appeal would raise an important point of principle or practice, but also the additional requirement that it would have "a real prospect of success". In addition, the scope of the rule is broadened so that it in terms covers a decision of the Upper Tribunal which was made on appeal from a decision of the First-tier Tribunal on a point of law where the Upper Tribunal has refused permission to appeal to the Court of Appeal. For commentary on the former rule (r.52.13), see para.52.13.1 et seq.

III. Permission to appeal – judicial review appeals, planning statutory review appeals and appeals from the Employment Appeal Tribunal

Judicial review appeals from the High Court

52n.8—(1) **Where permission to apply for judicial review has been refused 52n.8 at a hearing in the High Court, an application for permission to appeal may be made to the Court of Appeal.**

(2) **Where permission to apply for judicial review of a decision of the Upper Tribunal has been refused by the High Court on the papers or where permission to apply for judicial review has been refused on the papers and recorded as being totally without merit in accordance with rule 23.12, an application for permission to appeal may be made to the Court of Appeal.**

(3) **An application under paragraph (1) must be made within 7 days of the decision of the High Court to refuse to give permission to apply for judicial review.**

(4) **An application under paragraph (2) must be made within 7 days of service of the order of the High Court refusing permission to apply for judicial review.**

(5) **On an application under paragraph (1) or (2), the Court of Appeal may, instead of giving permission to appeal, give permission to apply for judicial review.**

(6) **Where the Court of Appeal gives permission to apply for judicial review in accordance with paragraph (5), the case will proceed in the High Court unless the Court of Appeal orders otherwise.**

Effect of rule

This rule replaces former r.52.15. Rule 52.8(1) states that this rule applies where an application **52n.8.1** for judicial review has been refused at a hearing in the High Court, and an application for permission to appeal is made to the Court of Appeal. It also applies in the circumstances stated in r.52.8(2). Rule 52.5 (Determination of application for permission to appeal to the Court of Appeal) applies to an application for permission to appeal under r.52.8. For commentary on the former rule (r.52.15), see para.52.15.1 et seq.

Judicial review appeals from the Upper Tribunal

52n.9—(1) **Where permission to bring judicial review proceedings has 52n.9 been refused by the Upper Tribunal at a hearing and permission to appeal has been refused by the Upper Tribunal, an application for permission to appeal may be made to the Court of Appeal.**

(2) **Where an application for permission to bring judicial review proceedings has been determined by the Upper Tribunal on the papers and recorded as being totally without merit and permission to appeal has been refused by the Upper Tribunal, an application for permission to appeal may be made to the Court of Appeal.**

(3) **An application under this rule to the Court of Appeal must be made within 7 days of—**

    (a)   the decision of the Upper Tribunal refusing permission to appeal to the Court of Appeal, where that decision was made at a hearing; or

    (b)   service of the order of the Upper Tribunal refusing permission to appeal to the Court of Appeal, where the decision to refuse permission was made on the papers.

Effect of rule

52n.9.1   This rule replaces former r.52.15A. Rule 52.9(1) states that this rule applies where (a) an application for judicial review has been refused by the Upper Tribunal at a hearing and (b) permission to appeal has been refused by the Upper Tribunal, and an application for permission to appeal is made to the Court of Appeal. It also applies in the circumstances stated in r.52.9(2). Rule 52.5 (Determination of application for permission to appeal to the Court of Appeal) applies to an application for permission to appeal under r.52.9. For commentary on the former rule (r.52.15A), see para.52.15A.1.

Planning statutory review appeals

52n.10   52n.10—(1) Where permission to apply for a planning statutory review has been refused at a hearing in the High Court, an application for permission to appeal may be made to the Court of Appeal.

    (See Part 8 and Practice Direction 8C.)

    (2) Where permission to apply for a planning statutory review has been refused by the High Court on the papers and recorded as totally without merit in accordance with rule 23.12, an application for permission to appeal may be made to the Court of Appeal.

    (3) An application under paragraph (1) must be made within 7 days of the decision of the High Court to refuse to give permission to apply for a planning statutory review.

    (4) An application under paragraph (2) must be made within 7 days of service of the order of the High Court refusing permission to apply for a planning statutory review.

    (5) On an application under paragraph (1) or (2) the Court of Appeal may, instead of giving permission to appeal, give permission to apply for a planning statutory review.

    (6) Where the Court of Appeal gives permission to apply for a planning statutory review in accordance with paragraph (5), the case will proceed in the High Court unless the Court of Appeal orders otherwise.

Effect of rule

52n.10.1   This rule replaces former r.52.15B. Rule 52.10(1) states that this rule applies where permission to apply for a planning statutory review has been refused at a hearing in the High Court, and an application for permission to appeal is made to the Court of Appeal. It also applies in the circumstances stated in r.52.10(2). Rule 52.5 (Determination of application for permission to appeal to the Court of Appeal) applies to an application for permission to appeal under r.52.10. For commentary on the former rule (r.52.15B), see para.52.15B.1.

Appeals from the Employment Appeal Tribunal

52n.11   52n.11—(1) Where on an appeal to the Employment Appeal Tribunal either—

    (a)   the appellant or special advocate has been given notice under rule 3(7) of the Employment Appeal Tribunal Rules 1993 ("the 1993 Rules") and an order has been made under rule 3(7ZA) of those Rules; or

    (b)   a direction has been made under rule 3(10) of the 1993 Rules that no further action shall be taken on the notice of appeal,

the appellant may apply to the Court of Appeal for permission to appeal.

    (2) An application under paragraph (1) must be made within 7 days of the date of—

(a)   service of the notice under rule 3(7) of the 1993 Rules; or

(b)   the direction made under rule 3(10) of those Rules,

as the case may be.

(3)   The Court of Appeal may, instead of giving permission to appeal, direct that the notice under rule 3(7) of the 1993 Rules or (as the case may be) the direction under rule 3(10) of those Rules shall be of no effect so that the appeal shall proceed in the Employment Appeal Tribunal as if the notice or direction had not been given or made, but such a direction shall not be given unless the test for the grant of permission to appeal under rule 52.6(2) is met.

Effect of rule

Rule 52.11(1) refers to three provisions in the Employment Tribunal Rules 1993, r.3(7), r.3(7ZA) **52n.11.1** and r.3.10, and states that an application for permission to appeal may be made to the Court of Appeal where notices, directions and orders have been given or made under those rules. Rule 52.5 (Determination of application for permission to appeal to the Court of Appeal) applies to an application for permission to appeal under r.52.11.

Put briefly, the substance of r.3(7), r.3(7ZA) and r.3.10 of the 1993 Rules is as follows. On an appeal from an Employment Tribunal to the Employment Appeal Tribunal in relation to national security proceedings, the EAT may require a party to provide a document setting out grounds of appeal. Rule 3(7) states that where it appears to a judge or the Registrar that a notice of appeal or a document provided accordingly (a) discloses no reasonable grounds for bringing the appeal, or (b) is an abuse of the Appeal Tribunal's process or is otherwise likely to obstruct the just disposal of proceedings, he shall notify the appellant or special advocate accordingly informing him of the reasons for his opinion and no further action shall be taken on the notice of appeal or document provided. Where a judge or the Registrar has taken a decision under r.3(7), and also considers that the notice of appeal or document provided is totally without merit, then judge or Registrar may order under r.3(7ZA) that the appellant or special advocate is not entitled to have the matter heard before a judge under another provision, that is under r.3(10), which states that an appellant or special advocate who expresses dissatisfaction in writing with the reasons given by the judge or Registrar for his opinion, he is entitled to have the matter heard before a judge, who shall make a direction as to whether any further action should be taken on the notice of appeal or document.

IV.   Additional rules

Appellant's notice

52n.12—(1)   Where the appellant seeks permission from the appeal court, **52n.12** it must be requested in the appellant's notice.

(2)   The appellant must file the appellant's notice at the appeal court within—

(a)   such period as may be directed by the lower court (which may be longer or shorter than the period referred to in sub-paragraph (b)); or

(b)   where the court makes no such direction, and subject to the specific provision about time limits in rules 52.8 to 52.11 and Practice Direction 52D, 21 days after the date of the decision of the lower court which the appellant wishes to appeal.

(3)   Subject to paragraph (4) and unless the appeal court orders otherwise, an appellant's notice must be served on each respondent—

(a)   as soon as practicable; and

(b)   in any event not later than 7 days,

after it is filed.

(4)   Where an appellant seeks permission to appeal against a decision to refuse to grant an interim injunction under section 41 of the Policing and Crime Act 2009, the appellant is not required to serve the appellant's notice on the respondent.

Effect of rule

This replaces former r.52.4, and is in substantially the same terms. For relevant commentary, **52n.12.1** see para.52.4.1 et seq.

Respondent's notice

52n.13   52n.13—(1)   A respondent may file and serve a respondent's notice.

(2)   A respondent who—

(a)   is seeking permission to appeal from the appeal court; or

(b)   wishes to ask the appeal court to uphold the decision of the lower court for reasons different from or additional to those given by the lower court,

must file a respondent's notice.

(3)   Where the respondent seeks permission from the appeal court it must be requested in the respondent's notice.

(4)   A respondent's notice must be filed within—

(a)   such period as may be directed by the lower court; or

(b)   where the court makes no such direction, 14 days after the date in paragraph (5).

(5)   The date referred to in paragraph (4) is—

(a)   the date the respondent is served with the appellant's notice where—

(i)   permission to appeal was given by the lower court; or

(ii)   permission to appeal is not required;

(b)   the date the respondent is served with notification that the appeal court has given the appellant permission to appeal; or

(c)   the date the respondent is served with notification that the application for permission to appeal and the appeal itself are to be heard together.

(6)   Unless the appeal court orders otherwise, a respondent's notice must be served on the appellant and any other respondent—

(a)   as soon as practicable; and

(b)   in any event not later than 7 days,

after it is filed.

(7)   This rule does not apply where rule 52.12(4) applies.

Effect of rule

52n.13.1   This replaces former r.52.5, and is in substantially the same terms. (Para.(2)(b) now reads "the decision of the lower court" and not "the order of the lower court".) For relevant commentary, see para.52.5.1 et seq.

Transcripts at public expense

52n.14   52n.14—(1)   Subject to paragraph (2), the lower court or the appeal court may direct, on the application of a party to the proceedings, that an official transcript of the judgment of the lower court, or of any part of the evidence or the proceedings in the lower court, be obtained at public expense for the purposes of an appeal.

(2)   Before making a direction under paragraph (1), the court must be satisfied that—

(a)   the applicant qualifies for fee remission or is otherwise in such poor financial circumstances that the cost of obtaining a transcript would be an excessive burden; and

(b)   it is necessary in the interests of justice for such a transcript to be obtained.

Effect of rule

52n.14.1   This replaces former r.52.5A, and is in the same terms. For relevant commentary, see para.52.5A.1.

Variation of time

52n.15   52n.15—(1)   An application to vary the time limit for filing an appeal notice must be made to the appeal court.

(2)   The parties may not agree to extend any date or time set by—
   (a)   these Rules;
   (b)   Practice Directions 52A to 52E; or
   (c)   an order of the appeal court or the lower court.
(Rule 3.1(2)(a) provides that the court may extend or shorten the time for compliance with any rule, practice direction or court order (even if an application for extension is made after the time for compliance has expired).)

   (Rule 3.1(2)(b) provides that the court may adjourn or bring forward a hearing.)

Effect of rule

This replaces former r.52.6, and is in the same terms. For relevant commentary, see para.52.6.1 et seq. **52n.15.1**

Stay[(GL)]

Unless—   **52n.16**
   (a)   the appeal court or the lower court orders otherwise; or
   (b)   the appeal is from the Immigration and Asylum Chamber of the
         Upper Tribunal,
an appeal shall not operate as a stay of any order or decision of the lower court.

Effect of rule

This rule replaces former r.52.7, and is in the same terms. For relevant commentary, see **52n.16.1** para.52.7.1 et seq.

Amendment of appeal notice

An appeal notice may not be amended without the permission of the appeal **52n.17** court.

Effect of rule

This rule replaces former r.52.8, and is in the same terms. For relevant commentary, see **52n.17.1** para.52.8.1 et seq.

Striking out[(GL)] appeal notices and setting aside[(GL)] or imposing conditions on permission to appeal

52n.18—(1)   The appeal court may—   **52n.18**
   (a)   strike out the whole or part of an appeal notice;
   (b)   set aside permission to appeal in whole or in part;
   (c)   impose or vary conditions upon which an appeal may be brought.
   (2)   The court will only exercise its powers under paragraph (1) where there is a compelling reason for doing so.
   (3)   Where a party was present at the hearing at which permission was given, that party may not subsequently apply for an order that the court exercise its powers under subparagraphs (1)(b) or (1)(c).

Effect of rule

This rule replaces former r.52.9, and is in substantially the same terms. For relevant commentary, see para.52.9.1 et seq. **52n.18.1**

Orders to limit the recoverable costs of an appeal

52n.19—(1)   In any proceedings in which costs recovery is normally **52n.19** limited or excluded at first instance, an appeal court may make an order that the recoverable costs of an appeal will be limited to the extent which the court specifies.

(2)   In making such an order the court will have regard to—
  (a)   the means of both parties;
  (b)   all the circumstances of the case; and
  (c)   the need to facilitate access to justice.

(3)   If the appeal raises an issue of principle or practice upon which substantial sums may turn, it may not be appropriate to make an order under paragraph (1).

(4)   An application for such an order must be made as soon as practicable and will be determined without a hearing unless the court orders otherwise.

Effect of rule

52n.19.1   This rule replaces former r.52.9A, and is in the same terms. For relevant commentary, see para.52.9A.1.

Appeal court's powers

52n.20   52n.20—(1)   In relation to an appeal the appeal court has all the powers of the lower court.

(Rule 52.1(4) provides that this Part is subject to any enactment that sets out special provisions with regard to any particular category of appeal. Where such an enactment gives a statutory power to a tribunal, person or other body, it may be the case that the appeal court may not exercise that power on an appeal.)

(2)   The appeal court has power to—
  (a)   affirm, set aside or vary any order or judgment made or given by the lower court;
  (b)   refer any claim or issue for determination by the lower court;
  (c)   order a new trial or hearing;
  (d)   make orders for the payment of interest;
  (e)   make a costs order.

(3)   In an appeal from a claim tried with a jury the Court of Appeal may, instead of ordering a new trial—
  (a)   make an order for damages; or
  (b)   vary an award of damages made by the jury.

(4)   The appeal court may exercise its powers in relation to the whole or part of an order of the lower court.

(Part 3 contains general rules about the court's case management powers.)

(5)   If the appeal court—
  (a)   refuses an application for permission to appeal;
  (b)   strikes out an appellant's notice; or
  (c)   dismisses an appeal,
and it considers that the application, the appellant's notice or the appeal is totally without merit, the provisions of paragraph (6) must be complied with.

(6)   Where paragraph (5) applies—
  (a)   the court's order must record the fact that it considers the application, the appellant's notice or the appeal to be totally without merit; and
  (b)   the court must at the same time consider whether it is appropriate to make a civil restraint order.

Effect of rule

52n.20.1   This rule replaces former r.52.10, and is in the same terms. For relevant commentary, see para.52.10.1 et seq.

Hearing of appeals

52n.21   52n.21—(1)   Every appeal will be limited to a review of the decision of the lower court unless—
  (a)   a practice direction makes different provision for a particular category of appeal; or

    (b)   the court considers that in the circumstances of an individual appeal it would be in the interests of justice to hold a re-hearing.

(2)   Unless it orders otherwise, the appeal court will not receive—

    (a)   oral evidence; or

    (b)   evidence which was not before the lower court.

(3)   The appeal court will allow an appeal where the decision of the lower court was—

    (a)   wrong; or

    (b)   unjust because of a serious procedural or other irregularity in the proceedings in the lower court.

(4)   The appeal court may draw any inference of fact which it considers justified on the evidence.

(5)   At the hearing of the appeal, a party may not rely on a matter not contained in that party's appeal notice unless the court gives permission.

Effect of rule

This rule replaces former r.52.11, and is in the same terms. For relevant commentary, see para.52.11.1 et seq.   **52n.21.1**

Non-disclosure of Part 36 offers and payments

52n.22—(1)   The fact that a Part 36 offer or payment into court has been **52n.22** made must not be disclosed to any judge of the appeal court who is to hear or determine—

    (a)   an application for permission to appeal; or

    (b)   an appeal,

until all questions (other than costs) have been determined.

(2)   Paragraph (1) does not apply if the Part 36 offer or payment into court is relevant to the substance of the appeal.

(3)   Paragraph (1) does not prevent disclosure in any application in the appeal proceedings if disclosure of the fact that a Part 36 offer or payment into court has been made is properly relevant to the matter to be decided.

(Rule 36.4 has the effect that a Part 36 offer made in proceedings at first instance will not have consequences in any appeal proceedings. Therefore, a fresh Part 36 offer needs to be made in appeal proceedings. However, this rule applies to a Part 36 offer whether made in the original proceedings or in the appeal.)

Effect of rule

This rule replaces former r.52.12, and is in substantially the same terms. For relevant commentary, see para.52.12.1.   **52n.22.1**

V.   Special provisions relating to the Court of Appeal

Assignment of appeals to the Court of Appeal

52n.23—(1)   Where the court from or to which an appeal is made or from **52n.23** which permission to appeal is sought ("the relevant court") considers that—

    (a)   an appeal which is to be heard by the County Court or the High Court would raise an important point of principle or practice; or

    (b)   there is some other compelling reason for the Court of Appeal to hear it,

the relevant court may order the appeal to be transferred to the Court of Appeal.

(The Master of the Rolls has the separate statutory power to direct that an appeal which would be heard by the County Court or the High Court should be heard instead by the Court of Appeal – see section 57 of the Access to Justice Act 1999.)

(2)   The Master of the Rolls or the Court of Appeal may remit an appeal to the court in which the original appeal was or would have been brought.

Effect of rule

52n.23.1   This rule replaces former r.52.14, and is in the same terms. For relevant commentary, see para.52.14.1 et seq.

Who may exercise the powers of the Court of Appeal

52n.24   **52n.24**—(1)   A court officer assigned to the Civil Appeals Office who is—

(a)   a barrister; or

(b)   a solicitor

may exercise the jurisdiction of the Court of Appeal with regard to the matters set out in paragraph (2) with the consent of the Master of the Rolls.

(2)   The matters referred to in paragraph (1) are—

(a)   any matter incidental to proceedings in the Court of Appeal;

(b)   any other matter where there is no substantial dispute between the parties; and

(c)   the dismissal of an appeal or application where a party has failed to comply with any order, rule or practice direction.

(3)   A court officer may not decide an application for—

(a)   permission to appeal;

(b)   bail pending an appeal;

(c)   an injunction$^{(GL)}$;

(d)   a stay$^{(GL)}$ of execution of any order or decision of the lower court other than a temporary stay over a period when the Court of Appeal is not sitting or cannot conveniently be convened;

(e)   a stay of proceedings in the lower court.

(4)   Decisions of a court officer will be made without an oral hearing, unless a court officer directs otherwise.

(5)   A party may request any decision of a court officer to be reviewed by a single judge, and—

(a)   the review will be determined on paper without an oral hearing; except that

(b)   the judge determining the review on paper may direct that the review be determined at an oral hearing, and must so direct if the judge is of the opinion that the review cannot be fairly determined on paper without an oral hearing.

(6)   A party may request a decision of a single judge made without a hearing (other than a decision made on a review under paragraph (5) and a decision determining an application for permission to appeal) to be reconsidered, and—

(a)   the reconsideration will be determined by the same or another judge on paper without an oral hearing; except that

(b)   the judge determining the reconsideration on paper may direct that the reconsideration be determined at an oral hearing, and must so direct if the judge is of the opinion that the reconsideration cannot be fairly determined on paper without an oral hearing.

(7)   A request under paragraph (5) or (6) must be filed within 7 days after the party is served with notice of the decision.

(8)   A single judge may refer any matter for a decision by a court consisting of two or more judges.

(Section 54(4) of the Access to Justice Act 1999 provides that there is no appeal from the decision of a single judge on an application for permission to appeal.)

(Section 58(2) of the Senior Courts Act 1981 provides that there is no appeal to the Supreme Court from decisions of the Court of Appeal that—

(a)   are taken by a single judge or any officer or member of staff of that court in proceedings incidental to any cause or matter pending before the civil division of that court; and

(b) do not involve the determination of an appeal or of an application for permission to appeal,

and which may be called into question by rules of court. Paragraphs (5) and (6) of this rule provide the procedure for the calling into question of such decisions.)

Effect of rule

52n.24.1

This rule replaces former r.52.16 in terms which differ in some material respects. Where a request was made under former r.52.16 before 3 October 2016, for (a) review of a decision of a court officer; or (b) reconsideration of a decision of a single judge or a court officer made without a hearing, the provisions of r.52.16 in force immediately before that date continue to apply for the purposes of that review or reconsideration (see r.16(2) of SI 2016/788).

Under the former rule it was provided (1) that decisions of a court officer "may be made" without a "hearing", (2) that a party may request any decision of a court officer to be reviewed "by the Court of Appeal", and (3) that, at the request of a party, a hearing will be held to reconsider a decision of a court officer made without a hearing. It is now provided (1) that decisions of a court officer "will be made" without an "oral hearing", unless a court officer directs otherwise, (2) that a party may request any decision of a court officer to be reviewed "by a single judge" (r.56.24(5)), and (3) that the review will be determined by the judge "on paper without an oral hearing" (a) unless the judge otherwise directs, or (b) is required to so direct by r.52.24(5)(b).

The former rule also stated that, at the request of a party, a hearing "will be held" to reconsider a decision of a single judge of the Court of Appeal, whether made when reviewing a decision of a court officer or otherwise. It is now provided (1) that a party may request a decision of a single judge made without a hearing, other than a decision reviewing a decision of a court officer or a decision determining an application for permission to appeal (as to which see r.52.5), to be reconsidered and (2) that the reconsideration will be determined by the same or another judge "on paper and without an oral hearing" (a) unless the judge otherwise directs, or (b) is required to so direct by r.52.24(6)(b).

VI.   Special provisions relating to statutory appeals

Statutory appeals – court's power to hear any person

52n.25

52n.25—(1)   In a statutory appeal any person may apply for permission—
(a)   to file evidence; or
(b)   to make representations at the appeal hearing.
(2)   An application under paragraph (1) must be made promptly.

Effect of rule

52n.25.1

This rule replaces former r.52.12A, and is in the same terms. For relevant commentary, see para.52.12A.1.

Appeals under the Law of Property Act 1922

52n.26

An appeal lies to the High Court against a decision of the Secretary of State under paragraph 16 of Schedule 15 to the Law of Property Act 1922.

Effect of rule

52n.26.1

This rule replaces former r.52.18, and is in the same terms. For relevant commentary, see para.52.18.1.

Appeals from certain tribunals

52n.27

52n.27—(1)   A person who was a party to proceedings before a tribunal referred to in section 11(1) of the Tribunals and Inquiries Act 1992 and is dissatisfied in point of law with the decision of the tribunal may appeal to the High Court.
(2)   The tribunal may, on its own initiative or at the request of a party to the proceedings before it, state, in the form of a special case for the decision of the High Court, a question of law arising in the course of the proceedings.

Effect of rule

52n.27.1

This rule replaces former r.52.19, and is in the same terms. For relevant commentary, see para.52.19.1 et seq.

Appeals under certain planning legislation

52n.28 52n.28—(1) Where the Secretary of State has given a decision in proceedings on an appeal under Part VII of the Town and Country Planning Act 1990 against an enforcement notice—

    (a) the appellant;

    (b) the local planning authority; or

    (c) another person having an interest in the land to which the notice relates,

may appeal to the High Court against the decision on a point of law.

    (2) Where the Secretary of State has given a decision in proceedings on an appeal under Part VIII of that Act against a notice under section 207 of that Act—

    (a) the appellant;

    (b) the local planning authority; or

    (c) another person (other than the appellant) on whom the notice was served,

may appeal to the High Court against the decision on a point of law.

    (3) Where the Secretary of State has given a decision in proceedings on an appeal under section 39 of the Planning (Listed Buildings and Conservation Areas) Act 1990 against a listed building enforcement notice—

    (a) the appellant;

    (b) the local planning authority; or

    (c) any other person having an interest in the land to which the notice relates,

may appeal to the High Court against the decision on a point of law.

Effect of rule

52n.28.1 This rule replaces former r.52.20, and is in the same terms. For relevant commentary, see para.52.20.1 et seq.

Appeals under certain legislation relating to pensions

52n.29 Where an appeal lies to the High Court—

    (a) under section 151(4) of the Pension Schemes Act 1993 from a determination or direction of the Pensions Ombudsman; or

    (b) under section 217(1) of the Pensions Act 2004 from a determination or direction of the Pension Protection Fund Ombudsman,

the permission of the High Court is required for such an appeal to be brought.

VII. Reopening final appeals

Reopening of final appeals

52n.30 52n.30—(1) The Court of Appeal or the High Court will not reopen a final determination of any appeal unless—

    (a) it is necessary to do so in order to avoid real injustice;

    (b) the circumstances are exceptional and make it appropriate to reopen the appeal; and

    (c) there is no alternative effective remedy.

    (2) In paragraphs (1), (3), (4) and (6), "appeal" includes an application for permission to appeal.

    (3) This rule does not apply to appeals to the County Court.

    (4) Permission is needed to make an application under this rule to reopen a final determination of an appeal even in cases where under rule 52.3(1) permission was not needed for the original appeal.

    (5) There is no right to an oral hearing of an application for permission unless, exceptionally, the judge so directs.

    (6) The judge must not grant permission without directing the application to be served on the other party to the original appeal and giving that party an

opportunity to make representations.

(7) There is no right of appeal or review from the decision of the judge on the application for permission, which is final.

(8) The procedure for making an application for permission is set out in Practice Direction 52A."

Effect of rule

This rule replaces former r.52.17, and is in the same terms. For relevant commentary, see para.52.17.1 et seq. | **52n.30.1**

PART 52

APPEALS

Editorial introduction

Add new paragraph at the beginning:

Rule 10 of, and the Schedule to, the Civil Procedure (Amendment No. 3) Rules 2016 (SI 2016/788) substituted for Pt 52 a new Pt 52. The rules in the new Part came into effect on 3 October 2016. | **52.0.1**

Rights of appeal—routes of appeal—"final" decision

Add new paragraph at the beginning:

The Access to Justice Act 1999 (Destination of Appeals) Order 2000 (SI 2000/1071) was revoked and replaced by the Access to Justice Act 1999 (Destination of Appeals) Order 2016 with effect from 3 October 2016, subject to transitional provisions. In its effects the 2016 Destination differs significantly to the 2000 Destination Order. In particular it makes no distinction between interim and final decisions and it removes the exceptions by which, under the 2000 Destination Order, appeals against certain final decisions would lie to the Court of Appeal. From 3 October 2016, appeals will generally be dealt with by the next tier of the judiciary. In this way, for example, an appeal from a County Court judge will be heard by a High Court judge and will no longer go to the Court of Appeal. See further, Vol.2 para. 9A-853 | **52.0.4**

I. General Rules about Appeals

Approach of appeal court to costs appeals

Delete the fourth paragraph (beginning with "That dictum has been adopted"). | **52.1.4**

After the sixth paragraph (beginning with "Where the issue on the appeal"), add as a new paragraph:

In *Patience v Tanner* [2016] EWCA Civ 158, 22 March 2016, CA, unrep., the Court explained the approach that an appeal court should take to an appeal against a costs order made by a trial court where the proceedings settled prior to trial.

Requirement for permission

Replace the second paragraph (where the citation for Michael Wilson & Partners Ltd v Emmott has changed) with:

An appeal from the High Court to the Court of Appeal invoking the Court's so-called "residual jurisdiction" (see Vol.2 paras 2F-268and 9A-55.1) is an "appeal" for the purposes of the Senior Courts Act 1981 s.16(1), and it follows from that that such an appeal is an appeal for which permission to appeal is required by r.52.3 (*Michael Wilson & Partners Ltd v Emmott* [2015] EWCA Civ 1285; [2016] 1 W.L.R. 857, CA). | **52.3.1**

The effect of refusal of permission

Add new paragraph at end:

Where a judge of the High Court grants a defendant's application to discharge a freezing order against it, and refuses permission to appeal, the judge has power to order that the discharge should take effect only after a prescribed period, sufficient to enable it to protect its position by making an application to the Court of Appeal for a freezing order pending an appeal to that Court (supplemental judgment in *Metropolitan Housing Trust Ltd v Taylor* [2015] EWHC 2897 (Ch), 23 October 2015, unrep. (Warren J)). See further Vol.2 para.15-9.1. | **52.3.8**

Application for permission to appeal "totally without merit"-reconsideration

Replace the second paragraph with:

52.3.8.1   Sub-rules (4A) and (4B) were originally added to r.52.3 by the Civil Procedure (Amendment) Rules 2006 (SI 2006/1689) for the purpose of enabling the Court of Appeal to make an order to the effect that a person refused permission to appeal may not request the decision to be reconsidered at a hearing. Such an order may be made if the appeal court considers that the application is "totally without merit". Sub-rule (4A) was significantly modified by the Civil Procedure (Amendment No.2) Rules 2012 (SI 2012/2208) for the purpose of extending the powers of the Court of Appeal in this respect to judges sitting at other levels in the appellate hierarchy and dealing with applications for permission to appeal. In this way, High Court Judges, Designated Civil Judges, and some Specialist Civil Judges have the jurisdiction to refuse an application for permission to appeal on the papers, and if they conclude that the appeal is "totally without merit", there is no right to a further oral hearing.

Add new paragraphs at end:

In circumstances where sub-rule (4A) of r.52.3 applies the judge "may make" an order that the person seeking permission to appeal may not request the decision to be reconsidered at a hearing; the loss of the right to a hearing is not an automatic consequence. This may be contrasted with the position where an applicant's application for permission to apply for judicial review is certified as TWM and r.52.15 or r.52.15A governs the applicant's application to the Court of Appeal for permission to appeal; in that event the application will be determined on paper without a hearing (see para.52.15.1 below).

No authoritative test has emerged for determining whether an application for permission to appeal should be certified as "totally without merit". In *R. (Grace) v Secretary of State for the Home Department* [2014] EWCA Civ 1091; [2014] 1 W.L.R. 3432, CA, and *R. (Wasif) v Secretary of State for the Home Department* [2016] EWCA Civ 82, 9 February 2016, CA, unrep., the Court of Appeal has given guidance on the approach to be adopted in the quite different context of applications for permission to apply for judicial review (see further para.54.12.1 below).

Permission will be granted more sparingly to appeal against case management decisions

Replace the last paragraph (where the citation for Abdulle v Commissioner of Police of the Metropolis has changed) with:

52.3.9   In *Abdulle v Commissioner of Police of the Metropolis* [2015] EWCA Civ 1260; [2016] 1 W.L.R. 898, CA the Court of Appeal re-affirmed that it would not lightly interfere with case management decisions of lower courts and stressed that that approach applied to decisions to grant or refuse relief from sanctions under r.3.9 and to decisions on whether to strike out under r.3.4(2)(c).

The role of respondents in relation to permission applications

Replace the first paragraph with:

52.3.17   In relation to appeals to the Court of Appeal the role of the respondent to an appeal is affected by provisions in Practice Direction 52C (Appeals to the Court of Appeal) as significantly amended by Update 79 with effect from 6 April 2015; in particular, by para.19 (Respondent's actions when served with the appellant's notice), and by para.20 (Respondent's costs of permission applications) (see paras 52CPD.19 and 52CPD.20 below). (Initially those directions reflected guidance given by the Court in *Jolly v Jay* [2002] EWCA Civ 277, 7 March 2002, CA, unrep.) It may be noted that, as amended, para.19(1)(a) states that a respondent "is permitted, and is encouraged" to file and serve "a brief statement" of any reasons why the appellant should be refused permission to appeal. (Before 6 April 2015, it was provided that a respondent "need not take any action" until notified that permission to appeal had been granted.)

Delete the second and third paragraphs.

Statutory time limits for filing notice of appeal

Replace the last paragraph (where the citation for Szegfu v Hungary has changed) with:

52.4.1.1   In relation to appeals under s.26(4) of the Extradition Act 2003, para.21.1(c) of PD52D stated that the appellant must serve a copy of the notice of appeal on the CPS, if they are not a party to the appeal, in addition to the persons to be served under r.52.4(3) "and in accordance with that rule". With effect from October 6, 2014, and subject to transitional provisions, rules of court for appeals to the High Court in extradition proceedings were included in Section 3 of Pt.17 in the Criminal Procedure Rules 2014 (SI 2014/1610) and by CPR Update 75 the whole of para.21.1 was omitted from PD52D. Cases dealing with the point that the court had no jurisdiction to extend the times limits for service of notices of appeal as required by para.21.1 are: *R. (Bajorek Sawczuk) v Poland* [2014] EWHC 1108 (Admin), March 21, 2014, unrep. (Collins J.); *Bugyo v Slovakia* [2014] EWHC 4230 (Admin), November 21, 2014, unrep. (Blake J.). Amendments made to Extradition Act 2003 effected by the Anti-social Behaviour, Crime and Policing Act 2014 s.160 altered the provisions imposing time limits on appeals for all cases in which notice of appeal was given on or after April 15, 2015. The effect of s.26(5) (as amended) is to require the High Court to refuse to entertain an application in a case in which notice was given outside a specified period of seven days unless the person concerned shows that he did everything reasonably possible to ensure that notice was given as soon as it could be given (*Szegfu v Hungary* [2015] EWHC 1764 (Admin); [2016] 1 W.L.R. 322, DC).

Date when time starts to run

In the last paragraph, replace "21 days" with:
   28 days
                                                                                          52.4.2

Skeleton argument

At the end of the first paragraph, replace "para.5.3" with:
   para.1(1)
                                                                                          52.4.5

To the end of the third paragraph (beginning with "As to form and content"), add:
   An appeal may be struck out and dismissed where the appellant fails to comply with the practice direction as to the preparation and filing of skeleton arguments (e.g. *Vaux v Solicitors Regulation Authority* [2015] EWHC 1365 (Admin), 31 March 2015, unrep., where the directions were reinforced by case management directions given by the appeal court).

At the end of the fifth paragraph (beginning with "The cost of preparing a skeleton"), replace "para.5.1(4)" with:
   para.5.1(5)

Compelling reason for setting aside permission to appeal

After the fourth paragraph (beginning with "In R. (Sabir)"), add new paragraph:
   In *R. (Khan) v. Secretary of State for the Home Department* [2016] EWCA Civ 416, 4 May 2016, CA, **52.9.2** unrep., the nature of the appellant's duty of candour when making an application for permission to appeal, and the contrasts between that duty and the similar duty arising on an application for permission to proceed with a judicial review claim or for an interim injunction, was exhaustively examined by the Court of appeal. In that case the appellant's application to the Court of Appeal for permission to appeal to the Court was granted by a single lord justice at a hearing, but on the respondent's application under r.52.9(1)(b) was set aside. The Court found that the application for permission to appeal was made on a factual basis which the appellant knew to be fundamentally false, and that amounted to a compelling reason for setting the permission to appeal aside in whole.

Imposition of conditions

To the end of the fifth paragraph (beginning with "In Société Générale SA v SAAD"), add:
   In *Goldtrail Travel Ltd v Aydin* [2016] EWCA Civ 20, 21 January 2016, unrep. (Patten LJ) it was **52.9.4** explained that, in deciding whether to impose the condition that the appellant should pay the judgment debt into court, there is no absolute bar against the court's taking into account the position of other entities or persons "close to the appellant", in particular, for example, where the appellant is a corporation, by taking into account that it has "wealthy owners" who could, if they were so minded, pay the judgment debt on its behalf.
   The relevant authorities were closely examined by a single lord justice in *Cruz City 1 Mauritius Holdings v Unitech Limited* [2013] EWCA Civ 1512, 22 November 2013, CA, unrep. (Gloster LJ), where, as a result of London-based arbitrations, one company (D) owed another (C) US$300m plus costs with interest, and for purposes of enforcement C issued an arbitration claim form, applying for an order requiring disclosure of assets by D. On D's application for permission to appeal to the Court of Appeal against the disclosure order, C applied for a condition to be attached to the permission to appeal to the effect that D should pay the whole or a substantial proportion of the sums due under the awards into court, or alternatively secure such payment. In granting C's application the single lord justice held: (1) in circumstances where a judgment debtor (in respect of a debt that is no longer subject to appeal), who has participated in liability proceedings in this jurisdiction, is able to pay a judgment debt, but has no intention of doing so, and is taking all possible steps to avoid enforcement of the judgment against its assets, whether in this jurisdiction or elsewhere, the court may well consider that it is appropriate, in exercise of its powers under r.52.3(7)(b), to attach a condition of payment in full of the judgment debt, to the grant of any permission to appeal against a post judgment enforcement order, (2) in circumstances where a judgment debtor is attempting to appeal the original judgment imposing liability upon him, is well able to pay the judgment debt, but is taking all steps open to him to avoid enforcement, there may well be a compelling reason for the imposition of a payment condition, (3) in the present case, factors combining to constitute a compelling reason for making D either pay the judgment debt or

secure it as a condition of permitting them to proceed with the appeal, included (a) that D were clearly in a position to pay the substantial sums which they owe C under the awards, without undue disruption to their business, or concerns about insolvency, but had deliberately taken the decision not to do so and to disobey orders of the English court requiring payment, and (b) that D had thwarted, and would continue to thwart, C's attempts at enforcement, in a variety of different jurisdictions by placing every obstacle in the latter's way.

The relevant authorities were again examined in detail by a single lord justice in *Merchant International Co Ltd v Natsionalna Aktsionerna Kompaniia Naftogaz Ukrainy* [2016] EWCA Civ 710, 7 July 2016, CA, unrep. (Christopher Clarke LJ), where, as a condition of the grant of permission to appeal the appointment of a receiver, a security for costs order was imposed in the sum of US$24.7m, being the whole of an unpaid judgment debt, interest, historic unpaid costs, and the estimated costs of the appeal. The judge said that, in the light of the authorities, five matters were clear ((a) to (e)) and was of the opinion that a sixth could be added to them. Those matters are:

(a)   the essential question is whether or not there is a compelling reason to make payment in of the judgment sum, plus costs and interest (or some part thereof) a condition of further pursuit of the appeal ("a security payment order");

(b)   whether there is a compelling reason is a value judgement to be made on the particular facts of the case under consideration;

(c)   the fact that a judgment had been entered against an appellant and no stay has been sought or granted does not mean that, as a matter of course, compliance with the judgment should be made a condition of appeal nor does it, alone, afford a compelling reason for a security payment order;

(d)   on the contrary, the power in r.52.9 was not designed to be no more than an alternative means of securing enforcement and is only to be exercised with caution;

(e)   whilst every case depends on its particular facts the court is likely to find there to be a compelling reason to make a security payment order which has that effect if the judgment debtor has in the past or is likely in the future to take steps to denude itself of assets or to put its assets beyond the reach of normal enforcement processes;

(f)   there may be a compelling reason to make a security payment order even if it is not established that the appellant as acted as in (e) above (this may be the case if there are considerable practical difficulties in effecting execution).

Replace title and paragraph with:

"party … may not subsequently apply for an order" (r.52.9(3))

52.9.5 Section 54(1) of the Access to Justice Act 1999 states that rules of court may provide that any right of appeal may be exercised "only with permission". Section 54(4) states that no appeal may be made against a decision of a court "under this section" giving or refusing permission, but that prohibition does not affect any right under rules of court to make a further application for permission "to the same or another court". Rules made in exercise of the rule-making power stated in s.54 include r.52.3(7), which states that an order giving permission to appeal, whether made by the lower court or the appeal court, may be made on terms limiting the issues to be heard and making it subject to conditions. Where an order giving permission is made on terms there is one composite decision, and the prohibition on an appeal imposed by s.54(4) applies to both the permission and to the terms *(R. (Medical Justice) v Secretary of State for the Home Department* [2011] EWCA Civ 269; [2011] 1 W.L.R. 2852, CA, at para.13, per Lord Neuberger MR).

However, although there is no appeal against the grant of permission and/or against any terms (if imposed), r.52.9(1) provides that the appeal court may set aside permission to appeal in whole or in part (r.52.9(1)(b)) and/or impose or vary conditions upon which the appeal may be brought (r.52.9(1)(c)). But this power is restricted by r.52.9(3) which states that, where permission to appeal was given at a hearing, a party "present at the hearing" may not subsequently apply for an order that the court exercise its powers to set aside permission or to impose or vary conditions, even where there has been a change of circumstances. The application of r.52.9(3) has occasioned some difficulty. The relevant authorities were examined by the Court of Appeal in *R. (Medical Justice) v Secretary of State for the Home Department* [2011] EWCA Civ 269; [2011] 1 W.L.R. 2852, CA, and subsequently by a single lord justice in *Spar Shipping AS v Grand China Logistics Holding (Group) Co Ltd* [2016] EWCA Civ 520, 12 April 2016, CA, unrep. (Longmore LJ).

The position is that r.52.9(3), despite examples of cases in which it has not been applied literally, or has been unnoticed or ignored, or has been regarded as subject to the court's general case management powers stated in r.3.1, means what it says, and it applies both where the hearing at which permission was granted was one held in a lower court as well as one held in an appeal court. Rule 52.9(3) is there for a purpose. Its purpose is to control costs and delays in the progressing and determination of appeals by denying parties, once they have had an opportunity of doing so, the further opportunity to make submissions about the matters referred to in sub-paras (1)(b) and (1)(c) of r.52.9 *(Spar Shipping AS v Grand China Logistics Holding (Group) Co Ltd* op cit at paras 15 & 27).

The restriction imposed by r.52.9(3) applies to a party who was present at the hearing at which permission was given (most likely the prospective appellant). In the Medical Justice case it was explained that r.52.9 seems implicitly to assume that a party making an application to an appeal invoking sub-paras (1)(b) and/or (1)(c) of r.52.9(1), and who had not been present at the hearing at which the terms were imposed (most likely the respondent), would not be appealing against the decision to impose terms; rather that party would be seeking to advance its case for the first time (at para.15 per Lord Neuberger MR). If that analysis is not right, and the party's application should properly characterised as an appeal, then to the extent that r.52.9(3) permits such application arguably it would be ultra vires as contrary to s.54(4) of the 1999 Act.

In the *Medical Justice* case, the Court of Appeal explained the procedural choices open to an appellant (1) who has been given permission to appeal by the lower court, but subject to conditions (limiting the issues and/or subject to conditions), (2) who is dissatisfied with the terms, and (3) who is (a) by operation of s.54(4) necessarily prevented from appealing, and (b) because present at the hearing where permission was given, by operation of r.52.9(3) is not permitted to make an application under r.52.9(1). The Court said the prospective appellant in such a case is put to an election. Either the appellant (1) accepts the terms, in which case he or she has permission to appeal, albeit on those terms, or (2) treats the conditional permission as a refusal, and pursues a fresh application to appeal to the appropriate appeal court (op cit at para.19 per Lord Neuberger MR).

II. Special Provisions Applying to the Court of Appeal

Skeleton and supplementary skeleton arguments

In the first paragraph, replace "Practice Direction 52A para.5.1(4)" with:
Practice Direction 52A para.5.1(5)

52.12.1.4

What constitute "first" and "second" appeals for these purposes

Add new paragraph at the beginning:
In *Handley v Lake Jackson Solicitors* [2016] EWCA Civ 465; 2016 W.L.R. 3138, CA, the Court of **52.13.2** Appeal said that the language used in s.55(1) of 1999 Act "is somewhat ambiguous" and held that the correct construction is as follows: (1) that the sub-section is applicable only in respect of the decision of the County Court on the appeal to it, (2) that it applies where an appeal is made to the County Court "in relation to any matter", by which is meant the subject matter of the appeal to that court, namely the decision of the district judge, (3) that when the sub-section then refers to a decision "in relation to that matter" it refers to the decision which the County Court makes as to the validity or otherwise of the decision of the district judge. Consequently, the second appeals test relates only to the decision of the County Court on that issue. The Court rejected the submission that the sub-section should be given a broader construction having the effect of applying it where there was an appeal to the County Court in relation to any decision of the County Court made on appeal, including a decision in respect of the costs of an appeal. In the Handley case, the Court considered appeals against costs orders in three unrelated cases, each raising issues as to whether the appeal lay to the High Court or to Court of Appeal and as to whether the second appeal test stated in r.52.13(2) applied.

Application for permission to appeal against refusal of permission below

Add new paragraph at end:
In *R. (Wasif) v Secretary of State for the Home Department* [2016] EWCA Civ 82, 9 February 2016, **52.15.1** CA, unrep., the Court of Appeal explained (para.7) that it is established that one consequence of certain provisions in r.52.15 (Judicial review appeals from the High Court) and r.52.15A (Judicial review appeals from the Upper Tribunal) is that, where an application for permission to apply for judicial review has been certified by the court or tribunal below as "totally without merit", a judge of the Court of Appeal is precluded from directing that an application for permission to appeal be heard orally, even if the judge believes that in the particular circumstances of the case a hearing would be desirable. The Court (1) commented that it is surprising, and sometimes inconvenient, that the hands of a judge of the Court of Appeal should be tied in this way by a decision taken at first instance, and (2) doubted whether this was the rule-makers' intention.

Effect of rule

Replace the third paragraph with:
An application for permission to appeal may be considered by an appeal court at an oral hear- **52.15A.1** ing or on paper. Paragraph (2) of this rule states, categorically, that in the circumstances provided for therein "the application will be determined on paper without an oral hearing". In this respect, r.52.15A accords with r.52.15.

PART 53

DEFAMATION CLAIMS

Direction to elect whether or not to make offer of amends

At the end of the paragraph replace "53PD.37" with:

53.2.3   53PD.27

PRACTICE DIRECTION 53—DEFAMATION CLAIMS

Pleading the meaning

Replace the last paragraph with:

53PD.6   Note that by s.1(1) of the Defamation Act 2013, a statement is not defamatory unless its publication has caused or is likely to cause serious harm to the reputation of the claimant. For the requirements of s.1(1), see *Cooke v MGN* [2014] EWHC 2831 (QB); [2015] W.L.R. 895, *Lachaux v Independent Print Ltd* [2016] Q.B. 402; [2015] EWHC 2242 (QB); [2016] 2 W.L.R. 437; [2015] E.M.L.R. 28, *Theedon v Nourish Training (t/a CSP Recruitment)* [2015] EWHC 3769 (QB); [2016] E.M.L.R. 10, and *Sobrinho v Impresa Publishing SA* [2016] EWHC 66 (QB); [2016] E.M.L.R. 12. Proof that the words complained of have caused or are likely to cause serious harm to reputation may be achieved by inference, but the claimant would be wise to plead all relevant circumstances, including the extent and nature of publication, the sort of people to whom the words were published, altered behaviour on the part of those who knew him, and adverse social media responses: see generally *Lachaux* at [101]ff. The bar is higher for bodies trading for profit, because by s.1(2) harm to reputation is not in their case "serious harm" unless they can show at least the likelihood of serious financial loss.

Damages

Replace the second paragraph (where the citation for Lachaux v Independent Print Ltd has changed) with:

53PD.24   However, in the light of Defamation Act 2013 s.1(1), the claimant must in every case show that publication of the words complained of has caused or is likely to cause serious damage to his or her reputation. (A higher threshold still applies to bodies trading for profit: s.1(2): harm to the reputation of a body that trades for profit is not "serious harm" unless it has caused or is likely to cause the body serious financial loss). It therefore appears that, whether or not Parliament envisaged it, the common law presumption of damage has been swept away: *Lachaux v Independent Print Ltd* [2016] Q.B. 402; [2015] EWHC 2422 (QB); [2016] 2 W.L.R. 437; [2015] E.M.L.R. 28 at [60].

Offer of amends and s.1, Defamation Act 2013

Replace the paragraph (where the citation for Lachaux v Independent Print Ltd has changed) with:

53PD.28.1   A defendant who wishes to resist a claim on the basis that it fails to meet the threshold of serious harm to reputation created by s.1 should not serve a defence before taking the serious harm point. If the application to determine the threshold issue fails, because no defence has been served the defendant can still consider making an offer of amends (*Lachaux v Independent Print Ltd* [2016] Q.B. 402; [2015] EWHC 2422 (QB); [2016] 2 W.L.R. 437; [2015] E.M.L.R. 28 at [169]).

Ruling on meaning

Replace with:

53PD.32   Defamation Act 2013, s.11 provides that trial will be without jury unless the court orders otherwise. The consequence is that jury trial in defamation will soon be as vanishingly rare as it has long been in personal injury cases. The new provision applies to cases begun on or after January 1, 2014 (see Defamation Act 2013, s.16(7)), so 53PD para.4 will continue to apply to any actions started before that date where jury trial has been ordered. For actions started on or after January 1, 2014, para.4 and the notes that follow are redundant: there will rarely if ever (but see *Al Alaoui v Elaph Publishing Ltd* [2015] EWHC 1084 (QB)) be any purpose in seeking a ruling as to what meanings the words complained of are capable of bearing. Instead, the court will be asked at an early stage to determine the actual meaning of the words by way of preliminary issue. For the advantages in terms of both speed and cost, of determining the actual meaning by way of preliminary issue, see *RBOS Shareholders Action Group v News Group Newspapers Ltd* [2014] EWHC 130 (QB); [2014] E.M.L.R. 15; and for a recent example of this practice and the considerations in play, see *Hiranandani-Vandrevala v Times Newspapers Ltd* [2016] EWHC 250 (QB); [2016] E.M.L.R. 16. In *Rufus v Elliott* [2015] EWCA Civ 121; [2015] E.M.L.R. 17, a pre-2013 Act case, the claimant would not agree to the defendant's proposal that the actual meaning should be determined by the judge, so the issue of capability had to go to the Court of Appeal and the issue of the actual meaning had then to be remitted to the judge: see [28].

PART 54

JUDICIAL REVIEW AND STATUTORY REVIEW

Editorial introduction

Replace the last paragraph with:

When brought into force, sub-section (1) of s.85 will amend SCA 1981 s.31(3) to provide that no **54.0.1**
application for judicial review may be made unless the claimant provides any information about the
financing of the claim which is required under any rules of court. Section 87 deals with interveners,
defined as persons who were granted permission to file evidence or make representations in
judicial review proceedings and were not, at that time, parties (see para. 9A–1311 below). That section came into force on April 13, 2015, subject to the same transitional provision as applied to
s.84(1) to (3) (see SI 2015/778 arts 3 and 4). The section states that a party may not be ordered to
pay an intervener's costs unless there are exceptional circumstances making it appropriate to do so.
There are also provisions in the section governing the circumstances in which interveners can be
made to pay costs incurred by other parties. There are provisions in ss.88 to 90 dealing with orders
limiting or removing the liability of a party to pay costs (these are currently known as protective
costs orders, although they are referred to in the 2015 Act as cost-capping orders) (see paras 9A–
1312 to 9A–1314 below). Sections 88 to 90 were brought into effect on August 8, 2016. The rules of
court necessary to support the jurisdiction of the High Court and the Court of Appeal to make
costs capping orders in judicial review proceedings in the circumstances permitted by ss.88 to 90
are contained in Section VI (rr.46.16 to 46.19) of CPR Part 46 (see further para.46.16.1 above).

Related sources

Replace list with:
- Senior Courts Act 1981 s.31 (Vol.2, para.9A-101.)   **54.0.4**
- CPR Pt 8
- CPR r.52.15 (judicial review appeals)
- Nationality, Immigration and Asylum Act 2002
- Tribunals, Courts and Enforcement Act 2007
- Criminal Justice and Courts Act 2015.

I. Judicial Review

Against whom does judicial review lie

Replace the fourth paragraph with:

The current approach is conveniently summarised in the decision of the Divisional Court in *R. v*   **54.1.2**
Insurance Ombudsman Bureau Ex p. Aegon Life Insurance Ltd, *The Times* January 7, 1994. The court
held that judicial review would not lie against a body whose birth and constitution owed nothing to
any exercise of governmental power; a body could be classed as public only if it had been woven
into the fabric of public regulation or into a system of governmental control, or was integrated into
a system of statutory regulation or, but for its existence, a governmental body would assume
control. Judicial review did not lie against a body whose powers derived from the agreement of the
parties and when private law remedies were available against the body concerned. The Insurance
Ombudsman Bureau fell into the latter category because it was a body whose jurisdiction was
dependent on the contractual consent of its members and its decisions were of a private law
arbitrative nature. The application of these principles is not always easy in practice. In *R. (Holmcroft
Properties Ltd) v KMPG LLP* [2016] EWHC 323 (Admin), the Divisional Court was dealing with a
system whereby the Financial Conduct Authority was concerned with redress for alleged mis-selling
of certain financial products by a particular bank. An agreement was entered into whereby a non-
statutory body (a limited liability partnership) was appointed as an independent reviewer to report
on the progress of the redress scheme and offers of redress to individual customers needed the approval of the independent reviewer. A decision of the independent reviewer was held not to be
amenable to judicial review. Although woven into the regulatory framework, the scheme of redress
was essentially voluntary and the independent reviewer's powers were confirmed by contract. See
generally, Ch.2 of Lewis, *Judicial Remedies in Public Law* (5th edn).

Replace r.54.5 with:

Time limit for filing claim form[1]

54.5   **54.5—(A1)   In this rule—**

"the planning acts" has the same meaning as in section 336 of the Town and Country Planning Act 1990

"decision governed by the Public Contracts Regulations 2015" means any decision the legality of which is or may be affected by a duty owed to an economic operator by virtue of regulations 89 or 90 of those Regulations (and for this purpose it does not matter that the claimant is not an economic operator); and

"economic operator" has the same meaning as in regulation 2(1) of the Public Contracts Regulations 2015.

(1)   The claim form must be filed—

(a)   promptly; and

(b)   in any event not later than 3 months after the grounds to make the claim first arose.

(2)   The time limits in this rule may not be extended by agreement between the parties.

(3)   This rule does not apply when any other enactment specifies a shorter time limit for making the claim for judicial review.

(4)   Paragraph (1) does not apply in the cases specified in paragraphs (5) and (6).

(5)   Where the application for judicial review relates to a decision made by the Secretary of State or local planning authority under the planning acts, the claim form must be filed not later than six weeks after the grounds to make the claim first arose.

(6)   Where the application for judicial review relates to a decision governed by the Public Contracts Regulations 2015, the claim form must be filed within the time within which an economic operator would have been required by regulation 92(2) of those Regulations (and disregarding the rest of that regulation) to start any proceedings under those Regulations in respect of that decision.

Time limits and delay

Replace the sixth paragraph with:

54.5.1   A court may grant an extension of time under CPR Pt 3.1(2)(a) (previously, RSC Ord.53 itself provided that the court could extend the time if there was good reason to do so). The likelihood is that the courts will continue to apply the previous case law on RSC Ord.53 on whether there was a good reason for extending the time in deciding whether or not to grant an extension of time under CPR r.3.1 in a judicial review claim. The courts have always recognised that public law claims are unlike ordinary civil litigation and require strict adherence to the time limits contained in the rules governing judicial review (*R. v Institute of Chartered Accountants in England and Wales Ex p. Andreou* (1996) 8 Admin L.R. 557). The courts are likely to require that there is a good reason or adequate explanation for the delay and that extending the time limit will not cause substantial hardship or substantial prejudice or be detrimental to good administration. Under the former provisions of RSC Ord.53 r.4 the courts refused to accept that there was good reason for extending the time for making a judicial review application where the delay was the fault of the applicant's lawyers (*R. v Secretary of State for Health Ex p. Furneaux* [1994] 2 All E.R. 652). The courts have accepted that there was good reason for the delay if the applicant was unaware of the decision provided that they applied expeditiously once they became aware of it (*R. v Secretary of State for the Home Department Ex p. Ruddock* [1987] 1 W.L.R. 1482; *R. v Secretary of State for Foreign and Commonwealth Affairs Ex p. World Development Movement Ltd* [1995] 1 W.L.R. 386 at p.402). The fact that the claim raises issues of general public importance may be a reason for extending the time-limit (*R. v Secretary of State for the Home Department Ex p. Ruddock* [1987] 1 W.L.R. 1482; *S (Application for Judicial Review), Re* [1998] 1 F.L.R. 790). In the past, delay arising out of the need to obtain legal

---

[1] Introduced by the Civil Procedure (Amendment No. 4) Rules 2000 (SI 2000/2092) and amended by the Civil Procedure (Amendment No. 4) Rules 2013 (SI 2013/1412), the Public Contracts Regulations 2015 (SI 2015/102), and the Civil Procedure (Amendment No.3) Rules (SI 2016/788).

aid was regarded as a sufficient justification for delay: see *R. v Stratford-upon-Avon DC Ex p. Jackson* [1985] 1 W.L.R. 1319. The Court of Appeal has now indicated, in a different context, that delay arising out of the need to obtain legal aid is unlikely, of itself, to justify compliance with relevant procedural rules: see *R. (Kigen) v Secretary of State for the Home Department* [2015] EWCA Civ 1286; [2016] 1 W.L.R. 723, CA. The Court of Appeal was dealing with an application for an extension of time for filing a request for reconsideration of a refusal of permission to apply for judicial review in the Upper Tribunal under the relevant statutory procedural rules but similar principles are likely to apply to a failure to comply with other provisions of the CPR: see *Kigen* at para.6.

Protective Costs Orders

Replace the last paragraph with:

For the procedure to be followed, and for the matters to be taken into account by the court in **54.6.3** other cases, where a party makes an application for an order limiting the amount of future costs (including disbursements) which a party may recover pursuant to an order for costs subsequently made (a "costs capping order"), see rr.3.19 to 3.21. That procedure does not apply to applications for protective costs orders (r.3.19(3)); see further rr.3.20 to 3.21 above, and note guidance on principles and procedure (both at first instance and on appeal) given by the Court of Appeal in *R. v (Corner House Research) v Secretary of State for Trade and Industry* [2005] EWCA Civ 192; [2005] 1 W.L.R. 2600, CA, and *R. (Buglife-the Invertebrate Conservation Trust) v Thurrock Thames Gateway Development Corp.* [2008] EWCA Civ 1209, November 4, 2008, CA, unrep.

Sections 88 to 90 of the Criminal Justice and Courts Act 2015 provide for a separate regime for the exercise by the High Court and the Court of Appeal of jurisdiction to make costs capping orders in judicial review proceedings (for texts of these sections, see Vol.2 paras 9A-1312 to 9A-1314). Those sections were brought into force on August 8, 2016. The rules of court necessary to support this jurisdiction are contained in Section VI (rr.46.16 to 46.19) of CPR Part 46; see further para.46.16.1 above.

Reconsideration of a refusal of permission

Replace the last paragraph with:

Applications for a request for reconsideration must be filed within even days of service of the **54.12.1** reasons for refusal of permission: see r.54.12(4). The Court of Appeal has indicated the appropriate approach to consideration of applications for an extension of time in the context of applications to renew in the Upper Tribunal (where the relevant rules provide for requests to made within nine days). The court should consider the seriousness and significance of the failure to comply with the rule, whether there is a satisfactory explanation for the failure and all the other circumstances. Delay arising out of the need to obtain legal aid is unlikely of itself to be a satisfactory explanation. Similar principles are likely to apply to applications for reconsideration in the Administrative Court. See *R. (Kigen) v Secretary of State for the Home Department* [2015] EWCA Civ 1286; [2016] 1 W.L.R. 723, CA at paras 6, 20, 25 to 29 and 32.

Interlocutory applications

To the end of the first paragraph, add:

See also *Jedwell v Denbighshire CC* [2015] EWCA Civ 1232 (justice required permitting cross- **54.16.2** examination to determine whether reasons given for an earlier decision were an ex post facto justification of the decision or gave an account the reasons existing at the time for taking the decision).

Costs

Add new paragraphs at end:

For the jurisdiction of the High Court and the Court of Appeal to make costs orders in judicial **54.16.7** review proceedings, as provided by ss.88 to 90 of the Criminal Justice and Courts Act 2015, and the rules of court regulating applications for such orders in those circumstances, see para.46.16.1 above.

As to the court's power to make a costs order against an intervener as provided by s.87 of the Criminal Justice and Courts Act 2015, see para.54.17.1 below.

PART 55

POSSESSION CLAIMS

II.   Accelerated Possession Claims of Property Let on an Assured Shorthold Tenancy

Defence

Replace "The Defence must" with:

55.14.1   The Defence should

PART 57

PROBATE, INHERITANCE AND PRESUMPTION OF DEATH

Add new paragraph at end:

Related Sources

57.1.1   The following new Chancery Forms are relevant to this Part:
   CH26 Order in Probate Claim involving compromise
   CH27 Handing out Testamentary Documents for examination
   CH28 Revocation or refusal of revocation of grant of probate
   CH29 Order pronouncing for some (testamentary) words, against others

I.   Probate Claims

Editorial note

Replace with:

57.7.1   In *O'Brien v Seagrave* [2007] EWHC 788 (Ch); [2007] 3 All E.R. 633 (Judge Mackie QC) it was held that the Claimant's right to bring proceedings under the 1975 Act was a sufficient interest to permit her to proceed with a probate claim seeking revocation of a grant in common form for the purposes of r.57.7(1).

In *Randall v Randall* [2016] EWCA Civ 494; the Court of Appeal held that a creditor of a beneficiary had a sufficient interest in an estate to bring a probate claim. In allowing the appeal, the court said that the Deputy Master had been wrong to assimilate the position of a creditor of a beneficiary with that of a creditor of an estate. The interests of the two types of creditor are fundamentally different. A creditor of an estate does not have sufficient interest in an estate to bring a probate claim. This is because the creditor of an estate is not interested in which beneficiary receives what. The interest of a creditor of an estate is to ensure that there is due administration of the estate. The position of a creditor of a beneficiary is to ensure that the beneficiary receives what is due to him or her under the will or on an intestacy. Thus H, a contingent creditor of W under a consent order in financial remedy proceedings following divorce, did have an interest in contesting the validity of a will made by W's mother, since if the will were invalid, H would be entitled to an equal split of W's inheritance from her mother in so far as it exceeded £100,000.

The requirement that a party to a probate claim must have an "interest" in the estate is a procedural matter not a matter of substantive law (per the Master of the Rolls and McCombe LJ). The probate courts have determined, on a pragmatic basis from case to case, which "interests" qualify and which do not. "It would be surprising (per McCombe LJ at para.32) if there were rigidity about the test."

PART 64

ESTATES, TRUSTS AND CHARITIES

Related sources

Replace the first list with: **64.0.2**
- Part 8 (Alternative Procedure for Claims)
- Part 23 (General Rules about Applications for Court Orders)
- Part 40 (Judgments, Orders, Sale of Land etc.)
- Part 52 (Appeals)
- Part 57 (Probate and Inheritance)
- Chancery Guide 2016 (Vol.2 para.1A–0)

Replace the second list with:
- **CH13** Executor's or administrator's account
- **CH14** Order stating results of proceedings on usual accounts and inquiries in administrative claim
- **CH38** Order for distribution of Lloyd's Estate
- **CH39** Lloyd's Estate form of witness statement

I. Claims Relating to the Administration of Estates and Trusts

Applications under r.64.2(a) to determine any question arising in the administration of the estate of a deceased person or execution of a trust

Replace with:
Examples of claims under r.64.2(a) are set out in PD 64 para.1. Applications for directions by **64.2.1** trustees or personal representatives must be made by Pt 8 claim form. The proceedings will normally be heard in private (BPD 64 para.3r.39.2(3)(f) and PD 39, para.1.5). The court will always consider whether such applications can be dealt with on paper without a hearing. If the trustees consider it appropriate they may apply to the court under r.8.2A for permission to issue the claim form without naming any defendants (BPD 64 para.4.2 Chancery Guide 7.15-7.16). Detailed guidance as to the procedure for applying to the court for directions in relation to the administration of a trust are given in the Practice Direction, BPD 64; see also Chancery Guide, paras 29.10–29.12.

Prospective Costs Orders in relation to applications under r.64.2(a)

At the end of the first paragraph, replace "para.25.9" with:
paras 29.18–29.19.   **64.2.2**

Beddoe applications under 64.2(a)

To the end of the paragraph, add:
(See also Chancery Guide para.29.17.)   **64.2.3**

Other more usual forms of application under 64.2(a)

Replace with:
These include: absence of power (the sanctioning of acts being done by trustees which they **64.2.4** themselves have no power to do); purchase by trustees of part of the trust estate; orders for partial distribution to known beneficiaries; kin inquiries; and Benjamin orders (authorising the distribution of the fund on the footing that a beneficiary predeceased the testator or intestate (*Re Benjamin, Neville v Benjamin* [1902] 1 Ch. 723).

Applications for permission to distribute the estate of a deceased Lloyd's name

Replace with:
These are made under r.64.2(a). The procedure for this is governed by a Practice Statement **64.2.5** dated May 25, 2001 ([2001] 3 All E.R. 765), following *Re Yorke (deceased)* [1997] 4 All E.R. 907, which enables the personal representatives of a deceased Lloyd's name to distribute the estate on the footing that no, or no further, provision need be made for Lloyd's creditors. The application must be made by Pt 8 claim form, which may be issued without naming any other party. Directions may be given without a hearing. The Practice Statement includes a form of witness statement and draft order, both of which should accompany the claim form. If the deceased was involved in underwriting activities through a limited liability vehicle, this should be drawn to the court's attention. (See Chancery Guide paras 29-41 and Forms **CH38** (Order for distribution of Lloyd's Estate) and **CH39** (Lloyd's Estate form of witness statement)).

Administration orders—r.64.2(b)

Replace the second and third paragraphs with:

64.2.6   Administration actions are of two kinds: creditor's administration actions and beneficiary's administration actions. Normally, a creditor's administration action is for the administration of a deceased person's estate. A beneficiary's administration action in respect of the estate of a deceased person or a trust may be brought by a beneficiary or by the executors, administrators or trustees as the case may be. All the executors, administrators or trustees must be made parties and any of them who does not consent to being joined as a claimant must be made a defendant.

Where the estate is insolvent the proceedings should be commenced by a creditor as claimant against the personal representative as defendant. The personal representative is not entitled to commence proceedings against a creditor who is unwilling to be made a defendant. In such a case the proper course is for the personal representative to present a petition under the Insolvency Act 1986. But, it would seem that the proceedings would be properly constituted if brought against a creditor who was willing to be joined as a defendant (*Re Bradley* [1956] Ch. 615; [1956] 3 All E.R. 113). Where the usual order has been made for administration in a beneficiary's action, and, by reason of insolvency, beneficiaries are no longer interested, the action must be reconstituted and carried on by creditors as claimants. See *Re Van Oppen* [1935] W.N. 51; 179 L.T.J. 255. The application is then treated on the same footing as any other application for a creditor's administration order in case of insolvency and is dealt with by the Master without reference to the judge.

Variation of Trusts Act 1958—r.64.2(c)

Replace with:

64.2.7   Applications under the Variation of Trusts Act must be made by Pt 8 claim form (CPR r.64.3). They may be heard by a judge or Master, following the changes in 2015 to PD2B. District Judges may not make final orders under s.1.1 of the Variation of Trusts Act, except in certain circumstances, without the consent of their Supervising Judge (PD2B para.7B 2(b)). If the application is to be heard by a judge, it will be listed in the General list. The previous practice of listing these applications before a judge without reference to the Master no longer applies (see Chancery Guide para.21.18). The Master will normally exercise jurisdiction and hear the case, unless it is appropriate for some reason (eg particular complexity or absence of authority) to refer the matter to the judge. Following the decision by *Morgan J in V v T* [2014] EWHC 3432 (Ch) it will be unusual for Variation of Trust cases to be heard in private. However, the Master or judge will consider at the hearing whether parts of the evidence should not be available for inspection on the file and whether additional safeguards are needed to protect children, born and unborn. The parties should, when they are ready to issue proceedings, attend the Master at an AWN, having lodged the papers beforehand. Provided that there are prima facie grounds for protecting confidentiality the Master will be likely to order that access to the court file should be restricted and that the parties should be anonymous until the hearing. In such a case the Claim Form should be issued on an anonymised basis. The Master will also consider at the AWN whether there is a reason why the application should be heard by a judge.

In every case a certificate of readiness, signed by the advocates for all the parties, must be lodged, stating that the evidence is complete and has been filed, the application is ready for hearing, and giving the estimated length of the hearing. PD 64 para.4 sets out the requirements as to the evidence that must be filed where any children or unborn beneficiaries will be affected by a proposed arrangement under the Act. A written opinion of the advocate who will appear at the hearing may be required, particularly in complicated cases. (See also Chancery Guide, paras 29.22–29.27). Attention is drawn to CPR r.64.4(2), which specifies the parties to be joined in such proceedings.

Administration of Justice Act 1985 s.48—r.64.2(d)

Replace with:

64.2.8   Claims under s.48 of the Administration of Justice Act (power of the High Court to authorise action to be taken in reliance on written legal opinion as to the construction of a will or trust document) must be made by Pt 8 claim form (CPR r.64.3) without naming the defendant under CPR r.8.2A and no separate application for permission under r.8.2A need be made (PD 64 para.5).The legal opinion must be given by a person who has a 10-year High Court qualification within the meaning of s.71 of the Courts and Legal Services Act 1990. The claim should be supported by a witness statement or affidavit stating the names of all persons affected by the order sought, the surrounding circumstances admissible and relevant to construction of the document, details of the qualification and experience of the writer of the opinion, the approximate value of the fund or property in question and the details of any dispute known to exist. There should be exhibited to the witness statement or affidavit copies of all relevant documents, instructions to the writer of the opinion, the opinion itself and a draft order. The Master will consider whether the evidence is complete and, if it is, will either deal with the matter or, if appropriate, send it to the Judge. If the Master or judge directs service of notices under r.19.8A and any acknowledgment of service is received, the claimant should apply to the Master, on notice to the parties who acknowledged service, for directions (see Chancery Guide, paras 29.28–29.34).

II.   Charity Proceedings

Editorial introduction

At the end of the last paragraph, replace "para.25.10" with:
   paras 29.20–29.21

64.5.1

PART 68

REFERENCES TO THE EUROPEAN COURT

Effect of rule

After the first paragraph, add new paragraph:
   In *Kernkraftwerke Lippe-Ems GmbH v Hauptzollamt Osnabruck* (C-5/14) EU:C:2015:354; [2016] 2 **68.2.1**
W.L.R. 369, ECJ, the German Finance Court referred to the ECJ the question whether art.267 of
TFEU must be interpreted as meaning that a national court which has doubts as to whether
national legislation is compatible with both EU law and with the constitution of the Member State
concerned loses the right or, as the case may be, is exempt from the obligation to submit questions
to the ECJ concerning the interpretation or validity of that law, on the ground that parallel
proceedings in the Finance Court had been stayed pending the conclusion of a reference to the
German Federal Constitutional Court for a ruling on the constitutionality of that legislation. The
ECJ ruled that in these circumstances a national court neither loses the right, nor is exempt from
submitting questions to the ECJ.

PART 71

ORDERS TO OBTAIN INFORMATION FROM JUDGMENT DEBTORS

"produce at court documents in his control" (r.71.2(6))

Replace with:
   The concept of "control" of documents for the purposes of the information-gathering exercise **71.2.9**
under Pt 71 to enable enforcement of a judgment is different from control in the context of
disclosure. Under Pt 71, a person may have sufficient control to be required to produce a document if he is likely to have "a real say" as to whether or not to produce the document (*North Shore
Ventures Ltd v Anstead Holdings Ltd* [2012] EWCA Civ 11, 18 January 2012, CA, unrep., per Toulson
LJ at [35]). If there are reasonable grounds to infer that the true nature of the relationship with a
third party (such as a trustee) is that there is some understanding or arrangement by which the latter is to shelter assets or follow instructions, the judge may be entitled to infer that such assets and
related documents are under the control of the person being examined (ibid at [38–40]). This is
consistent with the approach of the court to provision of information in orders ancillary to freezing
orders: the court can make an order under r.25.1(1)(g) for provision of information about relevant
assets. Such orders provide to the claimant an opportunity of investigating the truth of the claim,
for example, that assets are held on trust or by a third party for the defendant, in order to avoid
sophisticated or wily operators from making themselves immune to the court's orders (see *JSC
Mezhdunarodniy Promyshlenniy Bank v Pugachev* [2015] EWCA Civ 139; 2016 1 W.L.R. 160, CA, at
[58]).

PART 73

CHARGING ORDERS, STOP ORDERS AND STOP NOTICES

I.   Charging Orders

Effect of rule

Replace with:

73.5.1   This is a new provision introduced by reason of the delegation of powers to court officers to make interim charging orders (see r.73.4(3)). A request for reconsideration must be made in writing but there is no requirement for this to be by way of application under Pt 23 nor for an application fee to be paid. The party making a request for reconsideration should, however, include the reasons why a reconsideration is being sought. There is a degree of overlap between this rule and the provisions of r.73.10(2) which allows for a debtor to object to the making of a final order. In the latter case the objection will result in the transfer of the application to the debtor's home court for hearing. Rule 73.5(1) is intended to cover the situation in which a person applying raises an objection to the making of the interim order, e.g. on technical grounds or where the person served is not the judgment debtor or where it is alleged that the judgment debt has been satisfied.

Applications in the High Court

Replace with:

73.10C.4   Paragraph 4.2 of PD73 says "A claim in the High Court for an order for sale of land to enforce a charging order must be started in Chancery Chambers at the Royal Courts of Justice or a Chancery district registry". However, in *Packman Lucas Ltd v Mentmore Towers Ltd* [2010] EWHC 1037 (TCC), Coulson J at paras 9 and 10 (and affirming his earlier decision in *Harlow & Milner Ltd v Teasdale* [2006] EWHC 1708 (TCC)) pointed out that r.73.10C contains no such requirement and held that an order for sale could be made in the Technology and Construction Court. Thus although generally such orders are sought in the Chancery Division in an appropriate case the claim can be brought elsewhere. When applying the rule in r.73.10C, that claims for orders for sale should be made in the same court that had made the charging order, the High Court is one court. An argument that an order for sale in the Chancery Division was invalid where the charging order had been made in the Family Division therefore had no real prospect of success (*Harker v Reynolds* [2015] EWHC 3127 (Ch) Asplin J). See also PD73.4.2.

The Charging Orders (Orders for Sale: Financial Thresholds) Regulations 2013 (SI 2013/491)

Add new paragraph at end:

73.10C.10   The court has jurisdiction to make a charging order in respect of a judgment debtor's beneficial interest in a property registered in the sole name of a third party without first quantifying the precise extent of that beneficial interest. Under the Charging Orders Act 1979, a charging order could be made over a judgment debtor's beneficial interest in land, provided that the interest could be specified in the order (*Walton v Allman* [2015] EWHC 3325 (Ch) (Snowden J)). Since the property in the instant case was in the husband's sole name, there could be no presumption that the wife had any interest in it. However, that did not mean that the court could not make a charging order until it had quantified her interest. The purpose of a charging order was to give the judgment creditor the equivalent of an equitable charge to secure payment of the judgment debt. Since a debtor could voluntarily grant an equitable charge over his beneficial interest without quantifying the precise extent of that interest, it should be possible for the court to make a charging order in respect of a judgment debtor's beneficial interest without first quantifying the extent of that interest It was sufficient for the court to be satisfied that the judgment debtor had some beneficial interest in the relevant property, even though the precise extent of that interest could not be quantified when the charging order was made. The court would have to quantify the interest when the judgment creditor sought an order for sale, but there was no requirement for the interest to be quantified before a charging order can be made.

PRACTICE DIRECTION 73—CHARGING ORDERS, STOP ORDERS AND STOP NOTICES

Note

Replace with:

73PD.4.1   In reference to PD 73 para.4.2 see commentary at para.73.10C.4.

PART 74

ENFORCEMENT OF JUDGMENTS IN DIFFERENT JURISDICTIONS

Forms

Replace list with: 74.0.2
- **PF 154** Order for permission to register a foreign judgment
- **PF 156** Evidence in support of application for registration of a Community Judgment
- **PF 157** Order for registration of a Community judgment
- **PF 160** Order for registration of a Judgment of another contracting state
- **PF 163** Evidence in support of application for a certified copy of a judgment for enforcement in another contracting state
- **PF 165** Evidence in support of application for registration in the High Court of a Judgment of a court in another part of the United Kingdom containing non-money provisions

Note

Delete the penultimate paragraph (beginning with "Subparagraph (g) was added") and then add new paragraph at end:

Note that Singapore has ratified the 2005 Hague Convention which will apply between Singapore **74.1.1**
and the other contracting states from 1 October 2016.

I.   Enforcement in England and Wales of Judgments of Foreign Courts

Appeals

Add new paragraph at end:

In *Lebek v Domino (Case C-70/15)* the ECJ held that the concept of "proceedings to challenge a **74.8.1**
judgment" in article 34(2) of the 2001 Brussels Regulation (the previous Judgments Regulation)
includes applications for relief when the period for bringing an ordinary challenge has expired.
Under article 34(2), a default judgment is not recognised in another member state if the defendant
was not served with the originating process in time to arrange his defence. This does not apply if
he failed to commence proceedings to challenge the judgment when it was possible for him to do
so. The ECJ held that this proviso included an application for relief.

Public policy

Add new paragraph at end:

In *Meroni v Recoletos Ltd* (C-559/14) Advocate General Kokott delivered the Opinion that a freez- **74.10.5**
ing injunction from another member state did not infringe Article 34(1) of the 2001 Brussels
Regulation (public policy) where any third party affected had the right to apply to the original
court to vary or discharge the judgment. The appeal against enforcement of the freezing injunction in Latvia was on the basis that the party affected by the order had not been party to the
English proceedings, which was alleged to be contrary to its right to a fair trial. The Opinion,
which is likely to be followed by the ECJ, confirms the limited scope of public policy as a ground
for resisting enforcement of a judgment from another EU member state.

V.   European Enforcement Orders

Note

Add new paragraph at end:

In *Pebros Servizi srl v Aston Martin Lagonda Ltd (Case C-511/14)* the claimant in Italian proceedings **74.28.2**
applied to the court for certification of the judgment as an EEO. In the Italian legal system, a
failure to attend proceedings does not amount to acquiescence by the defendant to the action
brought against him, so it was not clear whether certification could be made. The ECJ was asked to
make a preliminary ruling on whether national law determines whether default of appearance
amounts to non-contestation. It held that a claim may be regarded as "uncontested" if the debtor
does nothing to object to it by failing to comply with an invitation from the court to give written
notice of intention to defend the case, or by failing to appear at the hearing. It must be assessed
solely in accordance with the EEO Regulation.

VI.   Recognition and enforcement of protection measures

Editorial introduction

Replace the first paragraph with:

This section (rr.74.34 to 74.50) was introduced by the Civil Procedure (Amendment No.8) Rules **74.34.1**

2014 (SI 2014/3299), and came into force on January 11, 2015. It contains rules necessary for the implementation of Regulation (EU) No. 606/2013 of the European Parliament and of the Council on mutual recognition of protection measures in civil matters, a Regulation (the "Protection Measures Regulation") coming into force on that date and having "direct effect" (see Official Journal L 181, 29.06.2013 p. 4).

Replace the third paragraph with:

Jurisdiction in relation to "incoming" protection measures for the purposes of the Regulation is conferred on the Family Court, the County Court and the High Court by reg.3(2) the Civil Jurisdiction and Enforcement (Protection Measures) Regulations 2014 (SI 2014/3298) (made under the European Communities Act 1972 s.2). By reg.3(3) of that statutory instrument para. 3 of Sch.1 of the Senior Courts Act 1981 (see Vol. 2 para.9A-400) was amended for the purpose of assigning to the Family Division business that comes to the High Court in relation to "incoming" protection measures. By the Family Court (Composition and Distribution of Business) (Amendment) Rules 2014 (SI 2014/3297) amendments were made to the Family Court (Composition and Distribution of Business) Rules 2014 (SI 2014/3297) to make provision in relation to the Family Court for certain proceedings under the Regulation. The implementation of the Regulation has required, not only the addition to CPR Part 74 of the rules contained in Section VI thereof, but also the addition of Part 38 (Recognition and Enforcement of Protection Measures) to the Family Procedure Rules 2010 (effected by the Family Procedure (Amendment No.4) Rules 2014 (SI 2014/3296)).

PART 81

APPLICATIONS AND PROCEEDINGS IN RELATION TO CONTEMPT OF COURT

The Committal Practice Direction—purpose and scope

Replace the last paragraph with:

81.0.2.1   Paragraph 1 of the Committal PD states that it applies to all proceedings for committal for contempt of court, including contempt in the face of the court, whether arising under any statutory or inherent jurisdiction. This wide scope is significantly affected by paras 7 to 17 of the Practice Guidance. Thus para.8 of the Practice Guidance (see para.B17A-004 below) states that the Committal PD does not apply to orders made on a written reference to a High Court judge or circuit judge under the procedure set out in paras.8(1) and 8(2) of CPR r.71.8 (Judgment debtor's failure to comply with order) and CPR PD71, paras 6 and 7 (see, respectively, para.71.8.1 and para.71PD.6 above), but for reasons given there does apply to any hearing under r.71(8)(4)(b). In terms, para.9 of the Practice Guidance states that the Committal PD applies to the attachment of earnings procedure under CCR Ord.27 r.7 and 7A as it does to CPR r.71.8. The effect of that was that the Committal PD only applied to the adjourned hearing referred to in CCR Ord.27 r.7B and to any further hearing to deal with a suspended committal order made under that provision. With effect from 6 April 2016, CCR Ord.27 was revoked and replaced by Pt 89 with the result that rr.7, 7A and 7B in Ord.27 referred to in the Guidance now stand as rr.89.7, 89.8 and 89.9 (see further para.89.8.2 below). Further, para.11 et seq of the Practice Guidance modifies the effect of the Committal PD in its application to proceedings under the Policing and Crime Act 2009 and the Antisocial Behaviour, Crime and Policing Act 2014.

II. *Committal for breach of a judgment, order or undertaking to do or abstain from doing an act*

Effect of notice of order

Replace with:

81.8.2   The court may dispense with personal service of a mandatory or a prohibitory judgment or order if it thinks just to do so. Where the judgment or order is prohibitory, the court may dispense with personal service if satisfied that the respondent has had notice of it. The court's discretion is a wide one (*Davy International Ltd v Tazzyman* [1997] 1 W.L.R. 1256, CA). Modern cases in which the relevant authorities were examined include: *Benson v Richards* [2002] EWCA Civ 1402, *The Times*, October 17, 2002, CA; *Hydropool Hot Tubs Ltd v Roberjot* [2011] EWHC 121 (Ch), February 4, 2011, unrep. (Arnold J.); *Gill v Darroch* [2010] EWHC 2347 (Ch), July 22, 2010, unrep. (Vos J). In *Sports Direct International Plc v Rangers International Football Club* [2016] EWHC 85 (Ch), 22 January 2016, unrep. (Peter Smith J), where the failure to serve the order personally was not mere oversight, the judge was not persuaded that in the circumstances he should exercise his discretion and dispense with the requirements of personal service retrospectively. Paragraph 16.2 of Practice Direction 81 refers to the court's power to waive procedural defects. In *JSC Mezhdunarodniy Promyshlenniy Bank v*

Pugachev [2016] EWHC 102 (Ch), 8 February 2016, unrep. (Rose J) concluded that, in the circumstances, it was in the interests of justice to waive the requirement for personal service (and thereby to dispense retrospectively with the requirements for a penal notice). In *Khawaja v Popat* [2016] EWCA Civ 362, 14 April 2016, CA, the Court of Appeal rejected the contemnor's submission that the judge was wrong to have waived the requirement of personal service, holding that the question is whether injustice has been caused, not whether the circumstances were sufficiently exceptional to justify that course. On the question whether failure to effect personal service is defect that can be waived, see further para.81.10.2 below. Where the court finds, in a case where the respondent has persistently failed to comply with a mandatory order, that there is no doubt at all that the respondent knew perfectly well what the order said and what its consequences were, any view other than that it was just to dispense with personal service would be an encouragement for persistent offenders to use technicalities to defeat the purpose of such orders (*Benson v Richards* op cit at [38]). Where a prohibitory order with a penal notice attached is made, the court has power to include in the order a method of service alternative to personal service. In committal proceedings, if the court is satisfied that the order was properly served through the alternative method stipulated within the order it may dispense with personal service (*Serious Organised Crime Agency v Hymans* [2011] EWHC 3599 (QB), October 18, 2011, unrep. (Kenneth Parker J)).

Effect of rule

To the end of the second paragraph (beginning with "The proposition that the lack"), add:

See also *In re L (A Child)* [2016] EWCA Civ 173, 22 March 2016, CA, unrep., at para.60 per Sir **81.9.1**
James Munby P.

Application notice under Part 23

Replace the eighth paragraph with:

An order for committal for breach of a judgment or order to do or abstain from doing an act is **81.10.2**
more than a form of execution available to one party to enforce an order against another, because the court itself has a very substantial interest in seeing that its orders are upheld. Where an application is made to commit a defendant for contempt of court, it is obviously important that great care is taken by the applicant to ensure that all the procedural requirements in this Section of Pt 81 are met. However, committal orders ought not to be set aside on purely technical grounds which having nothing to do with the justice of the case, because that would have the effect of undermining the system of justice and the credibility of court orders. (See *Nicholls v Nicholls* [1997] 1 W.L.R. 314, CA, *Bell v Tuohy* [2002] EWCA Civ 423; [2002] 1 W.L.R. 2703, CA, and authorities referred to there.) Accordingly, para.16.2 of Practice Direction 81 states that the court may waive any procedural defect in the commencement (or conduct) of a committal application if satisfied that no injustice has been caused to the respondent by the defect. As a practical matter, procedural defects are more likely to emerge through the applicant's failure to comply fully with the requirements of rr.81.4 and 81.5, rather than with the terms of r.81.10. In the Family Procedure Rules 2010, the comparable provision to para.16.2 of PD 81 is para.13.2 of PD 37. For a discussion of the authorities relevant to application of that provision, see *W v H* [2015] EWHC 2436 (Fam), 21 August 2015, unrep. (Parker J).

VI. Committal for making a false statement of truth (rule 32.14) or disclosure statement (rule 31.23)

Permission where collateral criminal proceedings

Replace (where the citation for First Capital East Ltd v Plana has changed) with:

It is conceivable that, in a given case, the material facts relevant to an application to commit a **81.18.2.1**
person for contempt of court may also expose that person to other forms of legal liability, in particular, for a criminal offence. In principle, where contempt proceedings have been taken and completed, any subsequent criminal charge cannot be met by a plea of autrefois acquit or autrefois convict. Conversely, the fact that criminal proceedings have been taken against a person is no bar to a committal application on the same facts (see Vol.2 para.3C-25). But where permission to proceed with the committal application is required it is unlikely to be granted where the respondent was acquitted in the criminal proceedings, except, for example, where there is material evidence that was not before the criminal court, or where important new evidence has since come to light (*First Capital East Ltd v Plana* [2015] EWHC 2982 (QB); [2016] 1 W.L.R. 1271, (Judge Hughes QC)).

VIII. General rules about committal applications, orders for committal and writs of sequestration

Grounds and evidence relied on

Replace the first paragraph with:

In committal proceedings it is important that applicants be clear and consistent about the allega- **81.28.4** tions they are making. And it is important that all involved should be clear about the type of contempt or contempts being alleged, for example, whether contempt for breach of court order, and/or contempt in the face of the court (see *In re L (A Child)* [2016] EWCA Civ 173, 22 March 2016, CA, unrep., where lack of clarity in this respect contributed to procedural error). A claim form or an application notice may be amended with the permission of the court but not otherwise (Practice Direction 81 paras 12(2) and 13.2(2)). Generally, the rule that, at the hearing, without the court's permission the applicant may not rely on any grounds or evidence not pleaded or served tends to be strictly applied by the courts. Too much leniency in that respect would lead to adjournments and prolonged trials. Obviously, as the relevant circumstances must vary enormously, apart from the consideration that the respondent must be treated fairly, there are no tests that could usefully be stated as to when the court may exercise its discretion.

Replace the fourth paragraph with:
   A person accused of contempt, like the defendant in a criminal trial, has the right to remain silent (*Comet Products UK Ltd v Hawkex Plastics Ltd* [1971] 2 QB 67, CA). It is the duty of the court to ensure that the accused person is made aware of that right and also of the risk that adverse inferences may be drawn from his silence (*Inplayer Limited v Thorogood* [2014] EWCA Civ 1511, November 25, 2014, CA, unrep., at para.41). The drawing of adverse inference in this context is consistent with the jurisprudence of the European Court of Human Rights (*Khawaja v Popat* [2016] EWCA Civ 362, 14 April 2016, CA, unrep., at para.30 per McCombe LJ). If the committal application is heard at the same time as other issues about which the alleged contemnor needs to give evidence, he is placed in the position where he is effectively deprived of the right of silence (ibid). That is a serious procedural error (see also *Hammerton v Hammerton* [2007] EWCA Civ 248; [2007] 2 F.L.R. 1133, CA). In the case of *In re L (A Child)* [2016] EWCA Civ 173, 22 March 2016, CA, unrep., in proceedings for enforcement of a collection order, the paternal uncle (D) of the child concerned was brought before the court on witness summons and gave evidence under compulsion (which was not believed). In proceedings brought by the local authority, in which it was alleged that D had not provided the court with all the information he had about the whereabouts of the child, D was committed for contempt. The Court of Appeal allowed D's appeal, principally on the ground that, at the committal hearing, use was made against him of "the evidence which had been extracted from him under compulsion".

In the fifth paragraph (beginning with "A person against whom a committal application"), replace "where the applicant does not seeks" with "where the applicant seek".

After the fifth paragraph (beginning with "A person against whom a committal application"), add as a new paragraph:
   In *Vis Trading Co Ltd v Nazarov* [2015] EWHC 3327 (QB), 18 November 2015, unrep. (Whipple J), where an application was made by the claimant (C) to commit for contempt a defendant (D) on the ground of his failure to comply with a disclosure order ancillary to a post-judgment freezing order, the judge explained (at para.31) that the fact that D had produced some documents, in purported compliance with the order, did not determine the compliance issue in his favour; nor did it require C to make any application for cross-examination. Rather, the position was that D was on notice of C's case of non-compliance and C was entitled to continue to advance that case, even in the face of purported compliance by D since the date of the application. The burden of proof remained on C throughout, to the criminal standard, and C could invite the court to conclude, on the basis of all the evidence in the case, that D had not yet complied with the order. If a respondent chose to remain silent in the face of such a submission, the court could draw an adverse inference against him, if the court considered that to be appropriate and fair, and recalling that silence alone cannot prove guilt. This is not to put the burden of proof on the respondent; the burden remains on the applicant.

Application to be discharged from prison

Add new paragraph at end:

81.31.1   In *Swindon BC v Webb* [2016] EWCA Civ 152, 16 March 2016, CA, a respondent contemnor (committed for breach of an injunction imposed on him under the Enterprise Act 2002 s.213 as "a rogue trader") made no application for discharge but, for purposes he did not comprehend, was taken before the court for a hearing scheduled on its own initiative, and of which the applicant had no notice, was told that in order to purge his contempt he should apologise to the court, dutifully did so, and was discharged. In effect the contemnor was released after he had served only 8 days of the four months sentence imposed. On appeal by the applicant (who submitted that the procedure adopted by the court was irregular) the Court of Appeal stressed the importance of ordinarily insisting in cases of this sort that the procedure provided by r.81.31 is followed where a contemnor seeks his discharge (para.24). Ordinarily an application for discharge should where possible be listed before the judge who imposed the order for committal (ibid).

Discharge of a person

Replace the second paragraph with:

81.31.4   In most cases, an application for discharge under r.81.31 by a contemnor who has been committed to prison involves the contemnor in "purging" his contempt by apologising to the court for his past misbehaviour. Further, in most cases, where the contempt consists of a breach of an order of the court, it will also involve a promise to comply in future with the court's orders. But a credible promise of future good behaviour is not always necessary as there may come a point where even the most obdurate refusal to comply will nonetheless not prevent a contemnor's discharge (see *Harris v Harris* [2001] Fam. 502, at [28] per Munby J, and authorities referred to there). Thus the court can effectively cut short a term of imprisonment imposed on a contemnor for coercive purposes, if satisfied that the desired end will not be achieved.

Add new paragraph at end:
In *Swindon BC v Webb* [2016] EWCA Civ 152, 16 March 2016, CA, for the purpose of drawing the attention of judges to the guidance available to them when considering whether contemnors should be released before the expiry of the term of their sentences, the Court of Appeal explained the relevant authorities.

PART 83

WRITS AND WARRANTS—GENERAL PROVISIONS

Forms

Replace list with: **83.0.20**
- **Form 53** Writ of control
- **Form 54** Writ of control on order for costs
- **Form 56** Writ of control (of Part)
- **Form 58** Writ of fieri facias de bonis ecclesiasticis
- **Form 59** Writ of sequestrari de bonis ecclesiasticis
- **Form 62** Writ of control to enforce Northern Irish or Scottish judgment
- **Form 63** Writ of control to enforce foreign registered judgment
- **Form 64** Writ of specific delivery: delivery of goods, damages and costs
- **Form 65** Writ of delivery of goods or value, damages and costs
- **Form 66** Combined writ of possession and control
- **Form 66A** Combined writ of possession and control for costs of action
- **Form 67** Writ of sequestration
- **Form 68** Writ of restitution
- **Form 69** Writ of assistance
- **Form 71** Notice of the extension of a writ of execution
- **N42** Warrant of control
- **N46** Warrant of delivery and of control for damages and costs
- **N49** Warrant for possession of land
- **N50** Warrant of restitution
- **N51** Warrant of Restitution (trespass)
- **N52** Warrant for Possession of Land (Trespassers)
- **N244** Application notice
- **N245** Application for suspension of warrant (and for variation of an instalment)
- **N246** Claimant's reply to defendant's application to vary instalment order
- **N246A** Claimant's reply to defendant's application to suspend warrant
- **N293A** Combined certificate of judgment and request for writ of control or writ of possession
- **N322** Order for recovery of money awarded by tribunal
- **N322A** Application for order to recover money awarded by tribunal or other body
- **N322H** Request to register a High Court judgment or order for enforcement
- **N323** Request for a warrant of control
- **N324** Request for warrant of delivery of goods
- **N325** Request for warrant of possession
- **N326** Notice of issue of warrant of control
- **N327** Notice of issue of warrant of control to enforce a judgment or order
- **N328** Notice of transfer of proceedings to the High Court
- **N444** Details of sale under a warrant of control
- PF 92 Order for permission to issue a writ of possession in the High Court to enforce a Judgment or Order for giving of possession of land in proceedings in the County Court (other than a claim against trespassers under Part 55) (Rule 83.13(2) and (8))

III.   Writs

Effect of rule

Replace the first paragraph with:

83.13.1   Under this rule, permission is required to enforce a judgment or order for the giving of posses-sion of land, subject to the important exceptions listed in r.83.13(3) and (5)—which in practice cover a minority of cases—and r.83.13(6), which deals with mortgages/security. Whilst rr.83.13(3) and (4) incorporate the position in respect of warrants in possession proceedings against trespass-ers into the body of the provision for possession, it is important to stress that in other cases permis-sion is required (r.83.13(2)). This is a point stressed by 'The Senior Master Practice Note 21.3.2016—Applications for transfers for enforcement of possession orders to the High Court', which recognises problems arising from the identified misuse of the procedure at r.83.19(1)(b). CPR r.83.19(1)(b) only applies to the enforcement of those possessions orders where the possession claim arises against trespassers. The Practice Note stresses this and reiterates that in possession claims the Queen's Bench Enforcement Section and court staff in District Registries will only accept **Form N293A** in respect of possession orders against trespassers. (Note this has no relevance to the use of **Form N293A** in respect of execution against goods—r.83.19(1)).

Replace the second paragraph with:

Rule 81.4 applies to the enforcement by committal orders of judgments, orders or undertakings to do or abstain ffrom doing an act, and r.81.20 applies to their enforcement by writs of sequestration. (As explained above, those rules replaced provisions formerly found in Ord.45.) A judgment or order to give possession of land will not be enforceable by an order of committal or by writ of sequestration unless it specifies the time within which this act is required to be done, and the defendant refuses or neglects to do it within that time (see r.81.4). Accordingly, as a judgment or order to give possession of land will not in practice specify the time within which this act is required to be done, it will not ordinarily be enforceable by an order of committal or by writ of sequestration, but only by a writ of possession, which will normally be sufficient to enforce the judgment. If, however, in an extreme case, it is desired to enforce the judgment against a recalcitrant defendant by an order of committal or writ of sequestration, it will be necessary first to apply to the court for an order to fix the time within which the defendant is required to give pos-session of the land, and to serve that order upon the defendant under r.81.5 (formerly r.7 of this Order), and then to apply under r.81.4 or r.81.20 for the order of committal or writ of sequestration.

Permission to issue writ of possession

Add new paragraphs at end:

83.13.6   Notice of any application for permission to issue a writ of possession under CPR r.83.13(2) must be given to the occupants of the property (r.83.13(8)). A failure to do so provides a sufficient ground upon which the court will set aside a writ of possession after it has been executed (see r.83.13.(8) and para.83.13.9 below and *Secretary of State for Defence v Nicholas* [2015] EWHC 4064 (Ch)).

From April 2016 there is a draft form of order (PF 92) for use when the court gives permission to enforce a judgment or order for giving possession of land in the County Court (other than in respect of trespassers)—see the commentary at para.83.13.9.

Notice of the proceedings

To the end of the first paragraph, add:

83.13.9   Failure to give notice of the application has been held to provide a sufficient ground upon which the court will set aside a writ of possession after it has been executed (see r.83.13(2) and para.83.13.6 above and *Secretary of State for Defence v Nicholas* [2015] EWHC 4064 (Ch)).

To the end of the second paragraph, add:

PF 92, introduced in April 2016, reinforces this, as it contains a standard paragraph that the court is satisfied that every person in occupation of the whole or part of the land has received such notice that "appears to the court sufficient to enable the occupant to apply to the court for any relief to which the occupant may be entitled".

IV.   Warrants

Procedure on Transfer

Replace with:

83.19.2   Note that r.83.19 only applies to requests to transfer for enforcement (i) by execution against goods (where the judgment is £600 or more) and/or (ii) of possession orders for possession of land made in claims against trespassers (cases where permission to issue writs of control or of possession is not required). **Form N293A** and this procedure is not required if the judgment creditor asks for, and receives, an order for transfer to the High Court under s 42 of the County Courts Act 1984 at the time judgment is given.

Add new paragraphs at end:

The grant of a certificate by the court takes effect as an order to transfer the proceedings to the High Court. Given identified misuse of this procedure (particularly in the case of orders for possession against tenants), the Senior Master issued a Practice Note 21.3.2016 'Applications for transfers for enforcement of possession orders to the High Court', clearly stating that the Queen's Bench Division Enforcement Section will not accept **Form N293A** for transfer to the High Court for enforcement of a possession order of the County Court other than in respect of possession orders against trespassers and requested that the same instructions were given to staff in the District Registries.

An earlier Practice Note from the Senior Master 14.12.2015 effectively brought to an end applications made 'not on notice' under s.41 of the County Courts Act 1984 (Transfer to High Court by order of the High Court) by High Court Enforcement Officers seemingly to avoid both perceived delays in the County Court and an apparent reluctance by that court to complete Form **N293A** without explanation. The note concluded '...that the QB Masters will not make Orders for Transfer for Enforcement under S.41 unless on notice, and therefore all applications for transfer of County Court Orders and Judgments for Enforcement should be made either by an application under S.42 to the District Judge making the order, or, if for a Writ of Control or of Possession in a claim against Trespassers, by lodging a properly completed Form N293A at a County Court Office.' The Practice Note in March 2016 took this a stage further by stating that the Queen's Bench Masters would not entertain any applications at all under s.41 in possession proceedings and that, where an order was required, applications should be made under s.42 to a judge of the hearing centre where the possession order was made.

For the procedure where permission is required to issue a writ of possession see the commentary to CPR r.83.13(2) and (8) above.

Add two new Practice Notes after Practice Direction 83:

SENIOR MASTER PRACTICE NOTE 14 DECEMBER 2015 TRANSFERS FOR ENFORCEMENT TO THE HIGH COURT

Form N293A (Combined Certificate for judgment and request for writ of **83PN.1** control or writ of possession)
(*http://hmctsformfinder.justice.gov.uk/courtfinder/forms/n293a-eng.pdf*) is used when a judgment creditor with a County Court judgment of £600 or more, or in receipt of a possession order against trespassers, wishes to transfer the claim to the High Court for enforcement, so that they can instruct a High Court Enforcement Officer, ("HCEO") (rather than the County Court bailiffs) to enforce the judgment either by a writ of control or a writ of possession.

The procedure to be adopted, (unless the judgment creditor/party with the benefit of a possession order asks the County Court District Judge for an order for transfer under S. 42 of the County Courts Act 1984 when judgment is given), is to use Form N293A. This is submitted to the County Court (and now that there is a single County Court in theory this can be done by any County Court Office), with Part 1 of the form completed by the Judgment Creditor's legal representative. Part 2 is then completed by a court officer. The HCEO then completes Part 3, and takes the completed and certified N293A to the Central Office or a District Registry of the High Court and obtains a Writ of Control and/or a Writ of Possession.

In the last 12 months, instead of the Claimant making an application under S.42 at the hearing, or submitting Form N293A, a number of HCEOs have been making applications on a regular basis to the Practice Master in QBD under S. 41 of the County Courts Act 1984 to transfer the County Court claim for enforcement to the High Court. The HCEOs have informed the Masters that that County Court officers are refusing to certify Form 293As, without explanation. We have also been told that when applications are made under S. 42, some County Courts can take some 6-8 weeks to deal with them, and in the case of possession orders this means a significant loss of rental income to the judgment creditors. Thus it is much more efficient for judgment creditors/ parties with the benefit of a possession order, to enforce through a HCEO rather than via County Court bailiffs, so the HCEOs have no alternative but to make applications under S.41, where they can get an immediate order and issue a Writ of Control/Possession straight away.

The QB Practice Masters have been dealing with such applications, and making S.41 orders. However, as the County Court file and log for the case is not available to the QB Masters, in a number of cases their orders have conflicted with orders made by judges in the County Court. This has caused considerable problems in some cases. Accordingly, after consultation with the Deputy Head of Civil Justice, the President of the Queen's Bench Division, and the appropriate policy officials of the Ministry of Justice and of HM Courts & Tribunal Services, I have determined that the QB Masters will not make orders for transfer for enforcement under S.41 unless on notice, and therefore all applications for transfer of county court orders and judgments for enforcement should be made either by an application under S. 42 to the District judge making the order, or, if for a Writ of Control or of Possession in a claim against trespassers, by lodging a properly completed Form N293A at a County Court office.

Barbara Fontaine
The Senior Master
14 December 2015

SENIOR MASTER PRACTICE NOTE 21 MARCH 2016 APPLICATIONS FOR TRANSFERS FOR ENFORCEMENT OF POSSESSION ORDERS TO THE HIGH COURT

83PN.2   I have received complaints that some High Court Enforcement Officers ("HCEOs") have been using Form N293A to transfer County Court Possession Orders against tenants for enforcement to the High Court. This procedure is wrong because:

1.   The Form is intended for enforcement of possession orders against trespassers only (as stated in the notes at the bottom of the form; and

2.   CPR 83.13(2) requires the permission of the High Court before a High Court Writ of Possession can be issued; and

3.   CPR 83.13(8) (a) requires sufficient notice to be given to all occupants of the premises to enable them to apply to the court for any relief to which they may be entitled.

There have also been recent decisions where the misuse of Form N293A has been identified, e.g. *Birmingham City Council v Mondhlani* [2015] EW Misc (CC) (6 Nov. 2015); and lack of notice required under CPR 83.13(8) e.g. *Nicholas v Secretary of State for Defence* [2015] EWHC 4064 (Ch) (24 August 2015) Rose J. (unrep.).

In order to ensure that this practice does not continue:

1.   The Queen's Bench Division Enforcement Section will not accept Form N293A for transfer to the High Court for enforcement of a possession order of the County Court other than for possession orders against trespassers. By distributing a copy of this note to Designated Civil Judges in District Registries I shall request that the same instructions be given to court staff in District Registries.

2.   The Queen's Bench Masters will not accept applications under Section 41 of the County Court Act 1984 for transfer of a County Court possession claim for enforcement and such applications must be made under Section 42 of the County Court Act 1984 to a judge of the hearing centre of the County Court where the possession order was made, so that judge can satisfy themselves that the appropriate notice has been given under CPR 83.13(8).

3.   The Civil Procedure Rule Committee ("CPRC") subcommittee on court forms has:

(i) re-drafted Form N293A with greater emphasis on the restriction of the use of the form to requests for writs of control and writs of possession against trespassers only; and

(ii) drafted a new form of draft order (PF92) giving permission to enforce a judgment or order for giving possession of land in the County Court (other than a claim against trespassers under Part 55), which make it clear that applications for such permission must provide evidence to satisfy the judge determining such application that the requirements of Rule 83.13(8) are met.

It is anticipated that these will be available for use in April 2016.

The Senior Master

SCHEDULE 1—RSC PROVISIONS

RSC Order 115—Confiscation and Forfeiture in Connection with Criminal Proceedings

I. Drug Trafficking Act 1994 and Criminal Justice (International Co-operation) Act 1990

"confiscation order"

Add new paragraph at end:

Any party to proceedings for a confiscation order must be familiar with the principles explained **sc115.2B.1** in the House of Lords and Supreme Court cases of *May* [2008] 1 A.C. 1028, *Waya* [2013] 1 A.C. 294, *Ahmad and Fields* [2015] A.C. 299 and *Harvey* [2016] 2 W.L.R. 37.

SECTION C   PRE-ACTION CONDUCT AND PROTOCOLS

The more pertinent case law

Broad application or where the case is sufficiently arguable

Add new paragraphs at end:

Jet Airways (India) v Barloworld Handling Ltd 2014 EWCA Civ 1311 In a case concerning **C1A-010** maintenance of forklift trucks for two years in a cargo handling depot prior to a fire which started in a truck that destroyed the premises the defendant argued that the cause of the fire was unlikely to be its maintenance so the claim was speculative, the Court of Appeal held that the first instance judge did have jurisdiction to order pre-action disclosure because one of the parties who designed built or maintained the truck could be responsible and the defendant's disclosure might assist in identifying with greater certainty the cause of the fire and help to resolve the dispute. They also said there was no "arguability threshold" test, only a "likely to be a party" test which meant something less than probable.

Personal Management Solutions Ltd v Gee 7 Group Ltd [2015] EWHC 3859 (Ch) decided that the court did not have jurisdiction to order preaction disclosure sought by the claimant when a case management hearing took place after the claim had been issued but not served. The claimant had the option to discontinue the proceedings, seek preaction disclosure and issue a second claim, provided this was not an abuse of process. *Anglia Research Services Ltd v Finders Genealogists Ltd* [2016] EWHC 297 (QB) followed this reasoning in a defamation case, and decided it was not an abuse of process to seek to bring a second claim while the initial claim remained live when the second claim was about publication, a separate cause of action, and the court could order preaction disclosure in that action.

The Pre-action Conduct PD

Replace the second paragraph with:

C1A-015   The Practice Direction was amended and came into force in April 2015. The new version is shorter and the main changes are:
- sections I, III and IV are omitted and the content of Sections III and IV are summarised into 4 short paragraphs (6-8 and 11);
- the aims are set out succinctly in paras 1–3 (consistent with the specific protocols);
- there are new paragraphs 4–5 on proportionality;
- there are new paragraphs 8–9 on settlement and ADR;
- there are new short paragraphs on expert evidence, 7, and the need for a stocktake, 12, to narrow the issues if the dispute does not resolve without proceedings;
- the section on compliance, paragraphs 13–16, is shortened.

PRE-ACTION PROTOCOL FOR LOW VALUE PERSONAL INJURY CLAIMS IN ROAD TRAFFIC ACCIDENTS FROM 31 JULY 2013

Section I — Introduction

Definitions

Replace paragraph 1.1 with:

C13-001 1.1   In this Protocol—
   (A1) "accredited medical expert" means a medical expert who—
   (a) prepares a fixed cost medical report pursuant to paragraph 7.8A(1) before 1 June 2016 and, on the date that they are instructed, the expert is registered with MedCo as a provider of reports for soft tissue injury claims; or
   (b) prepares a fixed cost medical report pursuant to paragraph 7.8A(1) on or after 1 June 2016 and, on the date that they are instructed, the expert is accredited by MedCo to provide reports for soft tissue injury claims;
   (1) "admission of liability" means the defendant admits that—
   (a) the accident occurred;
   (b) the accident was caused by the defendant's breach of duty;
   (c) the defendant caused some loss to the claimant, the nature and extent of which is not admitted; and
   (d) the defendant has no accrued defence to the claim under the Limitation Act 1980;
   (1A) "associate" means, in respect of a medical expert, a colleague, partner, director, employer or employee in the same practice and "associated with" has the equivalent meaning;
   (2) "bank holiday" means a bank holiday under the Banking and Financial Dealings Act 1971;
   (3) "business day" means any day except Saturday, Sunday, a bank holiday, Good Friday or Christmas Day;
   (4) "certificate of recoverable benefits" has the same meaning as in rule 36.22(1)(e)(i) of the Civil Procedure Rules 1998.
   (5) "child" means a person under 18;
   (6) "claim" means a claim, prior to the start of proceedings, for payment of damages under the process set out in this Protocol;
   (7) "claimant" means a person starting a claim under this Protocol unless the context indicates that it means the claimant's legal representative;
   (8) "CNF" means a Claim Notification Form;
   (9) "deductible amount" has the same meaning as in rule 36.15(1)(d) of the Civil Procedure Rules 1998;
   (10) "defendant" means the insurer of the person who is subject to the claim under this Protocol, unless the context indicates that it means—

(a) the person who is subject to the claim;

(b) the defendant's legal representative;

(c) the Motor Insurers' Bureau ('MIB'); or

(d) a person falling within the exceptions in section 144 of the Road Traffic Act 1988 (a "self-insurer");

(10A) "fixed cost medical report" means a report in a soft tissue injury claim which is from a medical expert who, save in exceptional circumstances—

(a) has not provided treatment to the claimant;

(b) is not associated with any person who has provided treatment; and

(c) does not propose or recommend treatment that they or an associate then provide;

(11) "legal representative" has the same meaning as in rule 2.3(1) of the Civil Procedure Rules 1998;

(12) "medical expert" means a person who is—

(a) registered with the General Medical Council;

(b) registered with the General Dental Council; or

(c) a Psychologist or Physiotherapist registered with the Health Care Professions Council;

(12A) "MedCo" means MedCo Registration Solutions;

(13) "motor vehicle" means a mechanically propelled vehicle intended for use on roads;

(14) "pecuniary losses" means past and future expenses and losses;

(15) "road" means any highway and any other road to which the public has access and includes bridges over which a road passes;

(16) "road traffic accident" means an accident resulting in bodily injury to any person caused by, or arising out of, the use of a motor vehicle on a road or other public place in England and Wales unless the injury was caused wholly or in part by a breach by the defendant of one or more of the relevant statutory provisions[1] as defined by section 53 of the Health and Safety at Work etc Act 1974;

(16A) "soft tissue injury claim" means a claim brought by an occupant of a motor vehicle where the significant physical injury caused is a soft tissue injury and includes claims where there is a minor psychological injury secondary in significance to the physical injury;

(17) "Type C fixed costs" has the same meaning as in rule 45.18(2) of the Civil Procedure Rules 1998; and

(18) "vehicle related damages" means damages for—

(a) the pre-accident value of the vehicle;

(b) vehicle repair;

(c) vehicle insurance excess; and

(d) vehicle hire.

---

[1] See — Control of Substances Hazardous to Health Regulations 2002 (S.I. 2002/2677) Lifting Operations and Lifting Equipment Regulations 1998 (S.I. 1998/2307) Management of Health and Safety at Work Regulations 1999 (S.I. 1999/3242) Manual Handling Operations Regulations 1992 (S.I. 1992/2793) Personal Protective Equipment at Work Regulations 1992 (S.I. 1992/2966) Provision and Use of Work Equipment Regulations 1998 (S.I. 1998/2306) Work at Height Regulations 2005 (S.I. 2005/735) Workplace (Health, Safety and Welfare) Regulations 1992 (S.I. 1992/3004). The Construction (Design and Management) Regulations 2007 (S.I 2007/320).

THE PROTOCOL FOR LOW VALUE PERSONAL INJURY CLAIMS IN ROAD TRAFFIC ACCIDENTS

The Stage 3 procedure

Add new paragraph at end:

C13A-003   In *Phillips v Willis* 2016 EWCA Civ 401 the Court of Appeal held at a hearing when the claimant's grounds of appeal had been drastically amended several times and when the court had an abundance of documents and an overflowing bundle of authorities, that a claim started under the protocol arising from an accident in July 2013, did not exit the protocol when the personal injury and vehicle damage claims were settled, leaving a contested small car hire claim. The District Judge, therefore, had no power to order that car hire claim should continue as a Pt 7 claim on the Small Claims Track, when no further evidence was necessary and Part 8 was the right route for an unsettled RTA claim of this type, as this was disproportionate including in costs. Jackson LJ noted, obiter, that the situation might be different if the car hire charges were high or there were complexities of law and fact.

VOLUME 2

SECTION A1   PROCEDURAL GUIDES

15.   INSOLVENCY

15.2   Proceedings under s.6 of the Company Directors Disqualification Act 1986 (CDDA 1986)

Report of office-holder

Replace entry with:

A1.15-002

CDDA 1986 s.6(1), s.7(3)   If it appears to the office holder acting in the company insolvency that the conditions in CDDA, s.6(1) are present (i.e. that a person has been a director of a company which has become insolvent, and that his conduct as a director (either taken alone or taken together with his conduct as a director of any other company or companies) makes him unfit to be concerned in the management of a company), he shall forthwith report the matter to the Secretary of State. Detailed provisions as to the form and timing of the report are set out in the Insolvent Companies (Reports on Conduct of Directors) (England and Wales) Rules 2016.

Notification of intention to apply for disqualification order

Replace entry with:

CDDA 1986 s.7(1), s.16(1)   A person intending to apply for the making of a disqualification order "shall give not less than 10 days' notice" of his intention to do so. Failure to give the proper notice is a procedural irregularity which does not nullify the application. The relevant person applying is normally the Secretary of State, but can also be the Official Receiver. References below to "the Secretary of State" herein should be treated as including both.

As a matter of current practice, once the Secretary of State has formed a preliminary view that it is expedient in the public interest that a disqualification order under s.6 should be made against a person, the Secretary of State will communicate that view to that person, and invite that person's comments.

Change title of paragraph from italic to bold:

Evidence

The first hearing of the disqualification application/directions hearing

Replace entry with:

Directors Disqualification Proceedings PD paras 4.3 and 9 Disqualification Rules 1987 r.7 Insolvency Rules 1986 r.13(2) Courts and Legal Services Act 1990 s.74   The first hearing is before a registrar in open court, and shall be not less than eight weeks from the date of issue of the claim form. The registrar can either determine the case (if it is uncontested, and does not merit a period of disqualification longer than five years), or give directions and adjourn it.

Where an uncontested case merits a period of disqualification of longer than five years it will be disposed of at the second hearing, provided there is sufficient time.

Evidence directions will normally simply provide for evidence in answer from defendants, and evidence in reply from the Secretary of State. Further rounds of evidence are possible, but unusual.

Expert evidence is rarely ordered, and expert evidence on questions such as whether a company was insolvent will almost never be appropriate.

In the context of the disqualification proceedings, "registrar" includes a district judge of a High Court District Registry or of a county court.

Add new Section 1BA:

SECTION 1BA   ADMINISTRATIVE COURT JUDICIAL REVIEW GUIDE

THE ADMINISTRATIVE COURT JUDICIAL REVIEW GUIDE 2016

CONTENTS

Foreword by the Right Honourable Sir Brian Leveson,
President of the Queen's Bench Division
Preface by the Honourable Mr Justice Cranston,
Lead Judge of the Administrative Court, the Honourable
Mr Justice Lewis and the Honourable Mrs Justice Whipple DBE

Foreword

1BA-1   I am very pleased to introduce this new guide to the Administrative Court. It is an invaluable roadmap to the practice and procedure of the Court which will greatly assist all who are involved in proceedings before it. Good practice is identified and pitfalls foreshadowed. I have no doubt as to its utility.

A very significant amount of work has gone into producing this guide and I am particularly indebted to Mr Justice Cranston (as lead Judge of the Court), Mr Justice Lewis and Mrs Justice Whipple for their input, to Natalie Ford who oversaw the production of the Guide, and to David Gardner, the Administrative Court Office lawyer based in Cardiff who did a large part of the research and drafting. A number of other Judges and court staff have had input and I am grateful to all those who played a part in the creation of such a comprehensive document.

The Right Honourable Sir Brian Leveson,

President of the Queen's Bench Division

Preface

1BA-2   This Guide provides a general explanation of the work and practice of the Administrative Court. It is designed to make it easier for parties to conduct judicial reviews in the Administrative Court, by drawing together into one place the relevant statutory provisions, rules of procedure, practice directions, and case law on procedural aspects of judicial review. It provides general guidance as to how litigation in the Administrative Court should be conducted in order to achieve the overriding objective of dealing with cases justly and at proportionate cost.

The Guide has been prepared with **all** Court users in mind, whether they are persons who lack legal representation (known as 'litigants in person') or persons who have legal representation. We invite all Court users to follow this Guide when they prepare and present their cases.

In recent years, the Administrative Court has become one of the busiest specialist Courts within the High Court. It is imperative that Court resources (including the time of the judges who sit in the Administrative Court) are used efficiently. That has not uniformly been the case to date. There have been particular problems in relation to applications claiming unnecessary urgency, over-long written arguments, and bundles of documents, authorities and skeleton arguments being filed very late (to name just a few problems). These and other bad practices must stop. This Guide therefore sets out in clear terms what is expected. Sanctions may be applied if parties fail to comply.

We welcome any constructive feedback on the Guide. That feedback should be sent to the Senior Legal Managers in the Administrative Court Office by email to administrativecourtoffice. guidefeedback@hmcts.x.gsi.gov.uk. We plan to update this Guide from time to time, as appropriate.

The Honourable Mr Justice Cranston, Lead Judge, Administrative Court

The Honourable Mr Justice Lewis

The Honourable Mrs Justice Whipple DBE

Royal Courts of Justice, July 2016

PART A:—PRELIMINARY MATTERS

1. Introduction

1.1 THE JUDICIAL REVIEW GUIDE

1BA-3   **1.1.1**   This Guide has been prepared under the direction of the lead Judge of the Administrative Court and provides a general explanation of the work and practice of the Administrative Court with particular regard to judicial review. The Guide is designed to make it easier for parties to conduct judicial reviews in the Administrative Court. The definition of public law and administrative law is beyond the scope of this Guide and reference should be made to the many academic and practitioner texts on the subject for further reading.

1.1.2 The Guide must be read with the Civil Procedure Rules ('CPR') and the supporting Practice Directions. Litigants and their advisers are responsible for acquainting themselves with the CPR; it is not the task of this Guide to summarise the CPR, nor should anyone regard this Guide as a substitute for the CPR.

1.1.3 The Guide does not have the force of law, but parties using the Administrative Court will be expected to act in accordance with it.

1.1.4 The Guide is intended to be applicable in the Administrative Court and the Administrative Court Offices across England and Wales.

1.1.5 The contents of the Guide, including any websites, email addresses, telephone numbers and addresses, are correct at the time of publication. The Guide will be updated from time to time.

1.2 THE CIVIL PROCEDURE RULES

1.2.1 The overriding objective set out in CPR 1.1(1) is central to civil proceedings, including **1BA-4** judicial reviews. It requires the parties and the Court to deal with cases justly and proportionately, including at proportionate cost.

1.2.2 The CPR are divided into Parts. A particular Part is referred to in the Guide as CPR Part 54, etc., as the case may be. Any particular rule within a Part is referred to, for example, as CPR 54.12(2). The current CPR can be viewed on the Government's website via *www.gov.uk/courts-tribunals/administrative-court*.

1.2.3 The judicial review procedure is mainly (but not exclusively) governed by CPR Part 54 and the associated practice directions. CPR Part 54 and the associated practice directions are required reading for any litigant considering judicial proceedings. More details on these provisions will be given throughout this Guide.

1.3 PRACTICE DIRECTIONS

1.3.1 Most Parts of the CPR have an accompanying practice direction or directions, and other **1BA-5** practice directions deal with matters such as the preaction Protocols.

1.3.2 The practice directions are made pursuant to statute, and have the same authority as the CPR themselves. However, in case of any conflict between a rule and a practice direction, the rule will prevail. Each practice direction is referred to in the Guide with the number of any part that it supplements preceding it; for example, one of the practice directions supplementing CPR Part 54 is referred to as CPR PD 54A. A reference to a particular subparagraph of a practice direction will be referred to as, for example, CPR PD 54A paragraph 5.1.

1.3.3 The key associated practice directions to CPR Part 54 are CPR PD 54A (Judicial Review Practice), CPR PD 54D (Venue for Claims), and CPR PD 54E (Planning Court). These practice directions are required reading for any litigant considering judicial proceedings. More details on these provisions will be given throughout this Guide.

1.4 FORMS

1.4.1 The CPR PD 4 lists the forms generally required to be used under the CPR. **1BA-6**

1.4.2 The Practice Direction contains 3 tables. Table 1 lists the 'N form' that are referred to and required by the CPR and the Practice Directions. Tables 2 and 3 list forms that are not relevant to this Guide. Other forms may be provided by the Administrative Court Office and are not available online (for example, form 86b – see paragraph 8.4 of this Guide).

1.4.3 The relevant N forms that are directly relevant to judicial review proceedings are:

N461	Judicial Review claim form
N461(PC)	Judicial Review claim form (Planning Court)
N462	Judicial Review acknowledgment of service
N462(PC)	Judicial Review acknowledgement of service (Planning Court)
N463	Judicial Review – application for urgent consideration
N463(PC)	Judicial Review – application for urgent consideration (Planning Court)

1.4.4 The following general N forms are also required in a judicial review application:

N215	Certificate of service
N244	Application notice
N260	Statement of costs (Summary Assessment)
N279	Notice of discontinuance
N434	Notice of change of legal representative

1.4.5   The forms contained in CPR PD 4 are available in the various practitioners' textbooks and at the Administrative Court website: *www.gov.uk/courts-tribunals/administrative-court*

1.4.6   There are a few forms which are not set out in the rules that practitioners must use. One form of importance in judicial review is that for an out of hours application (see paragraph 16.3 of this Guide).

1.5   FEES

1BA-7   **1.5.1**   By virtue of the Civil Proceedings (Fees) Order 2008 No. 1053 (L. 5) (as amended) the Administrative Court Office is required to charge fees at certain stages in proceedings or when a party requests an order from the Court. The relevant fees (at the time of publication) are outlined in annex 2.[1] Current fees can also be checked at the Administrative Court website at *www.gov.uk/courts-tribunals/administrative-court*

1.5.2   Some litigants may be entitled to the remission of fees.[2] Guidance on whether you may be entitled to fee remission can be found on form EX160A and litigants can apply online at *www.gov.uk/help-with-court-fees*.This Guide will only refer to fees, but a litigant should be aware that fee remission is potentially available for all fees save for copying charges (except for vexatious litigants and persons subject to Civil Restraint Orders where different rules apply, see paragraph 4.5 of this Guide).

1.5.3   Court fees should not be confused with costs between parties, which can be considerably more than the Court fees. Costs are discussed in this Guide in chapter 23.

1.5.4   A litigant in person will be expected to comply with the requirements to use the right form and to pay fees, just like a represented litigant. Litigants in person should therefore make themselves familiar with those parts of this Guide which are relevant to their claim and with the applicable requirements.

1.6   CALCULATING TIME LIMITS

1BA-8   **1.6.1**   Any reference to days in the CPR or in this Guide will be a reference to clear, calendar days, unless stated otherwise. Therefore, when calculating time limits, every day, including weekends and bank holidays, will count, except for the day of the act or order itself (see CPR 2.8 for more detail and examples).

1.6.2   Any reference in the CPR or in this Guide to service of a document does not mean the date that the document is actually received. The date of service is set as the second working day after the day that the document was sent.[3]

1.7   THE ADMINISTRATIVE COURT

1BA-9   **1.7.1**   The Administrative Court is part of the Queen's Bench Division of the High Court (one of the three divisions of the High Court, together with the Chancery Division and Family Division). The Administrative Court hears the majority of applications for judicial review[4] and also some statutory appeals and applications which fall outside the remit of this Guide.

1.7.2   Judicial review is the procedure by which an individual, company, or organisation may challenge the act or omission of a public body and ensure that the public body meets its legal obligations.

1.7.3   The Rt Hon Sir Brian Leveson is the President of the Queen's Bench Division. Mr. Justice Cranston is the Judge in charge of the Administrative Court.

1.7.4   Some cases in the Administrative Court come before a Divisional Court, usually consisting of one Lord Justice of Appeal (or the President) and one High Court Judge.

1.7.5   Judicial reviews which challenge planning decisions are heard in the specialist Planning Court, a part of the Administrative Court.

1.8   THE ADMINISTRATIVE COURT OFFICE

1BA-10   **1.8.1**   The administration of judicial review cases in the Administrative Court is dealt with by the Administrative Court Office ('ACO'). All documentation must be filed with the ACO and all enquiries on cases must be directed to the ACO (not directly to the judiciary).

1.8.2   The ACO and its staff are a part of Her Majesty's Courts and Tribunals Service ('HMCTS'), which in turn is an executive agency of the Ministry of Justice ('MOJ'). There are ACOs in Birmingham Civil Justice Centre, Cardiff Civil Justice Centre, Leeds Combined Court Centre, Manchester Civil Justice Centre, and in the Royal Courts of Justice in London. Contact details for the ACOs can be found in annex 1 to this Guide.

---

[1] The fees are set out in schedule 1 of the Civil Proceedings (Fees) Order 2008 (as amended).

[2] The fee remission provisions are set out in schedule 2 of the Civil Proceedings (Fees) Order 2008 (as amended).

[3] CPR 6.14 and CPR 6.26

[4] See paragraphs 5.5 and 5.6 of this Guide where the exceptions are discussed.

1.8.3   As outlined in CPR PD 2A paragraph 2 the ACO in London is open for business from 10 a.m. to 4.30 p.m. (10 a.m. to 4.00 p.m. for the other ACOs) on every day of the year except:

(a)   Saturdays and Sundays;

(b)   Good Friday;

(c)   Christmas Day;

(d)   A further day over the Christmas period determined in accordance with the table specifically annexed to the Practice Direction. This will depend on which day of the week Christmas Day falls;

(e)   Bank holidays in England and Wales;

(f)   Such other days as the Lord Chancellor, with the concurrence of senior judiciary, may direct.

1.9   THE JUDICIARY AND THE MASTER

1.9.1   The judiciary in the Administrative Court consists of the High Court Judges (The **1BA-11** Honourable Mr/Mrs Justice...) and other judges or practitioners who have been authorised to sit in the Administrative Court. This Guide will simply refer to judges rather than differentiating between these judges. The judges are addressed in Court as my Lord/my Lady.

1.9.2   In the Royal Courts of Justice there is also a Master of the Administrative Court, currently Master Gidden (addressed in Court as Master). Masters generally deal with interim and pre-action applications, and manage the claims so that they proceed without delay.

2.   THE PARTIES

2.1   This part of the Guide is intended to give guidance on who should be the parties in a claim **1BA-12** for judicial review. Identifying the parties correctly ensures that pre-action discussions are occurring between the proper persons (see reference to the pre-action Protocol at paragraph 5.2 of this Guide). It also ensures that the proper parties are referred to on any Court documents.

2.2   THE PARTIES

2.2.1   Claimant(s)

2.2.1.1   Claimants tend to be persons aggrieved by the public law decisions of public bodies **1BA-13** who wish to challenge those decisions in the Administrative Court (see reference to 'standing' at paragraph 5.3.2 of this Guide).

2.2.1.2   The claimant in judicial review proceedings can be any individual or incorporated company (also known as a corporation). Partnerships are able to bring proceedings in the name of the partnership.

2.2.1.3   The Court may allow unincorporated associations (which do not have legal personality) to bring judicial review proceedings in their own name. But it is sensible, and the Court may require, that proceedings are brought in the name of one or more individuals, such as an office-holder or member of the association, or by a private limited company formed by individuals. A costs order may be, and often is, made against the party or parties named as claimant(s).

2.2.1.4   Public bodies can be claimants in judicial review proceedings. The Attorney General has a common law power to bring proceedings. Local authorities may bring proceedings by virtue of s.222 of the Local Government Act 1972.

2.2.2   Defendant(s)

2.2.2.1   The Defendant in judicial review proceedings is the public body / public office which made the decision under challenge (or failed to make a decision where that failure is challenged), not the individual within that public body or public office.

2.2.2.2   Where the decision is made by a Government Department it is the relevant Secretary of State who is the defendant. Therefore, even if the decision challenged is that of a civil servant working in the Home Office, the defendant would still be the Secretary of State for the Home Department.

2.2.2.3   Where the decision maker is a Court or Tribunal it is the Court or Tribunal which must be the defendant. The opposing party in the underlying case is named as an 'Interested Party' (see below at 2.2.3).

2.2.3   Interested Parties

2.2.3.1   An interested party is defined as any person (including a corporation or partnership), other than the claimant or defendant, who is directly affected by the claim.[1] For example, where a claimant challenges the decision of a defendant local authority to grant planning permission to a third party, the third party has a direct interest in the claim and must be named as an interested

---

[1] CPR 54.1(2)(f).

party.

2.2.3.2   Where the defendant is a Court or Tribunal, any opposing party in the lower Court or Tribunal would be an interested party in the judicial review.[1]

2.2.3.3   Interested parties must be included in pre-action correspondence and named in the claim form. Interested parties must also be served with the claim form, as required by CPR 54.7(b).

2.2.4   Interveners

In judicial review proceedings the Court retains a power to receive evidence and submissions from any other persons. Any person can apply, under CPR 54.17(1), to make representations or file evidence in judicial review proceedings. Potential interveners should be aware that any application must be made promptly[2] and that there are costs considerations (see paragraph 23.6 of this Guide).

2.3   MULTIPLE CLAIMANTS / DEFENDANTS / INTERESTED PARTIES

1BA-14   **2.3.1**   A claim for judicial review may be brought by one claimant or, in appropriate circumstances, by more than one claimant. It may, for example, be appropriate for the claim to be brought by more than one claimant where a number of different individuals are affected by the decision challenged.

2.3.2   A claim may be brought against one defendant or, in appropriate circumstances, against two or more defendants. This may, for example, be appropriate where two or more bodies are responsible for the decision under challenge.

2.3.3   There may, exceptionally, be appropriate circumstances in which a number of different challenges by different claimants against different defendants can be combined within one single claim for judicial review. This will, generally, only be appropriate if the different challenges can be conveniently dealt with together.

2.3.4   If a claimant considers that any person is directly affected by the claim, they must identify that person as an interested party and serve the claim form on that person.[3] A defendant must also identify in its acknowledgement of service a person who the defendant considers is an interested party because the person is directly affected[4] and the Court will consider making that person an interested party when considering permission.

2.3.5   Where a person who is a potential defendant or interested party has not been named or served with the claim form, the Court may direct that the claim be served on that person and the person may make representations or lodge an acknowledgement of service if the person so wishes.[5][6][7]

2.3.6   In judicial review proceedings the case title differs from other civil proceedings to reflect the fact that judicial review is the modern version of a historical procedure whereby Her Majesty's Judiciary, on her behalf, acted in a supervisory capacity. Technically a judicial review is brought by the Crown, on the application of the claimant, to ensure that powers are being properly exercised. The case title reflects this:[8]

The Queen (on the application of Claimant X) -v- Defendant Y

2.3.7   The case title is sometimes written as follows:

R (on the application of Claimant X) -v- Defendant Y

Or

R (Claimant X) -v- Defendant Y

2.3.8   The Crown will not involve itself in any way in the claim on behalf of the Claimant. The inclusion of the Queen's name in the title is purely formal.

3.   LITIGANTS IN PERSON

3.1   GENERAL

1BA-15   **3.1.1**   Many cases in the Administrative Court are now conducted by parties who do not have professional legal representation and who represent themselves ('litigants in person'). It is important for litigants in person to be aware that the rules of procedure and of practice apply to

---

[1] CPR PD 54A

[2] CPR 54.17(2)

[3] CPR 54.6 and 54.7

[4] CPR 54.8(4) (1)

[5] CPR 19.2(2) & CPR 19.2(4). In an appropriate case, ACO lawyers would have power to make such an order under CPR 54.1A

[6] For the requirement to serve the papers on a new party, see CPR PD 5A paragraph 3.1

[7] For removal of parties, see CPR 19.2(3). In an appropriate case, ACO lawyers would have powers to make such an order under CPR 54.1A

[8] This form of the case title is stipulated in *Practice Direction (Administrative Court: Establishment)* [2000] 1 W.L.R. 1654.

them in the same way as to parties who are represented by lawyers. The Court will have regard to the fact that a party is unrepresented and will ensure that that party is treated fairly, as explained below. Many forms of help are available for individuals who wish to seek legal advice before bringing claims for judicial review.

3.1.2 Represented parties must treat litigants in person with consideration at all times during the conduct of the litigation. Represented parties are reminded of the guidance published by the Bar Council, CILEx and the Law Society (see: *http://www.lawsociety.org.uk/Support-services/Advice/ Articles/Litigants-in-person-new-guidelines-for-lawyers-June-2015/*)

3.1.3 Litigants in person must show consideration and respect to their opponents, whether legally represented or not, to their opponents' representatives, and to the Court.

3.2 OBLIGATION TO COMPLY WITH PROCEDURAL RULES

3.2.1 A litigant in person will be expected to comply with the Civil Procedure Rules ('CPR'), **1BA-16** and the provisions of this Guide apply to them. Litigants in person should therefore make themselves familiar with those parts of this Guide which are relevant to their claim and also with the applicable provisions of the CPR.

3.2.2 For example, the requirement to provide all relevant information and facts (described at paragraph 14.1 of this Guide under the heading 'Duty of Candour') applies to all litigants and includes documents and facts which are unfavourable to the litigant. This requirement applies to litigants in person in the same way as it applies to litigants with representation. Similarly, the requirement to set out grounds of challenge in a coherent and well-ordered Grounds of Claim (see paragraph 6.3.4.1 of this Guide) applies to litigants in person in the same way as it applies to litigants with representation. Litigants in person may be penalised if they do not comply with the rules.

3.2.3 Generally, it is the duty of all parties to litigation, whether represented or not, to bring relevant matters to the attention of the Court and not to mislead the Court. This means for example that parties must not misrepresent the law and must therefore inform the Court of any relevant legislation or previous Court decisions which are applicable to their case and of which they are aware (whether favourable or not to their case). In addition there is a particular duty when an application is made to the Court without the other party being present or notified in advance (usually in cases of urgency). Here the litigant is under a duty to disclose any facts or other matters which might be relevant to the Court's decision, even if adverse to their case, and specifically draw the Court's attention to such matters (described at paragraph 14.1 of this Guide under the heading 'Duty of Candour').

3.2.4 A litigant in person must give an address for service in England or Wales in the claim form. It is essential that any change of address is notified in writing to the Administrative Court Office ('ACO') and to all other parties to the case, otherwise important communications such as notices of hearing dates may not arrive.

3.3 THE HEARING

3.3.1 It is very important that litigants in person give copies of any written document which **1BA-17** sets out their arguments (known as a 'skeleton argument') which they intend to rely on, and any other material (for example, reports of cases) in support of their arguments, to the Court and to their opponents in good time before the hearing. Litigants in person should familiarise themselves with the rules about skeleton arguments at chapter 17 of this Guide. If they do not follow these rules, the Court may refuse to hear the case, or may adjourn the case to allow the other party or parties proper time to consider and respond to the late skeleton or material, in which case the litigant in person may be ordered to pay the costs incurred by the adjournment.

3.3.2 Litigants in person should identify in advance of the hearing the points which they consider to be their strongest points, and they should put those points first in their skeleton argument and in any oral submissions to the Court.

3.3.3 At the hearing, the litigant in person will be asked to give their name(s) to the usher or in-court support staff if they have not already done so.

3.3.4 The case name will be called out by the court staff. The hearing will then begin.

3.3.5 At the hearing, the claimant usually speaks first, then the defendant speaks, and then the claimant has an opportunity to comment on what the defendant has said. Sometimes the judge may think it is sensible, depending on the circumstances, to vary that order and, for example, let the defendant speak first.

3.3.6 At the hearing, the judge may make allowances for any litigant in person, recognising the difficulties that person faces in presenting his or her own claim. The judge will allow the litigant in person to explain his or her case in a way that is fair to that person. The judge may ask questions. Any other party in court, represented or not, will also have an opportunity to make submissions to the judge. At the end of the hearing, the judge will usually give a ruling, which may be short. The judge will explain the order he or she makes. Representatives for other parties should also explain the court's order after the hearing if the litigant in person wants further explanation.

3.4   PRACTICAL ASSISTANCE FOR LITIGANTS IN PERSON

1BA-18   **3.4.1**   Neither the court staff nor the judges are in a position to give advice about the conduct of a claim. There is however a great deal of practical help available for litigants in person.

3.4.2   The Personal Support Unit ('PSU') is a free and independent service based in a number of court buildings which support litigants going through the court process without legal representation. The PSU do not give legal advice and will not represent a litigant, but will assist by taking notes, discussing the workings of the court process, and providing assistance with forms. There are PSUs in each of the court centres in which the majority of judicial reviews are heard (Birmingham Civil Justice Centre, Bristol Civil Justice Centre, Cardiff Civil Justice Centre, Leeds Combined Court Centre, Manchester Civil Justice Centre, and the Royal Courts of Justice in London) as well as some other court buildings. For more information see *www.thepsu.org*

3.4.3   Citizens Advice ('CA') provides advice on a wide range of issues at drop in centres, by telephone, and online (see *www.citizensadvice.org.uk*).

3.4.4   There is a citizens advice at the Royal Courts of Justice which may be able to offer some advice. It is situated on the ground floor, on the left hand side of the main hall (see *www.rcjadvice.org.uk*)

3.4.5   There are a number of guides available designed to help litigants in person. Amongst these are: the Bar Council Guide to representing yourself in Court (see: *www.barcouncil.org.uk/media/203109/srl_guide_final_for_online_use.pdf*) and the QB Interim Applications Guide (see: *www.judiciary.gov.uk/publications/guide-self-represented-qbd/*)

3.5   LEGAL REPRESENTATION AND FUNDING

1BA-19   **3.5.1**   There are a number of solicitors firms in England and Wales that conduct judicial review litigation. Further, there are a number of barristers in both England and Wales that will give advice without referral by a solicitor, acting on a direct access basis. Details of these legal professionals can be found on the Law Society (*www.lawsociety.org.uk*) and Bar Council (*www.barcouncil.org.uk*) websites respectively.

3.5.2   There are three ways that legal representation can be provided: fee paid representation, legal aid, and Pro-bono representation (free legal representation).

3.5.3   Fee Paid Representation

3.5.3.1   Legal representatives will act for a party that will pay their fees directly. Fee paid representation is generally conducted at an agreed hourly rate or by agreeing a fixed fee in advance.

3.5.3.2   Alternatively, some legal representatives will act for a party under a conditional fee agreement ('CFA'). CFAs are commonly known as 'no win, no fee' agreements. The individual firm or barrister will be able to confirm the basis on which they will act.

3.5.3.3   Some lawyers will be prepared to undertake a specific piece of work for payment, short of representing the client for the whole of the case. For example, a lawyer may be prepared to draft a skeleton argument for the case, which the litigant in person can then use for the hearing, or appear at a particular hearing. This is sometimes called 'unbundled' work.

3.5.4   Legal Aid

3.5.4.1   The individual firm or barrister will be able to confirm whether they can work on a legal aid basis and whether a particular claimant will be entitled to apply for legal aid.

3.5.4.2   There are three types of legal aid: legal help, which can be used to give limited, initial advice and assistance; investigative representation, which can be used to investigate a potential claim in greater depth than that under legal help; and full representation, which can be used to issue and conduct judicial review proceedings.

3.5.4.3   Litigants in person who may be eligible for legal aid can contact Civil Legal Advice ('CLA'). Litigants can telephone the CLA helpline to find their nearest CLA Information Point on 0345 345 4 345. This service is funded by the Legal Aid Agency ('LAA'). The LAA is open from Monday to Friday, 9am to 8pm, and on Saturday, 9am to 12:30pm. Members of the public can also text 'legalaid' and their name to 80010 to get a call back. This costs the same as a normal text message. An online 'eForm' process for applying for legal aid is available. Telephone 0300 200 2020 or email mailto:contactcivil@legalaid.gsi.gov.uk.

3.5.4.4   To obtain full representations, and thus engage the legal representative to conduct the judicial review proceedings, the claimant will be required to pass two eligibility tests:

3.5.4.4.1   Financial Eligibility: The Legal Aid Agency will assess the claimant's disposable income and capital. If the claimant's income and/or capital amount to more than the set sum then legal aid will not be available.

3.5.4.4.2   Merits Criteria: The Legal Aid Agency will consider the merits of the proposed claim. If the Legal Aid Agency considers that the proposed claim lacks the requisite merit then legal aid will not be available.

3.5.5 Pro-Bono Advice and Representation

3.5.5.1 Some solicitors firms and barristers will offer limited free advice on the prospects of a claim. The individual solicitor or barrister will be able to confirm if they are prepared to give advice on such terms.

3.5.5.2 There are some specialist organizations that arrange for free advice and representation. The largest are:

3.5.5.2.1 The National Pro-Bono Centre *www.nationalprobonocentre.org.uk*

3.5.5.2.2 The Bar Pro-Bono Unit *www.barprobono.org.uk*

3.5.5.2.3 Law Works *www.lawworks.org.uk*

3.5.5.3 A potential litigant should note that pro-bono organizations are overwhelmed with applications and cannot offer assistance to everyone. Further, the application process can be lengthy. The Administrative Court is unlikely to stay a claim or grant an extension of time to file a claim to await the outcome of an application for pro-bono advice or representation.

3.6 MCKENZIE FRIENDS

3.6.1 A litigant in person may have the assistance of a non-legally qualified person, known as a 'McKenzie Friend'. Where a McKenzie friend assists, the litigant in person must be present at the hearing and will be responsible for the conduct of his case at that hearing. But the McKenzie friend may provide some assistance.   **1BA-20**

3.6.2 Guidance on McKenzie Friends was given in *Practice Guidance (McKenzie Friends: Civil and Family Courts)*[1] which established that a McKenzie Friend may:

3.6.2.1 Provide moral support for litigant(s) in person;

3.6.2.2 Take notes;

3.6.2.3 Help with case papers; and

3.6.2.4 Quietly give advice on any aspect of the conduct of the case.

3.6.3 The Practice Note also established that a McKenzie Friend may not:

3.6.3.1 Act as the litigant's agent in relation to the proceedings;

3.6.3.2 Manage litigants' cases outside Court, for example by signing Court documents; or

3.6.3.3 Address the Court, make oral submissions or examine witnesses

3.6.4 The Court can, however, give permission to a person who is not a party and who has no rights of audience to address the Court. But this is only done in exceptional cases, on an application being made, and where it is shown to be in the interests of justice that such permission should be given.

3.6.5 A litigant who wishes to attend a hearing with the assistance of a McKenzie Friend should inform the Court as soon as possible indicating who the McKenzie Friend will be. The proposed McKenzie Friend should produce a short curriculum vitae or other statement setting out relevant experience, confirming that he or she has no interest in the case and understands the McKenzie Friend's role and the duty of confidentiality.

3.6.6 The litigant in person and the McKenzie Friend must tell the Court if the McKenzie Friend is being paid for his or her assistance and be ready to give details of that remuneration. The Court may stop a McKenzie friend from assisting if the Court believes there is good reason to do so in any individual case. It is unlawful for a person who is not authorised to do so to give paid services in respect of immigration matters.

3.6.7 If the Court considers that a person is abusing the right to be a McKenzie friend (for example, by attending in numerous claims to the detriment of the litigant(s) and/or the Court) and this abuse amounts to an interference with the proper processes of the administration of justice, the Court may make an order restricting or preventing a person from acting as a McKenzie friend.[2]

4. VEXATIOUS LITIGANT ORDERS AND CIVIL RESTRAINT ORDERS

4.1 The Court has power to make a civil restraint order ('CRO') under CPR PD 3C in relation to any person, alternatively to make an order under s.42 of the Senior Courts Act 1981 (a 'vexatious litigant').   **1BA-21**

4.2 The effect of either of those orders is to require the person subject to that order to obtain the permission of the Court to start proceedings *before* they may commence a judicial review.

4.3 This application is distinct from the application for permission to apply for judicial review.

4.4 If a person who is subject to such an order fails to make an application for permission to start proceedings, the application for permission to apply for judicial review (or the application for an interim or pre-action order) will be dismissed without further order. The Court may also consider the filing of the application to be a contempt of Court.

---

[1] [2010] 1 W.L.R. 1881, [2010] 4 All ER 272, and see
https://www.judiciary.gov.uk/publications/mckenzie-friends/
[2] *Noueiri* [2001] 1 W.L.R. 2357

4.5   The application for permission to start proceedings must be made by filing an application notice (N244 or PF244)[1] with the Administrative Court Office with the relevant fee. This fee is not subject to fee remission and must be paid. If permission to start proceedings is later granted and the applicant is able to claim fee remission then the fee can be refunded.[2]

4.6   The application notice should state:[3]

4.6.1   The title and reference number of the proceedings in which the order was made;

4.6.2   The full name of the litigant and his/her address;

4.6.3   The fact that the litigant is seeking permission pursuant to the order to apply for permission to apply for judicial review (or whatever interim or pre-action order is sought);

4.6.4   Explain briefly why the applicant is seeking the order; and

4.6.5   The previous occasions on which the litigant has made an application for permission must be listed.[4]

4.7   The application notice must be filed together with any written evidence on which the litigant relies in support of his application.[5] Generally, this should be a copy of the claim papers which the litigant requests permission to file.

4.8   If the litigant is a vexatious litigant, there is no need to serve an application on any other intended litigants unless directed by the Court to do so.[6] It may be considered to be good practice to do so nonetheless.

4.9   If the litigant is subject to a CRO then notice of the application must be given to the other intended litigants, which must set out the nature and the grounds of the application, and they must be given 7 days to respond to the notice before the application for permission is filed. Any response must be included with the application.[7]

4.10   The application will be placed before a judge who may, without the attendance of the litigant:[8]

4.10.1   Make an order giving permission to start proceedings (this is not the same as permission to apply for judicial review, see chapter 8 of this Guide);

4.10.2   Give directions for further written evidence to be supplied by the litigant before an order is made on the application;

4.10.3   Make an order dismissing the application without a hearing; or

4.10.4   Give directions for the hearing of the application.

4.11   The Court will dismiss the application unless satisfied that the application is not an abuse of process and there are reasonable grounds for bringing the application.[9]

4.12   For vexatious litigants, an order dismissing the application, with or without a hearing, is final and may not be subject to reconsideration or appeal.[10]

4.13   For those subject to a CRO, there is a right of appeal to the Court of Appeal[11] (see chapter 26 of this Guide for appeals), unless the Court has ordered that the litigant has repeatedly made applications for permission pursuant to the CRO which were totally without merit, and the Court directs that if the litigant makes any further applications for permission which are totally without merit, the decision to dismiss the application will be final and there will be no right of appeal, unless the judge who refused permission grants permission to appeal.[12]

5.   Before Starting the Claim

5.1   GENERAL CONSIDERATIONS

1BA-22   **5.1.1**   Before bringing any proceedings, the intending claimant should think carefully about the implications of so doing. The rest of chapter 5 of this Guide considers the practical steps to be taken before issuing a claim form, but there are a number of general considerations, including personal considerations.

5.1.2   A litigant who is acting in person faces a heavier burden in terms of time and effort than

---

[1] CPR PD 3A paragraph 7.2, CPR PD 3C paragraph 2.6, CPR PD 3C paragraph 3.6, CPR PD 3C paragraph 4.6

[2] Paragraph 19, schedule 2, Civil Proceedings (Fees) Order 2008

[3] CPR PD 3A paragraph 7.3

[4] CPR PD 3A paragraph 7.5

[5] CPR PD 3A paragraph 7.4

[6] CPR PD 3A paragraph 7.7

[7] CPR PD 3C paragraph 2.4-2.6, CPR PD 3C paragraph 3.4-3.6, CPR PD 3C paragraph 4.4-4.6

[8] CPR PD 3A paragraph 7.6, CPR PD 3C paragraph 2.6, CPR PD 3C paragraph 3.6, CPR PD 3C paragraph 4.6

[9] s.42(3) of the Senior Courts Act 1981

[10] CPR PD 3A paragraph 7.6 and s.42(4) of the Senior Courts Act 1981

[11] CPR PD 3C, paragraphs 2.8, 3.8 and 4.8

[12] CPR PD 3C paragraph 2.3(2) and 2.6(3), CPR PD 3C paragraph 3.3(2) and 3.6(3), CPR PD 3C paragraph 4.3(2) and 4.6(3)

does a litigant who is legally represented, but all litigation calls for a high level of commitment from the parties. This should not be underestimated by any intending claimant.

5.1.3   The overriding objective of the CPR is to deal with cases justly and at proportionate cost. In all proceedings there are winners and losers; the loser is generally ordered to pay the costs of the winner and the costs of litigation can be large (see chapter 23 of this Guide for costs).

5.1.4   Part B of this Guide outlines the procedure when bringing a claim. This section will outline the considerations before bringing a claim, including the pre-action procedure, factors which may make bringing a claim inappropriate, costs protection, the timescales in which proceedings should be started, and the duties of the parties concerning the disclosure of documents.

5.2   THE JUDICIAL REVIEW PRE-ACTION PROTOCOL

5.2.1   So far as reasonably possible, an intending claimant should try to resolve the claim **1BA-23** without litigation. Litigation should be a last resort.

5.2.2   There are codes of practice for pre-trial negotiations. These are called 'Protocols'. The appropriate pre-action Protocol in judicial review proceedings is the Judicial Review Pre-action Protocol, which can be viewed on the Government's website via *www.gov.uk/courtstribunals/administrative-court*. This is a very important document which anyone who is considering bringing a claim should consider carefully.

5.2.3   It is very important to follow the Judicial Review Pre-action Protocol, if that is possible, before commencing a claim. There are two reasons for this. First of all, it may serve to resolve the issue without need of litigation or at least to narrow the issues in the litigation. Secondly, failure to follow the Protocol may result in costs sanctions being applied to the litigant who has not followed the Protocol.

5.2.4   A claim for judicial review must be brought within the relevant time limits fixed by the CPR. The Protocol process does not affect the time limits for starting the claim (see paragraph 5.4 of this Guide). The fact that a party is using the Protocol would not, of itself, be likely to justify a failure to bring a claim within the time limits set by the CPR or be a reason to extend time. Therefore, a party considering applying for judicial review should act quickly to comply with the Protocol but note the time limits for issue if the claim remains unresolved.

5.2.5   The Protocol may not be appropriate in urgent cases (e.g., where there is an urgent need for an interim order) but even in urgent cases, the parties should attempt to comply with the Protocol. The Court will not apply cost sanctions for non-compliance where it is satisfied that it was not possible to comply because of the urgency of the matter.

5.2.6   Stage one of the Protocol requires the parties to consider whether a method of alternative dispute resolution ('ADR') would be more appropriate. The Protocol mentions discussion and negotiation, referral to the Ombudsman and mediation (a form of facilitated negotiation assisted by an independent neutral party).

5.2.7   Stage two is to send the defendant a pre-action letter. The letter should be in the format outlined in Annex A to the Protocol. The letter should contain the date and details of the act or omission being challenged and a clear summary of the facts on which the claim is based. It should also contain the details of any relevant information that the claimant is seeking and an explanation of why it is considered relevant.

5.2.8   The defendant should normally be given 14 days to respond to the preaction letter and must do so in the format outlined in Annex B to the Protocol. Where necessary the defendant may request the claimant to allow them additional time to respond. The claimant should allow the defendant reasonable time to respond, where that is possible without putting the time limits to start the case in jeopardy.

5.3   SITUATIONS WHERE A CLAIM FOR JUDICIAL REVIEW MAY BE INAPPROPRIATE

5.3.1   There are situations in which judicial review will not be appropriate or possible. These **1BA-24** should be considered at the outset. Litigants should refer to the CPR and to the commentary in academic works on administrative law. The following are some of those situations in outline.

5.3.2   Lack of Standing (or Locus Standi)

5.3.2.1   A person may not bring an application for judicial review in the Administrative Court unless that person has a 'sufficient interest' in the matter to which the claim relates.[1]

5.3.2.2   The issue of standing will generally be determined when considering permission but it may be raised and determined at any stage.

5.3.2.3   The parties and/or the Court cannot agree that a case should continue where the claimant does not have standing.[2] Nor does the Court have a discretion. A party must have standing in order to bring a claim.

---

[1] s.31(3) of the Senior Courts Act 1981

[2] This principle has been confirmed in a number of other cases, for example in *R. v Secretary of State for Social Services ex parte Child Poverty Action Group* [1990] 2 Q.B. 540 at 556

5.3.2.4 The sufficient interest requirement is case specific and there is no general definition.[1] Those whom a decision directly and adversely affects will seldom (if ever) be refused relief for lack of standing. Some claimants may be considered to have sufficient standing where the claim is brought in the public interest.

5.3.3 Adequate Alternative Remedy

5.3.3.1 Judicial review is often said to be a remedy of last resort.[2] If there is another method of challenge available to the claimant, which provides an adequate remedy, the alternative remedy should generally be exhausted before applying for judicial review.

5.3.3.2 The alternative remedy may come in various guises. Examples include an internal complaints procedure or a statutory appeal.

5.3.3.3 If the Court finds that the claimant has an adequate alternative remedy, it will generally refuse permission to apply for judicial review.

5.3.4 The Claim is Academic

5.3.4.1 Where a claim is purely academic, that is to say that there is no longer a case to be decided which will directly affect the rights and obligations of the parties,[3] it will generally not be appropriate to bring judicial review proceedings. An example of such a scenario would be where the defendant has agreed to reconsider the decision challenged.

5.3.4.2 Only in exceptional circumstances where two conditions are satisfied will the Court proceed to determine an academic issue. These conditions are: (1) a large number of similar cases exist or are anticipated, or at least other similar cases exist or are anticipated; and (2) the decision in a judicial review will not be factsensitive.[4]

5.3.5 The Outcome is Unlikely to be Substantially Different.

The Courts have in the past refused permission to apply for judicial review where the decision would be the same even if the public body had not made the error in question. Section 31(3C)-(3F) of the Senior Courts Act 1981 now provides that the Courts must refuse permission to apply for judicial review if it appears to the Court highly likely that the outcome for the claimant would not be substantially different even if the conduct complained about had not occurred. The Court has discretion to allow the claim to proceed if there is an exceptional public interest in doing so.

5.3.6 The Claim Challenges a Decision of one of the Superior Courts.

5.3.6.1 The Superior Courts[5] are the High Court, the Court of Appeal, and the Supreme Court. They cannot be subject to judicial review.

5.3.6.2 Where the Crown Court is dealing with a trial on indictment it is a Superior Court and its actions are not subject to judicial review.[6] Otherwise, its functions are subject to judicial review.

5.4 TIME LIMITS

1BA-25 **5.4.1** The general time limit for starting a claim for judicial review requires that the claim form be filed promptly and in any event not later than 3 months after the grounds for making the claim first arose.[7] It must not be presumed that just because the claim has been lodged within the three month time that the claim has been made promptly, or within time.[8]

5.4.2 When considering whether a claim is within time a claimant should also be aware of two important points:

5.4.2.1 The time limit may not be extended by agreement between the parties (although it can be extended by the Court, see paragraphs 5.4.4 and 6.3.4.3 of this Guide);[9]

5.4.2.2 The time limit begins to run from the date the decision to be challenged was made (not the date when the claimant was informed about the decision).[10]

---

[1] *Inland Revenue Commissioners v National Federation of Self-Employed and Small Businesses Ltd* [1982] A.C. 617

[2] See *R. v Epping and Harlow General Commissioners ex parte Goldstraw* [1983] 3 All E.R. 257 at 262, *Kay v Lambeth London Borough Council* [2006] 2 A.C. 465 at 492, and more recently in *R. (Gifford) v Governor of Bure Prison* [2014] EWHC 911 (Admin) at paragraph 37.

[3] *R. v Secretary of State for the Home Department ex parte Salem* [1999] 1 AC 450

[4] *R. (Zoolife International Ltd) v The Secretary of State for Environment, Food and Rural Affairs* [2008] A.C.D. 44 at paragraph 36

[5] See the discussion of the differences between inferior and superior Courts in *R v Chancellor of St. Edmundsbury and Ipswich Diocese ex parte White* [1948] 1 K.B. 195.

[6] ss,1, 29(3), and 46(1) of the Senior Courts Act 1981.

[7] 54.5 (1)

[8] See for example *R. v Cotswold District Council ex parte Barrington Parish Council* [1998] 75 P. & C.R. 515

[9] CPR 54.5(2)

[10] *R. v Department of Transport ex parte Presvac Engineering* [1992] 4 Admin. L.R. 121

5.4.3 There are exceptions to the general time limit rule discussed above. These include the following:

5.4.3.1 Planning Law Judicial Reviews:[1] Where the claim relates to a decision made under planning legislation the claim must be started not later than six weeks after the grounds to make the claim first arose. Planning Legislation is defined as the Town and Country Planning Act 1990, the Planning (Listed Buildings and Conservation Areas) Act 1990, the Planning (Hazardous Substances) Act 1990 and the Planning (Consequential Provisions) Act 1990.

5.4.3.2 Public Contract Judicial Reviews:[2] Where the claim relates to a decision under the Public Contracts Regulations 2015 S.I. 2015/102, which governs the procedure by which public bodies may outsource public services (sometimes referred to as 'procurement'), the claim must be started within the time specified by r. 92 of those Regulations, which is currently 30 days from the date when the claimant first knew or ought to have known that grounds for starting the proceedings had arisen. (Note that this time limit begins to run from the date of knowledge, in contrast to the general rule where the relevant date is the decision date itself). For further guidance on Public Contract Judicial Reviews, see paragraph 5.7 of this Guide.

5.4.3.3 Judicial Review of the Upper Tribunal:[3] Where the defendant is the Upper Tribunal the claim must be started no later than 16 days after the date on which notice of the Upper Tribunal's decision was sent to the applicant. (Again, note the difference from the general rule, here the time limit is calculated from the date the decision was sent, not the date it was made).

5.4.3.4 Judicial Review of a decision of a Minister in relation to a Public Inquiry, or a member of an inquiry panel.[4] The time limit for these challenges is 14 days unless extended by the Court. That shorter time limit does not apply to any challenge to the contents of the inquiry report, or to a decision of which the claimant could not have become aware until publication of the report.[5]

5.4.4 Extensions of Time

5.4.4.1 CPR 3.1(2)(a) allows the Court to extend or shorten the time limit even if the time for compliance has already expired.

5.4.4.2 Where the time limit has already passed, the claimant must apply for an extension in section 8 of the claim form (form N461). The application for an extension of time will be considered by the judge at the same time as deciding whether to grant permission.

5.4.4.3 The Court will require evidence explaining the delay. The Court will only extend time if an adequate explanation is given for the delay, and if the Court is satisfied that an extension of time will not cause substantial hardship or prejudice to the defendant or any other party, and that an extension of time will not be detrimental to good administration.

5.5 JUDICIAL REVIEW OF IMMIGRATION AND ASYLUM DECISIONS

5.5.1 Since the 1st November 2013 the Upper Tribunal (Immigration and Asylum Chamber) **1BA-26** ('UT(IAC)') has been the appropriate jurisdiction for starting a judicial review in the majority of decisions relating to immigration and asylum, not the Administrative Court (see Annex 1 for UT(IAC) contact details).

5.5.2 The Lord Chief Justice's Practice Direction[6] requires filing in, or mandatory transfer to, the UT(IAC) of any application for permission to apply for judicial review and any substantive application for judicial review that calls into question the following:

5.5.2.1 A decision made under the Immigration Acts or any instrument having effect, whether wholly or partly, under an enactment within the Immigration Acts, or otherwise relating to leave to enter or remain in the UK. The Immigration Acts are defined as: Immigration Act 1971, Immigration Act 1988, Asylum and Immigration Appeals Act 1993, Asylum and Immigration Act 1996, Immigration and Asylum Act 1999, Nationality, Immigration and Asylum Act 2002, Asylum and Immigration (Treatment of Claimants, etc.) Act 2004, Immigration, Asylum and Nationality Act 2006, UK Borders Act 2007, the Immigration Act 2014; or

5.5.2.2 A decision made of the Immigration and Asylum Chamber of the First-tier Tribunal, from which no appeal lies to the Upper Tribunal.

5.5.3 All other immigration and asylum matters remain within the jurisdiction of the

---

[1] CPR 54.5(5).

[2] CPR 54.5(6),

[3] CPR 54.7A(3)

[4] s.38 (1) of the Inquiries Act 2005

[5] s. 38(3) of the Inquiries Act 2005

[6] Lord Chief Justice's Practice Direction; Jurisdiction of the Upper Tribunal under s.18 of the Tribunals, Courts and Enforcement Act 2007 and Mandatory Transfer of Judicial Review applications to the Upper Tribunal under s.31A(2) of the Senior Courts Act 1981, dated 21st August 2013 and amended on the 17th October 2014, available at: *https://www.judiciary.gov.uk/publications/lord-chiefjustices-direction-regarding-the-transfer-of-immigration-and-asylum-judicial-review-cases-to-the-uppertribunal-immigration-and-asylum-chamber/*

Administrative Court.[1] Even where an application comes within the classes of claim outlined at paragraph 5.5.2 above, an application which falls within any of the following classes must be brought in the Administrative Court:

5.5.3.1   A challenge to the validity of primary or subordinate legislation (or of immigration rules);

5.5.3.2   A challenge to the lawfulness of detention;

5.5.3.3   A challenge to a decision concerning inclusion on the register of licensed Sponsors maintained by the UKBA;

5.5.3.4   A challenge to a decision as which determines British citizenship;

5.5.3.5   A challenge to a decision relating to asylum support or accommodation;

5.5.3.6   A challenge to the decision of the Upper Tribunal;

5.5.3.7   A challenge to a decision of the Special Immigration Appeals Commission; and

5.5.3.8   An application for a declaration of incompatibility under the s.4 of the Human Rights Act 1998.

5.5.3.9   A challenge to a decision which is certified (or otherwise stated in writing) to have been taken by the Secretary of State wholly or partly in reliance on information which it is considered should not be made public in the interests of national security.

5.5.4   Challenges to decisions made under the National Referral Mechanism for identifying victims of human trafficking or modern slavery[2] are not immigration decisions. They fall within the jurisdiction of the Administrative Court.

5.6   JUDICIAL REVIEW OF FIRST-TIER TRIBUNAL DECISIONS

1BA-27   **5.6.1**   Since the 3rd November 2008 the Upper Tribunal (Administrative Appeals Chamber) ('UTAAC') has been the appropriate jurisdiction for starting a judicial review that challenges certain decisions of the First-tier Tribunal, not the Administrative Court (see Annex 1 for UT(AAC) contact details).

5.6.2   The Lord Chief Justice's Practice Direction[3] requires filing in, or mandatory transfer to, the UT(AAC) of any application for permission to apply for judicial review and any substantive application for judicial review that calls into question the following:

5.6.2.1   Any decision of the First-tier Tribunal on an appeal made in the exercise of a right conferred by the Criminal Injuries Compensation Scheme in compliance with s.5(1) of the Criminal Injuries Compensation Act 1995 (appeals against decisions on reviews); and

5.6.2.2   Decisions of the First-tier Tribunal where there is no right of appeal to the Upper Tribunal and that decision is not an excluded decision within paragraph (b), (c), or (f) of s.11(5) of the 2007 Act (appeals against national security certificates).

5.6.3   The direction does not have effect where an application seeks a declaration of incompatibility. In that case the Administrative Court retains the jurisdiction to hear the claim.

5.7   PUBLIC CONTRACT JUDICIAL REVIEWS

1BA-28   **5.7.1**   Where a decision made under the Public Contract Regulations 2015 is challenged, claimants may consider it necessary to bring proceedings for judicial review in the Administrative Court as well as issuing a claim in the Technology and Construction Court ('TCC'). Where this happens, the claim will, unless otherwise directed by the Judge in Charge of the Administrative Court or Judge in charge of the TCC, proceed in the TCC before a TCC judge who is also designated to sit in the Administrative Court.

5.7.2   If this occurs, the claimant must:

5.7.2.1   At the time of issuing the claim form in the ACO, by letter to the ACO, copied to the Judge in Charge of the Administrative Court and the Judge in Charge of the TCC, request transfer of the judicial review claim to the TCC;

5.7.2.2   mark that letter clearly as follows: 'URGENT REQUEST FOR TRANSFER OF A PUBLIC PROCUREMENT CLAIM TO THE TCC';

5.7.2.3   if not notified within 3 days of the issue of the claim form that the case will be transferred to the TCC, contact the ACO and thereafter keep the TCC informed of its position.

5.7.3   This procedure is to apply only when claim forms are issued by the same claimant against the same defendant in both the Administrative Court and the TCC simultaneously (ie within 48 hours of each other).

5.7.4   When the papers are transferred to the TCC by the ACO in accordance with the procedure outlined above, the Judge in Charge of the TCC will review the papers as soon as reasonably practicable. The Judge in Charge of the TCC will then notify the claimant and the ACO

---

[1] See paragraph.5.5.4 of this guide for an example.

[2] Published by the National Crime Agency at *http://www.nationalcrimeagency.gov.uk/about-us/whatwe-do/specialist-capabilities/uk-human-trafficking-centre/national-referral-mechanism*

[3] Lord Chief Justice's Practice Direction, Practice Direction (Upper Tribunal: Judicial Review Jurisdiction),[48] pursuant to s.18(6) of the Tribunals Courts and Enforcement Act 2007

whether he/she considers that the two claims should be case managed and/or heard together in the TCC.

5.7.5 If he or she decides that is so, the claim for judicial review will be case managed and determined in the TCC.

5.7.6 If he or she decides that the judicial review claim should not proceed in the TCC, he or she will transfer the judicial review claim back to the Administrative Court and give his/her reasons for doing so, and the claim for judicial review will be case managed and determined in the Administrative Court.

5.8 ABUSE OF PROCESS

5.8.1 It may be an abuse of process to file a judicial review in the Administrative Court, on the **1BA-29** basis that under the Lord Chief Justice's practice direction it falls within its jurisdiction and not the jurisdiction of UT(IAC). An example would be a judicial review which purports to fall within the detention exception where there is no obvious distinct merit to that aspect of the claim: see *R (Ashraf) v Secretary of State for the Home Department* [2013] EWHC 4028 (Admin).

PART B:—THE CLAIM

6. STARTING THE CLAIM

6.1 OVERVIEW OF JUDICIAL REVIEW PROCEDURE

6.1.1 Judicial review is a two stage process which is explained further in this Guide. First the **1BA-30** claimant must obtain permission (sometimes referred to as 'leave') to apply for judicial review from the Court. If permission is granted by the Court then the second stage is the substantive claim.

6.1.2 Unlike a number of other civil and criminal proceedings the judicial review process does not incorporate a case management conference, although one may be ordered by a judge. The Court expects the parties to liaise with each other and the ACO to ensure that the claim is ready for the Court. An open dialogue between the parties and the staff of the Administrative Court Office is essential to the smooth running of the case.

6.1.3 The following flow diagram may be used as a quick guide to the judicial review process. Full details of each stage are outlined later in this Guide:

Judicial Review Process[1]

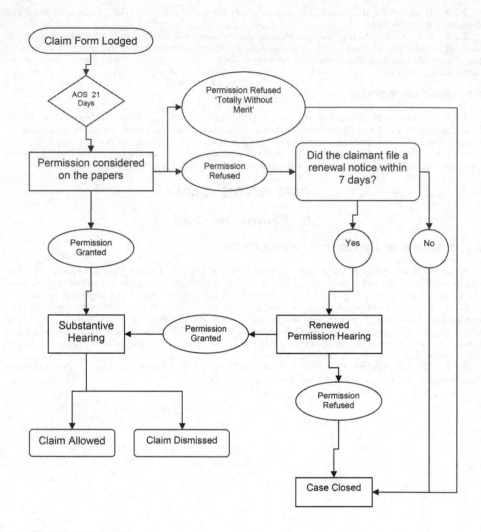

6.2 ISSUING THE CLAIM

1BA-31   **6.2.1**   All judicial review claims must be started by issuing a claim form in the ACO. Where a claim form is received in the ACO on an earlier date than the date of issue, then, for the purposes of the judicial review time limits (see paragraph 5.4 of this Guide), the claim is begun on the earlier date.[2] This earlier date will also be noted on the claim form by the ACO. All other relevant time limits will run from the date of issue shown by the Court seal.

6.2.2   If the claimant has lodged the claim in the ACO in Cardiff, the claim may be lodged in Welsh or English.

6.2.3   When issuing the claim form, it must be accompanied by the relevant fee. If the relevant fee is not paid, the claim form and any accompanying documentation will be returned.

6.2.4   If the claim form is returned in accordance with 6.2.3 above, it is not considered to have been issued for the purposes of the judicial review time limits (see paragraph 5.4 of this Guide).

---

[1] © David Gardner, reproduced with kind permission of The University of Wales Press from *Administrative Law and the Administrative Court in Wales*

[2] CRP PD 7A paragraphs 5.1 and 5.2

6.3 REQUIRED DOCUMENTATION

6.3.1   The claimant must file two copies of the completed judicial review claim form to be **1BA-32** retained by the ACO.

6.3.2   The claimant must also file an additional copy of the claim form for every defendant and interested party in the claim. The additional copies will be sealed and returned to the claimant to serve on the defendant(s) and interested parties (see paragraph 6.8 of this Guide for service, and see annex 3 for a list of addresses for service on government departments).

6.3.3   The claimant is required to apply for permission to apply for judicial review in the claim form. The judicial review claim form automatically includes this application in section 4 of the claim form. The claimant must also specify the judicial review remedies sought (see chapter 11 of this Guide for remedies). There is space for this in the claim form at section 7.

6.3.4   The claim form must be accompanied by certain documents, which must be with the claim form when it is filed. The required documents are:

6.3.4.1   A detailed statement of the claimant's grounds for bringing the claim for judicial review (which can be outlined in section 5 of the claim form or in an attached document). This document should be as short as possible, while setting out the claimant's arguments in full.

6.3.4.2   A statement of the facts relied on (which can be outlined in section 9 of the claim form, or in an attached document, or in an attached document incorporated with the grounds in a detailed statement of facts and grounds);

6.3.4.3   Any application to extend the time limit for filing the claim form (which can be made in section 8 of the claim form or in an attached document);

6.3.4.4   Any application for directions (which can be made in section 8 of the claim form or in an attached document);

6.3.4.5   Any written evidence in support of the claim or application to extend time;

6.3.4.6   A copy of any decision letter or order that the claimant seeks to have quashed;

6.3.4.7   Where the claim for judicial review relates to a decision of a Court or Tribunal, an approved copy of the reasons for reaching that decision;

6.3.4.8   Copies of any documents on which the claimant proposes to rely;

6.3.4.9   Copies of any relevant statutory material; and

6.3.4.10   A list of essential documents for advance reading by the Court (with page references to the passages relied on).

6.3.5   The documentation must be provided in an indexed and paginated bundle.

6.3.6   Two copies of the documentation bundle are to be provided to be retained by the Court.

6.3.7   Any request for the bundles to be returned when the claim has been closed must be made in writing before the end of the claim.

6.3.8   If the claim form is not accompanied by the documentation outlined at paragraph 6.3.4 above without explanation as to why and detail of when it will be provided, the ACO may, at its discretion, return the claim form without issuing it.

6.3.9   If the claim form is returned in accordance with 6.3.8 above, it is not considered to have been issued for the purposes of the judicial review time limits (see paragraph 5.4 of this Guide).

6.3.10   If the documentation required as outlined at paragraph 6.3.4 above is not filed with a claim form which is issued by the ACO, but at a later date, it has been filed out of time. As such, it must be accompanied by an application to extend time to file the documentation. Such an application must be made on an application notice with the relevant fee (see paragraph 12.7 of this Guide).

6.4   DUTY OF CANDOUR

6.4.1   There is a special duty which applies to parties to judicial review known as the 'duty of **1BA-33** candour' which requires the parties to ensure that all relevant information and all material facts are put before the Court.[1] This means that parties must disclose any information or material facts which either support or undermine their case.

6.4.2   **It is very important that you comply with the duty of candour. The duty is explained in more detail below at paragraph 14.1 of this Guide.**

6.5   DISCLOSURE

6.5.1   The duty of candour ensures that all relevant information is before the Court. The **1BA-34** general rules in civil procedure requiring the disclosure of documents do not apply to judicial review claims. However, the Court can order disclosure, exceptionally, in a particular claim.

6.5.2   An application may be made in the course of a judicial review claim for disclosure of specific documents or documents of a particular class or type. A Court may order disclosure (under

---

[1] See the discussion of this principle in *R. (Al-Sweady) v Secretary of State for Defence* [2010] H.R.L.R. 2 at 18; see also *R (Bancoult (No 2)) v Secretary of State for Foreign and Commonwealth Affairs* [2016] UKSC 35

CPR 31.12(1)) of documents where this is necessary to deal fairly and justly with a particular issue.[1] An application under CPR 31.12(1) is made in accordance with the principles discussed in paragraph 12.7 of this Guide

6.5.3   In practice, orders for disclosure of documents are rarely necessary in judicial review claims. The disclosure of documents may not, in fact, be necessary to allow the Court to consider a particular issue. Furthermore, a defendant may have disclosed the relevant documents (either before proceedings begin or as part of its evidence provided during proceedings (see paragraph 14.1 of this Guide on the duty of candour).

6.6   WHERE TO ISSUE THE CLAIM (APPROPRIATE VENUE)

1BA-35   **6.6.1**   There are five ACOs in England and Wales in which a claim may be issued. They are situated in Birmingham Civil Justice Centre, Cardiff Civil Justice Centre, Leeds Combined Court Centre, Manchester Civil Justice Centre, and in the Royal Courts of Justice in London. Contact details for the ACOs can be found in annex 1 to this Guide.

6.6.2   The general expectation is that proceedings will be administered and determined in the region with which the claimant has the closest connection.[2] As such the claim should be filed in the ACO with which the claimant has the closest connection.

6.6.3   Any claim started in Birmingham will normally be determined at an appropriate Court in the Midlands, in Cardiff in Wales, in Leeds in the North-East of England, in London at the Royal Courts of Justice; and in Manchester, in the North-West of England.

6.6.4   Claims where the claimant has the closest connection to the South West of England should be issued in the ACO in Cardiff Civil Justice Centre. The administration of the claim will take place in Cardiff, but all hearings will (unless there are exceptional circumstances) take place in the South West of England (principally in Bristol).

6.6.5   Whilst it is not encouraged, the claimant may issue a claim in a different region to the one with which he/she has the closest connection. The claimant should outline why the claim has been lodged in a different region in section 4 of the claim form. The decision should be justified in accordance with the following considerations:

6.6.5.1   Any reason expressed by any party for preferring a particular venue;

6.6.5.2   The region in which the defendant, or any relevant office or department of the defendant, is based;

6.6.5.3   The region in which the claimant's legal representatives are based;

6.6.5.4   The ease and cost of travel to a hearing;

6.6.5.5   The availability and suitability of alternative means of attending a hearing (for example, by videolink);

6.6.5.6   The extent and nature of media interest in the proceedings in any particular locality;

6.6.5.7   The time within which it is appropriate for the proceedings to be determined;

6.6.5.8   Whether it is desirable to administer or determine the claim in another region in the light of the volume of claims issued at, and the capacity, resources and workload of, the Court at which it is issued;

6.6.5.9   Whether the claim raises issues sufficiently similar to those in another outstanding claim to make it desirable that it should be determined together with, or immediately following, that other claim; and

6.6.5.10   Whether the claim raises devolution issues and for that reason whether it should more appropriately be determined in London or Cardiff.

6.6.6   There are a number of exceptions to the general rule on venue outlined in paragraph 6.6.2 above. The exceptions can be found in CPR PD 54D paragraph 3.1. They are not repeated here as they do not relate to judicial review proceedings.

6.6.7   If the claim is issued in an ACO thought not to be the most appropriate, it may be transferred by judicial order. The Court will usually invite the views of the parties if it is minded to transfer the claim to a different venue. The defendant and any interested party can address the issue of venue in their summary grounds.

6.7   FILING DOCUMENTS BY FAX AND EMAIL

1BA-36   **6.7.1**   The ACO will generally not accept the filing of documents by fax or email. However, the Administrative Court Office will accept the service of documents by email provided:

6.7.1.1   The document being filed does not require a fee;

6.7.1.2   The document, including attachments, does not exceed the maximum which the appropriate court office has indicated it can accept by email[3];

6.7.1.3   The email, including any attachments, is under 10Mb in size.

---

[1] As discussed in *R. v Secretary of State for Foreign and Commonwealth Affairs ex parte World Development Movement Ltd* [1995] 1 W.L.R. 386 at 396-397

[2] CPR PD 54D paragraph 5.2

[3] In many instances, 50 pages, but parties should check with the appropriate court office.

6.7.2 Where a document may be emailed it must be emailed to the appropriate ACO general inbox (see the contacts list at annex 1).[1] Any party filing a document by email should not also file a hard copy unless instructed;

6.7.3 A document may be filed by fax where it needs to be filed urgently. Hearing bundles and/or documents which require a fee should only be faxed in an emergency and must be accompanied by an undertaking to pay the fee. Any party filing a document by fax should not also file a hard copy unless instructed;[2]

6.7.4 Paragraph 6.7.1 above also applies to skeleton arguments, which must be sent to the dedicated skeleton arguments email address for the relevant ACO (see the contacts list at annex 1). Also see chapter 17 of this guide on skeleton arguments.

6.7.5 Any document filed by fax or email after 4pm will be treated as filed on the next day the ACO is open.[3] If any party intends to file documents by fax, that party should first telephone the relevant ACO to ensure that the fax machine is available, and that there is someone there to receive the document.

6.7.6 An email sent to the Court must include the name, telephone number and address / email address for contacting the sender and it (including attachments) must be in plain or rich text format rather than HTML.[4]

6.7.7 The ACO or a judge may give instructions or order that a document is to be filed by email or fax in circumstances other than those outlined above.

6.8 SERVING THE CLAIM FORM

6.8.1 The claimant must serve a sealed copy of the claim form with a copy of the bundle of documentation filed alongside the claim form on the defendant(s) and any interested parties within 7 days of lodging the claim.[5] **1BA-37**

6.8.2 All Government Departments should be served at the office as stipulated under the Crown Proceedings Act 1947 (reproduced at annex 3 of this Guide). Local authorities should be served at their main offices with a note that papers should be directed to the authority's legal department (see CPR PD 54A, paragraph 6.2(b)).

6.8.3 Once the claimant has served the papers on the defendant(s) and any interested party or parties the claimant must confirm this with the ACO by filing a certificate of service (form N215) within 21 days of service of the claim form.[6] If, after 28 days of lodging the claim form, the Administrative Court Office has not received a certificate of service or an acknowledgment of service from the defendant, then the case will be closed.

6.8.4 If a claim is closed because the claimant fails to file a certificate of service within time, the claim will only be reopened by judicial order. Such an order must be applied for on an application notice with the relevant fee (see paragraph 12.7 of this Guide). In the application the claimant must explain why the certificate of service was not filed on time, whether the failure caused any prejudice to any party or any delay to the judicial review process, and outline the reasons why the claim should be reopened.

6.9 ADDITIONAL PROVISIONS FOR VEXATIOUS LITIGANTS OR PERSONS SUBJECT TO A CIVIL RESTRAINT ORDER

6.9.1 If a claimant is subject to a civil proceedings order made under s.42 of the Senior Courts Act 1981 or is subject to a civil restraint order made under CPR 3.11 then the claimant must apply for permission to start proceedings before he/she may file an application for permission to apply for judicial review. **1BA-38**

6.9.2 Such an application must be made on form N244 or PF244 and be accompanied by the relevant fee. This fee is not subject to fee remission, but it can be refunded if permission to start proceedings is granted.

6.9.3 The requirements for vexatious litigants or persons subject to a civil restraint order are discussed in greater detail in chapter 4 of this Guide.

---

[1] CPR PD 5B paragraph 2.1 and 2.2
[2] CPR PD5A paragraph 5.3
[3] CPR PD5A paragraph 5.3(6) and CPR PD 5B paragraph 4.2
[4] CPR PD 5B paragraph 3
[5] CPR 54.7
[6] CPR 6.17(2)(a)

7.   THE ACKNOWLEDGEMENT OF SERVICE

7.1   THE ACKNOWLEDGEMENT OF SERVICE

1BA-39   **7.1.1**   Any defendant or interested party served with the claim form who wishes to take part in the application for permission to apply for judicial review must file and serve an acknowledgement of service.[1]

7.1.2   When filing an acknowledgement of service form N462 must be used.

7.1.3   Filing an acknowledgment of service is wise for any defendant and any interested party in order for the Court to know if that person intends to contest the claim, but it is not mandatory.

7.1.4   If a party fails to file an acknowledgment of service within the relevant time limit (see paragraph 7.2 below) this will have three effects on the claim:

7.1.4.1   The papers will be sent to a judge to consider whether to grant permission to the claimant to apply for judicial review without having heard from the party who has failed to file the acknowledgement of service;

7.1.4.2   In the event that the judge does not grant or refuse permission outright, but directs that permission falls to be considered at an oral hearing (see paragraph 8.2.5 of this Guide), or if the judge refuses permission and the claimant applies for reconsideration at an oral hearing (see paragraph 8.4 of this Guide), the party may not take part in that hearing without the permission of the Court;[2] and

7.1.4.3   The judge considering any substantive application for judicial review may consider that party's failure to submit an acknowledgement of service when considering costs (see chapter 23 of this Guide for costs).[3]

7.1.5   If the party does not file an acknowledgment of service and permission is subsequently granted (see paragraph 8.2.2 and chapter 10 of this Guide), the party may still take part in the substantive application for judicial review.[4]

7.1.6   If the claim was started in or has been transferred to the ACO in Cardiff, the acknowledgement of service and any evidence may be lodged in Welsh or English.

7.2   TIME LIMITS

1BA-40   **7.2.1**   The acknowledgment of service must be filed at the ACO within 21 days of the claim papers being served.[5] The 21 day time limit may be extended or shortened by judicial order. If appropriate, a judge may also consider permission to apply for judicial review without waiting for an acknowledgment of service.

7.2.2   The parties cannot agree between themselves to extend the deadline,[6] it can only be extended by an order of the Court. An application for an extension of time must be made in accordance with the interim applications procedure and on payment of the relevant fee (see paragraph 12.7 of this Guide). Alternatively, the application can be made retrospectively in the acknowledgement of service in section D, provided permission has not already been considered.

7.2.3   The acknowledgement of service must be served on all other parties no later than 7 days after it was filed with the ACO.

7.2.4   As soon as an acknowledgement of service has been filed by each party to the claim, or upon the expiry of the relevant time limit, the papers will be sent to a judge who will consider whether to grant permission to apply for judicial review by considering the papers alone (see chapter 8 of this Guide).

7.2.5   The judicial review procedure does not allow for the claimant to respond to the acknowledgement of service during the paper application process. The ACO will not delay consideration of permission on the basis that the claimant may wish to reply. Any replies that are received before a case is sent to a judge to consider permission will be put before the judge but it is a matter for the judge as to whether he/she is willing to consider the reply.

7.3   CONTENTS

1BA-41   **7.3.1**   The acknowledgment of service must:

7.3.1.1   Set out the summary grounds for contesting the claim, if the party does contest it.[7] These must be as concise as possible. The summary grounds of defence may be part of the acknowledgment of service in section C, or they may be included in an attached separate document.

7.3.1.2   State if the party is intending to contest the application for permission on the basis that

---

[1] CPR 54.8(2)
[2] CPR 54.9(1)(a)
[3] CPR 54.9(2)
[4] CPR 54.9(1)(b)
[5] CPR 54.8(2)(a)
[6] CPR 54.8(3)
[7] CPR 54.8(4)(a)(i)

it is highly likely that the outcome for the claimant would not have been substantially different if the conduct complained of had not occurred, by ticking the box in section A, and set out the summary of the grounds for doing so.[1]

7.3.1.3 State, in section B, the name and address of any person the party believes to be an interested party.[2]

7.3.1.4 State, in section E, if the party contests the claimant's application for an automatic costs limit under the Aarhus convention (see paragraph 24.4 of this Guide), if one was made.

7.3.2 Evidence may be filed with the acknowledgment of service but it is not required.

7.4 DEFENDANT'S APPLICATIONS

When lodging the acknowledgment of service the party may request further directions or an interim order from the Court in section D.[3] Examples of applications that may be made at this stage are for the party's costs of preparing the acknowledgment of service and for the discharge of any previously made injunctions.

1BA-42

8. PERMISSION TO APPLY FOR JUDICIAL REVIEW

8.1 THE APPLICATION

8.1.1 The claimant must obtain permission from the Court to apply for judicial review. If permission is granted, the claim will usually proceed to a full hearing (often referred to as the substantive hearing – see Chapter 10 of this Guide).

1BA-43

8.1.2 In the first instance the claim papers (comprising the papers filed by the claimant and any acknowledgment(s) of service) are sent to a judge. The judge will then consider the papers and determine whether to grant permission to apply for judicial review.

8.1.3 The Court will refuse permission to apply for judicial review unless satisfied that there is an arguable ground for judicial review having a realistic prospect of success,[4] although there are a number of orders the Court can make before ultimately determining this question (see paragraph 8.2 of this Guide).

8.1.4 Even if a case is thought to be arguable, the judge must refuse permission if the judge considers that the outcome for the applicant would not have been substantially different if the conduct complained of had not occurred.[5]

8.2 COURT ORDERS ON PERMISSION

8.2.1 There a number of different orders that may be made by the judge following consideration of the papers. The following are the most common orders made by judges considering permission to apply for judicial review, but they are not exhaustive.

1BA-44

8.2.2 Permission Granted

The judge has determined that there is an arguable case and that the case will proceed to a substantive hearing of the application for judicial review. In this event, the judge will usually give directions for the substantive hearing.

8.2.3 Permission Refused

The judge has determined that none of the grounds advanced by the claimant are arguable and as such the claim should not proceed to a substantive hearing. When permission is refused on the papers, the judge will record brief reasons for that decision in the order.[6] The judge may order the claimant to pay the defendant's costs of preparing an acknowledgement of service at this stage (see paragraph 23.4 of this Guide).

8.2.4 Permission Granted in Part

8.2.4.1 The judge has determined that some of the grounds advanced by the claimant are arguable. The judge will direct the matter to proceed to a substantive hearing on those grounds only.

8.2.4.2 The claimant can request that the refused grounds are reconsidered for permission at an oral hearing (see paragraph 8.4 of this Guide).

---

[1] CPR 54.8(4)(a)(ia)
[2] CPR 54.8(4)(a)(ii)
[3] CPR 54.8(4)(b)
[4] Description of the test taken from *Sharma v Brown-Antoine* [2007] 1 W.L.R. 780
[5] s.31(3F) of the Senior Courts Act 1981
[6] CPR 54.12(2)

8.2.5   Permission adjourned to an oral hearing on notice

The judge has made no determination on the application for permission. Instead the application for permission will be considered at an oral hearing in Court with the claimant and any other parties who wish to make representations to the Court attending. The hearing will take a similar form to that of a renewed permission hearing (see paragraph 8.4 of this Guide).

8.2.6   Permission adjourned to a 'rolled up hearing'

8.2.6.1   The judge has made no determination on the application for permission. Instead the application for permission will be considered in Court with the substantive hearing to follow immediately if permission is granted.

8.2.6.2   In practice, at the rolled up hearing the judge will not necessarily consider permission then the substantive hearing one after another formulaically. The judge is more likely to hear argument on both points together and give a single judgment, but the manner in which the hearing is dealt with is within the discretion of the judge.

8.2.6.3   When preparing documentation for a rolled up hearing the parties should apply the same rules as apply when preparing for a substantive hearing (see chapter 9 of this Guide). This is because, despite the fact that permission has not yet been granted or refused, substantive consideration of the application for judicial review will, if appropriate, take place on the same day. Thus, the documentation before the Court should be the same as if the hearing was the substantive hearing.

8.2.6.4   Where a rolled up hearing is ordered the claimant will be asked by the ACO to sign an undertaking to pay the fee for the substantive application for judicial review which would then become payable in the event that the judge later grants permission.

8.2.7   The application for permission is to be resubmitted

The judge has made no determination on the application for permission. Instead the judge will request the parties perform some act (such as file additional documents or representations) or await some other event (such as the outcome of a similar case). Once the act or event has been performed, or when the time limit for doing so has expired, the papers will be resubmitted to the judge to consider permission on the papers.

8.3   TOTALLY WITHOUT MERIT ORDERS

1BA-45   **8.3.1**   If the judge considers that the application for permission is 'totally without merit' then he/she may refuse permission and certify the claim as being totally without merit in the order.

8.3.2   The term 'totally without merit' has been defined broadly and applies to a case that it is bound to fail, not one that is necessarily abusive or vexatious.[1]

8.3.3   Where a case is certified as totally without merit there is no right to a renewed oral hearing[2] (see paragraph 8.4 of this Guide) and the claim is concluded in the Administrative Court, albeit appeal rights do apply (see paragraph 26.3 of this Guide).

8.4   RECONSIDERATION AT AN ORAL HEARING

1BA-46   **8.4.1**   If permission is refused the claimant should consider the judge's reasons for refusing permission on the papers before taking any further action.

8.4.2   If the claimant takes no further action then, seven days after service of the order refusing permission, the ACO will simply close the case. If the Court has directed the parties to file written submissions on costs or has given directions in relation to any other aspect of the case, the claim will remain open until the costs or that other aspect are resolved. If there is an interim or costs order in place at that time, and unless the Court has directed otherwise, it will continue in effect (even though the case is closed administratively) and the parties will have to apply to set aside that order (see paragraph 12.7 of this guide).

8.4.3   If, having considered the reasons, the claimant wishes to continue to contest the matter they may not appeal, but they may request that the application for permission to apply for judicial review be reconsidered at an oral hearing (often referred to as a renewed hearing).[3]

8.4.4   When the ACO serves an order refusing permission to apply for judicial review on the papers it will also include a renewal notice (form 86b). If the claimant wishes to have their application for permission to apply for judicial review reconsidered at an oral hearing they should complete and send this form back to the ACO within seven days[4] of the date upon which it is served. The claimant should send a copy of the 86b to any party that filed an acknowledgement of service.

8.4.5   The Claimant must provide grounds for renewing the application for permission, and

---

[1] *R. (Grace) v Secretary of State for the Home Department* [2014] 1 W.L.R. 3432, and *Samia W v Secretary of State for the Home Department* [2016] EWCA Civ 82

[2] CPR 54.12(7)

[3] CPR 54.12(3)

[4] CPR 54.12(4)

must in those grounds address the judge's reasons for refusing permission by explaining in brief terms why the claimant maintains those reasons are wrong. **It is not sufficient simply to state that renewal is sought on the original grounds, without seeking to explain the asserted error in the refusing judge's reasons.** If the refusing judge's reasons are not addressed, the judge may make an adverse costs order against the claimant at the renewal hearing and/or impose any other sanction which he/she considers to be appropriate.[1]

8.4.6 Upon receipt of the renewal notice the ACO will list an oral hearing (see paragraph 13.2.1 of this Guide on listing). The hearing cannot, without judicial order, take place without all parties being given at least two days notice of the hearing.[2] The ACO will send notice to all parties of the date of the hearing.

8.4.7 The renewed hearing is normally a public hearing that anyone may attend and observe and will take place in Court before a judge. The only issue at the hearing is the arguability of the claim or particular grounds, so hearings are expected to be short, with the parties making succinct submissions.

8.5 TIME ESTIMATE FOR RENEWED HEARING

8.5.1 The standard time estimate for a renewed permission hearing is 30 minutes to include **1BA-47** the Court giving judgment, if that is appropriate, at the end of the hearing.

8.5.2 If either party reasonably believes that the renewed hearing (including judgment) is likely to last more than 30 minutes, that party should inform the ACO as soon as possible of that fact, and of that party's revised time estimate (including judgment). Failure to inform the ACO may result in the hearing having to be adjourned on the hearing day for lack of Court time, in which event the Court will consider making a costs order against the party or parties which should have notified the Court of the longer time estimate.

8.5.3 Even where a party informs the Court that the renewed hearing is likely to take more than 30 minutes, the Court will only allocate such Court time as it considers appropriate, bearing in mind the pressure on Court time from other cases. In any event, it is rare that permission hearings will be allocated a time estimate over two hours.

8.6 PROCEDURE AT RENEWAL HEARINGS

8.6.1 The defendant and/or any interested party may attend the oral hearing. Unless the **1BA-48** Court directs otherwise, they need not attend.[3] If they have not filed an acknowledgement of service, they will have no right to be heard, although the Court may nonetheless permit them to make representations (see paragraph 7.1.4 of this Guide).[4]

8.6.2 Where there are a number of cases listed before a judge in any day, an attempt will be made to give a time marking for each case. This may be shown on the daily cause list or the judge's clerk may contact the parties and/or their representatives. Alternatively, at the start of the day's list, the judge may release the parties and/or their representatives until a specific time later in the day.

8.6.3 At the hearing, the judge retains discretion as to how the hearing will proceed. Subject to that discretion, generally, the hearing will follow a set pattern:

8.6.3.1 The claimant will speak first setting out his/her grounds and why he/she contends they are arguable;

8.6.3.2 The defendant(s) will speak second setting out why the grounds are not arguable or other reasons why permission should not be granted;

8.6.3.3 Any interested parties will speak third to support or contest the application for permission;

8.6.3.4 The claimant is usually given a right to a short reply;

8.6.3.5 The decision refusing or granting permission, and, if appropriate, any further directions or orders will usually be announced at the conclusion of the hearing.

8.6.4 Any party before a hearing in the Administrative Court in Wales has the right to speak Welsh or English. The guidance outlined at paragraph 10.3 of this Guide also applies to permission hearings.

8.6.5 The test for granting permission at an oral hearing is the same as the one applied by the judge considering permission on the papers (see paragraph 8.1.3 of this Guide).

8.6.6 In the event that permission is refused at the renewed hearing then the claim has ended in the Administrative Court (subject to any appeal – see paragraph 26.3 of this Guide). In the event that the judge does give permission then the case will proceed to the substantive hearing, which will take place on a later date (unless the hearing was 'rolled up' (see paragraph 8.2.6 of this Guide), in which case the substantive hearing will follow immediately). The date for the hearing may be ordered by the judge or listed by the ACO (see paragraph 13.2.2 of this Guide for listing).

---

[1] See, in an extradition context, *Roby Opalfvens v Belgium* [2015] EWHC 2808 (Admin), at [14]
[2] CPR 54.12(5)
[3] CPR PD 54A paragraph 8.5
[4] CPR 54.9(1)(a)

8.7 ALTERNATIVE PROCEDURE WHERE THE UPPER TRIBUNAL IS THE DEFENDANT

1BA-49 **8.7.1** In some claims the Upper Tribunal will be the appropriate defendant. This will generally only arise where the Upper Tribunal has refused permission to appeal against the decision of the First-tier Tribunal, because all other decisions of the Upper Tribunal are subject to a right of appeal, which should be exercised instead of applying for judicial review. Where the claimant wishes to challenge the decision of the Upper Tribunal when it has refused permission to appeal from a decision of the First-tier Tribunal the judicial review procedure is amended by CPR.54.7A. The claimant should read all of CPR 54.7A. The most important points are outlined below.

8.7.2 The Court will only grant permission to apply for judicial review if it considers:

8.7.2.1 That there is an arguable case which has a reasonable prospect of success that both the decision of the Upper Tribunal refusing permission to appeal and the decision of the First Tier Tribunal against which permission to appeal was sought are wrong in law; and

8.7.2.2 That either the claim raises an important point of principle or practice or there is some other compelling reason to hear the claim.[1]

8.7.3 The general procedure in CPR Part 54 will apply, save for the following amendments:

8.7.3.1 The application for permission may not include any other claim, whether against the Upper Tribunal or not and any such other claim must be the subject of a separate application;[2]

8.7.3.2 The claim form and the supporting documents must be filed no later than 16 days after the date on which notice of the Upper Tribunal's decision was sent to the applicant, not the normal three months;[3]

8.7.3.3 If the application for permission is refused on paper there is no right to a renewed oral hearing (see paragraph 8.4 of this Guide), albeit appeal rights do then apply (see paragraph 26.3 of this Guide).[4]

8.7.3.4 If permission to apply for judicial review is granted and if the Upper Tribunal or any interested party wishes there to be a hearing of the substantive application, it must make a request for such a hearing no later than 14 days after service of the order granting permission, in which case the ACO will list a substantive hearing. If no request for a hearing is made within that period, the Court will make a final order quashing the Upper Tribunal's decision without a further hearing.[5] The case will then return to the Upper Tribunal to consider permission to appeal again.

9. AFTER PERMISSION

9.1 DIRECTIONS FOR SUBSTANTIVE HEARING

1BA-50 **9.1.1** When permission to apply for judicial review is granted, the claim will proceed to the substantive hearing on a later date.

9.1.2 Unless the judge orders a particular date for the hearing, the ACO will list the substantive hearing as soon as practicable (see paragraph 13.2.2 of this Guide for listing).

9.1.3 When granting permission a judge will often give directions as to how the case will progress to the substantive hearing, including:

9.1.3.1 The time within which the defendant or interested party or parties should file detailed grounds of resistance and any evidence on which they intend to rely at the hearing;

9.1.3.2 Who should hear the case, and specifically whether it should be heard by a Divisional Court (a Court with two or more judges),

9.1.3.3 Other case management directions including a timetable for skeleton arguments, trial bundles and authorities bundles to be lodged.

9.1.4 Judicial directions will supersede any standard directions. If the judge does not make any directions, the following standard directions apply:

9.1.4.1 The claimant must pay the relevant fee to continue the application for judicial review. Failure to do so within 7 days of permission being granted will result in the ACO sending the claimant a notice requiring payment within a set time frame (normally 7 more days). Further failure will result in the claim being struck out without further order.[6]

9.1.4.2 Any party who wishes to contest or support the claim must file and serve any detailed grounds and any written evidence within 35 days of permission being granted;[7]

9.1.4.3 The claimant must file and serve a skeleton argument no less than 21 working days[8]

---

[1] CPR 54.7A(7)
[2] CPR 54.7A(2)
[3] CPR 54.7A(3)
[4] CPR 54.7A(8)
[5] CPR 54.7A(9)
[6] CPR 3.7(1)(d), (2), (3), & (4)
[7] CPR 54.14(1)
[8] CPR PD54A paragraph 15 refers to 'working' days. This is different from the normal presumption in the CPR that days means 'calendar' days, save for periods of time of less than 5 days, see

before the substantive hearing (see paragraph 17.2 of this Guide for the contents of the skeleton argument).[1]

9.1.4.4 The defendant and any other party wishing to make representations at the substantive hearing must file and serve a skeleton argument no less than 14 working days before the substantive hearing.[2]

9.1.4.5 The claimant must file a paginated and indexed bundle of all relevant documents required for the hearing of the judicial review when filing the skeleton argument[3] (21 working days before the hearing unless judicial order allows for a different time period). The bundle must include those documents required by the defendant and any other party who is to make representations at the hearing.[4] The parties should be liaising as far before the substantive hearing as possible to agree what is required in the agreed bundle.

9.2 AMENDING THE CLAIM

9.2.1 If the claimant wishes to file further evidence or rely on further grounds then the claimant must ask for the Court's permission to do so.[5] To seek permission the claimant must make an application in line with the interim applications procedure discussed at paragraph 12.7 of this Guide.

1BA-51

9.2.2 This rule also applies to other parties who are filing documents outside the 35 day time limit (discussed at paragraph 9.1.4.2 of this Guide).

9.2.3 The application may be dealt with in advance of the substantive hearing or at the hearing itself. The decision on when the application should be dealt with is ultimately a judicial one, but the parties should indicate a preference when lodging the application.

9.2.4 The Court retains a discretion as to whether to permit amendments. In *R (Bhatti) v Bury Metropolitan Borough Council* [2013] EWHC 3093 (Admin) the Court warned that, where the defendant has reconsidered the original decision challenged and has provided a fresh decision which it now relies on, it may not be appropriate to seek to amend the claim. Instead, it may be more appropriate to end the claim (see chapter 22 of this Guide) and, if the claimant seeks to challenge the new decision, to commence a new claim. The exceptions to this principle, where the Court may be prepared to consider the challenge to the initial decision, are narrow, and apply only where:

9.2.4.1 The case raises a point of general public importance; and

9.2.4.2 The point which was at issue in relation to the initial decision challenged remains an important issue in relation to the subsequent decision.[6]

9.3 ACTION IF AN INTERPRETER IS REQUIRED

9.3.1 If a party or witness requires an interpreter it is generally the responsibility of that party or the party calling the witness to arrange for the attendance of and to pay for the interpreter.

1BA-52

9.3.2 The ACO can arrange an interpreter to attend free of charge to the party seeking an interpreter's assistance where:

9.3.2.1 The party is a litigant in person who cannot address the Court in English (or Welsh if the case is proceeding in Wales) and the party cannot afford to pay for an interpreter, does not qualify for legal aid and does not have a friend or family member who the judge agrees can act as an interpreter; and

9.3.2.2 The judge agrees that an interpreter should be arranged free of charge to that party; or

9.3.2.3 In such other circumstances as ordered by the Court.

9.3.3 It is the responsibility of the party which requests an interpreter free of charge to that party to make the request in writing as soon as it becomes clear that a hearing will have to be listed and an interpreter is required.

9.3.4 The party which requests an interpreter free of charge must inform the ACO in writing that an interpreter is required and the party must state which language the interpreter will be required to translate into English and vice versa (or into Welsh and vice versa if the case is proceeding in Wales: see paragraph 10.3 of this Guide for use of the Welsh language).

9.3.5 Where the party does not notify the Court that an interpreter is required and a hearing

---

CPR2.8(3). It is a feature of the CPR that if the judge, when granting permission, expressly orders the skeleton argument to be filed '21 days' before the substantive hearing, then it must be provided 21 *calendar* days, not working days, before the substantive hearing. This is because CPR 2.8(3) applies to all judicial orders.

[1] CPR PD 54A paragraph 15.1
[2] See footnote 89 above
[3] CPR PD 54A paragraph 16.1
[4] CPR PD 54A paragraph 16.2
[5] CPR 54.15 and CPR 54.16(2) respectively.
[6] *R (Bhatti) v Bury Metropolitan Borough Council* [2013] EWHC 3093, and see *R (Yousuf) v Secretary of State for the Home Department* [2016] EWHC 663 (Admin)

has to be adjourned to arrange for an interpreter to attend on another occasion, the Court may make an adverse costs order against the party requiring an interpreter (see paragraph 23.1 of this Guide).

9.4   RESPONSIBILITY FOR PRODUCTION OF SERVING PRISONERS AND DETAINED PERSONS

1BA-53   **9.4.1**   Where a serving prisoner or a detained person is represented by counsel it is generally not expected that the serving prisoner or detained person will be produced at Court, unless the Court orders otherwise.

9.4.2   Where the serving prisoner or detained person is acting without legal representation, it is the responsibility of the serving prisoner or detained person to arrange for their attendance at Court or for a video-link to be arranged between the Court and prison or detention centre. The serving prisoner or detained person must make the request that they be produced at Court for the hearing or that a video-link should be arranged, to the prison or detention centre authorities, as soon as they receive notice of the hearing. The prison or detention centre authorities are responsible for considering requests for production, for arranging production of a person at Court, and for arranging video-links.

9.5   SPECIFIC PRACTICE POINTS

1BA-54   Reference should be made to the guidance contained under Part C of this Guide, Specific Practice Points, which gives detailed guidance on skeleton arguments (at chapter 17), documents (at chapter 18xx) and authorities (at chapter 19).

10.   Substantive Hearing

10.1   FORMAT OF THE HEARING

1BA-55   **10.1.1**   The hearing is generally a public hearing which anyone may attend and observe. The hearing normally takes place before a single judge, unless the Court orders the case to be heard by a Divisional Court (see paragraphs 1.7.4 and 13.3 of this Guide on Divisional Courts).

10.1.2   The Court will decide how the hearing should proceed. But most hearings follow the following sequence:

10.1.2.1   The claimant will speak first setting out the arguments in support of the grounds of claim.

10.1.2.2   The defendant will speak second setting out the arguments in support of the grounds of defence;

10.1.2.3   Any interested parties and/or interveners will speak third to support, contest, or clarify anything that has been said; and

10.1.2.4   The claimant will have a right to reply to the other parties' submissions.

10.2   EVIDENCE

1BA-56   **10.2.1**   Evidence before the Court will nearly always consist of witness statements and written evidence without allowing oral evidence to be given and without cross examination of witnesses.

10.2.2   The Court retains an inherent power to hear from witnesses.[1] If a party seeks to call or cross-examine a witness, an application should be made in accordance with the interim applications procedure outlined in section 12.7 of this Guide. As a matter of practice, it is only in very exceptional cases that oral evidence is permitted in a judicial review. Permission will be given only where oral evidence is necessary to dispose of the claim fairly and justly[2].

10.3   USE OF THE WELSH LANGUAGE

1BA-57   **10.3.1**   A hearing before the Administrative Court in Wales is subject to the provisions of s.22 of the Welsh Language Act 1993 and as such any person addressing the Court may exercise their right to speak in Welsh. This right applies only to hearings in Wales and so, if the party seeks to exercise this right they should start the claim in the ACO in Cardiff or seek transfer of the claim to the ACO in Cardiff.

10.3.2   Under the Practice Direction Relating to the Use of the Welsh Language in Cases in the Civil Courts in Wales, the Court may hear any person in Welsh without notice of the wish to speak in Welsh, providing all parties and the Court consent.[3]

---

[1] See the comments of Munby J (as he then was) in *R. (PG) v London Borough of Ealing* [2002] A.C.D. 48 at paragraphs 20 and 21.

[2] *R (Bancoult) v Secretary of State for Foreign and Commonwealth Affairs* [2012] EWHC 2115 at 14;

[3] Paragraph 1.2 of the Practice Direction Relating to the Use of the Welsh Language in Cases in the Civil Courts in Wales

10.3.3 In practice, the parties should inform the Court as soon as possible,[1] preferably when lodging the claim papers, if any person intends to speak in Welsh. This will allow the Court to make proper directions and allow the ACO in Cardiff to make practical arrangements.

10.3.4 There are bi-lingual judges who can consider such claims, but nonetheless, it is likely that an order will be made for simultaneous translation, where a translator appears in Court translating into English and Welsh.[2]

10.4 JUDICIAL REVIEW WITHOUT A HEARING

If all parties agree, the substantive consideration may take place without a hearing, and the judge will decide the claim by considering the papers alone. The parties should inform the ACO in writing if all parties have agreed to this course of action. The judge, on consideration of the papers, may refuse to make a decision on the papers and order an oral hearing.

1BA-58

10.5 THRESHOLD FOR RELIEF

10.5.1 To succeed in the claim the claimant must show that the defendant has acted unlawfully.

1BA-59

10.5.2 Even if a claimant establishes that the defendant has acted unlawfully, the Court has a discretion whether to grant a remedy or not.

10.6 JUDGMENT AND ORDERS

10.6.1 When the hearing is concluded the Court will usually give judgment in one of two ways:

1BA-60

10.6.1.1 Orally, then and there, or sometimes after a short adjournment (this is referred to as an 'ex tempore' judgment).

10.6.1.2 The Court may give judgment in writing some time after the hearing (this is referred to as a 'reserved' judgment).

10.6.2 A reserved judgment will be 'handed down' at a later date. The hand down procedure is governed by CPR PD 40E. Unless the Court otherwise directs, at least two working days before the hand down date the judge will provide a copy of the judgment to legal representatives in the case.[3] That draft is confidential and any breach of that confidentiality is a contempt of court. The legal representatives may then propose any typographical corrections.[4]

10.6.3 After the draft judgment has been circulated the parties are obliged to attempt to agree the form of the final order and any consequential orders[5] (usually costs and permission to appeal – see chapters 23 and 26 of this Guide). The parties should submit an agreed order, which should include the terms of any orders made by the judge in Court and the terms of any agreed consequential orders, by 12 noon the day before the hand down date.[6] If the parties can agree a final order then they need not attend the hand down hearing.[7]

10.6.4 If consequential orders cannot be agreed then the Court will decide consequential orders by considering representations. This may be done in one of two ways:

10.6.4.1 The parties may attend Court on the date of handing down and make representations orally. The Court will then decide on consequential orders. The parties should inform the ACO in good time if they intend to do this as time will need to be allocated for the judge to hear representations. Such a hearing would usually last for 30 minutes, rather than the 5 minutes set aside for a simple hand down; or

10.6.4.2 The parties may agree a final order that allows them to make written representations within a set time period on consequential orders, which the Court will then consider and, at a later date, make an order based on those written representations alone.

10.6.5 The final judgment will then be handed down in Court. In practice this is a short hearing at which the judge makes the final copy of the judgment available and endorses it. The judge will not read the judgment verbatim. The judge will adjourn any consequential matters which remain to be dealt with at a later date.

10.6.6 The ACO will send sealed copies of any orders approved by the judge to the parties. Until an order has been approved and sealed the parties should not assume that any agreed orders will be approved. It is the sealed order itself that holds legal force as opposed to the judgment and it is the order that must be enforced if a party fails to comply with the terms.

---

[1] Paragraph 1.3 of the Practice Direction Relating to the Use of the Welsh Language in Cases in the Civil Courts in Wales

[2] This was the format ordered in *R. (Welsh Language Commissioner) v National Savings and Investments* [2014] P.T.S.R. D8 and is in line with HMCTS's Welsh language scheme 2013-2016, paragraph 5.26.

[3] CPR PD 40E paragraph 2.3

[4] Ibid, paragraph 3.1

[5] Ibid, paragraph 4.1

[6] CPR PD 40E, paragraph 4.2

[7] Ibid, paragraph 5.1

10.6.7 All substantive judgments are made publicly available at the website *www.bailii.org* which does not charge a fee for access.

11. REMEDIES

11.1.

1BA-61 When the claimant starts a claim he/she must state in section 7 of the claim form what remedy he/she seeks from the Court in the event that he/she is successful. There are six remedies available to a successful claimant in judicial review proceedings, all of which are listed in sections 31(1) and 31(4) of the Senior Courts Act 1981 as well as CPR part 54. This section of the Guide will discuss those remedies.

11.2 MANDATORY ORDER

1BA-62 **11.2.1** A mandatory order is the order the Court can make to compel a public body to act in a particular way.

11.3 QUASHING ORDER

1BA-63 **11.3.1** A quashing order quashes, or sets aside, the decision, thereby confirming that the challenged decision has no lawful force and no legal effect.
11.3.2 After making a quashing order the Court will generally remit the matter to the public body decision maker and direct it to reconsider the matter and reach a fresh decision in accordance with the judgment of the Court.[1]
11.3.3 The Court has power to substitute its own decision for the decision which has been quashed.[2] This power is only exercisable against the decisions of the inferior Courts or Tribunals, only on the grounds of error of law, and only where there is only one possible decision now open to the decision maker.

11.4 PROHIBITING ORDER

1BA-64 **11.4.1** A prohibiting order prohibits a public body from taking an action that the public body has indicated an intention to take, but has not yet taken.

11.5 ORDINARY DECLARATIONS

1BA-65 **11.5.1** A declaration is a statement by the Court as to what the law on a particular point is or is not. Using the declaratory remedy the Administrative Court can examine an act (including an act announced but not yet taken) of a public body and formally declare that it is lawful, or unlawful.
11.5.2 A declaration does not have any coercive effect although a public body is expected to comply with the declaration. A declaration can be a remedy on its own,[3] or can be granted in combination with other remedies.
11.5.3 A declaration will not be granted where the question under consideration is a hypothetical question, nor where the person seeking the declaration has no real interest in it, nor where the declaration is sought without proper argument (e.g. in default of defence or on admissions or by consent).[4]

11.6 DECLARATION OF INCOMPATIBILITY

1BA-66 **11.6.1** If the Court determines that any Act of Parliament is incompatible with a Convention right, that is a right derived from the European Convention on Human Rights 1950 ('ECHR') which in incorporated into the law of the United Kingdom by the Human Rights Act 1998, it may make a declaration of incompatibility.[5]
11.6.2 A declaration of incompatibility may be made in relation to subordinate legislation if the Court is satisfied that (disregarding any possibility of revocation) the Act of Parliament concerned prevents removal of the incompatibility.[6]
11.6.3 The principles behind ordinary declarations (see paragraph 11.5 of this Guide above), such as the requirement that a declaration will not be made in hypothetical circumstances, apply.[7]

---

[1] As outlined in s.31(5)(a) of the Senior Courts Act 1981 and CPR 54.19(2)(a)
[2] Under s.31(5)(b) of the Senior Courts Act 1981 and CPR 54.19(2)(b)
[3] CPR 40.20
[4] *Re F* [1990] 2 A.C. 1
[5] ss.4(1) and 4(2) of the Human Rights Act 1998
[6] ss.4(3) and 4(4) of the Human Rights Act 1998.
[7] See, for example, *Taylor v Lancashire County Council* [2005] 1 W.L.R. 2668

11.6.4 A declaration of incompatibility does not affect the validity, continuing operation or enforcement of the provision in respect of which it is given and it is not binding on the parties to the proceedings in which it is made.[1] The declaration acts to inform Parliament of the incompatibility of that provision with a Convention right.

11.6.5 The claimant must state in the remedies section of the claim form (section 7) if they are applying for a declaration of incompatibility, giving precise details of the Convention right which has allegedly been infringed, and the domestic law provision which is said to be incompatible.[2]

11.6.6 The claimant should consider making the Crown, via the relevant Secretary of State, an interested party, if a declaration of incompatibility is sought. In any event, where an application for a declaration of incompatibility has been made the Court may order that notice should be given to the Crown.[3] If the Court is considering making a declaration of incompatibility and the Crown is not already a party, the Court must inform the relevant Secretary of State and allow him/her at least 21 days[4] to consider whether to intervene and make representations.[5]

11.7 INJUNCTIONS

11.7.1 An injunction is an order to act in a particular way (a positive injunction) or to refrain from acting in a particular way (a negative injunction). It is a remedy that is not confined to judicial review, although it is available in judicial review.
1BA-67

11.8 DAMAGES

11.8.1 Whilst primarily a private law remedy, the Administrative Court has power to award damages.
1BA-68

11.8.2 The right to seek damages in judicial review proceedings is subject to two provisos:

11.8.2.1 The claimant may only seek damages if they are also seeking another remedy, not just damages alone;[6] and

11.8.2.2 The claimant may only seek damages if a private law claim for damages on the same basis would have succeeded (had it been brought in the County Court or appropriate division of the High Court).[7]

11.8.3 Where the assessment and award of damages is likely to be a lengthy procedure the general practice of the Administrative Court is to determine the judicial review claim, award the other remedy sought (if appropriate), and then transfer the claim to either the County Court or appropriate division of the High Court to determine the question of damages.

11.9 MULTIPLE REMEDIES

11.9.1 The Court may grant more than one remedy where it is deemed appropriate.
1BA-69

11.10 REMEDIES WHERE THE OUTCOME WOULD NOT BE SUBSTANTIALLY DIFFERENT

11.10.1 If the claimant is successful in judicial review proceedings, but the Court considers that it is highly likely that the outcome for the claimant would not be substantially different even if the unlawful decision by the public body was set aside or remedied, the Court must refuse to grant any form of relief and must not award damages, except in exceptional public interest cases.[8]
1BA-70

11.11 DISCRETIONARY REMEDIES

11.11.1 Remedies in judicial review proceedings are within the discretion of the Court.
1BA-71

11.11.2 Even where a claimant shows that a defendant has acted unlawfully, the Court may refuse to grant a remedy, in particular where:[9]

11.11.2.1 The claimant has delayed in filing the application for judicial review and the Court considers that the granting of the remedy sought would be likely to cause substantial hardship to, or would substantially prejudice the rights of any person, or would be detrimental to good administration.

11.11.2.2 The error of law made by the public body was not material to the Court's decision.

11.11.2.3 The remedy would serve no useful practical purpose.

---

[1] s.4(6) of the Human Rights Act 1998
[2] CPR PD 16 paragraphs 15.1(2)(a), (c)(i), & (d)
[3] CPR 54A PD paragraph 8.2 & CPR PD 19A paragraph 6.1
[4] CPR 19.4A(1)
[5] s.5(1) of the Human Rights Act 1998
[6] CPR 54.3(2).
[7] s.31(4) of the Senior Courts Act 1981
[8] s31(2A) Senior Courts Act 1981 and s31(2B) Senior Courts Act 1981
[9] See R. (Baker) v Police Appeals Tribunal [2013] EWHC 718 (Admin)

11.11.2.4 The claimant has suffered no harm or prejudice.

11.11.3 The principles on discretionary remedies discussed above do not apply to the award of damages.

12. CASE MANAGEMENT

12.1 CASE MANAGEMENT IN THE ADMINISTRATIVE COURT

1BA-72   **12.1.1** All proceedings in the Administrative Court, from the start of the claim to the end, are subject to the overriding objective outlined in CPR 1.1. The overriding objective requires all cases to be dealt with justly and at proportionate cost.

12.1.2 Dealing with a case justly and at proportionate cost includes:[1]

12.1.2.1 Ensuring that the parties are on an equal footing;

12.1.2.2 Saving expense;

12.1.2.3 Dealing with it in ways which are proportionate to the amount of money involved, to the importance of the case, to the complexity of the issues, and to the financial position of each party;

12.1.2.4 Ensuring that it is dealt with expeditiously and fairly;

12.1.2.5 Allotting to it an appropriate share of the Court's resources, while taking into account the need to allot resources to other cases; and

12.1.2.6 Ensuring compliance with rules, practice directions and orders.

12.1.3 In ensuring that the overriding objective is complied with, the Court must actively manage cases,[2] which includes (but is not limited to) the following:

12.1.3.1 Encouraging the parties to co-operate with each other in the conduct of the proceedings;

12.1.3.2 Identifying the issues at an early stage;

12.1.3.3 Deciding promptly which issues need full investigation and trial and accordingly disposing summarily of the others;

12.1.3.4 Deciding the order in which issues are to be resolved;

12.1.3.5 Encouraging the parties to use an alternative dispute resolution procedure if the Court considers that appropriate and facilitating the use of such procedure;

12.1.3.6 Helping the parties to settle the whole or part of the case;

12.1.3.7 Fixing timetables or otherwise controlling the progress of the case;

12.1.3.8 Considering whether the likely benefits of taking a particular step justify the cost of taking it;

12.1.3.9 Dealing with as many aspects of the case as it can on the same occasion;

12.1.3.10 Dealing with the case without the parties needing to attend at Court;

12.1.3.11 Making use of technology; and

12.1.3.12 Giving directions to ensure that the trial of a case proceeds quickly and efficiently.

12.1.4 The parties are required to help the Court to further the overriding objective.[3]

12.1.5 This chapter of the Guide is intended to provide more detail on what is expected from the Court, the ACO, and the parties in order to further the overriding objective.

12.2 DUTIES OF THE PARTIES

1BA-73   **12.2.1** The parties must make efforts to settle the claim without requiring the intervention of the Court. This is a continuing duty and whilst it is preferable to settle the claim before it is started, the parties must continue to evaluate the strength of their case throughout proceedings, especially after any indication as to the strength of the case from the Court (such as after the refusal or grant of permission to apply for judicial review). The parties should consider using alternative dispute resolution (for example, mediation) to explore settlement of the case, or at least to narrow the issues in the case.

12.2.2 CPR Part 54 does not provide for a formal case management hearing in judicial review proceedings, although the parties may apply for an interim order or the Court may make case management orders with or without a hearing. It is not uncommon for the first time the parties appear in Court before the judge to be the final hearing of the claim. As such, the parties have a duty to ensure that they maintain effective, constructive, and regular communication with each other and the ACO (see also paragraph 14.1 of this Guide on the Duty of Candour).

12.2.3 The parties must comply with the procedural provisions in the CPR, the relevant Practice Directions and orders of the Court (including orders by an ACO lawyer). If a party knows they will not be able to do so they should inform the ACO and the other parties as soon as possible and make the application to extend the time limit as soon as possible (in accordance with the interim applications procedure in 12.7 of this Guide).

---

[1] CPR 1.1(2)
[2] CPR 1.4
[3] CPR 1.3

12.2.4 If a party is aware that they may need to apply for an interim order (extending time as per paragraph 12.2.3 above or for interim relief in accordance with chapter 15 of this Guide) they should inform the other parties and the ACO as soon as they know they may need to make the application. The application should then be made as quickly as possible. Delay in making an application and/or a failure to put the ACO and the other parties on notice, especially where it requires urgent consideration, is a factor which may weigh against the granting of the order.

12.2.5 The parties should, if possible, agree the form of any case management order and/or interim relief and file an agreed consent order, which will be subject to the Court's approval. A fee is payable when submitting a consent order and the reasons for requesting the order should be included in an accompanying application notice (N244 or PF244).

12.2.6 The parties should also comply with any requests from ACO staff members (such as requests for documents or information). Whilst these requests do not have the force of an order of the Court, failure to comply with such a request may be a factor considered by a judge or ACO lawyer that weighs against granting an interim order, permission to apply for judicial review, substantive relief, or costs.

12.2.7 If the parties are aware that a case is likely to settle without the further involvement of the Court they should inform the ACO as soon as possible.

12.2.8 The parties and their legal representatives should ensure compliance with the CPR, Practice Directions and rules. Of particular importance are: the duty of candour, the requirement to make full disclosure of all material facts (see paragraph 14.1 of this Guide), and the procedures for bringing urgent cases before the Court, see chapter 16 of this Guide.

12.3 ROLE OF THE ADMINISTRATIVE COURT OFFICE STAFF

12.3.1 The staff members in the ACO handle the day to day running of the ACO from the start **1BA-74** of the process to the finish. One of their duties is to ensure that the cases are properly managed by requesting missing or late documents from the parties and by referring problematic issues to an ACO lawyer, the Master, or a judge.

12.3.2 The ACO staff members are not legally qualified, and cannot give legal advice on the merits of the claim. Staff members may be able to assist with the basic judicial review procedure. However, any advice from a member of staff as to procedure must not be considered to circumvent any legal provision (be that provision in statute, case law, the CPR, or a Court order) or the provisions of this Guide. Parties and the Court are responsible for the conduct of proceedings and the parties will not be able to rely on the advice of the ACO as a reason for not complying with legal provisions.

12.3.3 The ACO staff may contact the parties to request information or specific documents if that information or document is required under the CPR or is thought to be necessary to allow the Court to properly consider or case manage the claim. The parties should comply with any requests unless they are unable to do so, when written reasons should be given for the failure.

12.3.4 The ACO staff have a duty to ensure that cases are being managed in accordance with the overriding objective. As such, where it appears that a case is not being managed in accordance with the overriding objective they have a duty to either make enquiries of the parties to establish the proper further course of action and/or to refer the case to an ACO lawyer or judge to consider further case management. Examples (but not an exhaustive list) of scenarios in which ACO staff may act as such are:

12.3.4.1 The claim appears to have been filed and/or issued in the Administrative Court under the judicial review provisions when it appears the claim should properly have been filed and/or issued in another Court or under a different provision;

12.3.4.2 The parties have failed to comply with procedural provisions in the CPR or a Court order;

12.3.4.3 The claim has been stayed for some time without a satisfactory update from the parties;

12.3.4.4 The staff member has concerns over the conduct of the parties.

12.4 ROLE OF THE ADMINISTRATIVE COURT OFFICE LAWYERS

12.4.1 An ACO lawyer must be a qualified solicitor or barrister. The role of the ACO lawyer is **1BA-75** as a non-partisan lawyer, subject to the duties of an officer of the Court (as all lawyers are). Therefore, whilst employed by HMCTS, their primary duty is to the Court. The role in itself is three fold:

12.4.1.1 To provide advice on practice and procedure in the Administrative Court to whoever requires it; be that judges, ACO staff, practitioners, or litigants;

12.4.1.2 To provide legal research and updates for the judges of the Administrative Court; and

12.4.1.3 To communicate with the parties and exercise delegated judicial powers to ensure that cases in the Administrative Court are managed properly.

12.4.2 As an ACO lawyer is independent of the parties he/she cannot give advice on the merits of the claim. An ACO lawyer may draw the parties' attention to provisions or precedents that may have an impact on the claim. If this is done the parties should consider what is said, but this should not be considered to be formal legal advice or a determination on the law. The parties have responsibility for the conduct of their own claim and the decision on the law is the preserve of the judge who considers the claim.

12.4.3 An ACO lawyer has a duty to ensure that the case is managed in accordance with the overriding objective and may enter into discussions with the parties or make case management orders (when applied for, when a case is referred to them by an ACO staff member, or of his/her own volition) to further the overriding objective and properly manage the case. Any order of an ACO lawyer will always be made after consideration of the papers without a hearing.

12.4.4 The specific powers that the ACO lawyer may use are delegated by the President of the Queen's Bench Division[1] and include:

12.4.4.1 Extending or abridging time for filing documents;

12.4.4.2 Making orders giving directions;

12.4.4.3 Adding to or removing parties from the claim;

12.4.4.4 Varying a Judge's order for directions;

12.4.4.5 Considering applications for abridgement of time for acknowledgment of service;

12.4.4.6 Determining applications for an extension of time in which to file a renewal notice;

12.4.4.7 Ordering a claim issued in Cardiff is to be heard in Bristol or elsewhere on the Western Circuit;

12.4.4.8 Transferring a case to the Upper Tribunal (Immigration Asylum Chamber); and

12.4.4.9 Approving consent orders (including orders to quash and costs).

12.4.5 An Administrative Court Office lawyer may not make any orders in judicial review proceedings which relate to criminal causes or matters;

12.4.6 If a party is not content with an order of the ACO lawyer then CPR 54.1A(5) provides that the party may request that the order is reviewed by a High Court Judge. Such a review may take place on the papers or by way of an oral hearing in Court.[2] The choice of how the review takes place is the choice of the party requesting the review. The request for a review must be made by filing the request in writing (a letter or application notice may be used) within 7 days of the date on which the party was served with the ACO lawyer's order.[3] As long as the request is filed within 7 days (or such time as allowed by the order) there is no fee. If it is filed out of time then an application must be made to file the request out of time and it must be made on an application notice (N244 or PF244) with the relevant fee.

12.5 ROLE OF THE MASTER OF THE ADMINISTRATIVE COURT

1BA-76

12.5.1 The Master has the power to make any order allowed under the CPR unless the CPR expressly states that the Master may not make such an order. In judicial review proceedings this means that the Master generally deals with interim applications that do not come within the powers delegated to the ACO lawyers.[4] This includes, but is not limited to:[5]

12.5.1.1 Making interim orders relating to case management or interim remedies (including those claims for judicial review relating to criminal causes and applications to vary bail conditions, provided the prosecutor does not oppose the variation);

12.5.1.2 Determining liability for costs and making summary assessments of costs (see chapter 23. of this Guide for costs); and

12.5.1.3 Making orders relating to applications from vexatious litigants for permission to start or continue claims for judicial review (see paragraphs 4.10 and 4.11 of this Guide).

12.5.2 The Master may make orders with or without a hearing.[6]

12.5.3 The Master is under a duty to case manage the claim in accordance with the overriding objective. To this end the Master may request enquires are made of the parties by an ACO lawyer or ACO staff member or he/she may make case management orders (when applied for, when a case is referred to him/her by an ACO staff member or ACO lawyer, or of his/her own volition).

12.5.4 Any challenge to the terms of an order made by the Master without a hearing must be made by applying for reconsideration of the order at an oral hearing.[7] The application must be made on form N244 or PF244 and the relevant fee is payable. The hearing will be listed before a judge in Court. See paragraph 15.4 of this Guide for further details.

12.5.5 A challenge to an order made by the Master at an oral hearing must be made by appealing to a High Court judge (see paragraph 26.6 of this Guide on appeals).[8]

---

[1] CPR 54.1A(1)

[2] CPR 54.1A(5) & (6)

[3] CPR 54.1A(7)

[4] CPR 2.4(a) and CPR PD 2B paragraph 3.1(c)

[5] CPR PD 2B paragraph 3.1A

[6] CPR 23.8

[7] *R. (MD (Afghanistan) v Secretary of State for the Home Department* [2012] 1 W.L.R. 2422

[8] CPR PD 52A paragraph 4.3

12.6 ROLE OF THE JUDICIARY

12.6.1 Judges of the Administrative Court have all the powers of the High Court under **1BA-77**
statute, the CPR, and under the inherent jurisdiction of the Court.
12.6.2 In ensuring that the overriding objective is complied with, the Court must actively manage cases (see paragraph 12.1 of this Guide).
12.6.3 Any challenge to the terms of a case management order made without a hearing must
be made by applying for reconsideration at a hearing (see paragraph 15.5 of this Guide). Any challenge to an order made at an oral hearing must be appealed (see paragraph 26.6 of this Guide).

12.7 APPLICATIONS ONCE A CLAIM HAS COMMENCED

12.7.1 An application for directions or an interim order can be made at any time after com- **1BA-78**
mencement of the Claim.[1] For pre-commencement applications, see paragraph 16.4 of this Guide;
for applications for interim relief, chapter 15 of this Guide.
12.7.2 To make such an application:
12.7.2.1 The application must be filed with the ACO on an application notice (N244 or PF244
are the most commonly used).
12.7.2.2 The application must be accompanied by payment of the relevant fee.
12.7.2.3 The application must be accompanied by evidence stating why the direction or order
is required.
12.7.2.4 A draft order should be enclosed with the application.
12.7.3 Where possible, a copy of the application, evidence and accompanying draft order
should be sent to the proposed defendants and interested parties to give them notice that the application is being made. Where the application has been made without giving notice to the other
parties then the evidence supporting the application should explain why the application has been
made without giving notice.
12.7.4 In the application notice the applicant may request the application be considered at a
hearing or by a judge considering the papers. In either event, the ACO will send the papers to a
judge, master, or ACO lawyer to consider in the first instance. A judicial order may be made on the
papers alone if it is thought that a hearing would not be appropriate. Otherwise, a hearing may be
listed to hear the application. Such a hearing is usually listed at short notice (see paragraph 13.2.3
of this Guide).
12.7.5 It is the responsibility of each party to indicate the likely length of the hearing to
determine the application (if the application is determined at a hearing). The length of hearing
should include time for giving judgment.

12.8 APPLICATIONS FOR THE CLAIM TO BE STAYED

12.8.1 If either party wishes to stay a Claim, an application must be made to the Court for that **1BA-79**
to occur (see paragraph 12.7 of this Guide for the procedure for making applications). Save in
exceptional circumstances, an application for stay should be made on notice to the other parties,
and their agreement to it should be sought before the application is made.
12.8.2 The duration of the proposed stay must be made clear in the application notice. Usually, a stay is sought pending the outcome of a particular event (for example, the conclusion of a
related Tribunal appeal or a lead case in the Court of Appeal) or for a specific period of time (not
usually exceeding a few weeks or months).
12.8.3 A stay will not normally be permitted to enable the defendant to reconsider the decision
under challenge in the claim. Where the defendant agrees to reconsider, the judicial review should
generally be withdrawn. A fresh claim can then be brought if the claimant wishes to challenge the
reconsideration.[2] In any event, the Court's permission will be required to amend the claim form in
light of any subsequent decision (see paragraph 9.2 of this Guide).

12.9 RELIEF FROM SANCTIONS

12.9.1 Where a party has failed to comply with a provision under the CPR, Practice Direction **1BA-80**
or an order of the Court, which specifies a sanction for non-compliance, that party must apply for
relief from sanction.[3] If they do not then the Court may refuse to consider that party's case[4] and/or
make an adverse costs order against the party.[5]
12.9.2 An application for relief from sanction must be made in line with the interim applica-

---

[1] CPR 23
[2] See *R (Bhatti) v Bury Metropolitan Borough Council* [2013] EWHC 3093, and *R (Yousuf) v Secretary
of State for the Home Department* [2016] EWHC 663 (Admin)
[3] CPR 3.8(1)
[4] CPR 3.4(1)(c)
[5] CPR 44.2(4)(a), CPR 44.2(5)(c), and CPR 44.4(3)(a)(i)

tions procedure (see paragraph 12.7 of this Guide). The application for relief from sanction may be considered by an ACO lawyer, the Master, or a judge.

12.9.3   When considering whether to grant an application for relief from sanction, the ACO lawyer, the Master, or a judge, must consider the principles outlined in *Mitchell v News Group Newspapers Ltd* [2013] EWCA Civ 1537, *Denton v T.H. White Ltd* [2014] EWCA Civ 906,.[1] These cases should be considered if making such an application, but, in summary, the Court will consider the application in three stages:

12.9.3.1   Identify and assess the seriousness and significance of the failure to comply with any rule or Court order. If the breach is neither serious nor significant, the Court is likely to grant relief.

12.9.3.2   Consider why the default occurred. If there is a good reason for it, the Court will be likely to decide that relief should be granted, but merely overlooking the deadline is unlikely to constitute a good reason.

12.9.3.3   Evaluate all the circumstances of the case, so as to enable the Court to deal justly with the application including consideration of the first two factors. Particular weight is to be given to the need for litigation to be conducted efficiently and at proportionate cost and to enforce compliance with rules, practice directions and orders.

12.10   ABUSE OF THE COURT'S PROCESS

1BA-81   **12.10.1**   The Court has a duty to ensure that the Court's process is not abused. If a party, a legal representative, or any other person acts in a way thought to be inappropriate the Court may, in an appropriate case:

12.10.1.1   Strike out statements of case;[2]

12.10.1.2   Make an adverse costs order requiring the person to pay a party's costs (see paragraph 23.1 of this Guide);[3]

12.10.1.3   Make a wasted costs requiring a legal representative to pay a party's costs (see paragraph 23.12 of this Guide);[4]

12.10.1.4   Refer a legal representative to their regulatory body to consider further sanctions;[5]

12.10.1.5   Make a Civil Restraint Order (see chapter 4 of this Guide).[6]

12.10.2   Before making any of the above orders, the Court will usually give the relevant party, legal representative, or third party the opportunity to make representations on the appropriateness of such an order.

12.10.3   Scenarios which may be considered to be an abuse of process include, but are not limited to:[7]

12.10.3.1   Acting in bad faith or with an improper purpose.

12.10.3.2   Attempting to re-litigate a decided issue.

12.10.3.3   Raising in subsequent proceedings matters which could and should have been litigated in earlier proceedings.

12.10.3.4   Starting proceedings or applying for an order after improper delay.

12.10.3.5   Persistent failure to comply with rules or orders of the Court.

12.10.3.6   Knowingly starting proceedings in the Administrative Court which ought to be issued in another Court or Tribunal.

12.10.3.7   Proceedings which are frivolous, vexatious, harassing or manifestly groundless.

12.11   COMMUNICATIONS WHICH ARE ABUSIVE OR WITHOUT PROPER PURPOSE

1BA-82   **12.11.1**   The ACO is generally in a position to communicate with the parties in person at the public counter, by telephone, email, or post (see annex 1 for details) and will respond to communications if the communication so requires. The exception to this principle will apply if a person has been made subject to a notification of restricted communication.

12.11.2   Such a notification will be sent by the manager of the ACO if it is considered that the person has been communicating with the ACO in a manner which is:

12.11.2.1   Aggressive, intimidating, or harassing; or

12.11.2.2   Persistent, time consuming, and without proper purpose.

12.11.3   Such a notification will inform the persons that the form in which they may com-

---

[1] See *Hysaj v Secretary of state for the Home Department* [2014] EWCA Civ 1633 and *Altomart Ltd v Salford Estates (No.2) Ltd* [2014] EWCA Civ 1408 which suggest that relief from sanction may be appropriate even where no sanction is specified.

[2] CPR 3.4(1)(c)

[3] CPR 44.2(4)(a), CPR 44.2(5)(c), and CPR 44.4(3)(a)(i)

[4] Section 51(6) Senior Courts Act 1981 and CPR 46.8

[5] *R (Hamid) v SSHD* [2012] EWHC 3070 (Admin)

[6] CPR 3.11, CPR PD 3C, and CPR 23.12

[7] Examples taken from *Halsbury's Laws of England*, Vol.11 Civil Procedure (2015), Part 19, paragraph 1044, and from *R (Ashraf) v SSHD* [2013] EWHC 4028 (Admin)

municate with the ACO is restricted to the manner outlined in the notice, all other forms of communication will be ignored, and that a response to the permitted form of communication will only be made if the communication raises a new issue that requires the response of the ACO.

12.11.4 Notifications of restricted communication will be sent in writing to the last known address for the person subject to the notification.

12.11.5 The person subject to the notification may request in writing at any time that the ACO manager rescinds the notification at his/her discretion. Such a request should include reasons for the request and will be responded to in writing.

12.11.6 A notification of restricted communication is made by the manager of the ACO as an employee of HMCTS. Any complaint against such a notification must be made in accordance with the HMCTS complaints policy.

12.11.7 The Court, under its inherent jurisdiction to control its own proceedings, may also make, rescind, or vary a notification of restricted communication.

13. LISTING

13.1 LISTING POLICIES

13.1.1 The Administrative Court has a listing policy that will be followed by the ACO when it **1BA-83** lists any hearing. This policy can be found on the Administrative Court website: *www.gov.uk/courts-tribunals/administrative-court*.

13.1.2 The ACO in Cardiff has a supplementary listing policy that supplements the general listing policy. This policy can be made available on request from the ACO in Cardiff.

13.1.3 This section of the Guide will summarise the procedure in the policies, but the policies themselves should be referred to for full details.

13.1.4 The policies are intended to be applied flexibly. The ACO may, where it considers it appropriate to do so, list cases otherwise than in accordance with the policies.

13.1.5 A particular case may be listed in a particular way by reason of a judicial order.

13.2 LISTING PROCEDURE

13.2.1 For permission hearings, hearings will usually be fixed for a date without seeking the **1BA-84** views of representatives. Several weeks' notice of the hearing will normally be given.

13.2.2 For substantive hearings, the ACO will usually consult with counsel's clerks to attempt to agree a suitable date for the hearing. This will generally occur in one of two ways:

13.2.2.1 In the ACO in London, the ACO will telephone or email either counsel's clerks and/or solicitors to arrange an appointment to fix the hearing. Five working days' notice will be given of the appointment. At the appointment if parties are unable to agree a date that is also acceptable to the Court, the ACO will list the matter for first available date convenient to the Court. Failure to attend the appointment will mean the matter will be listed without consultation.

13.2.2.2 In the other ACOs, the ACO will either email or telephone counsel's clerks for all parties to request the dates of availability for counsel on the Court record (that is to say the Court has been informed counsel is/are acting). Unless availability is provided over the telephone at the time of the initial contact the clerk will be informed that they must provide availability within 48 hours otherwise the ACO will list the matter for first available date convenient to the Court. If parties are unable to agree a date that is also acceptable to the Court, the ACO will list the matter for first available date convenient to the Court.

13.2.3 Interim relief hearings are usually listed in the same way as renewal hearings, but where interim relief is required urgently the hearing may be listed at short notice with little or no consultation as to the availability of the parties. The application will usually be fixed on the basis that it will take no longer than 30 minutes to hear, unless a different time estimate is required by a judge, master, or ACO lawyer. If a party considers that the application will require a longer hearing, the suggested time estimate must be confirmed as soon as possible, in writing with reasons.

13.2.4 Due to limited judicial time the ACO is unable to routinely take into account the availability of litigants representing themselves (litigants in person) or instructing solicitors. However, if there are dates when a litigant in person is unable to attend and there are good reasons for not being able to attend then the litigant in person may inform the ACO in writing in advance and the ACO may be able to take this into account when listing.

13.2.5 A substantive hearing will be allocated a hearing time estimate by either the judge granting permission or the ACO. If a party considers that the application will require a longer hearing, the suggested time estimate must be confirmed as soon as possible, in writing with reasons.

13.2.6 Once the hearing has been listed, all parties will be sent a listing notice by the ACO which confirms the date, location, and time estimate for the hearing. The start time of the hearing will not be in the listing notice. Generally, Administrative Court hearings start at 10.30am, but this may be changed up until 2.00pm the day before the hearing. The parties should check the hearing time on the day before the hearing by telephoning the ACO or checking the hearing time online at *www.gov.uk/courts-tribunals/administrative-court.*.

13.3 DIVISIONAL COURTS

1BA-85   **13.3.1** Divisional Courts may be convened for any case in the High Court.[1] A Divisional Court means that two or more judges sit together.

13.3.2 If a judicial review is allocated to the Divisional Court, the listing arrangements will be different, particularly if the case is considered to be urgent. The ACO will not be able to offer as many suitable available dates for a hearing and will not generally take account of the availability of each party's counsel when listing the hearing.

13.4 APPLYING TO ADJOURN A LISTED HEARING

1BA-86   **13.4.1** If a party wishes to apply to adjourn a listed hearing then the application must be made in one of the following ways:

13.4.1.1 By agreeing with all other parties that the hearing should be adjourned and filing a draft consent order for the approval of the Court,[2] one of terms of which is that the hearing is adjourned. Such an order must be signed by all parties and must be accompanied by the relevant fee (although see paragraph 13.4.1.2 below). The parties may also include further directions sought in such a draft order. The parties should not assume that a hearing has been adjourned unless they have been informed by the ACO that the consent order has been approved. A consent order should also include reasons for the hearing being adjourned, which should be included in an accompanying application notice (form N244 or PF244).

13.4.1.2 If the parties agree a consent order to adjourn the hearing, which does not seek other directions, and they file the draft consent order with the ACO more than 14 days before the hearing, then no fee is payable. The other provisions noted at paragraphs 13.4.1.1 and 22.4 of this Guide will still apply.

13.4.1.3 If the parties cannot agree a consent order, then a party may make an application to adjourn the hearing in line with the interim applications procedure (see paragraph 12.7 of this Guide). Such an application must be made on form N244 or PF244 and be accompanied by the relevant fee. The application notice should include the reasons for the request, any attempts made to agree the request with the other parties, and any responses from the other parties to that request. A draft of the order sought should also be attached to the application.

13.4.2 The decision to adjourn a listed hearing is a judicial decision and cannot be taken by the ACO. The hearing will generally not be adjourned unless there are good reasons to do so, even where all parties agree that the hearing should be adjourned. Where the sole reason for seeking the adjournment is that counsel is/are not available for the hearing the application to adjourn will rarely be granted. Where the matter has been listed to be heard by a Divisional Court the Court will be very reluctant to grant an adjournment.

PART C:—SPECIFIC PRACTICE POINTS

14. Duty of Candour

1BA-87   **14.1.1** There is a special duty which applies to parties to judicial review known as the 'duty of candour' which requires the parties to ensure that all relevant information and facts are put before the Court.[3] This means that parties must disclose any information or material facts which either support or undermine their case.

14.1.2 This rule is needed in judicial review claims, where the Court's role is to review the lawfulness of decisions made by public bodies, often on an urgent request being made, where the ordinary rules of disclosure of documents do not apply (see paragraph 6.5 and chapter 20 of this Guide on evidence) and where the witness statements are usually read (rather than being subject to cross examination by witnesses who are called to give their evidence orally).

14.1.3 The rule is particularly important where the other party has not had the opportunity to submit its own evidence or make representations (usually an urgent application – see chapter 16 of this Guide).

14.1.4 The Court will take seriously any failure or suspected failure to comply with the duty of

---

[1] s. 66 of the Senior Courts Act 1981

[2] See paragraph 22.4 of this Guide for the procedure for filing a consent order in the context of ending a claim – the procedure is identical.

[3] See the discussion of this principle in *R. (Al-Sweady) v Secretary of State for Defence* [2010] H.R.L.R. 2 at 18; see also *R (Bancoult (No 2)) v Secretary of State for Foreign and Commonwealth Affairs* [2016] UKSC 35

candour. The parties or their representatives may be required to explain why information or evidence was not disclosed to the Court, and any failure may result in sanctions.

14.1.5 Specifically, claimants in judicial review proceedings must ensure that the Court has the full picture. In some circumstances, to ensure this, it is not sufficient simply to provide the relevant documents. Instead, a specific explanation of a document or an inconsistency must be given, usually by witness statement attested by the claimant.[1]

14.1.6 The duty of candour is a continuing duty. The claimant must reassess the viability and propriety of a challenge in light of the defendant's Acknowledgement of Service and Summary Grounds.[2]

15. INTERIM RELIEF

15.1 WHEN IS INTERIM RELIEF APPROPRIATE?

15.1.1 A party (usually the Claimant) may request an interim remedy whilst the case is pending. **1BA-88** Common examples are:

15.1.1.1 An interim order stopping the action the defendant plans to take (e.g – to prevent removal from the UK, assuming that UTIAC has no jurisdiction in the matter, see paragraph 5.5 of this Guide);

15.1.1.2 An interim order requiring the defendant to act in a certain way (e.g – to provide the claimant with accommodation).

15.1.2 Interim relief is usually requested in the claim form. But it can be applied for at any stage of proceedings and in exceptional cases can be applied for before proceedings are commenced. The procedure is outlined in CPR Part 23, supplemented in places by CPR Part 25 and CPR Part 54.

15.1.3 The Court may require the claimant to give undertakings as a condition of any interim relief:

15.1.3.1 The claimant may be required to give an undertaking in damages, so that if the defendant succeeds at the end of the day, and has suffered financial loss as a result of the relief ordered in the claimant's favour in the meanwhile, the claimant will have to compensate that loss; and

15.1.3.2 An undertaking operates as if it was a Court order, and breach of an undertaking is equivalent to breaching a Court order, which the Court can sanction by imposing an adverse costs order on the party in default, refusing to hear the application, striking out the claim and proceeding to consider committal for contempt of Court.

15.2 INTERIM RELIEF WHEN LODGING THE CLAIM

15.2.1 Interim relief is usually applied for at the same time as lodging the claim papers (see **1BA-89** chapter 6 of this Guide on starting proceedings).

15.2.2 Such an application can be made by making the application in section 8 of the claim form (form N461). As with the statement of facts and grounds, the substance of the application can be contained in a separate document to which section 8 of the claim form refers.

15.2.3 The application for interim relief will be considered by the judge on the papers, usually at the same time as the application for permission to apply for judicial review. The advantage for all parties is that this process reduces paperwork, reduces Court time, and does not require an additional fee.

15.2.4 The judge considering the application for interim relief alongside permission may either make an order based on the papers alone or order that the application for interim relief be dealt with at a hearing in Court (see paragraph 13.2.3 of this Guide for listing of such hearings).

15.2.5 Where the circumstances of the case require urgent consideration of the application for permission to apply for judicial review and/or any interim relief, a different procedure applies. This is dealt with separately in this Guide (see chapter 16).

15.3 INTERIM RELIEF BEFORE COMMENCEMENT OF PROCEEDINGS

15.3.1 In exceptionally urgent circumstances a person may apply for interim relief before **1BA-90** starting proceedings. See paragraph 16.4 of this Guide for the procedure where an urgent application is made before proceedings have been commenced.

---

[1] *R (Mohammed Shahzad Khan) v Secretary of State for the Home Department* [2016] EWCA Div 416 at 45

[2] Ibid, 48

15.4 INTERIM RELIEF IN ONGOING PROCEEDINGS

1BA-91   **15.4.1** Where a claim has already been lodged but it subsequently becomes clear that an interim order is required, the party seeking interim relief should issue an application on form N244 or PF244. If the application is urgent, the party should make that clear in the application form, and indicate the timescale within which the judge is requested to consider the application in that application and, preferably, in a covering letter as well. Such an application, whether it is made urgently or not, should always, unless it is impracticable, be served on all the other parties. The Court is unlikely to consider the application unless the opposing party has been given an opportunity to respond to the application in writing.

15.5 RECONSIDERATION IF INTERIM RELIEF IS REFUSED

1BA-92   **15.5.1** Where an application for an interim order has been refused without a hearing (that is to say that the judge made the order considering the papers alone), a party may request the decision be reconsidered.[1]

15.5.2 Reconsideration is requested by lodging an application notice (N244 or PF244) with the relevant fee. The application must be served on all other parties.

15.5.3 If an application is made for reconsideration after refusal on the papers then reconsideration must take place at an oral hearing in Court (see paragraph 13.2.3 of this Guide on listing).

15.5.4 If reconsideration is required within a set time frame the application must make the relevant timescale clear in the application and, preferably, in a covering letter as well.

15.5.5 Where reconsideration of an order made on the papers is extremely urgent and cannot wait until the Court's sitting hours, then the application for reconsideration can be made to out of hours judge in accordance with paragraph 16.3 of this Guide. In such circumstances the practitioner will be asked to undertake to pay the relevant fee on the next working day.

15.5.6 A party who wishes to challenge a decision made on the papers must apply for reconsideration in the Administrative Court before they can appeal (see chapter 26 of this Guide for appeals).[2]

15.6 CRITERIA FOR THE GRANT OF INTERIM RELIEF

1BA-93   **15.6.1** When considering whether to grant interim relief while a judicial review claim is pending, the judge will consider:[3]

15.6.1.1 Whether there is a real issue to be tried. In practice, in judicial review claims, that involves considering whether there is a real prospect of succeeding at the substantive hearing, that is to say a more than fanciful prospect of success;

15.6.1.2 Whether the balance of convenience lies in granting the interim order;

15.6.1.3 Any other factors the Court considers to be relevant.

15.6.2 Generally, there is a strong public interest in permitting a public authority's decision to continue, so the applicant for interim relief must make out a strong case for relief in advance of the substantive hearing.

15.6.3 The Court will be reluctant to grant any form of interim relief without establishing the defendant's response to the application. The Court is likely, if time permits, to permit the defendant an opportunity to respond to the application. In an urgent case, this may be by abridging time for service of the Acknowledgement of Service or calling the matter in for a hearing on short notice.

15.6.4 If time does not permit the defendant to be heard, then the Court will consider granting relief for a very short period until the defendant has been able to make its submissions (in writing or at a hearing).

15.6.5 Sometimes, if the merits of the underlying claim are unclear and there is no particular urgency in granting relief, the Court will give directions for an 'expedited' (speedy) determination of permission, or trial of the claim (possibly on the basis that permission should be 'rolled up' with the substantive hearing – see paragraph 8.2.6 of this Guide). In this way, the Court can be sure that both parties have had a chance to put their arguments before the Court before any form of order granting (or refusing) relief is made.

---

[1] *R. (MD (Afghanistan) v Secretary of State for the Home Department* [2012] 1 W.L.R. 2422

[2] *R. (MD (Afghanistan)) v Secretary of State for the Home Department* [2012] 1 W.L.R. 2422 at paragraph 21

[3] *R. (Medical Justice) v Secretary of State for the Home Department* [2010] A.C.D. 70 and *American Cyanamid Company v Ethicon Limited* [1975] AC 396

15.7 REMOVALS CASES

15.7.1 There are particular rules relating to cases where a claimant challenges a decision to **1BA-94** remove him or her from the jurisdiction, see CPR PD 54A, paragraph 18. Such challenges would now generally fall within the jurisdiction of UTIAC. A person who makes an application for permission to apply for judicial review of a removal decision must file a claim form which must:

15.7.1.1 Indicate on the face of the claim form that the practice direction applies;

15.7.1.2 Attach to the claim form a copy of the removal directions and the decision to which the application relates;

15.7.1.3 Attach any document served with the removal directions including any document which contains the UK Border Agency's factual summary of the case; and

15.7.1.4 Contain or be accompanied by the detailed statement of the claimant's grounds for bringing the judicial review (or give the reasons why compliance with the last two conditions is not possible)

15.7.2 That person must send copies of the claim form to the UK Border Agency.

15.7.3 The Court has set out certain principles to be applied when such applications are made in *R (Madan) v Secretary of State for the Home Department* [2007] EWCA Civ 770:

15.7.3.1 Such applications must be made promptly on the intimation of a deportation decision and not await the actual fixing of removal arrangements;

15.7.3.2 The detailed statement of grounds must include a statement of all previous applications made in respect of that applicant's immigration status and indicate how the present state of the case differs from previous applications;

15.7.4 Counsel and solicitors appearing on the application, in the absence of the defendant, are under professional obligations to draw the judge's attention to any matter adverse to their client's case, including in particular any previous adverse decisions, and to take a full note of the judge's judgment or reasons, which should then be submitted to the judge for approval.

16. URGENT CASES

16.1 GENERAL

16.1.1 The Administrative Court often deals with urgent cases. This is a very important part of **1BA-95** the Court's work, and the availability of the Court to deal with urgent cases is in the public interest. However, the Court's experience in recent years is that some litigants and practitioners are misusing, and even abusing, the procedures for seeking urgent adjudication. The consequence of this is or may be that those claimants with genuinely urgent cases have had to wait longer than they needed to, because wholly unmeritorious and/or non-urgent cases are ahead of them in the queue.

16.1.2 All litigants and their advisers are reminded of the rules relating to urgent applications which are summarised below. In particular,

16.1.2.1 It is very important that litigants and their advisors state clearly on the Court forms what are the reasons for urgency (see paragraph 16.2 below).

16.1.2.2 It is very important that litigants and their advisors comply with their duty of candour which requires them to disclose all relevant material to the Court (see paragraph 14.1 of this Guide)

16.1.3 The CPR, Practice Directions and other obligations owed to the Court must be complied with. If they are not complied with, the party in default is likely to be made subject to an adverse costs order (for example, being made to pay some or all of the other party's legal costs, or being unable to recover their own legal costs, even if successful), and risks having their claim dismissed for non-compliance. Professional representatives may face applications for wasted costs, or be referred to their Regulator for consideration of disciplinary action, for failure to comply with their professional obligations.

16.1.4 Professional representatives are reminded of the following passage from *R (Hamid) v Secretary of State for the Home Department* [2012] EWHC 3070 (Admin):

> "[7]   ... If any firm fails to provide the information required on the form and in particular explain the reasons for urgency, the time at which the need for immediate consideration was first appreciated, and the efforts made to notify the defendant, the Court will require the attendance in open court of the solicitor from the firm who was responsible, together with his senior partner. It will list not only the name of the case but the firm concerned. ..."

16.2 URGENT CONSIDERATION – FORM N463

16.2.1 Where the circumstances of the case require urgent consideration of the application for **1BA-96** permission to apply for judicial review and/or any interim relief (which is not so urgent that it has been sought pre-action, but still sufficiently urgent that the Court is being asked to deal with it within a shortened timeframe), the Claimant may apply for urgent consideration at the same time as issuing the claim form.[1] These situations will generally be those where some irreversible action will take place if the Court does not act to prevent it, or where an expedited judicial review is required.

16.2.2   The claimant must complete form N463, providing the following information (which is required to be inserted in the relevant boxes on that form):

16.2.2.1   The circumstances giving rise to the urgency. If the form is filed only shortly before the end of the working day, an explanation should also be provided as to why the application was not made earlier in the day;

16.2.2.2   The timescale sought for the consideration of the application;

16.2.2.3   The date by which any substantive hearing should take place;

16.2.2.4   Efforts taken to put the defendant on notice of the application for urgent consideration;

16.2.2.5   The grounds on which any interim order is sought.

16.2.3   A draft of the order sought should be attached which sets out the relief sought and any directions for an expedited hearing.

16.2.4   The full claim papers (see chapter 6 of this Guide on starting proceedings, ie claim form and required supporting documents) must be filed alongside the urgent application. Where the application for urgent consideration is filed at the same time as the claim papers there is no additional fee for the urgent application, it is covered by the fee to start proceedings.

16.2.5   The claimant should serve the claim papers and the Form N463 with supporting documentation on the defendant and interested parties, advising them of the application and that they may make representations.

16.2.6   The Administrative Court Office will have a judge available to consider any urgent application received between 10am and 4pm (4.30pm in London), Monday to Friday, excluding public holidays (See CPR PD 2A, paragraph 2.1). The judge may either make an order based on the papers alone or order that the application (or part of it) be dealt with at a hearing in Court (see paragraph 13.2.3 for listing of such hearings). In appropriate situations the Master or an ACO lawyer may consider the application and request further information or make an order.

16.2.7   It is not appropriate for any urgent application arising in relation to a judicial review to be put before the judge in charge of the interim applications Court ('Court 37'). The Administrative Court has a judge available to deal with immediate applications in the context of a judicial review: see paragraph 16.2.6 above. Court 37 deals with other Queen's Bench Division matters.

16.2.8   Wherever possible the Court will want representations from the defendant before determining the application. In cases where interim relief is sought, the Court will generally make an order allowing the defendant a short time to file written submissions before deciding the application, unless irreversible prejudice would be caused to the claimant in the meanwhile; alternatively, the judge may list the matter for a hearing on notice to the defendant (see paragraph 13.2.3 of this Guide for listing). In cases where an expedited substantive hearing is sought, the Court may abridge time for service of the defendant's acknowledgement of service and request the defendant's views on the order sought, to enable the Court to take an early view on permission and any consequential case management directions.

16.2.9   If the matter is put before a judge who concludes that the application was not urgent, and is suitable for disposal according to the ordinary procedures of the Court, he or she may refuse to deal with the matter on an urgent basis, and may make an adverse costs order against the applicant or his legal representatives (see paragraph 23.1 of this Guide on costs).

16.3   OUT OF HOURS APPLICATIONS

1BA-97

16.3.1   In the event that an urgent application needs to be made outside the sitting hours of the Administrative Court (see paragraph 16.2.6 of this Guide) and the application cannot wait until the sitting hours recommence, then the claimant may make the application to the out of hours High Court Judge. A High Court Judge is on call at all times to deal with very urgent applications which cannot wait until the next working day.

16.3.2   If a party needs to make an out of hours application to the Court, the acting barrister or solicitors should telephone 020 7947 6000[2] and speak to security who will take certain details for forwarding onto the Queen's Bench Division out of hours duty clerk.

16.3.3   The out of hours duty clerk will require the practitioner to complete the out of hours form, which can be downloaded from the Government website (*http://hmctsformfinder.justice.gov.uk/HMCTS/GetForm.do?court_forms_id=3007*) and emailed to QBDutyClerk@hmcts.gsi.gov.uk. (Emails must not be sent to this address unless the out of hours duty clerk has invited you to do so.)

16.3.4   The out of hours judge may deal with the application on paper. Alternatively, the out of hours judge may telephone the representatives acting for the claimant to enable them to make their submissions orally before deciding the application. The representatives will be required to

---

[1] *Practice Statement (Administrative Court: Listing and Urgent Cases)* [2002] 1 W.L.R. 810
[2] As required by CPR PD 54D paragraph 4.2 and CPR PD 25A paragraph 4.5

provide a telephone number on which they can be reached. The out of hours judge may also telephone any other party to the application if he or she considers that to be appropriate (this is often done in immigration cases where the application seeks a stay on removal).

16.3.5 The fact that a judge is being asked to make an order out of hours, usually without a hearing, and often without any representations from the defendant's representatives and in a short time frame, means that the duty of candour (to disclose all material facts to the judge, even if they are not of assistance to the claimant's case) is particularly important, see paragraph 14.1 of this Guide.

16.3.6 Legal representatives must consider very carefully whether an out of hours application really is required and should only make such an application if the matter really cannot wait until the next working day.

16.3.7 **The out of hours service is not available to litigants in person.**

16.4 PRE-ACTION APPLICATIONS

16.4.1 In exceptionally urgent circumstances, a person may apply, typically for interim relief, **1BA-98** before starting judicial review proceedings. The Court may only grant a pre-action order where:

16.4.1.1 The matter is urgent; or

16.4.1.2 It is otherwise necessary to do so in the interests of justice.[1]

16.4.2 The claimant should carefully consider whether the matter is really so urgent that an application should be made before the claim is started. It is much better to apply at the same time as lodging the claim papers if that is possible: this will make it easier for the Court to understand the issues and is likely to conserve legal costs.

16.4.3 The claimant should always try to reach an agreement with the public authority, even for a short period, before applying for pre-action interim relief. The Court will expect to be told about such efforts and why they have not succeeded, if the matter is brought before the Court instead.

16.4.4 If the matter really is urgent and no short-term compromise can be reached, then the claimant can make an application for a pre-action relief by filing an application notice (N244 or PF244) with the ACO[2]. The application must be accompanied by the relevant fee, must be supported by evidence establishing why the order is required[3], and should enclose a copy of the draft order. Where possible a copy of the application, evidence, and draft order should be sent to the proposed defendants and interested parties to give them notice that the application is being made.[4] Where the application has been made without giving notice to the other parties then the evidence supporting the application should explain why the application has been made without giving notice.[5]

16.4.5 In the application notice the applicant may request the application be considered at a hearing or by a judge considering the papers. In either event, the ACO will send the papers to a judge, master, or ACO lawyer to consider in the first instance. A judicial order may be made on the papers alone if it is thought that a hearing would not be appropriate.[6] Otherwise, a hearing will be listed to consider the application. Such a hearing is usually listed at short notice.

16.4.6 Wherever possible the Court will want representations from the defendant before determining any application made in advance of issuing the claim form. Unless, by not granting that order, irreversible prejudice would be caused to the claimant, the Court will generally make an order allowing the defendant a short time period to file written representations or the Court will direct that the application should be dealt with at a hearing listed with notice being provided to the defendant.

16.4.7 The claimant will usually be required to undertake to file a claim form and grounds of claim, usually within a short period, or, if no satisfactory undertaking is offered, will be directed by the Court to do so.[7]

16.5 ABUSE OF THE PROCEDURES FOR URGENT CONSIDERATION

16.5.1 Where an application for urgent consideration or an out of hours application is made **1BA-99** which does not comply with this Guide and/or it is manifestly inappropriate, the Court may make a wasted costs order or some other adverse costs order (see paragraphs 23.1 and 23.12 of this Guide respectively).[8]

16.5.2 In *R. (Hamid) v Secretary of State for the Home Department* [2012] EWHC 3070 (Admin)

---

[1] CPR 25.2(2)(b).
[2] CPR 23.3(1)
[3] CPR 25.3(2)
[4] CPR 23.4(1)
[5] CPR 25.3(3)
[6] CPR 23.8(c)
[7] CPR 25.2(3)
[8] *Practice Statement (Administrative Court: Listing and Urgent Cases)* [2002] 1 W.L.R. 810 at 811

(see paragraph 16.1.4 above) the Court held that where urgent applications are made improperly the Court may summon the legal representative to Court to explain his or her actions and would consider referring that person, or their supervising partner (if different) to the relevant regulator. Examples (but not an exhaustive list) of applications which have been held to be inappropriate under the Hamid rule are:

16.5.2.1   The claimant's solicitor had delayed making the urgent application until the last minute and had not disclosed the full facts of the case in an attempt to use the urgent process to prevent his client's removal from the UK.[1]

16.5.2.2   The claimant's solicitor requested urgent interim relief against a decision that had been made three years earlier.[2]

16.5.2.3   A practitioner advanced arguments that his client was suicidal and psychotic when they knew or ought to have known were false and/or inconsistent with their own medical evidence.[3]

16.5.2.4   A practitioner lodged an application with grounds that were opaque and brief and failed to set out any of the claimant's history of criminality.[4]

16.5.3   Practitioners should be aware that the Court can identify those who are responsible for abusing the Court's processes by making adverse costs orders (see paragraph 23.1 of this Guide) or by activating the Hamid procedure outlined above which may lead to those practitioners being disciplined by their Regulator. Also see paragraph 12.10 of this Guide on abuse of the Court's process.

17.   Skeleton Arguments

17.1   GENERAL

1BA-100   **17.1.1**   A skeleton argument is a written document setting out a summary of the party's arguments in the case.

17.1.2   The rules require each party to prepare a skeleton argument before any substantive hearing.

17.1.3   Parties should also prepare skeleton arguments before any interim hearing in the course of a judicial review (including any hearing for interim relief or directions), even where the issue is straightforward.

17.2   CONTENT OF SKELETON ARGUMENT

1BA-101   **17.2.1**   The skeleton argument must include the following:[5]

17.2.1.1   A time estimate for the complete hearing, including delivery of judgment.

17.2.1.2   A list of issues.

17.2.1.3   A list of the legal points to be taken (together with any relevant authorities with page references to the passages relied on)

17.2.1.4   A chronology of events with page references to the bundle of documents.

17.2.1.5   A list of essential documents for the advance reading of the Court (with page references to the passages relied on);

17.2.1.6   A time estimate for the advance reading suggested; and

17.2.1.7   A list of persons referred to in the claim.

17.2.2   It is helpful if the skeleton argument sets out the points to be made as clearly and as concisely as possible. Ideally, the skeleton argument should be in the following form:

17.2.2.1   The decision under challenge should be clearly identified, or the relevant failure to make a decision if that is what is under challenge.

17.2.2.2   The relevant facts should be summarised including any relevant change of facts or circumstances since the claim form and supporting documentation were lodged.

17.2.2.3   The grounds for seeking judicial review (or interim relief, or any other order) should be set out under numbered headings.

17.2.2.4   Relevant legal principles should be set out. Lengthy extracts from EU Directives, international Conventions, statutes, case law and other sources should be avoided if possible. It is much more helpful to the Court if the skeleton states the proposition of law which the party contends for, and then refers to the source of or authority for that proposition, with short extracts quoted if that is appropriate. It is not usually necessary or helpful to cite more than one case in support of each proposition of law.

---

[1] *R. (Hamid) v Secretary of State for the Home Department* [2012] EWHC 3070 (Admin)

[2] *R. (Butt) v Secretary of State for the Home Department* [2014] EWHC 264 (Admin)

[3] *R (Okondu) v Secretary of State for the Home Department (wasted costs; SRA referrals; Hamid) IJR* [2014] UKUT 377 (IAC)

[4] *R (Okondu) v Secretary of State for the Home Department (wasted costs; SRA referrals; Hamid) IJR* [2014] UKUT 377 (IAC)

[5] CPR PD 54A paragraph 15.3

17.2.2.5 The remedy sought should be identified.

17.2.2.6 Any urgency, other matter relevant to the timing of the case, and any other relevant point, such as alternative remedy, should be identified.

17.3 FORMAT OF SKELETON ARGUMENT

17.3.1 A skeleton argument should be clearly typed and properly spaced. A font style of not less than 11-point should be used, and lines should be reasonably spaced (1.5 or double spacing is ideal). **1BA-102**

17.3.2 Paragraphs should be numbered sequentially.

17.3.3 Pages should be numbered. It is rarely necessary for skeleton arguments to be any longer than 20 pages in length.

17.4 METHOD OF SERVICE

17.4.1 Skeleton arguments may be lodged with the Court by email on the relevant email address set out in annex 1 so long as they do not exceed the maximum which the appropriate court office has indicated it can accept by email (see paragraph 6.7 of this Guide).[1] Otherwise, they should be lodged at the Court in hard copy. However, service by email is encouraged, wherever possible, and is likely to be of greatest assistance to the Court. **1BA-103**

17.4.2 Skeleton arguments should always be served on the other party or parties to the case, whether or not that party is in a position to provide a skeleton by way of exchange.

17.5 TIMING OF SERVICE OF SKELETON ARGUMENTS

17.5.1 Skeleton arguments must be served in good time before any hearing. **1BA-104**

17.5.2 That means that the skeleton argument must be served on or before the date set by the Court, if directions are in place. The standard direction usually ordered by the Court for substantive hearings is that the claimant's skeleton argument is to be filed with the Court and served on the other parties not less than 21 days before the date of the hearing of the claim, and the defendant's skeleton argument is to be filed with the Court and served on the other parties not less than 14 days before the hearing date. (But see paragraph 9.1.4 of this Guide for computation of time for service of skeleton arguments.)

17.5.3 These standard directions may be varied by the Court, in which case the parties must comply with those specific directions.

17.5.4 For all other hearings where there are no standard directions (for example, hearings for renewal of permission), and in the absence of specific directions, skeleton arguments should be served **at least 2 working days** before the hearing is listed. If there is or may be a problem with compliance with that deadline, the ACO should be alerted as soon as possible.

17.5.5 **Failure to lodge a skeleton argument in good time before the hearing may result in the Court having insufficient time to read the skeleton before the hearing which may lead to the hearing being adjourned and/or a costs sanction being imposed on the party in default.**

17.6 SANCTION FOR NON-COMPLIANCE

17.6.1 If the skeleton argument does not comply with this guidance, or is served late, the Court may refuse to permit the party in default to rely on the skeleton; alternatively, the Court make an adverse costs order against the party in default (see paragraph 23.1 of this Guide on costs). **1BA-105**

18. DOCUMENTS

18.1 BUNDLES FOR SUBSTANTIVE HEARINGS

18.1.1 The rules require the claimant to file a bundle of documents at the same time as the claimant files his or her skeleton argument for the substantive hearing.[2] The bundle of documents should contain all relevant documents, including any documents required to be included by the defendant and any other party who is to make representations at the hearing. **1BA-106**

18.1.2 The Court expects, therefore, to have a joint bundle of documents for the judicial review which includes all the documents to which any party present at the hearing will refer. The Court does not expect to have documents handed up to it during the course of the hearing, save in exceptional circumstances (and always subject to the Court's permission to adduce documents or evidence in that way).

---

[1] CPR PD5B, paragraph 2.2(b)
[2] 54APD.16

18.2 OTHER HEARINGS

1BA-107   **18.2.1**   In some instances, there will be no directions about the production of bundles (for example, where an urgent application is made by one party), but that party should still make sure that all relevant documents are before the Court. Any bundle containing documents which are to be put before the Court should be served on the Court and the other party or parties in good time before the hearing.

18.2.2   Good time means at least three clear days before most ordinary hearings.

18.2.3   If the matter is urgent, the bundle should be served on the Court and the other party or parties no later than 1pm on the day before the hearing.

18.3 FORMAT OF COURT BUNDLES

1BA-108   **18.3.1**   Any collection of documents to go before the Court is a 'bundle'. Bundles should ideally be secured in files which are sufficiently large to accommodate the documents contained in them. The pages should be numbered sequentially and indexed.

18.3.2   The bundle spines should be clearly marked with the reference number of the case and name of the parties.

18.3.3   Photocopying should be 2-sided in portrait format (not landscape).

18.3.4   Photocopies must be legible.

18.3.5   Documents should be presented in chronological order.

18.3.6   In cases where the documents are extensive (as a guideline, more than 500 pages), the parties should endeavour to agree a 'core bundle' of key documents. In those cases, consideration should be given to including only the important and relevant parts of a long document in the Court bundle and not copying the whole of that document.

18.3.7   The judge may refuse to read a bundle which does not comply with these requirements, or direct that a revised bundle is submitted which does comply, in which event the judge may disallow the costs of preparing the bundle or make a different adverse costs order.

18.4 TIMING OF LODGING OF TRIAL BUNDLES

1BA-109   **18.4.1**   Trial bundles must be lodged in good time before any hearing.

18.4.2   That means that the trial bundle must be lodged on or before the date set by the Court if directions are in place. The direction usually ordered by the Court for substantive hearings is that the trial bundle must be filed and served not less than 4 weeks before the date of the hearing.

18.4.3   For substantive hearings, where there are no direction, trial bundles must be lodged when the claimant is due to lodge a skeleton argument (see paragraph 9.1.4.5 of this Guide for more detail) For all other hearings, or where there are no specific directions in place, any documents must be filed at Court as soon as possible and in good time before the hearing.

18.4.4   Any unavoidable submission of late bundles should clearly state the date of the hearing on the bundles. The bundles should be accompanied by a letter to the ACO setting out the reasons for late submission. Failure to make it clear that the bundles relate to an imminent hearing may result in the bundles not being placed before the judge in advance of the hearing.

18.5 SANCTION FOR NON-COMPLIANCE

1BA-110   **18.5.1**   If the trial bundle or bundle of documents does not comply with this guidance, or is served late, the Court may refuse to allow the party in default to rely on the bundle of documents; alternatively, it may make an adverse costs order against the party in default (see paragraph 23.1 of this Guide on costs).

19.   AUTHORITIES

19.1 GENERAL

1BA-111   **19.1.1**   Parties are encouraged to limit the number of authorities (ie cases) cited, to those which are really necessary for the fair disposal of the claim, and which establish the particular principle of law contended for. In most cases, it is unnecessary to adduce more than 10 authorities, and some cases will require fewer, if any, authorities.

19.1.2   Where extensive authorities are cited, it is preferable to agree a core bundle of authorities, itself not exceeding 10 authorities.

19.2 FORMAT OF AUTHORITIES BUNDLES

1BA-112   **19.2.1**   Bundles of authorities should be paginated or tabbed, and indexed.

19.2.2   Photocopying should be 2-sided in portrait format (not landscape).

19.2.3   Copies should be legible.

19.2.4 Authorities which have been reported should be produced in their reported form. Transcripts are only acceptable where the case has not been reported.

19.3 AGREEMENT OF CONTENTS, AND SERVICE OF AUTHORITIES BUNDLES

19.3.1 A party should always notify the other party or parties of any authorities on which he or she intends to rely at the hearing, in good time before the hearing, and ensure that copies of those authorities are available for that party at the hearing. **1BA-113**

19.3.2 The Court will usually give directions for a joint bundle of authorities to be filed in advance of any substantive hearing. But if there are no such directions in place, the parties are required to work together to arrive at a joint list of authorities, and to ensure that a bundle of those authorities is filed at Court in good time before any hearing. If agreement cannot be reached, separate bundles will have to be filed by each party in which event there should be no duplication in the two sets of bundles.

19.3.3 All authorities on which the parties intend to rely at the substantive hearing should be included in the bundles of authorities, even if those authorities were filed at Court with the Claim Form, Acknowledgement of Service or Detailed Grounds. The Court will not necessarily have the permission or earlier bundles available at the substantive hearing.

19.4 SANCTION FOR NON-COMPLIANCE

19.4.1 If the bundle of authorities does not comply with this guidance, or is served late, the Court may refuse to allow the party in default to rely on those authorities, may require the bundle to be adjusted to meet the Court's requirements, and/or may make an adverse costs order against the party in default (see paragraph 23.1 of this Guide on costs). **1BA-114**

20. EVIDENCE

20.1 WITNESS EVIDENCE

20.1.1 Witness statements must comply with Court rules[1]. Specifically, they must **1BA-115**
20.1.1.1 Be in the witness' own words;
20.1.1.2 State that person's full name and address;
20.1.1.3 State which of the statements in it are made from the witness' own knowledge, and which are matters of information or belief (also stating what is the source of matters of information or belief);
20.1.1.4 Be produced on A4 paper, and legible, with numbered pages and paragraphs.

20.1.2 Witness statements must include a statement of truth in the following terms: "*I believe that the facts stated in this witness statement are true*". The witness must not sign that statement of truth unless he or she holds an honest belief in the truth of the statements made in the witness statement.

20.1.3 Proceedings for contempt of Court may be brought against a person if he or she makes or causes to be made a false statement in a document verified by a statement of truth, without an honest belief in its truth.[2]

20.1.4 In judicial review proceedings, it is rare for a witness to be called to give oral evidence: see paragraph 10.2 of this Guide.

20.2 EXPERT EVIDENCE

20.2.1 Sometimes a party will wish to rely on expert evidence to advance its case although this is unusual in judicial review. **1BA-116**

20.2.2 Expert evidence must be restricted to that which is reasonably required to resolve the proceedings.[3]

20.2.3 Experts owe an overriding duty to the Court. It is the duty of an expert to help the Court on matters which are within their expertise. That duty overrides any obligation owed to the person from whom the expert received instructions or by whom the expert was paid.[4]

---

[1] CPR PD32.17-25
[2] CPR 32.14
[3] CPR 35.1
[4] CPR 35.3

21. SANCTIONS

21.1 OVERVIEW

1BA-117   **21.1.1**   The Court has at its disposal various means to enforce compliance with the CPR, Practice Directions and rules. The following is a summary. Details of the various means, and when they may be used, are set out elsewhere in this Guide.

21.2 COSTS SANCTIONS

1BA-118   **21.2.1**   So far as costs sanctions are concerned, the Court has a discretion on whether to award costs to or against a party. The Court can sanction noncompliance by ordering the party in default to pay the other side's costs, or by disallowing the costs by the party in default even if that party is successful in the claim (see paragraph 23.1 of this Guide).

21.2.2   The Court can make a wasted costs order in appropriate circumstances, if the non-compliance has been the fault of the party's legal representatives. A wasted costs order falls to be paid by those legal representatives (see paragraph 23.12 of this Guide).

21.2.3   If the Court does make a costs order in favour of one of the parties, the Court can order that costs should be paid on the 'indemnity' basis, which means that in quantifying those costs, the party in whose favour the order has been made gets the benefit of the doubt on any question going to the reasonableness or proportionality of those costs (see paragraph 23.2.4 of this Guide).

21.3 PROCEDURAL SANCTIONS

1BA-119   **21.3.1**   If Court documents are filed out of time according to the Court's directions, that party must file an application for an extension of time. The Court will only grant that extension if it is satisfied that it is appropriate to do so, according to the rules (see paragraphs 12.7 and 12.9 of this Guide)

21.3.2   If no extension of time is granted, the party in default will not be able to rely on the late-filed documents, and that may be to that party's disadvantage. If the Court does grant an extension of time, it may be on the basis that the party in default should pay some or all of the other party's costs (see paragraph 23.1 of this Guide).

21.3.3   If there are no directions in place relating to the serving and filing of documents, but nonetheless documents are filed late (for example a skeleton argument on an application for directions), then the Court may refuse to consider those documents, which may disadvantage the party which seeks to rely on them (see, for example, paragraphs 17.5 and 18.4 of this Guide).

21.4 OTHER SANCTIONS

1BA-120   **21.4.1**   The Court can summon before it professional representatives who appear to have abused the procedure for urgent consideration pursuant to *Hamid*, and if not satisfied of the explanation given, may refer those professional representatives to their disciplinary body with a view to further action being taken (see paragraph 16.5 of this Guide).

PART D:—ENDING THE CLAIM

22. ENDING A CLAIM

22.1 INTRODUCTION

1BA-121   Once a claim has been started then there are a set number of ways to end the claim. They broadly fit into three categories: where the case is determined by the Court, where the case is discontinued and where the case is settled by consent. A claim cannot be ended by simply writing to the Court asking to withdraw the claim.

22.2 DETERMINED BY THE COURT

1BA-122   Where the Court makes a final determination, and produces a Court order, the case will have concluded in the Administrative Court (subject only to an appeal to the Court of Appeal, see CPR Part 52 and chapter 26 of this Guide). Such a determination will generally be one of the following:

22.2.1   Permission to apply for judicial review is refused (either at an oral hearing or on the papers where the claim is held to be totally without merit or reconsideration is not requested).

22.2.2   The substantive claim is dismissed.

22.2.3   The substantive claim is allowed.

22.3 DISCONTINUANCE

22.3.1 A case may be ended by discontinuing the claim, which may be done at any point in the **1BA-123** proceedings.[1]

22.3.2 Discontinuance requires the claimant to file a notice of discontinuance (form N279) and serve it on all parties.[2] There is no Court fee payable when discontinuing.

22.3.3 The claimant may discontinue the claim in relation to all or some of the parties.[3]

22.3.4 The Court's permission is required to discontinue where the claimant has obtained an interim injunction[4] or any party has given an undertaking to the Court.[5] This can be done by filing the notice of discontinuance, referring to the fact that permission is required, and the ACO will forward the notice to a judge to give permission without a hearing (unless the judge orders a hearing and representations). In other cases, permission is not required.

22.3.5 The discontinuance will take effect from the date on which the notice of discontinuance is served on the defendant(s).[6]

22.3.6 By filing a notice of discontinuance the claimant accepts that he/she is liable for the defendant's costs up until that date[7] and a costs order will be deemed to have been made on the standard basis[8] (see paragraph

23.2.3 of this Guide).[9] The claimant may apply to reverse the general rule that they are liable for costs and /or may claim their costs. Any such application must demonstrate a good reason for departing from the general rule. A good reason will normally exist if the Defendant has behaved unreasonably. Any such application must be made in accordance with the interim applications procedure (see paragraph 12.7 of this Guide).

22.4 CONSENT ORDERS AND UNCONTESTED PROCEEDINGS

22.4.1 Subject to the approval of the Court, the parties may agree to end the claim by filing **1BA-124** two copies of a draft, agreed order with the ACO, accompanied by the relevant fee.[10] The Court will only approve the order if it is satisfied that the order should be made; if not so satisfied, the Court may make any further or different order which it considers to be appropriate.

22.4.2 The terms of the order can include anything that the parties wish the Court to approve, but will generally include the following:

22.4.2.1 The draft order must note (often in the header to the order as well as in the recitals) that the order is made 'By Consent'.[11]

22.4.2.2 The draft order must be signed by the legal representative for every party to the claim (including interested parties), or by the party themselves where they are acting in person.[12]

22.4.2.3 Where the claim has been finally determined the consent order must detail the manner of determination, which includes:

22.4.2.3.1 The claim is 'withdrawn'. The effect of this is to leave the challenged decision in place (unless the defendant has voluntarily withdrawn the decision, thus removing the claimant's need to obtain the relief of the Court).

22.4.2.3.2 The parties agree that the decision challenged should be quashed (see paragraph 11.3 of this Guide). Where the parties do agree that the order should be quashed they must also supply a schedule to the consent order detailing the reasons, including legal provisions, outlining why the decision should be quashed.[13]

22.4.3 The consent order should make provision for determining costs, otherwise a deemed costs order will apply (see paragraph 23.7 of this Guide for deemed costs orders). This is generally done in one of three ways:

22.4.3.1 By providing for an agreed, set sum to be paid between the parties.

22.4.3.2 By allowing the parties to agree the quantum of costs after the consent order has been finalised, with a fallback option of applying for detailed assessment of costs, for example – the Claimant is to pay the Defendant's reasonable costs, to be subject to detailed assessment if not agreed (see paragraph

---

[1] CPR 38.2(1)
[2] CPR 38.3(1)
[3] CPR 38.2(3)
[4] CPR 38.2(2)(i)
[5] CPR 38.2(2)(ii)
[6] CPR 38.5(1)
[7] CPR 38.6(1)
[8] CPR 44.9(1)(c)
[9] CPR 44.3(2)(a)
[10] CPR PD 54A paragraph 17
[11] CPR 40.6(7)(b)
[12] CPR 40.6(7)(c)
[13] Paragraph 1 of the *Practice Direction (Administrative Court: Uncontested Proceedings)* [2008] 1 W.L.R. 1377 23.3.4 of this Guide for detailed assessment).

22.4.3.3   By making provision for summary assessment of costs on the papers. Such a provision should follow the ACO Costs Guidance, which is outlined at paragraph 23.5 of this Guide.

22.5   SETTLEMENTS ON BEHALF OF CHILDREN AND PROTECTED PARTIES

1BA-125   **22.5.1**   Where a claim is made by or on behalf of, or against, a child or a protected party[1] no settlement, compromise or payment and no acceptance of money paid into Court shall be valid without the approval of the Court.[2]

22.5.2   To obtain the Court's approval, an application must be made in accordance with the procedure described at paragraph 12.7 of this Guide.

22.6   OTHER POINTS OF PRACTICE

1BA-126   **22.6.1**   The parties have an obligation to inform the Court if they believe that a case is likely to settle as soon as they become aware of the possibility of settlement.[3] Such information allows judges and staff to allocate preparation time and hearing time accordingly. Failure to do so may result in the Court making an adverse costs order against the parties (see paragraph 23.1 of this Guide for costs).

22.6.2   When a case is closed by the ACO the file may be immediately reduced in size for storage (or 'broken up'). Particulars of claim and witness statements are retained on the closed file but all exhibits, written evidence, and authorities are confidentially destroyed. The reduced file is retained for three years after the case is closed before it too is confidentially destroyed. If the parties believe there is a need to keep fuller papers on file, or would like full bundles returned to them once the case has been closed, then they should inform the ACO before the case is closed.

23.   COSTS

23.1   LIABILITY FOR COSTS

1BA-127   **23.1.1**   The Court has a discretion as to whether costs are payable by one party to another.[4] There are provisions which guide this discretion.

23.1.2   Where the Court decides to make an order for costs, the general rule is that the unsuccessful party will be ordered to pay the costs of the successful party, subject to the abovementioned discretion of the Court.[5]

23.1.3   In deciding whether to make an order contrary to the general rule, the Court must have regard to all the circumstances of the case, including the conduct of the parties and whether a party has succeeded on part of his or her case even if he/she has not been wholly successful.

23.1.4   The conduct of the parties includes (but is not limited to):[6]

23.1.4.1   Conduct before as well as during the proceedings, and in particular the extent to which the parties followed the pre-action Protocol (see paragraph 5.2 of this Guide).

23.1.4.2   Whether it was reasonable for a party to raise, pursue or contest a particular allegation or issue.

23.1.4.3   The manner in which a party has pursued or defended his/her case and whether he/she has wholly or partly exaggerated his claim.

23.1.5   As a result of the provisions above, where a party has failed to comply with orders of the Court or other procedural rules (such as those outlined in this Guide) the Court may reduce the amount of costs to which a successful party would normally be entitled. Further, in such a scenario, a liable party may be required to pay more than would normally be considered to be reasonable had the breach of the provision not occurred.

23.1.6   Liability to pay costs is not necessarily an all or nothing decision and a judge may require one party to pay a percentage of the other party's costs, thus deciding that the losing party is, for example, liable to pay 80% of the other party's costs.

23.1.7   The Court does not generally order an unsuccessful claimant to pay two sets of costs (typically the costs incurred by the defendant and an interested party), although the Court may order two sets of costs to be paid where the defendant and the interested party deal with separate

---

[1] CPR 21.1

[2] CPR 21.10

[3] *Yell Ltd v Garton* [2004] C.P. Rep. 29

[4] s.51(1) of the Senior Courts Act 1981 and CPR 44.2(1)

[5] CPR 44.2(2)(a) and *R. (M) v Croydon London Borough Council* [2012] 1 W.L.R. 2607, at paragraphs 58 – 65

[6] *R (KR) v Secretary of State for the Home Department* [2012] EWCA Civ 1555

issues, or have different interests and so require separate representation.[1] The Court may order an unsuccessful claimant to pay two sets of costs of preparing Acknowledgements of Service.[2]

23.2 REASONABLE COSTS AND THE BASIS OF THE ASSESSMENT

23.2.1 The Court will not allow costs which have been unreasonably incurred or are unreason- **1BA-128** able in amount.[3] In determining if costs are reasonable the Court will have regard to all the circumstances of the case.[4]

23.2.2 The basis of the assessment is important when determining whether the costs claimed are reasonable. In determining the basis of the assessment the Court has two options; the standard basis or on an indemnity basis.

23.2.3 The Standard Basis

23.2.3.1 Most costs orders are made on the standard basis. Where a Court is silent as to the basis on which it is assessing costs, the presumption is that assessment is on the standard basis.[5]

23.2.3.2 Where the amount of costs is to be assessed on the standard basis, the Court will only allow costs which are proportionate to the matters in issue. Where there is doubt as to whether costs were reasonable and proportionate in amount the Court will determine the question in favour of the paying party.[6] Costs incurred are proportionate[7] if they bear a reasonable relationship to:

23.2.3.2.1 The sums in issue in the proceedings;

23.2.3.2.2 The value of any non-monetary relief in issue in the proceedings;

23.2.3.2.3 The complexity of the litigation;

23.2.3.2.4 Any additional work generated by the conduct of the paying party; and

23.2.3.2.5 Any wider factors involved in the proceedings, such as reputation or public importance.

23.2.4 The Indemnity Basis

23.2.4.1 This basis is reserved as a sanction. The Court will apply indemnity costs in those cases where the losing party has acted unreasonably in bringing or maintaining the claim or in any other way.

23.2.4.2 Where the amount of costs is to be assessed on an indemnity basis, the Court will resolve any doubt which it may have as to whether costs were reasonably incurred or were reasonable in amount in favour of the receiving party.[8] There is no requirement that the costs be proportionate, as appears in the standard basis assessment.

23.3 MANNER OF ASSESSMENT AND POTENTIAL COSTS ORDERS

23.3.1 Where the Court orders a party to pay costs to another party, it may either make a **1BA-129** summary assessment of the costs or order detailed assessment of the costs.[9]

23.3.2 Where the Court does not proceed to summary assessment and does not mention the manner of assessment in a costs order then the costs order is presumed to order detailed assessment.[10]

23.3.3 Summary Assessment

23.3.3.1 Summary assessment involves a judge determining the amount of costs payable by the liable party. The judge will then make an order for the amount of costs to be paid, for example: The Claimant is to pay the Defendant's costs in the sum of £5,000.

23.3.3.2 The parties must lodge a statement of costs not less than 24 hours before the hearing at which costs will be assessed or with the papers where an application is to be determined without a hearing (unless a judge has ordered a different timescale).[11]

23.3.3.3 The Court is not entitled to summarily assess the costs of a receiving party who is a child or protected party unless the legal representative acting for the child or protected party has

---

[1] See *Bolton MDC v Secretary of State for the Environment* [1995] 1 WLR 1176)
[2] See *R (Luton Borough Council) v Central Bedfordshire Council* [2014] EWHC 4325 (Admin).
[3] CPR 44.3(1)
[4] CPR 44.4(1)
[5] CPR 44.3(4)(a)
[6] CPR 44.3(2)
[7] According to CPR 44.3(5)
[8] CPR 44.3(3)
[9] CPR 44.6(1)
[10] CPR PD 44 paragraph 8.2
[11] CPR PD 44 paragraph 9.5(4)(b)

waived the right to further costs.[1]

23.3.3.4 Unless a judge orders otherwise, any costs order must be complied with within 14 days of the costs order,[2] although the parties may vary this time limit and agree their own payment terms without seeking the agreement of the Court.

23.3.4 Detailed Assessment

23.3.4.1 Detailed assessment involves a costs judge considering the claim for costs in accordance with the procedure in CPR Part 47. An outline of the procedure can be found in the Senior Courts Costs Office Guide, which can be found online at the following website;
https://www.gov.uk/government/publications/seniorcourts-costs-office-guide.

23.3.4.2 Where detailed assessment has been ordered by the Administrative Court in London, the application for detailed assessment of costs must be started at the Senior Courts Costs Office in London.

23.3.4.3 Where detailed assessment has been ordered by any of the Administrative Courts outside of London, the application for detailed assessment of costs must be started in the District Registry associated with the relevant ACO. For example, a judicial review determined by the Administrative Court in Cardiff would result in any detailed costs assessment being started in the District Registry in Cardiff Civil Justice Centre.[3] Western Circuit cases administered by the ACO in Cardiff but heard on the Western Circuit must also be lodged in the District Registry in Cardiff.

23.3.4.4 It should be noted that detailed assessment proceedings cease to be Administrative Court proceedings and a new case number will be assigned to the proceedings. The ACO will not have any further involvement with the case.

23.4 COSTS AT THE PERMISSION STAGE

1BA-130

23.4.1 There is a discrete procedure on applying for and considering costs when a judge is considering permission to apply for judicial review, although this procedure may be varied by judicial order:[4]

23.4.1.1 If permission has not been granted, either on the papers or at an oral hearing, then the claimant's costs are deemed to be costs in the case, and the question of whether the claimant will be able to recover those costs will depend on the outcome of the case.

23.4.1.2 Where a proposed defendant or interested party wishes to seek costs at the permission stage, the acknowledgement of service should include an application for costs and should be accompanied by a schedule setting out the amount claimed;

23.4.1.3 The judge, if refusing permission on the papers, should include in the refusal a decision whether to award costs in principle, and an indication of the amount which he/she proposes to assess summarily.

23.4.1.4 The claimant should be given 14 days to respond in writing and should serve a copy on the defendant.

23.4.1.5 The defendant will normally have 7 days to reply in writing to any such response, and to the amount proposed by the judge;

23.4.1.6 The judge will then decide and make an award on the papers.

23.4.1.7 In the event that the claimant requests an oral hearing for reconsideration of refusal of permission, the Court at that hearing may also consider the question of costs of the permission stage.

23.4.2 If permission to apply for judicial review is refused there are additional principles which the Court will generally apply:[5]

23.4.2.1 A successful defendant or other party at the permission stage who has filed an acknowledgment of service should generally recover the costs of doing so from the claimant, whether or not they attend any permission hearing.

23.4.2.2 A defendant or other party who attends and successfully resists the grant of permission at a renewal hearing should not generally recover from the claimant the costs of attending, but will still be entitled to the costs of preparing the acknowledgment of service.[6]

23.4.2.3 A Court, in considering an award of costs against an unsuccessful claimant at a permission hearing, should only depart from the general principles above if it is considered that there are exceptional circumstances for doing so.

23.4.2.4 Exceptional circumstances may consist in the presence of one or more of the features in the following non-exhaustive list:

23.4.2.4.1 The hopelessness of the claim.

---

[1] CPR PD 44 paragraph 9.9

[2] CPR 44.7(1)(a)

[3] *Public Services Ombudsman for Wales v Heesom* [2015] EWHC 3306 (QB)

[4] *R. (Ewing) v Office of the Deputy Prime Minister* [2006] 1 W.L.R. 1260

[5] *R. (Mount Cook Land Ltd) v Westminster City Council* [2004] C.P. Rep. 12

[6] See *R (Davey) v Aylesbury Vale DC (Practice Note)* [2008] 1 WLR 878

23.4.2.4.2 The persistence in it by the claimant after having been alerted to facts and/or of the law demonstrating its hopelessness.

23.4.2.4.3 The extent to which the Court considers that the claimant, in the pursuit of his application, has sought to abuse the process of judicial review (see paragraph 12.10.3 of this Guide for examples of abuse of process).

23.4.2.4.4 Whether, as a result of the deployment of full argument and documentary evidence by both sides at the hearing, the unsuccessful claimant has had, in effect, the advantage of an early substantive hearing of the claim.

23.4.2.4.5 Whether the unsuccessful claimant has substantial resources which it has used to pursue the unfounded claim and which are available to meet an order for costs.

23.4.2.4.6 Whether the permission was refused at a rolled up hearing, in which event the defendant, who has prepared for a substantive hearing, may be awarded costs.

23.5 COSTS AFTER SETTLING

23.5.1 The onus lies on the parties to reach agreement on costs wherever possible and in advance of asking the Court to resolve costs, in order to support the overriding objective and ensure that efficient use is made of Court time. The parties should not, therefore, make submissions to the Court on costs following a compromise of proceedings without first seeking to agree costs through reasoned negotiation, mindful of the overriding objective to the CPR, the amount of costs actually at stake, and the principles set out in *M v Croydon* [2012] EWCA Civ 595, paragraphs 59-63.

1BA-131

23.5.2 Where a clam has settled (see paragraph 22.4 of this Guide) but the parties have been unable to agree costs, the parties may use the procedure for assessing costs outlined in the ACO Costs Guidance (*http://www.justice.gov.uk/courts/rcj-rolls-building/administrative-court/applying-for-judicial-review*).

23.5.3 The costs section of the consent order should state:

23.5.3.1 Within 28 days of the order, the defendant may file with the Court and serve on all other parties, submissions as to what the appropriate costs order should be. If the defendant does not file submissions, the order will be that the defendant will pay the claimant's costs of the claim on the standard basis, to be the subject of detailed assessment if not agreed.

23.5.3.2 Where the defendant does file submissions within 28 days, the claimant or any other party may file and serve submissions within 14 days of service of those submissions. If neither the claimant nor any other party files such submissions in response, the costs order will be in the terms sought by the defendant.

23.5.3.3 Where submissions are filed by the claimant or any other party, the defendant shall have 7 days in which to file and serve a reply. The matter shall then be put before the judge for a decision on costs or further order.

23.5.4 In accordance with the costs guidance, the submissions must:

23.5.4.1 Confirm that the parties have used reasonable endeavours to negotiate a costs settlement.

23.5.4.2 Identify what issues or reasons prevented the parties agreeing costs liability.

23.5.4.3 State the approximate amount of costs likely to be involved in the case.

23.5.4.4 Identify the extent to which the parties complied with the preaction Protocol.

23.5.4.5 State the relief the claimant sought (i) in the claim form and (ii) obtained.

23.5.4.6 Address specifically how the claim and the basis of its settlement fit the principles in *M v Croydon London Borough Council* and *Tesfay* [2016] EWCA Civ 415 (see paragraph 23.5.6 below), including the relationship of any step taken by the defendant to the claim.

23.5.5 In accordance with the costs guidance, the submissions must be made in documentation as outlined below:

23.5.5.1 Submissions should be of a normal print size and should not normally exceed two A4 pages in length unless there is good reason to exceed this, which is properly explained in the submissions.

23.5.5.2 Submissions should be accompanied by the pre-action Protocol correspondence (where this has not previously been included as part of the documents supporting the claim), the correspondence in which the costs claim is made and defended, along with any other correspondence necessary to demonstrate why the claim was brought in the light of the pre-action Protocol correspondence or why the step which led to settlement was not taken until after the claim was issued.

23.5.5.3 Unless advised otherwise, the parties should assume that the Court has the claim papers originally lodged by the parties. Further copies of these should not be provided unless requested by the Court.

23.5.6 The following is a short summary of how the Court will consider what order on costs to make, based on *M v Croydon London Borough Council* and *Tesfay*:

23.5.6.1 Where a claimant has been wholly successful in terms of the relief sought the claimant will generally recover all his/her costs, unless there is some good reason to the contrary.

23.5.6.2 Where a claimant has only succeeded in part the judge will normally determine how reasonable the claimant was in pursuing the unsuccessful relief (the defendant has refused to adhere to the demands of the claimant but the claim has settled anyway), how important the unsuccessful relief was compared with the successful relief, and how much the costs were increased as a result of the claimant pursuing the unsuccessful relief.

23.5.6.3   Where there has been some compromise which does not actually reflect the claimant's claims the default position will generally be no order for costs. However, in some cases, the judge may look at the underlying claim and inquire whether it was tolerably clear who would have won if the matter had not settled. If it is, then that may well strongly support the contention that the party who would have won did better out of the settlement, and therefore did win.

23.6   INTERVENERS AND COSTS

1BA-132   **23.6.1**   A person may apply to file evidence or make representations at a hearing[1] (see paragraph 2.2.4 of this Guide). Such a person is commonly referred to as an intervener and there are specific rules governing whether an intervener can recover its costs or be ordered to pay costs, summarised below.[2]

23.6.2   A relevant party, that is to say a claimant or defendant in substantive or permission judicial review proceedings,[3] cannot be ordered to pay an intervener's costs[4] unless there are exceptional circumstances that make such a costs order appropriate.[5]

23.6.3   If the Court is satisfied that any one of four conditions is met, the Court must order the intervener to pay any costs specified in an application by a claimant or defendant that the Court considers have been incurred by them as a result of the intervener's involvement in that stage of the proceedings.[6] The four conditions are:

23.6.3.1   The intervener has acted, in substance, as the sole or principal applicant, defendant, appellant or respondent.

23.6.3.2   The intervener's evidence and representations, taken as a whole, have not been of significant assistance to the Court.

23.6.3.3   A significant part of the intervener's evidence and representations relates to matters that it is not necessary for the Court to consider in order to resolve the issues that are the subject of the stage in the proceedings.

23.6.3.4   The intervener has behaved unreasonably.

23.6.4   If the intervener becomes a party, the costs provisions above no longer apply and are deemed never to have applied.[7]

23.7   ORDERS WHICH DO NOT MENTION COSTS

1BA-133   **23.7.1**   Where an order does not mention costs then a deemed costs order is presumed to have been made. There are two scenarios in the Administrative Court where deemed costs orders apply. Those two scenarios are:

23.7.1.1   Subject to paragraph 23.7.1.2 below, where an order is silent as to costs and makes no provision for how costs are to be assessed, then the Court is deemed to have ordered that there be no order for costs.[8]

23.7.1.2   Where the Court makes an order granting permission to appeal, an order granting permission to apply for judicial review, or any other order or direction sought by a party on an application without notice, and its order does not mention costs, it will be deemed to include an order that the costs are in the case, and will be determined according to the outcome of the claim.[9]

23.7.2   A party may apply to set aside the deemed costs order at any point.[10] Such an application must be made in accordance with the interim orders procedure (see paragraph 12.7 of this Guide).

23.8   SETTING ASIDE COSTS ORDERS

1BA-134   **23.8.1**   Save for deemed costs orders (see paragraph 23.7 above) any costs order where the parties have had the opportunity to make representations before the order was made, be that a costs order on the papers or after an oral hearing, is a final costs order.[11] The Administrative Court may

---

[1] CPR 54.17
[2] s.87 of the Criminal Justice and Courts Act 2015
[3] See above, s.87(9) and (10)
[4] See above, s.87(3)
[5] See above, s.87(4)
[6] See above, s.87(5)
[7] See above, s.87(11)
[8] CPR 44.10(1)(a)(i)
[9] CPR 44.10(2)
[10] CPR 44.10(3)
[11] *R. (Jones) v Nottingham City Council* [2009] A.C.D. 42 and *R. (Bahta) v Secretary of State for the Home Department* [2011] C.P. Rep. 43

not set it aside or reconsider the order at a hearing. If challenged, the order must be appealed (see chapter 26 of this Guide for appeals).

23.9 COSTS WHEN THE CLAIMANT HAS THE BENEFIT OF LEGAL AID

23.9.1 Costs orders can be made against persons who have the benefit of legal aid (subject to the principles discussed earlier in this section of the Guide). Where the Court does make such an order it will order that the person with the benefit of legal aid must pay the costs of the requesting party and the Court may set the amount to be paid, but the Court will note that the person with the benefit of legal aid is subject to costs protection in accordance with s.26 of the Legal Aid, Sentencing, and Punishment of Offenders Act 2012. **1BA-135**

23.9.2 As a result of the costs protection, the person with the benefit of legal aid is not automatically liable for the costs. If the person awarded costs wishes to require the person with the benefit of legal aid to pay those costs they must apply for an order from the Senior Courts Costs Office or, where the costs order was made by an Administrative Court not in London, he/she must apply to the relevant associated District Registry.

23.10 COSTS FROM CENTRAL FUNDS (CRIMINAL CASES)

23.10.1 In judicial reviews relating to a criminal cause or matter, where a claimant is successful, a Divisional Court may make a costs order, which shall be for payment out of central funds (that is to say, it will be paid by the Ministry of Justice).[1] **1BA-136**

23.10.2 The costs order is made in such amount as the Court considers reasonably sufficient to compensate for any expenses properly incurred in the proceedings, unless the Court considers that there are circumstances that make it inappropriate to recover the full amount when the Court may order a lesser amount in a sum the Court considers just and reasonable.

23.10.3 The costs order may not require the payment out of central funds of an amount that includes legal costs unless those costs were incurred in proceedings in the Court below (Magistrates' Court or Crown Court on appeal against conviction or sentence).

23.10.4 There is no power for a single judge to order costs be paid out of central funds. Where a claimant seeks an order for costs from central funds when appearing before a single judge, the judge will adjourn the matter to be considered on the papers by a Divisional Court, constituted of the single judge who heard the case and another judge.

23.10.5 When making the costs order, the Court will fix the amount to be paid out of central funds in the order if it considers it appropriate to do so.[2] Where the Court does not fix the amount to be paid out of central funds in the order it must describe in the order any reduction required and the amount must be fixed by means of a determination made by or on behalf of the Court by the Senior Courts Costs Office.[3]

23.10.6 If the claimant has the benefit of a representation order or a legal aid certificate (see paragraph 3.5.4 of this Guide) then he/she cannot claim costs out of central funds.[4]

23.10.7 Where an order for costs from central funds has been made the claimant must forward the order to the Senior Courts Costs Office, which will arrange for payment of the amount specified.

23.11 COSTS AGAINST COURTS OR TRIBUNALS

23.11.1 Where the defendant in judicial review proceedings is a Court or Tribunal the Administrative Court will generally not impose costs orders against the Court or Tribunal where the Court has not acted obstructively or improperly and only makes representations neutrally on the procedure or law applied by the lower Court. Where the Court or Tribunal contests the claim the Court or Tribunal may become liable for costs, subject to the principles discussed in this section of the Guide.[5] **1BA-137**

23.12 WASTED COSTS ORDERS

23.12.1 In appropriate cases the Court has power to order that a legal representative should pay the costs of an opposing party or that a specified sum for costs is disallowed.[6] These orders are referred to as wasted costs orders. **1BA-138**

23.12.2 A wasted costs order may be made against the receiving party's own legal representatives or against those of the paying party.[7]

---

[1] s16(6) and 17 of the Prosecution of Offences Act 1985
[2] See above, s.16(6C)
[3] See above, s.16(6D)
[4] See above, s.21(4A)
[5] *R (Davies) v Birmingham Deputy Coroner* [2004] EWCA Civ 207
[6] s.51(6) of the Senior Courts Act 1981 and CPR 46.8
[7] *Brown v Bennett* [2002] 2 All ER 273

23.12.3 An application for a wasted costs order may be made by the party who suffered the wasted costs or may be ordered of the Court's own volition.

23.12.4 When considering whether to make a wasted costs order, the Court will consider three points:[1]

23.12.4.1 Did the legal representative (or any employee of the representative) act improperly, unreasonably or negligently?

23.12.4.2 If so, did the conduct cause the party who incurred the costs to incur unnecessary costs or has the conduct caused costs incurred by a party prior to the conduct to be wasted?

23.12.4.3 If so, is it just in all the circumstances to order the legal representative to compensate the subject of the wasted costs for the whole or part of the relevant costs?

23.12.5 The Court will give the legal representative a reasonable opportunity to make written submissions or, if the legal representative prefers, to attend a hearing before it makes such an order.[2]

23.12.6 Unless there is good reason otherwise, wasted costs applications should generally be considered by the Court at the end of proceedings.[3]

23.13 COSTS WHERE A PARTY IS REPRESENTED PRO BONO

1BA-139   **23.13.1** Section 194 of the Legal Services Act 2007 makes provision for the recovery of costs where the representation has been provided pro bono (free of charge to the represented party), see paragraph 3.5.5 of this Guide.[4] Where such an order is made, the costs awarded in favour of that party will not be payable to the party's legal representatives but to a charity, the Access to Justice Foundation.

24.   PROTECTIVE COSTS ORDERS AND JUDICIAL REVIEW COSTS CAPPING ORDERS

24.1 LEGISLATIVE CHANGE

1BA-140   **24.1.1** Sections 88–90 of the Criminal Justice and Courts Act 2015 introduce a new comprehensive code for cost capping in judicial reviews, including a new form of cost capping order for judicial review ("judicial review cost capping order" or "JRCCO")[5]. The JRCCO replaces Protective Costs Orders(see below) and removes cost capping orders under CPR Part 3 from judicial review claims (see chapter 25 of this Guide for "old" style cost capping orders).

24.1.2 Sections 88–90 of the 2015 Act come into force on 8 August 2016. Accordingly, for claims issued before 8 August 2016, the old rules apply. For claims issued on or after that date, the new rules apply. Both sets of rules are outlined below.

24.2 BEFORE 8 AUGUST 2016: PROTECTIVE COSTS ORDERS

1BA-141   **24.2.1** A Protective Costs Order (or 'PCO') may take a number of forms. Frequently, the order may specify a limit on the amount that a claimant can be ordered to pay in respect of the other side's cost if the claimant loses (e.g the claimant's liability for costs will be limited to £5,000). Often, that order is coupled with an order placing a limit on the amount that a claimant who is successful can recover from a defendant even if the claimant ultimately wins the case.[233]

24.3 PCO: GENERAL PRINCIPLES

1BA-142   **24.3.1** The lead case on when a PCO should be granted is *R (Corner House Research) v Trade and Industry Secretary* [2005] EWCA Civ 192. In Corner House the Court of Appeal stated that the following matters were relevant threshold criteria:

24.3.1.1 The issues raised must be of general public importance;

24.3.1.2 The public interest requires that those issues should be resolved;

24.3.1.3 The applicant must have no private interest in the outcome of the case;

24.3.1.4 Having regard to the financial resources of the applicant and the respondent(s) and to the amount of costs that are likely to be involved, it is fair and just to make the order;

24.3.1.5 If the order is not made the applicant will probably discontinue the proceedings and will be acting reasonably in so doing.

24.3.2 If those acting for the applicant are doing so pro bono this will be likely to enhance the merits of the application for a PCO.

---

[1] CPR PD 46 paragraph 5.5 and *Re a Barrister (Wasted Costs Order) (No 1 of 1991)* [1993] QB 293
[2] CPR 46.8(2)
[3] *Filmlab Systems International Ltd v Pennington* [1994] 4 All ER 673
[4] CPR 46.7
[5] For implementation, see the Civil Procedure (Amendment No 2) Rules 2016, SI 2016/707; and see the Criminal Justice and Courts Act 2015 (Commencement No. 4 and Transitional provisions) Order 2016, SI 2016/717

24.4 PCO: PROCEDURE

24.4.1 *Corner House* gave guidance on the appropriate procedure for applying for a PCO in the **1BA-143** Administrative Court. The Court of Appeal confirmed the Corner House procedural principles in *R (Buglife) v Thurrock Thames Gateway Development Corp* [2008] EWCA Civ 1209 and clarified them. The *Corner House / Buglife* principles can be summarised as:

24.4.1.1 A PCO should, in normal circumstances, be sought on the claim form (in section 8).

24.4.1.2 The application must be supported by evidence establishing the principles outlined in *Corner House*, and should include a schedule of the claimant's future costs of and incidental to the full judicial review application.

24.4.1.3 If the defendant wishes to resist the making of the PCO, or any of the sums set out in the claimant's schedule, it should set out its reasons in the acknowledgment of service. Similarly, if the defendant wishes to request a reciprocal PCO (thus capping both parties costs), such a request should also be made in the acknowledgment of service.

24.4.1.4 The claimant will be liable for the Court fee(s) for pursuing the claim, and it will also be liable for the defendant's costs incurred in a successful resistance to an application for a PCO.

24.4.1.5 The judge will consider whether to make the PCO on the papers (usually alongside permission to apply for judicial review) and if he or she decides a PCO is appropriate, will decide its terms including the level of the cap on the recoverable costs.

24.4.1.6 If the judge refuses to grant the PCO and the claimant requests that his decision is reconsidered at a hearing (see paragraph xx of this Guide) the hearing should be limited to an hour and the claimant will face liability for costs if the PCO is again refused. The paper decision should only be revisited in exceptional circumstances.

24.4.1.7 The Court should not set aside a PCO unless there is an exceptional reason for doing so.

24.4.2 A PCO can be made at any time, although the above procedure is preferred to ensure that any PCO is in place at an early stage of the claim. But a party can still apply for a PCO after the claim has been started, in which the application should be made in accordance with the interim applications procedure (see paragraph 12.7 of this Guide), but taking into account the requirements above.

24.5 ON OR AFTER 8 AUGUST 2016: JUDICIAL REVIEW COSTS CAPPING ORDERS

24.5.1 Judicial Review Costs Capping Orders ("JRCCOs") replace PCOs (see paragraphs 24.2– **1BA-144** 24.4 above). The name and procedure was changed with the coming into force of the relevant provisions in the Criminal Justice and Courts Act 2015 on 8 August 2016.[1] A JRCCO may take a number of forms. The order may specify a limit on the amount that a claimant can be ordered to pay in respect of the other side's cost if the claimant loses (e.g *A costs capping order is granted. The claimant's liability for costs will be limited to £5,000*). That order must be coupled with an order placing a limit on the amount that a claimant who is successful can recover from a defendant even if the claimant ultimately wins the case (sometimes called a reciprocal costs capping order).[2]

24.6 JRCCOS: GENERAL PRINCIPLES

24.6.1 A JRCCO may only be granted after permission to apply for judicial review has been **1BA-145** granted (see paragraph 8.2.2 of this Guide);[3]

24.6.2 A JRCCO may only be applied for by a claimant, not a defendant, interested party, or intervener;[4]

24.6.3 The court may only make a JRCCO if it is satisfied that:[5]

24.6.3.1 The proceedings are public interest proceedings. Public interest proceedings are defined[6] as an issue that is the subject of the proceedings which is of general public importance. Further, the public interest requires the issue to be resolved and the proceedings are likely to provide an appropriate means of resolving it. When considering this issue, the court must have regard[7] to the number of people likely to be directly affected if relief is granted, how significant the effect on those people is likely to be, and whether the proceedings involve consideration of a point of law of general public importance.

24.6.3.2 In the absence of the order, the claimant would withdraw the application for judicial

---

[1] The new provisions apply to all claims lodged after the 8th August 2016. See the Criminal Justice and Courts Act 2015 (Commencement No. 4 and Transitional Provisions) Order 2016 SI 2016/717. And see Civil Procedure (Amendment No 2) Rules 2016, SI 2016/707.

[2] s.89(2) of the Criminal Justice and Courts Act 2015

[3] s.88(3) of the Criminal Justice and Courts Act 2015

[4] s.88(4) of the Criminal Justice and Courts Act 2015

[5] Further to s.88(6) of the Criminal Justice and Courts Act 2015

[6] s.88(7) of the Criminal Justice and Courts Act 2015

[7] Under s.88(8) of the Criminal Justice and Courts Act 2015

review or cease to participate in the proceedings and it would be reasonable to do so.

24.6.4   The court must have regard,[1] when considering whether to make a JRCCO, to the following:

24.6.4.1   The financial resources of the parties to the proceedings, including the financial resources of any person who provides, or may provide, financial support to the parties;

24.6.4.2   The extent to which the claimant is likely to benefit if relief is granted (see chapter 11 of this guide for final remedies);

24.6.4.3   The extent to which any person who has provided, or may provide, the applicant with financial support is likely to benefit if relief is granted;

24.6.4.4   Whether legal representatives for the applicant for the order are acting free of charge; and

24.6.4.5   Whether the claimant is an appropriate person to represent the interests of other persons or the public interest generally.

24.7   JRCCOS: PROCEDURE[2]

1BA-146

24.7.1   An application for a JRCCO must normally be contained in the claim form at section 8 or it must accompany the claim form in a separate document.[3]

24.7.2   The application must be supported by evidence setting out:[4]

24.7.2.1   Why a JRCCO should be made, having regard, in particular, to the matters at paragraph 24.6.3 and 24.6.4 above.

24.7.2.2   A summary of the claimant's financial resources, unless the court has dispensed with this requirement.[5] The summary must provide details of the following:[6]

24.7.2.2.1   The claimant's significant assets, liabilities, income and expenditure; and

24.7.2.2.2   In relation to any financial support which any person has provided or is likely to provide to the claimant, the aggregate amount which has been provided and which is likely to be provided.

24.7.2.3   The costs (and disbursements) which the claimant considers the parties are likely to incur in the future conduct of the proceedings.

24.7.2.4   If the claimant is a body corporate, whether it is able to demonstrate that it is likely to have financial resources available to meet liabilities arising in connection with the proceedings. Where it cannot the court must consider giving directions for the provision of information about the body's members and their ability to provide financial support for the purpose of the proceedings.[7]

24.7.3   If the defendant wishes to resist the making of the JRCCO it should set out its reasons in the acknowledgment of service. Similarly, any representations on a reciprocal costs capping order (capping both parties' costs) should be made in the acknowledgment of service.

24.7.4   The claimant will usually be liable for defendant's costs incurred in a successful resistance to an application for a JRCCO.

24.7.5   If the judge grants permission to apply for judicial review on the papers the judge will then consider whether to make the JRCCO on the papers and if so, in what terms. If the judge does not grant permission the judge cannot make a JRCCO (see paragraph 24.6.1 above).

24.7.6   If the judge grants permission to apply for judicial review, but refuses to grant the JRCCO, and the claimant requests that the decision is reconsidered at a hearing (see paragraph 15.5 of this Guide for the procedure), that hearing should be limited to an hour and the claimant will face liability for costs if the JRCCO is again refused. The paper decision should only be revisited in exceptional circumstances.

24.7.7   The court should not set aside a JRCCO unless there is an exceptional reason for doing so.

24.7.8   An application for a JRCCO can be made at any time, not just when lodging the claim, although it is discouraged. When the preferred procedure, outlined above, cannot be utilised, a party may still apply for a JRCCO. In such circumstances the application should be made in accordance with the application procedure outlined at paragraph 12.7 of this Guide.

---

[1] Further to s.89(1) of the Criminal Justice and Courts Act 2015

[2] The relevant procedure is outlined in the Criminal Justice and Courts Act 2015 and supplemented where appropriate by the pre-existing procedural provisions on protective costs order in *R. (Corner House Research) v Trade and Industry Secretary* [2005] 1 W.L.R. 2600 and *R. (Buglife) v Thurrock Thames Gateway Development Corp* [2009] C.P. Rep. 8 at paragraphs 29 – 31

[3] CPR PD 46 paragraph 10.2 and *R. (Corner House Research) v Trade and Industry Secretary* [2005] 1 W.L.R. 2600

[4] CPR 46.17(1)(b)

[5] CPR 46.17(3)

[6] CPR PD 46 paragraph 10.1

[7] CPR 46.18

24.8 ENVIRONMENTAL LAW CASES

24.8.1 There are limits on the amount of costs that a party may be ordered to pay in what are **1BA-147** known as Aarhus Convention claims (that is, certain claims involving environmental issues).

24.8.2 An Aarhus Convention claim is a claim which deals with subject matter within the scope of the Convention on Access to Information, Public Participation in Decision Making and Access to Justice in Environmental Matters (' the Aarhus Convention'). The Aarhus Convention defines what constitutes ' the environment':

"Art.2(3) - Environmental information means any information...on:

(a) The state of elements of the environment, such as air and atmosphere, water, soil, land, landscape and natural sites, biological diversity and its components, including genetically modified organisms, and the interaction among these elements;

(b) Factors, such as substances, energy, noise and radiation, and activities or measures, including administrative measures, environmental agreements policies, legislation, plans and programmes, affecting or likely to affect the elements of the environment within the scope of subparagraph (a) above, and cost-benefit and other economic analyses and assumptions used in environmental decision-making;

(c) The state of human health and safety, conditions of human life, cultural sites and built structures, inasmuch as they are or may be affected by the state of the elements of the environment or, through these elements, by the factors, activities or measures referred to in subparagraph (b) above."

24.8.3 Where the claimant believes that his or her claim comes within the terms of the Aarhus Convention then they should note it in part 6 of the claim form. Where the claimant contends that the Aarhus Convention applies, unless the defendant challenges that assertion, the costs limit is automatically in place.[1]

24.8.4 The current costs limit is £5,000 where the claimant is claiming only as an individual and not as or on behalf of, a business or other legal person. In all other cases the limit is £10,000. Where a defendant is ordered to pay costs, the limit is £35,000.[2]

24.8.5 Where the defendant intends to challenge the assertion that the Aarhus Convention applies and, therefore, that the costs limit does not apply, the procedure to challenge the assertion can be found at CPR 45.44:

24.8.5.1 The defendant must indicate if he refutes the assertion in the acknowledgment of service at section E.

24.8.5.2 The defendant must set out the defendant's grounds for such denial.

24.8.5.3 Where the defendant argues that the claim is not an Aarhus Convention claim, the Court will determine that issue at the earliest opportunity, usually at the same time as considering permission to apply for judicial review on the papers.

24.8.6 In any proceedings to determine whether the claim is an Aarhus Convention claim:

24.8.6.1 If the Court holds that the claim is not an Aarhus Convention claim, it will normally make no order for costs in relation to the application for a costs cap;

24.8.6.2 If the Court holds that the claim is an Aarhus Convention claim, it will normally order the defendant to pay the claimant's costs in relation to the application on an indemnity basis (see paragraph 23.2.4 of this Guide), and that order may be enforced notwithstanding that this would increase the costs payable by the defendant beyond the £35,000 limit (see paragraph 24.8.4 above).

24.8.7 The automatic costs limit provisions also apply where the claimant is a public body.[3]

24.8.8 A claimant may indicate on the claim form that they wish to opt out of the automatic costs limit. If the claimant does not indicate on the claim form that the Aarhus Convention applies, the claimant is taken to have opted out.[4]

25. "OLD-STYLE" COSTS CAPPING

25.1 LEGISLATIVE CHANGE

From 8 August 2016, a new comprehensive code for costs capping in judicial review will apply. **1BA-148** The new "judicial review costs capping order" or "JRCCO" is outlined above, see paragraph 24.5–24.7 of this Guide. The rest of this chapter concerns "old-style" costs capping orders which remain available only in relation to cases issued before 8 August 2016.

---

[1] CPR 45.43(1)
[2] CPR PD 45 paragraph 5.1
[3] *R. (HS2 Action Alliance Ltd) v Secretary of State for Transport* [2015] 2 Costs L.R. 411
[4] CPR 45.42

25.2   OLD-STYLE COSTS CAPPING

1BA-149   A costs capping order is an order limiting the amount of future costs (including disbursements) which a party may recover pursuant to an order for costs subsequently made.[1]

25.3   OLD-STYLE COSTS CAPPING: PROCEDURE

1BA-150   **25.3.1**   A costs capping order may be made in respect of the whole litigation, or any issues which are to be tried separately.

25.3.2   The Court may make a costs capping order if it is:

25.3.2.1   In the interests of justice to do so;

25.3.2.2   There is a substantial risk that without such an order costs will be disproportionately incurred; and

25.3.2.3   The Court is not satisfied that the risk identified in the forgoing paragraph can be adequately controlled by case management directions, or order, and/or detailed assessment of costs.

25.3.3   In considering whether to exercise its discretion to make a costs capping order, the Court will consider all the circumstances of the case, including

25.3.3.1   Whether there is a substantial imbalance between the financial position of the parties;

25.3.3.2   Whether the costs of determining the amount of the cap are likely to be proportionate to the overall costs of the litigation;

25.3.3.3   The stage which the proceedings have reached; and

25.3.3.4   The costs which have been incurred to date and future costs.

25.3.4   A costs capping order, once made, will limit the costs recoverable by the party subject to the order unless a party successfully applies to vary the order. No variation will be made unless:

25.3.4.1   There has been a material and substantial change of circumstances since the date when the order was made; or

25.3.4.2   There is some other compelling reason why a variation should be made.

25.3.5   An application for a costs capping order must be made by way of application on notice to the other party or parties (see paragraph 12.7 of this Guide). The application must set out what order is sought, and why a costs capping order should be made. The application should be accompanied by a budget setting out the costs and disbursements incurred by the applicant to date, and the costs and disbursements which the applicant is likely to incur in the future conduct of the proceedings.[2]

25.3.6   The Court may fix directions for the hearing of the application (see paragraph 13.2.3 for listing).

25.3.7   Any application to vary a costs capping order must be made by application on notice to the other party or parties.[3]

26.   APPEALS

26.1   APPEALS IN CIVIL CASES

1BA-151   **26.1.1**   All parties have a right to seek to appeal to the Court of Appeal (Civil Division) against a substantive decision or against refusal of permission to apply for judicial review. Permission to appeal is required.

26.2   CHALLENGING THE GRANT OF PERMISSION

1BA-152   **26.2.1**   Where permission to bring a judicial review has been granted:

26.2.1.1   Neither the defendant nor any other person served with the claim form may apply to the Administrative Court to set aside an order giving permission to bring a judicial review.[4]

26.2.1.2   If the defendant or another interested party has not been served with the claim form, they may apply to the Administrative Court to set aside permission, but the power to set aside permission is exercised sparingly and only in a very plain case.[5]

26.3   APPEALS AGAINST THE REFUSAL OF PERMISSION

1BA-153   **26.3.1**   Where permission has been refused after a hearing in the Administrative Court, the person seeking permission may apply to the Court of Appeal.[6]

---

[1] CPR 3.19(1), and see PD 3F
[2] CPR 3.20 and PD 3F
[3] CPR 3.21
[4] CPR 54.13
[5] See *R v Secretary of State ex p Chinoy* (1992) 4 Admin L Rep 457
[6] CPR 52.15

26.3.2 Where permission has been refused on the papers and there is no right to renewal, the person can apply to the Court of Appeal for permission to appeal, and that application will be determined on paper without a hearing.[1]

26.3.3 An appeal (including any application for permission to appeal) against the refusal of permission to apply for judicial review must be lodged with the Court of Appeal within 7 days of the date of the decision, or within the time limit ordered by the Administrative Court.[2] This is also the case where permission has been refused and the right to renewal has been removed (cases where the Upper Tribunal is the defendant (see paragraph 8.7 of this Guide) and totally without merit cases (see paragraph 8.3 of this Guide)),[3] although in these cases the 7 days begins from the date of service of the order, not the date of the decision.[4]

26.3.4 The Court of Appeal may, instead of giving permission to appeal, give permission to apply for judicial review, in which event the case will proceed in the Administrative Court unless the Court of Appeal orders otherwise.

26.4 APPEALS AGAINST SUBSTANTIVE DECISIONS

26.4.1 Permission to appeal against the Court's decision following the substantive hearing is required and it can be granted by the Administrative Court at the hearing where the decision being appealed is made. The application must be made at the hearing; there is no provision to allow for it to be made once the hearing has concluded. The Court may adjourn the question of permission to another date or to be considered on written representations, but it must make an order doing so at the time of the hearing.[5] **1BA-154**

26.4.2 In the event that permission to appeal is refused by the Administrative Court, a second application can be made to the Court of Appeal itself in the appellant's notice (form N161).[6] The application for permission can be made to the Court of Appeal even if permission to appeal was not sought from the Administrative Court.

26.4.3 An appeal (including any application for permission to appeal) against a substantive decision of the Administrative Court must be lodged with the Court of Appeal within 21 days of the date of the decision,[7] or within the time limit ordered by the Administrative Court.

26.4.4 Permission to appeal will only be granted if the Court finds that the appeal would have a real prospect of success or there is some other compelling reason why the appeal should be heard.[8]

26.4.5 Further information on appeals to the Court of Appeal can be provided by the Civil Appeals Office (see annex 1 for contact details).

26.5 APPEALS IN CRIMINAL CASES

26.5.1 There is no right of appeal from the Administrative Court to the Court of Appeal in cases relating to any criminal cause or matter.[9] **1BA-155**

26.5.2 The only route of appeal from the Administrative Court is to the Supreme Court. An appeal to the Supreme Court is only possible where two conditions are satisfied. First, the Administrative Court must certify that the case raises a point of law of general public importance.[10] The second is that permission to appeal must be granted. An application for permission to appeal to the Supreme Court and for a certificate of a point of law must be made to the Administrative Court within 28 days of the decision challenged or the date when reasons for the decision are given.[11]

26.5.3 The application for a certificate of a point of law and for permission to appeal may be made in the same application. The procedure is the same as the interim applications procedure (see paragraph 12.7 of this Guide).

26.5.4 The right of appeal to the Supreme Court applies only to substantive decisions. There is no appeal from the decision of the Court if permission to apply for judicial review is refused.[12]

26.5.5 Further information on appeals to the Supreme Court can be obtained from the Supreme Court (see annex 1 for contact details).

---

[1] CPR 52.15(1A)
[2] CPR 52.15(2)
[3] CPR 52.15(1A)
[4] CPR 52.15(2)
[5] CPR 52.3(2)(a)
[6] CPR 52.3(3)
[7] CPR 52.4(2)(b)
[8] CPR 52.3(6)
[9] s.18(1)(a) of the Senior Courts Act 1981
[10] s.1(2) of the Administration of Justice Act 1960
[11] s.2(1) of the Administration of Justice Act 1960
[12] *Re Poh* [1983] 1 All ER 287

26.6 APPEALING CASE MANAGEMENT ORDERS

1BA-156   **26.6.1**   The principles applied above at paragraphs 26.1 – 26.4 (for civil cases) and 26.5 (for criminal cases) apply for appeals against case management orders, although paragraph 15.5 of this Guide on reconsideration of interim orders made without a hearing should be considered before appealing.

26.6.2   The time limit for appealing remains 21 days in civil cases, but the proceedings in the Administrative Court will not necessarily await the decision of the Court of Appeal. If the parties wish the Administrative Court proceedings to be stayed pending the decision of the Court of Appeal they must apply for a stay (see paragraph 12.8 of this Guide).

26.6.3   Permission to appeal is generally granted more sparingly in appeals against case management orders as not only will the Court consider whether the appeal would have a real prospect of success or there is some other compelling reason why the appeal should be heard, but it will generally also consider the significance of the decision, the costs involved in appealing, the delay or disruption likely to be caused to the Administrative Court proceedings, and whether the point would be better dealt with at or after the substantive hearing.[1]

26.7 APPEALS AGAINST AN INTERIM ORDER MADE BY THE MASTER

1BA-157   **26.7.1**   An appeal against the order of the Master made at an oral hearing may be appealed to a High Court Judge.[2] If the Master's decision is made on the papers the provisions on reconsideration at paragraph 15.5 of this Guide should be considered.

26.7.2   The application for permission to appeal must be filed on form N161 and lodged with the Administrative Court Office. The parties should also consider the guidance in paragraphs 26.1 – 26.4 above, which, save for any references to the Court of Appeal, would equally apply to appeals against the Master's decisions.

Annex 1

Contact Details

1BA-158   The Administrative Court Offices
Website: *www.gov.uk/courts-tribunals/administrative-court*

Birmingham

The Administrative Court Office
Birmingham Civil and Family Justice Hearing Centre
Priory Courts
33 Bull Street
Birmingham
West Midlands
B4 6DS
DX 701987 Birmingham 7

Telephone Number: 0121 681 4441
General Email: administrativecourtoffice.birmingham@hmcts.x.gsi.gov.uk
Skeleton Arguments Email: administrativecourtofficebirmingham.skeletonarguments@hmcts.x.gsi.gov.uk

Leeds

The Administrative Court Office
Leeds Combined Court Centre
The Courthouse
1 Oxford Row
Leeds
West Yorkshire
LS1 3BG
DX: 703016 Leeds 6

Telephone Number: 0113 306 2578

---

[1] CPR PD 52A paragraph 4.6
[2] CPR PD 52A paragraph 4.3

General Email: administrativecourtoffice.leeds@hmcts.x.gsi.gov.uk
Skeleton Arguments Email: administrativecourtofficeleeds.skeletonarguments@hmcts.x.gsi.gov.
uk

London

The Administrative Court Office
Royal Courts of Justice
Strand
London
WC2A 2LL
DX 44450 Strand

Telephone Number: 020 7947 6655
General Email: administrativecourtoffice.generaloffice@hmcts.x.gsi.gov.uk
Skeleton Arguments Email: administrativecourtofficelondon.skeletonarguments@hmcts.x.gsi.
gov.uk

Manchester

The Administrative Court Office
Manchester Civil and Family Justice Centre
1 Bridge Street West
Manchester
M60 9DJ
DX 724783 Manchester 44

Telephone Number: 0161 240 5313
General Email: administrativecourtoffice.manchester@hmcts.x.gsi.gov.uk
Skeleton Arguments Email: administrativecourtofficemanchester.skeletonarguments@hmcts.x.
gsi.gov.uk

Wales and Western Circuit

The Administrative Court Office
Cardiff Civil Justice Centre,
2 Park Street,
Cardiff,
CF10 1ET
DX 99500 Cardiff 6

Telephone Number: 029 20376460
General Email: administrativecourtoffice.cardiff@hmcts.x.gsi.gov.uk
Skeleton Arguments Email: administrativecourtofficecardiff.skeletonarguments@hmcts.x.gsi.gov.
uk

Upper Tribunal (Administrative Appeals Chamber)

Upper Tribunal (Administrative Appeals Chamber)
5th Floor Rolls Building
7 Rolls Buildings,
Fetter Lane
London
EC4A 1NL
DX 160042 STRAND 4

Email: adminappeals@hmcts.gsi.gov.uk
Telephone Number: 020 7071 5662

Upper Tribunal (Immigration and Asylum Chamber)
For the UT(IAC) – Judicial Reviews Only:
For London:

Upper Tribunal (Immigration and Asylum Chamber)
IA Field House
15 Breams Buildings

London
EC4A 1DZ

For UT(IAC) judicial reviews in Birmingham, Cardiff, Leeds, or Manchester, see the contact details for the Administrative Court Office in that area above.

For UT(IAC) – All non judicial review cases:
Lodging Appeals:

Upper Tribunal (Immigration and Asylum Chamber)
IA Field House
15 Breams Buildings
London
EC4A 1DZ

Unless advised otherwise, all other correspondence to:

Upper Tribunal (Immigration and Asylum Chamber)
Arnhem Support Centre
PO Box 6987
Leicester
LE1 6ZX

Fax: 0116 249 4130
Customer Service Centre (Enquiry Unit) telephone: 0300 123 1711

Senior Courts Costs Office

Senior Courts Costs Office
Royal Courts of Justice
Strand
London
WC2A 2LL
DX 44454 Strand

Telephone Number: 020 7947 6469/ 6404 / 7818
Email: SCCO@hmcts.gsi.gov.uk
Website: *https://www.gov.uk/courts-tribunals/senior-courts-costs-office*

Court of Appeal (Civil Division)

Civil Appeals Office
Room E307
Royal Courts of Justice
Strand
London
WC2A 2LL
DX: 44450 Strand
Telephone Number: 020 7947 7677

Supreme Court

The Supreme Court
Parliament Square
London
SW1P 3BD
DX 157230 Parliament Sq 4
Telephone Number: 020 7960 1500 or 1900
Facsimile: 020 7960 190

ANNEX 2

FORMS AND FEES

Act / Application	Form*	Fee**	Ref**
Application for permission to apply for judicial review	N461 (Judicial Review Claim Form)	£154.00	1.9(a)
Reconsideration of permission at an oral hearing	86b	£385.00	1.9(aa)
Continuing judicial review after permission has been granted Any fee paid under 1.9(aa) is deducted	-	£770.00	1.9(b)
Appeal	N161 (Appellant's Notice)	£240.00	2.4
Acknowledgment of Service	N462 (JR)	£0.00	-
Interim Application	N244 (Application Notice)	£255.00	2.6
Consent Order	N244 & Consent Order	£100.00	2.7
Discontinuance	N279 (Notice of Discontinuance)	£0.00	-
Urgent Consideration (within 48 hours of lodging claim)	N463 (Application for Urgent Consideration)	£255.00 (unless made when lodging when the fee is £0.00)	2.6

1BA-159

*= current forms can be found at *www.gov.uk/courts-tribunals/administrative-court*
**=schedule 1, Civil Proceedings Fee Order 2008 (as amended). The fees above were correct on the 25 July 2016.

ANNEX 3

ADDRESSES FOR SERVICE OF CENTRAL GOVERNMENT DEPARTMENTS[1]

Government Department	Solicitor for Service
Advisory, Conciliation and Arbitration Service, Board of Trade, Cabinet Office, Commissioners for the Reduction of National Debt, Crown Prosecution Service, Department for Business, Innovation and Skills, Department for Communities and Local Government, Department for Culture, Media and Sport, Department for Education, Department of Energy and Climate Change, Department for Environment, Food and Rural Affairs, Department for Health, Department for International Development, Department for Transport, Department for Work and Pensions, Foreign and Commonwealth Office, Forestry Commissioners, Government Actuary's Department, Government Equalities Office, Health and Safety Executive, Her Majesty's Chief Inspector of Education and Training in Wales, Her Majesty's Treasury, Home Office, Ministry of Defence, Ministry of Justice, National Savings and Investments, Northern Ireland Office, Office for Standards in Education, Children's Services and Skills, Ordnance Survey, Privy Council Office, Public Works Loan Board, Revenue and Customs Prosecutions Office, Royal Mint, Serious Fraud Office, Statistics Board (UK Statistics Authority), The National Archives, Wales Office (Office of the Secretary of State for Wales)	The Government Legal Department, One Kemble Street, London, WC2B 4TS, DX 123242 Kingsway

1BA-160

[1] Taken from published list by Sir Francis Maude, Cabinet Secretary, on the 26 October 2012. Also found at annex 2 to CPR PD 66. The above table has been amended from the 2012 published version to add the Department of Health and the Department for Work and Pensions to the Government Legal Department's remit, thus reflecting the current position for those departments. It also updates by replacing the Treasury Solicitor's Department with the Government Legal Department.

1BA-160

Government Department	Solicitor for Service
Crown Estate Commissioners	Legal Director, The Crown Estate, 16 New Burlington Place, London, W1S 2HX
Export Credits Guarantee Department	The General Counsel, Export Credits Guarantee Department, P.O. Box 2200, 2 Exchange Tower, Harbour Exchange Square, London, E14 9GS
Food Standards Agency	Director of Legal Services, Food Standards Agency, Aviation House, 125 Kingsway, London, WC2B 6NH
Gas and Electricity Markets Authority	Senior Legal Director, Office of Gas and Electricity Markets, 9 Millbank, London, SW1P 3GE
Her Majesty's Revenue and Customs	General Counsel and Solicitor to Her Majesty's Revenue and Customs, HM Revenue and Customs, South West Wing Bush House, Strand London, WC2B 4RD
Office of Fair Trading	General Counsel, Fleetbank House, 2-6 Salisbury Square, London, EC4Y 8JX
Office of Qualifications and Examinations Regulation (Ofqual)	Head of Legal Ofqual, 1410 Spring Place, Herald Avenue, Coventry Business Park, Coventry, West Midlands, CV5 6UB
Office of Rail Regulation	Director of Legal Services ORR, One Kemble Street, London, WC2B 4AN
Water Services Regulation Authority (OFWAT)	Director of Legal Services and Board Secretary, Water Services Regulation Authority (OFWAT), Centre City Tower, 7 Hill Street, Birmingham, B5 4UA
Welsh Assembly Government	The Director of Legal Services to the Welsh Assembly Government, Cathays Park, Cardiff, CF10 3NQ

SECTION 2 SPECIALIST PROCEEDINGS
SECTION 2A COMMERCIAL COURT

PART 58—COMMERCIAL COURT

Related sources

2A-3 *Replace "The Admiralty and Commercial Courts Guide 9th edn 2011 (updated January 2016), (see para.2A-39 et seq)." with:*

- The Admiralty and Commercial Courts Guide 9th edn 2011 (updated March 2016), (see para.2A-39 et seq).

PRACTICE DIRECTION 58—COMMERCIAL COURT

Note

After "been updated in", replace "January" with:
  March

2A-39.0

ADMIRALTY AND COMMERCIAL COURTS GUIDE

APPENDIX 5

FORMS OF FREEZING INJUNCTION AND SEARCH ORDER
adapted for use in the Commercial Court

** FREEZING INJUNCTION **

PENAL NOTICE

FREEZING INJUNCTION

[FOR EITHER FORM OF INJUNCTION]

Replace paragraph (where the citation for JSC BTA Bank v Ablyazov in the first footnote has changed) with:
6. Paragraph 5 applies to all the Respondent's assets[1] whether or not they are in his own name, whether they are solely or jointly owned [and whether the Respondent is interested in them legally, beneficially or otherwise][2]. For the purpose of this order the Respondent's assets include any asset which he has the power, directly or indirectly, to dispose of or deal with as if it were his own. The Respondent is to be regarded as having such power if a third party holds or controls the asset in accordance with his direct or indirect instructions.

2A-162

ADDRESSES AND CONTACT DETAILS

Replace paragraph with:
  The individual telephone and fax numbers are as follows:

2A-215

The Admiralty Marshal:
Tel: 020 7947 6111
Fax: 020 7947 7671

The Admiralty & Commercial Registry:
Tel: 020 7947 6112
Fax: 020 7947 6245
DX 160040 Strand 4

The Admiralty & Commercial Court Listing Office:
Tel: 020 7947 6826
Fax: 020 7947 7670
DX 160040 Strand 4

The Secretary to the Commercial Court Committee:

---

[1] In *JSC BTA Bank v Ablyazov* [2015] UKSC 64; [2015] 1 W.L.R. 4754; [2016] 1 All E.R. 608; [2016] 1 All E.R. (Comm) 97; [2015] 2 Lloyd's Rep. 546 the Supreme Court held that the proceeds of a loan agreement were "assets" within the definition contained in the standard Commercial Court form of freezing order. Under that definition, the term "assets" included any asset which a defendant had power, directly or indirectly, to dispose of, or deal with as if it were his own. A loan agreement gave a borrower the power to dispose of or deal with the assets as if they were his own and a borrower who instructed a lender to pay the lender's money to a third party was dealing with the lender's assets as if they were his own.

[2] Whether this wider wording should be included in relation to the Order and/or the provision of information will be considered on a case by case basis—see generally *JSC BTA Bank v Kythreotis and Others* [2010] EWCA Civ 1436.

Mr Joseph Quinn
Tel: 020 7947 6826
Fax: 020 7947 7670
DX 160040 Strand 4[1]

SECTION 2B   MERCANTILE COURTS

MERCANTILE COURT GUIDE

APPENDIX A

COURT ADDRESSES AND OTHER INFORMATION

1.   LONDON AND SOUTH EAST

Judge

Replace "Clerk—Adham Harker" with:
2B-35   Clerk—Adam Wilcox

Replace "Email: Adham.Harker@hmcts.gsi.gov.uk" with:
Email: adam.wilcox@hmcts.gsi.gov.uk

2.   MIDLANDS (BIRMINGHAM)

Judge

Replace "His Honour Judge Brown QC (Court 5 on 2nd floor)" with:
2B-36   Acting Mercantile Judge HHJ Martin McKenna (Court 5 on 2nd floor)

Users' Committee

Replace "Chair: HHJ Brown QC" with:
Chair: Acting Mercantile Judge HHJ Martin McKenna

3.   NORTH EAST (LEEDS)

Judges

2B-37   *Delete "His Honour Judge Kaye QC".*

4.   NORTH EAST (NEWCASTLE UPON TYNE)

Judges

Replace paragraph with:

2B-38
His Honour Judge Raeside QC
His Honour Judge Behrens
Clerk—Richard Marsland
Email: richard.marsland@hmcts.gsi.gov.uk
Tel: 0191 2012029
Fax: 0191 2012001

---

[1] The Secretary to the Commercial Court Committee is now Joseph Quinn. Contact details are unchanged.

5. NORTH WEST (LIVERPOOL)

Judges

Replace paragraph with:

Her Honour Judge Moulder **2B-39**
His Honour Judge Bird

6. NORTH WEST (MANCHESTER)

Judges and Listing

Replace paragraph with:

Her Honour Judge Moulder **2B-40**
His Honour Judge Bird
Manager of Mercantile Listing—Lesley Armstrong
Clerk to Mercantile Judges: 0161 240 5305
Email: manchester.mercantile@hmcts.gsi.gov.uk
Fax (Goldfax): 01264 785034

7. SOUTH WEST (BRISTOL)

Address

Replace paragraph with:

The Bristol Civil and Family Justice Centre **2B-41**
2 Redcliff Street
Bristol England
BS1 6GR
DX 95903 Bristol 3

Judge and Listing

Replace paragraph with:

His Honour Judge Havelock-Allan QC (Court 12 on the 3rd floor)
Specialist Listing Officers—Debbie Thal-Jantzen and Amy Smallcombe
Telephone number 0117 366 4866 and 4833
Email: bristolmercantilelisting@hmcts.gsi.gov.uk
General switchboard: 0117 366 4860
Fax: 0117 366 4801 (not a dedicated fax so clearly mark "Mercantile Court")
Dedicated email: bristolmercantilelisting@hmcts.gsi.gov.uk

8. WALES (CARDIFF)

Judge

Replace paragraph with:

His Honour Judge Keyser QC **2B-42**
Clerk—Barry Sharples
Email: barry.sharples@hmcts.gsi.gov.uk
Tel: 02920 376411
Fax: 02920 376475
Listing Clerk—Amanda Barrago
Email: amanda.barrago@hmcts.gsi.gov.uk
Tel: 029 20376412
Fax: 029 20376475

9. WALES (MOLD)

Delete paragraph "Address".

Change title of paragraph "Postal Address" to: **2B-43**

Address

Judge and Listing

Replace paragraph with:

His Honour Judge Keyser QC
Listing: Clerk—Beth Sear
Tel: 01978 317406
Fax: 01978 358213
Email: northwalescivillisting@wrexham.countycourt.gsi.gov.uk

SECTION 2E   ARBITRATION PROCEEDINGS

PART 62—ARBITRATION CLAIMS

Add new paragraph 2E–6.1:

Family Court claims

2E-6.1   Pending rule/practice direction amendments special provision has been made for arbitration claims arising out of family court cases. On 23 November 2015 the President of the Family Court, Sir James Munby, issued *Practice Direction (Family Court: Interface with Arbitration)* [2016] 1 W.L.R. 59. This concerns the interface between the Family Court and arbitrations conducted in accordance with the provisions of the Arbitration Act 1996 where the parties to a post-relationship breakdown financial dispute have agreed to submit issues for decision by an arbitrator whose award is to be binding upon them. The text of the guidance is at:
https://www.judiciary.gov.uk/publications/practice-guidance-arbitration-in-the-family-court/ [Accessed 17 May 2016].

Arbitration Act 1996

Onus of showing that claim should proceed

Replace the second paragraph (where the citation for Salford Estates (No.2) Ltd v Altomart Ltd has changed) with:

2E-112   In *Wealands v C.L.C. Contractors Ltd* [1998] C.L.C. 808, the court held on an application by a sub-contractor for third party proceedings against it by the contractor to be stayed under s.9 of the Arbitration Act 1996 that despite the disadvantages of the claim against the third party going to arbitration (if the plaintiff did not join the third party as a defendant) the 1996 Act gave priority to party autonomy and entitled the third party as of right to the stay which is sought (affirmed [1999] 2 Lloyd's Rep. 739, CA. However, in *Salford Estates (No.2) Ltd v Altomart Ltd* [2014] EWCA Civ 1575; [2015] Ch. 589; [2015] 3 W.L.R. 491; [2015] B.C.C. 306, the Court of Appeal held that where a number of disputes concerning liability for the payment of service charges and insurance rent were referred to arbitration under the provisions of a lease, the Arbitration Act 1996 s.9 did not apply to a winding-up petition presented by the lessor based on the lessee company's inability to pay its debts, because the substance of the dispute was the existence of a particular debt mentioned in the petition.

Application of section

Add new paragraph after the quotation:

2E-167   In *HC Trading Malta Ltd v Tradeland Commodities SL* [2016] EWHC 1279 (Comm) HHJ Waksman QC held that where a party intended to commence arbitration on the basis of the disputed existence of a contract containing an arbitration clause, it would be wrong in principle for the court to intervene and entertain an application for a declaration that the parties had entered into a binding arbitration agreement; it could not have been the legislative intention that a party to a disputed arbitration agreement could obtain the decision of the courts on its existence without being subject to the restrictions contained in s.32 by the simple step of not appointing an abitrator.

Unless otherwise agreed ... the following provisions apply

Add new paragraph at end:

2E-184   In *Pearl Petroleum Co Ltd v Kurdistan Regional Government of Iraq* [2015] EWHC 3361 (Comm) Burton J held that when making a peremptory order under s.41(5), arbitrators did not have to state that the order was necessary for the "proper and expeditious conduct of the arbitral proceedings". Section 41(5) could be invoked for a failure to comply with "any" order of the tribunal and was not to be construed only in the context of s.41(1) of the Act.

Scope of section 47

Replace the second paragraph with:

In *Sucafina SA v Nicola Rotenberg* [2012] EWCA Civ 637; [2012] 2 Lloyd's Rep. 54; [2012] 2 All **2E-207** E.R. (Comm) 952; [2013] Bus. L.R. 158; [2012] 2 C.L.C. 203 the Court of Appeal upheld the decision of Eder J that a failure to pay arbitral fees did not affect the nature of two interim awards as awards which were final and binding on those issues with which they dealt. In *Enterprise Insurance Co Plc v U-Drive Solutions (Gibraltar) Ltd* [2016] EWHC 1301 (QB) Judge Moulder QC held that an arbitral tribunal's refusal to strike out a claim was not finally determinative of the claim and was not an "award" for the purposes of the Arbitration Act 1996 s.68 and s.69. The court therefore had no jurisdiction to hear an appeal against such a decision under s.68 or s.69.

Note

Replace the third paragraph (where the citation for Emirates Trading Agency LLC v Sociedade de Fomento Industrial Private Ltd has changed) with:

Arbitrators have to be appointed in compliance with any applicable procedure for appointment. **2E-256** Any irregularity in appointment invalidates the arbitration. There is no room in arbitration for the common law doctrine which can sometimes validate the acts of an apparent or reputed judge. See *Sumukan Ltd v Commonwealth Secretariat* [2007] EWCA Civ 1148; [2008] Bus L.R. 858; [2008] 2 All E.R. (Comm); [2008] 1 Lloyd's Rep. 40, CA; [2007] 2 C.L.C. 821; *Dallah Estate and Tourism Holding Co v Ministry of Religious Affairs of the Government of Pakistan* [2010] UKSC 46; [2011] 1 A.C. 763; [2011] 1 All E.R. 485; [2011] 1 All E.R. (Comm) 383; [2010] 2 Lloyd's Rep. 691; [2010] 2 C.L.C. 793. In *Emirates Trading Agency LLC v Sociedade de Fomento Industrial Private Ltd* [2015] EWHC 1452 (Comm); [2016] 1 All E.R. (Comm) 517; [2015] 2 Lloyd's Rep. 487 Popplewell J held that an application under this section to set aside a final merits award for lack of jurisdiction should be refused where the tribunal had already made a partial award on jurisdiction which was binding and had not been challenged.

"On the ground of serious irregularity"

In the first paragraph, after "813, Flaux J.", delete ", Flaux J.". **2E-262**

After the second paragraph (beginning "In BV Scheepswerf Damen Gorinchem v Marine Institute"), add as a new paragraph:

In *Larus Australia v Agrocorp International Pte Ltd* [2015] EWHC 3774 (Comm) Knowles J rejected a submission that arbitrations had committed misconduct within s.68(2)(a) where they did not invite a defendant to make an application under s.41 of the Act having considered the point and concluded that had such an application been made they would have concluded that the delay was not inexcusable.

Replace the eighth paragraph (where the citation for Maass v Musion Events Ltd has changed) with:

In cases under s.68(2)(d), there are four questions for the court: (i) whether the relevant point or argument was an "issue" within the meaning of the sub-section; (ii) if so, whether the issue was "put" to the tribunal; (iii) if so, whether the tribunal failed to deal with it; and (iv) if so, whether that failure has caused substantial injustice. Per Andrew Smith J in *Petrochemical Industries Co v Dow Chemical* [2012] EWHC 2739 (Comm); [2012] 2 Lloyd's Rep 691 at [15], *Primera Maritime Hellas v Jiangsum Eastern Heavy Industry* [2013] EWHC 3066 (Comm); [2014] 1 Lloyd's Rep. 255; [2013] 2 C.L.C. 901; [2014] 1 All E.R. (Comm) 813 Flaux J., *Transition Feeds LLP (formerly Advanced Liquid Feeds LLP) v Itochu Europe Plc* [2013] EWHC 3629 (Comm); [2013] 2 C.L.C. 920 Field J. The test for whether such an irregularity caused, or would cause, a substantial injustice was whether the irregularity caused the arbitrator to reach a conclusion which, but for the irregularity, he might not have reached, as long as the alternative was reasonably arguable: *Maass v Musion Events Ltd* [2015] EWHC 1346 (Comm); [2016] 1 All E.R. (Comm) 292; [2015] 2 Lloyd's Rep. 383 (Andrew Smith J). For there to be a serious irregularity under s.68(2)(d) because the arbitrators failed to deal with an issue put to them, it was necessary to establish that they had failed to deal at all with a fundamental issue which was essential to the decision: *Abuja International Hotels Ltd v Meridien SAS* [2012] EWHC 87 (Comm); [2012] 1 Lloyd's Rep. 461, Hamblen J. See also *Fidelity Management SA v Myriad International Holdings BV* [2005] EWHC 1193 (Comm); [2005] 2 All E.R. (Comm) 312. A failure to address central issue by GAFA constituted a serious irregularity within s.68(2)(d), see *Ascot Commodities NV v Olam International Ltd* [2002] C.L.C 277. An issue is not "put to" the arbitrator when the question of fact is not supported by any evidence sufficient to require a conclusion and without a relevant factual finding, the point of law is of hypothetical interest only: *Cordoba Holdings v Ballymore Properties* [2011] EWHC 1636 (Ch) per Morritt C. Likewise a failure to make a declaratory award thereby depriving a party of a set off will not be a serious irregularity where it was clear to the parties that a money award was to be made, and the set off would have come too late: *L v R* [2012] EWHC 2894 (Comm), Hamblen J.

Appeal to the High Court

To the end of the third paragraph, add:

2E-266   However in *Enterprise Insurance Co Plc v U-Drive Solutions (Gibraltar) Ltd* [2016] EWHC 1301 (QB) Judge Moulder QC held that the consent of the parties to an appeal on a strike out decision, which was not as a matter of law an award, could not confer jurisdiction on the Court.

Appeals to the Court of Appeal

Replace the last paragraph (where the citation for Michael Wilson & Partners Ltd v Emmott has changed) with:

2E-268   In *CGU International Insurance plc v Astra Zeneca Insurance Co Ltd* [2006] EWCA Civ 1340; [2007] 1 Lloyd's Rep. 142; [2007] 1 All E.R. (Comm) 501; [2006] 2 C.L.C. 441, and *Philip Hanby Ltd v Clarke* [2013] EWCA Civ 647, March 20, 2013, CA the court has held that there is a residual discretion to permit an appeal despite the judge's refusal of leave where the refusal could be challenged on the ground that the decision had been arrived at as the result of some unfair or improper process such that that decision could not properly be called a decision at all or on the ground of unfairness under art.6 of the European Convention on Human Rights. Courts would however not allow such power which existed to ensure that injustice was avoided to become itself an unfair instrument for subverting statute and undermining the process of arbitration. See too *ASM Shipping Ltd of India v TTMI Ltd of England* [2006] EWCA Civ 1341; [2007] 1 Lloyd's Rep. 136; [2006] 2 C.L.C. 471 (residual discretion not involved; no overarching principle in Human Rights Convention that an award tainted by apparent bias must be set aside: application of margin of appreciation in domestic court). The recent cases of *Philip Hanby* (above) and *Bunge SA v Kyla Shipping Co Ltd* [2013] EWCA Civ 734; [2013] 3 All E.R. 1006; [2013] 2 All E.R. (Comm) 577; [2013] 2 Lloyd's Rep. 463 confirm that this is "an extraordinarily high hurdle to surmount" (per Longmore LJ in the latter case) and has never, to date, been surmounted. An appeal from the High Court to the Court of Appeal based on this "residual jurisdiction" is an "appeal" for the purposes of s.16(1) of the Senior Courts Act 1981 (para.9A-57 below), and it follows from that that such an appeal is an appeal for which permission to appeal is required by r.52.3 (*Michael Wilson & Partners Ltd v Emmott* [2015] EWCA Civ 1285; [2016] 1 W.L.R. 857).

Note

Add new paragraph at end:

2E-278   It will only be in exceptional cases that a court faced with proceedings which require it to determine the jurisdiction of arbitrators will be justified in exercising its inherent power to stay those proceedings to enable the arbitrators themselves to decide the question: *Albon (t/a NA Carriage Co) v Naza Motor Trading Sdn Bhd* [2007] EWHC 665 (Ch) approved *Hashwani v OMV Maurice Energy Ltd* [2015] EWCA Civ 1171.

Section 80(5)

Replace with:

2E-292   Paragraph (2)(a) of CPR r.3.1 (The court's general powers of court management) states that the court may "extend or shorten the time for compliance with any rule, practice direction or court order (even of the application is made after the time for compliance has expired)" (for commentary, see Vol.1, para.3.1.2). The manner in which this discretion should be exercised for the purpose of extending time limits for proceedings under the 1996 Act to which s.80(5) relates (in particular in ss.67 to 69) was considered by Colman J in *Kalmneft JSC v Glencore International AG* [2002] 1 All E.R. 76; [2002] 1 Lloyd's Rep.128. In *Nagusina Naviera v Allied Maritime Inc* [2002] EWCA Civ 1147; [2003] 2 C.L.C. 1, CA, the Court of Appeal was referred to the guidance given by Colman J and did not dissent from it. Since then that guidance given by Colman J has been followed by the Commercial Court; see *The Joanna V* [2003] EWHC 1655 (Comm); [2003] 2 Lloyd's Rep. 617 (Thomas J); *DDT Trucks of North America Ltd v DDT Holdings Ltd* [2007] EWHC 1542 (Comm); [2007] 2 Lloyd's Rep. 213 (Cooke J), *The Amer Energy (Note)* [2009] 1 Lloyd's Rep. 293 (Flaux J), *Broda Agro Trade (Cyprus) Ltd v Alfred C. Toepfer International GmbH* [2009] EWHC 3318 (Comm); [2010] 1 Lloyd's Rep. 533 (Teare J) and *Terna Bahrain Holding Company WLL v Al Shamsi* [2012] EWHC 3283 (Comm); [2013] 1 Lloyd's Rep. 86, where the principles derived from this line of authority were summarised. However in *S v A* [2016] EWHC 846 (Comm); [2016] 1 Lloyd's Rep. 604 Eder J questioned whether this approach was consistent with the principles in given the recent decisions of the Court of Appeal in *Mitchell v News Group Newspapers Ltd* [2013] EWCA Civ 1537 and *Denton v TH White Ltd* [2014] EWCA Civ 906.

Subsection (5)

Replace with:

2E-361   On an application to adjourn an application for leave to enforce a foreign arbitration award because of a legal challenge to the validity of the award in a foreign jurisdiction, the court should consider the strength or otherwise of the argument for setting aside the award and the ease or difficulty of enforcing the award if an order for security was not made, together with any other relevant considerations (*Soleh Boneh International Ltd v Government of the Republic of Uganda* [1993] 2 Lloyd's Rep. 208). See also *Dowans Holdings SA v Tanzania Electric Supply Co Ltd* [2011] EWHC 1957 (Comm); [2012] 1 All E.R. (Comm) 820; [2011] 2 Lloyd's Rep. 475 and *IPCO (Nigeria) v Nigerian National Petroleum* [2015] EWCA Civ 1144; [2016] 1 Lloyd's Rep. 5 where the Court of Appeal considered the circumstances in which a decision to adjourn an enforcement decision in the face of allegations of fraud will be made. In a supplementary judgment [2015] EWCA Civ 1145; [2016] 1 Lloyd's Rep. 36 the Court rejected the argument that there was no application for security on the facts and the court therefore lacked jurisdiction.

Replace s.105(6) with:

PART IV

GENERAL PROVISIONS

Meaning of "the court": jurisdiction of High Court and county court

(6)   An order under this section for Northern Ireland shall be a statutory rule for the purposes of the [S.I. 1979/1573 (N.I. 12).] Statutory Rules (Northern Ireland) Order 1979 which shall be subject to negative resolution (within the meaning of section 41(6) of the Interpretation Act (Northern Ireland) 1954). **2E-364**

Note

Add new paragraph at end:
Subsection (6) amended by the Northern Ireland Act 1998 (Devolution of Policing and Justice Functions) Order 2010 (SI 2010/976) Sch.18(1) para.50(2), with effect from 12 April 2010 subject to transitional provisions specified in SI 2010/976 art.28. **2E-365**

SECTION 2F   INTELLECTUAL PROPERTY PROCEEDINGS

PART 63—INTELLECTUAL PROPERTY CLAIMS

V.   Intellectual Property Enterprise Court

Replace r.63.19 with:

Enterprise judges and District Judges[1]

63.19—(1)   Subject to paragraph (2), proceedings in the Intellectual Property Enterprise Court will be dealt with by an enterprise judge. **2F-17.12**

(1A)   [Omitted]

(2)   Unless the court otherwise orders, the following matters will be dealt with by a District Judge—

(a)   allocation of claims to the small claims track or multi-track in accordance with rule 63.27(3);

(b)   claims allocated to the small claims track; and

(c)   all proceedings for the enforcement of any financial element of an Intellectual Property Enterprise Court judgment.

(3)   For the purposes of the Practice Direction 52A—Appeals: General Provisions, a decision of a District Judge shall be treated as a decision by a District Judge hearing a claim in the County Court. An appeal from such a decision shall be heard by an enterprise judge.

---

[1] Amended by the Civil Procedure (Amendment) Rules 2014 (SI 2014/407) and the Civil Procedure (Amendment No.3) Rules 2016 (SI 2016/788).

SECTION 2FA FINANCIAL LIST

PART 63A—FINANCIAL LIST

Editorial introduction

Replace the first paragraph with:

2FA-1.1 As is explained in the CPR Glossary, for administrative purposes, cases are allocated to different "lists" depending on the subject-matter of the case and may have their own procedures and judges. CPR r.2.3 (Interpretation) para.(2) states that a reference in the CPR to a "specialist list" is a reference to a list that has been designated as such by a rule or practice direction (see further Vol.1 para.2.3.14). Part 63A (rr.63A.1 to 63A.4) was inserted in the CPR by the Civil Procedure (Amendment No.4) Rules 2015 (SI 2015/1569). Rule 63A.2 creates a new "specialist list" known as the Financial List. Part 63A is supplemented by Practice Direction 63AA (Financial List) published in CPR Update 81 (August 2015). The rules and the Practice Direction came into effect on 1 October 2015.

The objectives of the Financial List

Replace the first paragraph with:

2FA-1.2 The Guide to the Financial List at para.1.2 states that its objectives include providing a forum whereby "cases which would benefit from being heard by judges with particular expertise in the financial markets or which raise issues of general importance to the financial markets are dealt with by judges with suitable expertise and experience." To this end, the Financial List seeks to allow the two parts of the High Court, the Commercial Court and Chancery Division, to work together to offer specialist judges on a range of financial service disputes. The dovetailing of the two parts of the High Court is reflected in the rules governing the Financial List in CPR 63A. These include that a "Financial List claim" (as defined under CPR r.63A.1(2)) shall be allocated to a designated "Financial List judge" who is a judge of the Chancery Division or the Commercial Court who has been authorised to try claims in the Financial List (CPR r.63A.4(2) and (3)), "Financial List claims" may be commenced in the Chancery Division or Commercial Court (CPR r.63A.2(1)) and that the Chancellor and the Judge in charge of the Commercial Court have joint overall responsibility for all "Financial List claims" (CPR r.63A.2(2)).

Replace the fourth paragraph with:

A "Financial List claim" is a claim exhibiting the features stated in r.63A.1(2). Such a claim "may be started in the Financial List" (r.63A.4(1)). The "administrative office" for a particular Financial List claim will be the Admiralty and Commercial Registry in the Royal Courts of Justice if it is commenced in the Commercial Court, or the Chancery Registry if it is commenced in the Chancery Division (Practice Direction 63AA para.1.4).

Sources

In the third paragraph, after "(ACCG). In that,", replace "Practice Direction 63AA" with:

2FA-1.3 the Guide

In the fourth paragraph (beginning "The objective of retaining the procedures"), after "answers is: https://www.judiciary.gov.uk/publications/financial-list-faq [Accesssed", replace "December 6, 2015" with

18 July 2016

In the last paragraph, replace "Royal Courts of Justice on October 21, 2015" with:

Rolls Building on 20 October 2015

Delete the sixth paragraph (beginning "In Part 30 (Transfer)").

Forms

Replace list with:

2FA-1.4
- **N1(CCFL)** Claim form (Part 7, Commercial Court Financial List)
- **N1(CHFL)** Claim form (Part 7, Chancery Division Financial List)
- **N1C(CCCHFL)** Notes for the defendant replying to a Part 7 claim form—Chancery Division / Commercial Court Financial List
- **N208(CCFL)** Claim form (Part 8, Commercial Court Financial List)
- **N208(CHFL)** Claim form (Part 8, Chancery Division Financial List)
- **N211(CCFL)** Claim form (Part 20, Commercial Court Financial List)
- **N211(CHFL)** Claim form (Part 20, Chancery Division Financial List)
- **N9(CCFL)** Acknowledgment of service (Part 7, Commercial Court Financial List)

- **N9(CHFL)** Acknowledgment of service (Part 7 Chancery Division Financial List)
- **N210(CCFL)** Acknowledgment of service (Part 8 Commercial Court Financial List)
- **N210(CHFL)** Acknowledgment of service (Part 8, Chancery Division Financial List)
- **N213(CCFL)** Acknowledgment of service (Part 20, Commercial Court Financial List)
- **N213(CHFL)** Acknowledgment of service (Part 20, Chancery Division Financial List)
- **N244(CCFL)** Application Notice (Commercial Court Financial List)
- **N244(CHFL)** Application Notice (Chancery Division Financial List)
- **N265(CCFL)** Standard Disclosure (Commercial Court Financial List)
- **N265(CHFL)** Standard Disclosure (Chancery Division Financial List)

Background

Replace the last paragraph with:

The Financial List opened its door to the public on 1 October 2015 and a formal launch event **2FA-1.5** was held at the Rolls Building on 20 October 2015. At the event, attended by leading figures in the fields of finance, government and law, the Lord Chancellor Michael Gove described the Financial List as one of the most "exciting innovations in the field of British justice". The Bank of England Deputy Governor Sir Jon Cunliffe said the bank ""wholeheartedly supports" the initiative and that "[t]his isn't just something that matters for the UK and the UK's financial stability. It is something that matters [for] international financial stability as well"" (reported at (2015) LS Gaz 6, 26 Oct.).

Financial List claims

To the end of the first paragraph, add:

Paragraph 2.3 of the Financial List Guide recognises that whilst an insurance, professional **2FA-2.1** negligence or Companies Court case will not generally fall within the definition of Financial List claims, if such a case were to require financial market expertise to resolve the matter or raise issues of general market importance, then it may be appropriate for the claim to be considered in the Financial List.

Replace the second paragraph with:

At the time of writing and based on public information, an estimated twenty cases have been issued or transferred into the Financial List, with five cases recently leading to judgment although certain cases are now subject to appeal. The Royal Bank of Scotland Group issued the first four cases on 21 October 2015. The proceedings consist of claims against four energy companies and the case type is described as "derivative and financial products". There is currently limited publically available information on the matters.

Replace the third paragraph with:

The first substantive judgment in the Financial List was handed down on 29 January 2016. *GSO Credit v Barclays Bank Plc* [2016] EWHC 146 (Comm) was the second case transferred into the Financial List. The judgment illustrates that the Financial List will be a suitable forum for cases requiring guidance on the interpretation of standard form documentation for financial transactions, with the decision clarifying the meaning of several terms used in the Loan Market Association (the "LMA") facility documentation. Given that the LMA documentation is widely used to govern the secondary trading of debt, the judgment provides welcome guidance and is likely to have wider significance on financial markets.

After the fourth paragraph (beginning "There were two key issues in the case"), add as a new paragraph:

Mr Justice Blair handed down the second substantive in the Financial List 4 March 2016. In *Banco Santander Totta SA v Companhia Carris de Ferro de Lisboa SA* [2016] EWHC 465 (Comm), the Defendant public sector Portuguese transport companies raised various defences to claims by the Claimant bank under swap agreements. The Court had made findings in favour of the Claimant and findings in favour of the Defendants but the overall decision was in favour of the Claimant. The decision sets out helpful clarification on the construction of the terms of "exotic" snowball swaps, an area where there hereto been limited legal authority. In addition, the decisions clarifies the scope of the Article 3.3 of the Convention on the Law Applicable to Contractual Obligations 1980 (the Rome Convention) in light of the *Dexia Crediop Spa v Comune di Prato* [2015] EWHC 1746 (Comm) decision.

Replace the fifth paragraph with:

When Financial List claims start to lead to a wider body of published judgments, it should provide further clarification on the types of cases that are suitable for determination in the Financial List. The Financial List judgments are published on the Judiciary's website dedicated to the Financial List at the following webpage: *https://www.judiciary.gov.uk/court/financial-list/* [Accessed 18 July 2016].

Delete the sixth and seventh paragraphs (beginning "The Royal Bank of Scotland Group" and "The first case to be transferred").

Replace the last paragraph with:

The Judiciary intends to use the Claims Information Form to be completed by claimants issuing Financial List claims to gather statistics on Financial List Claims to improve the Financial List (Financial List Guide at para.10.2). The Judiciary may also publish this information to provide guidance to users. In the interim, parties have the opportunity to raise queries by writing to the Financial List Users' Committee (Committee), which will provide a forum in which the High Court will listen and respond to matters raised by litigators and others concerned with the financial markets (Financial List Guide at para.4.1). Anyone having views concerning the improvement of financial markets litigation is invited to make his or her views known to the Committee, preferably through the relevant professional representative on the Committee or its secretary. The Committee held its first meeting in early 2016. The matters discussed included the types of cases suitable for determination using the Financial Markets Test Case Scheme introduced under Practice Direction 51M. The introduction of the Committee reflects the Judiciary's commitment to listen to users so as to improve the Financial List where possible. An aim endorsed by the comments of the Lord Chief Justice Lord Thomas, who has been at the vanguard of the Financial List, at the official launch event on October 20, 2015 who explained that the procedure would be kept under review and that "I do hope this initial experiment will work and we will try and improve it wherever possible" (reported at (2015) 6 LS Gaz, 26 Oct.).

Add new paragraph 2FA-2.2:

Transfer of claims

2FA-2.2   The Financial List Guide provides at para.2.3 that the parties may apply to transfer a case into the Financial List under CPR 30, including where the case falls "within the spirit but not the letter" of the specified criteria.

CPR 30 (Transfer), r.30.5(2) states that a judge dealing with claims in a specialist list may order proceedings "to be transferred to or from that list". Under r.63A.4(4), the provision of r.30.5 applies to proceedings in the Financial List and a judge dealing with claims in that List may order, not only that claims be transferred to or from it, but also that a claim be transferred from it "to any other specialist list". Particular provisions as to the transfer of claims to or from the Financial List are contained in paras 4.1 to 4.6 of Practice Direction 63A. CPR r.30.3, to which reference is made in para.4.6 of PD63AA, provides that various matters should be taken into account by the court when considering whether to make an order for the transfer of proceedings. These include:

(1)   the financial value of the claim;

(2)   whether it would be more convenient or fair for hearings, including the trial, to be held in some other court;

(3)   the availability of a judge specialising in the type of claim in question;

(4)   whether the facts, legal issues, remedies or procedures involved are simple or complex;

(5)   the importance of the outcome of the claim to the public in general; and

(6)   the facilities available to the court at which the claim is being dealt with.

In deciding whether or not to transfer a case into a specialist list, including in the Financial List, regard is also given to the overriding objective in CPR Pt 1.

One of the most recent cases transferred into the Financial List is *Property Alliance Group Ltd v Royal Bank of Scotland* [2016] EWHC 207 (Ch). In considering the Defendant's application for the case to be transferred, the Chancellor, Sir Justice Etherton, set out useful guidance in an interlocutory judgment on the issues that judges are likely to consider when deciding whether to accede to applications to transfer existing proceedings into the Financial List. The issues included ten matters which are likely to be of particular significance in deciding whether to accede to a contested application to transfer existing proceedings into the Financial List:

(1)   the extent to which the case concerns matters of market significance, as distinct from factual and other matters relevant only to the case and the parties in question;

(2)   the relative importance of the issues of market significance;

(3)   whether the case has already been assigned to a judge;

(4)   whether, if transferred into the Financial List, the proceedings would require a change of judge;

(5)   the length of time in which the proceedings have already been on foot;

(6)   the extent to which an assigned judge has already conducted hearings and delivered judgments in the pending proceedings, and his or her general familiarity with the case;

(7)   the extent to which the familiarity of the existing assigned judge with the case would enable judicial trial pre-reading, and the trial itself, to be conducted in a more efficient and timely way than if a new Financial List judge were to be appointed;

(8)   whether or not the trial date has been fixed, and, if so, the proximity to the trial date;

(9)   whether the trial timetable would be disrupted by the transfer into the Financial List; and

(10)   whether, and if so, assigning a new Financial List judge would be disruptive to one or more other cases in the other lists, because the new judge would no longer be able to conduct those other proceedings, or for any other reason.

On the facts of the case, it was found to be appropriate to transfer the case into the Financial List. This was even though the transfer involved a change of judge. It was considered that the case would benefit from being determined by a Financial List Judge, representing a relatively small cadre of judges who are not only particularly expert in the law applicable to financial markets, but also abreast of important developments in financial markets.

A further reason for concluding that it would be appropriate to transfer the case into the Financial List was that the case involved issues of general market significance regarded as clearly relevant to other participants in the market. Allied to those considerations, was that the case could be viewed in a general sense as a test or lead case, which would therefore make it desirable for a Financial List judge to determine the case so that the judgment carries appropriate weight in the future. Another important consideration was that it was possible for an alternative Financial List judge, also from the Chancery Division, to conduct both the Pre-Trial Review and the trial. Sir Justice Etherton noted that it would have been preferable and possible for the Defendant to apply to transfer the case at an earlier time and that delay may carry consequences that are more significant on the facts of other cases.

Effect of rule

Replace with:
    CPR r.63A.4(4) sets out several two unique features of the Financial List. These are that: **2FA-5.1**
(1)   a docketed Financial List judge will generally preside over the matter from the commencement of the proceeding to the trial, through to enforcement if necessary (see further the Financial List Guide at paras 6.1 and 6.2 and Financial List website FAQ at para.14); and
(2)   the Financial List judges are those authorised from the Chancery Division or Commercial Court to try claims in the Financial List.

After the first paragraph, add as a new paragraph:
    The rule that a docketed judge will preside over a Financial List claim from start to finish is not an inflexible procedure. In that, in certain cases there may be good reason to allow a Financial List claim to be assigned from one Financial List judge to another. For example, to allow a trial at an earlier date when requested by the parties for reasons of expediency.

The Financial List judges

In the third paragraph, replace "may preside other" with
    may preside over

Replace "Mr Justice Richards;" with:
    Mr Justice Hildyard;

Replace the fifth paragraph with:
    The Judge in charge of the Commercial Court, currently Mr Justice Blair;
        Mr Justice Flaux;
        Mr Justice Leggatt;
        Mr Justice Knowles,
        Mr Justice Popplewell; and
        Mr Justice Phillips.

Replace the sixth paragraph with:
    The Judiciary's dedicated website for the Financial List contains a webpage that has an updated list of Financial List judges and the address is:
https://www.judiciary.gov.uk/you-and-the-judiciary/going-to-court/high-court/financial-list/judges/ [Accessed 18 July 2016].

GUIDE TO THE FINANCIAL LIST
Issued 1st October 2015

By authority of The Chancellor of the High Court, Sir Terence Etherton, and The Hon. Mr Justice Flaux, Judge in charge of the Commercial Court

A   General

2   JURISDICTION

Replace paragraph 2.3 with:
2.3   The court has the general power to transfer proceedings into the Financial List under CPR   **2FA-14** Part 30. This permits the court to order cases into the Financial List which fall within the spirit but not the letter of the three criteria. Cases which fall outside the subject matter definition and/or the financial markets definition may nevertheless require comparable expertise or may be of comparable general importance. Thus, a case concerning insurance, re-insurance or professional

negligence, or a case falling within the normal specialist jurisdiction of the Companies Court (insolvencies, capital reductions, schemes of arrangement as well as shareholder disputes like unfair prejudice petitions and equitable petitions) will not generally fall within the definition of Financial List Claims but if issues arising in such a case were to require financial market expertise or were issues of general market importance, then it may be appropriate to issue the claim in the Financial List or transfer such a case or part of it into the Financial List.

Editorial

To the end of the second paragraph, add:

2FA-21.1   At the time of writing, no parties have yet issued proceedings using the procedure. If this remains the case at the end of the two-year period, it is expected that the scheme will nonetheless remain open for application.

Qualifying claim

Replace with:

   Practice Direction 51M defines a "qualifying claim" as a "claim started in the Financial List which raises issues of general importance to the financial markets in relation to which immediately relevant authoritative English law guidance is needed" (Practice Direction 51M at para.2.1). For example, the procedure may be a vehicle to consider the consequences of the exit of the United Kingdom from the European Union on finance contracts. The definition of a "qualifying claim" provides that the claim has to be "started in the Financial List". It may therefore not be possible to transfer a claim from another division or list to the Financial List for determination under the Test Case Scheme. The two year pilot scheme will hopefully address this point and other aspects of uncertainty in respect of the relatively new procedure (for further commentary on the areas of uncertainty see L Feldman and D Flack, (2015) 11 JIBFL 700). Parties may request guidance on points of uncertainty from the Financial List Users' Committee (the Financial List Guide at para.4.1). The current secretary of the Committee is Vannina Ettori, Legal Advisor to the Chancellor of the High Court, who may be contacted at vannina.ettori@judiciary.gsi.gov.uk (see the Financial List Guide at para.12.3).

Procedure

In the first paragraph, after "these differences are that judge will need to", delete "be".

C   General Arrangements

12   CONTACT

Replace paragraph 12.3 with:

2FA-24 12.3   The secretary of the Financial List Users' Committee is Vannina Ettori, Legal Advisor to the Chancellor of the High Court. She may be contacted at vannina.ettori@judiciary.gsi.gov.uk.

SECTION 3   OTHER PROCEEDINGS
SECTION 3A   HOUSING

Protection from Eviction Act 1977

Note

Replace with:

3A-78   Added by the Housing Act 1988 s.31. Amended by the Local Government (Wales) Act 1994 Sch.8 para.4(1); the Housing Act 1996 (Consequential Provisions) Order 1996 (SI 1996/2325) art.5, Sch.2 para.7; the Government of Wales Act 1998 s.140 and Sch.16, para.2 and Sch.18 Pt IV the Asylum and Immigration Act 1996 Sch.14 para.73; Greater London Authority Act 1999 Sch.29 para.27; by the Nationality, Immigration and Asylum Act 2002 s.32(5) (SI 2005/1379); and by the Immigration, Asylum and Nationality Act 2006 s.43(4)(a); the Housing and Regeneration Act 2008, s.56 and Sch.8 para.24, with effect from 1 April 2010; and (subject to transitional and saving provisions in Sch.3 thereof) by the Housing and Regeneration Act 2008 (Consequential Provisions) Order 2010 (SI 2010/866) Sch.2 para.13, with effect from 1 April 2010; and the Local Democracy, Economic Development and Construction Act 2009 Sch.6 para.47, with effect from 17 December 2009 and the Localism Act 2011 s.195, Sch.19 para.6, with effect (subject to transitional, transitory and saving provisions in arts 9, 11, 14, 15, 17) from 1 April 2012 (SI 2012/628 art.6(i)) and s.222,

Sch.22 para.6, with effect from 15 January 2012 (s.240(1)(l)). Protection from Eviction Act 1977 s.3A has been amended by Immigration Act 2016 s.40, which inserted a new subsection (7D). The amendment will be implemented by a Commencement Order and is not yet in force, but is printed at 3A-1864. The amendment applies in relation to a tenancy or a licence entered into before or after the coming into force of the section.

Replace s.8(6) with:

Part III

Supplemental Provisions

Interpretation

(6)   Any reference in subsection (5) above to a variation affecting the amount **3A-86** of the rent which is payable under a tenancy or licence does not include a reference to—

    (a)   a reduction or increase effected under Part III or Part VI of the Rent Act 1977 (rents under regulated tenancies and housing association tenancies), section 78 of that Act (power of tribunal in relation to restricted contracts) or sections 11 to 14 of the Rent (Agriculture) Act 1976; or

    (b)   a variation which is made by the parties and has the effect of making the rent expressed to be payable under the tenancy or licence the same as a rent for the dwelling which is entered in the register under Part IV or section 79 of the Rent Act 1977.

Note

Replace with:

Amended by the Agricultural Holdings Act 1986 Sch.14 para.61; the Housing Act 1988 s.33; the **3A-87** Local Government and Housing Act 1989 Sch.11 para.54; and the Agricultural Tenancies Act 1995 Sch. para.29; and the Transfer of Tribunal Functions Order 2013 (SI 2013/1036) Sch.1(1) para.35, with effect from 1 July 2013 subject to transitional provisions and savings specified in SI 2013/1036 art.6(3) and Sch.3.

Rent Act 1977

Add new paragraph 3A–256.1:

Rent Act 1977 Pt 1 of Sch.15 (grounds for possession of dwelling-houses let on or subject to **3A-256.1** protected or statutory tenancies) has been amended by Immigration Act 2016 s.41 by inserting a new Case 10A. The amendment will be implemented by a Commencement Order and is not yet in force, but is printed at 3A-1864.

Housing Act 1985

Add new paragraphs 3A–342.1 to 3A–342.15:

New English secure tenancies to be between 2 and 10 years in general

81A.—(1)   A person may grant a secure tenancy of a dwelling-house in **3A-342.1** England only if it is a tenancy for a fixed term that is—

    (a)   at least 2 years, and

    (b)   no longer than the permitted maximum length.

(2)   The permitted maximum length is 10 years, unless subsection (3) applies.

(3)   If the person granting the tenancy has been notified in writing that a child aged under 9 will live in the dwelling-house, the permitted maximum length is the period—

    (a)   beginning with the day on which the tenancy is granted, and

    (b)   ending with the day on which the child will reach the age of 19.

(4)   If a person purports to grant a secure tenancy in breach of subsection (1), it takes effect as a tenancy for a fixed term of 5 years.

(5)   In deciding what length of tenancy to grant in a case to which this section applies a person must have regard to any guidance given by the Secretary of State.

(6)   This section does not apply to the grant of an old-style secure tenancy (as to which, see section 81B).

3A-342.2   *Commencement* —This section was inserted by Housing and Planning Act 2016 Sch.7. It will be implemented by a Commencement Order and is not yet in force.

Editorial introduction

3A-342.3   The aim of Housing and Planning Act 2016 Sch.7 is to amend the Housing Act 1985 and the Housing Act 1996 to phase out lifetime tenancies. Secure tenancies will generally have to be for a fixed term and will not automatically be renewed. Sections 81A to 81C provide that local authorities may generally only grant secure tenancies for a fixed term of between 2 and 10 years, or where a child under 9 years lives in the property until the child turns 19. Local authorities must have regard to any guidance issued by the Secretary of State when deciding what length of tenancy to grant and a tenant may request a review of the landlord's decision as to the length of the fixed term. If a landlord tries to grant a lifetime tenancy or a tenancy shorter than 2 years or longer than the maximum permitted period, the tenancy defaults to a 5 year fixed term. Existing lifetime tenants must be given a further lifetime tenancy if they are required to move by the landlord and the landlord has discretion to grant a lifetime tenancy in other circumstances to be set out in regulations. If a local authority takes on a property with a tenant who has a periodic tenancy or one that is less than 2 years or more than 5 years, the tenancy becomes a non-secure tenancy and the local authority must offer the tenant a new fixed term tenancy.

Secure tenancy

3A-342.4   See Housing Act 1985 s.79.

Cases where old-style English secure tenancies may be granted

3A-342.5   **81B.**—(1)   A person may grant an old-style secure tenancy of a dwelling-house in England only—

(a)   in circumstances specified in regulations made by the Secretary of State,

(b)   in accordance with subsection (2), or

(c)   if required to do so by section 158(9B) of the Localism Act 2011 (which relates to transfer requests made before section 121 of the Housing and Planning Act 2016 comes into force).

(2)   A local housing authority that grants a secure tenancy of a dwelling-house in England must grant an old-style secure tenancy if—

(a)   the tenancy is offered as a replacement for an old-style secure tenancy of some other dwelling-house, and

(b)   the tenant has not made an application to move.

(3)   Other provisions of this Part set out the consequences of a tenancy being an old-style secure tenancy.

(4)   Regulations under subsection (1) may include transitional or saving provision.

(5)   Regulations under subsection (1) are to be made by statutory instrument.

(6)   A statutory instrument containing regulations under subsection (1) may not be made unless a draft of the instrument has been laid before and approved by a resolution of each House of Parliament.

3A-342.6   *Commencement* —This section was inserted by Housing and Planning Act 2016 Sch.7. It will be implemented by a Commencement Order and is not yet in force.

Secure tenancy

3A-342.7   See Housing Act 1985 s.79.

Regulations

3A-342.8   At present there are no regulations.

Duty to offer new secure tenancy in limited circumstances

3A-342.9   **81C.**—(1)   This section applies where a change in circumstances means that a tenancy that is not a secure tenancy would become a secure tenancy but for the exception in paragraph 1ZA of Schedule 1.

(2) The landlord must, within the period of 28 days, make the tenant a written offer of a secure tenancy in return for the tenant surrendering the original tenancy.

(3) If the tenant accepts in writing within the period of 28 days beginning with the day on which the tenant receives the offer, the landlord must grant the secure tenancy on the tenant surrendering the original tenancy.

Commencement —This section was inserted by Housing and Planning Act 2016 Sch.7. It will be **3A-342.10** implemented by a Commencement Order and is not yet in force.

Secure tenancy
See Housing Act 1985 s.79. **3A-342.11**

Review of decisions about length of secure tenancies in England

81D.—(1) A person who is offered a secure tenancy of a dwelling-house in **3A-342.12** England (under section 81C or otherwise) may request a review under this section, unless the tenancy on offer is an old-style secure tenancy.

(2) The sole purpose of a review under this section is to consider whether the length of the tenancy is in accordance with any policy that the prospective landlord has about the length of secure tenancies it grants.

(3) The request must be made before the end of—
    (a) the period of 21 days beginning with the day on which the person making the request first receives the offer, or
    (b) such longer period as the prospective landlord may allow in writing.

(4) On receiving the request the prospective landlord must carry out the review.

(5) On completing the review the prospective landlord must —
    (a) notify the tenant in writing of the outcome,
    (b) revise its offer or confirm its original decision about the length of the tenancy, and
    (c) if it decides to confirm its original decision, give reasons.

(6) The Secretary of State may by regulations make provision about the procedure to be followed in connection with a review under this section.

(7) The regulations may, in particular—
    (a) require the review to be carried out by a person of appropriate seniority who was not involved in the original decision;
    (b) make provision as to the circumstances in which the person who requested the review is entitled to an oral hearing, and whether and by whom that person may be represented.

(8) Regulations under this section may include transitional or saving provision.

(9) Regulations under this section are to be made by statutory instrument which is subject to annulment in pursuance of a resolution of either House of Parliament.

Commencement —This section was inserted by Housing and Planning Act 2016 Sch.7. It will be **3A-342.13** implemented by a Commencement Order and is not yet in force.

Secure tenancy
See Housing Act 1985 s.79. **3A-342.14**

Regulations
At present there are no regulations. **3A-342.15**

Note

Replace with:
Section 82 has been amended by Anti-Social Behaviour Act 2003 s.14(1). This amendment was **3A-344** brought into force in England on 30 June 2004 by the Anti-Social Behaviour Act 2003 (Commencement No.3 and Savings) Order 2004 (SI 2004/1502) (c.61). It does not have effect in relation to any

proceedings for the possession of a dwelling-house begun before 30 June 2004. It was brought into force in Wales on 30 April 2005 by the Anti-Social Behaviour Act 2003 (Commencement No.4) (Wales) Order 2005 (SI 2005/1225) (w.83) (c.55). The amendment allows a secure tenancy to be brought to an end by a demotion order. This section has also been amended by the Housing and Regeneration Act 2008 Sch.11 Pt I para.2 (for transitional provisions see para.14) with effect from 20 May 2009 (SI 2009/1261) (c.66). Housing Act 1985 s.82 has been amended by Housing and Planning Act 2016 s.119. The amendment will be implemented by a Commencement Order and is not yet in force, but is printed at 3A-1902.

Note

Replace with:

3A-350   Inserted by the Anti-Social Behaviour Act 2003 s.14(2) and brought into force in relation to England on 30 June 2004 (SI 2004/1502) and in relation to Wales on 30 April 2005 (the Anti-Social Behaviour Act 2003 (Commencement No.4) (Wales) Order 2005 (SI 2005/1225)); amended by the Police and Justice Act 2006 s.52 and Sch.14 para.12; and (subject to transitional and saving provisions in Sch.2, para.19(5) and Sch.3 thereof) by the Housing and Regeneration Act 2008 (Consequential Provisions) Order 2010 (SI 2010/866) Sch.2 para.20, with effect from 1 April 2010. Subsection (2) amended, subject to savings and transitional provisions, by the Crime and Courts Act 2013 Sch.9 para.52, with effect from 22 April 2014 (see SI 2014/954); for savings and transitional provisions see Sch.8 to the Act. Further amended by Anti-social Behaviour, Crime and Policing Act 2014 Sch.11 para.6. The amendment was brought into force on 23 March 2015 by the Anti-social Behaviour, Crime and Policing Act 2014 (Commencement No.8, Saving and Transitional Provisions) Order 2015 (SI 2015/373). Housing Act 1985 s.82A has been amended by Housing and Planning Act 2016 Sch.7. The amendments will be implemented by a Commencement Order and are not yet in force, but are printed at 3A-1902 and 3A-1903.

Note

Replace the second paragraph with:

3A-359   Section 83 has been amended by Anti-Social Behaviour Act 2003 s.14(3) and Sch.1. The amendments were brought into force in England on 30 June 2004 by the Anti-Social Behaviour Act 2003 (Commencement No.3 and Savings) Order 2004 (SI 2004/1502) (c.61). It was brought into force in Wales on 30 April 2005 by the Anti-Social Behaviour Act 2003 (Commencement No.4) (Wales) Order 2005 (SI 2005/1225) (w.83) (c.55). Amended by the Localism Act 2011 s.155(1), with effect (subject to transitional, transitory and saving provisions in arts 9, 11, 14, 15, 17) from 1 April 2012 (SI 2012/628, art.6(a)). Further amended by Anti-social Behaviour, Crime and Policing Act 2014 Sch.11 para.7. The amendment was brought into force in England on 20 October 2014 by the Anti-social Behaviour, Crime and Policing Act 2014 (Commencement No.7, Saving and Transitional Provisions) Order 2014 (SI 2014/2590). It was brought into force in Wales on 21 October 2014 by the Anti-social Behaviour, Crime and Policing Act 2014 (Commencement No 2 and Transitional Provisions) (Wales) Order 2014 (SI 2014/2830). Housing Act 1985 s.83 has been amended by Housing and Planning Act 2016 s.119 and Sch.7. The amendments will be implemented by a Commencement Order and are not yet in force, but are printed at 3A-1902 and 3A-1903.

Note

Replace with:

3A-367   Amended by the Housing Act 1996 s.147. Amended by the Localism Act 2011 s.155(2), with effect (subject to transitional, transitory and saving provisions in arts 9, 11, 14, 15, 17) from 1 April 2012 (SI 2012/628, art.6(a)). Further amended by the Anti-social Behaviour, Crime and Policing Act 2014 Sch.11 para.9. The amendment was brought into force in England on 20 October 2014 by the Anti-social Behaviour, Crime and Policing Act 2014 (Commencement No.7, Saving and Transitional Provisions) Order 2014 (SI 2014/2590). It was brought into force in Wales on 21 October 2014 by the Anti-social Behaviour, Crime and Policing Act 2014 (Commencement No.2 and Transitional Provisions) (Wales) Order 2014 (SI 2014/2830). Housing Act 1985 s.84 has been amended by Housing and Planning Act 2016 s.119 and Sch.7. The amendments will be implemented by a Commencement Order and are not yet in force, but are printed at 3A-1902 and 3A-1903.

"reasonable"—nuisance and annoyance

Serious or continuing conduct

After the first paragraph, add as a new paragraph:

3A-375   In *City West Housing Trust v Massey* [2016] EWCA Civ 704; 7 July 2016, the Court of Appeal considered what amounts to 'cogent' evidence for the hope that the previous conduct will cease. Arden LJ stated "'Cogent' evidence that there is a sound basis for hope that the previous conduct will cease is not simply evidence which shows there is some basis on which it could be said that the tenant will observe the terms of his tenancy in future. ... To be 'cogent', the evidence must be more than simply credible: it must be persuasive. There has to be evidence which persuades the court that there is a sound basis for the hope that the previous conduct will cease or not recur. ...

[W]hen making an SPO the court has to make a judgment about the future and that the focus at this stage is on the future and not the past ... By stating the requirement to be 'cogent' evidence that there is a sound basis for hope for the future, the standard is pitched at a realistic level. On the one hand, the tenant does not have to give a cast-iron guarantee. On the other hand, a social landlord does not have to accept a tenant who sets out to breach the terms of his tenancy and disables the landlord from providing accommodation in more deserving cases. There is no principle that the cogent evidence regarding future compliance must stem solely from the tenant himself, without any regard to how others might behave. The likelihood or possibility of action by others, or even the perception that others might take action, may in an appropriate case be evidence which supports an overall assessment that there is a real hope of compliance in the future. For example, a tenant who has mental health problems affecting his ability to comply might be able to show that his compliance in future is made likely because of support received from others. Similarly, the inclusion of an inspection condition in a SPO might provide support for an assessment that the tenant will comply in future, if his fear of being evicted is sufficiently strong and he thinks the risk of inspection is real rather than illusory." [paras 47 to 49]

At the beginning of the second paragraph, replace "Similarly, where" with:
   Where

Add new paragraph 3A–393.1:
   Housing Act 1985 s.86 has been amended by Housing and Planning Act 2016 s.119 and Schs 7 and 8. The amendments will be implemented by a Commencement Order and are not yet in force, but are printed at 3A-1902, 3A-1903 and 3A-1904.   **3A-393.1**

Note

Replace with:
   Inserted by the Localism Act 2011 s.160(1), with effect (subject to transitional, transitory and saving provisions in arts 9, 11, 14, 15, 17 and savings in the 2011 Act s.160(6)) from1 April 2012 (SI 2012/628 art.(6)(a)). Existing s.86A (persons qualified to succeed: England) as inserted by the Localism Act 2011 will be renumbered s.86G (so that it follows on from s.86F as inserted by Housing and Planning Act 2016 Sch.7 without making the numbering more complex than it has to be), and amended further. See Housing and Planning Act 2016 Sch.8 para.3, printed at 3A-1904. These amendments are not yet in force.   **3A-395.2**

Add new paragraphs 3A–395.7 to 3A–395.25:

ENGLISH SECURE TENANCIES: REVIEW, RENEWAL AND POSSESSION

English tenancies: review to determine what to do at end of fixed term

86A.—(1)   The landlord under a fixed term secure tenancy of a dwelling-   **3A-395.7** house in England must carry out a review to decide what to do at the end of the term, unless one of the following exceptions applies.

(2)   The landlord under a fixed term secure tenancy of a dwelling-house in England must carry out a review to decide what to do at the end of the term, unless one of the following exceptions applies.

(3)   Exception 2 is where the tenancy is a flexible tenancy the term of which ends within the period of 9 months beginning with the day on which paragraph 4 of Schedule 7 to the Housing and Planning Act 2016 comes fully into force.

(4)   A review under this section must be carried out while the term has 6 to 9 months left to run.

(5)   On a review under this section the landlord must decide which of the following options to take.

Option 1: offer to grant a new secure tenancy of the dwelling-house at the end of the current tenancy.

Option 2: seek possession of the dwelling house at the end of the current tenancy but offer to grant a secure tenancy of another dwelling-house instead.

Option 3: seek possession of the dwelling-house at the end of the current tenancy without offering to grant a secure tenancy of another dwelling-house.

(6)   The landlord must also—
   (a)   offer the tenant advice on buying a home if the landlord considers that to be a realistic option for the tenant, and

> (b) in appropriate cases, offer the tenant advice on other housing options.

3A-395.8 *Commencement* —This section was inserted by Housing and Planning Act 2016 Sch.7. It will be implemented by a Commencement Order and is not yet in force.

Editorial introduction

3A-395.9 Sections 86A to 86F deal with the process for reviewing, renewing and terminating fixed term tenancies. A landlord must carry out a review between 6 and 9 months before the end of the fixed term to decide whether to grant a new tenancy in the same or a different dwelling house or to end the tenancy without offering another. Where appropriate, the local authority must provide advice on buying a home or other housing options. The landlord must notify the tenant of the outcome of the review and the tenant may ask the landlord to reconsider a decision to terminate the tenancy. Local authorities may not issue a demoted tenancy within 1 year and 9 months of the end of a fixed term tenancy, to allow time to carry out the review. A demoted tenancy is a tool to tackle anti-social behaviour; it puts the tenant on notice to improve their behaviour and lasts for 12 months at the end of which the tenancy reverts to its original type. If the landlord does not grant a new tenancy at the end of the old one, or seeks possession of the property, the default position is that a new 5 year tenancy arises automatically at the end of the tenancy. This does not prevent the landlord from recovering possession of the property but ensures that the tenancy does not become a lifetime tenancy at the end of the term.

Secure tenancy

3A-395.10 See Housing Act 1985 s.79.

Notification of outcome of review under section 86A

3A-395.11 **86B.**—(1) On completing a review under section 86A the landlord must notify the tenant in writing of the outcome of the review.

(2) The notice must be given by no later than 6 months before the end of the term of the current tenancy.

(3) The notice must state which of the options mentioned in section 86A the landlord has decided to take.

(4) If the landlord has decided to seek possession of the dwelling-house at the end of the secure tenancy the notice must also—

(a) inform the tenant of the right under section 86C to request the landlord to reconsider, and

(b) inform the tenant of the right under section 86C to request the landlord to reconsider, and

(5) If the notice states that the landlord has decided to offer a new tenancy and the tenant accepts in writing before the end of the current tenancy, the landlord must grant the new tenancy in accordance with the offer.

3A-395.12 *Commencement* —This section was inserted by Housing and Planning Act 2016 Sch.7. It will be implemented by a Commencement Order and is not yet in force.

Reconsideration of decision not to grant a tenancy

3A-395.13 **86C.**—(1) Where a tenant is notified that the outcome of a review under section 86A is that the landlord has decided to seek possession of the dwelling-house at the end of the current tenancy, the tenant may request the landlord to reconsider its decision.

(2) The request must be made before the end of the period of 21 days beginning with the day on which tenant was notified of the decision.

(3) On receiving the request, the landlord must reconsider its decision.

(4) The landlord must, in particular, consider whether the original decision is in accordance with any policy that the landlord has about the circumstances in which it will grant a further tenancy on the coming to an end of an existing fixed term tenancy.

(5)   Once the landlord has reconsidered the decision the landlord must—
  (a)   notify the tenant in writing of the outcome,
  (b)   revise or confirm its original decision, and
  (c)   if it decides to confirm its original decision, give reasons.

(6)   The Secretary of State may by regulations make provision about the procedure to be followed in connection with reconsidering a decision for the purposes of this section.

(7)   The regulations may, in particular—
  (a)   require the original decision to be reconsidered by a person of appropriate seniority who was not involved in the original decision, and
  (b)   make provision as to the circumstances in which the person who requested the landlord to reconsider the original decision is entitled to an oral hearing, and whether and by whom that person may be represented.

(8)   Regulations under this section may include transitional or saving provision.

(9)   Regulations under this section are to be made by statutory instrument which is subject to annulment in pursuance of a resolution of either House of Parliament.

Commencement —This section was inserted by Housing and Planning Act 2016 Sch.7. It will be **3A-395.14** implemented by a Commencement Order and is not yet in force.

Regulations
At present there are no regulations.   **3A-395.15**

Fixed term tenancy arising on termination of previous fixed term

86D.—(1)   This section applies to a secure tenancy of a dwelling-house in **3A-395.16** England other than—
  (a)   an old-style secure tenancy, or
  (b)   a flexible tenancy the term of which ends within the period of 9 months beginning with the day on which paragraph 4 of Schedule 7 to the Housing and Planning Act 2016 comes fully into force.

(2)   If the tenancy comes to an end by virtue of the term expiring, or by virtue of an order under section 82(3), a new tenancy of the same dwelling-house arises by virtue of this subsection.

(3)   Where the landlord has offered the tenant a new tenancy of the same dwelling-house following a review under section 86A but the tenant has failed to accept, the new tenancy that arises by virtue of subsection (2) is a fixed term tenancy of whatever length the landlord offered.

(4)   In any other case, the new tenancy that arises by virtue of subsection (2) is a 5 year fixed term tenancy.

(5)   The parties and other terms of a new tenancy that arises by virtue of subsection (2) are the same as those of the tenancy that it replaces, except that the terms are confined to those which are compatible with a tenancy of the length determined in accordance with subsection (3) or (4).

(6)   A new tenancy does not arise by virtue of subsection (2) if the tenant has been granted another secure tenancy of the same dwelling-house to begin at the same time as the earlier tenancy ends.

Commencement —This section was inserted by Housing and Planning Act 2016 Sch.7. It will be **3A-395.17** implemented by a Commencement Order and is not yet in force.

Secure tenancy
See Housing Act 1985 s.79.   **3A-395.18**

Recovery of possession of secure tenancies in England

3A-395.19   **86E.**—(1)   The landlord under a secure tenancy of a dwelling-house in England may bring proceedings for possession under this section if—

    (a)   the landlord has decided on a review under section 86A to seek possession at the end of the tenancy, and

    (b)   the landlord has not subsequently revised the decision under section 86C.

(2)   If the landlord brings proceedings under this section the court must make an order for possession if satisfied that—

    (a)   the landlord has complied with all of the requirements of sections 86A to 86C,

    (b)   the tenancy that was the subject of the review section 86A has ended,

    (c)   the proceedings were commenced before the end of the period of 3 months beginning with the day on which the tenancy ended, and

    (d)   the only fixed term tenancy still in existence is a new secure tenancy arising by virtue of section 86D.

(3)   But the court may refuse to grant an order for possession under this section if the court considers that a decision of the landlord under section 86A or 86C was wrong in law.

(4)   Where a court makes an order for possession of a dwelling-house under this section, any fixed term tenancy arising by virtue of section 86D on the coming to an end of the tenancy that was the subject of the review under section 86A comes to an end (without further notice) in accordance with section 82(2).

(5)   This section does not limit any right of the landlord under a secure tenancy to recover possession of the dwelling-house let on the tenancy in accordance with other provisions of this Part.

3A-395.20   *Commencement* —This section was inserted by Housing and Planning Act 2016 Sch.7. It will be implemented by a Commencement Order and is not yet in force.

Editorial note

3A-395.21   Section 86E provides for the process by which a landlord may recover possession of a property at the end of the fixed term. A tenant may terminate a fixed term tenancy on giving 4 weeks' notice. See s.86F below.

Secure tenancy

3A-395.22   See Housing Act 1985 s.79.

Termination of English secure tenancies by tenant

3A-395.23   **86F.**—(1)   It is a term of every secure tenancy of a dwelling-house in England, other than an old-style secure tenancy, that the tenant may terminate the tenancy in accordance with the following provisions of this section.

(2)   The tenant must serve a notice in writing on the landlord stating that the tenancy will be terminated on the date specified in the notice.

(3)   That date must be after the end of the period of four weeks beginning with the date on which the notice is served.

(4)   The landlord may agree with the tenant to dispense with the requirement in subsection (2) or (3).

(5)   The tenancy is terminated on the date specified in the notice or (as the case may be) determined in accordance with arrangements made under subsection (4) only if on that date—

    (a)   no arrears of rent are payable under the tenancy, and

    (b)   the tenant is not otherwise materially in breach of a term of the tenancy.

3A-395.24   *Commencement* —This section was inserted by Housing and Planning Act 2016 Sch.7. It will be implemented by a Commencement Order and is not yet in force.

Secure tenancy

3A-395.25   See Housing Act 1985 s.79.

Note

Add at end:
    Section 88 has been amended by Housing and Planning Act 2016 Sch.8 para.4, printed at 3A- **3A-404**
1904. This amendment is not yet in force.

Note

Add new paragraph at end:
    Section 89 has been amended by Housing and Planning Act 2016 Sch.8, printed at 3A-1904. **3A-410**
This amendment is not yet in force.

Note

Add at end:
    This section will be omitted when Housing and Planning Act 2016 Sch.7 para.14 is implemented **3A-440.2**
by a commencement order and replaced by a new section. These amendments are not yet in force.

Note

Add at end:
    This section will be omitted when Housing and Planning Act 2016 Sch.7 para.14 is implemented **3A-440.9**
by a commencement order and replaced by a new section. These amendments are not yet in force.

Note

Add at end:
    This section will be omitted when Housing and Planning Act 2016 Sch.7 para.14 is implemented **3A-440.14**
by a commencement order and replaced by a new section. These amendments are not yet in force.

Note

Add at end:
    This section will be omitted when Housing and Planning Act 2016 Sch.7 para.14 is implemented **3A-440.17**
by a commencement order and replaced by a new section. These amendments are not yet in force.

Note

Add at end:
    This section will be omitted when Housing and Planning Act 2016 Sch.7 para.14 is implemented **3A-440.21**
by a commencement order and replaced by a new section. These amendments are not yet in force.

Add new paragraphs 3A–463.1 to 3A–463.4:

Meaning of "flexible tenancy"
115B.—(1)   For the purposes of this Act, a flexible tenancy is a secure **3A-463.1**
tenancy to which any of the following subsections applies.
    (2)   This subsection applies to a secure tenancy if—
        (a)   it was granted by a landlord in England for a fixed term of not less
              than two years,
        (b)   it was granted before the day on which paragraph 4 of Schedule 7
              to the Housing and Planning Act 2016 came fully into force, and
        (c)   before it was granted the person who became the landlord under
              the tenancy served a written notice on the person who became the
              tenant under the tenancy stating that the tenancy would be a flex-
              ible tenancy.
    (3)   This subsection applies to a secure tenancy if—
        (a)   it became a secure tenancy by virtue of a notice under paragraph
              4ZA(2) of Schedule 1 (family intervention tenancies becoming secure
              tenancies),
        (b)   the notice was given before the day on which paragraph 4 of
              Schedule 7 to the Housing and Planning Act 2016 came fully into
              force,
        (c)   the landlord under the family intervention tenancy in question was
              a local housing authority in England,

(d) the family intervention tenancy was granted to a person on the coming to an end of a flexible tenancy under which the person was a tenant,

(e) the notice states that the tenancy is to become a secure tenancy that is a flexible tenancy for a fixed term of the length specified in the notice, and sets out the other express terms of the tenancy, and

(f) the length of the term specified in the notice is at least two years.

(4) The length of the term of a flexible tenancy that becomes such a tenancy by virtue of subsection (3) is that specified in the notice under paragraph 4ZA(2) of Schedule 1.

(5) The other express terms of the flexible tenancy are those set out in the notice, so far as those terms are compatible with the statutory provisions relating to flexible tenancies; and in this subsection "statutory provision" means any provision made by or under an Act.

(6) This subsection applies to a secure tenancy if—

(a) it is created by virtue of section 137A of the Housing Act 1996 (introductory tenancies becoming flexible tenancies), or

(b) it arises by virtue of section 143MA or 143MB of that Act (demoted tenancies becoming flexible tenancies).

3A-463.2   *Commencement* —This section has been inserted by Housing and Planning Act 2016 Sch.7 para.15. It will be implemented by a commencement order. It is not yet in force.

Meaning of "old-style secure tenancy" in England

3A-463.3   **115C.—** In this Part "old-style secure tenancy" means a secure tenancy of a dwelling-house in England that—

(a) is a secure tenancy, other than a flexible tenancy, granted before the day on which paragraph 4 of Schedule 7 to the Housing and Planning Act 2016 came fully into force,

(b) is a secure tenancy granted on or after that date that contains an express term stating that it is an old-style secure tenancy, or

(c) is a tenancy that arose by virtue of section 86 on the coming to an end of a secure tenancy within paragraph (a) or (b).

3A-463.4   *Commencement* —This section has been inserted by Housing and Planning Act 2016 Sch.7 para.15. It will be implemented by a commencement order. It is not yet in force.

Note

Replace with:

3A-466   Amended by the Housing and Planning Act 1986 s.24(1), (2), Sch.5; the Housing Act 1988 s.140, Sch.17; the Housing Act 1996 s.141(1), Sch.14 para.4; the Housing Act 1996 (Consequential Provisions) Order 1996 (SI 1996/2325) art.5, Sch.2 para.14 and the Government of Wales Act 1998 Sch.16 para.11 and Sch.18 Pt VI; and the Localism Act 2011 s.155(5), with effect (subject to transitional, transitory and saving provisions in arts 9, 11, 14, 15, 17) from 1 April 2012 (SI 2012/628 art.(6)(a)). Section 117 has been amended by Housing and Planning Act 2016 Schs 7 and 8. The amendments will be implemented by a Commencement Order and are not yet in force, but are printed at 3A-1903 and 3A-1904.

Note

Replace with:

3A-497   Amended by the Housing Act 1988 s.83; the Planning (Consequential Provisions) Act 1990, the Charities Act 1992; the Agricultural Holdings Act 1986 Sch.14; the Education Reform Act 1988 Sch.12; the Housing Act 1996 Schs 16 and 17; the Education Act 1996 Sch.7; the Agricultural Tenancies Act 1995 s.40, Sch.; the Police Act 1996 s.103, Sch.7, para.40; the Government of Wales Act 1998 Sch.18, Pt IV; the Immigration and Asylum Act 1999 Sch.14, para.81; the Anti-Social Behaviour Act 2003 s.14(5) and Sch.1; and by the Fire and Rescue Services Act 2004 s.53(1), Sch.1, para.62(1), (3); the Licensing Act 2003 Sch.6, paras 102, 104; the Fire and Rescue Services Act 2004 s.53(1), Sch.1, para.62(1), (3); theImmigration, Asylum and Nationality Act 2006 s.43(4); the Housing and Regeneration Act 2008 (Consequential Provisions) Order 2008 (SI 2008/3002) para.28; the Housing and Regeneration Act 2008 s.297 with effect from January 1, 2009 (CO 2008/3068); the Localism Act 2011 s.222, Sch.22, para.15, with effect from January 15, 2012 (s.240(1)(l));

and the Anti-social Behaviour, Crime and Policing Act 2014 Sch.11, para.12, with effect from May 13, 2014 and Housing (Wales) Act 2014 Sch.3 para.1, with effect from 27 April 2015 (SI 2015/1271). Schedule 1 has been amended by Housing and Planning Act 2016 Sch.7 para 17. The amendment will be implemented by a Commencement Order and is not yet in force, but is printed at 3A-1903.

Note

Add new paragraph at end:
Ground 15A is Ground 16 in Wales.   **3A-524**

After paragraph 28, add:

SECTION 84A(9)   SCHEDULE 2A

ABSOLUTE GROUND FOR POSSESSION FOR ANTI-SOCIAL BEHAVIOUR: SERIOUS OFFENCES

Drug-related offences
29.   An offence under section 6 of that Act (restrictions of cultivation of cannabis plant) where the cultivation is for profit and the whole or a substantial part of the dwelling-house concerned is used for the cultivation.
29A   An offence under either of the following sections of the Modern Slavery Act 2015—
    (a)   section 1 (slavery, servitude and forced or compulsory labour),
    (b)   section 2 (human trafficking).

Note

Add new paragraph at end:
Paragraph 29A inserted, in relation to Wales by the Housing Act 1985 (Amendment of Schedule   **3A-533** 2A) (Serious Offences) (Wales) Order 2016 (SI 2016/173) art.2(2), with effect from 16 February 2016; and in relation to England by the Modern Slavery Act 2015 (Consequential Amendments) Regulations 2016 (SI 2016/244) reg.7, with effect from 17 March 2016.

Landlord and Tenant Act 1985

Note

Replace with:
Subsections (1A), (1B) inserted by the Localism Act 2011, s.166, with effect (subject to transitional,   **3A-565.1** transitory and saving provisions in arts 9, 11, 14, 15, 17) from April 1, 2012 (SI 2012/628 art(6)(ci)). Section 13 has been amended by Housing and Planning Act 2016 Sch.7 para 18. The amendment will be implemented by a Commencement Order and is not yet in force, but is printed at 3A-1903.

Housing Act 1988

Note

Replace with:
Amended by the Housing Act 2004 s.222(1) and (2). This section has also been amended by the   **3A-749** Housing and Regeneration Act 2008 Sch.11 Pt I para.6 (for transitional provisions see para.14) with effect from 20 May 2009 (SI 2009/1261) (c.66). Housing Act 1988 s.5 has been amended by Housing and Planning Act 2016 s.63. The amendment will be implemented by a Commencement Order and is not yet in force, but is printed at para 3A-1898. Housing Act 1988 s.5 has been amended by Immigration Act 2016 s.40. The amendment will be implemented by a Commencement Order and is not yet in force, but is printed at para 3A-1864. The amendment applies in relation to a tenancy or a licence entered into before or after the coming into force of the section.

Note

Replace with:
Amended by the Local Government and Housing Act 1989 Sch.11. This section has also been   **3A-770** amended by the Housing and Regeneration Act 2008 Sch.11 Pt I para.7 (for transitional provisions see para.14) with effect from 20 May 2009 (SI 2009/1261) (c.66); and the Localism Act 2011 s.162(4), with effect (subject to transitional, transitory and saving provisions in arts 9, 11, 14, 15, 17) from 1 April 2012 (SI 2012/628 art.(6)(b)). It was further amended by the Anti-social Behaviour, Crime and Policing Act 2014 Sch.11 para.18. The amendment was brought into force in England on 20 October 2014 by the Anti-social Behaviour, Crime and Policing Act 2014 (Commencement No.7, Saving and Transitional Provisions) Order 2014 (SI 2014/2590). It was brought into force in Wales on 21 October 2014 by the Anti-social Behaviour, Crime and Policing Act 2014 (Commencement No.2 and Transitional Provisions) (Wales) Order 2014 (SI 2014/2830). Housing Act 1988 s.7

has been amended by Immigration Act 2016 s.41. The amendment will be implemented by a Commencement Order and is not yet in force, but is printed at para.3A-1866.

Note

Replace with:

3A-785 Amended by the Housing Act 1996 s.151. Further amended by the Anti-social Behaviour, Crime and Policing Act 2014 s.97. The amendment was brought into force in England on 20 October 2014 by the Anti-social Behaviour, Crime and Policing Act 2014 (Commencement No.7, Saving and Transitional Provisions) Order 2014 (SI 2014/2590). It was brought into force in Wales on 21 October 2014 by the Anti-social Behaviour, Crime and Policing Act 2014 (Commencement No.2 and Transitional Provisions) (Wales) Order 2014 (SI 2014/2830) (subject to transitional provisions in art.3). Housing Act 1988 s.8(5) has been amended by Immigration Act 2016 s.41. The amendment will be implemented by a Commencement Order and is not yet in force, but is printed at para.3A-1866.

Notice of proceedings for possession

Replace the first paragraph with:

3A-791 Before bringing possession proceedings against assured tenants, landlords must either serve a "notice of proceedings for possession" in accordance with the Housing Act 1988 s.8, or (in cases other than Ground 8) persuade the court that it is just and equitable to dispense with that requirement. The relevant form is contained in the Assured Tenancies and Agricultural Occupancies (Forms) (England) (Amendment) Regulations 2016 (SI 2016/443). The relevant form (Form 3) states that the landlord must, inter alia, "give the full text ... of each ground which is being relied upon". It is similar to the form of notice used in connection with public sector secure tenancies (Housing Act 1985 s.83). An earlier form provided that "Particulars of the grounds relied upon have to be included as well as the ground itself. The current form requires a full explanation of why each ground is being relied upon".

Add new paragraph 3A–815.1:

3A-815.1 *Note* —Housing Act 1988 has been amended by Immigration Act 2016 s.41 by inserting a new s.10A "Power to order transfer of tenancy in certain cases". The amendment will be implemented by a Commencement Order and is not yet in force, but is printed at para.3A-1866.

Note

Replace with:

3A-827 Amended by the Regulatory Reform (Assured Periodic Tenancies) (Rent Increases) Order 2003 (SI 2003/259) and the Transfer of Tribunal Functions Order 2013 (SI 2013/1036) Sch.1 para.82 with effect from July 1, 2013. The amendment made by SI 2003/259 was designed to overcome the argument that a strict interpretation of former s.13(2)(c) rendered many rent increases made by registered social landlords invalid because, although increases may have occurred annually, in some years they may have purported to take effect a few days earlier than "the first anniversary of the date" when the last increase took effect. The effect of the amendment is to enable landlords to set a fixed day (e.g. the first Monday in April) on which rent increases are to take effect. The first time that the rent is increased after the Order came into force on February 10, 2003, the increase may take effect not less than 52 weeks after the start of the tenancy or, if the rent has already been increased, not less than 52 weeks after the date of the last increase. On the second and subsequent occasions, the increase may take effect not less than 52 weeks after the last increase, unless that would result in the increase taking effect on a date falling a week or more before the anniversary of the first increase after the date on which the Order comes into force. In such a case the increase may not take effect until 53 weeks after the date of the last increase. In England, the prescribed forms to be used by landlords when proposing new rents under s.13(2) are contained in the Assured Tenancies and Agricultural Occupancies (Forms) (England) (Amendment) Regulations 2016 (SI 2016/443). The Assured Tenancies and Agricultural Occupancies (Forms) (Amendment) (Wales) Regulations 2003 (SI 2003/307) (w.46) prescribe the forms to be used in Wales.

3A-851.1 *Change title of paragraph:*

Transfer of tenancies under Localism Act 2011

Note

Replace "October 2015" with:

3A-897.8 1 October 2015

Add new paragraph 3A–999.2:

3A-999.2 *Note* —Housing Act 1988 Sch.2 Pt 1 (assured tenancies: grounds on which court must order possession) has been amended by Immigration Act 2016 s.41 by inserting a new Ground 7B. The amendment will be implemented by a Commencement Order and is not yet in force, but is printed at para.3A-1866.

Housing Act 1996

Note

Replace with:

Amended (subject to transitional and saving provisions in Sch.3 thereof) by the Housing and **3A-1063.1** Regeneration Act 2008 (Consequential Provisions) Order 2010 (SI 2010/866) Sch.2 para.96, with effect from 1 April 2010. The law relating to introductory tenancies has been amended by Housing and Planning Act 2016 Schs 7 and 8. The amendments will be implemented by a Commencement Order and are not yet in force, but are printed at paras 3A-1903 and 3A-1904.

Replace s.185(2A) with:

ELIGIBILITY FOR ASSISTANCE

Persons from abroad not eligible for housing assistance

(2A)   No person who is excluded from entitlement to universal credit or housing benefit by section 115 of the Immigration and Asylum Act 1999 (exclusion from benefits) shall be included in any class prescribed under subsection (2).

Note

Add new paragraph at end:

Subsection (2A) amended by the Universal Credit (Consequential, Supplementary, Incidental **3A-1290** and Miscellaneous Provisions) Regulations 2013 (SI 2013/630) reg.12(5), with effect from 29 April 2013.

Persons from abroad and priority need

Add at end:

In relation to this section, see *Mirga v Secretary of State for Work and Pensions* [2016] UKSC 1, 27 **3A-1297** January 2016.

Commonhold and Leasehold Reform Act 2002

Replace s.168 with:

No forfeiture notice before determination of breach

168.—(1)   A landlord under a long lease of a dwelling may not serve a **3A-1593** notice under section 146(1) of the Law of Property Act 1925 (c.20) (restriction on forfeiture) in respect of a breach by a tenant of a covenant or condition in the lease unless subsection (2) is satisfied.

(2)   This subsection is satisfied if—
- (a)   it has been finally determined on an application under subsection (4) that the breach has occurred,
- (b)   the tenant has admitted the breach, or
- (c)   a court in any proceedings, or an arbitral tribunal in proceedings pursuant to a post-dispute arbitration agreement, has finally determined that the breach has occurred.

(3)   But a notice may not be served by virtue of subsection (2)(a) or (c) until after the end of the period of 14 days beginning with the day after that on which the final determination is made.

(4)   A landlord under a long lease of a dwelling may make an application to the appropriate tribunal for a determination that a breach of a covenant or condition in the lease has occurred.

(5)   But a landlord may not make an application under subsection (4) in respect of a matter which—

(a)   has been, or is to be, referred to arbitration pursuant to a post-
dispute arbitration agreement to which the tenant is a party,

(b)   has been the subject of determination by a court, or

(c)   has been the subject of determination by an arbitral tribunal pursuant to a post-dispute arbitration agreement.

(6)   For the purposes of subsection (4), "appropriate tribunal" means—

(a)   in relation to a dwelling in England, the First-tier Tribunal or,
where determined by or under Tribunal Procedure Rules, the Upper Tribunal; and

(b)   in relation to a dwelling in Wales, a leasehold valuation tribunal.

Add new paragraph 3A-1593.1:

3A-1593.1   *Note* —Amended by the Transfer of Tribunal Functions Order 2013 (SI 2013/1036) Sch.1
para.141 with effect from 1 July 2013.

Policing and Crime Act 2009

Replace s.34(7)-(8) with:

PART 4

INJUNCTIONS: GANG-RELATED VIOLENCE

POWER TO GRANT INJUNCTIONS

Injunctions to prevent gang-related violence and drug-dealing activity

3A-1719   (7)   In this Part "drug-dealing activity" means—

(a)   the unlawful production, supply, importation or exportation of a
controlled drug, or

(b)   the unlawful production, supply, importation or exportation of a
psychoactive substance.

(8)   In subsection (7)—

(a)   in paragraph (a), "production", "supply" and "controlled drug"
have the meaning given by section 37(1) of the Misuse of Drugs Act
1971;

(b)   in paragraph (b), "production", "supply" and "psychoactive
substance" have the meaning given by section 59 of the Psychoactive
Substances Act 2016.

Note

Replace with:

3A-1719.1   This section was substituted, and the words in the Pt 4 heading were inserted by, the Serious
Crime Act 2015 s.51, Sch.4 para.83, with effect from 1 June 2015 (SI 2015/820). Subsections (7)
and (8) substituted for subs.(7) by the Psychoactive Substances Act 2016 Sch.5 para.10, with effect
from 26 May 2016. It has been held at first instance that the use of the civil standard of proof on
the balance of probabilities when deciding applications for gang-related injunctions under s.34 is
compatible with art.6 of the ECHR (*Chief Constable of Lancashire v Wilson* [2015] EWHC 2763 (QB),
14 July 2015, unrep. (Kerr J)).

Add new paragraph 3A–1719.2:

Interim injunctions

3A-1719.2   As to the variation and discharge of interim injunctions, see *Murray v Chief Constable of Lancashire*
[2015] EWCA Civ 1174 (18 November 2015).

Note

After "Sub-section", add:

3A-1720.1   (2)(e)

Replace s.43(7) with the following, and add para.3A 1728.1:

Arrest without warrant

(7)   In this Part "relevant judge", in relation to an injunction, means a judge **3A-1728**
of the court that granted the injunction, except that where—
>   (a)   the respondent is aged 18 or over, but
>   (b)   the injunction was granted by a youth court,

it means a judge of the county court.

Note —Subsection (7) was amended by the Crime and Courts Act 2013 s.18(3), with effect from 1 **3A-1728.1**
June 2015 (SI 2015/813) subject to savings and transitional provisions specified in 2013 c.22 s.15
and Sch.8.

Add new paragraphs 3A–1732.2 and 3A–1732.3:

Appeals against decisions of youth courts

46B.—(1)   An appeal lies to the Crown Court against a decision of a youth **3A-1732.2**
court made under this Part.
(2)   On an appeal under this section the Crown Court may make—
>   (a)   whatever orders are necessary to give effect to its determination of
>   the appeal;
>   (b)   whatever incidental or consequential orders appear to it to be just.

(3)   An order of the Crown Court made on an appeal under this section
(other than one directing that an application be re-heard by a youth court) is to
be treated for the purposes of section 42 as an order of a youth court.

Note —Inserted, together with preceding crossheading, by the Crime and Courts Act 2013 **3A-1732.3**
Sch.12 para.2 with effect from 1 June 2015 (SI 2015/813).

Replace para.3A–1734 with paras 3A–1734 and 3A–1734.1:

Supplemental

48.—(2)   Rules of court may provide that an appeal from a decision to **3A-1734**
which this subsection applies may be made without notice being given to the
respondent.
(3)   Subsection (2) applies—
>   (a)   to a decision under section 39(4)(a) that an application without
>   notice be dismissed, and
>   (b)   to a decision to refuse to grant an interim injunction under section
>   41.

(4)   In relation to a respondent attaining the age of 18 after the commencement of proceedings under this Part, rules of court may—
>   (a)   provide for the transfer of the proceedings from a youth court to
>   the High Court or the county court;
>   (b)   prescribe circumstances in which the proceedings may or must
>   remain in a youth court.

Note —Subsection (1) was repealed by the Crime and Courts Act 2013 Sch.9 para.51(2), with ef- **3A-1734.1**
fect from 22 April 2014 (SI 2014/954) subject to transitional provision specified in SI 2014/954
art.3.
   Subsections (2) and (3) were amended by the Crime and Courts Act 2013 Sch.12 para.3, with effect from 1 June 2015 (SI 2015/813) subject to savings and transitional provisions specified in 2013
c.22 s.15 and Sch.8.
   Subsection (4) was inserted by the Crime and Courts Act 2013 s.18(4), with effect from 1 June
2015 (SI 2015/813).

Interpretation

Replace s.49(1) with:

3A-1735
(1)   In this Part—
"application without notice" has the meaning given by section 39(2);
"consultation requirement" has the meaning given by section 38(2);
"court" (except in Schedule 5A)—
(a)   in the case of a respondent aged under 18, means a youth court, and
(b)   in any other case, means the High Court or the county court, but this is subject to any provision in rules of court that is or could be made under section 48(4);
"drug-dealing activity" has the meaning given by section 34(7).
"judge", in relation to a youth court, means a person qualified to sit as a member of that court;
"local authority" has the meaning given by section 37(2);
"relevant judge" has the meaning given by section 43(7);
"respondent" means the person in respect of whom an application for an injunction is made or (as the context requires) the person against whom such an injunction is granted;
"review hearing" has the meaning given by section 36(5);
"specify", in relation to an injunction, means specify in the injunction;
"violence" includes violence against property.

Note

Replace with:
3A-1735.1   Definition "court" substituted by the Crime and Courts Act 2013 s.18(2), with effect from 1 June 2015 (SI 2015/813).
Definition "drug dealing activity" inserted by the Serious Crime Act 2015 Sch.4 para.85, with effect from 1 June 2015.
Definition "judge" inserted by the Crime and Courts Act 2013 Sch.12 para.4, with effect from 1 June 2015 (SI 2015/813) subject to savings and transitional provisions specified in 2013 c.22 s.15 and Sch.8.

Replace para.3A–1737 with paras 3A–1737 and 3A–1737.1:

SECTION 46   SCHEDULE 5

INJUNCTIONS: POWERS TO REMAND

Injunctions: Power to remand
3A-1737   1.—(1)   The provisions of this Schedule apply where the court has power to remand a person under section 43(5) or 44(4).
(2)   In this Schedule, "the court" means the High Court, the county court or a youth court and includes—
(a)   in relation to the High Court, a judge of that court,
(b)   in relation to the county court, a judge of that court, and
(c)   in relation to a youth court, a judge of that court.

3A-1737.1   *Note* —Paragraph 1(2) was amended by the Crime and Courts Act 2013 Sch.9 para.51(3), with effect from 22 April 2014 (SI 2014/954) subject to savings and transitional provisions specified in 2013 c.22 s.15 and Sch.8 and transitional provision specified in SI 2014/954 arts 2(c) and 3. Paragraph 1(2) further amended by the Crime and Courts Act 2013 Sch.12 para.5(a), with effect from 1 June 2015 (SI 2015/813) subject to savings and transitional provisions specified in 2013 c.22 s.15 and Sch.8.

Replace Part 1 of Schedule 5A with:

SECTION 46

SCHEDULE 5A

BREACH OF INJUNCTION: POWERS OF COURT IN RESPECT OF UNDER-18S

PART 1

INTRODUCTORY

Power to make supervision order or detention order

1.—(1)   Where—
    (a)   an injunction under Part 4 has been granted against a person under the age of 18,
    (aa)   the person is still under the age of 18, and
    (b)   on an application made by the injunction applicant, a youth court is satisfied beyond reasonable doubt that the person is in breach of any provision of the injunction,
that court may make one of the orders specified in sub-paragraph (2) in respect of the person.
  (2)   Those orders are—
    (a)   a supervision order (see Part 2 of this Schedule);
    (b)   a detention order (see Part 3 of this Schedule).
  (4)   Before making an application under paragraph 1(1)(b) the injunction applicant must consult—
    (a)   the youth offending team consulted under section 38(1) or 39(5) in relation to the injunction, and
    (b)   any other person previously so consulted.
  (5)   In considering whether and how to exercise its powers under this paragraph, the court must consider a report made to assist the court in that respect by the youth offending team referred to in subparagraph (4)(a).
  (6)   An order under sub-paragraph (1) may not be made in respect of a person aged 18 or over.
  (7)   The court may not make a detention order under sub-paragraph (1) unless it is satisfied, in view of the severity or extent of the breach, that no other power available to the court is appropriate.
  (8)   Where the court makes a detention order under sub-paragraph (1) it must state in open court why it is satisfied as specified in sub-paragraph (7).
  (9)   In this Schedule—
    "defaulter", in relation to an order under this Schedule, means the person in respect of whom the order is made;
    "injunction applicant", in relation to an injunction under Part 4 or an order under this Schedule made in respect of such an injunction, means the person who applied for the injunction.

3A-1744

Note

Add new paragraph at end:
  Paragraph 1 amended by the Crime and Courts Act 2013 Sch.12 para.7, with effect from 1 June 2015 (SI 2015/813) subject to savings and transitional provisions specified in 2013 c.22 s.15 and Sch.8.

3A-1744.1

Replace paras 3A–1745 to 3A–1756 with paras 3A–1745 to 3A–1756.1:

PART 2

SUPERVISION ORDERS

Supervision orders

2.—(1)   A supervision order is an order imposing on the defaulter one or more of the following requirements—
    (a)   a supervision requirement;
    (b)   an activity requirement;
    (c)   a curfew requirement.
  (2)   Before making a supervision order the court must obtain and consider information about the defaulter's family circumstances and the likely effect of such an order on those circumstances.
  (3)   Before making a supervision order imposing two or more requirements, the court must consider their mutual compatibility.
  (4)   The court must ensure, as far as practicable, that any requirement imposed by a supervision order is such as to avoid—
    (a)   any conflict with the defaulter's religious beliefs,
    (b)   any interference with the times, if any, at which the defaulter normally works or attends school or any other educational establishment, and

3A-1745

(c) any conflict with the requirements of any other court order or injunction to which the defaulter may be subject.

(5) A supervision order must for the purposes of this Schedule specify a maximum period for the operation of any requirement contained in the order.

(6) The period specified under sub-paragraph (5) may not exceed six months beginning with the day after that on which the supervision order is made.

(7) A supervision order must for the purposes of this Schedule specify a youth offending team established under section 39 of the Crime and Disorder Act 1998.

(8) The youth offending team specified under sub-paragraph (7) is to be—

(a) the youth offending team in whose area it appears to the court that the respondent will reside during the period specified under sub-paragraph (5), or

(b) where it appears to the court that the respondent will reside in the area of two or more such teams, such one of those teams as the court may determine.

Supervision requirements

3A-1746 3.—(1) In this Schedule, "supervision requirement", in relation to a supervision order, means a requirement that the defaulter attend appointments with—

(a) the responsible officer, or

(b) another person determined by the responsible officer, at such times and places as may be instructed by the responsible officer.

(2) The appointments must be within the period for the time being specified in the order under paragraph 2(5).

Activity requirements

3A-1747 4.—(1) In this Schedule, "activity requirement", in relation to a supervision order, means a requirement that the defaulter do any or all of the following within the period for the time being specified in the order under paragraph 2(5)—

(a) participate, on such number of days as may be specified in the order, in activities at a place, or places, so specified;

(b) participate in an activity or activities specified in the order on such number of days as may be so specified;

(c) participate in one or more residential exercises for a continuous period or periods comprising such number or numbers of days as may be specified in the order;

(d) in accordance with sub-paragraphs (6) to (9), engage in activities in accordance with instructions of the responsible officer on such number of days as may be specified in the order.

(2) The number of days specified in a supervision order in relation to an activity requirement must not, in aggregate, be less than 12 or more than 24.

(3) A requirement referred to in sub-paragraph (1)(a) or (b) operates to require the defaulter, in accordance with instructions given by the responsible officer, on the number of days specified in the order in relation to the requirement—

(a) in the case of a requirement referred to in sub-paragraph (1)(a), to present himself or herself at a place specified in the order to a person of a description so specified, or

(b) in the case of a requirement referred to in sub-paragraph (1)(b), to participate in an activity specified in the order, and, on each such day, to comply with instructions given by, or under the authority of, the person in charge of the place or the activity (as the case may be).

(4) Where the order includes a requirement referred to in sub-paragraph (1)(c) to participate in a residential exercise, it must specify, in relation to the residential exercise—

(a) a place, or

(b) an activity.

(5) A requirement under sub-paragraph (1)(c) to participate in a residential exercise operates to require the defaulter, in accordance with instructions given by the responsible officer—

(a) if a place is specified under sub-paragraph (4)(a)—

(i) to present himself or herself at the beginning of the period specified in the order in relation to the exercise, at the place so specified to a person of a description specified in the instructions, and

(ii) to reside there for that period;

(b) if an activity is specified under sub-paragraph (4)(b), to participate, for the period specified in the order in relation to the exercise, in the activity so specified, and, during that period, to comply with instructions given by, or under the authority of, the person in charge of the place or the activity (as the case may be).

(6) Subject to sub-paragraph (8), instructions under sub-paragraph (1)(d) relating to any day must require the defaulter to do either of the following—

(a) present himself or herself to a person of a description specified in the instructions at a place so specified;

(b) participate in an activity specified in the instructions.

(7) Any such instructions operate to require the defaulter, on that day or while participating in that activity, to comply with instructions given by, or under the authority of, the person in

202

charge of the place or, as the case may be, the activity.

(8) If the supervision order so provides, instructions under sub-paragraph (1)(d) may require the defaulter to participate in a residential exercise for a period comprising not more than seven days, and, for that purpose—

(a) to present himself or herself at the beginning of that period to a person of a description specified in the instructions at a place so specified and to reside there for that period, or

(b) to participate for that period in an activity specified in the instructions.

(9) Instructions such as are mentioned in sub-paragraph (8)—

(a) may not be given except with the consent of a parent or guardian of the defaulter, and

(b) operate to require the defaulter, during the period specified under that sub-paragraph, to comply with instructions given by, or under the authority of, the person in charge of the place or activity specified under paragraph (a) or (b) of that sub-paragraph.

(10) Instructions given by, or under the authority of, a person in charge of a place under sub-paragraph (3), (5), (7) or (9)(b) may require the defaulter to engage in activities otherwise than at that place.

(11) Where a supervision order contains an activity requirement, a youth court may on the application of the injunction applicant or the defaulter amend the order by substituting for any number of days, place, activity, period or description of persons specified in the order a new number of days, place, activity, period or description (subject, in the case of a number of days, to sub-paragraph (2)).

(12) A court may only include an activity requirement in a supervision order or vary such a requirement under sub-paragraph (11) if—

(a) it has consulted the youth offending team which is to be, or is, specified in the order,

(b) it is satisfied that it is feasible to secure compliance with the requirement or requirement as varied,

(c) it is satisfied that provision for the defaulter to participate in the activities proposed can be made under the arrangements for persons to participate in such activities which exist in the area of the youth offending team which is to be or is specified in the order, and

(d) in a case where the requirement or requirement as varied would involve the co-operation of a person other than the defaulter and the responsible officer, that person consents to its inclusion or variation.

(13) For the purposes of sub-paragraph (9) "guardian" has the same meaning as in the Children and Young Persons Act 1933 (subject to sub-paragraph (14)).

(14) If a local authority has parental responsibility for a defaulter who is in its care or provided with accommodation by it in the exercise of any social services functions, the reference to "guardian" in sub-paragraph (9) is to be read as a reference to that authority.

(15) In sub-paragraph (14)—

(a) "parental responsibility" has the same meaning as it has in the Children Act 1989 by virtue of section 3 of that Act;

(b) "social services functions" has the same meaning as it has in the Local Authority Social Services Act 1970 by virtue of section 1A of that Act.

3A-1748

5.—(1) In this Schedule, "curfew requirement", in relation to a supervision order, means a requirement that the defaulter remain, for periods specified in the order, at a place so specified.

(2) A supervision order imposing a curfew requirement may specify different places or different periods for different days.

(3) The periods specified under sub-paragraph (1)—

(a) must be within the period for the time being specified in the order under paragraph 2(5);

(b) may not amount to less than two or more than eight hours in any day.

(4) Before specifying a place under sub-paragraph (1) in a supervision order, the court making the order must obtain and consider information about the place proposed to be specified in the order (including information as to the attitude of persons likely to be affected by the enforced presence there of the defaulter).

(5) Where a supervision order contains a curfew requirement, a youth court may, on the application of the injunction applicant or the defaulter amend the order by—

(a) substituting new periods for the periods specified in the order under this paragraph (subject to sub-paragraph (3)); or

(b) substituting a new place for the place specified in the order under this paragraph (subject to sub-paragraph (4)).

3A-1749

6.—(1) A supervision order containing a curfew requirement may also contain a requirement (an "electronic monitoring requirement") for securing the electronic monitoring of compliance with the curfew requirement during a period—.

(a)   specified in the order, or

(b)   determined by the responsible officer in accordance with the order.

(2)   In a case referred to in sub-paragraph (1)(b), the responsible officer must, before the beginning of the period when the electronic monitoring requirement is to take effect, notify—

(a)   the defaulter,

(b)   the person responsible for the monitoring, and

(c)   any person falling within sub-paragraph (3)(b),

of the time when that period is to begin.

(3)   Where—

(a)   it is proposed to include an electronic monitoring requirement in a supervision order, but

(b)   there is a person (other than the defaulter) without whose cooperation it will not be practicable to secure that the monitoring takes place,

the requirement may not be included in the order without that person's consent.

(4)   A supervision order imposing an electronic monitoring requirement must include provision for making a person responsible for the monitoring.

(5)   The person who is made responsible for the monitoring must be of a description specified in an order under paragraph 26(5) of Schedule 1 to the Criminal Justice and Immigration Act 2008.

(6)   An electronic monitoring requirement may not be included in a supervision order unless the court making the order—

(a)   has been notified by the youth offending team for the time being specified in the order that arrangements for electronic monitoring are available in the area where the place which the court proposes to specify in the order for the purposes of the curfew requirement is situated, and

(b)   is satisfied that the necessary provision can be made under the arrangements currently available.

(7)   Where a supervision order contains an electronic monitoring requirement, a youth court may, on the application of the injunction applicant or the defaulter, amend the order by substituting a new period for the period specified in the order under this paragraph.

(8)   Sub-paragraph (3) applies in relation to the variation of an electronic monitoring requirement under sub-paragraph (7) as it applies in relation to the inclusion of such a requirement.

3A-1750   7.—(1)   For the purposes of this Part of this Schedule, the "responsible officer", in relation to a supervision order, means—

(a)   in a case where the order imposes a curfew requirement and an electronic monitoring requirement, but does not impose an activity or supervision requirement, the person who under paragraph 6(4) is responsible for the electronic monitoring;

(b)   in any other case, the member of the youth offending team for the time being specified in the order who, as respects the defaulter, is for the time being responsible for discharging the functions conferred by this Schedule on the responsible officer.

(2)   Where a supervision order has been made, it is the duty of the responsible officer—

(a)   to make any arrangements that are necessary in connection with the requirements contained in the order, and

(b)   to promote the defaulter's compliance with those requirements.

(3)   In giving instructions in pursuance of a supervision order, the responsible officer must ensure, so far as practicable, that any instruction is such as to avoid the matters referred to in paragraph 2(4).

(4)   A defaulter in respect of whom a supervision order is made must—

(a)   keep in touch with the responsible officer in accordance with such instructions as the responsible officer may from time to time give to the defaulter, and

(b)   notify the responsible officer of any change of address.

(5)   The obligations imposed by sub-paragraph (4) have effect as a requirement of the supervision order.

3A-1751   8.—(1)   A youth court may, on the application of the injunction applicant or the defaulter, amend a supervision order by substituting a new period for that for the time being specified in the order under paragraph 2(5) (subject to paragraph 2(6)).

(2)   A youth court may, on amending a supervision order pursuant to sub-paragraph (1), make such other amendments to the order in relation to any requirement imposed by the order as the court considers appropriate.

3A-1752   9.—(1)   This paragraph applies where, on an application made by the injunction applicant or the defaulter in relation to a supervision order, a youth court is satisfied that the defaulter proposes to reside, or is residing, in the area of a youth offending team other than the team for the time being specified in the order.

(2)   If the application is made by the defaulter, the court to which it is made may amend the order by substituting for the youth offending team specified in the order the youth offending team for the area referred to in sub-paragraph (1) (or, if there is more than one such team for that area, such of those teams as the court may determine).

(3)   If the application is made by the injunction applicant, the court to which it is made must, subject as follows, so amend the order.

(4)   Where a court amends the supervision order pursuant to sub-paragraph (2) or (3) but the order contains a requirement which, in the opinion of the court, cannot reasonably be complied with if the defaulter resides in the area referred to in subparagraph (1), the court must also amend the order by—

(a)   removing that requirement, or

(b)   substituting for that requirement a new requirement which can reasonably be complied with if the defaulter resides in that area.

(5)   Sub-paragraph (3) does not require a court to amend the supervision order if in its opinion sub-paragraph (4) would produce an inappropriate result.

(6)   The injunction applicant must consult the youth offending team for the time being specified in the order before making an application under sub-paragraph (1).

10.—(1)   Where a supervision order is made, the injunction applicant or the defaulter may apply to a youth court— **3A-1753**

(a)   to revoke the order, or

(b)   to amend the order by removing any requirement from it.

(2)   If it appears to the court to which an application under sub-paragraph (1)(a) or (b) is made to be in the interests of justice to do so, having regard to circumstances which have arisen since the supervision order was made, the court may grant the application and revoke or amend the order accordingly.

(3)   The circumstances referred to in sub-paragraph (2) include the conduct of the defaulter.

(4)   If an application made under sub-paragraph (1) in relation to a supervision order is dismissed, no further such application may be made in relation to the order by any person without the consent of a youth court.

(5)   The injunction applicant must consult the youth offending team for the time being specified in the order before making an application under sub-paragraph (1).

11.   If the responsible officer considers that the defaulter has complied with all the requirements of the supervision order, the responsible officer must inform the injunction applicant. **3A-1754**

12.—(1)   If the responsible officer considers that the defaulter has failed to comply with any requirement of the supervision order, the responsible officer must inform the injunction applicant. **3A-1755**

(2)   On being informed as specified in sub-paragraph (1) the injunction applicant may apply to a youth court.

(3)   Before making an application under sub-paragraph (2) the injunction applicant must consult—

(a)   the youth offending team for the time being specified in the order, and

(b)   any person consulted by virtue of section 38(2)(a) or (b).

(4)   If on an application under sub-paragraph (2) the court to which it is made is satisfied beyond reasonable doubt that the defaulter has without reasonable excuse failed to comply with any requirement of the supervision order, the court may—

(7)   The court to which an application under sub-paragraph (2) is made must consider representations made by the youth offending team for the time being specified in the order before exercising its powers under this paragraph.

13.—(1)   The court by which a supervision order is made must forthwith provide a copy of the order to— **3A-1756**

(a)   the defaulter, and

(b)   the youth offending team for the time being specified in the order.

(2)   Where a supervision order is made, the injunction applicant must forthwith provide a copy of so much of the order as is relevant—

(a)   in a case where the order includes an activity requirement specifying a place under paragraph 4(1)(a), to the person in charge of that place;

(b)   in a case where the order includes an activity requirement specifying an activity under paragraph 4(1)(b), to the person in charge of that activity;

(c)   in a case where the order includes an activity requirement specifying a residential exercise under paragraph 4(1)(c), to the person in charge of the place or activity specified under paragraph 4(4) in relation to that residential exercise;

(d)   in a case where the order contains an electronic monitoring requirement, to—

(i)   any person who by virtue of paragraph 6(4) will be responsible for the electronic monitoring, and

(ii)   any person without whose consent that requirement could not have been included in the order.

(3)   The court by which a supervision order is revoked or amended must forthwith provide a copy of the revoking order, or of the order as amended, to—

(a)   the defaulter, and

(b)   the youth offending team for the time being specified in the order.

(4)   Where—

(a)   a copy of a supervision order (or part of a supervision order) has been given to a person under sub-paragraph (2) by virtue of any requirement contained in the order, and

(b)   the order is revoked, or amended in respect of that requirement,

the injunction applicant must forthwith give a copy of the revoking order, or of so much of the order as amended as is relevant, to that person.

3A-1756.1   *Note* —Paragraph 4(11) amended by the Crime and Courts Act 2013 Sch.12 para.8, with effect from 1 June 2015 (SI 2015/813) subject to savings and transitional provisions specified in 2013 c.22 s.15 and Sch.8.

Paragraph 5(5) amended by the Crime and Courts Act 2013 Sch.12 para.9, with effect from 1 June 2015 (SI 2015/813) subject to savings and transitional provisions specified in 2013 c.22 s.15 and Sch.8.

Paragraph 6(7) amended by the Crime and Courts Act 2013 Sch.12 para.10, with effect from 1 June 2015 (SI 2015/813) subject to savings and transitional provisions specified in 2013 c.22 s.15 and Sch.8.

Paragraph 8 amended by the Crime and Courts Act 2013 Sch.12 para.11, with effect from 1 June 2015 (SI 2015/813) subject to savings and transitional provisions specified in 2013 c.22 s.15 and Sch.8.

Paragraph 9(1) amended by the Crime and Courts Act 2013 Sch.12 para.12, with effect from 1 June 2015 (SI 2015/813) subject to savings and transitional provisions specified in 2013 c.22 s.15 and Sch.8.

Paragraph 10(1), (4) amended by the Crime and Courts Act 2013 Sch.12 para.13, with effect from 1 June 2015 (SI 2015/813) subject to savings and transitional provisions specified in 2013 c.22 s.15 and Sch.8.

Paragraph 12(2) amended and para.12(5), (6) repealed by the Crime and Courts Act 2013 Sch.12 para.14, with effect from 1 June 2015 (SI 2015/813) subject to savings and transitional provisions specified in 2013 c.22 s.15 and Sch.8.

Replace Part 3 of Schedule 5A with:

PART 3

DETENTION ORDERS

Detention orders

3A-1757   **14**(1)   A detention order is an order that the defaulter be detained for a period specified in the order in such youth detention accommodation as the Secretary of State may determine.

(2)   The period specified under sub-paragraph (1) may not exceed the period of three months beginning with the day after that on which the order is made.

(3)   In sub-paragraph (1) "youth detention accommodation" means—

(a)   a secure training centre;

(aa)   a secure college;

(b)   a young offender institution;

[(c)   a secure children's home, as defined by section 102(11) of the Legal Aid, Sentencing and Punishment of Offenders Act 2012.]

(4)   The function of the Secretary of State under sub-paragraph (1) is exercisable concurrently with the Youth Justice Board.

(5)   A person detained under a detention order is in legal custody.

Revocation of detention order

15(1)   Where a detention order is made, the injunction applicant or the defaulter may apply to a youth court to revoke it.

(2)   If it appears to the court to which an application under sub-paragraph (1) is made to be in the interests of justice to do so, having regard to circumstances which have arisen since the detention order was made, the court may grant the application and revoke the order accordingly.

(3)   The circumstances referred to in sub-paragraph (2) include the conduct of the defaulter.

(4)   If an application made under sub-paragraph (1) in relation to a detention order is dismissed, no further such application may be made in relation to the order by any person without the consent of a youth court.

(5)   Before making an application under sub-paragraph (1) the injunction applicant must consult—

(a)   in the case of a detention order made under paragraph 1(1), the youth offending team referred to in paragraph 1(4)(a); or

(b)   in the case of a detention order made under paragraph 12(4)(b), the youth offending team referred to in paragraph 12(3)(a).

Note

Add new paragraph at end:

3A-1758.1   Paragraph 15(1), (4) amended by the Crime and Courts Act 2013 Sch.12 para.15, with effect from 1 June 2015 (SI 2015/813) subject to savings and transitional provisions specified in 2013 c.22 s.15 and Sch.8.

Add new paragraphs 3A-1845.1 to 3A-1845.9:

Immigration Act 2014

(2014 c.22)

Termination of agreement where all occupiers disqualified

33D.—(1) The landlord under a residential tenancy agreement relating to premises in England may terminate the agreement in accordance with this section if the condition in subsection (2) is met.   **3A-1845.1**

(2) The condition is that the Secretary of State has given one or more notices in writing to the landlord which, taken together,—

    (a) identify the occupier of the premises or (if there is more than one occupier) all of them, and

    (b) state that the occupier or occupiers are disqualified as a result of their immigration status from occupying premises under a residential tenancy agreement.

(3) The landlord may terminate the residential tenancy agreement by giving notice in writing and in the prescribed form to the tenant or, in the case of a joint tenancy, all of the tenants specifying the date on which the agreement comes to an end.

(4) That date must not be earlier than the end of the period of 28 days beginning with the day specified in the notice as the day on which it is given.

(5) The notice may be given—

    (a) by delivering it to the tenant or tenants,

    (b) by leaving it at the premises,

    (c) by sending it by post to the tenant or tenants at the address of the premises, or

    (d) in any other prescribed manner.

(6) The notice is to be treated as a notice to quit in a case where a notice to quit would otherwise be required to bring the residential tenancy agreement to an end.

(7) The notice is enforceable as if it were an order of the High Court.

(8) In this section "occupier", in relation to premises to which a residential tenancy agreement applies, means—

    (a) a tenant,

    (b) a person who, under the agreement, otherwise has the right to occupy the premises and is named in the agreement, and

    (c) any other person who the landlord knows is occupying the premises.

Commencement —This section was inserted by Immigration Act 2016 s.40. It is not yet in force. It will be brought into force by Regulations. See Immigration Act 2016 s.94. It applies to residential tenancy agreements entered into before or after the coming into force of this section—see Immigration Act 2016 s.40(3).   **3A-1845.2**

Editorial introduction

This section enables certain landlords to terminate tenancies if occupants (as defined in subs.(8)) are disqualified from occupying premises under Immigration Act 2014 s.21. Occupants are disqualified if they are not relevant nationals (i.e. a British citizen, a national of an EEA State, or a national of Switzerland) and do not have a "right to rent", viz. if they require leave to remain in the UK and do not have it, or they have leave to enter or remain in the UK but such leave is subject to a condition preventing them from occupying the premises. In those circumstances, their occupation may   **3A-1845.3** be terminated by notice, which operates as if it is a notice to quit. However, that may only be done if the Secretary of State has first given notice to the landlord that the occupant is disqualified. The resulting right to possession may be enforced as if it were an order of the High Court.

"a residential tenancy agreement"

3A-1845.4   A tenancy or a sub-tenancy which is not a Rent Act 1977 statutory tenancy or a Housing Act 1988 assured tenancy.

"notice in writing and in the prescribed form"

3A-1845.5   At present there is no prescribed form. The notice must give a minimum of twenty-eight days notice.

Other procedures for ending agreement

3A-1845.6   **33E.**—(1)   It is an implied term of a residential tenancy agreement to which this subsection applies that the landlord may terminate the tenancy if the premises to which it relates are occupied by an adult who is disqualified as a result of their immigration status from occupying premises under a residential tenancy agreement.

(2)   Subsection (1) applies to a residential tenancy agreement relating to premises in England if—

(a)   it is a tenancy or sub-tenancy or an agreement for a tenancy or sub-tenancy, but

(b)   it is not a protected or statutory tenancy within the meaning of the Rent Act 1977 or an assured tenancy within the meaning of the Housing Act 1988.

(3)   For provision relating to a residential tenancy agreement which is a protected or statutory tenancy where a tenant or occupier is disqualified as a result of their immigration status from occupying premises under a residential tenancy agreement, see Case 10A in Part 1 of Schedule 15 to the Rent Act 1977.

(4)   For provision relating to a residential tenancy agreement which is an assured tenancy where a tenant or occupier is disqualified as a result of their immigration status from occupying premises under a residential tenancy agreement, see Ground 7B in Part 1 of Schedule 2 to the Housing Act 1988.

3A-1845.7   *Commencement* —This section was inserted by Immigration Act 2016 s.40. It is not yet in force. It will be brought into force by Regulations. See Immigration Act 2016 s.94. It applies to residential tenancy agreements entered into before or after the coming into force of this section—see Immigration Act 2016 s.40(3).

"a residential tenancy agreement"

3A-1845.8   A tenancy or a sub-tenancy which is not a Rent Act 1977 statutory tenancy or a Housing Act 1988 assured tenancy.

"disqualified"

3A-1845.9   Occupants are disqualified from occupying premises under Immigration Act 2014 s.21 if they are not relevant nationals (i.e. a British citizen, a national of an EEA State, or a national of Switzerland) and do not have a "right to rent", viz. if they require leave to remain in the UK and do not have it, or they have leave to enter or remain in the UK but such leave is subject to a condition preventing them from occupying the premises.

Add now paragraphs 3A-1864 to 3A-1870:

Immigration Act 2016

(2016 c.19)

PART 2

ACCESS TO SERVICES

RESIDENTIAL TENANCIES

Eviction

40.—(3)   In section 35 (transitional provision) after subsection (6) (inserted **3A-1864**
by section 39(3)) insert—

"(7)   Sections 33D and 33E apply in relation to a residential tenancy
agreement entered into before or after the coming into force of section 40
of the Immigration Act 2016 (which inserted those sections into this Act)."

(4)   In section 37(4)(a) (provisions in which references to the landlord are to
any of them) after sub-paragraph (iv) (inserted by section 39(5)(b)) insert—

"(v)   section 33D, and
(vi)   section 33E,".

(5)   In section 3A of the Protection from Eviction Act 1977 (excluded tenancies and licences) after subsection (7C) insert—

"(7D)   A tenancy or licence is excluded if—
(a)   it is a residential tenancy agreement within the meaning of
Chapter 1 of Part 3 of the Immigration Act 2014, and
(b)   the condition in section 33D(2) of that Act is met in relation to
that agreement."

(6)   In section 5 of the Housing Act 1988 (security of tenure)—
(a)   in subsection (1) omit the "or" at the end of paragraph (b) and at
the end of paragraph (c) insert ", or (d) in the case of an assured
tenancy—
(i)   which is a residential tenancy agreement within the meaning
of Chapter 1 of Part 3 of the Immigration Act 2014, and
(ii)   in relation to which the condition in section 33D(2) of that
Act is met, giving a notice in accordance with that section,",
and
(b)   in subsection (2) omit the "or" at the end of paragraph (a) and at
the end of paragraph (b) insert ", or
(c)   the giving of a notice under section 33D of the Immigration Act
2014,".

(7)   The amendments made by subsections (5) and (6) apply in relation to a tenancy or (in the case of subsection (5)) a licence entered into before or after the coming into force of this section.

3A-1865   *Commencement* —This section is not yet in force. It will be brought into force by Regulations.

Order for possession of dwelling-house
3A-1866   41.—(1)   The Housing Act 1988 is amended in accordance with subsections (2) to (5).

(2)   In Part 1 of Schedule 2 (assured tenancies: grounds on which court must order possession) after Ground 7A insert—

"Ground 7B
Both of the following conditions are met in relation to a dwelling-house in England.
Condition 1 is that the Secretary of State has given a notice in writing to the landlord or, in the case of joint landlords, one or more of them which identifies—

(a)   the tenant or, in the case of joint tenants, one or more of them, or

(b)   one or more other persons aged 18 or over who are occupying the dwelling-house,

as a person or persons disqualified as a result of their immigration status from occupying the dwelling-house under the tenancy.
Condition 2 is that the person or persons named in the notice—

(a)   fall within paragraph (a) or (b) of condition 1, and

(b)   are disqualified as a result of their immigration status from occupying the dwelling-house under the tenancy.

For the purposes of this ground a person ("P") is disqualified as a result of their immigration status from occupying the dwelling-house under the tenancy if—

(a)   P is not a relevant national, and

(b)   P does not have a right to rent in relation to the dwelling-house.

P does not have a right to rent in relation to the dwelling-house if—

(a)   P requires leave to enter or remain in the United Kingdom but does not have it, or

(b)   P's leave to enter or remain in the United Kingdom is subject to a condition preventing P from occupying the dwelling-house.

But P is to be treated as having a right to rent in relation to a dwelling-house if the Secretary of State has granted P permission for the purposes of this ground to occupy a dwelling-house under an assured tenancy.
In this ground "relevant national" means—

(a)   a British citizen,

(b)   a national of an EEA State other than the United Kingdom, or

(c)   a national of Switzerland."

(3)   In section 7 (orders for possession)—

(a)   in subsection (3) after "subsections (5A) and (6)" insert "and section 10A",

(b)   in subsection (5A)(a) for "and 7A" substitute ", 7A and 7B",

(c)   in subsection (6)(a) after "Ground 7A" insert ", Ground 7B", and

(d)   after subsection (6A) insert—

"(6B)   The requirement in subsection (6)(b) that would otherwise apply to an order for possession of a dwelling-house let on an assured fixed term tenancy does not apply where the ground for possession is Ground 7B in Part 1 of Schedule 2 to

210

this Act."

(4)   In section 8(5) (cases where court may not dispense with notice of proceedings for possession) after "Ground 7A" insert ", 7B".

(5)   After section 10 insert—

Power to order transfer of tenancy in certain cases

"**10A**(1)   This section applies on an application for an order for possession of a dwelling-house let on an assured tenancy if the court is satisfied that—

(a)   Ground 7B in Schedule 2 is established,

(b)   no other ground in that Schedule is established, or one or more grounds in Part 2 of that Schedule are established but it is not reasonable to make an order for possession on that ground or those grounds,

(c)   the tenancy is a joint tenancy, and

(d)   one or more of the tenants is a qualifying tenant.

(2)   In subsection (1)(d) "qualifying tenant" means a person who (within the meaning of Ground 7B) is not disqualified as a result of the person's immigration status from occupying the dwelling-house under the tenancy.

(3)   The court may, instead of making an order for possession, order that the tenant's interest under the tenancy is to be transferred so that it is held—

(a)   if there is one qualifying tenant, by the qualifying tenant as sole tenant, or

(b)   if there is more than one qualifying tenant, by all of them as joint tenants.

(4)   The effect of an order under this section is that, from the time the order takes effect, the qualifying tenant or tenants—

(a)   are entitled to performance of the landlord's covenants under the tenancy, and

(b)   are liable to perform the tenant's covenants under the tenancy.

(5)   The effect of an order under this section is that, from the time it takes effect, any other person who was a tenant under the tenancy before the order took effect—

(a)   ceases to be entitled to performance of the landlord's covenants under the tenancy, or

(b)   ceases to be liable to perform the tenant's covenants under the tenancy.

(6)   Subsection (5) does not remove any right or liability of the person which accrued before the order took effect.

(7)   An order under this section does not operate to create a new tenancy as between the landlord and the qualifying tenant or tenants.

(8)   In particular, if the tenancy is a fixed term tenancy, the term comes to an end at the same time as if the order had not been made."

(6)   In Part 1 of Schedule 15 to the Rent Act 1977 (grounds for possession of dwelling-houses let on or subject to protected or statutory tenancies) after Case 10 insert—

"Case 10A

Both of the following conditions are met in relation to a dwelling-house in England.

Condition 1 is that the Secretary of State has given a notice in writing to the landlord or, in the case of joint landlords, one or more of them which identifies—

(a)   the tenant or, in the case of joint tenants, one or more of them, or

(b)   one or more other persons aged 18 or over who are occupying the dwelling-house,

as a person or persons disqualified as a result of their immigration status from occupying the dwelling-house under the tenancy.

Condition 2 is that the person or persons named in the notice—

(a)   fall within paragraph (a) or (b) of condition 1, and

(b)   are disqualified as a result of their immigration status from occupying the dwelling-house under the tenancy.

For the purposes of this case a person ("P") is disqualified as a result of their immigration status from occupying the dwelling-house under the tenancy if—

(a)   P is not a relevant national, and

(b)   P does not have a right to rent in relation to the dwelling-house.

P does not have a right to rent in relation to the dwelling-house if—

(a)   P requires leave to enter or remain in the United Kingdom but does not have it, or

(b)   P's leave to enter or remain in the United Kingdom is subject to a condition preventing P from occupying the dwelling-house.

But P is to be treated as having a right to rent in relation to a dwelling-house if the Secretary of State has granted P permission for the purposes of this case to occupy a dwelling-house which is for the time being let on a protected tenancy or subject to a statutory tenancy.

In this case "relevant national" means—

(a)   a British citizen,

(b)   a national of an EEA State other than the United Kingdom, or

(c)   a national of Switzerland."

(7)   The amendments made by this section apply in relation to a tenancy entered into before or after the coming into force of this section.

3A-1867   *Commencement* —This section is not yet in force. It will be brought into force by Regulations.

Extension to Wales, Scotland and Northern Ireland

3A-1868   **42.**—(1)   The Secretary of State may by regulations make such provision as the Secretary of State considers appropriate for enabling any of the residential tenancies provisions to apply in relation to Wales, Scotland or Northern Ireland.

(2)   The Secretary of State may by regulations make provision which—

(a)   has a similar effect to any of the residential tenancies provisions, and

(b)   applies in relation to Wales, Scotland or Northern Ireland.

(3)   Regulations under subsection (1) or (2) may—

(a)   amend, repeal or revoke any enactment;

(b)   confer functions on any person.

(4)   Regulations under subsection (1) or (2) may not confer functions on—

(a)   the Welsh Ministers,

(b)   the Scottish Ministers,

(c)   the First Minister and deputy First Minister in Northern Ireland,

(d)   a Northern Ireland Minister, or

(e)   a Northern Ireland department.

(5)   In this section—

"enactment" includes—

(a)   an enactment contained in subordinate legislation within the meaning of the Interpretation Act 1978;

(b)   an enactment contained in, or in an instrument made under, an Act or Measure of the National Assembly for Wales;

(c)   an enactment contained in, or in an instrument made under, an Act of the Scottish Parliament;

(d) an enactment contained in, or in an instrument made under, Northern Ireland legislation;

"the residential tenancies provisions" means sections 39 to 41 and the amendments made by those sections.

Commencement —This section is not yet in force. It will be brought into force by Regulations. **3A-1869**

Commencement

94.—(1) Subject to subsections (3) to (5) this Act comes into force on such **3A-1870** day as the Secretary of State appoints by regulations.

(2) Regulations under subsection (1) may appoint different days for different purposes or areas.

(3) Subsections (3) to (5) of section 61 come into force on the day on which this Act is passed.

(4) Section 85 comes into force at the end of the period of two months beginning with the day on which this Act is passed.

(5) This Part comes into force on the day on which this Act is passed.

Add new paragraphs 3A-1872 to 3A-1904:

Housing and Planning Act 2016

(2016 c.22)

ARRANGEMENT OF SECTIONS

PART 3

RECOVERING ABANDONED PREMISES IN ENGLAND

PART 3

RECOVERING ABANDONED PREMISES IN ENGLAND

Recovering abandoned premises

57. A private landlord may give a tenant a notice bringing an assured **3A-1872** shorthold tenancy to an end on the day on which the notice is given if—

(a)   the tenancy relates to premises in England,

(b)   the unpaid rent condition is met (see section 58),

(c)   the landlord has given the warning notices required by section 59, and

(d)   no tenant, named occupier or deposit payer has responded in writing to any of those notices before the date specified in the warning notices.

3A-1873   *Commencement* —The section will be implemented by a Commencement Order and is not yet in force.

Editorial introduction

3A-1874   This Part of the Act sets out a procedure which a landlord may follow to recover possession of a property which has been abandoned, without the need for a court order. Section 57 provides that a private landlord may give a tenant notice which brings the tenancy to an end on that day, if the tenancy relates to premises in England and certain conditions are met. These conditions are that
*   a certain amount of rent is unpaid (i.e. the 'unpaid rent condition' set out in s.58 has been met),
*   the landlord has given a series of warning notices as required by s.59; and
*   neither the tenant or a named occupier or deposit payer has responded in writing to those warning notices before the date specified in the notices.

"private landlord"

3A-1875   See s.62—viz a landlord who is not within s.80(1) of the Housing Act 1985 (the landlord condition for secure tenancies).

"assured shorthold tenancy"

3A-1876   See the Housing Act 1988 Pt 1.

Deposit and deposit payer

3A-1877   See ss.59 and 62. A deposit is any money intended to be held (by the landlord or otherwise) as security for—
(a)   the performance of any obligations of the tenant arising under or in connection with the tenancy, or
(b)   the discharge of any liability of the tenant arising under or in connection with the tenancy.

"unpaid rent condition"

3A-1878   See s.59.

"warning notice"

3A-1879   See s.58.

The unpaid rent condition

3A-1880   58.—(1)   The unpaid rent condition is met if—

(a)   rent is payable weekly or fortnightly and at least eight consecutive weeks' rent is unpaid,

(b)   rent is payable monthly and at least two consecutive months' rent is unpaid,

(c)   rent is payable quarterly and at least one quarter's rent is more than three months in arrears, or

(d)   rent is payable yearly and at least three months' rent is more than three months in arrears.

(2)   If the unpaid rent condition has been met and a new payment of rent is made before the notice under section 57 is given, the unpaid rent condition ceases to be met (irrespective of the period to which the new payment of rent relates).

(3)   In this section "rent" means rent lawfully due from the tenant.

3A-1881   *Commencement* —The section will be implemented by a Commencement Order and is not yet in force.

Editorial introduction

3A-1882   This section sets out the periods for which lawfully due rent must be unpaid for the unpaid rent condition to be met. It also provides that if any payment of rent (irrespective of the period it relates to) is received after a warning notice has been served, then the unpaid rent condition ceases to apply.

Warning notices

59.—(1) Before bringing a tenancy to an end under section 57 the landlord **3A-1883**
must give three warning notices, at different times, in accordance with this
section.

(2) The first two warning notices must be given to the following using one
of the methods in section 61(2) or (3)—

(a) the tenant,

(b) any named occupiers, and

(c) any deposit payers.

(3) The third warning notice must be given by fixing it to some conspicuous
part of the premises to which the tenancy relates.

(4) Each warning notice must explain—

(a) that the landlord believes the premises to have been abandoned,

(b) that the tenant, a named occupier or a deposit payer must respond
in writing before a specified date if the premises have not been
abandoned, and

(c) that the landlord proposes to bring the tenancy to an end if no tenant, named occupier or deposit payer responds in writing before
that date.

(5) The date specified under subsection (4)(b) must be after the end of the
period of 8 weeks beginning with the day on which the first warning notice is
given to the tenant.

(6) The first warning notice may be given even if the unpaid rent condition
is not yet met.

(7) The second warning notice may be given only once the unpaid rent
condition has been met.

(8) The second warning notice must be given at least two weeks, and no
more than 4 weeks, after the first warning notice.

(9) The third warning notice must be given before the period of 5 days
ending with the date specified in the warning notices under subsection (4)(b).

(10) The Secretary of State may make regulations setting out the form that
the third warning notice must take.

(11) In this Part—

"deposit payer" means a person who the landlord knows paid a tenancy
deposit in relation to the tenancy on behalf of the tenant;

"named occupier" means a person named in the tenancy as a person who
may live at the premises to which the tenancy relates.

Commencement —The section will be implemented by a Commencement Order and is not yet in **3A-1884**
force.

Editorial introduction

This section describes warning notices that landlords may give to tenants and any named oc- **3A-1885**
cupiers and deposit payers, if they believe the premises have been abandoned. The section provides
that if they wish to rely on the procedure contained in this Part of the Act, they must give three
warning notices, at different times, before bringing the tenancy to an end. The first two warning
notices must be addressed to the tenant and any other person named on the tenancy agreement as
well as the deposit payer and served in accordance with s.61(2) or (3). Each of those warning
notices must explain that the landlord believes that the premises have been abandoned and that
the tenant or named occupier must respond in writing before a specified date if the premises have
not been abandoned. The notices must also state that the landlord proposes to bring the tenancy to
an end if neither the tenant nor a named occupier or deposit payer responds in writing before that
date. The proposed tenancy end date specified in the notices must be at least eight weeks after the
date on which the first warning notice is given to the tenant. The first warning notice may be given
even if the unpaid rent condition has not been met, but the second warning notice may only be
given after the unpaid rent condition has been met. There must also be at least two weeks but not
more than four weeks between the first and second warning notices being given. The third warning notice must be affixed to a conspicuous part of the premises, for example the front door. It

must be given at least 5 days before the end of the warning period for the tenant or named occupier in which to respond.

Regulations

3A-1886   At present there are no regulations.

3A-1887   *"named occupier"* —See s.59.

3A-1888   *"tenancy deposit"* —See s.62, viz any money intended to be held (by the landlord or otherwise) as security for—

(a)   the performance of any obligations of the tenant arising under or in connection with the tenancy, or

(b)   the discharge of any liability of the tenant arising under or in connection with the tenancy.

Reinstatement

3A-1889   **60.**—(1)   Where a tenancy is brought to an end by a notice under section 57 the tenant may apply to the county court for an order reinstating the tenancy if the tenant has a good reason for having failed to respond to the warning notices.

(2)   If the county court finds that the tenant had a good reason for failing to respond to the warning notices it may make any order it thinks fit for the purpose of reinstating the tenancy.

(3)   An application under this section may not be made after the end of the period of 6 months beginning with the day on which the notice under section 57 is given.

3A-1890   *Commencement* —The section will be implemented by a Commencement Order and is not yet in force.

Editorial introduction

3A-1891   This section provides that tenants may apply for reinstatement if a tenancy has been brought to an end by a notice under s.57 if they had a good reason for failing to respond to the warning notices. They must apply to the county court, within 6 months of the notice bringing the tenancy to an end.

Methods for giving notices under sections 57 and 59

3A-1892   **61.**—(1)   This section sets out the methods for giving—

(a)   a notice under section 57;

(b)   the first or second warning notice under section 59.

(2)   The notice may given by delivering it to the tenant, named occupier or deposit payer in person.

(3)   If the notice is not delivered to the tenant, named occupier or deposit payer in person it must be given by—

(a)   leaving it at, or sending it to, the premises to which the tenancy relates,

(b)   leaving it at, or sending it to, every other postal address in the United Kingdom that the tenant, named occupier or deposit payer has given the landlord as a contact address for giving notices,

(c)   sending it to every email address that the tenant, named occupier or deposit payer has given the landlord as a contact address for giving notices, and

(d)   in the case of a tenant, leaving it at or sending it to every postal address in the United Kingdom of every guarantor, marked for the attention of the tenant.

(4)   In subsection (3) "guarantor", in relation to a tenant, means a person who has agreed with the landlord to guarantee the performance by the tenant of any of the tenant's obligations under the tenancy.

3A-1893   *Commencement* —The section will be implemented by a Commencement Order and is not yet in force.

Editorial introduction

3A-1894   Section 61 sets out methods of service of notices given under ss.57 and 59. They may be given by delivering the notice to the tenant or a named occupier or the deposit payer in person. Where such a notice is not delivered in person, it must be given by leaving it at, or sending it to, the premises to which the tenancy relates; leaving it at, or sending it to, every other postal address in the UK that the tenant or named occupier has given the landlord as a contact address for giving notices; and sending it to every email address that the tenant or named occupier gave the landlord as a contact email address for giving notices. It must also be sent, in the case of the tenant, care of any person who has agreed with the landlord to guarantee the performance of the tenancy.

Deposit and deposit payer

See ss.59 and 62. A deposit is any money intended to be held (by the landlord or otherwise) as **3A-1895** security for—

(a) the performance of any obligations of the tenant arising under or in connection with the tenancy, or

(b) the discharge of any liability of the tenant arising under or in connection with the tenancy.

Interpretation of Part

62. In this Part— **3A-1896**

"assured shorthold tenancy" has the same meaning as in Part 1 of the Housing Act 1988;

"named occupier" has the meaning given by section 59;

"private landlord" means a landlord who is not within section 80(1) of the Housing Act 1985 (the landlord condition for secure tenancies);

"tenancy deposit", in relation to a tenancy, means any money intended to be held (by the landlord or otherwise) as security for—

(a) the performance of any obligations of the tenant arising under or in connection with the tenancy, or

(b) the discharge of any liability of the tenant arising under or in connection with the tenancy;

"warning notice" means a notice under section 59.

Commencement — The section will be implemented by a Commencement Order and is not yet in **3A-1897** force.

Consequential amendment to Housing Act 1988

63. In section 5 of the Housing Act 1988 (security of tenure), in subsection (1)—

(a) omit "or" at end of paragraph (b); **3A-1898**

(b) at the end of paragraph (c) insert ", or

(d) in the case of an assured shorthold tenancy, serving a notice in accordance with section 57 of the Housing and Planning Act 2016,".

Commencement —The section will be implemented by a Commencement Order and is not yet in **3A-1899** force.

PART 4

SOCIAL HOUSING IN ENGLAND

CHAPTER 6

SECURE TENANCIES ETC.

Secure tenancies etc: phasing out of tenancies for life

118. Schedule 7 changes the law about secure tenancies, introductory tenan- **3A-1900** cies and demoted tenancies to phase out tenancies for life.

Commencement —The section will be implemented by a Commencement Order and is not yet in **3A-1901** force.

Termination of fixed-term secure tenancies without need to forfeit

3A-1902   **119.**—(1)   The Housing Act 1985 is amended as follows.

(2)   In section 82 (security of tenure)—

(a)   before subsection (1) insert—

> "(A1)   A fixed-term secure tenancy of a dwelling-house in England that is granted on or after the day on which paragraph 4 of Schedule 7 to the Housing and Planning Act 2016 comes fully into force cannot be brought to an end by the landlord except by—
>
>> (a)   obtaining—
>>
>>> (i)   an order of the court for the possession of the dwelling-house, and
>>>
>>> (ii)   the execution of the order, or
>>
>> (b)   obtaining a demotion order under section 82A.
>
> (A2)   A secure tenancy can be brought to an end by the landlord as mentioned in subsection (A1)(a) whether or not the tenancy contains terms for it to be brought to an end."

(b)   in subsection (1)(b), for "but" substitute ", other than one to which subsection (A1) applies, that is";

(c)   in subsection (2), after "subsection" insert "(A1)(a) or".

(3)   In section 83 (proceedings for possession), in subsection (A1), for "82(1A)" substitute "82(A1) or (1A)".

3A-1902.1   *Commencement* —The section will be implemented by a Commencement Order and is not yet in force. This section ensures that local authorities can terminate new fixed-term tenancies on the statutory fault grounds without the need to take action to forfeit in parallel.

Succession to secure tenancies and related tenancies

3A-1902.2   **120.**   Schedule 8 changes the law about succession to secure tenancies, introductory tenancies and demoted tenancies.

3A-1902.3   *Commencement* —The section will be implemented by a Commencement Order and is not yet in force.

Commencement

3A-1902.4   **216.**—(1)   The following come into force on the day on which this Act is passed—

(a)   this Part;

(b)   Chapter 2 of Part 4;

(c)   sections 136 and 137 and Schedule 10;

(d)   sections 139, 140, 149, 151, 152(1) and 157;

(e)   sections 161 to 168.

(2)   The following come into force at the end of the period of two months beginning with the day on which this Act is passed—

(a)   section 124;

(b)   section 130;

(c)   sections 150(1) to (3) and 153.

(3)   The other provisions of this Act come into force on such day as the Secretary of State may by regulations appoint.

(4)   Different days may be appointed for different purposes.

(5)   In respect of sections 181 and 183, and Schedule 15, different days may be appointed for different areas.

SCHEDULE 7

Secure tenancies etc: phasing out of tenancies for life

Housing Act 1985 (c. 68)

2   The Housing Act 1985 is amended as follows.   **3A-1903**

3   For the italic heading before section 79 substitute—

"*Secure tenancies*".

...

5   In section 82 (security of tenure), in subsection (3), for the words from "section 86" to the end substitute "section 86 or 86D shall apply".

...

6   After section 82 insert—

"*Orders for possession and expiry of term etc*".

7(1)   Section 82A (demoted tenancy) is amended as follows.

(2)   After subsection (4) insert—

"(4A)   The court may not make a demotion order in relation to a secure tenancy of a dwelling-house in England if—
    (a)   the landlord is a local housing authority or housing action trust, and
    (b)   the term has less than 1 year and 9 months left to run
(4B)   But subsection (4A) does not apply to a tenancy to which an exception in section 86A(2) or (3) applies."

(3)   In subsection (5), for paragraph (b) substitute—

"(b)   the period or term of the tenancy (but see subsection (6));".

(4)   For subsection (6) substitute—

"(6)   Subsection (5)(b) does not apply if—
    (a)   the secure tenancy was for a fixed term and was an old-style secure tenancy or a flexible tenancy, or
    (b)   the secure tenancy was for a fixed term and was a tenancy of a dwelling-house in Wales,
and in such a case the demoted tenancy is a weekly periodic tenancy."

....

8   In section 83 (proceedings for possession or termination: general notice requirements), in subsection (A1), for paragraph (b) substitute—

"(b)   proceedings for possession of a dwelling-house under section 86E (recovery of possession on expiry of certain English secure tenancies)."

9   In section 84 (grounds and orders for possession), in subsection (1), for "section 107D (recovery of possession on expiry of flexible tenancy)" substitute "section 86E (recovery of possession on expiry of certain English secure tenancies)".

10(1)   Section 86 (periodic tenancy arising on termination of fixed term) is amended as follows.

(2)   In subsection (1), after "secure tenancy" insert "to which this section applies".

(3)   After subsection (1) insert—

"(1A)   This section applies to a secure tenancy of a dwelling-house in Wales.
(1B)   This section also applies to a secure tenancy of a dwelling-house in England that is—
    (a)   an old-style secure tenancy, or
    (b)   a flexible tenancy the term of which ends within the period of 9 months beginning with the day on which paragraph 4 of Schedule 7 to the Housing and Planning Act 2016 comes fully into force,
unless it is a tenancy excluded by subsection (1C)."

(4)   In subsection (2), for "this section" substitute "subsection (1)".

...

16(1)   Section 117 (index of defined expressions) is amended as follows.

(2)   In the entry relating to flexible tenancies, for "section 107A" substitute "section 115B".

(3)   At the appropriate place insert—

"old-style secure tenancy | section 115C"

17(1)   Schedule 1 (tenancies which are not secure tenancies) is amended as follows.

(2)   After paragraph 1 insert—

"Certain English tenancies that were not secure tenancies when originally granted

1ZA   A tenancy of a dwelling-house in England cannot become a secure tenancy if—

(a)   it was granted on or after the day on which paragraph 4 of Schedule 7 to the Housing and Planning Act 2016 came fully into force,

(b)   it was not a secure tenancy or an introductory tenancy at the time it was granted, and

(c)   it is a periodic tenancy or a tenancy for a fixed term of less than 2 years or more than 5 years."

(3)   In paragraph 4ZA, after sub-paragraph (2) insert—

"(2A)   A notice under sub-paragraph (2) that relates to a tenancy of a dwelling-house in England must—

(a)   state that the tenancy is to become a secure tenancy for a fixed term of a length specified in the notice, and

(b)   set out the other express terms of the tenancy.

(2B)   The length of the term specified in a notice in accordance with sub-paragraph (2A) must not be—

(a)   less than 2 years, or

(b)   more than the permitted maximum length.

(2C)   The permitted maximum length is 10 years, unless sub-paragraph (2D) applies.

(2D)   If the landlord has been notified in writing that a child aged under 9 will live in the dwelling-house, the permitted maximum length is the period—

(a)   beginning with the day on which the tenancy becomes a secure tenancy, and

(b)   ending with the day on which the child will reach the age of 19.

(2E)   In deciding what length to specify in a notice under sub-paragraph (2A)(a) the landlord must have regard to any guidance given by the Secretary of State.

(2F)   Where a notice is given in accordance with sub-paragraph (2A) the length of the secure tenancy, and the other terms, are those set out in the notice.

(2G)   Sub-paragraphs (2A) to (2F) do not apply to notices given before the day on which paragraph 4 of Schedule 7 to the Housing and Planning Act 2016 comes fully into force."

Landlord and Tenant Act 1985 (c. 70)

18(1)   Section 13 of the Landlord and Tenant Act 1985 is amended as follows.

(2)   After subsection (1A) insert—

"(1AB)   Section 11 also applies to a lease of a dwelling-house in England which is an introductory tenancy for a fixed term of seven years or more granted on or after the day on which paragraph 4 of Schedule 7 to the Housing and Planning Act 2016 comes fully into force."

(3)   In subsection (1B)—

(a)   for "In subsection (1A)" substitute "In this section", and

(b)   after the definition of "assured tenancy" insert—

""introductory tenancy" has the same meaning as in Chapter 1 of Part 5 of the Housing Act 1996;".

Housing Act 1996 (c. 52)

19   The Housing Act 1996 is amended as follows.

20(1)   Section 124 (introductory tenancies) is amended as follows.

(2)   After subsection (1) insert—

"(1A)   When such an election is in force, every fixed term tenancy of a dwelling-house in England entered into or adopted by the authority or trust shall, if it would otherwise be a secure tenancy, be an introductory tenancy, unless section 124A(7) applies or immediately before the tenancy was entered into or adopted the tenant or, in the case of joint tenants, one or more of them was—

(a)   a secure tenant of the same or another dwelling-house, or

(b)   a tenant under a relevant assured tenancy, other than an assured shorthold tenancy, of the same or another dwelling-house."

(3)   In subsection (2), in the words before paragraph (a), after "dwelling-house" insert "in Wales".

(4)   In subsection (2A), for "subsection (2)(b)" substitute "subsections (1A)(b) and (2)(b)".

(5)   In subsection (3), for "subsection (2)" substitute "subsections (1A) and (2)".

(6)   After subsection (5) insert—

"(6)   In relation to a tenancy entered into or adopted by a local housing authority or a housing action trust before the day on which paragraph 4 of Schedule 7 to the Housing and Planning Act 2016 comes fully into force, this section has effect—
  (a)   as if subsection (1A) were omitted, and
  (b)   as if, in subsection (2), the words "in Wales" were omitted."

21   After section 124 insert—

New introductory tenancies in England: overall length

124A.—(1)   A local housing authority or a housing action trust may enter into an introductory tenancy of a dwelling-house in England only if it is a tenancy for a fixed term that is—
  (a)   at least 2 years, and
  (b)   no longer than the permitted maximum length.
  (2)   The permitted maximum length is 10 years, unless subsection (3) applies.
  (3)   If the person entering into the tenancy has been notified in writing that a child aged under 9 will live in the dwelling-house, the permitted maximum length is the period—
  (a)   beginning with the day on which the tenancy is entered into, and
  (b)   ending with the day on which the child will reach the age of 19.
  (4)   If a local housing authority or a housing action trust purports to enter into an introductory tenancy in breach of subsection (1), it takes effect as a tenancy for a fixed term of 5 years.
  (5)   In deciding what length of tenancy to enter into in a case to which subsection (1) applies, the local housing authority or housing action trust must have regard to any guidance given by the Secretary of State.
  (6)   Subsections (1) and (4) apply only to tenancies entered into on or after the day on which paragraph 4 of Schedule 7 to the Housing and Planning Act 2016 comes fully into force.
  (7)   A tenancy of a dwelling-house in England that is adopted by a local housing authority or a housing action trust does not become an introductory tenancy if—
  (a)   it is adopted on or after the day on which paragraph 4 of Schedule 7 to the Housing and Planning Act 2016 came fully into force, and
  (b)   the tenancy is a periodic tenancy or it is a tenancy for a fixed term of less than 2 years or more than 5 years.
  (8)   Subsections (9) and (10) apply where a tenancy that has been adopted by a local housing authority or a housing action trust is not an introductory tenancy but would (on adoption or at any later time) become a secure tenancy but for subsection (7).
  (9)   The local housing authority or housing action trust must, within the period of 28 days, make the tenant a written offer of an introductory tenancy in return for the tenant surrendering the original tenancy.
  (10)   If the tenant accepts in writing within the period of 28 days beginning with the day on which the tenant receives the offer, the local housing authority or housing action trust must grant an introductory tenancy on the tenant surrendering the original tenancy.

Review of decisions about length of introductory tenancies in England

124B(1)   A person who is offered an introductory tenancy of a dwelling-house in England may request a review under this section.
  (2)   The sole purpose of a review under this section is to consider whether the length of the tenancy is in accordance with any policy that the prospective landlord has about the length of introductory tenancies it grants.
  (3)   The request must be made before the end of—
  (a)   the period of 21 days beginning with the day on which the person making the request first receives the offer, or
  (b)   such longer period as the prospective landlord may allow in writing.
  (4)   On receiving the request the prospective landlord must carry out the review.
  (5)   On completing the review the prospective landlord must —
  (a)   notify the tenant in writing of the outcome,
  (b)   revise its offer or confirm its original decision about the length of the tenancy, and
  (c)   if it decides to confirm its original decision, give reasons.
  (6)   The Secretary of State may by regulations make provision about the procedure to be followed in connection with a review under this section.
  (7)   The regulations may, in particular—
  (a)   require the review to be carried out by a person of appropriate seniority who was not involved in the original decision;
  (b)   make provision as to the circumstances in which the person who requested the review is entitled to an oral hearing, and whether and by whom that person may be represented."

22(1)   Section 125A (extension of trial period by 6 months) is amended as follows.
(2)   In subsection (1), for "both" substitute "each".
(3)   After subsection (3) insert—

"(3A)   The third condition must be met only if the introductory tenancy —
(a)   is one to which section 124A(1) or (2) applies, or
(b)   is adopted by a local housing authority or housing action trust on or after the day on which paragraph4 of Schedule 7 came fully into force.

(3B)   The third condition is that the new expiry date would be before the period mentioned in section 86A(3) of the Housing Act 1985 (review to determine what to do at end of fixed term secure tenancy); and for this purpose "the new expiry date" means the last day of the 6 month extension period mentioned in subsection (1)."

23   In section 128 (notice of proceedings for possession), in subsection (4), for the second sentence substitute—

"The date so specified—
(a)   in a case where the introductory tenancy is a periodic tenancy, must not be earlier than the date on which the tenancy could, apart from this Chapter, be brought to an end by notice to quit given by the landlord on the same date as the proceedings, and
(b)   in a case where the introductory tenancy is a fixed term tenancy, must not be earlier than the end of the period of 6 weeks beginning with the date on which the notice of proceedings is served."

24   In section 137A (introductory tenancies that are to become flexible tenancies), in subsection (2), for ", before entering into or adopting the introductory tenancy" substitute "the introductory tenancy was entered into or adopted before the day on which paragraph 4 of Schedule 7 to the Housing and Planning Act 2016 came fully into force and, before entering into or adopting it,".
25   In section 143A (demoted tenancies), in subsection (1), omit "periodic".
26   In section 143E (notice of proceedings for possession), for subsection (3) substitute—

"(3)   The date specified under subsection (2)(c)—
(a)   in a case where the demoted tenancy is a periodic tenancy, must not be earlier than the date on which the tenancy could, apart from this Chapter, be brought to an end by notice to quit given by the landlord on the same date as the proceedings, and
(b)   in a case where the demoted tenancy is a fixed term tenancy, must not be earlier than the end of the period of 6 weeks beginning with the date on which the notice of proceedings is served."

27(1)   Section 143MA (demoted tenancies that are to become flexible tenancies) is amended as follows.
(2)   In subsection (1), for "section 107A of the Housing Act 1985" substitute "section 115B of the Housing Act 1985 (certain tenancies granted etc before the day on which paragraph 4 of Schedule 7 to the Housing and Planning Act 2016 came fully into force)".
(3)   After subsection (3) insert—

"(3A)   If the notice is given on or after the day on which paragraph 4 of Schedule 7 to the Housing and Planning Act 2016 comes fully into force, the period specified under subsection (3)(b) must be no longer than the permitted maximum length.

(3B)   The permitted maximum length is 10 years, unless subsection (3C) applies.

(3C)   If the landlord has been notified in writing that a child aged under 9 will live in the dwelling-house, the permitted maximum length is the period—
(a)   beginning with the day on which the tenancy becomes a secure tenancy, and
(b)   ending with the day on which the child will reach the age of 19.

(3D)   In deciding what length to specify in a notice under paragraph (3)(b) the landlord must have regard to any guidance given by the Secretary of State."

28   After section 143MA insert—

Default flexible tenancies when no notice given under section 143MA

"**143MB**(1)   This section applies where—
(a)   a landlord has the power to serve a notice under section 143MA on the tenant under a demoted tenancy but fails to do so, and
(b)   the tenancy comes to an end on or after the day on which paragraph 4 of Schedule 7 to the Housing and Planning Act 2016 comes fully into force.

(2)   On ceasing to be a demoted tenancy, the tenancy becomes a secure tenancy for a fixed term of 5 years that is a flexible tenancy.

(3)   The terms of the new tenancy are the same as those of the tenancy that it replaces, so far as those terms are compatible with—

(a) a tenancy for a fixed term of 5 years, and

(b) the statutory provisions relating to flexible tenancies (within the meaning given by section 143MA(5)."

....

SCHEDULE 8

SUCCESSION TO SECURE TENANCIES AND RELATED TENANCIES

Housing Act 1985 (c. 68)

1 The Housing Act 1985 is amended as follows.

3A-1904

2 In section 86 (periodic tenancy arising on termination of fixed term), after subsection (1B) (inserted by Schedule 7) insert—

"(1C) This section does not apply to a secure tenancy of a dwelling-house in England if—

(a) the original secure tenant has died,

(b) the tenancy has been vested in, or otherwise disposed of to, the current tenant in the course of the administration of the original tenant's estate, and

(c) the current tenant qualified to succeed the original tenant under section 86G(2) or (4)."

3(1) Section 86A (persons qualified to succeed: England) as inserted by the Localism Act 2011—

(a) is renumbered section 86G (so that it follows on from section 86F as inserted by Schedule 7 without making the numbering more complex than it has to be), and

(b) is amended as follows.

(2) After subsection (7) insert

"(8) This section applies to a tenancy that was granted before 1 April 2012, or that arose by virtue of section 86 on the coming to the end of a secure tenancy granted before 1 April 2012, as it applies to a secure tenancy granted on or after that day."

4 In section 88 (cases where the tenant is a successor), in subsection (1), after paragraph (b) insert—

"(ba) the tenancy arose by virtue of section 89(2A) (fixed term tenancy arising in certain cases following succession to periodic tenancy), or".

5(1) Section 89 (succession to periodic tenancy) is amended as follows.

(2) In subsection (1A), for "section 86A" substitute "section 86G".

(3) After subsection (2) insert—

"(2A) Where the tenancy vests in a person qualified to succeed the tenant under section 86G(2) or (4) and continues to be a secure tenancy—

(a) the periodic tenancy ("the old tenancy") comes to an end immediately after vesting, and

(b) a new tenancy of the same dwelling-house arises by virtue of this subsection for a fixed term of 5 years.

(2B) The parties and terms of a tenancy arising by virtue of subsection (2A) are the same as those of the tenancy that it replaces, except that the terms are confined to those which are compatible with a tenancy for a fixed term of 5 years.

(2C) Where a possession order was in force in relation to the old tenancy—

(a) the possession order is to be treated, so far as possible, as if it applied in relation to the new tenancy, and

(b) any other court orders made in connection with the possession order are also to be treated, so far as possible, as if they applied in relation to the new tenancy.

(2D) In subsection (2C) "possession order" means an order for possession of the dwelling house."

6 In section 117 (index of defined expressions), in the entry relating to persons qualified to succeed, for "section 87" substitute "sections 86G and 87".

Housing Act 1996 (c. 52)

7 Before section 131 (but after the italic heading) insert—

Persons qualified to succeed to introductory tenancy: England

"**130A**(1) A person is qualified to succeed the tenant under an introductory tenancy of a dwelling-house in England if—

(a) the person occupies the dwelling-house as his or her only or principal home at the time of the tenant's death, and

(b)   the person is the tenant's spouse or civil partner.

(2)   A person is qualified to succeed the tenant under an introductory tenancy of a dwelling-house in England if—

(a)   at the time of the tenant's death the dwelling-house is not occupied by a spouse or civil partner of the tenant as his or her only or principal home,

(b)   an express term of the tenancy makes provision for a person other than such a spouse or civil partner of the tenant to succeed to the tenancy, and

(c)   the person's succession is in accordance with that term.

(3)   Subsection (1) or (2) does not apply if the tenant was a successor as defined in section 132.

(4)   In such a case, a person is qualified to succeed the tenant if—

(a)   an express term of the tenancy makes provision for a person to succeed a successor to the tenancy, and

(b)   the person's succession is in accordance with that term.

(5)   For the purposes of this section a person who was living with the tenant as the tenant's wife or husband is to be treated as the tenant's spouse.

(6)   Subsection (7) applies if, on the death of the tenant, there is by virtue of subsection (5) more than one person who fulfils the condition in subsection (1)(b).

(7)   Such one of those persons as may be agreed between them or as may, where there is no such agreement, be selected by the landlord is for the purpose of this section to be treated as the fulfilling that condition."

8(1)   Section 131 (persons qualified to succeed tenant) is amended as follows.

(2)   At the end of the heading for "tenant" substitute "to introductory tenancy: Wales".

(3)   After "introductory tenancy" insert "of a dwelling-house in Wales".

9(1)   Section 133 (succession to introductory tenancy) is amended as follows.

(2)   After subsection (1) insert—

"(1A)   Where there is a person qualified to succeed the tenant under section 130A, the tenancy vests by virtue of this section—

(a)   in that person, or

(b)   if there is more than one such person, in such one of them as may be agreed between them or as may, where there is no agreement, be selected by the landlord."

(3)   In subsection (2), after ""tenant" insert "under section 131".

10   Before section 143H (but after the italic heading) insert—

Persons qualified to succeed to demoted tenancy: England

"**143GA**(1)   A person is qualified to succeed the tenant under a demoted tenancy of a dwelling-house in England if—

(a)   the person occupies the dwelling-house as his or her only or principal home at the time of the tenant's death, and

(b)   the person is the tenant's spouse or civil partner.

(2)   A person is qualified to succeed the tenant under a demoted tenancy of a dwelling-house in England if—

(a)   at the time of the tenant's death the dwelling-house is not occupied by a spouse or civil partner of the tenant as his or her only or principal home,

(b)   an express term of the tenancy makes provision for a person other than such a spouse or civil partner of the tenant to succeed to the tenancy, and

(c)   the person's succession is in accordance with that term.

(3)   Subsection (1) or (2) does not apply if the tenant was a successor as defined in section 132.

(4)   In such a case, a person is qualified to succeed the tenant if—

(a)   an express term of the tenancy makes provision for a person to succeed a successor to the tenancy, and

(b)   the person's succession is in accordance with that term.

(5)   For the purposes of this section a person who was living with the tenant as the tenant's wife or husband is to be treated as the tenant's spouse.

(6)   Subsection (7) applies if, on the death of the tenant, there is by virtue of subsection (5) more than one person who fulfils the condition in subsection (1)(b).

(7)   Such one of those persons as may be agreed between them or as may, where there is no such agreement, be selected by the landlord is for the purpose of this section to be treated as fulfilling that condition.

(8)   This section applies to a tenancy that became a demoted tenancy before or after Schedule 8 of the Housing Act 2015 comes into force.

Succession to demoted tenancy: England

143GB(1)   This section applies if the tenant under a demoted tenancy of a dwelling-house in England dies.

(2)   Where there is a person qualified to succeed the tenant under section 143GA, the tenancy vests by virtue of this section—

(a)   in that person, or

(b)   if there is more than one such person, in such one of them as may be agreed between them or as may, where there is no agreement, be selected by the landlord.

(3)   Where a periodic demoted tenancy vests in a person qualified to succeed the tenant under section 143GA(2) or (4) and continues to be a demoted tenancy—

(a)   the tenancy comes to an end immediately after vesting, and

(b)   a new tenancy of the same dwelling-house arises by virtue of this subsection for a fixed term of 5 years.

(4)   The parties and terms of a tenancy arising by virtue of subsection (3) are the same as those of the tenancy that it replaces, except that the terms are confined to those which are compatible with a tenancy for a fixed term of 5 years.

(5)   Where a demoted tenancy comes to an end and a new tenancy arises by virtue of subsection (3), as from that time the demotion order is to be treated for all purposes as it had been made in relation to the new tenancy (and the demotion period remains the same)."

11(1)   Section 143H (succession to demoted tenancy) is amended as follows.

(2)   At the heading insert ": Wales".

(3)   In subsection (1), after "tenancy" insert "of a dwelling-house in Wales".

12   In section 143I (no successor tenant: termination), after "section" insert "143GA or".

13(1)   Section 143J of the Housing Act 1996 (demoted tenancies: successor tenants) is amended as follows.

(2)   After subsection (3) insert—

"(3A)   The tenancy arose by virtue of section 89(2A) of the Housing Act 1985."

(3)   For subsection (7) substitute—

"(7)   A person is the successor to a demoted tenancy if—

(a)   the tenancy vests in the person by virtue of section 143GB(2) or 143H(4) or (5), or

(b)   the tenancy arose by virtue of section 143GB(3)."

SECTION 3B   BUSINESS TENANCIES

Landlord and Tenant Act 1954

s.30(1)(g) intention of landlord to occupy the holding for the purposes of a business or as his residence

Before the third paragraph (beginning "The landlord need not intend"), add as a new paragraph:

Compare *Gulf Agencies Ltd v Ahmed* [2016] EWCA Civ 44, where the Court of Appeal held that **3B-183** two years occupation on the facts of that case would be more than "fleeting or illusory" and more than "short term" (para.42).

"rent"

Add at end:

For an example where there was no adequate evidence of the market rent and the Court of Ap- **3B-207** peal held that the judge was entitled to give weight to the passing rent see *Flanders Community Centre Ltd v London Borough of Newham* [2016] EWHC 1089 (Ch).

Replace s.63 with:

PART IV

MISCELLANEOUS AND SUPPLEMENTARY

Jurisdiction of court for purposes of Parts I and II and of Part I of Landlord and Tenant Act 1927

3B-280   63.—(1)   Any jurisdiction conferred on the court by any provision of Part I of this Act shall be exercised by the county court.

(2)   Any jurisdiction conferred on the court by any provision of Part II of this Act or conferred on the tribunal by Part I of the Landlord and Tenant Act 1927, shall, subject to the provisions of this section, be exercised [by the High Court or the county court]

(3)   [...]

(4)   The following provisions shall have effect as respects transfer of proceedings from or to the High Court or the county court, that is to say—

(a)   where an application is made to the one but by virtue of [an Order under section 1 of the Courts and Legal Services Act 1990] cannot be entertained except by the other, the application shall not be treated as improperly made but any proceedings thereon shall be transferred to the other court;

(b)   any proceedings under the provisions of Part II of this Act or of Part I of the Landlord and Tenant Act 1927, which are pending before one of those courts may by order of that court made on the application of any person interested be transferred to the other court, if it appears to the court making the order that it is desirable that the proceedings and any proceedings before the other court should both be entertained by the other court.

(5)   In any proceedings where in accordance with the foregoing provisions of this section the county court exercises jurisdiction the powers of the judge of summoning one or more assessors under subsection (1) of section 91 of the County Courts Act 1959, may be exercised notwithstanding that no application is made in that behalf by any party to the proceedings.

(6)   Where in any such proceedings an assessor is summoned by a judge under the said subsection (1),—

(a)   he may, if so directed by the judge, inspect the land to which the proceedings relate without the judge and report to the judge in writing thereon;

(b)   the judge may on consideration of the report and any observations of the parties thereon give such judgment or make such order in the proceedings as may be just;

(c)   the remuneration of the assessor shall be at such rate as may be determined by the Lord Chancellor with the approval of the Treasury and shall be defrayed out of moneys provided by Parliament.

(7)   In this section the expression "the holding"—

(a)   in relation to proceedings under Part II of this Act, has the meaning assigned to it by subsection (3) of section twenty-three of this Act,

(b)   in relation to proceedings under Part I of the Landlord and Tenant Act 1927, has the same meaning as in the said Part I.

(8)   [...]

(9)   Nothing in this section shall prejudice the operation of section 41 of the County Courts Act 1984 (which relates to the removal into the High Court of proceedings commenced in the county court).

(10)   In accordance with the foregoing provisions of this section, for section

21 of the Landlord and Tenant Act 1927, there shall be substituted the following section—
The Tribunal
21. The tribunal for the purposes of Part I of this Act shall be the court exercising jurisdiction in accordance with the provisions of section sixty-three of the Landlord and Tenant Act 1954.

Note

Add new paragraph at end:
Subsections (2), (9) amended by the Crime and Courts Act 2013 Sch.9 para.52(1)(b), with effect **3B-281** from 22 April 2014 (SI 2014/954) subject to savings and transitional provisions specified in 2013 c.22 s.15 and Sch.8 and transitional provision specified in SI 2014/954 arts 2(c) and 3.

SECTION 3C   CONTEMPT OF COURT

A. AN OUTLINE OF THE LAW OF CONTEMPT OF COURT

2.   Principal forms of contempt liability

(c)   Interference with the due administration of justice

After the third paragraph (beginning "Instances of contempt which involve"), add as new paragraphs:
In *Solicitor General v Cox* [2016] EWHC 1241 (QB), 27 May 2016, DC, unrep., a Divisional Court **3C-9** held that the deliberate taking of photographs in court, in breach of notices prohibiting such conduct, was a contempt of court as well as an offence under the Criminal Justice Act 1925 s.41 (prohibition on taking photographs etc in court), and explained that a specific intent to interfere with the administration of justice was not required before such a contempt could be proven, as it was sufficient that the act was deliberate and in breach of the criminal law or a court order of which the contemnor was aware.
In the case of *In re West* [2014] EWCA Crim. 1480; [2015] 1 W.L.R. 109, CA, a judge sitting in the Crown Court found a barrister to be in contempt of court by failing (a) to attend an adjourned preliminary hearing as directed, and (b) to assist with the case management requests that were made of him. The Court of Appeal (Criminal Division) allowed the barrister's appeal for want of procedural irregularity (in particular, lack of compliance with rules in Pt 62 of the Criminal Procedure Rules 2011), but in doing so acknowledged (after reviewing the relevant authorities) that a failure by a party's legal representative to co-operate with the court or a refusal to attend court conceivably may amount to contempt of court, being conduct that interferes with the due administration of justice.

(e)   Contempt of court and enforcement of judgments etc by order of committal

Replace the second paragraph with:
See further, CPR r.70.2 (and 70PD para.1.2), and rr.81.4, 81.20, 83.13 and 83.14. **3C-18**

To the end of the seventh paragraph (beginning "This dictum was applied by the House of Lords"), add:
The principle derived from these authorities was confirmed and applied by the Court of Appeal **3C-19** in *Khawaja v Popat* [2016] EWCA Civ 362, 14 April 2016, CA, unrep., at para.30 per McCombe LJ).

3.   Jurisdiction

(c)   County courts

Replace the fourth paragraph with:
In *Ex p Martin* (1879) 4 Q.B.D. 212, D.C., sub nom *Martin v Bannister* (1879) 4 Q.B.D. 491, CA, **3C-33** it was held that, by the Supreme Court of Judicature Act 1873 s.89, county courts (being inferior courts within the meaning of that section) were invested with the power to grant injunctions and to enforce obedience of them by committal "in as full and ample a manner" (as the section said) as the same power invested in the High Court. Nowadays, those powers are invested in county courts by the County Courts Act 1984 s.38(1) (see para.9A-468). By that sub-section (subject to exceptions), in any proceedings in a county court the court may make any order which could be made by the High Court if the proceedings were in the High Court. It follows that, so far as orders made by county court judges are concerned, those judges have the same power and authority to commit for their breach as a High Court judge would have in respect of the breach of any order made by him

(*Jennison v Baker*, op cit, at 65 to 66 per Salmon LJ). (Before Pt 81 was inserted in the CPR (particularly Section II thereof) the existence of such jurisdiction was recognised by CCR Ord.29.)

B. DEBTORS ACTS 1869 & 1878

General Note

Replace the seventh paragraph with:

3C-41   The scope of the jurisdiction exercisable under s.5 was considerably restricted by the Administration of Justice Act 1970 (c.31) s.11 (see para.9B-39+ below). That section states that the jurisdiction is exercisable only (a) by the High Court in respect of a High Court maintenance order, and (b) by a county court in respect of (i) a High Court or a county court maintenance order, or (ii) a judgment or order which is enforceable by a court in England and Wales and is for the payment of any of the taxes, contributions or liabilities specified in Sch.4 to that Act. (As to meaning of "maintenance order" in this context, see *ZUK v ZUK* [2012] EWCA Civ 1871, [2013] 2 F.L.R. 1466, CA.) The liabilities specified in Sch.4 include "an order for periodical or other payments made, or having effect as if made, under Part II of the Matrimonial Causes Act 1973" (para.2A). It has been explained that a wide, flexible definition is given to the phrase "or having effect as if made" (*Migliaccio v Migliaccio* [2016] EWHC 1055 (Fam); [2016] 4 W.L.R. 90 (Mostyn J) at para.33). The result is that the power of committal provided by r.5 (which should be distinguished from other committal powers exercisable by the courts for the purpose of the enforcement of judgments or orders but not falling within s.5) is very limited. A creditor wishing to enforce a judgment for a debt which would have fallen within s.5 before the 1970 Act came into force but which was excluded from the scope of the section by that statute, is restricted to enforcement against the debtor's property, or (if the debtor is an employee) through an attachment of earnings order.

Replace the eighth paragraph with:

The jurisdiction under s.5 may be invoked in the County Court by the judgment summons procedure for which rules are provided in CPR Sch.2 CCR Ord.28 (see Vol.1 para.cc28.1 and following). The jurisdiction may also be invoked in family proceedings in the High Court and in the Family Court by the judgment summons procedure provided by Pt 33 of the Family Procedure Rules 2010 (SI 2010/2955). In terms less elaborate than those found in CCR Ord.28, but similar in effect, r.33.14 of the FPR 2010 states that no person may be committed on an application for a judgment summons unless the judgment creditor proves that the debtor has, or has had, since the date of the order the means to pay the sum in respect of which the debtor has made default, and has refused or neglected, or refuses or neglects to pay that sum. Rule 33.14(2) provides that the debtor may not be compelled to give evidence. In *Prest v Prest* [2014] EWHC 3430 (Fam), 29 July 2014, unrep. (Moylan J), the modern authorities on the principles to be applied at the hearing of a judgment summons brought by a wife seeking her husband's committal to prison for failing to pay sums due by way of periodical payments order were reviewed at first instance. See also *Migliaccio v Migliaccio* [2016] EWHC 1055 (Fam); [2016] 4 W.L.R. 90 (Mostyn J) at para.22 et seq. Proceedings under s.5 are criminal proceedings within art.6 of the Convention and, after the Human Rights Act 1998 came into effect, the proceedings referred to above were modified in certain respects to ensure compliance with the requirements of that article.

Replace para.3C–43 with paras 3C–43 and 3C–43.1:

Saving of power of committal for small debts

3C-43   **5.** Subject to the provisions herein-after mentioned, and to the prescribed rules, any court may commit to prison for a term not exceeding six weeks, or until payment of the sum due, any person who makes default in payment of any debt or instalment of any debt due from him in pursuance of any order or judgment of that or any other competent court. Provided—

(1)   That the jurisdiction by this section given of committing a person to prison shall, in the case the county court—

    (a)   Be exercised only by a judge of the court, and by an order made in open court and showing on its face the ground on which it is issued.

    (b)   [Repealed by Bankruptcy Act 1883 (c.52), Sch.5.]

(2)   That such jurisdiction shall only be exercised where it is proved to the satisfaction of the court that the person making default either has or has had since the date of the order or judgment the means to pay the sum in respect of which he has made default, and has refused or neglected, or refuses or neglects, to pay the same.-

Proof of the means of the person making default may be given in such manner as the court thinks just.

For the purpose of considering whether to commit a debtor to prison under this section, the debtor may be summoned in accordance with the prescribed rules.

Any jurisdiction by this section given to the High Court or family court may be exercised by a judge sitting in chambers, or otherwise, in the prescribed manner.

For the purposes of this section any court may direct any debt due from any person in pursuance of any order or judgment of that or any other competent court to be paid by instalments, and may from time to time rescind or vary such order.

This section, so far as it relates to the county court, shall be deemed to be substituted for sections ninety-eight and ninety-nine of the County Courts Act 1846, and that Act and the Acts amending the same shall be construed accordingly, and shall extend to orders made by the county court with respect to sums due in pursuance of any order or judgment of any court other than the county court.

No imprisonment under this section shall operate as a satisfaction or extinguishment of any debt or demand or course of action, or deprive any person of any right to take out execution against the lands, goods, or chattels of the person imprisoned, in the same manner as if such imprisonment had not taken place.

Any person imprisoned under this section shall be discharged out of custody upon a certificate signed in the prescribed manner to the effect that he has satisfied the debt or instalment of a debt in respect of which he was imprisoned, together with the prescribed costs (if any).

Section 31E(1)(b) of the Matrimonial and Family Proceedings Act 1984 (family court has county court's powers) does not apply in relation to the powers given by this section to the county court.

Note —Amended by the Crime and Courts Act 2013 Sch.9(3) para.78, Sch.10(2) para.2, with ef- **3C-43.1**
fect from 22 April 2014 (SI 2014/954) subject to savings and transitional provisions specified in 2013 c.22 s.15 and Sch.8 and transitional provision specified in SI 2014/954 arts 2(c), (d) and 3.

C. Contempt of Court Act 1981

Add new paragraph 3C–68.1:

Enabling the making, and use, of films and other recordings of proceedings
Section 32 of the Crime and Courts Act 2013 (see para.9B-1427 below) states that the Lord **3C-68.1**
Chancellor may by Order provide that s.9 does not apply, and that the Criminal Justice Act 1925 s.41, which makes it an offence to film in court, does not apply, to the making of recordings (by which is meant visual or sound recordings) as prescribed in the Order. The Crown Court (Recording) Order 2016 (SI 2016/612) was made in exercise of that power and came into effect on 27 May 2016.

"in any case where a court has power to commit"

Replace the last paragraph with:
Where there are several proceedings, the first court to sentence must not allow for or anticipate **3C-86**
a likely further sentence. It is for the second court to reflect the prior sentence to ensure that the defendant is not punished twice for the same act (*Lomas v Parle* [2003] EWCA Civ 1804; [2004] 1 W.L.R. 1642, CA (breach of non-molestation orders)). Further, there is an obligation on the first court to ensure that the basis of its sentence is fully expressed and that a transcript of its judgment is made available to the second court (ibid at para.48). Where proceedings in a criminal court are followed by proceedings in a civil court, and the civil judge regards the punishment given by the criminal court for certain conduct as too lenient, it would be improper for him to use his power of committal in respect of that self-same conduct in order to top up the punishment to what he regarded as a proper level; instead the judge should sentence only for such conduct as was not the subject of the criminal proceedings (*Slade v Slade* [2009] EWCA Civ 748; [2010] 1 W.L.R. 1262, CA). In *Gill v Birmingham City Council* [2016] EWCA Civ 608, 28 June 2016, CA, unrep., whilst the defendant (D) was on bail awaiting sentence by a magistrates' court, a County Court judge commit-

ted him for breaches of an anti-social behaviour injunction and imposed a sentence of imprisonment. On D's appeal, the Court of Appeal held that the County Court judge was entitled to sentence D, notwithstanding that he had already pleaded guilty to the criminal offences constituted by the breaches for which he was committed, but reduced the sentence to 12 months, principally on the ground that the judge had failed to take into account the fact that D had pleaded guilty in the magistrates' court to the most serious offences with which he was charged.

Term of imprisonment or fine for contempt

3C-87

Replace the second paragraph with:
Frequently, in judgments imposing sentences for contempt judges, as a preliminary to reaching their conclusions, seek to outline the principles involved; see, e.g., at para.9 of the judgment in *Revenue and Customs Commissioners v Munir* [2015] EWHC 1366 (Ch); [2015] B.C.C. 425 (Norris J); Appendix 1 attached to the judgment in *Otkritie International Investment Management Ltd v Gersamia* [2015] EWHC 821 (Comm), 25 March 2015, unrep. (Eder J). The sentencing guidance given by the Court of Appeal in *JSC BTA Bank v Solodchenko* [2011] EWCA Civ 1241; [2012] 1 W.L.R. 350, CA, and the guidance to be derived from other decisions was helpfully collated in *Power v Hodges* [2015] EWHC 2931 (Ch); [2016] B.P.I.R. 140 (Judge Simon Baker QC) at paras 60 to 69.

Replace the sixth paragraph (where the citation for VIS Trading Co Ltd v Nazarov has changed) with:
Where the court is required to distinguish between the element of sentence to reflect punishment for past failures, and the element which reflects continuing non-compliance, it must make findings about whether one or both aspects are proven, before arriving at the appropriate sentence (and giving reasons for that sentence), and if there is a dispute about whether there is continuing non-compliance, that issue must be resolved on the evidence (*VIS Trading Co Ltd v Nazarov* [2015] EWHC 3327 (QB); [2016] 4 W.L.R. 1 (Whipple J) at para.29). A claimant is entitled to continue to advance the case that the respondent is in breach, even in the face of purported compliance by the respondent since the date of the committal application (ibid).

After the twenty-fourth paragraph (beginning "In South Wales Fire and Rescue Service v Smith"), add as a new paragraph:
Where under a statutory provision the High Court has power to punish a person for an act or omission which, if it had been an act or omission in the High Court, would have been contempt of court (see CPR r.81.15), the purpose of the statutory provision should determine the appropriate penalty. See, for example, *Secretary of State for Business, Innovation and Skills v Marshall* [2015] EWHC 3874 (Ch), 30 October 2015, unrep. (Judge Pelling QC), where it was said that, as the primary purpose of proceedings under the Companies Act 1985 s.453C was not to imprison people for contempt but to enable the secretary of state to make progress in an investigation that had to be carried out in the public interest, the appropriate course to adopt where a company director had failed to comply with various demands for delivery up of documents was to impose a prison term, suspended on condition that he produced the relevant documents by a specified date.

Add new paragraph 3C–87.1:

Personal injury claim dismissed for "fundamental dishonesty" – sentence in subsequent proceedings for contempt

3C-87.1
In the circumstances provided for by the Criminal Justice and Courts Act 2015 s.57, a court should dismiss a personal injury claim in which the court has found that the claimant is entitled to damages where, on the application of the defendant, the court is satisfied on the balance of probabilities that the claimant has been "fundamentally dishonest" in relation to the claim, unless the court is satisfied that the claimant would suffer substantial injustice if the claim were dismissed. Where a court dismisses a claim for these reasons it must record the amount of damages that the claimant would have been awarded. It is expressly provided that if in any subsequent proceedings for contempt of court against the claimant in respect of that dishonesty the claimant is found guilty, then in sentencing the claimant or otherwise disposing of the proceedings the court "must have regard" to the dismissal of the claim (s.57(6) and (7)).

Replace s.19 with:

SUPPLEMENTAL

Interpretation

3C-96
19. In this Act—
"court" includes any tribunal or body exercising the judicial power of the State, and"legal proceedings" shall be construed accordingly;
"publication" has the meaning assigned by subsection (1) of section 2, and"publish" (except in section 9) shall be construed accordingly;

"Scottish proceedings" means proceedings before any court, including the Courts-Martial Appeal Court and Employment Appeal Tribunal, sitting in Scotland, and includes proceedings before the Supreme Court in the exercise of any appellate jurisdiction over proceedings in such a court;

"the strict liability rule" has the meaning assigned by section 1;

"superior court" means Supreme Court, the Court of Appeal, the High Court, the Crown Court, the Courts-Martial Appeal Court, the Employment Appeal Tribunal and any other court exercising in relation to its proceedings powers equivalent to those of the High Court.

Note

After "2009 (SI 2009/1604", add:

); and the Competition Act 1998 (Consequential Provisions) Order 2013 (SI 2013/294) Sch.1, **3C-97** with effect from 10 March 2013.

Replace Schedule 1 with:

SCHEDULE 1

TIMES WHEN PROCEEDINGS ARE ACTIVE FOR PURPOSES OF SECTION 2

Preliminary

1.   In this Schedule "criminal proceedings" means proceedings against a person in respect of **3C-102** an offence, not being appellate proceedings or proceedings commenced by motion for committal or attachment in England and Wales or Northern Ireland; and "appellate proceedings" means proceedings on appeal from or for the review of the decision of a court in any proceedings.

1ZA.   Proceedings under the Double Jeopardy (Scotland) Act 2011 (asp 16) are criminal proceedings for the purposes of this Schedule.

2.   Criminal, appellate and other proceedings are active within the meaning of section 2 at the times respectively prescribed by the following paragraphs of this Schedule; and in relation to proceedings in which more than one of the steps described in any of those paragraphs is taken, the reference in that paragraph is a reference to the first of those steps.

Criminal proceedings

3.   Subject to the following provisions of this Schedule, criminal proceedings are active from **3C-103** the relevant initial step specified in paragraph 4 or 4A until concluded as described in paragraph 5.

4.   The initial steps of criminal proceedings are—
   (a)   arrest without warrant;
   (b)   the issue, or in Scotland the grant, of a warrant for arrest;
   (c)   the issue of a summons to appear, or in Scotland the grant of a warrant to cite;
   (d)   the service of an indictment or other document specifying the charge;
   (e)   except in Scotland, oral charge.
   (f)   the making of an application under section 2(2) (tainted acquittals), 3(3)(b) (admission made or becoming known after acquittal), 4(3)(b) (new evidence), 11(3) (eventual death of injured person) or 12(3) (nullity of previous proceedings) of the Double Jeopardy (Scotland) Act 2011 (asp 16).

4A.   Where as a result of an order under section 54 of the Criminal Procedure and Investigations Act 1996 (acquittal tainted by an administration of justice offence) proceedings are brought against a person for an offence of which he has previously been acquitted, the initial step of the proceedings is a certification under subsection (2) of that section; and paragraph 4 has effect subject to this.

5.   Criminal proceedings are concluded—
   (a)   by acquittal or, as the case may be, by sentence;
   (b)   by any other verdict, finding, order or decision which puts an end to the proceedings;
   (c)   by discontinuance or by operation of law.
   (d)   where the initial steps of the proceedings are as mentioned in paragraph 4(f)—
      (i)   by refusal of the application;
      (ii)   if the application is granted and within the period of 2 months mentioned in section 6(3) of the Double Jeopardy (Scotland) Act 2011 (asp 16) a new prosecution is brought, by acquittal or, as the case may be, by sentence in the new prosecution.

6.   The reference in paragraph 5(a) to sentence includes any order or decision consequent on conviction or finding of guilt which disposes of the case, either absolutely or subject to future events, and a deferment of sentence under section 1 of the Powers of Criminal Courts (Sentencing)

Act 2000, s.219 or 432 of the Criminal Procedure (Scotland) Act 1975 or Article 14 of the Treatment of Offenders (Northern Ireland) Order 1976.

7.   Proceedings are discontinued within the meaning of paragraph 5(c)—

(a)   in England and Wales or Northern Ireland, if the charge or summons is withdrawn or a *nolle prosequi* entered;

(aa)   in England and Wales, if they are discontinued by virtue of section 23 of the Prosecution of Offences Act 1985;

(ab)   in England and Wales, if they are discontinued by virtue of paragraph 11 of Schedule 17 to the Crime and Courts Act 2013 (deferred prosecution agreements);

(b)   in Scotland, if the proceedings are expressly abandoned by the prosecutor or are deserted *simpliciter*;

(c)   in the case of proceedings in England and Wales or Northern Ireland commenced by arrest without warrant, if the person arrested is released, otherwise than on bail, without having been charged.

(d)   where the initial steps of the proceedings are as mentioned in paragraph 4(f) and the application is granted, if no new prosecution is brought within the period of 2 months mentioned in section 6(3) of the Double Jeopardy (Scotland) Act 2011 (asp 16).

9.   Criminal proceedings in England and Wales or Northern Ireland cease to be active if an order is made for the charge to lie on the file, but become active again if leave is later given for the proceedings to continue.

9A.   Where proceedings in England and Wales have been discontinued by virtue of section 23 of the Prosecution of Offences Act 1985, but notice is given by the accused under subsection (7) of that section to the effect that he wants the proceedings to continue, they become active again with the giving of that notice.

10.   Without prejudice to paragraph 5(b) above, criminal proceedings against a person cease to be active—

(a)   if the accused is found to be under a disability such as to render him unfit to be tried or unfit to plead or, in Scotland, is found to be insane in bar of trial; or

(b)   if a hospital order is made in his case under section 51(5) of the Mental Health Act 1983 or Article 57(5) of the Mental Health (Northern Ireland) Order 1986 or, in Scotland, where an assessment order or a treatment order ceases to have effect by virtue of sections 52H or 52R respectively of the Criminal Procedure (Scotland) Act 1995

but become active again if they are later resumed.

11.   Criminal proceedings against a person which become active on the issue or the grant of a warrant for his arrest cease to be active at the end of the period of twelve months beginning with the date of the warrant unless he has been arrested within that period, but become active again if he is subsequently arrested.

Other proceedings at first instance

3C-104   12.   Proceedings other than criminal proceedings and appellate proceedings are active from the time when arrangements for the hearing are made or, if no such arrangements are previously made, from the time the hearing begins, until the proceedings are disposed of or discontinued or withdrawn; and for the purposes of this paragraph any motion or application made in or for the purposes of any proceedings, and any pre-trial review in the county court, is to be treated as a distinct proceeding.

13.   In England and Wales or Northern Ireland arrangements for the hearing of proceedings to which paragraph 12 applies are made within the meaning of that paragraph—

(a)   in the case of proceedings in the High Court for which provision is made by rules of court for setting down for trial, when the case is set down;

(b)   in the case of any proceedings, when a date for the trial or hearing is fixed.

14.   [*Proceedings in Scotland.*]

Appellate proceedings

3C-105   15.   Appellate proceedings are active from the time when they are commenced—

(a)   by application for leave to appeal or apply for review, or by notice of such an application;

(b)   by notice of appeal or of application for review;

(c)   by other originating process,

until disposed of or abandoned, discontinued or withdrawn.

16.   Where, in appellate proceedings relating to criminal proceedings, the court—

(a)   remits the case to the court below; or

(b)   orders a new trial or a *venire de novo*, or in Scotland grants authority to bring a new prosecution,

any further or new proceedings which result shall be treated as active from the conclusion of the appellate proceedings.

Note

Replace with:
Amended by the Mental Health Act 1983 Sch.4 paras 57(c) and 59(c); the Prosecution of Of- **3C-106**
fences Act 1985 s.31, Sch.1 paras 4 and 5; the Mental Health (Scotland) Act 1984 s.17, s.127(1),
Sch.3 para.48; the Criminal Procedure and Investigations Act 1996 s.57; the Powers of Criminal
Courts (Sentencing) Act 2000; and by the Double Jeopardy (Scotland) Act 2011 Sch.1 paras 2, 3, 4;
the Armed Forces Act 2006 Sch.17 para.1, with effect from 31 October 2009 (SI 2009/1167); and by
the Crime and Courts Act 2013 Sch.17 para.34, with effect from 24 February 2014 subject to
transitional provisions and savings specified in 2013 c.22 s.15, Sch.8 and Sch.17 para.39.

SECTION 3E   INSOLVENCY PROCEEDINGS

Jurisdiction and distribution of business

Company insolvency

Replace "The county courts have concurrent jurisdiction where the company's registered office is within the
relevant insolvency district and the capital paid up or credited as paid up does not exceed £120,000 (s.117(2)
Insolvency Act 1986)." with:
  •   The county court has concurrent jurisdiction where the company's registered office is **3E-22**
        within the relevant insolvency district and the capital paid up or credited as paid up does
        not exceed £120,000 (s.117(2) Insolvency Act 1986).

Bankruptcy

Replace the third paragraph (from "Petitions in the London Insolvency District" to "r.6.9(2) Insolvency Rules
1986.") with:
  NB: Debtors' petitions
  With effect from 6 April 2016 debtors' petitions are no longer dealt with by the courts but by
  an official known as the adjudicator. Debtors' applications for a bankruptcy order must now
  be made to the adjudicator online. See the Enterprise and Regulatory Reform Act 2013
  (Commencement No.9 and Savings Provisions) Order 2016 (SI 2016/191) which brought into
  force s.71 Enterprise and Regulatory Reform Act 2013 which repealed ss.272–274A Insolvency
  Act 1986 and inserted a new Chapter A1 into Part IX of the Act. The new provisions do not
  affect debtors' petitions presented before 6 April 2016 or petitions presented under the
  Administration of Insolvent Estates of Deceased Persons Order 1986 (SI 1986/1999) or the
  Insolvent Partnerships Order 1994 (SI 1994/2421).
  Petitions in the London Insolvency District are presented to the High Court (in the Rolls Build-
ing, Fetter Lane, London EC4A 1NL) or the County Court at Central London (sitting in the
Thomas More Building, Royal Courts of Justice, Strand, London WC2A 2LL). The work is split
between the High Court and the County Court at Central London as follows: With effect from 6
April 2011 where the petition debt is £50,000 or more, the debtor has not resided or had a place of
business in England or Wales for six months preceding the date of presentation of the petition, the
debtor's residence or place of business cannot be ascertained or the petition is presented against a
member of a partnership that is being wound up by the High Court, the petition should be
presented to the High Court. Where the petition debt is less than £50,000, subject to the exceptions mentioned, the petition should be presented to the County Court at Central London. NB
Some county court hearing centres have no insolvency jurisdiction.

Add new paragraph 3E–27:

Insolvency Express Trials
  From 6 April 2016 a new regime for insolvency cases began as a two year pilot in the registrars' **3E-27**
courts in the Chancery Division of the High Court at the Rolls Building. Practitioners are referred
to the Practice Direction 51P—Pilot for Insolvency Express Trials (Vol.1 para.51PPD.1).

Company voluntary arrangements (Part I Insolvency Act 1986)

Company voluntary arrangements without moratorium

Replace the first paragraph with:
  The directors of a company, its administrator (where an administration order is in force) or its **3E-31**
liquidator (where the company is being wound up) may propose to the creditors of the company a
composition in satisfaction of its debts or a scheme of arrangement (a company voluntary arrange-

ment) (s.1). The proposal must be made to all the company's creditors, and it must be for a composition of debts or a scheme of arrangement (as to which see *March Estates plc v Gunmark Ltd* [1996] 2 B.C.L.C. 1). Within 28 days (or any longer period the courts allow) the nominee must submit a report to the court stating whether a meeting of creditors and members of the company should be summoned to consider the proposal (s.2). The meetings must then be held at the time, date and place proposed (s.3). The chairman of the meetings must report to the court the result of the meetings (s.4(6)). Members vote according to the rights attaching to their shares (r.1.18(1)) but are entitled to vote even where no voting rights attach to their shares (r.1.18(2)). A resolution may be passed by a majority of creditors in value, but any resolution to approve or modify the proposal must be passed by a majority of three-quarters or more in value of creditors present and voting in person or by proxy (r.1.19(1) and (2)).

Individual voluntary arrangements (Part VIII Insolvency Act 1986)

Replace the first paragraph with:

3E-91   The Insolvency Act 2000 ss.3 and 4 and Sch.3, and the Insolvency (Amendment) (No.2) Rules 2002 (SI 2712/2002) which came into force on 1 January 2003, enable the debtor to choose whether or not to apply for an interim order. If the debtor needs protection from his creditors, which now includes protection against peaceable reentry by his landlord or distress (except with the permission of the court), then an interim order will be required and an application will need to be made to the court as before. The procedure has not changed and is set out in Pt 5 of the Insolvency Rules 1986. If protection is not required then the debtor may submit his proposal, which must comply with r.5.3 (as amended) and statement of affairs to the intended nominee who, if he is of the opinion that the debtor is an undischarged bankrupt or is able to petition for his own bankruptcy and is prepared to act, can call the meeting of creditors. The nominee must within 14 days (or such longer period as the court may allow) after receiving the proposal and statement of affairs submit a report to the court in which he must state whether in his opinion the voluntary arrangement has a reasonable prospect of being approved and implemented, whether a meeting of creditors should be summoned and if so the date, time and venue. This must be filed along with a copy of the proposal, the statement of affairs and form 5.5 (which contains the statement that it is not intended to apply for an interim order). The court will not read the report unless an application is made under the Act or Rules in relation to the proposal, for example to challenge the decision of the creditors' meeting under s.262 of the Insolvency Act 1986.

Replace the last paragraph with:

The appropriate court in which to file is the court in which the debtor would be entitled to make an application in accordance with r.6.50A, or if an undischarged bankrupt the court with the conduct of the bankruptcy. Where the debtor is an undischarged bankrupt the nominee must send copies of his report, the proposal and the statement of affairs to the official receiver or trustee and to any petitioning creditor if a petition has been filed (r.5.14A(3)).

Replace the second paragraph with:

3E-92   In his report the nominee must state whether in his opinion the proposal has a reasonable prospect of being approved and implemented (s.256A(3)). An application may be made to the court for an order replacing a nominee where it is impractical or inappropriate for the nominee to continue to act. Section 260(2) provides that approval of a voluntary arrangement binds every person who in accordance with the rules was entitled to vote at the meeting (whether or not he was present or represented at it), or would have been so entitled had he had notice of it. The classes of person who may challenge the outcome of the meeting under s.262 of the Insolvency Act 1986 includes any person who was entitled, in accordance with the rules, to vote at the creditors' meeting or would have been so entitled had he had notice of it. The content of the debtor's proposal must now state how it is proposed to deal with the claims of any person who is bound by the arrangement by virtue of this provision.

The Proposal

Replace with:

3E-93   The debtor must ensure that his proposal complies with the requirements of r.5.3 of the Insolvency Rules 1986 as amended. In particular it must deal with the EC Regulation on Insolvency Proceedings (see para.3E-23) and give details of the debtor's centre of main interests and/or his establishment (r.5.3(2)(r)). It is also necessary to set out not only the fees to be charged by the intended nominee but also to list the disbursements (r.5.3(2)(h)).

Application for interim order

Replace the first paragraph with:

3E-94   If the debtor decides that he needs the protection of an interim order then the steps set out in Pt 5 of the Insolvency Rules must be followed. The debtor must give written notice of his proposal together with a copy of the proposal to the intended nominee (r.5.4(1)). If he is an undischarged bankrupt then he must also give notice to the or his trustee (r.5.4(5)). If the nominee is prepared to act he endorses his consent on the notice (r.5.4(3)) and returns it to the debtor. The debtor then has 7 days, or such longer period as the nominee may allow, to give the nominee his statement of affairs (r.5.5(1)).

Replace the last paragraph with:

The application may be made by the debtor where he is not bankrupt or by the debtor, the official receiver or his trustee where he is (s.253(3) of the Insolvency Act 1986). The application is by way of originating application accompanied by a witness statement in support. The evidence must comply with r.5.7(1) of the Insolvency Rules 1986: it should give the reason for the application, details of any execution or other legal process, state whether the debtor is an undischarged bankrupt or able to file his own petition, confirm that there has been no other application within the last 12 months, name the nominee and confirm that he is qualified to act and is willing to act. A copy of the notice served upon the nominee endorsed with his consent to act must be exhibited to the written evidence (r.5.7(2)). If the nominee has completed his enquiries the application may be accompanied by his report.

Interim order

Replace the first paragraph with:

Where it is not necessary to give any other party notice the court will often deal with the ap- **3E-95** plication in the absence of the parties and will only require a hearing if the papers are not in order. In the absence of a nominee's report the court will make an interim order for 14 days commencing the day following the making of the order and will fix a hearing date within the 14 day period to consider the nominee's report (r.5.9(3)). At the adjourned hearing if the nominee's report has not been filed the court may extend the 14 day period in certain circumstances, if appropriate. Where it has been filed and a date, time and venue have been given for the meeting of creditors (which is not less than 14 days from the date on which it was filed and not more than 28 days from the date on which it is considered by the court) the court will extend the interim order to a date 7 weeks after the proposed date of the meeting and adjourn the application to a date about 3 weeks after the date of the meeting for consideration of the chairman's report. The time scale allows for possible adjournment of the meeting. If the nominee's report accompanies the application the court may make a "concertina order" which combines the two orders set out above. The nominee must state in his report whether the debtor's proposal has a reasonable prospect of being approved (s.256 as amended). As to the obligations of a nominee in reporting to the court see *Greystoke v Hamilton-Smith* [1996] 2 B.C.L.C. 429; [1997] B.P.I.R. 24).

Chairman's report

Replace with:

The chairman's report must state whether the proposal was approved, with or without modifica- **3E-96** tions, or rejected, set out the resolutions and the decision on each one, list the creditors who were present and how they voted, indicate whether it is governed by the E.C. Regulation on Insolvency Proceedings and if so whether the proceedings are main or territorial proceedings and include any other information he thinks should be made known to the court (r.5.27(2)). As to the chairman's obligations in conducting the meeting of creditors see *Re a Debtor (No.222 of 1990) Ex p. Bank of Ireland* [1992] B.C.L.C. 137; [1993] B.C.L.C. 233; as to his obligations in reporting to the court see *Re N (a debtor)* [2002] B.P.I.R. 1024.

Bankruptcy (Part IX Insolvency Act 1986)

After "creditor or creditors,", delete "the debtor,". **3E-98**

Presentation of petition

Replace with:

A creditor's petition is normally presented to the court in whose insolvency district the debtor **3E-99** has carried on business; this may be different from the insolvency district in which the debtor resides. Petitions presented by government departments are always presented in the London Insolvency district and will either be in the High Court or the Central London County Court depending on the size of the debt, see IR6.9A. IR 7.10ZA (a)(v) and (c) identifies the circumstances when a creditor must present the petition in the High Court, namely, where the debtor is not resident in England and Wales and within the six months immediately prior to presentation of the petition he has neither carried on business nor resided in England and Wales; where the petitioner cannot ascertain where the debtor resides or if he carries on business in England and Wales both where the debtor resides and where he caries on business; and where the debtor is the member of a partnership and the partnership is being wound up by the High Court in London.

Grounds of a creditor's petition

Replace with:

The grounds for a creditor's petition are set out in s.267(2) of the Insolvency Act 1986. A credi- **3E-100** tor may present a petition where the amount of the debt or debts is equal to or greater than the bankruptcy level, currently £5,000, the debt or debts are for a liquidated sum payable either immediately or at some future time and are unsecured and the debtor appears either to be unable to pay or to have no reasonable prospect of paying the debt or debts. Also there must be no outstanding application to set aside a statutory demand. It is possible for creditors to join in the presentation of a creditor's petition: the debts do not need to be interrelated but can be entirely separate. The creditor has a duty to disclose whether he holds any security though he may undertake in the petition to give it up for the benefit of all the creditors (s.269(1)(a)).

Application to set aside statutory demand

In the second paragraph, replace "Paragraph 13.4.4" with:

3E-103   Paragraph 13.3.4

Hearing of the petition

In the third paragraph, after "not less than", replace "7 days before the hearing" with:

3E-107   5 business days before the hearing

Change title of paragraph:

Debtor's Bankruptcy Application

Replace with:

3E-109   Since 1 April 2016 the process by which a debtor can apply for a bankruptcy order is no longer to the court but is made by way of a Bankruptcy Application to an adjudicator. Please refer to Pt 6 Ch.3 of the Insolvency Rules.

Annulment

Replace the first paragraph with:

3E-111   The jurisdiction to annul a bankruptcy order is found in ss.261 and 282 of the Insolvency Act. Section 261(2)(a) allows a bankrupt to apply for the annulment of the bankruptcy order if his creditors have at a meeting called for the purpose approved a proposal for a voluntary arrangement. The court cannot make the order before the end of the period of 28 days beginning with the day on which the chairman's report was made to the court (s.261(3)). The official receiver and trustee (if appointed) are necessary parties and must be given notice of the application but they are not required to file any report. If the court feels that a relevant obligation under the arrangement has yet to be fulfilled, for example if a third party is to make a single lump sum payment, then the court may adjourn the annulment application until the payment has been received.

Discharge

Replace with:

3E-112   Section 279 of the Insolvency Act 1986 provides for automatic discharge for the majority of bankrupts after one year (s.279(1)). The official receiver may still apply to suspend discharge if a bankrupt fails to comply with his obligations. Section 279(3) provides that the official receiver may apply to suspend discharge until the end of a specified period or until the fulfilment of a specified condition (see also r.6.215).

Appeal

In the first paragraph, replace "Paragraph 19" with:

3E-115   Paragraph 20

SECTION 3F   PERSONAL INJURY

Add new paragraphs 3F–32.3 to 3F–32.5:

Criminal Justice and Courts Act 2015

(2015 c.2)

ARRANGEMENT OF SECTIONS

Personal injury claims: cases of fundamental dishonesty

57.—(1) This section applies where, in proceedings on a claim for damages **3F-32.3**
in respect of personal injury ("the primary claim")—

    (a) the court finds that the claimant is entitled to damages in respect of
        the claim, but

    (b) on an application by the defendant for the dismissal of the claim
        under this section, the court is satisfied on the balance of prob-
        abilities that the claimant has been fundamentally dishonest in rela-
        tion to the primary claim or a related claim.

(2) The court must dismiss the primary claim, unless it is satisfied that the
claimant would suffer substantial injustice if the claim were dismissed.

(3) The duty under subsection (2) includes the dismissal of any element of
the primary claim in respect of which the claimant has not been dishonest.

(4) The court's order dismissing the claim must record the amount of damages that the court would have awarded to the claimant in respect of the
primary claim but for the dismissal of the claim.

(5) When assessing costs in the proceedings, a court which dismisses a claim
under this section must deduct the amount recorded in accordance with subsection (4) from the amount which it would otherwise order the claimant to pay in
respect of costs incurred by the defendant.

(6) If a claim is dismissed under this section, subsection (7) applies to—

    (a) any subsequent criminal proceedings against the claimant in respect
        of the fundamental dishonesty mentioned in subsection (1)(b), and

    (b) any subsequent proceedings for contempt of court against the claim-
        ant in respect of that dishonesty.

(7) If the court in those proceedings finds the claimant guilty of an offence
or of contempt of court, it must have regard to the dismissal of the primary
claim under this section when sentencing the claimant or otherwise disposing
of the proceedings.

(8) In this section—

"claim" includes a counter-claim and, accordingly, "claimant" includes a
counter-claimant and "defendant" includes a defendant to a counterclaim;
"personal injury" includes any disease and any other impairment of a
person's physical or mental condition;
"related claim" means a claim for damages in respect of personal injury
which is made—

        (a) in connection with the same incident or series of incidents in
            connection with which the primary claim is made, and

        (b) by a person other than the person who made the primary
            claim.

(9) This section does not apply to proceedings started by the issue of a
claim form before the day on which this section comes into force.

Commencement

    13 April 2015 by Sch.1 to the Criminal Justice and Courts Act 2015 (Commencement No.1, Sav- **3F-32.4**
ing and Transitional Provisions) Order 2015 (SI 2015/778).

General Note

    By subss.(1)-(3) a Claimant who is found by the court in a personal injury claim (namely either **3F-32.5**
his or her own claim, counterclaim or a "related" personal injury claim such as that of a relative
arising from the same incident or series of incidents) to have have acted in a fundamentally dishonest way in relation to that claim may face an application under this section for dismissal of the
claimant's own claim (referred to as the "primary" claim in the section). If the court is satisfied that
the test of fundamental dishonesty is met, and the court finds that the claimant is entitled to damages in respect of the claim, then the court must dismiss the primary claim unless to do so "would"
cause the claimant to suffer "substantial injustice" if the claim were dismissed. The entire claim

must be dismissed, not merely the part affected by the dishonesty in question.

The dismissal under this section does not, it appears, bring matters to an end entirely because the court must nonetheless make a decision (subs.(4)) as to the sum of damages which it would (but for the application under s.57) have awarded to the Claimant, and (by subs.(5)) must then deduct that amount from the sum of costs it orders the Claimant to pay to the Defendant, when detailed assessment takes place. In any criminal or committal proceedings the court dealing with the criminal proceedings or the committal must have regard to the dismissal of the primary claim when deciding sentence (subss.(6)-(7)). Note that the power under s.57 is similar but not identical to that in CPR r.44.16 which provides that in relation to Qualified One Way Costs Shifting, "orders for costs made against the claimant may be enforced to the full extent of such orders with the permission of the court where the claim is found on the balance of probabilities to be fundamentally dishonest".

Case law: in relation to s.57 see *Hughes, Kindon and Jones v KGM*, 1 April 2016, unrep., county court at Taunton, a decision at Deputy District Judge level in which three claimants alleged they had suffered injuries whose effects lasted for 12 months. The court concluded that such injuries as had been suffered would have lasted around two weeks and awarded the two remaining claimants £750 in damages. On application under s.57 the court held that the two claims in question had been fundamentally dishonest (the claim of the third claimant had been struck out for other reasons) and that there would be no substantial injustice in dismissing the claims in their entirety, triggering the removal of QOCS protection.

In *Gosling v Hailo*, 29 April 2014, unrep. (county court at Cambridge, circuit judge decision of HHJ Maloney, claim no. UD17868, Lawtel AC0142747) the court made use of the similar powers under CPR r.44.16 (which, notably, apply even where a claim has been discontinued). It held that investigate the question of fundamental dishonesty in relation to liability, raised after discontinuance of a claim, it would be inappropriate to proceed on the papers without oral hearing and that holding an oral hearing would be disproportionate. However the case on quantum was capable of being found to be fundamentally dishonest based on the evidence without the need for further hearing. It was observed that "fundamental dishonesty" should be considered purposively and contextually and that the test determined whether or not the claimant had the protection of QOCS put in place for social policy reasons. Collateral or minor matters not going to the heart of the claim should not expose the claimant to the costs penalty. Where a case was not a plain one the court would have to consider whether it was proportionate to pursue the allegation but in some cases the dishonesty would be sufficiently plain that an oral hearing was unnecessary. The Claimant was ordered to pay the Defendants' costs in full.

SECTION 3G   DATA PROTECTION ACT 1998

INTRODUCTION

Replace the first paragraph with:

3G-1   The Data Protection Act ("the Act" or "DPA") was passed to implement Directive 95/46 of October 24, 1995 on the protection of individuals with regard to the processing of personal data and the free movement of such data ("Directive 95/46"). It repealed the Data Protection Act 1984 which had been passed to enable the UK to ratify the Convention for the Protection of Individuals with regard to automatic processing of Personal Data ("Treaty 108"). Directive 95/46 will be replaced by the General Data Protection Regulation and the accompanying Directive applicable to personal data in the criminal justice system. Both instruments were approved in April 2016, and must be implemented by 2018. The position of the UK post the referendum result is not known but some form of equivalent legislature change will be necessary. The UK courts have referred to the Directive, Treaty 108 and the Convention Rights under the European Convention on Human Rights and Fundamental Freedoms, particularly art.8, in interpreting cases on the Act. In case law since the Act came into force the courts have tended to consider the tort of misuse of private information and rights under art.8 in conjunction with the Act. The CJEU has increasingly referred to the European Union Charter of Fundamental Rights when considering data protection cases. Further specific rights in relation to telecommunications services and electronic marketing are contained in the Privacy and Electronic Communications (EC Directive) Regulations 2003 (see para.3G-17). Retention of personal data derived from public telecommunications services was mandated by Directive 2006/24 EC. That directive was ruled to be invalid by the CJEU in April 2014 because it breaches Articles 7 and 8 of the EU Charter of Fundamental Rights, in joined cases C-293/12 and C-594/12. The UK has enacted the Data Retention and Investigatory Powers Act 2014 (DRIPA) to replace its earlier legislation. DRIPA is currently subject to legal challenge in the UK.

Exemptions

Replace the first paragraph with:
Class exemptions apply to personal dataprocessed only for domestic and recreational purposes **3G-11**
(s.36) (see para.3G-9 above), information available to the public by or under any enactment (s.34),
references provided in confidence when in the hands of the giver only (para.1 Sch.7), judicial appointments and honours (para.3 Sch.7), certain Crown Offices exempt under Data Protection
(Crown Appointments) Order 2000 (SI 2000/416), examination scripts (para.9 Sch.7) and where
legal professional privilege or the equivalent privilege in Scotland, would apply (para.10 Sch.7).
The extent of this exception was considered in *Dawson-Damer v Taylor Wessing LLP* [2015] EWHC
2366 (Ch). In *Ranger v House of Lords Appointments Commission* [2015] EWHC 45 (QB) the High
Court confirmed a refusal of subject access by the Lords Appointment Commission on the basis of
Sch.7 para.3. In *Guriev v Community Safety Development (UK) Ltd* [2016] EWHC 643 (QB) the High
Court rejected an argument that personal data was exempt under legal professional privilege or
the exemption in s.29(1)(b) in respect of the prevention or detection of crime.

To the end of the twenty-third paragraph (beginning "The courts have however proved reluctant"), add:
This approach was confirmed in *Gurieva v Community Safety Development (UK) Ltd* [2016] EWHC
643 (QB).

Editorial note

*After the fourth paragraph (beginning "Additional provisions apply to marketing by telephone"), add as a new
paragraph:*
The maximum fine for breach of this provision has been a fine of £200,000.00 imposed by the **3G-17**
Information Commissioner on the LMLd for making unlawful automated calls, September 2015.

The eighth principle

Replace the last paragraph with:
The decision of the CJEU left a serious lacunae in the arrangements of many major businesses **3G-62.0.24**
for sending personal data to the US. In February 2016 agreement was reached between the Commission and the US Government over replacement arrangements, called the 'Privacy Shield'. The
proposed agreement has been subject to criticism and subsequent revision. However in May the
EU authorised the signing of an EU/US agreement on data protection in law enforcement
exchanges (Decision 8505/16) which may resolve some areas of difficulty. The final authorisation
has not been given for this replacement arrangement but is expected by the end of 2016.

SECTION 3H CONSUMER CREDIT AND CONSUMER LAW

Introductory note about procedure in consumer credit cases

Unenforceable agreements

Change title of sub-paragraph: **3H-17.3.1**

Agreements made before 1 April 2014

Change title of sub-paragraph:

Agreements made on or after 1 April 2014

Add new paragraph at end:
The Designated Professional Body (Consumer Credit) Handbook became effective from 1 April
2016.

Consumer Credit Act 1974

Meaning of credit

Subsection (1)

Add new paragraph at end:
See *Burrell v Helical (Bramshott Place) Ltd* [2015] EWHC 3727 (Ch). This was an interesting claim **3H-26**

brought by residents of a retirement village under leases contending that transfer fee provisions amounted to the provision of credit and that the leases are consumer credit agreements within the meaning of ss.8 and 9 of the Act. In giving summary judgment in favour of the Defendants thereby rejecting these contentions David Casement QC Sitting as a Deputy High Court Judge considered ss.8 and 9 of the Act and the authorities as to the meaning of credit and his judgment from para.22 onwards helpfully summarises the relevant law.

Unfair relationships

Add new paragraphs at end:

3H-329   See *Axton v G E Money Mortgages Ltd* [2015] EWHC 1343 (QB) concerning PPI mis-selling—brokers as agents.

Swift Advances Plc v Okokenu [2015] C.T.L.C. 302 lending to elderly consumers and loan sustainability—relevance of OFT guidance.

Burden of proof/adducing evidence/summary judgment

Add new paragraph at end:

3H-331.1   It is suggested that whilst in principle it is enough for the debtor merely to allege an "unfair relationship" for the issue to be raised, if the debtor is the claimant (as was the case in *Carey*) then in practice he will need to provide supporting evidence if a Pt 18 request for "further information" is served by the defendant creditor. Moreover, even if the debtor is the defendant, it is suggested that if the creditor's evidence provides no suggestion that the relationship is unfair; the court is likely to regard the creditor as having discharged the burden and to dismiss the debtor's claim. [See *Coldunell v Gallon* [1986] Q.B. 1184 as to discharge of burden of proof by a creditor.] It is suggested that Datum Finance is of doubtful authority in the light of *Axton v GE Money Mortgages Ltd* and *Bluestone Mortgages Ltd v Faith Momoh (920160CA)* [2016] C.C.L.R. 4. At the end of this case it is noted that this decision together with *Axton v GE Money Mortgages Ltd* shows that the court can determine cases summarily where an allegation of unfair relationship (even with the reverse burden of proof) is raised. It is also suggested that it must be doubted if *Bevin v Datum Finance Limited* would be decided the same way now. Note also that HHJ Platts in *Plevin v Paragon Personal Finance Ltd* [2016] C.C.L.R. 5 said the decision in *Bevin* was of limited assistance in assessing remediation in an unfair relationship case.

Unfair Contract Terms Act 1977

Note

Replace with:

3H-549   Amended by the Occupiers' Liability Act 1984 s.2; and by the Consumer Rights Act 2015 Sch.4 para.3 with effect from 1 October 2015 (other than for the purposes of a contract to supply a consumer transport service) subject to transitional provisions and savings specified in SI 2015/1630 arts 6–8, and from 1 October 2016 (for the purposes of a contract to supply consumer transport service) subject to transitional provisions and savings specified in SI 2015/1630 art.6.

Note

Replace with:

3H-552.1   Subsection (4) inserted by the Consumer Rights Act 2015 Sch.4 para.4 with effect from 1 October 2015 (other than for the purposes of a contract to supply a consumer transport service) subject to transitional provisions and savings specified in SI 2015/1630 arts 6–8, and from 1 October 2016 (for the purposes of a contract to supply consumer transport service) subject to transitional provisions and savings specified in SI 2015/1630 art.6.

Note

Replace with:

3H-555.1   Subsection (1) amended and subs.(3) inserted by the Consumer Rights Act 2015 Sch.4 para.5 with effect from 1 October 2015 (other than for the purposes of a contract to supply a consumer transport service) subject to transitional provisions and savings specified in SI 2015/1630 arts 6–8, and from 1 October 2016 (for the purposes of a contract to supply consumer transport service) subject to transitional provisions and savings specified in SI 2015/1630 art.6.

Note

Replace with:

3H-557.1   Repealed by the Consumer Rights Act 2015 Sch.4 para.6 with effect from 1 October 2015 (other than for the purposes of a contract to supply a consumer transport service) subject to transitional provisions and savings specified in SI 2015/1630 arts 6–8, and from 1 October 2016 (for the purposes of a contract to supply consumer transport service) subject to transitional provisions and savings specified in SI 2015/1630 art.6.

Note

Replace with:
Repealed by the Consumer Rights Act 2015 Sch.4 para.10 with effect from 1 October 2015 **3H-568**
(other than for the purposes of a contract to supply a consumer transport service) subject to
transitional provisions and savings specified in SI 2015/1630 arts 6–8, and from 1 October 2016
(for the purposes of a contract to supply consumer transport service) subject to transitional provisions and savings specified in SI 2015/1630 art.6.

Note

Replace with:
Repealed by the Consumer Rights Act 2015 Sch.4 para.11 with effect from 1 October 2015 **3H-574**
(other than for the purposes of a contract to supply a consumer transport service) subject to
transitional provisions and savings specified in SI 2015/1630 arts 6–8, and from 1 October 2016
(for the purposes of a contract to supply consumer transport service) subject to transitional provisions and savings specified in SI 2015/1630 art.6.

Note

Replace with:
Amended by the Consumer Rights Act 2015 Sch.4 para.12 with effect from 1 October 2015 **3H-576.1**
(other than for the purposes of a contract to supply a consumer transport service) subject to
transitional provisions and savings specified in SI 2015/1630 arts 6–8, and from 1 October 2016
(for the purposes of a contract to supply consumer transport service) subject to transitional provisions and savings specified in SI 2015/1630 art.6.

Note

Replace with:
Amended by the Sale of Goods Act 1979 s.63(2) and Sch.2; and by the Consumer Rights Act **3H-579**
2015 Sch.4 para.13 with effect from 1 October 2015 (other than for the purposes of a contract to
supply a consumer transport service) subject to transitional provisions and savings specified in SI
2015/1630 arts 6–8, and from 1 October 2016 (for the purposes of a contract to supply consumer
transport service) subject to transitional provisions and savings specified in SI 2015/1630 art.6.

Note

Replace with:
Amended by the Consumer Rights Act 2015 Sch.4 para.27 with effect from 1 October 2015 **3H-580.1**
(other than for the purposes of a contract to supply a consumer transport service) subject to
transitional provisions and savings specified in SI 2015/1630 arts 6–8, and from 1 October 2016
(for the purposes of a contract to supply consumer transport service) subject to transitional provisions and savings specified in SI 2015/1630 art.6.

Consumer Rights Act 2015

Add new paragraph 3H–1112:

Editorial note
See *Makdessi v Cavendish Square Holdings BV* [2015] UKSC 67 and *ParkingEye Ltd v Beavis* [2015] **3H-1112**
EWCA Civ 402.
Although the *ParkingEye Ltd v Beavis* [2015] EWCA Civ 402 case raises issue under the Unfair
Terms in Consumer Contracts Regulations 1999 (SI 1999/2083) replaced by the Consumer Rights
Act 2015, this case is still of relevance to Schedule 2—Consumer Contract Terms which may be
Regarded as Unfair at para.3H–1102.

SECTION 3I DISCRIMINATION

EQUALITY ACT 2010

Notes on Parts 9 and 11 of the Equality Act 2010

Enforcement and Remedies

Replace with:

3I-95   The unlawful acts created by the Equality Act 2010 are statutory torts and in general terms the courts will address their enforcement and remedies in much the same way as with any other statutory tort. As to remedies under the Equality Act 2010, the county courts may make any order as would be available in the High Court in proceedings in tort or on a claim for judicial review (s.119(2)). In particular, a court may award compensation, including for injury to feelings (*Vento v Chief Constable of West Yorkshire Police* [2002] EWCA Civ 1871; [2003] I.C.R. 318; *Da'Bell v National Society for the Prevention of Cruelty to Children* [2010] I.R.L.R. 19; *Taylor v XLN Telecom Ltd* [2010] I.R.L.R. 499), aggravated and exemplary damages (*Ministry of Defence v Fletcher* [2010] I.R.L.R. 25) and "stigma" damages (*Chagger v Abbey National plc* [2010] I.R.L.R. 47). General damages should be uplifted by 10% following *Simmons v Castle* [2012] EWCA Civ 1039 (see, *Summers v Bundy* [2016] EWCA Civ 126). There are competing decisions from the Employment Appeal Tribunal as to whether in the context of general damages for discrimination in the employment field, the 10% uplift applies. The Court of Appeal is due to determine this issue in December 2016 in the case of *Pereira de Souza v Vinci Construction UK Ltd* [2015] UKEAT/0328/14/; [2015] I.R.L.R. 536 but this is unlikely to bear on the question whether general damages in discrimination claims outside the employment sphere should be uplifted following *Simmons v Castle*. In determining whether any particular losses are recoverable the test to be applied is whether such losses are caused by (or arise naturally and directly from) the discrimination found proved. There is no requirement of foreseeabilty (*Essa v Laing Ltd* [2004] EWCA Civ 2; [2004] I.C.R. 746, CA). In claims of indirect discrimination (Equality Act 2010 s.19), a county court or sheriff court must not make an award of damages unless it first considers whether to make any other disposal in cases where it is satisfied that the provision, criterion or practice was not applied with the intention of discriminating against the claimant (Equality Act 2010 s.119(5) and (6)). However, a court may infer that a defendant had the requisite intention where he knew when he applied the offending requirement or condition that the discriminatory consequences would follow (*London Underground Limited v Edwards* [1995] I.R.L.R. 355, EAT; *JH Walker Ltd v Hussain* [1996] I.C.R. 291, EAT).

SECTION 3J DIRECTORS DISQUALIFICATION PROCEEDINGS

PRACTICE DIRECTION—DIRECTORS DISQUALIFICATION PROCEEDINGS

Appeals

In the first paragraph, replace "para.35" with:

3J-63   para.32

SECTION 3K CIVIL RECOVERY PROCEEDINGS

PRACTICE DIRECTION—CIVIL RECOVERY PROCEEDINGS

Replace with:

3K-1   This Practice Direction (set out from para.3K-7) was published in HMSO CPR Update 30, February 2003. It does not supplement any particular Part of the CPR, or Schedule rule, but is a consequence of the Proceeds of Crime Act 2002. See further Vol.1 para.sc115.0.2.1.

Editorial note

Add new paragraphs at end:
The Practice Direction, unlike the Act and the Regulations, is not made with statutory authority. **3K-2**
It must however be recognised and applied subject to any conflict with primary and secondary
legislation and, if relevant, the exercise of case management powers (*Serious Organised Crime Agency
v Azam* [2013] EWCA Civ 970; [2013] 1 W.L.R. 3800).
A practice note was issued by the Senior Master of the Queen's Bench Division on 15 April 2016
("the Practice Note") (set out from para.3K-29). This lays down a procedure for the commencement and initial case management of claims for civil recovery in cases where there is likely to be a
dispute of fact. It makes provision for points of claim, defence and reply.

Part 5 powers—power to make a recovery order

Replace the first paragraph with:
The power in Pt 5 is for the High Court to make a "recovery order" against property if satisfied **3K-3**
that the property is the proceeds of crime (see s.266(1) combined with ss.241, 242 and 304(1) of
the 2002 Act). For whether property can properly be said to be the proceeds of crime (defined by
304(1) as property obtained "by or in return for" crime) see *Director of the Assets Recovery Agency v
John* [2007] EWHC 360, QB; *Director of the Assets Recovery Agency v Olupitan* [2008] EWCA Civ 104;
R. (Greater Manchester Police) v Salford Magistrates' Court [2008] EWHC 1651 (Admin); *Serious
Organised Crime Agency v Matthews* [2009] EWHC 1544 (Admin)); and *Serious Organised Crime Agency
v Namli* [2014] EWCA Civ 411. A recovery order is an order which forfeits the interests in the
property to the State by vesting the property rights in a "trustee for civil recovery", a creature of
the 2002 Act (see ss.266(2) and 267). Property may be traced and recovered from persons who did
not carry out the crime, but there are various defences set out in Pt 5, the principal one of which is
that the holder of the property is a good faith purchaser for value without notice of the unlawful
origin of the property (s.308(1)). For the effect on third parties, particularly in a domestic context,
see *National Crime Agency v Azam* [2015] EWCA Civ 1234. In domestic and European Convention of
Human Rights law, civil recovery proceedings are civil proceedings, not criminal (*Gale and another v
Serious Organised Crime Agency* [2011] UKSC 49; [2011] 1 W.L.R. 2760). Civil recovery proceedings
are independent of criminal proceedings. They may properly be brought even though there has
been an acquittal in criminal proceedings on the same evidence (*Gale* (above)). The claimant does
have to specify which *type* of crime generated the proceeds but does not have to identify a *particular*
crime (*Director of Assets Recovery Agency v Green* [2005] EWHC 3168 (Admin)). The mere fact of a
lack of lawful income to support lifestyle is insufficient; but a failure to account for how a lifestyle is
maintained or a false explanation for lifestyle may well lead to an inference that property is
recoverable: *Director of Assets Recovery Agency v Olupitan* [2008] EWCA Civ 104. In *Director of the Assets Recovery Agency v Olupitan* the Court of Appeal explained that to comply with the requirements
identified in *Green* it was not necessary for the claimant to plead the facts in the same manner as in
a civil case alleging fraud. All that was necessary was for the type of crime to be identified in the
most general terms. The claimant may be able to allege money laundering. If so, he does not have
to identify the type of crime which generated the proceeds which were laundered, provided he can
establish an "irresistible inference" that they were criminally derived (*Serious Organised Crime Agency
v Gale* [2009] EWHC 1015 (QB)).

Replace the second paragraph with:
The nature of the claim is neither proprietary nor in personam, but sui generis (*Director of the
Assets Recovery Agency v Creaven* [2006] 1 W.L.R. 622). Statements in the Supreme Court in *Gale*
(above) suggest that civil recovery proceedings are in rem. For a full discussion see *Serious Fraud
Office v Saleh* [2015] EWHC 2119 (QB).

Part 5 powers—procedure on application for a recovery order

Replace the first paragraph with:
The Practice Direction (para.3K-7 at 3K-10) and the Practice Note (from para.3K-29) set out **3K-4**
how the claimant should make a claim for a recovery order. This must be read with the requirements in the Act. The claimant may bring proceedings against any person that it "thinks" holds
recoverable property (s.243(1) of the 2002 Act). For the definition of "property" and holding
property see s.316 of the 2002 Act. Such a person is called a "respondent" by the 2002 Act and the
claim form must be served on that person (s.243(2) combined with s.316(1)). The claim form
should also be served upon any person holding associated property, unless the court dispenses
with service (s.243(2)). Associated property is property which is not itself recoverable property, but
is another interest in recoverable property (s.245). The claim form should therefore be served on
all persons with an interest in the property (*Director of the Assets Recovery Agency v Charrington* [2004]
EWHC 2345 (Admin)). The proceedings "must be made using the Part 8 procedure" (PD para.4.1).
This is a curious choice made by the draftsman of the Practice Direction as civil recovery proceedings almost always involve substantial disputes of fact. They are better suited to the Pt 7 procedure.
This is recognised by the court which will order a case to proceed under Pt 7 where appropriate

(*Director of the Assets Recovery Agency v Creaven* [2006] 1 W.L.R. 622; *Director of the Assets Recovery Agency v Szepietowski* [2007] EWCA Civ 766; *SOCA v Pelekanos* [2009] EWHC 2307 (QB) and *SOCA v Bosworth* [2010] EWHC 645 (QB)).

After the first paragraph, add as a new paragraph:
The Senior Master of the QBD has now issued a Practice Note (para.3K-29) to ameliorate this problem, making provision for points of case to be filed by the parties where there is likely to be a dispute of fact. Reference should be made to the Practice Note for the detail, but in summary i) if the facts may be contested, before issuing the claim, the claimant should seek directions from the court, ii) if oral directions are appropriate, the court will list the case for a 30 minute directions hearing and notify the parties (Although not provided for by the Practice Note, in such a case it will normally be sensible for the claimant to serve a draft claim form under Pt 8, accompanied by a short witness statement and the directions it seeks), iii) if the claimant considers that directions can be given on the papers without a hearing, it must issue and serve the Pt 8 claim form, a short witness statement, draft points of claim and draft initial directions providing for the exchange of points of case and a directions hearing thereafter, and iv) the court may make these directions on the papers or may direct an oral hearing.

In the second paragraph, after "It will often have", add:
sensitive

Part 5 powers—making a recovery order

After the first paragraph, add as a new paragraph:
3K-5   Victims of the respondent's crime may intervene in civil recovery proceedings in order to secure the return of their property and avoid its forfeiture to the state (s.281). For guidance as to the scope of s.281, see *National Crime Agency v Robb* [2014] EWHC 4384 (Ch); [2015] Ch. 520.

Part 5 powers—interim powers to preserve assets

Replace the second paragraph with:
3K-6   The second type of interim order is for the appointment of a "civil recovery management receiver". This power is conferred by s.245E, inserted by s.83 of the Serious Crime Act 2007. Such a receiver is akin to a receiver appointed under the equitable jurisdiction of the High Court in civil litigation to manage assets and prevent dissipation. The powers which may be conferred on such a receiver are set out in s.245F of the 2002 Act. Such a receiver will be an officer of the court (as to which, in a different context, see *Re Andrews* [1999] 1 W.L.R. 1236). The costs of such a receiver ought normally to be met out of the assets under management (*Capewell v Customs and Excise Commissioners* [2007] UKHL 2; [2007] 1 W.L.R. 386). There are exceptional circumstances where the claimant may be liable to meet them (*Crown Prosecution Service v Eastenders Group* [2014] UKSC 26; [2015] A.C. 1). The Court of Appeal has issued guidelines to keep costs under control (*Capewell v Customs and Excise Commissioners* [2004] EWCA Civ 1628; [2005] 1 All E.R. 900).

To the end of the third paragraph, add:
The investigative costs of such a receiver are recoverable as legal costs in the case (*Serious Organised Crime Agency v Gale* [2011] UKSC 49; [2011] 1 W.L.R. 2760). The management costs fall to be determined as set out above in respect of the costs of a management receiver.

Replace the fourth paragraph with:
These specific statutory interim powers are not the limit of the court's powers. The CPR applies and so any of the interim remedies in Pt 25 are available to the Court (see s.243(5) of the 2002 Act, inserted by Sch.6 of the Serious Organised Crime and Police Act 2005). Part 25 will be required where a property freezing order has utility after the making of a recovery order. In such a case, the Act does not permit a PFO to continue (*Serious Organised Crime Agency v O'Docherty* [2013] EWCA Civ 518; [2013] C.P. Rep. 35).

In the fifth paragraph, replace "The use of the word "may"" to "this approach is correct" with:
Consequently, unlike conventional civil proceedings, the making of interim orders is not linked to the commencement of a claim. However PD para.5A requires the court to specify a period within which the claimant must commence proceedings or apply for a continuation of the order, failing which the order shall be set aside

Add new paragraph at end:
As to the procedure for interim orders see paras 2 and 5-7 of the PD. In summary, pre-action applications for interim orders must be made in the Administrative Court. Any claim will commence in the QBD, so thereafter all applications should be made there (or where the claim is thereafter progressing) (para.2). A pre-action without notice application in the Administrative Court will normally be made on the papers without a hearing, but one may be sought by the claimant, or directed by the court when the papers are lodged (*National Crime Agency v Simkus* [2016]

EWHC 255 (Admin)) The application should be made by application notice in accordance with Pt 23 and supported by a witness statement (PD para.5.1/5.4). See para.5.4 for guidance as to the contents of such a witness statement. As with any application made without notice, the claimant is under a duty to make full disclosure of facts which undermine the application (generally see *Brink's-MAT Ltd v Elcombe* [1988] 1 W.L.R. 1350, *Re Stanford* [2010] EWCA Civ 137, *Jennings v CPS* [2005] EWCA Civ 746; [2006] 1 W.L.R. 182, *R. (Rawlinson and Hunter) v Central Criminal Court* [2012] EWHC 2254 (Admin); [2013] 1 W.L.R. 1634 and *NCA v Simkus* (above) (Admin). The witness statement should set out what approach has been taken to these disclosure obligations and what has been done in execution of them (*NCA v Simkus* (above)).

Varying and setting aside interim orders

After the first paragraph, add as a new paragraph:

See para.7.1 of the PD for the procedure to vary or discharge an order. Such an application **3K-6.1** should also be made in accordance with CPR Pt 23 supported by a witness statement.

Exclusions for legal costs

Replace with:

As originally enacted, the 2002 Act did not permit any exception to an interim order preventing **3K-6.2** disposition of assets to be made for meeting the respondent's own legal costs. It was intended that legal aid funding would be made available.

This proved unworkable and, as a result, the Serious Organised Crime and Police Act 2005 inserted various provisions in the 2002 Act allowing "exclusions" to be made to property freezing orders and interim receiving orders to pay legal costs.

The primary legislation (ss.245C, 252, 266(8A), 266(8B), 268A, 268B, 280), the Proceeds of Crime Act 2002 (Legal Expenses in Civil Recovery Proceedings) Regulations 2005 (SI 2005/3382) ("the Regulations") and paragraphs 5B, 7.1-7.3, 7A and 7B of the Practice Direction must be read together for comprehensive guidance. Respondents sued by the claimant and third parties who intervene to recover their property which may otherwise be forfeited (*National Crime Agency v Robb* [2014] EWHC 4384 (Ch)) may obtain exclusions from interim orders under these provisions.

Summary—In summary, on a without notice application for a property freezing order ("PFO") or interim receiving order ("IRO") the court may exclude a modest amount to deal with the immediate consequences of the order. Then on application or by consent the court can earmark an amount for exclusion from the PFO or IRO on the basis of a prospective costs budget. The court must identify a maximum amount for this exclusion. Once the costs have been incurred, the litigant with the benefit of the exclusion may apply under the Regulations for payment of that amount to his lawyers. The Regulations prescribe hourly rates for solicitors and counsel. If the amount is agreed between the claimant and the litigant, the Regulations provide that it may be paid. If it is not agreed, the litigant may be paid 65% of the amount claimed with the balance left over for later assessment if a civil recovery order is made.

Initial exclusion on the ex parte application for the PFO or IRO—In the first instance and on the making of a PFO or IRO without notice, the court will "normally" exclude the sum of up to £3,000. This is for the initial limited purposes laid down in PD para.5B.1. If the PFO or IRO only applies to limited property and the claimant explains in the application for it that the respondent has substantial other assets which could be used to pay legal costs, then the order should not make provision for legal costs (PD para.7A.4(1)).

If any further exclusion is sought, a discretionary order from the court is required (ss.245C(1); 252(2)). An exclusion does not guarantee payment but is a necessary step towards it.

When to apply—An application for exclusion for legal costs ought to be made before they are incurred (*Serious Organised Crime Agency v Azam* [2013] EWHC 1480 (QB), reversed on appeal on another issue and *National Crime Agency v Simkus* [2016] EWHC 728 (Admin)).

The court must consider whether to make or vary an exclusion whenever it makes an order or gives directions; but (save the initial without notice application) such an order is dependent on the applicant filing a statement of assets (PD para.7A.1-2).

An application to exclude will not succeed if there are other assets to pay legal costs (PD para.7A.4). As to the correct approach to deciding this issue, see *Serious Organised Crime Agency v Azam* [2013] EWCA Civ 970; [2013] 1 W.L.R. 3800. This may involve a trial of issue with the applicant being cross-examined on his statement of assets (*Serious Organised Crime Agency v Surin* [2013] EWHC 3137 (QB) and [2013] EWHC 3784 (QB) provides an example).

The exercise of the discretion to exclude was considered by Edis J in *National Crime Agency v Simkus* [2016] EWHC 728 (Admin). The starting point is that it is desirable that the respondent be represented (s.245C(6)(a)). The issue would normally be whether the amount sought to be excluded is reasonable. Since the Regulations provide for mandatory hourly rates, the only issue was whether the work proposed was reasonable. Exclusions cannot be made for extravagant work or hopeless exaggerations.

On an application for exclusion, the applicant must (for the 1st application) file a witness statement setting out his assets, their value and location (PD para.7A.3). Each application must comply with the requirements in para.7.3 of the Practice Direction. In summary, these require details of the stage or stages to which the costs apply, include an estimate of the costs incurred or to be incurred in the form of the Precedent for Estimate of Costs in relation to Civil Recovery Proceedings, using Precedent Q (see the PD to Pt 47) and say whether the claimant agrees those costs. Where the court has previously made an exclusion in relation to the stage concerned, the witness statement must contain an explanation of why the costs have exceeded the amount previously allowed.

After the exclusion is made, the litigant's solicitor must notify the claimant if the legal expenses have or may exceed the amount specified under the exclusion or an amount specified in any stage in an exclusion (reg.5 of the Regulations).

Form of order for exclusion—The order for exclusion must specify the amount of the exclusion and the stage in the proceedings to which it relates. If the exclusion relates to more than one stage, the exclusion must specify the amount for each stage (ss.245C(5); 252(4), reg.4 of the Regulations and the Practice Direction para.7A.7). The property which is excluded must be specified in the order, at least in general terms (ss.245C(7); 252(5)). The court has a general discretion to impose conditions to an exclusion (ss.245C(4) and (5)(c) and 252(3) and (4)(c)) but these must be consistent with the mandatory requirements identified above.

Obtaining payment of an excluded sum—To obtain release of an excluded sum engages the Regulations. Interim payments can be made out of excluded sums before trial or upon a settlement by complying with Pt 3 of the Regulations. This requires the respondent to provide the claimant with details of the work done including evidence in support (reg.8(1)). The respondent can only make one request every two months (reg.10). The claimant then has 21 days to respond. If the claimant agrees the amount, the sum can be released (reg.10). In deciding whether to agree, the claimant must have regard to the rates set out in reg.17 of the Regulations. If the claimant does not agree the amount, it is entitled to limit the release to between 65% and 100% of the claimed amount.

A release under Pt 3 is not a final irreversible payment. If a recovery order is made in relation to assets which were previously the subject of a PFO or IRO but excluded for legal costs, in order to recover any amount due from the forfeited assets, the recovery order must make provision for assessment of all of the respondent's own costs (whether made by interim payments or releases under Pt 3 or yet to be considered) (s.266(8A)/(8B) and para.7B.1 of the PD). Paragraph 7B.2 of the Practice Direction requires the court to order an assessment of those costs. In the absence of these orders, the effect of regs 13 and 14 seems to be that all of the interim payments must be repaid by the solicitor to the trustee for civil recovery to be paid on to the Treasury (*Serious Organised Crime Agency v Szepeitowski* [2009] EWHC 1560 (Ch)).

In the absence of agreement by the claimant to the amount of costs, the respondent must then start an assessment process under CPR Pt 47 within 2 months of the recovery order being made (reg.13 and para.7B.5 of the Practice Direction). If there is an assessment, Pt 5 of the Regulations (reg.13(3)) and paras 7B.3-7B.7 of the Practice Direction apply. Part 5 of the Regulations sets out mandatory sliding scale rates for solicitors and counsel. Note that the QC rate can only be paid if the court determines that the case involves substantial novel or complex issues of law or fact (reg.17(2)). This determination should be made at the stage of initial exclusion (*National Crime Agency v Simkus* [2016] EWHC 728 (Admin)). If the case does not fall into this category, a silk may only be paid at the maximum junior standard rate (*Simkus* (above)).

If the solicitor has, by interim releases, been paid more than the assessed amount, he must pay the excess to the trustee for civil recovery. If he has been paid less, then assuming the recovery order makes provision for it, the trustee must pay the balance from the proceeds of the assets which are subject to the recovery order (reg.14).

Partial civil recovery and trustees—If a partial civil recovery order is made (whether by settlement or otherwise), the respondent may have free assets with which to pay costs. In such circumstances, the court could well set aside the exclusions, thus requiring all sums excluded (and released to the solicitor as interim payments) to be paid back by the solicitor to the trustee for civil recovery. This then leaves the solicitor to pursue his client, if he can, for outstanding costs from the free assets (*Serious Organised Crime Agency v Szepietowski* (above)).

For the position of respondents sued in their capacity as a trustee see *Serious Organised Crime Agency v Szepietowski* [2009] EWHC 344 (Ch).

Add new Practice Note at end of Section 3K.

SENIOR MASTER PRACTICE NOTE 15 APRIL 2016 POCA CIVIL RECOVERY CLAIMS UNDER CPR PART 8

Civil Recovery Proceedings Practice Direction

Introduction

1. Civil Recovery claims commenced under Part 5 of the Proceeds of Crime **3K-29** Act 2002 ("POCA") must be brought under CPR 8 in accordance with paragraph 4.1 of the Civil Recovery Proceedings Practice Direction.

2. Part 8 is primarily designed for matters that are not factually contentious. There are normally no statements of case and claims are litigated purely by way of witness evidence.

3. Whilst this remains an appropriate procedure for civil recovery claims that are unlikely to be disputed, where facts may be contested the Part 8 procedure is not necessarily suitable. See for example the note in the White Book Vol 2 3K-4 (end of page 1996 to beginning page 1997) and the cases mentioned; particularly *Director of Assets Recovery Agency v Creaven* [2006] 1 WLR 633 at [11] per Stanley Burnton J. (as he then was); *SOCA v Bosworth* [2010] EWHC 645 (QB) at [26] to [29] per HHJ Seymour; *SOCA v Pelekanos* [2009] EWHC 2307 per Hamblen J. at [3].

4. The court has power to order a case to proceed under Part 7 where appropriate under CPR 3.3 (see Hamblen J. in *SOCA v Pelekanos*). However, that would not assist in civil recovery cases, as many are suitable for the usual Part 8 procedure, and for those where facts are in issue the Part 7 procedure would be likely to unduly delay progress to trial.

5. To resolve these issues, a procedure has been put in place in the Queen's Bench Division under the court's case management powers in CPR 3.3 to take effect from 3 May 2016 for the case management of POCA civil recovery claims, as set out in the Schedule to this Practice Note.

The Senior Master

Schedule

1. Before issuing the Part 8 Claim Form, the enforcement authority (as defined in s.316 (1) of POCA) will consider whether to ask the court to make directions ("Initial Directions") on the papers or at a hearing.

2. If the enforcement authority decides to seek Initial Directions without a hearing, it will

(1) serve on the Defendant (unless evidence is provided to the court that there is good reason not to do so before Initial Directions are given) and

(2) lodge at court

the issued Part 8 Claim Form, accompanied by a short witness statement, with the following exhibits:

(i) Draft Points of Claim; and

(ii) Draft Initial Directions providing for:

    a) The serving and filing of Points of Claim, Points of Defence and Points of Reply;

    b) A directions hearing to be listed after service and filing of statements of case;

    c) Permission to the Defendant(s) to apply to court to vary any of the Initial Directions.

3. Where either:

(i) the draft Initial Directions have been agreed with the Defendant(s) or their legal representatives; or

(ii)   the court considers that a hearing is not required;

the court will make Initial Directions without a hearing ("the Initial Directions Order").

4.   If the court makes the Initial Directions Order, the enforcement authority will serve on the Defendant(s) within 7 days of receipt of the Initial Directions Order from the court:

(i)   Part 8 Claim Form and witness statement with exhibits (unless previously served);

(ii)   Points of Claim;

(iii)   the Initial Directions Order.

5.   If either:

(i)   the court considers it is not appropriate to make Initial Directions without a hearing; or

(ii)   the enforcement authority considers that it is not appropriate to ask the court to deal with the matter without a hearing;

the court will list a directions hearing for 30 minutes (or longer if requested by either party) and will serve notice of the hearing on all parties.

SECTION 3L   EUROPEAN PROCEDURES (CPR PART 78)

PART 78—EUROPEAN PROCEDURES

Editorial introduction

3L-1   *Add new sub-paragraph at end:*

(iii)   Future amendments—Both the EOP Regulation (see Annex 1 and section I of this Part) and the ESCP Regulation (see Annex 2 and section II of this Part) are amended by Regulation (EU) 2015/2421 in part from 14 January 2017 and otherwise from 14 July 2017.

Section I—European Order for Payment Procedure

Making a claim

Add new paragraph at end:

3L-5   The scope and effect of art.20 (Review in exceptional cases) (see para.3L-76 below) was considered by the ECJ in *Thomas Cook Belgium NV v Thurner Belgium GmbH* (C-245/14) EU:C:2015:715; [2016] 1 W.L.R. 878, ECJ, where it was argued by the judgment debtor that the court issuing the EOP lacked jurisdiction due to the possible existence of a jurisdiction clause agreed between the parties and not referred to in the application form for the order. The ECJ ruled that this did not constitute "exceptional circumstances" within art.20(2) such as to justify a review of the order by the competent court in the Member State of origin.

SECTION 3M   PREVENTION OF TERRORISM PROCEEDINGS (CPR PARTS 76, 79 AND 80)

Part 76—Proceedings under the Prevention of Terrorism Act 2005

III.   Permission Applications, References and Appeals to the High Court Relating to Non-Derogating Control orders

Replace r.76.12(2) with:

Modification of Part 52 (appeals)[1]

(2)   The following rules do not apply to appeals under section 10 of the **3M-16** Act—

    (a)   rules 52.3, 52.4 and 52.6 (permission);

    (b)   rule 52.12 (appellant's notice);

    (c)   rule 52.13 (respondent's notice); and

    (d)   rule 52.21 (hearing of appeals).

IV.   Appeals to the Court of Appeal

Replace r.76.16(2) with:

Modification of Part 52 (appeals)[2]

(2)   The following rules do not apply to appeals to the Court of Appeal—   **3M-20**

    (a)   rule 52.12 (appellant's notice); and

    (b)   rule 52.13 (respondent's notice); but

the provisions of rules 76.13 and 76.15 shall apply with appropriate modifications.

Part 79—Proceedings Under the Counter-Terrorism Act 2008 and Part 1 of the Terrorist Asset-Freezing Etc. Act 2010

IV.   General Provisions applicable to Sections 2 and 3 of this Part

Effect of rule

Add new paragraph at end:

    In *Bank Mellat v HM Treasury* [2015] EWCA Civ 1052; [2016] 1 W.L.R. 1187, the Court of Ap-   **3M-95** peal rejected an argument that, in the light of *Tariq v Home Office* [2011] UKSC 35; [2012] 1 A.C. 452, the AF standard of disclosure should be held to apply only where either personal liberty or an equally fundamental interest is at stake. Applying *Kiani v Secretary of State for the Home Department* [2015] EWCA Civ 776; [2016] 2 W.L.R. 788, at [23], the Court of Appeal held that the question whether the AF standard of disclosure applied depended on the context and circumstances. In the particular context of proceedings under the Counter-Terrorism Act 2008 by Bank Mellat, the exercise of the power to impose financial retractions would have extremely serious and possibly ir-reversible consequences and involved a sufficiently serious restriction on the Bank's freedom of ac-

---

[1] Amended by the Civil Procedure (Amendment No.2) Rules 2009 (SI 2009/3390), the Civil Procedure (Amendment No.2) Rules 2012 (SI 2012/2208) and the Civil Procedure (Amendment No.3) Rules 2016 (SI 2016/788).

[2] Amended by the Civil Procedure (Amendment No.2) Rules 2009 (SI 2009/3390), the Civil Procedure (Amendment No.2) Rules 2012 (SI 2012/2208) and the Civil Procedure (Amendment No.3) Rules 2016 (SI 2016/788).

tion and business that the application of the AF standard of disclosure was called for (*Bank Mellat v HM Treasury*, at [23]-[25]).

Part 80—Proceedings Under the Terrorism Prevention and Investigation Measures Act 2011

I Application of this Part

Effect of rule

After "withhold disclosed material.", add:

3M-106 CPR r.80.7.

II Permission Applications, References and Appeals to the High Court Relating to TPIM Notices

Add new paragraph 3M–110.1:

Review hearings and appeals

3M-110.1 In *EB v Secretary of State for the Home Department* [2016] EWHC 137 (Admin), 29 January 2016, unrep. (Cranston J), where an individual (D) was subject to a TPIM notice and a review under s.9 of the 2011 Act was pending, D appealed under s.16 of that Act against the Secretary of State's refusal to vary measures set out in the notice. The judge directed that the appeal should not be heard forthwith (as D submitted) but should be joined with the review (due to be heard some time hence) so that both could be properly and justly determined.

Replace s.80.8(2) with:

Modification of Part 52 (appeals)[1]

3M-111 (2) The following rules do not apply to appeals under section 16 of the Act—

    (a)   rules 52.3, 52.4 and 52.6 (permission);

    (b)   rule 52.12 (appellant's notice);

    (c)   rule 52.13 (respondent's notice); and

    (d)   rule 52.21 (hearing of appeals).

III Appeals to the Court of Appeal

Replace r.80.12(2) with:

Modification of Part 52 (appeals)[2]

3M-116 (2) The following rules do not apply to appeals to the Court of Appeal—

    (a)   rule 52.12(1) (appellant's notice); and

    (b)   rule 52.13 (respondent's notice), but

the provisions of rules 80.9 and 80.11 shall apply with appropriate modifications.

---

[1] Amended by the Civil Procedure (Amendment No.2) Rules 2012 (SI 2012/2208) and the Civil Procedure (Amendment No.3) Rules 2016 (SI 2016/788).

[2] Amended by the Civil Procedure (Amendment No.2) Rules 2012 (SI 2012/2208) and the Civil Procedure (Amendment No.3) Rules 2016 (SI 2016/788).

PART 88—PROCEEDINGS UNDER THE COUNTER-TERRORISM AND SECURITY ACT 2015

III. Modification of Part 52 (appeals)

Replace r.88.15(2) with:

Modification of Part 52 (appeals)[1]
(2) The following rules do not apply to appeals to the Court of Appeal—   **3M-161**
   (a) rule 52.12(1) (appellant's notice); and
   (b) rule 52.13 (respondent's notice).

SECTION 3O EMPLOYMENT

Employment Tribunals (Constitution and Rules of Procedure) Regulations 2013

Forms of Costs and Preparation Time Orders

Replace the fifth paragraph with:
Note that if, as frequently occurs, representation arrangements change during the course of the   **3O-2.1**
litigation, the type of order available may differ in respect of each period. But the Tribunal cannot
make both types of order in favour of the same party in the same proceedings. However, a party
whose representation status has changed may apply for both types of order, leaving the Tribunal to
decide entitlement to each, and, as appropriate, which to make. See: *Duhoe v Support Services Group
Ltd (In Liquidation)* UKEAT/0102/15, 13 August 2015.

SECTION 4 SUPREME COURT OF THE UNITED KINGDOM AND JUDICIAL COMMITTEE OF THE PRIVY COUNCIL

SECTION 4A SUPREME COURT OF THE UNITED KINGDOM APPEALS

SUPREME COURT OF THE UNITED KINGDOM APPEALS

Doctrine of precedent

Add at end:
For discussion of the circumstances in which the Judicial Committee of the Privy Council may   **4A-0.5**
formally overrule or depart from a judgment of the House of Lords, Supreme Court or Court of
Appeal, see *Willers v Joyce* [2016] UKSC 44.

---

[1] Amended by the Civil Procedure (Amendment No.3) Rules 2016 (SI 2016/788).

Supreme Court Rules 2009

Effect of rule

Replace the third paragraph with:

4A-23.1   Parties granted permission to appeal on or after 1 October 2014 must follow the Court's publicised guidelines for electronic submission of their bundles, in addition to filing hard copies. The guidelines set out at *https://www.supremecourt.uk/procedures/electronic-bundle-guidelines.html* [Accessed 1 August 2016] are in addition to Practice Direction 14 and oblige parties to prepare their electronic bundles through a centralised system.

Effect of rule

Replace the third paragraph with:

4A-24.1   For filing of volumes of authorities in electronic form, see Practice Direction 14 (Filing Documents in the Registry of the Supreme Court by electronic means). The parties must file electronic bundles and the practice direction is highly prescriptive. Supplemental authorities should also be provided electronically. Parties granted permission to appeal on or after 1 October 2014 must follow the Court's publicised guidelines for electronic submission of their authorities bundles, in addition to filing hard copies. The guidelines set out at *https://www.supremecourt.uk/procedures/electronic-bundle-guidelines.html* [Accessed 1 August 2016] are in addition to Practice Direction 14 and oblige parties to prepare their electronic bundles through a centralised system.

Application to reopen judgment

Add new paragraph at end:

4A-28.1   The Supreme Court has an inherent jurisdiction to correct any injustice caused by an unfair procedure which led to an earlier judgment of itself or of the House of Lords. On an application for an appeal to be re-opened, the test is that it must be clearly established that a significant injustice has probably occurred and that there is no alternative effective remedy. The jurisdiction extends to situations in which further evidence, including evidence of non-disclosure, is discovered after a judgment is rendered which is not susceptible of appeal: *R v Bow Street Metropolitan Stipendiary Magistrate, ex p Pinochet Ugarte (No.2)* [2000] 1 AC 119; *Bain v The Queen* [2009] UKPC 4; *R (Bancoult) v Secretary of State for Foreign and Commonwealth Affairs (No.4)* [2016] UKSC 35; [2016] 3 W.L.R. 157.

Effect of rule

Replace the first paragraph with:

4A-45.1   The fees which are payable in the Court are prescribed by the Supreme Court Fees Order 2009 (SI 2009/2131) made under s.52 of the 2005 Act. (The Order was amended by SI 2011/1737, by SI 2013/534, by SI 2013/2302 and by SI 2014/590, along with other minor amendments made to Sch.2 by additional statutory instruments.) For fees payable, see Annex 2 to Practice Direction 7 (Applications, Documents, Forms and Orders) (replicating Sch.1 to the 2009 Order). The Registry will not issue an application for permission to appeal or other document unless (amongst other things) the prescribed fee is paid or a request for fee remission from court fees is made (Practice Direction 2 (The Registry of the Supreme Court) para.2.1.11).

PRACTICE DIRECTION 1—GENERAL NOTE AND JURISDICTION

Section 2 The Jurisdiction of the Supreme Court

Civil Appeals

Replace paragraph 1.2.2 with:

4A-57   **1.2.2**   The principal provisions relating to civil appeals from Scotland are in section 40 of the Court of Session Act 1988 as amended by the Act. (But see also sections 24, 27(5), 32(5), 41, 42, 43 and 52(3) as amended for further matters of detail and para.1.2.25).

Devolution Matters

Replace paragraph 1.2.24 with:

4A-62   **1.2.24**   Devolution matters raise issues of constitutional importance as to the purported or proposed exercise of a function by a member of the Scottish

Executive, a Minister in Northern Ireland or a Northern Ireland department or the Welsh Ministers or as to the legislative competence of the Scottish Parliament under the Scotland Act 1998, the Northern Ireland Assembly under the Northern Ireland Act 1998, and the National Assembly for Wales under the Government of Wales Act 2006. Under these Acts, as amended by Part 2 of Schedule 9 to the Act, the Supreme Court has an appellate jurisdiction in proceedings for the determination of a devolution issue and special statutory powers to consider referred questions, including questions referred by the relevant law officer or Ministers. See rule 41 and Practice Direction 10 (Devolution Issues).

Civil appeals from Scotland

Replace paragraph 1.2.25 with:

1.2.25   Where judgment is pronounced after 22 September 2015 on a deci-   **4A-62.1**
sion of the Inner House of the Court of Session which is
1.   A decision constituting final judgment in any proceedings,
2.   A decision in an exchequer cause,
3.   A decision, on an application under s.29 of the Court of Session Act 1988, to grant or refuse a new trial in any proceedings,
4.   Any other decision in any proceedings if:
     i.   is a difference of opinion among the judges making the decision, or
     ii.   the decision is one sustaining a preliminary defence and dismissing the proceedings;
an appeal may be made to the Supreme Court
1.   With the permission of the Inner House, or
2.   If the Inner House has refused permission, with the permission of the Supreme Court.
   •   "final judgment", in relation to any proceedings, means a decision which, by itself or taken along with prior decisions in the proceedings, disposes of the subject matter of the proceedings on its merits, even though judgment may not have been pronounced on every question raised or expenses found due may not have been modified, taxed or decerned for,
   •   "preliminary defence", in relation to any proceedings, means a defence that does not relate to the merits of the proceedings.
In the case of any other decision of the Inner House, an appeal may be made to the Supreme Court only with the permission of the Inner House.

No appeal may be taken to the Supreme Court against any decision of a Lord Ordinary.

An application to the Inner House for permission to take an appeal must be made:
1.   Within the period of 28 days beginning with the date of the decision against which the appeal is to be taken, or
2.   Within such longer period as the Inner House considers equitable having regard to all the circumstances.

An application to the Supreme Court for permission to appeal must be made:
1.   Within the period of 28 days beginning with the date on which the Inner House refuses permission for the appeal, or
2.   Within such longer period as the Supreme Court considers equitable having regard to all the circumstances.

The Inner House or the Supreme Court may grant permission for an appeal only if the Inner House or, as the case may be, the Supreme Court considers that the appeal raises an arguable point of law of general public importance which ought to be considered by the Supreme Court at that time.

PRACTICE DIRECTION 4—NOTICE OF APPEAL

Form of notice of appeal

Replace paragraph 4.2.2 with:

4A-85   **4.2.2**   The notice of appeal must be signed by the appellants or their agents. In appeals where permission to appeal is not required (for example, in most Scottish appeals) the notice of appeal must be certified as reasonable by two counsel from the relevant jurisdiction and signed by them.[1]

References to the European Court

Replace paragraph 4.2.13 with:

4.2.13   If an appellant seeks a reference to the Court of Justice of the European Union, this should be stated clearly in the notice of appeal and special provisions apply: see rule 42 and Practice Direction 11. The appellant must also notify the Registrar in writing.

PRACTICE DIRECTION 6—THE APPEAL HEARING

The core volumes and authorities volumes

Replace paragraph 6.4.1 with:

4A-101   **6.4.1**   As soon as the parties' cases have been exchanged and in any event not later than 14 days before the date fixed for the hearing the appellant must file core volumes in accordance with paragraph 6.4.3 and (if necessary) additional volumes containing further parts of the appendix and 10 copies of every case filed by the parties or any intervener. These copies of the cases must contain cross-references (in a footnote or in the body of the text) to the Appendix and authorities volumes.

Judgment

Conditions under which judgments are released in advance

Replace paragraph 6.8.5 with:

4A-106   **6.8.5**   Accredited members of the media may on occasion also be given a copy of the judgment in advance by the Court's communications team. The contents of this document are subject to a strict embargo, and are not for publication, broadcast or use on club tapes before judgment has been delivered. The documents are issued in advance solely at the Court's discretion, and in order to form later reporting, on the strict understanding that no approach is made to any person or organisation about their contents before judgment is given.

---

[1] In such cases, counsel's signatures are required even if the appellants propose to conduct the appeal in person. The term "counsel" is defined by rule 2 and, for the purposes of this provision,"counsel" includes an enrolled solicitor with a right of audience in the Supreme Court: see the Solicitors (Scotland) Act 1980, s.25A as amended by the Constitutional Reform Act 2005, Sch 9 para 32).

PRACTICE DIRECTION 10—DEVOLUTION JURISDICTION

General note

Replace paragraph 10.1.3 with:
10.1.3 Questions of the kind referred to in paras 10.1.1 and 10.1.2 can reach **4A-135** the Supreme Court in four ways.

Add new paragraph 10.1.7:
10.1.7 In cases where the Court is asked to consider the provisions of Bills passed by devolved legislatures, it will usually be desirable for special directions to be given, particularly if there is some urgency. It is helpful if at an early stage the relevant officer making the reference notifies any relevant officer and any other person or body who has a potential interest in the proceedings, of the making of the reference and of any request for directions. All parties to the proceedings are expected to co-operate with one another in order that the Court can ensure that the proceedings are conducted efficiently and expeditiously.

PRACTICE DIRECTION 11—THE COURT OF JUSTICE OF THE EUROPEAN UNION

Add new paragraph 11.1.11:

Papers for the Court of Justice
11.1.11 Parties should be aware that the Court of Justice will not translate **4A-142** documents which are longer than 20 pages; only summaries are made.

PRACTICE DIRECTION 12—CRIMINAL PROCEEDINGS

Section 2 Applications for Permission

5. Costs

Replace paragraph 12.5.1 with:
12.5.1 Where an application for permission to appeal is determined without **4A-147** an oral hearing, costs may be awarded as follows:
  (a) to a publicly funded or legally aided appellant, reasonable costs incurred in preparing papers for the Appeal Panel;
  (b) to a publicly funded or legally aided respondent, only those costs necessarily incurred in attending the client, attending the appellant's solicitors, considering the application, filing notice of objection and, where applicable, preparing respondent's objections to the application;
  (c) to an unassisted respondent where the appellant is publicly funded or legally aided, payment in accordance with the relevant statutory provisions[1])[2] of costs as specified at (b) above;
  (d) to an appellant or respondent, payment out of central funds, pursuant to s 16 or s 17 of the Prosecution of Offences Act 1985, of costs incurred at (a) or (b) above, as the case may be;
  (e) to a respondent where neither party is publicly funded or legally aided, costs as specified at (b) above to be paid by the appellant.

---

[1] Also pursuant to r.5(2) Community Legal Service (Cost Protection) Regulations 2000 and in accordance with the procedural requirements of rr.9, 10 Community Legal Service (Costs) Regulations 2000(as amended).
[2] Or s.18 Legal Aid Act 1988; or, in Scotland, pursuant to s.19 Legal Aid (Scotland) Act 1986 or, in Northern Ireland, pursuant to Article 16 Legal Aid Advice and Assistance (N.I.) Order 1981.

PRACTICE DIRECTION 13—COSTS

Section 2: Form 5: (Bill of Costs)

Replace form with:

4A-176

Section 2 – Form 5 (Bill of Costs)

This form covers all Supreme Court proceedings. Please delete rows or sections
as appropriate.

UKSC Form 5
Part 1 APPELLANT'S RESPONDENT'S BILL OF COSTS (delete as appropriate)
Case title/UKSC reference
Parties
Summary of UKSC decision
Brief outline of proceedings below
Brief outline of UKSC proceedings
Outline of funding arrangements
Fee earners and hourly rates
Other useful information
VAT number if appropriate

1

Item	Description/date etc	Profit costs	Counsel's fees	Other disbursements	VAT
PERMISSION TO APPEAL					
Counsel's fees					
1					
2					
3					
Attendances on and communications with the court including fees paid					
4					
5					
6					
Attendances on and communications with counsel					
7					
8					
9					
Attendances on and communications with client					
10					
11					
12					
Attendances on and communications with opponent					
13					
14					
15					
Attendances on and communications with others (please specify)					
16					
17					
18					
Attendance at oral hearing					
19					
20					
21					
Work done on documents (itemise at Part 3)					
22					
23					
24					
Other work done/disbursements					
25					
26					
27					
Costs claimed against legal aid provider where party and party costs also claimed					
28					
29					
30					
NOTICE OF APPEAL					
Counsel's fees					
31					
32					
33					
34					
35					
36					
Attendances on and communications with the court including fees paid					
37					
38					

2

Item	Description/date etc	Profit costs	Counsel's fees	Other disbursements	VAT
39					
40					
41					
42					
43					
Attendance at appeal hearing					
44					
45					
46					
47					
Attendances on and communications with counsel					
48					
49					
50					
51					
52					
53					
Attendances on and communications with client					
54					
55					
56					
57					
58					
59					
Attendances on and communications with opponent					
60					
61					
62					
63					
64					
65					
Attendances on and communications with others (please specify)					
66					
67					
68					
69					
70					
71					
Work on documents (itemise at Part 3)					
72					
73					
74					
75					
76					
77					
Other work done/disbursements					
78					
79					
80					
81					
82					
83					
Costs claimed against legal aid provider where party and party costs also claimed					
84					
85					
86					
87					
88					

3

Item	Description/date etc	Profit costs	Counsel's fees	Other disbursements	VAT
89					
90					

COSTS OF ASSESSMENT

Attendances on and communications with the court

Item	Description/date etc	Profit costs	Counsel's fees	Other disbursements	VAT
91					
92					
93					
94					

Attendances on and communications with counsel

95					
96					
97					
98					

Attendances on and communications with opponent

99					
100					
101					
102					

Work done drawing the bill

103					
104					
105					
106					

Costs claimed against legal aid provider where party and party costs also claimed

107					
108					
109					
110					

Other work done/disbursements

111					
112					
113					
114					

Detailed assessment costs schedule

115					
116					
117					
118					
119					

TOTAL COSTS CLAIMED excluding costs of assessment

	Profit costs	Counsel's fees	Other disbursements	VAT
Profit costs				
VAT on profit costs				
Counsel's fees				
VAT on counsel's fees				
Other disbursements				
VAT on other disbursements				

TOTAL COSTS CLAIMED AGAINST LEGAL AID PROVIDER where party and party costs also claimed

Profit costs				
VAT on profit costs				
Counsel's fees				
VAT on counsel's fees				
Other disbursements				
VAT on other disbursements				

TOTAL COSTS OF ASSESSMENT

Profit costs				

4

Item	Description/date etc	Profit costs	Counsel's fees	Other disbursements	VAT
VAT on profit costs					
Counsel's fees					
VAT on counsel's fees					
Other disbursements					
VAT on other disbursements					
Totals					
Grand total					

Part 2 SUMMARY AND AGREED AMOUNT TO BE CERTIFIED					
	Claimed	Assessed off	Allowed	VAT	Total £ (Allowed + VAT)
Profit costs					
Counsels' fees					
Other disbursements					
Filing fee					
Assessment fee					
Total amount to be certified					
Signed for receiving party					
Signed for paying party					

This Part should first be completed and signed by the receiving party and then (if appropriate) by the paying party. The receiving party should then return the bill to the Court along with the assessment fee.

Cont'd overleaf

5

Part 3 DOCUMENTS SCHEDULE				
Grade	Date	Description of work done	Hours claimed	Amount claimed

Cont'd overleaf

6

Part 4 CERTIFICATES – DELETE OR AMEND AS APPROPRIATE	
CERTIFICATE OF SERVICE This bill was served on the appellant/respondent [NAME] on [DATE] This document was served on the [NAME OF SOLICITORS] by the following method: [METHOD OF SERVICE] I believe that the facts stated in this certificate are true	Y/N
CERTIFICATE AS TO INTEREST OF LEGALLY AIDED PARTY PURSUANT TO REGULATION 119 OF THE CIVIL LEGAL AID (GENERAL) REGULATIONS 1989 The legally aided party has no financial interest in the detailed assessment **OR** A copy of this bill has been sent to the legally aided party in accordance with Regulation 119 of the Civil Legal Aid General Regulations 1989 with an explanation of his/her interest in the detailed assessment and the steps which can be taken to safeguard that interest in the assessment. He/she has/has not requested that the costs officer be informed of his/her interest and has/has not requested that notice of the detailed assessment hearing be sent to him/her.	Y/N Y/N
CERTIFICATES AS TO ACCURACY, INTEREST, PAYMENTS AND VAT (i) **Accuracy** This bill is both accurate and complete *(where the receiving party was legally aided)* All the work claimed as payable by a legal aid provider was done under a certificate issued by the legal aid provider granted to [legall aided party] *(where costs are claimed for work done by an employed solicitor)* The work claimed at items [ ] was conducted by a solicitor who is an employee of the receiving party *(other cases where costs are claimed for work done by a solicitor)* The costs claimed in this bill do not exceed the costs which the receiving party is required to pay me/my firm.	Y/N Y/N Y/N Y/N
(ii) **Interest and Payments** No rulings have been made in this case which affects the receiving party's entitlement to interest on costs **OR** The only rulings made in this case as to interest are as follows *[give brief details as to the date of such ruling]* **AND** No payments have been made by the paying party on account of costs included in this bill of costs **OR** The following payments have been made on account of costs included in this bill of costs *[give brief details of such payments]*	Y/N Y/N Y/N Y/N
(iii) **Disbursements** All disbursements listed in this bill which individually do not exceed £500 (other than those relating to Counsel's fees) have been duly discharged.	Y/N
(iv) **VAT** With reference to the pending assessment of the appellant's/respondent's costs and disbursements which are payable by the appellant/respondent— the appellant/respondent, on the basis of its last completed VAT return, would [not] be entitled to recover/would be entitled to recover only X percent of the Value Added Tax on such costs and disbursements as input tax pursuant to Section 14 of the Value Added Tax Act 1983.	Y/N
I, Grade solicitor at the firm , certify that the above statements are true Signed Date	Y/N

7

PRACTICE DIRECTION 14—FILING DOCUMENTS IN THE REGISTRY OF THE SUPREME COURT BY ELECTRONIC MEANS

Submission of electronic documents to the Registry

Replace paragraph 14.3.1 with:

4A-192.1 **14.3.1**   Unless otherwise directed or permitted by the Registrar, or where the circumstances in paragraph 14.5.5 apply, the means of submitting electronic documents to the Registry is via e-mail at registry@supremecourt.uk.

FORM3

Replace Forms 1–3 with:

Form 1 (Application for permission/notice of appeal)

4A-197

| Save form | Print form | Reset form |

In the Supreme Court of the United Kingdom

Notice of appeal
(or application for permission to appeal)

On appeal from

———— v ————

Appeal number

Date of filing

D D / M M M / Y Y Y Y

Appellant's solicitors

Respondent's solicitors

SC001 Notice of appeal (05.14)

© Crown copyright 2014

1. Appellant

Appellant's full name

Original status

☐ Claimant   ☐ Defendant

☐ Petitioner   ☐ Respondent

☐ Pursuer   ☐ Defender

Solicitor

Name

Address

Telephone no.

Fax no.

DX no.

Postcode

Ref.

Email

How would you prefer us to communicate with you?

☐ DX   ☐ Email

☐ Post   ☐ Other *(please specify)*

Is the appellant in receipt of public funding/legal aid?

☐ Yes   ☐ No

If Yes, please give the certificate number

Counsel

Name

Address

Telephone no.

Fax no.

DX no.

Postcode

Email

Page 2

SC001 Notice of appeal

Counsel

Name

Address

Telephone no.

Fax no.

DX no.

Postcode

Email

2. Respondent

Respondent's full name

Original status

☐ Claimant   ☐ Defendant

☐ Petitioner   ☐ Respondent

☐ Pursuer   ☐ Defender

Solicitor

Name

Address

Telephone no.

Fax no.

DX no.

Postcode

Ref.

Email

How would you prefer us to communicate with you?

☐ DX   ☐ Email

☐ Post   ☐ Other *(please specify)*

Is the respondent in receipt of public funding/legal aid?

☐ Yes   ☐ No

If Yes, please give the certificate number

Page 3

SC001 Notice of appeal

Counsel

Name

Address   Telephone no.

Fax no.

DX no.

Postcode

Email

Counsel

Name

Address   Telephone no.

Fax no.

DX no.

Postcode

Email

3. Decision being appealed

Name of Court

Names of Judges

Date of order/
interlocutor/decision

D D / M M M / Y Y Y Y

Page 4

SC001 Notice of appeal

4. Permission to appeal

If you have permission to appeal complete **Part A** or complete **Part B** if you require permission to appeal.

PART A

Name of Court granting permission

Date permission granted

D D / M M M / Y Y Y Y

Conditions on which permission granted

PART B

☐ The appellant applies to the Supreme Court for permission to appeal.

267

5. Information about the decision being appealed

Please set out

- Narrative of the facts
- Statutory framework
- Chronology of proceedings
- Orders made in the Courts below
- Issues before the Court appealed from
- Treatment of issues by the Court appealed from
- Issues in the appeal

268

6. Grounds of appeal

Counsel's name or signature:

7. Other information about the appeal

Are you applying for an
extension of time?

☐ Yes ☐ No

If Yes, please explain why

What order are you asking the Supreme Court to make?

Order being appealed ☐ set aside ☐ vary

Original order ☐ set aside ☐ restore ☐ vary

**Does the appeal raise
issues under the:**

Human Rights Act 1998? ☐ Yes ☐ No

Are you seeking a declaration of incompatibility?

☐ Yes ☐ No

Are you challenging an act of a public authority?

☐ Yes ☐ No

If you have answered Yes to any of the questions above please give details below:

Court's devolution
jurisdiction? ☐ Yes ☐ No

If Yes, please give details below:

Are you asking the Supreme Court to:

depart from one of its own decisions or from one made by the House of Lords?

☐ Yes   ☐ No

If Yes, please give details below:

make a reference to the European Court of Justice of the European Communities?

☐ Yes   ☐ No

If Yes, please give details below:

Will you or the respondent request an expedited hearing?

☐ Yes   ☐ No

If Yes, please give details below:

8. Certificate of Service

Either complete this section or attach a separate certificate

The date on which this form was served on the

1st Respondent ☐☐ / ☐☐☐☐ / ☐☐☐☐
                D D   M M M   Y Y Y Y

2nd Respondent ☐☐ / ☐☐☐☐ / ☐☐☐☐
                D D   M M M   Y Y Y Y

I certify that this document was served on

by

by the following method

Signature

9. Other relevant information

Neutral citation of the judgment appealed against e.g. [2009] EWCA Civ 95

References to Law Report in which any relevant judgment is reported.

Subject matter catchwords for indexing.

Please return your completed form to:

The Supreme Court of the United Kingdom, Parliament Square, London SW1P 3BD
DX 157230 Parliament Square 4

Telephone: 020 7960 1991/1992   Fax: 020 7960 1901
email: registry@supremecourt.uk
www.supremecourt.uk

Save form   Print form

Page 11

SC001 Notice of appeal

Page 12

SC001 Notice of appeal

Form 2 (Application form)

4A-198

Save form	Print form	Reset form

In the Supreme Court of the United Kingdom

Application form

On appeal from

_____ V _____

Appeal number

Date of filing

D D   M M M   Y Y Y Y

Applicant's solicitors

Appellant's solicitors

Respondent's solicitors

SC002 Application form (05.14)

© Crown copyright 2014

1. Details of the applicant

Applicant's full name

Original status

- [ ] Claimant
- [ ] Petitioner
- [ ] Pursuer
- [ ] Defendant
- [ ] Respondent
- [ ] Defender
- [ ] Intervener

Solicitor

Name

Address

Telephone no.

Fax no.

DX no.

Postcode

Ref.

Email

How would you prefer us to communicate with you?

- [ ] DX
- [ ] Post
- [ ] Email
- [ ] Other *(please specify)*

Counsel

Name

Address

Telephone no.

Fax no.

DX no.

Postcode

Email

Page 2

SC002 Application form

276

Counsel

Name

Address

Telephone no.

Fax no.

DX no.

Postcode

Email

2. Nature of the application

The applicant applies for

☐ Extension of time   ☐ Permission to intervene

☐ Security   ☐ Order for substituted service

☐ Expedited hearing   ☐ Review of Registrar's decision

☐ Other order *(please specify)*

3. Grounds on which application made

On what grounds are you
making this application?

4. Consent to application

The following parties **consent** to this application

See attached letter(s) dated

The following parties **object** to this application

See attached letter(s) dated

5. Other relevant information

6. Details of the appellant

Appellant's full name

Original status

☐ Claimant   ☐ Defendant

☐ Petitioner   ☐ Respondent

☐ Pursuer   ☐ Defender

Solicitor

Name

Address   Telephone no.

Fax no.

DX no.

Postcode ☐☐☐☐ ☐☐☐☐   Ref.

Email

Counsel

Name

Address   Telephone no.

Fax no.

DX no.

Postcode ☐☐☐☐ ☐☐☐☐

Email

Counsel

Name

Address

Telephone no.

Fax no.

DX no.

Postcode

Email

7. Details of the respondent

Respondent's full name

Original status
- [ ] Claimant
- [ ] Petitioner
- [ ] Pursuer
- [ ] Defendant
- [ ] Respondent
- [ ] Defender

Solicitor

Name

Address

Telephone no.

Fax no.

DX no.

Postcode

Ref.

Email

Counsel

Name

Address

Telephone no.

Fax no.

DX no.

Postcode

Email

Counsel

Name

Address

Telephone no.

Fax no.

DX no.

Postcode

Email

8. Certificate of Service

Either complete this section or attach a separate certificate

On what date was this
form served on the

Appellant

D D / M M M / Y Y Y Y

Respondent

D D / M M M / Y Y Y Y

I certify that this document was served on

by

by the following method

Signature

9. Details of Registrar's order/decision being appealed

Date of order/decision

D D / M M M / Y Y Y Y

Save form   Print form

Page 10

SC002 Application form

Page 11

SC002 Application form

Please return your completed form to:

The Supreme Court of the United Kingdom, Parliament Square, London SW1P 3BD
DX 157230 Parliament Square 4

Telephone: 020 7960 1991/1992   Fax: 020 7960 1901
email: registry@supremecourt.uk
www.supremecourt.uk

Page 12

SC002 Application form

Form 3 (Notice of objection/acknowledgment by respondent)

Save form   Print form   Reset form

In the Supreme Court of the United Kingdom

Notice of objection/ Acknowledgement

——— v ———

Appeal number

Date of filing

| D | D | | M | M | M | | Y | Y | Y | Y |

Name of respondent

Respondent's solicitors

Name of appellant

Appellant's solicitors

SC003 Notice of objection/Acknowledgement (05.14)

© Crown copyright 2014

1. Respondent

Respondent's full name

The respondent was served with the
- [ ] application for permission to appeal
- [ ] notice of appeal
- [ ] application

On date

D D / M M M / Y Y Y Y

The respondent intends to ask the Court to:
- [ ] refuse to grant permission to appeal
- [ ] order the appellant to give security for costs if permission to appeal is granted
- [ ] dismiss the appeal
- [ ] give the respondent permission to cross-appeal
- [ ] allow the appeal for reasons which are different from, or additional to, those given by the court below
- [ ] Other *(please specify)*

The respondent wishes to receive notice of any hearing date and to be advised of progress. The respondent's details are:

Solicitor

Name

Address

Telephone no.

Fax no.

DX no.

Postcode

Ref.

Email

How would you prefer us to communicate with you?
- [ ] DX
- [ ] Email
- [ ] Post
- [ ] Other *(please specify)*

Page 2

SC003 Notice of objection/Acknowledgement

288

Counsel

Name

Address

Telephone no.

Fax no.

DX no.

Postcode

Email

Counsel

Name

Address

Telephone no.

Fax no.

DX no.

Postcode

Email

2. Certificate of Service

Either complete this section or attach a separate certificate

On what date was this form served on the

Appellant

D D / M M M / Y Y Y Y

Other

D D / M M M / Y Y Y Y

I certify that this document was served on

by

by the following method

Signature

3. Other information about the respondent

☐ The respondent is in receipt of public funding/legal aid

Certificate number

[   ]

☐ The respondent is applying for public funding/legal aid

Information about the respondent's case

Set out here the respondent's grounds of appeal, reasons why permission to appeal should be refused or why the appeal should be allowed. Include information to explain what the respondent intends to ask the Court to do.

290

Is the respondent seeking a declaration of incompatibility?

☐ Yes ☐ No

☐ The respondent will seek to raise issues under the Human Rights Act 1998
(please give brief details)

☐ The respondent will ask the court to make a reference to the
European Court of Justice *(please give brief details)*

Save form   Print form

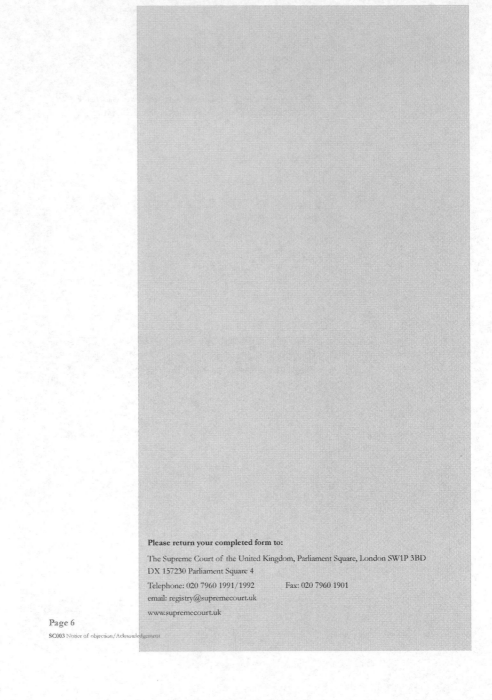

Please return your completed form to:

The Supreme Court of the United Kingdom, Parliament Square, London SW1P 3BD
DX 157230 Parliament Square 4

Telephone: 020 7960 1991/1992   Fax: 020 7960 1901
email: registry@supremecourt.uk

www.supremecourt.uk

Page 6

SC003 Notice of objection/Acknowledgement

SECTION 4B   JUDICIAL COMMITTEE OF THE PRIVY COUNCIL APPEALS

Judicial Committee (Appellate Jurisdiction) Rules 2009

Replace the last paragraph with:

4B-0.2   The rule in Pt 7 of the Rules (r.53) applies to appeals to the Judicial Committee under the Veterinary Surgeons Act 1966 s.17; and the rule in Pt 8 (r.54) applies to appeals to the Judicial

Committee under the Brunei (Appeals) Act 1989 s.1. The rule in Pt 9 (r.55) provides for appeals against draft Pastoral Schemes under the Mission and Pastoral Measure 2011; and the rule in Pt 10 (r.56) provides for references under s.4 of the Judicial Committee Act 1833. For a recent example of a s.4 reference see: *Re Baronetcy of Pringle of Stichill* [2016] UKPC 16.

Leave and special leave to appeal

In the first paragraph, replace "Ross v Bank of Commerce (St Kitts Nevis) Trust and Savings Association Ltd [2010] UKPC 28; [2011] 1 W.L.R. 125, PC," with:

    Ross v Bank of Commerce (St Kitts Nevis) Trust and Savings Association Ltd [2010] UKPC 28; [2011] 1 W.L.R. 125   **4B-0.3**

Practice Directions

Add new paragraph at end:

    In *Willers v Joyce* [2016] UKSC 44 the Supreme Court clarified that where a party on appeal to **4B-0.4** the Judicial Committee wishes to invite the Judicial Committee to depart from a decision of the Court of Appeal of England and Wales, that should be expressly drawn to the Committee's attention. This will allow the Committee to consider empanelling a suitable number of Justices to consider the matter, and to direct that the judgment of the Judicial Committee is to represent the law of England and Wales.

SECTION 6   ADMINISTRATION OF FUNDS, PROPERTY AND AFFAIRS
SECTION 6A   COURT FUNDS

Administration of Justice Act 1982

Replace s.38(1) with:

PART VI

FUNDS IN COURT

Management and investment of funds in court

38.—(1)   Subject to rules made under subsection (7) below, all sums of **6A-5** money, securities and effects paid and deposited in, or under the custody of—

    (a)   the High Court;
    (aa)   the family court;
    (b)   the county court; or
    (c)   such other courts and tribunals as the Lord Chancellor may by rules made under that subsection prescribe,

shall be vested in the Accountant General.

Note

Replace with:

    Subsection (1)(aa) inserted by the Crime and Courts Act 2013 (Family Court: Consequential **6A-5.1** Provision) Order 2014 (SI 2014/605), art.17, with effect from 22 April 2014 (being the date on which s.17(3) of the Crime and Courts Act 2013 is brought fully into force. Subsection (1)(b) amended by the Crime and Courts Act 2013 Sch.9(3) para.52(1)(b), with effect from 22 April 2014 subject to savings and transitional provisions specified in 2013 c.22 s.15 and Sch.8 and transitional provision specified in SI 2014/954 arts 2(c) and 3.

INVESTMENTS ON BEHALF OF CHILDREN AND PROTECTED BENEFICIARIES

Protected beneficiaries

Replace "Form 320PB is available via the following link: http://www.justice.gov.uk/global/forms/cfo.htm [Accessed 28 January 2016]." with:

6A-207   Form 320PB is available via the following link:
https://www.gov.uk/government/publications/court-funds-manage-a-protected-beneficiarys-fund [Accessed 1 August 2016].

Birth, marriage and death certificates

In the first paragraph, replace "certificate.service@gro.gsi.gov.uk" with:

6A-214   certificate.services@gro.gsi.gov.uk

Funds held in court in Scotland

In the second paragraph, replace "National Archives of Scotland" with:

6A-217   National Records of Scotland

Funds in court in Ireland

After "353 1 8886", replace "746" with:

6A-219   211

Special and Basic rates from October 1, 1965

6A-220   *Replace table with:*

High Court Special (formerly S.T.I.)			High Court Basic (formerly M.O.D.)		
Date	Rate	SI	Date	Rate	SI
1.11.88	12¼	Lord Chancellor's direction d/d 22.10.88	1.8.99	5¼	Lord Chancellor's direction d/d 14.7.99
			1.2.02	4	Lord Chancellor's direction d/d 7.1.02
1.1.89	13	Lord Chancellor's direction d/d 21.12.88	1.2.09	2	Lord Chancellor's direction d/d 8.12.08
1.11.89	14¼	Lord Chancellor's direction d/d 27.10.89	1.6.09	1	Lord Chancellor's direction d/d 2.2.09
1.4.91	12	Lord Chancellor's direction d/d 25.3.91	1.7.09	0.3	Lord Chancellor's direction d/d 3.6.09
1.10.91	10¼	Lord Chancellor's direction d/d 20.9.91	6.6.16	0.1	Approved with the concurrence of Treasury in May 2016
1.2.93	8	Lord Chancellor's direction d/d 27.1.93			
1.8.99	7	Lord Chancellor's direction d/d 14.7.99			
1.2.02	6	Lord Chancellor's direction d/d 7.1.02			

High Court Special (formerly S.T.I.)			High Court Basic (formerly M.O.D.)		
Date	Rate	SI	Date	Rate	SI
1.2.09	3	Lord Chancellor's direction d/d 8.12.08			
1.6.09	1.5	Lord Chancellor's direction d/d 2.2.09			
1.7.09	0.5	Lord Chancellor's direction d/d 3.6.09			

Replace table with:

County Court Special (formerly S.T.I.)			County Court Basic (formerly M.O.D.)		
Date	Rate	SI	Date	Rate	SI
1.10.65	5	65/1500	1.10.65	2½	65/1500
1.9.66	5½	66/875	1.3.71	3½	71/260
1.3.68	6	68/107	1.3.73	4	73/230
1.3.69	6½	69/204	1.3.77	5	76/2234
1.3.70	7	70/228	1.4.83	9½	83/291
1.3.71	7½	71/260	1.4.84	8	84/285
1.3.73	8	73/230	1.8.86	7½	86/1142
1.3.74	9	74/206	1.1.87	8½	86/2115
1.3.77	10	76/2234	1.12.87	8	Lord Chancellor's direction d/d 23.11.87
1.3.79	12½	79/105			
1.1.80	15	79/1619			
1.1.81	12½	80/1857	1.5.88	7½	Lord Chancellor's direction d/d 22.4.88
1.12.81	15	81/1588			
1.03.82	14	82/124			
1.7.82	13	82/786	1.8.88	9	Lord Chancellor's direction d/d 19.7.88
1.4.83	12½	83/291			
1.4.84	12	84/285			
1.8.86	11½	86/1142	1.11.88	10¼	Lord Chancellor's direction d/d 22.10.88
1.1.87	12¼	86/2115			
1.4.87	11¾	Lord Chancellor's direction d/d 30.3.87			
			1.1.89	10¾	Lord Chancellor's direction d/d 20.12.88
1.11.87	11¼	Lord Chancellor's direction d/d 19.10.87	1.11.89	11¼	Lord Chancellor's direction d/d 27.10.89
1.12.87	11	Lord Chancellor's direction d/d 23.11.87	1.4.91	9½	Lord Chancellor's direction d/d 25.3.91
1.5.88	9½	Lord Chancellor's direction d/d 22.4.88	1.10.91	8	Lord Chancellor's direction d/d 20.9.91

County Court Special (formerly S.T.I.)			County Court Basic (formerly M.O.D.)		
Date	Rate	SI	Date	Rate	SI
1.8.88	11	Lord Chancellor's direction d/d 19.7.88	1.2.93	6	Lord Chancellor's direction d/d 27.1.93
1.11.88	12¼	Lord Chancellor's direction d/d 22.10.88	1.8.99	5¼	Lord Chancellor's direction d/d 14.7.99
1.1.89	13	Lord Chancellor's direction d/d 21.12.88			
1.11.89	14¼	Lord Chancellor's direction d/d 27.10.89	1.2.02	4	Lord Chancellor's direction d/d 7.1.02
1.4.91	12	Lord Chancellor's direction d/d 25.3.91	6.6.16	0.1	Approved with the concurrence of Treasury in May 2016
1.10.91	10¼	Lord Chancellor's direction d/d 20.9.91			
1.2.93	8	Lord Chancellor's direction d/d 27.1.93			
1.8.99	7	Lord Chancellor's direction d/d 14.7.99			
1.2.02	6	Lord Chancellor's direction d/d 7.1.02			
1.2.09	3	Lord Chancellor's direction d/d 8.12.08	1.2.09	2	Lord Chancellor's direction d/d 8.12.08
1.6.09	1.5	d/d 2.2.09	1.6.09	1	d/d 2.2.09
1.7.09	0.5	d/d 3.6.09	1.7.09	0.3	d/d 3.6.09

SECTION 7   LEGAL REPRESENTATIVES—COSTS AND LITIGATION FUNDING
SECTION 7A1   LITIGATION FUNDING BEFORE APRIL 1, 2013

Access to Justice Act 1999

Add new paragraph 7A1–11:

Editorial introduction

7A1-11   Sections 29 and 30 have been repealed with effect from 1 April 2013 by the Legal Aid, Sentencing and Punishment of Offenders Act 2012 ss.46(2), 47 save in relation to proceedings relating to a claim for damages in respect of diffuse mesothelioma and publication and privacy proceedings: Legal Aid, Sentencing and Punishment of Offenders Act 2012 (Commencement No.5 and Saving Provision) Order 2013 (SI 2013/77). The repeals were deferred until 6 April 2016 in relation to certain insolvency proceedings: the Legal Aid, Sentencing and Punishment of Offenders Act 2012 (Commencement No.12) Order 2016 (SI 2016/345) art.2 (see further Vol.1 para.48.0.2.4). Section 29 continues to apply in relation to a costs order made in favour of a party to proceedings who took out a costs insurance policy in relation to the proceedings before 1 April 2013. Section 30 continues to apply in relation to a costs order made in favour of a person to whom a body gave an undertaking before 1 April 2013 if the undertaking was given specifically in respect of the costs of other parties to proceedings relating to the matter which is the subject of the proceedings in which the costs order is made.

FUNDING ARRANGEMENTS

Conditional Fees

Success fees

Add new paragraph at end:

A conditional fee agreement provided that it covered work done by the claimant's solicitors **7A1-58** before the date of the agreement. In disallowing success fees claimed on the work done before the date of the agreement on the basis that the risk assessment when instructions were given was different to that at the date of the agreement, the costs judge had erred: *Ghising v Secretary of State for the Home Department* [2015] EWHC 3706 (QB).

Insurance Premiums

Add new paragraph 7A1–64.1:

Transferring from Legal Aid

In claims for damages for clinical negligence the claimants, who had the benefit of legal aid, **7A1-64.1** entered into conditional fee agreements and purchased after the event insurance shortly before 1 April 2013. They had not been advised by their solicitors that in doing so they would lose the 10 per cent increase in general damages to which they would have been entitled following *Simmons v Castle* [2012] EWCA Civ 1039. The defendants contended that the claimants' decisions were unreasonable in that they were not the subject of informed consent and that the claimants should not be entitled to recover any additional liabilities. It was held that the failure to mention the 10 per cent increase was not likely to have made a difference to the claimants' decisions and which were not therefore unreasonable. Accordingly the additional liabilities were recoverable in principle: *Surrey v Barnet and Chase Farm Hospitals NHS Trust* [2016] EWHC 1598 (QB).

SECTION 7A2   LITIGATION FUNDING AFTER APRIL 1, 2013

INTRODUCTION

Replace the second paragraph with:

The amendments made by the 2012 Act will not apply to claims for damages in respect of dif- **7A2-1** fuse mesothelioma until the Lord Chancellor has carried out a review of the likely effect of the amendments in relation to such proceedings, and published a report of the conclusions of the review. The commencement of the amendments has also been deferred in relation to publication and privacy proceedings: see the Legal Aid, Sentencing and Punishment of Offenders Act 2012 (Commencement No.5 and Saving Provision) Order 2013 (SI 2013/77), which lists the proceedings excluded and provides a definition of "publication and privacy proceedings". The commencement of the amendments was deferred until 6 April 2016 in relation to certain insolvency proceedings: the Legal Aid, Sentencing and Punishment of Offenders Act 2012 (Commencement No.12) Order 2016 (SI 2016/345) art.2 (see further Vol.1 para.48.0.2.4).

Replace the sixth paragraph with:

Premiums for after the event insurance policies are not recoverable save insofar as provided by regulations made under s.58C of the Courts and Legal Services Act 1990 and save in limited classes of cases in respect of which the commencement of the amendments has been deferred. Sections 29 and 30 of the Access to Justice Act 1999 have been repealed (s.29 is repealed except in respect of claims for damages in respect of diffuse mesothelioma and publication and privacy proceedings). The repeal of s.29 was deferred until 6 April 2016 in respect of certain insolvency proceedings. The Recovery of Costs Insurance Premiums in Clinical Negligence Proceedings (No.2) Regulations 2013 (SI 2013/739) permit the recovery of that part of a premium which insures against the liability to pay for experts' reports on liability and causation in clinical negligence proceedings if the financial value of the claim for damages exceeds £1,000. The Supreme Court has confirmed that, in the absence of agreement or specific statutory provision to the contrary, a party cannot recover an ATE premium as part of the costs of legal expenses: *McGraddie v McGraddie* [2015] UKSC 1.

Courts and Legal Services Act 1990

Note

Replace the first paragraph with:

7A2-4   Substituted, together with s.58A, by the Access to Justice Act 1999 s.27. Amended by SI 2003/1887, SI 2005/3429 and (with effect from 1 April 2013) by the Legal Aid, Sentencing and Punishment of Offenders Act 2012 s.44 which inserted ss.58(4A) and (4B). The amendments made by the 2012 Act will not apply to claims for damages in respect of diffuse mesothelioma until the Lord Chancellor has carried out a review of the likely effect of the amendments in relation to such proceedings, and published a report of the conclusions of the review. The amendments made by the 2012 Act have also not been brought into force in relation to publication and privacy proceedings and, in respect of certain insolvency proceedings, were deferred until 6 April 2016. All proceedings which can be the subject of an enforceable conditional fee agreement under s.58, other than proceedings under s.82 of the Environmental Protection Act 1990, are specified for the purposes of s.58(4)(a) by r.2 of the Conditional Fee Agreements Order 2013. For the purposes of s.58(4)(c), r.3 of that Order prescribes a maximum success fee of 100 per cent. Regulations 4 and 5 of the Order provide that the additional conditions shall apply to claims for personal injuries and that the maximum limit of the success fee in such claims shall be 25 per cent in proceedings at first instance and 100 per cent in all other proceedings of general damages for pain, suffering, and loss of amenity and damages for pecuniary loss, other than future pecuniary loss, net of any sums recoverable by the CRU. The amendments made by the Legal Aid, Sentencing and Punishment of Offenders Act 2012 s.44 were brought into force for certain purposes by the Legal Aid, Sentencing and Punishment of Offenders Act 2012 (Commencement No.12) Order 2016 (SI 2016/345) art.2, with effect from 6 April 2016.

Note

Replace the penultimate sentence with;

7A2-6   The amendments made the 2012 Act have also not been brought into force in relation to publication and privacy proceedings and, in respect of certain insolvency proceedings, were deferred until 6 April 2016.

Note

Replace with:

7A2-12   Inserted by the Legal Aid, Sentencing and Punishment of Offenders Act 2012 s.46(1) with effect from April 1, 2013, except in respect of claims for damages in respect of diffuse mesothelioma, certain insolvency proceedings and publication and privacy proceedings: The Legal Aid, Sentencing and Punishment of Offenders Act 2012 (Commencement No.5 and Saving Provision) Order 2013, SI 2013/77. Subsequently, the saving in relation to insolvency proceedings was removed, with effect from 6 April 2016, by the Legal Aid, Sentencing and Punishment of Offenders Act 2012 (Commencement No.12) Order 2016 (SI 2016/345) (see further Vol.1 para.48.0.2.4). The insertion of this section by the Legal Aid, Sentencing and Punishment of Offenders Act 2012 s.46(1) was brought into force for certain purposes by the Legal Aid, Sentencing and Punishment of Offenders Act 2012 (Commencement No.12) Order 2016 (SI 2016/345) art.2, with effect from 6 April 2016.

Editorial note

Replace the first paragraph with:

7A2-13   The Access to Justice Act 1999 s.29 (Recovery of insurance premiums by way of costs) is revoked by the Legal Aid, Sentencing and Punishment of Offenders Act 2012 s.46(2) with effect from 1 April 2013, subject to savings in ss.46(3) and 48. Costs orders made in favour of a party to proceedings who took out a costs insurance policy in relation to the proceedings before the commencement day are not affected by the repeal (s.46(3)). The repeal is postponed in respect of proceedings relating to claims for damages for diffuse mesothelioma pending a review by the Lord Chancellor (s.48). By the Legal Aid, Sentencing and Punishment of Offenders Act 2012 (Commencement No.5 and Saving Provision) Order 2013 (SI 2013/77) the amendments made by the 2012 Act were not brought into force in relation to certain insolvency proceedings and publication and privacy proceedings, but subsequently the exception in relation to insolvency proceedings was removed, with effect from 6 April 2016, by the Legal Aid, Sentencing and Punishment of Offenders Act 2012 (Commencement No.12) Order 2016 (SI 2016/345) (see further Vol.1 para.48.0.2.4).

SECTION 7C SOLICITORS ACT 1974

Add new paragraph 7C–58.1:

Subsection (5)—"Unfair or unreasonable"
See para.7C-83.

7C-58.1

Subsection (2)—"Fair and reasonable"

Add new paragraph at end:
When considering what is unfair and unreasonable for the purposes of s.57(5) (non-contentious **7C-83**
business agreements) the court must consider fairness and reasonableness separately: *Bolt Burdon
Solicitors v Tariq* [2016] EWHC 811 (QB) (following *Re Stuart*). A non-contentious business agreement under which the solicitors would receive 50 per cent of the compensation received under the
Financial Conduct Authority Redress Scheme was held not to be unfair or unreasonable even
though they would recover fees of about £400,000 for work valued at about £50,000 if billed at
hourly rates.

SECTION 8 LIMITATION

Limitation Act 1980

Change title of paragraph:

Knowledge of claimant in negligence actions

*To the end of the eighth paragraph (beginning "In applying the test propounded in Nash v Eli Lilly & Co"),
add:*
In *Lenderink-Woods v Zurich Assurance Ltd* [2015] EWHC 3634 (Ch) it was held that the claim **8-43**
would be statute-barred if someone with the characteristics of a person in the claimant's position
might reasonably be expected to have acquired knowledge (a) of the material facts; (b) that the
financial adviser could have considered alternatives, but had not made enquiries or recommended
things that other competent financial advisers would have recommended; (c) that what the financial
adviser had or had not done was causally relevant to her predicament. That knowledge would
need to have been accompanied by enough confidence to prompt her to embark upon prepara-
tions for litigation.

Section 21—actions for breach of trust and actions for breach of fiduciary duty

Replace the first paragraph with:
In *Haysport Properties Ltd v Ackerman* [2016] EWHC 393 (Ch) a director was in breach of his **8-60**
fiduciary duty by causing two of his companies to grant security over their properties and/or make
a substantial unsecured loan to enable a third company, which he also ran, to acquire a property.
He had failed to ensure that his companies were properly advised and had failed to deal with the
obvious conflict of interest. The limitation period for bringing a claim against him was disapplied
by virtue of the Limitation Act 1980 s.21(1)(b). In *Green v Gaul* [2006] EWCA Civ 1124 the Court of
Appeal held that the 12-year period under s.22(a) of the Act to bring an action in respect of any
claim to the personal estate of a deceased had no application to a claim to remove a personal
representative of the estate. Claims against the representative to provide an account of the
deceased's assets and make payment due were claims that fell within s.21(1)(b) of the Act, and
although the defence of laches to the claims was not excluded by s.21(1)(b), it was not made out on
the facts.

Add new paragraph at end:
In *Burnden Holdings (UK) Ltd v Fielding* [2016] EWCA Civ 557 no limitation period applied to a
claim for breach of fiduciary duty by reason of the s.21(1)(b). Alternatively, the availability of a
postponed limitation period, such that the proceedings had been started in time under s.32, could
not be determined on an application for summary judgment.

Discretion to disapply relevant limitation period

Replace the fifth paragraph with:
The Act of 1980 does not lay down any specific procedure whereby the statutory power under **8-92**

s.33 ("to override time limits") is to be invoked. In order to preclude any undue prolongation of an action which it may not be equitable to permit to proceed and in seeking to limit the burden of costs which may be imposed on the defendant, an application by him to stay the claim under CPR r.3.1(f) would, provided that the plaintiff has given due notice of his intention to rely on the section, serve to initiate the investigation contemplated by s.33. In a clear case, the defendant may apply for summary judgment under CPR r.24.2(a)(i), though in some situations the substantive issues may be so intimately and inextricably bound up with the questions arising under s.33 as to make any summary resolution of the question impracticable (see per Shaw LJ in *Walkley v Precision Forgings Ltd* [1979] 1 W.L.R. 606 at 1238; [1979] 1 All E.R. 102, CA). It has however been observed that there is a "danger in the section 33 exercise of putting the cart before the horse, that is, determining the claim and relying on that determination in undertaking the balance of prejudice as to whether the claim should have preceded at all": see *KR v Bryn Alyn Community (Holdings) Ltd* [2003] EWCA Civ 85; [2003] Q.B. 1441; [2003] 3 W.L.R. 107; [2004] 2 All E.R. 7116, CA, at paras 74(viii) and 309. It was also held at para.74(vi), that "Whenever the judge considers it feasible to do so, he should decide the limitation point by a preliminary hearing by reference to the pleading and written witness statements and, importantly, the extent and content of discovery ... It may not always be feasible or produce savings in time and cost for the parties to deal with the matter by way of preliminary hearing, but a judge should strain to do so whenever possible." In *Blue Water Recoveries Ltd v Secretary of State for Transport* [2014] QBD (TCC) 27 June 2014 it was held that it was not appropriate to order a hearing of preliminary issues in relation to limitation because such a hearing would concern contentious issues of fact that could only be determined by calling witnesses from each side to be cross-examined, all the issues would have to be decided in the defendant's favour for the case to be brought to an end, and it was unlikely that costs would be reduced. In *Re Kenyan Emergency Group Litigation* [2016] EWHC 600 (QB) numerous claimants were seeking damages for trespass to the person arising from the alleged actions of employees and agents of the British colonial administration in Kenya during a state of emergency in 1952. It was held that although it was appropriate for certain issues of limitation to be determined as preliminary issues, it was not appropriate for the court to decide, at a preliminary stage, whether to exercise its discretion under the Limitation Act 1980 s.33 to disapply the limitation period. If limitation was decided in the defendant's favour, there might be an appeal that could hold up the litigation for two to three years. That would be extremely unsatisfactory. The rest of the evidence, including doctors, corroborative witnesses and the defendant's evidence would probably be compromised. The vast majority of lay witnesses for both sides were very elderly and might not be capable of giving evidence in three to four years' time.

After the thirteenth paragraph (beginning "In Davidson v Aegis Defence Services"), add as a new paragraph:

In *F v TH* [2016] EWHC 1605 (QB), a case of historic sexual abuse, Langstaff J held that even if the evidence had been sufficient to satisfy the burden of proof (which it was not), such were the difficulties caused by the considerable delay in taking action that it would not have been appropriate to exercise discretion to extend time to permit the claim to continue. Even after the claimants were able to freely discuss the abuse, there was unexplained delay in excess of three years in bringing the claim.

Dissolution of a company defendant

Replace the second paragraph (where the citation for County Leasing Asset Management Ltd v Hawkes has changed) with:

8-95 In *County Leasing Asset Management Ltd v Hawkes* [2015] EWCA Civ 1251; [2016] B.C.C. 102 it was held that the starting point to achieve the purpose of the discretion under s.1032(3) of the 2006 Act was to recognise that time would have run against the company if it had not been dissolved in exactly the same way as it had in fact run, while it was dissolved. The court had to ask itself whether had it not been dissolved, the company would have commenced the relevant proceedings within time; there must be a causative link between the company's dissolution and the failure to bring proceedings in time. The court then had to ask itself whether it would be just to provide the opportunity, after the event, by a limitation direction.

SECTION 9   JURISDICTIONAL AND PROCEDURAL LEGISLATION
SECTION 9A   MAIN STATUTES

Senior Courts Act 1981

Replace s.9(4) with:

OTHER PROVISIONS

Assistance for transaction of judicial business [...]

(4)   Without prejudice to section 24 of the Courts Act 1971 (temporary appointment of deputy Circuit judges [...]), if it appears to the Lord Chief Justice, after consulting the Lord Chancellor, that it is expedient as a temporary measure to make an appointment under this subsection in order to facilitate the disposal of business in the High Court or the Crown Court or any other court or tribunal to which persons appointed under this subsection may be deployed, he may appoint a person qualified for appointment as a puisne judge of the High Court to be a deputy judge of the High Court during such period or on such occasions as the Lord Chief Justice, after consulting the Lord Chancellor, thinks fit; and during the period or on the occasions for which a person is appointed as a deputy judge under this subsection, he may act as a puisne judge of the High Court. **9A-31**

Judicial bias—"incapable" and "apparent"

After the twelfth paragraph (beginning "In Locabail (UK) Ltd v Bayfield Properties Ltd"), add as a new paragraph:

In *Davidson v Scottish Ministers (No.2)* [2004] UKHL 34; [2004] S.L.T. 895 HL, Lord Bingham **9A-48** explained (at para.19) that it is routine for judges, before or at the outset of a hearing, to disclose a previous activity or association which would or might provide the basis for a reasonable apprehension of lack of impartiality and added that it is very important that proper disclosure should be made in such cases, first, because it gives the parties an opportunity to object and, secondly, because the judge shows, by disclosure, that he or she has nothing to hide and is fully conscious of the factors which might be apprehended to influence his or her judgment. In *Bhardwaj v FDA* [2016] EWCA Civ 800, 28 July 2016, CA, unrep., the appointment of a particular person as one of the lay members of an employment tribunal, in the circumstances, arguably gave rise to a real possibility of bias on the part of the tribunal affecting the claimant (C). Upon being alerted to this by disclosures made by the tribunal concerning past connections between the member and C, C's counsel made no objection to the tribunal continuing to hear C's claim as constituted. Following the dismissal of C's claim, the EAT, and on C's further appeal, the Court of Appeal, rejected C's submission that the tribunal should have recused itself on the grounds of apparent bias, holding that C had made a valid and irrevocable waiver of her right to object to the continued hearing of her case by the tribunal. In particular, C's submission that, prior to its disclosure the tribunal ought to have made a fuller inquiry into the relevant background facts was rejected. The Court of Appeal explained that the appropriate level of disclosure by a tribunal depended in large measure on the stage that the matter had reached. If a tribunal was alerted to matters after a hearing had commenced, then its only obligation was to disclose what it knew. That was in contrast to where a possibility of bias was raised before, or at the outset, of a hearing where the duty was to inquire into the full facts, as far as they were ascertainable.

Replace the twenty-second paragraph with:

As to bias in arbitrators, see *Save and Prosper Pensions Ltd v Homebase Ltd* [2001] L. & T.R. 11; *AT&T Corp v Saudi Cable Co* [2000] 2 Lloyd's Rep. 127, CA; *Sierra Fishing Co v Farran* [2015] EWHC 140 (Comm); [2015] 1 All E.R. (Comm) 560 (Popplewell J). In an arbitration claim brought under the Arbitration Act 1996 s.68, challenging an award on ground of serious irregularity, specifically alleging apparent bias in the arbitrator based on alleged conflict of interest, the court explained that the 2014 edition of the International Bar Association Guidelines on Conflicts of Interest in International Arbitration do not bind the Court, but they can be of assistance (*W Ltd v M Sdn Bhd* [2016] EWHC 422 (Comm), 2 March 2016, unrep. (Knowles J), where stated that some of the provisions in the Guidelines dealing with non-waiver of certain conflict of interest situations were weak and could not be given judicial approval).

To the end of the last paragraph, add:
   Bhardwaj v FDA [2016] EWCA Civ 800, 28 July 2016, CA, unrep. (informed waiver of objection to member of tribunal valid and irrevocable).

Civil jurisdiction of the Court of Appeal

9A-51   *Replace list (where the citation for In re X (Court of Protection: Deprivation of Liberty) (Nos 1 and 2) has changed) with:*
   (1)   *High Court*—Subject to exceptions, the Court of Appeal has jurisdiction to hear and determine any appeals from any judgment or order of any Division of the High Court (including the Family Division and including any part of a Division, e.g. the Commercial Court or the Patents Court (s.16)) (see para.9A-57 below). Statutory provisions in addition to s.16 affecting rights of appeal from the High Court to the Court of Appeal include the Insolvency Act 1986 s.375 (Appeals etc from courts exercising insolvency jurisdiction) (see para.3E-661+ above), and the Patents Act 1977 s.97 (Appeals from the comptroller).
   (2)   *County Court*—Subject to exceptions, the Court of Appeal has jurisdiction to hear and determine appeals from determinations of the County Court (County Courts Act 1984 s.77) (see para.9A-568 below)
   (3)   *Family Court*—Subject to exceptions, an appeal lies to the Court of Appeal from a decision of the Family Court (Matrimonial and Family Proceedings Act 1984 s.31K(1)).
   (4)   *Court of Protection*—Section 53(1) of the Mental Capacity Act 2005 states that an appeal lies to the Court of Appeal "from any decision" of the Court of Protection. This is qualified by s.53(2) which states that Court of Protection Rules may provide that appeals from certain decisions of the court lie "to a prescribed higher judge of the court and not to the Court of Appeal" (s.53(2)). Such rules qualifying s.53(1) are found in Part 20 of the Court of Protection Rules 2007 (rr.169 to 182). For explanation of their effects on the Court of Appeal's jurisdiction under s.53(1), see commentary on r.169 (para.6B-399+ above). It is noteworthy that, unlike the statutory provisions providing for appeals to the Court of Appeal from the High Court or from the County Court, s.53(1) does not speak of appeals from "any judgment or order" or from "any determination", but from "any decision". In the case of *In re X (Court of Protection: Deprivation of Liberty) (Nos 1 and 2))* [2015] EWCA Civ 599; [2016] 1 W.L.R. 227, CA, the Court of Appeal held (contrary to the submission of all parties to the appeal) that the word "decision" in s.53(1) did not include a decision made by a judge of the Court of Protection in determining, not an issue in a case before him, but a hypothetical issue. For there to be a "decision" capable of supporting an appeal there must be the determination of an issue arising between two or more parties to proceedings before the court (at para.42 per Black LJ, and at para.156 per Moore-Bick LJ).
   (5)   *Upper Tribunal*—By the Tribunal, Courts and Enforcement Act 2007 s.13 (para.9A-994 below), where the Court of Appeal is "the relevant appeal court" (see s.13(13)), an appeal lies to that Court, with permission, on a point of law arising from a decision made by the Upper Tribunal, other than an "excluded decision" (as defined, see s.3(8)). (By the 2007 Act the functions of several tribunals and bodies were transferred to the First-tier tribunal and the Upper Tribunal created by that Act. Thereafter any statutory rights of appeal that lay to the Court of Appeal from the decisions of such tribunals or bodies (e.g. the Lands Tribunal and the Social Security Commissioner) under particular statutory provisions were incorporated within the arrangements for appeals from the Upper Tribunal to the Court of Appeal, and the particular statutory provisions granting rights of appeal were amended as necessary (e.g. the Social Security Act 1998 s.15).)
   (6)   *Employment Appeal Tribunal*—An appeal lies to the Court of Appeal on any question of law from any decision or order of the Employment Appeal Tribunal in proceedings in England and Wales (Employment Tribunals Act 1996 s.37).

Residual discretion to permit an appeal

Replace paragraph (where the citation for Michael Wilson & Partners Ltd v Emmott has changed) with:
9A-55.1   The Court of Appeal has recognised that it has a residual discretion to permit an appeal, despite the lower court's refusal of permission to appeal, where that refusal can be challenged on the grounds of unfairness pursuant to art.6 of the Convention on Human Rights, that is to say in those rare cases when it can be said that there was no decision at all or "misconduct or unfairness (or even mischance) in the decision-making process" such that the decision was so flawed as to be in breach of art.6 (see *CGU International Insurance Plc v Astrazeneca Insurance Co Ltd* [2006] EWCA Civ 1340; [2007] Bus. L.R. 1340, CA; *Patel v Mussa* [2015] EWCA Civ 434; [2015] 1 W.L.R. 4788. Most of the authorities on the scope of this discretion are concerned with appeals to the Court in arbitration claims (see para.2E-268 above). An appeal from the High Court to the Court of Appeal invoking this "residual jurisdiction" is an "appeal" for the purposes of s.16(1) of the Senior Courts Act 1981 (para.9A-57below) and it follows from that that such an appeal is an appeal for which permission to appeal is required by CPR r.52.3 (*Michael Wilson & Partners Ltd v Emmott* [2015] EWCA Civ 1285; [2016] 1 W.L.R. 857, CA, where single lord justice on the papers refused permission and recorded that the application was totally without merit with the result that, pursuant to

r.52.3(1A)(a), the appellants, though invoking the residual jurisdiction, were not entitled to ask for the decision to be reconsidered at an oral hearing.

Court of Appeal jurisdiction to hear appeals from High Court

Add new paragraph at end:
CPR r.52.15(1A) states that where permission to apply for judicial review has been refused by **9A-59** the High Court, and recorded by that Court as totally without merit (TWM) in accordance with r.23.12, an application by the applicant to the Court of Appeal for permission to appeal to it will be determined on paper without an oral hearing. Section 16(1) does not confer any right of appeal to the Court of Appeal against the High Court's TWM certification as such (*R. (Wasif) v Secretary of State for the Home Department* [2016] EWCA Civ 82, 9 February 2016, CA, unrep.).

Appeals are against orders, not reasoned judgments—"appeals from any judgment or order"

Replace the first paragraph (where the citation for In re X (Court of Protection: Deprivation of Liberty) (Nos 1 and 2) has changed) with:
Section 16 of the Senior Courts Act 1981 states that the Court of Appeal shall have jurisdiction **9A-59.3** to hear and determine appeals "from any judgment or order of the High Court". Section 77 of the County Courts Act 1984 states that if any party to any proceedings in a county court "is dissatisfied with the determination of the judge" that party may "appeal from it" to the Court of Appeal (see para.9A-568 below). (In this context, "determination" has the same meaning as "judgment or order".) These statutory provisions are given effect to by r.52.10 which states, in para.(2)(a), that an appeal court has power to "affirm, set aside or vary any order or judgment made or given by the lower court". (See further "Meaning of 'judgment' and 'order'" Vol. 1 para.40.1.1). The use of the word "decision" in para.(1) of CPR r.53.2 (Permission) does not imply that the Court of Appeal has a jurisdiction to entertain appeals other than from judgments or orders or from determinations (*In re X (Court of Protection: Deprivation of Liberty) (Nos 1 and 2)*) [2015] EWCA Civ 599; [2016] 1 W.L.R. 227, CA, at para.43 per Black LJ).

Jurisdiction where proceedings raising "academic" or "hypothetical" point of law

Replace the fifth paragraph with:
In modern times, the appellate courts have indicated a greater willingness to entertain proceed- **9A-77** ings which raise points of law which, although "academic" or "hypothetical", are points of general public interest (see cases cited arguendo in *R. v Canons Park Mental Health Review Tribunal Ex p. A* [1995] Q.B. 60, op. cit. at 63) but no general principle to this effect has emerged (see also *Don Pasquale v Customs & Excise* [1990] 1 W.L.R. 1108, CA; *Watford BC v Simpson* (2000) 32 H.L.R. 9901; (2000) 80 P. & C.R. D37; *Prudential Assurance Co Ltd v McBains Cooper* [2000] 1 W.L.R. 2000, CA; *Callery v Gray (No.2)* [2001] EWCA Civ 1246; [2001] 1 W.L.R. 2142, CA (Court deciding not to resolve hypothetical questions as to recovery of insurance premiums as costs)). The law is not settled. In *R. v Secretary of State for the Home Department Ex p. Salem* [1999] 2 W.L.R. 483, HL, it was held that the House of Lords has a discretion, to be exercised sparingly, to hear an appeal on an "academic" issue of public law involving a public authority where there was good reason in the public interest for doing so. Note also *R. v Secretary of State for Health, Ex p. Imperial Tobacco Ltd* [2001] 1 W.L.R. 127, HL; *R. v Secretary of State for Employment Ex p. Equal Opportunities Commission* [1995] 1 A.C. 1, HL; *R. (Barron) v Surrey CC* [2002] EWCA Civ 713; [2002] 20 E.G. 225 (C.S.); [2002] N.P.C. 78 (and cases cited therein); *Pridding v Secretary of State for Work and Pensions* [2002] EWCA Civ 306; *R. (Customs and Excise Commissioners) v Canterbury Crown Court*, 2002 S.L.T. 834 (court declaring that Crown Court judge had no jurisdiction to make order even though matter had become academic); *R. (W.) v Commissioner of Police for the Metropolis* [2006] EWCA Civ 458; [2006] All E.R. (D.) 144 (May), CA (Court determining meaning and effect of statutory provision affecting powers of police). It is not unusual for the Court of Appeal, especially in public law proceedings, to give permission to appeal in a case raising a short point of some practical importance set in a context in which there is some uncertainty as to related issues with the intention that the court should not only determine the short point, but also should carry out an authoritative review of the whole position and give guidance on matters which are (strictly speaking) academic (e.g. *R. (Davey) v Aylesbury Vale DC* [2007] EWCA Civ 1166; *The Times,* 21 November 2007, CA (successful respondent's recovery of pre-permission costs in judicial review proceedings)). In *R. (MD (Afghanistan)) v Secretary of State for the Home Department* [2012] EWCA Civ 194; [2012] 1 W.L.R. 2422, CA, where, before the hearing of an appeal to the Court of Appeal the parties had agreed a settlement of the proceedings, the Court, having of its own initiative raised certain jurisdictional and procedural issues of general importance affecting its own jurisdiction, gave judgment dealing with those issues (making certain assumptions). In *Portland Gas Storage Ltd v Revenue and Customs* [2015] EWCA Civ 559; [2015] B.T.C. 20, CA, the Court of Appeal ruled that it was not appropriate for the Court to proceed to hear an appeal brought by the Revenue in respect of the First-tier Tribunal's jurisdiction to consider a claim for repayment of stamp duty land tax where the underlying claim had since been withdrawn by the taxpayer. In the circumstances, although the appeal might raise points of some general significance, it could not be said that it was unlikely

that the Court would again have the chance to consider the points raised on a proper inter partes basis. In *R. (Sisangia) v Director of Legal Aid Casework* [2016] EWCA Civ 24; [2016] 1 W.L.R. 1373, CA, the defendant's decision to refuse the claimant legal aid on the ground that her proposed action was not within the scope of the Legal Aid, Sentencing and Punishment of Offenders Act 2012 (in particular para.21 of Sch.1 to that Act) was quashed by a judge, whereupon the claimant was granted legal aid to pursue her claim. Though the matter had become academic, the Court of Appeal entertained an appeal by the defendant because of the wider implications of the judge's decision and, in the event, allowed the appeal.

Replace the tenth paragraph with:

In the case of *In re X (Court of Protection: Deprivation of Liberty) (Nos 1 and 2))* [2015] EWCA Civ 599; [2016] 1 W.L.R. 227, CA, where two mental health patients and an intervening party appealed to the Court of Appeal against rulings of the President of the Court of Protection made in managing unrelated deprivation of liberty cases, in particular a decision on the question whether a person lacking capacity must be joined as a party to any application for approval of measures depriving him of his liberty, the Court held that the President had no jurisdiction to proceed as he did and that the Court had no jurisdiction to entertain an appeal against his determinations. The particular decision of the President related to a "generic academic issue" and it was one which raised a question of considerable general importance. The Court considered whether it should as a matter of discretion hear the appeal, even though it had no jurisdiction, but in the event, after reviewing the modern authorities on the power of appeal courts to entertain "academic appeals", declined to do so; see para.46 and following per Black LJ, and para.157 and following per Moore-Bick LJ. Black LJ said that the authorities do not go so far as to establish that the Court of Appeal should entertain an appeal in a case in which the lower court was itself only ever engaged upon a determination of hypothetical or academic issues, and do not constitute a licence to ignore jurisdictional and procedural rules completely or permit the courts to be used to determine issues "just because it would be useful to have an authoritative answer" (ibid).

Effect of this section

Replace the first paragraph with:

9A-130   Section 37(1) puts on a statutory basis the High Court's jurisdiction to grant injunctions and to appoint receivers. In *Masri v Consolidated Contractors International (UK) Ltd (No. 2)* [2008] EWCA Civ 303; [2009] Q.B. 450, CA, the Court of Appeal held that there was no rule that the court could not ever make a receivership order by way of equitable execution in relation to foreign debts. Before that decision it had long been thought that the power in (what is now) s.37(1) could only be exercised in circumstances which would have enabled the court to appoint a receiver prior to 1873 when it was first put on a statutory basis. The *Masri (No.2)* case confirmed or established the following principles: (1) the demands of justice are the overriding consideration in considering the scope of the jurisdiction under s.37(1); (2) the court has power to grant injunctions and appoint receivers in circumstances where no injunction would have been granted or receiver appointed before 1873; (3) a receiver by way of equitable execution may be appointed over an asset whether or not the asset is presently amenable to execution at law; and (4) the jurisdiction to appoint receivers by way of equitable execution can be developed incrementally to apply old principles to new situations. In addition, the *Masri (No.2)* case confirmed that s.37(1) does not confer an unfettered power. The injunctive power is circumscribed by judicial authority dating back many years, and modern authorities confirm that the power to appoint receivers is also not unfettered. See further *Tasarruf Mevduati Signorta Fonu v Merrill Lynch Bank and Trust Company (Cayman) Ltd* [2011] UKPC 17; [2011] 1 W.L.R. 1721, PC, and extensive citation of authorities there at [55] to [58]. It has been said that the power to grant an injunction, while placed on a statutory footing by s.37, does not derive solely from the legislature. Rather it is "a hybrid creation of the old equitable power and 19th century statutory intervention" and it is not a solecism to refer to the power as deriving from the inherent jurisdiction of the court, though it is a power clearly defined and regulated by s.37 of the 1981 Act alone, and therefore its exercise can only be effected under that section and the authorities decided under it (*L v K (Freezing Orders: Principles and Safeguards)* [2013] EWHC 1735 (Fam); [2014] 2 W.L.R. 914 (Mostyn J) at para.14). The extent of the court's powers under s.37(1) was examined in detail in *Holyoake v Candy* [2016] EWHC 970 (Ch); [2016] 3 W.L.R. 357 (Nugee J), where it was held that it included power to make a free-standing order (a "notification order"), that is to say, an order not ancillary to another order, requiring a party to proceedings to notify another prior to (or shortly after) entering into a transaction by which property is disposed of.

Add new paragraph at end:

For a comparison of the powers granted to the court by s.37 of the 1981 Act and of the powers granted by the Matrimonial Causes Act 1973 s.37 (Avoidance of transactions intended to prevent or reduce financial relief), and of the relationship between those powers and their respective functions, see *C v C* [2015] EWHC 2795 (Fam), 30 September 2015, unrep. (Roberts J) at para.49 et seq.

"costs ... shall be in the discretion of the court"

Replace the third paragraph with:

9A-202   The modern law of protective costs orders may be traced to decisions of the Court of Appeal emphasising the breadth of the discretion contained in s.51; e.g. *McDonald v Horn* [1995] I.C.R. 685, CA (where held that, notwithstanding the general principle that costs followed the event, the discretion extended to the granting of a pre-emptive costs order in favour of beneficiaries under a company pension scheme bringing a claim against the company and the scheme's trustees). The leading authorities on protective costs orders were explained, and the particular question of the granting of PCOs in closed material cases was considered, in *Begg v HM Treasury* [2015] EWHC 1851 (Admin), 29 June 2015, unrep. (Cranston J) in the context of an appeal under the Terrorist Asset-Freezing etc. Act 2010 s.26. In that case the judge refused the application for a PCO made by a person appealing against a designation order made under s.2(1) of the 2010 Act. The Court of Appeal held that the judge had been wrong to conclude that the consideration of the application should await the disclosure by the defendants of their evidence ([2016] EWCA Civ 568, 23 June 2016, CA, unrep.).

After the fourth paragraph (beginning "The breadth of the discretion was emphasised"), add as a new paragraph:

For a survey of the authorities concerning the making of orders for costs against insurers who fund the defence of a claim (beginning with *TGA Chapman Ltd v Christopher* [1998] 1 W.L.R. 12, CA), see *Legg v Sterte Garage Ltd* [2016] EWCA Civ 97, 23 February 2016, C.A., unrep., at para.49 et seq per David Richards LJ).

County Courts Act 1984

Add new paragraph 9A–449.2:

"proceedings for relief against fraud or mistake"

In *Salekipour v Parmar* [2016] EWHC 1466 (QB), 23 June 2016, unrep. (Garnham J), at the trial **9A-449.2** of a claim brought by tenants (C) against their landlords (D) in the County Court, the Court dismissed the claim and gave D judgment on their counterclaim, and there was no appeal. Subsequently, C brought new proceedings against D for rescission of the judgment on the ground that it had been obtained by fraud, alleging perjury and subordination of a witness. A district judge struck out the claim as an abuse of process and a Circuit judge dismissed D's application to set aside that order, holding that the County Court has no jurisdiction to rescind a previous judgment of the Court. A High Court judge dismissed C's appeal from that decision, holding that, although it is established that a decision of the High Court may be challenged by a collateral action in that Court on the ground that it was obtained by fraud rather than by an appeal, no comparable jurisdiction is conferred on the County Court, either by s.23 (in particular by para.(g) of that section), or by s.38 (which merely describes the remedies available to the Court but does not purport to give jurisdiction). The words in para.(g) of s.23 are appropriate to describe an original action for relief against fraud which itself causes damage below the relevant limits and contemplate the Court having jurisdiction to try fraud cases where the amount in issue is below the relevant limit. But they are "inapt to create a mechanism by which a prior judgment can be set aside".

Add new paragraph 9A–481.1:

Transfer for enforcing orders for possession

Part 83 (Writs and Warrants—General Provisions) was inserted in the CPR with effect from 6 **9A-481.1** April 2014, and replaced Orders formerly found in the RSC and CCR (see Vol.1 para.83 0.1). Rule 83.13 therein provides for the enforcement in the High Court of a judgment or order for the possession of land. Rule 83.19 makes particular provision for transfer to the High Court of certain County Court judgments for enforcement at the request of a creditor (and applies where the creditor makes a request for a certificate of judgment under r.40.14A(1) for the purpose of enforcement in the High Court). Following upon the emergence of some practical problems concerning the transfer of County Court possession orders to the High Court for enforcement, the Senior Master issued two detailed Practice Notes. They are: Senior Master's Practice Note—Transfers for Enforcement to the High Court (14 December 2015), and Senior Master's Practice Note—Applications for Transfer for Enforcement of Possession to the High Court (21 March 2016). The texts of these Practice Notes may be found in Vol.1 at, respectively, para.83PN.1 and para.83PN.2. See further relevant commentary in CPR Part 83.

Transfer of proceedings to High Court

After the second paragraph (beginning "For transfer of proceedings under the Arbitration Act 1996"), add as a new paragraph:

For transfer to High Court for enforcement of County Court possession orders, see para.9A- **9A-485** 481.1 above.

Power to enforce undertakings of solicitors

To the end of the last paragraph, add:

9A-705   For law on solicitors' liability on undertakings enforceable in the High Court generally, see Jackson & Powell on Professional Liability (7th edn 2015) Ch.11.

Access to Justice Act 1999

Altering destination of appeals by Order

Replace with:

9A-847   The Access to Justice 1999 (Destination of Appeals) Order 2000 (SI 2000/1071) was made by the Lord Chancellor in exercise of the power to alter the normal routes for the exercise of rights of appeal granted by s.56, principally for the purpose of providing that certain appeals which would normally lie to the Court of Appeal (Civil Division) from County Court decisions should lie instead to the High Court. The 2000 Destination Order was revoked and replaced by the Access to Justice Act 1999 (Destination of Appeals) Order 2016 with effect from 3 October 2016; see para.9A-853.0 below. The Senior Courts Act 1981 s.16 (Appeals to High Court) (para.9A-57 above) and the County Courts Act 1984 s.77 (Appeals: general provisions) (para.9A-568 above) take effect subject to any order made under s.56. The Matrimonial and Family Proceedings Act 1984 s.31K(1), which provides for appeals from the Family Court to the Court of Appeal, also takes effect subject to any such order. Orders made under s.56 affecting the destination of appeals in family proceedings (including appeals under s.31K(1)) are the Access to Justice Act 1999 (Destination of Appeals) (Family Proceedings) Order 2014 (SI 2014/602), and the Access to Justice Act 1999 (Destination of Appeals) (Family Proceedings) Order 2011 (SI 2011/1044), as amended by SI 2014/602.

Add new paragraphs 9A-853.0 to 9A-863:

The Access to Justice Act 1999 (Destination of Appeals) Order 2016

ARRANGEMENT OF ARTICLES

Editorial Note

9A-853.0   The version of the Access to Justice Act 1999 (Destination of Appeals) Order 2016 printed at para.9A-854 is draft. A final version was not available at the time of publication. We will publish the final version in the next Supplement or Main Work.

Introductory Note

9A-853   Section 56 of the Access to Justice Act 1999 states that the Lord Chancellor may by Order provide that appeals which would otherwise lie to the County Court, the Family Court, the High Court or the Court of Appeal, shall lie instead to another of those courts; see para.9A-847 above. This Order was made by the Lord Chancellor in exercise of power conferred by s.56, and came into effect on 3 October 2016. Article 7 of this Order revoked the Access to Justice 1999 (Destination of Appeals) Order 2000 (SI 2000/1071). Article 6 (Appeals where decision was itself made on appeal) replicates art.5 in the 2000 Order. The consequential amendments in arts 9 and 10 replicate arts 7 and 8 of the 2000 Order. Article 7 contains a transitional provision.

Article 3 (replicating art.1(4) in the 2000 Order) states that the operational articles in the Order do not apply to an appeal in family proceedings and are subject to any enactment that provides a different "route of appeal" and any requirement to obtain permission to appeal.

The principal purpose of this Order (as of its predecessor) is to divert to the High Court appeals which would otherwise (by operation of statutory provisions) lie within the jurisdiction of the Court of Appeal, in particular appeals from the County Court. In the 2000 Order it was provided that certain appeals which, by operation of provisions in that Order modifying statutory provisions, would lie to the High Court rather than to the Court of Appeal would nevertheless lie to the Court of Appeal; for example, a "final decision" of the County Court in a claim made under Pt 7 of the CPR and allocated to the multi-track. The provisions in the 2016 Order differ in that they make no distinction between interim and final decisions and remove the exceptions by which under the 2000 Order appeals against certain final decisions would lie to the Court of Appeal.

It remains the case that appeals from Masters, Registrars and District Judges of the High Court lie to a judge of the High Court (art.4(1)). But in proceedings which have been allocated to the small claims track of the Intellectual Property Enterprise Court an appeal will lie from a decision of a District Judge to a judge authorised to sit in that Court (see CPR r.63.1(2)(h)).

When the CPR came into effect, the County Courts Act 1984 s.5 (Judges of county courts) stated that, by virtue of their offices, every judge of the Court of Appeal, every judge of the High Court (or deputy), every Circuit Judge (or deputy), and every recorder (or assistant) were capable of sitting as judges of a county court. By the time the 2016 Destination Order came into effect, the list in s.5 of persons capable of sitting as judges of the County Court had been extended considerably (for text of s.5, see Vol.2 para.9A-419+). As extended the list includes, for example, High Court Masters and Registrars (s.5(2)(l)), District Judges (or deputies) (s.5(1)(b) & s.5(2)(m)), District Judges (Magistrates' Courts) (s.5(2)(r)), and various First-tier and Upper Tribunal judges (s.5(2)(n) to (u)). Article 5 (Appeals from the county court) provides that certain appeals will lie from a decision of the County Court to the High Court and that others will lie to a specified judge of the County Court. This article is elaborate and draws distinctions between judges of various levels as specified in s.5 of the 1984 Act. The distinction between, on the one hand, Circuit Judges and judicial officers of comparable rank, and, on the other, judicial officers of lower rank than Circuit Judges, is of particular importance for an understanding of art.5.

Article 5(1) states that an appeal will lie from a decision of a Circuit Judge (or deputy) made in proceedings in the County Court to the High Court, as will an appeal from a decision of judge of higher rank, or of a High Court Master or a recorder (s.5(2)(a) to (l)), or of certain First-tier and Upper Tribunal judges (s.5(2)(n) to (q)). Article 5(1) is qualified by art.5(2) for the purpose of taking account of the fact that some persons qualified to sit as Tribunal judges hold office as District Judges. An appeal from a decision of such a judge does not lie to the High Court under art.5(1), but follows the route of appeal for appeals from District Judges provided for by art.5(3). Article 5(1) is made subject to art.6 (Appeals where decision was itself made on appeal). Article 6 replicates art.5 in the 2000 Order (for explanation, see para.9A-905.7 below).

Although, in terms, art.5(3) is not confined to an appeal from a decision of a District Judge (or deputy) to a Circuit Judge (or deputy) sitting as a judge of the County Court, its principal practical effect is that it provides that such an appeal should allow such a route. This is subject to the qualification that where the decision relates to non-insolvency company law, the appeal shall lie to the High Court.

Where, at the hearing at which a judgment or order is made, a party applies for permission to appeal against the judgment or order, the judgment or order shall state whether an appeal lies from the judgment or order and if so to which appeal court, with an indication of the decision of the High Court where the High Court is the appeal court (CPR r.40.2(4)(b)). If at such hearing permission to appeal is refused the judgment or order shall state the appropriate appeal court, including the appropriate division where relevant, to which any further application for permission may be made (CPR r.40.2(4)(d)).

Citation, commencement and interpretation

1.—(1) This Order may be cited as the Access to Justice Act 1999 (Destination of Appeals) Order 2016. **9A-854**

(2) This Order comes into force on the twenty-first day after the day on which it is made.

2. In this Order— **9A-855**

"the 1981 Act" means the Senior Courts Act 1981;

"the 1984 Act" means the County Courts Act 1984;

"the Companies Acts" means the Companies Act 1985, the Companies Act 1989 and the Companies Act 2006;

"decision" includes any judgment, order or direction of the High Court or the county court;

"enterprise judge" has the meaning assigned to it by rule 63.1(2)(h) of the Civil Procedure Rules 1998;

"family proceedings" has the meaning assigned to it by section 32 of the Matrimonial and Family Proceedings Act 1984; and

"a judge of the county court" has the meaning assigned to it by section 5 of the 1984 Act.

9A-856   3.   Articles 4 to 6 and 8—
    (a)   do not apply to an appeal in family proceedings; and
    (b)   are subject to—
        (i)   any enactment that provides a different route of appeal; and
        (ii)   any requirement to obtain permission to appeal.

Appeals to the High Court
9A-857   4.—(1)   Subject to paragraph (2), an appeal shall lie to a judge of the High Court where the decision to be appealed is made by—
    (a)   a person holding an office referred to in Part 2 of Schedule 2 to the 1981 Act;
    (b)   a District Judge of the High Court; or
    (c)   a person appointed to act as a deputy for any person holding an office referred to in subparagraph (a) or (b) or to act as a temporary additional officer in any such office.

(2)   In proceedings which have been allocated to the small claims track of the Intellectual Property Enterprise Court pursuant to rule 63.7 of the Civil Procedure Rules 1998, an appeal shall lie from a decision of a District Judge to an enterprise judge.

Appeals from the county court
9A-858   5.—(1)   Subject to paragraphs (2) to (4) and article 6, an appeal shall lie from a decision of the county court to the High Court, if the decision is made by—
    (a)   a judge of the county court specified in section 5(1)(a) of the 1984 Act;
    (b)   a deputy appointed pursuant to section 24 of the Courts Act 1971; or
    (c)   a judge of the county court specified in—
        (i)   section 5(2)(a) to (l); or
        (ii)   section 5(2)(n) to (q),
    of the 1984 Act.

(2)   Paragraph (1)(c)(ii) shall not apply if the decision is made by a judge of the county court who is also a judge of the county court specified in section 5(1)(b) or (2)(m) or (r) of the 1984 Act.

(3)   Subject to paragraph (4), an appeal shall lie to a judge of the county court specified in paragraph (1) if—
    (a)   that judge is sitting as a judge of the county court; and
    (b)   the decision to be appealed is made by a judge of the county court specified in section 5(1)(b) or (2)(m) or (r) to (v) of the 1984 Act.

(4)   In proceedings brought pursuant to the Companies Acts, an appeal from a decision of a judge of the county court specified in section 5(1)(b) or (2)(m) or (r) to (v) of the 1984 Act shall lie to the High Court.

Appeals where decision was itself made on appeal
9A-859   6.   Where—
    (a)   an appeal is made to the county court or the High Court (other than from the decision of an officer authorised to assess costs by the Lord Chancellor); and
    (b)   on hearing the appeal the court makes a decision,
an appeal shall lie from that decision to the Court of Appeal and not to any other court.

Revocation
9A-860   7.   The Access to Justice Act 1999 (Destination of Appeals) Order 2000 is revoked.

Transitional provision

8.   Where a person has filed a notice of appeal or applied for permission to   **9A-861**
appeal before the date on which this Order comes into force—
   (a)   this Order shall not apply to the appeal to which that notice or application relates; and
   (b)   that appeal shall lie to the court to which it would have lain before that date.

Consequential amendments

9.   In section 16(1) of the 1981 Act, before "the Court of Appeal", the second   **9A-862**
time it appears, insert "or as provided by any order made by the Lord Chancellor under section 56(1) of the Access to Justice Act 1999,".

10.   In section 77(1) of the 1984 Act, after "Act" insert "and to any order   **9A-863**
made by the Lord Chancellor under section 56(1) of the Access to Justice Act
1999".

Access to Justice Act 1999 (Destination of Appeals) Order 2000

Introductory note

To the beginning of the paragraph, add:
   This Order was revoked and replaced by the Access to Justice Act 1999 (Destination of Appeals)   **9A-897**
Order 2016 with effect from 3 October 2016.

Appeals where decision was itself made on appeal (2000 Destination Order art. 5) ("second" appeals to Court of Appeal)

After the second paragraph (beginning "Article 5 comes into play"), add as a new paragraph:
   In *Rubric Lois King v Lane*, 13 March 2012, unrep. (Stadlen J) a district judge sitting in the   **9A-905.7**
County Court (1) ordered the trial of a dispute that had arisen as to whether a sum paid by the
defendant (D) to the claimant (C) was in full and final settlement of actions by C against D in which
C had obtained default judgments, but (2) refused C's application for disclosure of certain documents by D. A county court judge granted C permission to appeal against that refusal and allowed
the appeal, but declined to give C their costs of the appeal to him. A High Court judge held that
an appeal by C against the county court judge's order as to costs lay, not to the Court of Appeal,
but to the High Court, because an order as to costs made in relation to an appeal which has been
allowed or dismissed could not be categorised as a decision which the court makes "on hearing the
appeal" within the meaning of art.5(b). In *Handley v Lake Jackson Solicitors* [2016] EWCA Civ 465;
[2016] 1 W.L.R. 3138, CA, the Court of Appeal disapproved that decision. The Court held that the
correct analysis was (1) that the county court judge had allowed C's appeal and declined to give C
their costs of it, (2) that circumstance fell within art. 5 since the judge had heard the appeal and
"on hearing the appeal" had made two decisions (a) that the appeal should be allowed, and (b) that
C should not recover its costs of the appeal. Consequently, C's appeal against the second decision
lay to the Court of Appeal.

Tribunals, Courts and Enforcement Act 2007

"appeal...from a decision made by the Upper Tribunal"

Replace with:
   In *Sarfraz v Disclosure and Barring Service* [2015] EWCA Civ 544; [2015] 1 W.L.R. 4441, the Court   **9A-1007.2**
of Appeal stated that it is a principle of long-standing derived from authority (in particular from
Lane v Esdaile [1891] A.C. 210, HL) that, in the absence of express statutory language to the
contrary, a provision giving a court the power to grant or refuse permission to appeal should be
construed as not extending to an appeal against a refusal of permission to appeal. The Court, in
applying that principle to s.13, held that there was no jurisdiction in the Court for it to give
permission to appeal against the refusal by the UT of permission to appeal to itself. In doing so the
Court rejected that submission of the would-be appellant that the exceptions to the right of appeal
provided by s.13(1) are set out exhaustively in s.13(8) and there is no room for a further exception,
whether based on the principle or on some other ground, outside s.13(8). CPR r.52.15A(2) states
that where permission to apply for judicial review has been refused by the Upper Tribunal, and
recorded by that Tribunal as totally without merit (TWM), in accordance with the Tribunal
Procedure (Upper Tribunal) Rules 2008 r.30(4A), an application by the applicant to the Court of
Appeal for permission to appeal to it will be determined on paper without an oral hearing. Section
13 does not confer any right of appeal to the Court of Appeal against the Tribunal's TWM certification as such (*R. (Wasif) v Secretary of State for the Home Department* [2016] EWCA Civ 82, 9 February
2016, CA, unrep.).

Add new paragraphs 9A–1008.1 to 9A–1008.6:

Appeal to Supreme Court: grant of certificate by Upper Tribunal

9A-1008.1   **14A.—**(1)   If the Upper Tribunal is satisfied that—

(a)   the conditions in subsection (4) or (5) are fulfilled in relation to the Upper Tribunal's decision in any proceedings, and

(b)   as regards that decision, a sufficient case for an appeal to the Supreme Court has been made out to justify an application under section 14B,

the Upper Tribunal may grant a certificate to that effect.

(2)   The Upper Tribunal may grant a certificate under this section only on an application made by a party to the proceedings.

(3)   The Upper Tribunal may grant a certificate under this section only if the relevant appellate court as regards the proceedings is—

(a)   the Court of Appeal in England and Wales, or

(b)   the Court of Appeal in Northern Ireland.

(4)   The conditions in this subsection are that a point of law of general public importance is involved in the decision of the Upper Tribunal and that point of law is—

(a)   a point of law that—

(i)   relates wholly or mainly to the construction of an enactment or statutory instrument, and

(ii)   has been fully argued in the proceedings and fully considered in the judgment of the Upper Tribunal in the proceedings, or

(b)   a point of law—

(i)   in respect of which the Upper Tribunal is bound by a decision of the relevant appellate court or the Supreme Court in previous proceedings, and

(ii)   that was fully considered in the judgments given by the relevant appellate court or, as the case may be, the Supreme Court in those previous proceedings.

(5)   The conditions in this subsection are that a point of law of general public importance is involved in the decision of the Upper Tribunal and that—

(a)   the proceedings entail a decision relating to a matter of national importance or consideration of such a matter,

(b)   the result of the proceedings is so significant (whether considered on its own or together with other proceedings or likely proceedings) that, in the opinion of the Upper Tribunal, a hearing by the Supreme Court is justified, or

(c)   the Upper Tribunal is satisfied that the benefits of earlier consideration by the Supreme Court outweigh the benefits of consideration by the Court of Appeal.

(6)   Before the Upper Tribunal decides an application made to it under this section, the Upper Tribunal must specify the court that would be the relevant appellate court if the application were an application for permission (or leave) under section 13.

(7)   In this section except subsection (6) and in sections 14B and 14C, "the relevant appellate court", as respects an application, means the court specified as respects that application by the Upper Tribunal under subsection (6).

(8)   No appeal lies against the grant or refusal of a certificate under subsection (1).

9A-1008.2   *Note* —Sections 14A–14C inserted by the Criminal Justice and Courts Act 2015 s.64, with effect from 8 August 2016 subject to transitional provision specified in SI 2016/717 art.4.

Appeal to Supreme Court: permission to appeal

14B.—(1)   If the Upper Tribunal grants a certificate under section 14A in **9A-1008.3** relation to any proceedings, a party to those proceedings may apply to the Supreme Court for permission to appeal directly to the Supreme Court.

(2)   An application under subsection (1) must be made—

    (a)   within one month from the date on which that certificate is granted, or

    (b)   within such time as the Supreme Court may allow in a particular case.

(3)   If on such an application it appears to the Supreme Court to be expedient to do so, the Supreme Court may grant permission for such an appeal.

(4)   If permission is granted under this section—

    (a)   no appeal from the decision to which the certificate relates lies to the relevant appellate court, but

    (b)   an appeal lies from that decision to the Supreme Court.

(5)   An application under subsection (1) is to be determined without a hearing.

(6)   Subject to subsection (4), no appeal lies to the relevant appellate court from a decision of the Upper Tribunal in respect of which a certificate is granted under section 14A until—

    (a)   the time within which an application can be made under subsection (1) has expired, and

    (b)   where such an application is made, that application has been determined in accordance with this section.

Note —Sections 14A–14C inserted by the Criminal Justice and Courts Act 2015 s.64, with effect **9A-1008.4** from 8 August 2016 subject to transitional provision specified in SI 2016/717 art.4.

Appeal to Supreme Court: exclusions

14C.—(1)   No certificate may be granted under section 14A in respect of a **9A-1008.5** decision of the Upper Tribunal in any proceedings where, by virtue of any enactment (other than sections 14A and 14B), no appeal would lie from that decision of the Upper Tribunal to the relevant appellate court, with or without the permission (or leave) of the Upper Tribunal or the relevant appellate court.

(2)   No certificate may be granted under section 14A in respect of a decision of the Upper Tribunal in any proceedings where, by virtue of any enactment, no appeal would lie from a decision of the relevant appellate court on that decision of the Upper Tribunal to the Supreme Court, with or without the permission (or leave) of the relevant appellate court or the Supreme Court.

(3)   Where no appeal would lie to the relevant appellate court from the decision of the Upper Tribunal except with the permission (or leave) of the Upper Tribunal or the relevant appellate court, no certificate may be granted under section 14A in respect of a decision of the Upper Tribunal unless it appears to the Upper Tribunal that it would be a proper case for giving permission (or leave) to appeal to the relevant appellate court.

(4)   No certificate may be granted under section 14A in respect of a decision or order of the Upper Tribunal made by it in the exercise of its jurisdiction to punish for contempt.

Note —Sections 14A–14C inserted by the Criminal Justice and Courts Act 2015 s.64, with effect **9A-1008.6** from 8 August 2016 subject to transitional provision specified in SI 2016/717 art.4.

Note

Add at end:

, with effect from 8 August 2016 subject to transitional provision specified in SI 2016/717 art.6.   **9A-1009.1**

Note

Replace "That amendment is not yet in force." with:

9A-1010.1   Subsections (3C)–(3G), (6A) and (6B) were brought into force on 8 August 2016 (SI 2016/717); the remaining amendments are not yet in force.

Criminal Justice and Courts Act 2015

Note

Replace with:

9A-1311.1   This section was brought into force on 13 April 2015 by the Criminal Justice and Courts Act 2015 (Commencement No.1, Saving and Transitional Provisions) Order 2015 (SI 2015/778). Relevant rules of court are contained in Section V (Costs in Claims for Judicial Review) (r.46.15) of CPR Pt 46 (Costs—Special Cases); see further Vol.1 para.46.15.1.

Note

Replace with:

9A-1312.1   This section, together with ss.89 and 90, was brought into force on 8 August 2016 by the Criminal Justice and Courts Act 2015 (Commencement No.4 and Transitional Provisions) Order 2016 (SI 2016/717) arts 3(d) to (f).

Add new paragraph 9A–1312.2:

Costs capping in judicial review proceedings

9A-1312.2   In the CPR the exercise of the powers of the High Court and the Court of Appeal to make costs capping orders (formerly known as protective costs orders) is regulated by the rules in Section III of Part 3 (The Court's Case and Costs Management Powers) (rr.3.19 & 3.20). In a consultation launched by the Justice Secretary in December 2013 views were sought on removing the availability of protective costs orders (PCOs) in judicial review proceedings where there is an individual or private interest, on modifying the principles for determining when PCOs may be made and on whether in such proceedings there should be a presumption of a cross cap (limiting, generally at a higher level than the claimant's cap) an unsuccessful defendant's liability for the claimant's costs. In its response to that consultation the Government announced that it intended to bring forward "a tough package" of reform to financial provisions in respect of judicial review to deter weak claims from being brought or pursued (*Judicial Review—proposals for further reform: the Government Response* (Cm 8811, February 2014) para.41). In relation to PCOs specifically the Government stated (1) that it recognised that some PCOs would undoubtedly be made in cases where there is a strong public interest in resolving an issue, (2) that therefore it did not intend to remove the availability of PCOs entirely in non-environmental cases, but (3) that it did wish to make sure that in future PCOs were reserved for cases where there are serious issues of the highest public interest in cases granted permission and which otherwise would not be able to be taken forward without a PCO (ibid para.57). The legislation in ss.88 to 90 of the Criminal Justice and Courts Act 2015 is designed to implement that policy. Section 88, along with ss.89 and 90 of this Act, removes the ability of the High Court and the Court of Appeal to make costs capping orders in judicial review proceedings except as provided by those sections. In subss.(4) and (5) of s.88 it is stated that an application for a costs capping order must be made in accordance with rules of court and that rules of court may, in particular, specify information that must be contained in the application. Sections 88 to 90 were brought into force on 8 August 2016. By Regulation the Lord Chancellor may amend s.88 and s.89 as provided in s.88(9) and s.89(3), and may provide that s.88 and s.89 do not apply in relation to judicial review proceedings which have as their subject an issue relating entirely or partly to the environment (s.90). Relevant rules of court are found in Section VI (rr.46.16 to 46.19) (Judicial Review Costs Capping Orders under Part 4 of the Criminal Justice and Courts Act 2015) of CPR Pt 46 (Costs—Special Cases); see further Vol.1 para.46.16.1.

Note

Replace with:

9A-1313.1   This section was brought into force on 8 August 2016; see further para.9A-1312.1 above.

Note

Replace with:

9A-1314.1   This section was brought into force on 8 August 2016; see further para.9A-1312.1 above. The effect of this section is to enable the Lord Chancellor by Regulations to provide that ss.88 and 89 do not apply in relation to judicial review proceedings which, in the Lord Chancellor's opinion, have as their subject an issue relating entirely or partly to the environment.

SECTION 9B   OTHER STATUTES AND REGULATIONS

Civil Liability (Contribution) Act 1978

Note

Replace the first paragraph with:

The similarity in the language used in s.2(1) and in the Law Reform (Contributory Negligence) **9B-1092**
Act 1945 s.1(1) (see para.9B-1198.1 below) is striking and there is no reason why the principles applicable under the two provisions should be different in cases where the facts are themselves similar
(*J (A Child) v Wilkins* [2001] R.T.R. 19). An apportionment made under s.2(1) by a trial judge will
only be interfered with on appeal where it is clearly wrong or there has been an error of principle
or mistake of fact (ibid.). As the discretion as to costs granted by the Senior Courts Act s.51 is not
limited so as to exclude an order in contribution proceedings in respect of a sum paid to the
original claimants in respect of their costs, the court is entitled to order a contribution in respect of
the full sum paid by the person applying for contribution inclusive of any part referable to costs
(*B.I.C.C. Ltd v Cumbrian Industrials Ltd* [2001] EWCA Civ 1621; October 30, 2001, unrep., CA). The
ex turpi defence is not available against a claim under s.1(1) (*K v P* [1993] Ch 140 (Ferris J)).

*After the fourth paragraph (beginning "Section 2(1) requires the court to have regard"), add as a new
paragraph:*

In *Mohidin v Commissioner of Police of the Metropolis* [2016] EWHC 105 (QB); [2016] 1 Costs L.R.
71 (Gilbart J), where individual claimants (C) brought proceedings for false imprisonment etc
against the police, the defendant Commissioner (D) issued claims against the police officers
concerned under s.1 of the 1978 Act and successfully applied to join them as additional parties
pursuant to CPR r.20.7. After judgment had been given for C at trial (during which D adopted a
neutral stance on the issue of liability to C) and damages awarded, D's application for an order
against the additional parties indemnifying him for the damages and costs he was liable to pay to
and in respect of C, was resisted by them on various grounds. In granting the orders sought
against some of the additional parties the judge (1) explained (a) that while the issue of what is
"just and equitable" is relevant, it is so within the confines of the discretion set out in s.2(1), that is
to say, having regard to the extent of the responsibility of the person from whom contribution is
claimed for the damage in question (para.27), and (b) that that discretion is not unfettered, and the
court's power to exempt granted by s.2(2) is governed by the context set out in s.2(1) (para.35),
and (2) ruled that the current financial means of the person from whom contribution is sought cannot be relevant to the issue of the contribution to the damages claim (ibid para.28). In *Dawson v
Bell* [2016] EWCA Civ 96, 19 February 2016, CA, unrep. the Court of Appeal dismissed an appeal
by the claimant for contribution made by one director (C) of a company against another (D) in a
commercial dispute between them, holding that in the circumstances it was not just and equitable
that D should pay a share of what C owed to the company having regard to the extent of her
responsibility for the damage in question, even though she knew of the practice of unlawful use of
the company's funds and, in breach of her own duty to the company, had failed to put a stop to it.

Crime and Courts Act 2013

Effect of section

To the end of the third paragraph, add:

The Crown Court (Recording) Order 2016 (SI 2016/612) was made under this section and came **9B-1428**
into effect on 27 May 2016. The Order makes, subject conditions, provision for the recording of
sentencing remarks in Crown Court cases.

SECTION 10   COURT FEES

Civil Proceedings Fees Order 2008

Add new paragraph 10–1.2:

Editorial note

Fees are regularly reviewed. The most recent increases were effected by the Civil Proceedings, **10-1.2**
Family Proceedings and Upper Tribunal Fees (Amendment) Order 2016 (SI 2016/402) which was
made on 17 March 2016 and came into force on 21 March 2016.

Replace paras 10–5 and 10–5.1 with:

Remissions and part remissions

10-5   **5.**(1)   Subject to paragraph (2), Schedule 2 applies for the purpose of ascertaining whether a party is entitled to a remission or part remission of a fee prescribed by this Order.

   (2)   Schedule 2 does not apply to—

   (a)   fee 1.2 if the fee relates to proceedings to recover a sum of money in cases brought by Money Claim OnLine users; or

   (b)   fee 8.8 (fee payable on a consolidated attached of earnings order or an administration order).

10-5.1   *Note* —Substituted by the Courts and Tribunals Fee Remissions Order 2013 (SI 2013/2302) art.6(2) with effect from 7 October 2013 (for transitional provisions see art.13(1) thereof). Subsection (2)(a) substituted by Civil Proceedings and Family Proceedings Fees (Amendment) Order 2015 (SI 2015/576) art.2(2) with effect from 1 March 2015.

Replace Schedule 1 with:

ARTICLE 3

SCHEDULE 1

FEES TO BE TAKEN

10-7

Column 1 Number and description of fee	Column 2 Amount of fee (or manner of calculation)
1 Starting proceedings (High Court and County Court)	
1.1 On starting proceedings (including proceedings issued after permission to issue is granted but excluding CCBC cases brought by Centre users or cases brought by Money Claim OnLine users) to recover a sum of money where the sum claimed:	
(a) does not exceed £300;	£35
(b) exceeds £300 but does not exceed £500;	£50
(c) exceeds £500 but does not exceed £1,000;	£70
(d) exceeds £1,000 but does not exceed £1,500;	£80
(e) exceeds £1,500 but does not exceed £3,000;	£115
(f) exceeds £3,000 but does not exceed £5,000;	£205
(g) exceeds £5,000 but does not exceed £10,000;	£455
(h) exceeds £10,000 but does not exceed £200,000;	5% of the value of the claim
(i) exceeds £200,000 or is not limited.	£10,000
1.2 On starting proceedings in CCBC cases brought by Centre users or cases brought by Money Claim OnLine users, to recover a sum of money where the sum claimed:	
(a) does not exceed £300;	£25
(b) exceeds £300 but does not exceed £500;	£35
(c) exceeds £500 but does not exceed £1,000;	£60
(d) exceeds £1,000 but does not exceed £1,500;	£70
(e) exceeds £1,500 but does not exceed £3,000;	£105
(f) exceeds £3,000 but does not exceed £5,000;	£185
(g) exceeds £5,000 but does not exceed £10,000;	£410
(h) exceeds £10,000 but does not exceed £100,000.	4.5% of the value of the claim
Fee 1.1	
Where the claimant does not identify the value of the claim when starting proceedings to recover a sum of money, the fee payable is the one applicable to a claim where the sum is not limited.	

Column 1 Number and description of fee	Column 2 Amount of fee (or manner of calculation)
Fees 1.1 and 1.2.	
Where the claimant is making a claim for interest on a specified sum of money, the amount on which the fee is calculated is the total amount of the claim and the interest.	
1.4 On starting proceedings for the recovery of land:	
(a) in the High Court;	£480
(b) in the County Court, other than where fee 1.4(c) applies;	£355
(c) using the Possession Claims Online website.	£325
1.5 On starting proceedings for any other remedy (including proceedings issued after permission to issue is granted):	
in the High Court	£528
in the County Court	£308
Fees 1.1, 1.4 and 1.5. Recovery of land or goods. Where a claim for money is additional or alternative to a claim for recovery of land or goods, only fee 1.4 or 1.5 is payable.	
Fees 1.1 and 1.5. Claims other than recovery of land or goods. Where a claim for money is additional to a non money claim (other than a claim for recovery of land or goods), then fee 1.1 is payable in addition to fee 1.5.	
Where a claim for money is alternative to a non money claim (other than a claim for recovery of land or goods), only fee 1.1 is payable in the High Court, and, in the County Court, whichever is greater of fee 1.1 or fee 1.5 is payable.	
Fees 1.1 and 1.5. Where more than one non money claim is made in the same proceedings, fee 1.5 is payable once only, in addition to any fee which may be payable under fee 1.1.	
Fees 1.1 and 1.5 are not payable where fee 1.8(b), fee 1.9(a), fee 3 or fee 10.1 applies.	
Fees 1.1 and fee 1.5. Amendment of claim or counterclaim. Where the claim or counterclaim is amended, and the fee paid before amendment is less than that which would have been payable if the document, as amended, had been so drawn in the first instance, the party amending the document must pay the difference.	
1.6 On the filing of proceedings against a party or parties not named in the proceedings.	£55
Fee 1.6 is payable by a defendant who adds or substitutes a party or parties to the proceedings or by a claimant who adds or substitutes a defendant or defendants.	
1.7 On the filing of a counterclaim.	The same fee as if the remedy sought were the subject of separate proceedings
No fee is payable on a counterclaim which a defendant is required to make under rule 57.8 of the CPR (a) (requirement to serve a counterclaim if a defendant makes a claim or seeks a remedy in relation to a grant of probate of a will, or letters of administration of an estate, of a deceased person).	
1.8(a) On an application for permission to issue proceedings.	£55
(b) On an application for an order under Part 3 of the Solicitors Act 1974 (b) for the assessment of costs payable to a solicitor by a client or on starting costs only proceedings.	£55
1.9(a) For permission to apply for judicial review.	£154

Column 1 Number and description of fee	Column 2 Amount of fee (or manner of calculation)
1.9(b) On applying for a request to reconsider at a hearing a decision on permission.	£385
Where fee 1.9(b) has been paid and permission is granted at a hearing, the amount payable under fee 1.9(c) is £385.	
Where the court has made an order giving permission to proceed with a claim for judicial review, there is payable by the claimant within 7 days of service on the claimant of that order:	
1.9(c) if the proceedings have been started by an application for permission to apply for judicial review.	£770
1.9(d) if the claim for judicial review was started otherwise than by an application for permission to apply for judicial review.	£154
2 General Fees (High Court and County Court)	
2.1 On the claimant filing a pre-trial check list (listing questionnaire); or where the court fixes the trial date or trial week without the need for a pre-trial check list; or where the claim is on the small claims track, within 14 days of the date of despatch of the notice (or the date when oral notice is given if no written notice is given) of the trial week or the trial date if no trial week is fixed a fee payable for the hearing of:	
(a) a case on the multi-track;	£1,090
(b) a case on the fast track.	£545
(c) a case on the small claims track where the sum claimed:	
(i) does not exceed £300;	£25
(ii) exceeds £300 but does not exceed £500;	£55
(iii) exceeds £500 but does not exceed £1,000;	£80
(iv) exceeds £1,000 but does not exceed £1,500;	£115
(v) exceeds £1,500 but does not exceed £3,000;	£170
(vi) exceeds £3,000.	£335
Fee 2.1 is payable by the claimant except where the action is proceeding on the counterclaim alone, when it is payable by the defendant: or	
within 14 days of the date of despatch of the notice (or the date when oral notice is given if no written notice is given) of the trial week or the trial date if no trial week is fixed.	
Where a case is on the multi-track or fast track and, after a hearing date has been fixed, the court receives notice in writing from the party who paid the hearing fee that the case has been settled or discontinued then the following percentages of the hearing fee will be refunded:	
(i) 100% if the court is notified more than 28 days before the hearing;	
(ii) 75% if the court is notified between 15 and 28 days before the hearing;	
(iii) 50% if the court is notified between 7 and 14 days before the hearing.	
Where a case is on the small claims track and, after a hearing date has been fixed, the court receives notice in writing from the party who paid the hearing fee, at least 7 days before the date set for the hearing, that the case has been settled or discontinued the hearing fee will be refunded in full.	
Fee 2.1 is not payable in respect of a case where the court fixed the hearing date on the issue of the claim.	
2.2 In the High Court on filing:	£240
an appellant's notice: or	

Column 1 Number and description of fee	Column 2 Amount of fee (or manner of calculation)
a respondent's notice where the respondent is appealing or wishes to ask the appeal court to uphold the order of the lower court for reasons different from or additional to those given by the lower court:	
2.3 In the County Court on filing:	
an appellant's notice, or	
a respondent's notice where the respondent is appealing or wishes to ask the appeal court to uphold the order of the lower court for reasons different from or additional to those given by the lower court:	
(a) in a claim allocated to the small claims track;	£120
(b) in all other claims.	£140
Fees 2.2 and 2.3 do not apply on appeals against a decision made in detailed assessment proceedings.	
2.4(a) On an application on notice where no other fee is specified, except for applications referred to in fee 2.4(b).	£255
2.4(b) On an application on notice where no other fee is specified made—	£155
(i) under section 3 of the Protection from Harassment Act 1997; or (ii) for a payment out of funds deposited in court.	
2.5(a) On an application by consent or without notice where no other fee is specified, except for applications referred to in fee 2.5(b).	£100
2.5(b) On an application made by consent or without notice where no other fee is specified made—	£50
(i) under section 3 of the Protection from Harassment Act 1997; or (ii) for a payment out of funds deposited in court.	
For the purpose of fee 2.5 a request for a judgment or order on admission or in default does not constitute an application and no fee is payable.	
Fee 2.5 is not payable in relation to an application by consent for an adjournment of a hearing where the application is received by the court at least 14 days before the date set for that hearing.	
Fees 2.4(a) and 2.5(b) are not payable in proceedings to which fees 3.11 and 3.12 apply.	
2.6 On an application for a summons or order for a witness to attend court to be examined on oath or an order for evidence to be taken by deposition, other than an application for which fee 7.2 or 8.3 is payable.	£50
2.7 On an application to vary a judgment or suspend enforcement, including an application to suspend a warrant of possession.	£50
Where more than one remedy is sought in the same application only one fee is payable.	
2.8 Register of judgments, orders and fines kept under section 98 of the Courts Act 2003:	
On a request for the issue of a certificate of satisfaction.	£15
3 Companies Act 1985 , Companies Act 2006 **and** Insolvency Act 1986 **(High Court and County Court)**	
3.1 On entering a bankruptcy petition:	
(a) if presented by a debtor or the personal representative of a deceased debtor;	£180
(b) if presented by a creditor or other person.	£280
3.2 On entering a petition for an administration order.	£280
3.3 On entering any other petition.	£280

Column 1 Number and description of fee	Column 2 Amount of fee (or manner of calculation)
One fee only is payable where more than one petition is presented in relation to a partnership.	
3.4 (a) On a request for a certificate of discharge from bankruptcy.	£70
(b) after the first certificate, for each copy.	£10
3.5 On an application under the Companies Act 1985 (c), the Companies Act 2006 (d) or the Insolvency Act 1986 (e) other than one brought by petition and where no other fee is specified.	£280
Fee 3.5 is not payable where the application is made in existing proceedings.	
3.6 On an application for the conversion of a voluntary arrangement into a winding up or bankruptcy under Article 37 of Council Regulation (EC) No 1346/2000.	£160
3.7 On an application, for the purposes of Council Regulation (EC) No 1346/2000, for an order confirming creditors' voluntary winding up (where the company has passed a resolution for voluntary winding up, and no declaration under section 89 of the Insolvency Act 1986 has been made).	£50
3.8 On filing: a notice of intention to appoint an administrator under paragraph 14 of Schedule B1 to the Insolvency Act 1986 (f) or in accordance with paragraph 27 of that Schedule; or a notice of appointment of an administrator in accordance with paragraphs 18 or 29 of that Schedule.	£50
Where a person pays fee 3.8 on filing a notice of intention to appoint an administrator, no fee is payable on that same person filing a notice of appointment of that administrator.	
3.9 On submitting a nominee's report under section 2(2) of the Insolvency Act 1986.	£50
3.10 On filing documents in accordance with paragraph 7(1) of Schedule A1(g) to the Insolvency Act 1986.	£50
3.11 On an application by consent or without notice within existing proceedings where no other fee is specified.	£50
3.12 On an application with notice within existing proceedings where no other fee is specified.	£155
3.13 On a search in person of the bankruptcy and companies records, in a County Court.	£45
Requests and applications with no fee: No fee is payable on a request or on an application to the Court by the Official Receiver when applying only in the capacity of Official Receiver to the case (and not as trustee or liquidator), or on an application to set aside a statutory demand.	
4 Copy Documents (Court of Appeal, High Court and County Court)	
4.1 On a request for a copy of a document (other than where fee 4.2 applies):	
(a) for ten pages or less;	£10
(b) for each subsequent page.	50p
Note: The fee payable under fee 4.1 includes:	
where the court allows a party to fax to the court for the use of that party a document that has not been requested by the court and is not intended to be placed on the court file;	
where a party requests that the court fax a copy of a document from the court file; or	

Column 1 Number and description of fee	Column 2 Amount of fee (or manner of calculation)
where the court provides a subsequent copy of a document which it has previously provided.	
4.2 On a request for a copy of a document on a computer disk or in other electronic form, for each such copy.	£10
5 Determination of costs (Senior Court and County Court) Fee 5 does not apply to the determination in the Senior Courts of costs incurred in the Court of Protection.	
5.1 On the filing of a request for detailed assessment where the party filing the request is legally aided, is funded by the Legal Aid Agency or is a person for whom civil legal services have been made available under arrangements made by the Lord Chancellor under Part 1 of the Legal Aid, Sentencing and Punishment of Offenders Act 2012 and no other party is ordered to pay the costs of the proceedings.	£220
5.2 On the filing of a request for detailed assessment in any case where fee 5.1 does not apply, or on the filing of a request for a hearing date for the assessment of costs payable to a solicitor by a client pursuant to an order under Part 3 of the Solicitors Act 1974 where (in either case) the amount of the costs claimed:	
(a) does not exceed £15,000;	£369
(b) exceeds £15,000 but does not exceed £50,000;	£743
(c) exceeds £50,000 but does not exceed £100,000;	£1,106
(d) exceeds £100,000 but does not exceed £150,000;	£1,480
(e) exceeds £150,000 but does not exceed £200,000;	£1,848
(f) exceeds £200,000 but does not exceed £300,000;	£2,772
(g) exceeds £300,000 but does not exceed £500,000;	£4,620
(h) exceeds £500,000.	£6,160
Where there is a combined assessment of costs: party and party costs and legal aid costs; party and party costs and Legal Aid Agency costs; party and party costs and Lord Chancellor costs; or party and party costs and one or more of legal aid costs, Legal Aid Agency costs or Lord Chancellor determination of costs, fee 5.2 must be attributed proportionately to the party and party, legal aid, Legal Aid Agency or Lord Chancellor (as the case may be) portions of the bill on the basis of the amount allowed.	
5.3 On a request for the issue of a default costs certificate.	£66
5.4 On commencing an appeal against a decision made in detailed assessment proceedings.	£231
5.5 On a request or application to set aside a default costs certificate.	£121
6 Determination in the Senior Court of costs incurred in the Court of Protection	
6.1 On the filing of a request for detailed assessment:	
(a) where the amount of the costs to be assessed (excluding VAT and disbursements) does not exceed £3,000;	£115
(b) in all other cases.	£225
6.2 On an appeal against a decision made in detailed assessment proceedings.	£65
6.3 On a request or application to set aside a default costs certificate.	£65
7 Enforcement in the High Court	
7.1 On sealing a writ of control/possession/delivery.	£66
Where the recovery of a sum of money is sought in addition to a writ of possession and delivery, no further fee is payable.	
7.2 On an application for an order requiring a judgment debtor or other person to attend court to provide information in connection with enforcement of a judgment or order.	£55

Column 1 Number and description of fee	Column 2 Amount of fee (or manner of calculation)
7.3(a) On an application for a third party debt order or the appointment of a receiver by way of equitable execution.	£110
(b) On an application for a charging order.	£110
Fee 7.3(a) is payable in respect of each third party against whom the order is sought. Fee 7.3(b) is payable in respect of each charging order applied for.	
7.4 On an application for a judgment summons.	£110
7.5 On a request or application to register a judgment or order, or for permission to enforce an arbitration award, or for a certificate or a certified copy of a judgment or order for use abroad.	£66
8 Enforcement in the county court	
8.1 On an application for or in relation to enforcement of a judgment or order of the County Court or through the County Court, by the issue of a warrant of control against goods except a warrant to enforce payment of a fine:	
(a) in CCBC cases, or cases in which a warrant of control is requested in accordance with paragraph 11.2 of Practice Direction 7E to the Civil Procedure Rules (Money Claim Online cases);	£77
(b) in any other case.	£110
8.2 On a request for a further attempt at execution of a warrant at a new address following a notice of the reason for non-execution (except a further attempt following suspension and CCBC cases brought by Centre users).	£33
8.3 On an application for an order requiring a judgment debtor or other person to attend court to provide information in connection with enforcement of a judgment or order.	£55
8.4(a) On an application for a third party debt order or the appointment of a receiver by way of equitable execution.	£110
(b) On an application for a charging order.	£110
Fee 8.4(a) is payable in respect of each third party against whom the order is sought. Fee 8.4(b) is payable in respect of each charging order applied for.	
8.5 On an application for a judgment summons.	£110
8.6 On the issue of a warrant of possession or a warrant of delivery.	£121
Where the recovery of a sum of money is sought in addition, no further fee is payable.	
8.7 On an application for an attachment of earnings order (other than a consolidated attachment of earnings order) to secure payment of a judgment debt.	£110
Fee 8.7 is payable for each defendant against whom an order is sought. Fee 8.7 is not payable where the attachment of earnings order is made on the hearing of a judgment summons.	
8.8 On a consolidated attachment of earnings order or on an administration order.	For every £1 or part of a £1 of the money paid into court in respect of debts due to creditors - 10p
Fee 8.8 is calculated on any money paid into court under any order at the rate in force at the time when the order was made (or, where the order has been amended, at the time of the last amendment before the date of payment).	
8.9 On an application for the enforcement of an award for a sum of money or other decision made by any court, tribunal, body or person other than the High Court or the County Court.	£44
8.10 On a request for an order to recover a sum that is:	

Column 1 Number and description of fee	Column 2 Amount of fee (or manner of calculation)
a specified debt within the meaning of the Enforcement of Road Traffic Debts Order 1993; or pursuant to an enactment, treated as a specified debt for the purposes of that Order.	£8
No fee is payable on: an application for an extension of time to serve a statutory declaration or a witness statement in connection with any such order; or a request to issue a warrant of control to enforce any such order.	
8A Service in the county court	
8A.1 On a request for service by a bailiff of an order to attend court for questioning.	£110
9 Sale (County Court only)	
9.1 For removing or taking steps to remove goods to a place of deposit.	The reasonable expenses incurred
Fee 9.1 is to include the reasonable expenses of feeding and caring for any animals.	
9.2 For the appraisement of goods.	5p in the £1 or part of a £1 of the appraised value
9.3 For the sale of goods (including advertisements, catalogues, sale and commission and delivery of goods).	15p in the £1 or part of a £1 on the amount realised by the sale or such other sum as the district judge may consider to be justified in the circumstances
9.4 Where no sale takes place by reason of an execution being withdrawn, satisfied or stopped.	(a) 10p in the £1 or part of a £1 on the value of the goods seized, the value to be the appraised value where the goods have been appraised or such other sum as the district judge may consider to be justified in the circumstances; and in addition (b) any sum payable under fee 9.1 and 9.2.
FEES PAYABLE IN HIGH COURT ONLY	
10 Miscellaneous proceedings or matters	
Bills of Sale	
10.1 On filing any document under the Bills of Sale Acts 1878 and the Bills of Sale Act (1878) Amendment Act 1882 or on an application under section 15 of the Bills of Sale Act 1878 for an order that a memorandum of satisfaction be written on a registered copy of the bill.	£28
Searches	
10.2 For an official certificate of the result of a search for each name, in any register or index held by the court; or in the Court Funds Office, for an official certificate of the result of a search of unclaimed balances for a specified period of up to 50 years.	£50
10.3 On a search in person of the court's records, including inspection, for each 15 minutes or part of 15 minutes.	£11
Judge sitting as arbitrator	
10.4 On the appointment of:	
(a) a judge of the Commercial Court as an arbitrator or umpire under section 93 of the Arbitration Act 1996 (l); or	£2,455

Column 1 Number and description of fee	Column 2 Amount of fee (or manner of calculation)
(b) a judge of the Technology and Construction Court as an arbitrator or umpire under section 93 of the Arbitration Act 1996.	£2,455
10.5 For every day or part of a day (after the first day) of the hearing before:	
(a) a judge of the Commercial Court; or	£2,455
(b) a judge of the Technology and Construction Court, so appointed as arbitrator or umpire.	£2,455
Where fee 10.4 has been paid on the appointment of a judge of the Commercial Court or a judge of the Technology and Construction Court as an arbitrator or umpire but the arbitration does not proceed to a hearing or an award, the fee will be refunded.	
11 Fees payable in Admiralty matters	
In the Admiralty Registrar and Marshal's Office:	
11.1 On the issue of a warrant for the arrest of a ship or goods.	£225
11.2 On the sale of a ship or goods	
Subject to a minimum fee of £205:	
(a) for every £100 or fraction of £100 of the price up to £100,000;	£1
(b) for every £100 or fraction of £100 of the price exceeding £100,000.	50p
Where there is sufficient proceeds of sale in court, fee 11.2 will be payable by transfer from the proceeds of sale in court.	
11.3 On entering a reference for hearing by the Registrar.	£70
FEES PAYABLE IN HIGH COURT AND COURT OF APPEAL ONLY	
12 Affidavits	
12.1 On taking an affidavit or an affirmation or attestation upon honour in lieu of an affidavit or a declaration except for the purpose of receipt of dividends from the Accountant General and for a declaration by a shorthand writer appointed in insolvency proceedings: for each person making any of the above.	£12
12.2 For each exhibit referred to in an affidavit, affirmation, attestation or declaration for which fee 12.1 is payable.	£2
FEES PAYABLE IN COURT OF APPEAL ONLY	
13 Fees payable in appeals to the Court of Appeal	
13.1(a) Where in an appeal notice, permission to appeal or an extension of time for appealing is applied for (or both are applied for): on filing an appellant's notice, or where the respondent is appealing, on filing a respondent's notice.	£235
13.1(b) Where permission to appeal is not required or has been granted by the lower court: on filing an appellant's notice, or on filing a respondent's notice where the respondent is appealing.	£465
13.1(c) On the appellant filing an appeal questionnaire (unless the appellant has paid fee 13.1(b), or the respondent filing an appeal questionnaire (unless the respondent has paid fee 13.1(b)).	£465
13.2 On filing a respondent's notice where the respondent wishes to ask the appeal court to uphold the order of the lower court for reasons different from or additional to those given by the lower court.	£235
13.3 On filing an application notice.	£235
Fee 13.3 is not payable for an application made in an appeal notice.	

Note

Add new paragraphs at end:

Entries 1.4(b), 1.4(c), 2.4, 2.5 and the entry beginning "Fees 2.4 and 2.5 are not payable" **10-7.1** amended by the Civil Proceedings, Family Proceedings and Upper Tribunal Fees (Amendment) Order 2016 (SI 2016/402) art.2, with effect from 21 March 2016.

Entries 1.5, 1.6, 1.8(a)-(b), 1.9(a)-(d), 5.1, 5.2, 5.3, 5.4, 5.5, 7.1, 7.2, 7.3, 7.4, 7.5, 8.1, 8.1(a)-(b), 8.2, 8.3, 8.4, 8.4(a)-(b), 8.5, 8.6, 8.7, 8.9, 8.10, 10.2, 10.2, 10.3 and 12.1 amended by the Civil Proceedings, First-tier Tribunal, Upper Tribunal and Employment Tribunals Fees (Amendment) Order 2016 (SI 2016/807), with effect from 25 July 2016.

SECTION 11   OVERRIDING OBJECTIVE OF CPR

E.   DUTY OF THE PARTIES (R.1.3)

To the end of the seventh paragraph (beginning "There is no general duty upon one party"), add:

And see *OOO Abbott v Econowall UK Ltd* [2016] EWHC 660 (IPEC), 23 March 2016, unrep. (HHJ **11-15** Hacon), where it was noted that while parties are not required to inform their opponents of mistakes they have made, this is subject to the overriding objective and the obligation to ensure that parties and the court have a clear, common understanding of the real issues in dispute and as to the proper procedural arrangements for the effective progress of the claim. A failure to ensure this is the case can lead to unnecessary and disproportionate cost and delay to the parties, to the court, and have an adverse effect on other litigants. Where parties become aware of a genuine misunderstanding on a significant issue they should take reasonable steps to dispel it.

SECTION 12   CPR: APPLICATION, AMENDMENTS AND INTERPRETATION

C.   STATUTORY INSTRUMENTS AMENDING CPR

4.   Amendments and Transitional Arrangements in Amending Statutory Instruments

(b)   2014 to date

Add new paragraphs at the beginning:

The Civil Procedure (Amendment No.3) Rules 2016 (SI 2016/788) comes into force on 3 October **12-34** 2016, subject to transitional provisions. It amends r.2.4(a), inserts a new r.26.2A(5A), amends r.40.2(4), r.54.5(6), and r.63.19. It further substitutes a new Pt 52 in place of the previously in force Pt 52. This latter amendment is subject to transitional provisions that maintain the pre-3 October 2016 in force for appeals where the appellant's notice was issued before 3 October 2013.

The Civil Procedure (Amendment No.2) Rules 2016 (SI 2016/707) contained amendments to the following rules: r.3.19; the Table following r.46.14; and rr.46.16-46.19. It came into force on 8 August 2016, subject to transitional provisions concerning the continuing application of the pre-8 August 2016 provisions to judicial review proceedings where the judicial review claim form was filed prior to that date.

The Civil Procedure (Amendment) Rules 2016 (SI 2016/234) contained amendments to the following rules: Pt 3, r.45.8 Table 5; Pt 66; Pt 70; Pt 73; Pt 75; and RSC Ord.115 rule 4(4). It introduced a new Pt 89 (attachment of earnings) and deleted CCR Ord.27. It came into force on 6 April 2016, subject to transitional provisions which provide for that the amendments to the following only take effect as to proceedings commended on or after 6 April 2016: rules 3.13; 45.8; 66.6(1), 70.1; 70.5; 73.17; 75.6(d); 75.10; RSC Ord.115 r.4(4); and Pts 73, 89 and CCR Ord.27.

SECTION 13   RIGHTS OF AUDIENCE

G.   RIGHT OF AUDIENCE GRANTED BY THE COURT IN RELATION TO THE PROCEEDINGS (SCH.3, PARA.1(2))

4.   *Exercise of the Discretion*

(c)   McKenzie friend

Replace the fifth paragraph with:

13-19   McKenzie friends do not have a right to conduct litigation or a right of audience. However, once a party acting in person is allowed to have the assistance of a McKenzie friend, the question might then arise whether the court should exercise its discretion under para.1(2) of Sch.3 and grant the assistant a right of audience. Guidance in the Practice Note deals with the considerations which then arise. The High Court has inherent jurisdiction to grant a right of audience on an ad hoc basis to a party's McKenzie Friend even where that party is a body corporate if the body corporate would otherwise have no one capable of speaking for it; see per Hildyard J in *Bank of St Petersburg PJSC v Arkhangelsky* [2015] EWHC 2997 (Ch); [2016] 1 W.L.R. 1081.

SECTION 14   ALTERNATIVE DISPUTE RESOLUTION

A.   INTRODUCTION

1.   *Negotiation, Mediation and Other Dispute Resolution Procedures*

Replace the last paragraph with:

14-2   With reference to the Government's proposals on legal aid in 2011 Lord Neuberger, Master of the Rolls, as he then was, expressed concern about what some see as the prospect of replacing legal aid-funded cases with alternative dispute resolution. Lord Neuberger warned: "If we expand mediation beyond its proper limits as a complement to justice we run the risk of depriving particular persons or classes of person of their right to equal and impartial justice under the law." (See *http://webarchive.nationalarchives.gov.uk/20131202164909/http://judiciary.gov.uk/Resources/JCO/ Documents/Speeches/moj-speech-mediation-lectureA.pdf* [Accessed 15 April 2016]).

2.   *Appellate Judges' Statements and Speeches on ADR—The Jackson Report—Proposals for Reform*

Replace the second paragraph with:

14-3   Between 2007 and 2009, Lightman J, Lord Phillips CJ and Sir Anthony Clarke M.R. (as they then were) each delivered speeches, out of court, all of which were predicated on the greater use of ADR. They will be referred to collectively below as the "Judicial Speeches" and the speech on May 8, 2008 will be referred to as Sir Anthony Clarke's Birmingham Speech. The speeches are available at *http://www.cedr.com/articles/?item=Mediation-an-approximation-to-justice-a-speech-by-The-Honour- able-Mr-Justice-Lightman* [Accessed 15 April 2016] (Lightman J); *http://webarchive.nationalarchives.gov. uk/20131202164909/http://judiciary.gov.uk/Resources/JCO/Documents/Speeches/lcj__adr__india__290308. pdf* [Accessed 15 April 2016] (Lord Phillips CJ); *http://webarchive.nationalarchives.gov.uk/ 20131202164909/http:/judiciary.gov.uk/media/speeches/2008/speech-clarke-lj-mor-11042008* [Accessed 15 April 2016] (Sir Anthony Clarke M.R., Brighton); *http://webarchive.nationalarchives.gov.uk/ 20131202164909/http://judiciary.gov.uk/Resources/JCO/Documents/Speeches/mr__mediation__conference__ may08.pdf* [Accessed 15 April 2016] (Sir Anthony Clarke M.R., Birmingham); *http://webarchive. nationalarchives.gov.uk/20131202164909/http://judiciary.gov.uk/Resources/JCO/Documents/Speeches/mr- littleton-chambers-080609.pdf* [Accessed 15 April 2016] (Lord Clarke of Stone-Cum-Ebony M.R.). In 2011 Lord Dyson responded to some of the issues arising in the Judicial Speeches in a speech subsequently published under title of "A word on Halsey v Milton Keynes" (Arbitration 2011, 77(3), 337-341).

In the sixth paragraph (beginning "Lord Neuberger of Abbotsbury"), replace the quoted section with:
". better able to achieve a just or fair outcome for the parties, provided that they both have the will to settle their differences. Fair here not because the outcome necessarily reflects the substantive legal merits of the underlying dispute but rather because the parties have both participated in a consensual process and reached a mutually agreeable resolution" (*http://webarchive.nationalarchives.gov.uk/20131202164909/http://www.judiciary.gov.uk/Resources/ JCO/Documents/Speeches/mr-keating-lecture-19052010.pdf* [Accessed 15 April 2016]).

Replace the last paragraph with:
Also in 2011 the Ministry of Justice announced the Dispute Resolution Commitment. This requires government departments and agencies to be proactive in the management of disputes, and to use effective, proportionate and appropriate forms of dispute resolution to avoid expensive legal costs or court actions. (See *https://www.gov.uk/government/news/government-supports-more-efficient-dispute-resolution* [Accessed 15 April 2016]).

B.   ADR IN THE CONTEXT OF THE CPR

1.   Case Management

(c)   Voluntary v compulsory/mandatory ADR and case management

Replace the first paragraph with:
It is often said that the hallmark of ADR procedures, and perhaps the key to their effectiveness **14-6** in individual cases, is that they are processes voluntarily entered into by the parties in dispute with outcomes, if the parties so wish, which are non-binding. Indeed, it is also a popular view that the voluntary nature of mediation lies at the very heart of mediation and that compulsory mediation is an oxymoron. Authoritative commentators such as Lord Phillips of Worth Matravers, Lord Chief Justice (as he then was) and Professor Dame Hazel Genn, have remarked that compulsory mediation has always been a controversial subject that promotes strong views and more than a little confusion. It is, however, clear beyond doubt, and this was noted in the Judicial Speeches referred to in para.14-3 above, that some jurisdictions (with more experience than our own in the deployment of ADR) do use compulsory mediation. Also, the fact that compulsory mediation is used in Europe can be inferred from the EU Mediation Directive 2008 which includes a provision that nothing in the Directive should prejudice a Member State making the use of mediation compulsory. (Directive 2008/52/EC of the European Parliament and of the Council of 21 May 2008 on certain aspects of mediation in civil and commercial matters, para.(14) of the preamble: *http://eur-lex.europa.eu/LexUriServ/LexUriServ.do?uri=OJ:L:2008:136:0003:0008:EN:PDF* [Accessed 28 January 2016]). More information about how and where compulsory mediation is used may be obtained from a most comprehensive review of ADR in the "*Consultation Paper on Alternative Dispute Resolution*" published by the Law Reform Commission in Ireland in July 2008 (see *http://www.lawreform.ie/2008/consultation-paper-on-alternative-dispute-resolution.186.html* [Accessed 28 January 2016]). One of the most controversial aspects of compulsory mediation is whether it is successful. There is evidence to suggest that compulsory mediation schemes can (fairly obviously) increase the rate of take up of mediation, but that this is at the expense of lowering both the success rate in relation to settlements and the client satisfaction rate in the process (see "Twisting arms: court referred and court linked mediation under judicial pressure" *https://www.ucl.ac.uk/laws/judicial-institute/files/Twisting_arms_mediation_report_Genn_et_al_1.pdf* [Accessed 15 April 2016]). Against that, however, Lord Phillips has commented that "Statistics show that settlement rates in relation to parties who have been compelled to mediate are just about as high as they are in the case of those who resort to mediation of their own volition." (See the Judicial Speeches referred to in para.14-3 above.) The Irish Consultation Paper (see above) assists our understanding of these issues by suggesting that the issue of "voluntary" or "compulsory" is not an "either, or" choice but that there is a range of options along a spectrum. The options identified by the Commission were:
1.   The parties themselves propose the idea for mediation as an option;
2.   The court encourages the parties to consider mediation;
3.   The court encourages the parties to consider mediation and warns of the possible imposition of cost sanctions for an unreasonable refusal to consider ADR;
4.   Access to court is denied, where mediation has not first been attempted.

(f)   Judicial speeches—ADR case management post Halsey—power to direct ADR

To the end of the first paragraph, add:
See also para.14–20.

14-9

(h)   Case management and cost sanctions

At the end of the fourth paragraph (beginning "Jackson L.J. reviewed costs sanctions"), replace "November 13, 2015" with:

14-11   15 April 2016

Replace the sixth paragraph with:
   In *Lewicki v Nuneaton & Bedworth BC* [2013] UKUT 120 (LC) the court stated, in agreement with the view of Jackson L.J. immediately above, that in principle, the refusal of a party to participate in mediation might justify an adverse costs order on the indemnity basis. Indemnity costs were awarded by way of a sanction in *Garritt-Critchley v Ronnan* [2014] EWHC 1774 (Ch), *Reid v Buckinghamshire Healthcare NHS Trust*, 28 October 2015, unrep., WL 8131473 and *Bristow v Princess Alexandra Hospital NHS Trust*, 4 November 2015, unrep., WL 9298774. In *PGF II SA v OMFS Co* [2013] EWCA Civ 1288 the Court of Appeal clearly contemplated that an unreasonable refusal to mediate might be met by a range of sanctions. The court suggested that the otherwise successful party might be ordered to pay part of the unsuccessful party's costs, and only in the event of the most serious and flagrant failures to engage would it be appropriate to adopt the draconian sanction of depriving it of all of its costs.

(i)   Case management: facilitation of ADR procedures and criteria for referral to ADR

Replace list with:
14-12   (i)   By ensuring that the opportunity to explore ADR prospects is not prejudiced by the rigours of case management procedures generally. (For example, see *Electrical Waste Recycling Group Ltd v Philips Electronics UK Ltd* [2012] EWHC 38 (Ch) where the court considered how ordering a split trial might impact on the prospects of mediating the matter.) In *CIP Properties (AIPT) Ltd v Galliford Try Infrastructure Ltd* [2014] EWHC 3546 (TCC) Coulson J. suggested "A timetable for trial that allows the parties to take part in ADR along the way is a sensible case management tool."
   (ii)   By acting as a source of information about professional and commercial bodies providing ADR services (for example, see *http://www.civilmediation.justice.gov.uk* [Accessed 28 January 2016] and paras 14–22, 14–24 and 14–27 below).
   (iii)   By verbally encouraging the parties to consider ADR at a hearing or telephone conference, such as a case management conference or a pre-trial review. (see para.14-11)
   (iv)   By ordering a stay of the whole or part of the proceedings, for mediation or some other ADR procedure, pursuant to the application of the parties or one of them (r.3.1(2)(f) and r.3.3(1) and see para.14-13 below).
   (v)   By ordering such a stay of its own initiative (r.3.1(2)(f) and r.3.3(1)). An appropriate time to make such an order might be upon perusal of the parties' statements about ADR in their directions questionnaires. (See para. 14-13 below.)
   (vi)   By ordering such a stay upon the written request of a party or of its own initiative when considering completed directions questionnaires (r.26.4). (See also Standard Directions Model Paragraph B05-stay for settlement which provides:
         "1)   ....
         2)   The claim is stayed until xxxx, during which period the parties will attempt to settle the matter or to narrow the issues.
         3)   By 4pm on xxxx the Claimant must notify the court in writing of the outcome of negotiations (without disclosing any matters which remain subject to 'without prejudice' terms) and what, if any, further directions are sought. Failure to comply with this direction or to engage properly in negotiations may result in the application of sanctions. If settlement has been reached, the parties must file a consent order signed by all of them." (See *http://www.justice.gov.uk/courts/procedure-rules/civil/standard-directions/list-of-cases-of-common-occurrence/menu-of-sd-paragraphs* (B05-ADR.doc) [Accessed 28 January 2016]).
   (vii)   By ordering the parties to consider ADR (including Mediation) using, for example a direction in the form of Standard Directions Model Paragraph A03-ADR.doc, whether at the time of giving standard directions or otherwise as follows:
         "1)   ....
         2)   At all stages the parties must consider settling this litigation by any means of Alternative Dispute Resolution (including Mediation); any party not engaging in any such means proposed by another must serve a witness statement giving reasons within 21 days of that proposal; such witness statement must not be shown to the trial judge until questions of costs arise.
      '21 days' can be altered manually.
      The words 'and not less than 28 days before trial' can always be added after the word 'proposal' by the managing judge if appropriate. Not necessary for every Order." (See *http://www.justice.gov.uk/courts/procedure-rules/civil/standard-directions/list-of-cases-of-common-occurrence/menu-of-sd-paragraphs* (A03-ADR.doc) [Accessed 28 January 2016]).
      It might be particularly appropriate to consider directions of the type referred to im-

mediately above when considering cost budgets and proportionality during the costs management and case management process. Such directions might be combined with directions designed to facilitate the holding of an immediate mediation. For example, provision could be made for early disclosure of a particular category of documents that would facilitate a mediation prior to full disclosure. See *SM v DAM* [2014] EWHC 537 (Fam) 2014 WL 795215 at para.525. In respect of directions for a stay in boundary disputes see the observations about *Bradley v Heslin* [2014] EWHC 3267 (Ch) in para.14-9.1 above.

(viii)   By making an order, whether on directions for allocation or a later stage, of the type referred to in the Multi-Track Practice Direction (sometimes referred to as an "Ungley Order"). (29PD4.10(9) and see para.14-13 below.)

(ix)   By making an ADR order on the basis of the draft in App.7 to the Admiralty and Commercial Courts Guide (see para.14-22). The draft order includes the following paragraph: "4. The parties shall take such serious steps as they may be advised to resolve their disputes by ADR procedures before the neutral individual or panel so chosen by no later than [*]." See para.14-9 above regarding the issue of the court's power to order parties to take part in a mediation process.

(x)   By making an ADR order on the basis of the draft order in App.F to and Section 7 of the Technology and Construction Court Guide (see para.14-22). Although these Guides refer to their particular courts there appears to be no reason why the type of ADR orders made in these courts could not be made, where appropriate, in other courts. Again, see para.14-9 above regarding the issue of the court's power to order parties to take part in a mediation process. See also paras 14-22 and 14-23 below regarding ADR in the Commercial Court and the Technology and Construction Court.

(xi)   By arranging, in the Admiralty and Commercial Court or the Technology and Construction Court, for the court to provide Early Neutral Evaluation (see the references to the respective Court Guides in sub-paras (vii) and (viii) immediately above). Further, in the Technology and Construction Court the court can provide a judge to act as a mediator. (See *http://www.justice.gov.uk/downloads/courts/tech-court/tech-con-court-guide.pdf* [Accessed October 31, 2014].)

(xii)   By, in a case which is suitable to be resolved by an ADR procedure except for one sticking point, ordering the hearing of that point as a preliminary issue with a view to the case then being referred to ADR (see s.8 of the Technology and Construction Court Guide, para.14-22, although, again, there is no reason why the approach taken by the Technology and Construction Court cannot be taken by other courts, where appropriate).

(xiii)   By referring a Small Claim to the Small Claims Mediation Service (see para.14-24).

(xiv)   By making an appropriate costs order (or advising that such an order might be made in the future) in respect of failure to give adequate consideration to ADR prior to the commencement of proceedings (para.14-21) or during proceedings (see paras 14-11 and 14-17).

3.   *Costs where ADR Declined*

Replace the fifth paragraph with:

In *Vale of Glamorgan Council v Roberts* [2008] EWHC 2911 an unsuccessful litigant claimed costs against the successful defendant local authority. His application did not succeed. The court noted that the defendant had not positively suggested mediation and said that it would be going too far to disallow costs incurred by a local authority because that authority did not initiate suggestions for a mediation. Making contact with a mediation provider does not amount to an offer to mediate: *Park Promotion Ltd v Welsh Rugby Union Ltd* [2012] EWHC 2406 (QB).   **14-17**

Replace the eleventh paragraph with:

This was in fact the approach taken by the Court of Appeal in *Bray (t/a Building Co) v Bishop* 2009 WL 1657212 when it considered conduct in relation to costs and took into account a number of factors, including one party's rejection of a Pt 36 offer and the other's refusal to engage with a suggestion of mediation. See also *Sonmez v Kebabery Wholesale Limited* [2009] EWCA Civ 1386; 2009 WL 3197559; *Fitzroy Robinson Ltd v Mentmore Towers Ltd* [2010] EWHC 98 (TCC); 2010 WL 308605; *Brookfield Construction (UK) Limited, (formerly Multiplex Constructions (UK) LIMITED) v Mott MacDonald Limited* [2010] EWHC 659; (TCC) 2010 WL 910166; *Kayll v Rawlinson* [2010] EWHC 1789 (Ch); [2010] W.T.L.R. 1479; *Oliver v Symons* [2011] EWHC 1250 (Ch); 2011 WL 1151625*Camertown Timber Merchants Ltd v Sidhu* [2011] EWCA Civ 1041; 2011 WL 2748531, *Nelson's Yard Management Co v Eziefula* [2013] EWCA Civ 235, *Bristow v The Princess Alexander Hospital NHS Trust*, 4 November 2015, unrep., WL 9298774 and *Flanagan v Liontrust Investment Partners LLP* [2016] EWHC 446 (Ch).

Delete paragraph 14–17A.

Add new section 3A:

3A.   *Disputes about costs*

ADR is as relevant to disputes about costs as it is to all other types of litigation. In particular an unreasonable refusal to mediate a costs dispute may, and in a number of cases has, resulted in a   **14-17A** costs sanction. In *Lakehouse Contracts Ltd v UPR Services Ltd* [2014] EWHC 1223 (Ch) a failure to mediate was taken into account in dealing with the costs of a winding-up petition. In *Morris v Thay County Court*, 2 February 2015, unrep. (Kingston upon Hull) the defendant paying party received two CPR r.47.20 offers prior to a detailed assessment but did not respond to them. The District Judge found that the defendant failed to failure to make any offer and/or to actively consider dispute resolution and concluded that this was a conduct issue. He said, following *Halsey v Milton Keynes General NHS Trust* [2004] EWCA Civ 576; [2004] 1 W.L.R. 3002 and *PGF II SA v OMFS Co 1 Ltd* [2013] EWCA Civ 1288; [2014] 1 W.L.R. 1386, that the parties were expected to engage in alternative dispute resolution. He considered it likely that further mediation could have achieved a far speedier conclusion and at less cost and concluded that the defendant's conduct was also conduct contrary to the overriding objective.

See also *Reid v Buckinghamshire Healthcare NHS Trust*, 28 October 2015, unrep., WL 8131473 and *Bristow v The Princess Alexandra Hospital NHS Trust*, 4 November 2015, unrep., WL 9298774.

The fact that disputes about costs are being mediated is demonstrated by *Sugar Hut Group Ltd v A J Insurance Service* [2016] EWCA Civ 46; WL 00386250: the Court of Appeal judgment noted that Property Damage costs in the matter were agreed at a mediation.

4.   Confidentiality, without Prejudice and "Mediation Privilege" in Relation to Mediation

(c)   Confidentiality

Replace the fourth paragraph with:

14-18.2   Another particular point clarified by this case was the finding that the mediator could enforce the provisions relating to confidentiality, as against the parties. This means that where, as in *Farm Assist 2*, the parties have waived without prejudice privilege the mediator may nevertheless be able to require that confidentiality will be maintained. (As in *Farm Assist Ltd*, the Court may not always treat the mediator's word on this issue as decisive: see the comment by Nicol J in *Commodities Research Unit International (Holdings) Ltd v King and Wood Mallesons LLP* [2016] EWHC 63 (QB) at para.21.)

(d)   Without prejudice

Replace the fourth paragraph with:

14-18.3   See also *Youlton v Charles Russell* 2010 WL 1649039, *Curtis v Pulbrook* 2011 WL 291736 and *Commodities Research Unit International (Holdings) Ltd v King and Wood Mallesons LLP* [2016] EWHC 63 (QB). These are solicitor's professional negligence claims where it was necessary for the court to enquire into the detail of proceedings of a prior mediation to deal with the subsequent claim against the solicitors.

6.   Miscellaneous Matters

Add new paragraph at end:

14-20   Any agreement reached at mediation needs to be recorded carefully and arrangements need to be made to implement the agreement in a manner that reflects the outcome intended to be agreed between the parties. This involves consideration of all aspects relating to implementation eg the impact of any taxation provisions that may arise during implementation. See *Moore v Revenue and Customs Commissioners* [2016] UKFTT 115 (TC); 2016 WL 00750585.

7.   Mediation and EU Directives

At the end of the fifth paragraph (beginning "An EU Directive on alternative dispute resolution"), replace "November 13, 2015" with:

14-20.1   15 April 2016

Change title of part:

C.   ADR IN PRE-ACTION PROTOCOLS, COURT GUIDES AND HANDBOOKS

Change title of section:

2.   ADR in Court Guides and Handbooks

Replace the first paragraph with:

14-22   Several Court Guides make reference to ADR procedures. To an extent the Guides repeat what is said in CPR provisions and in practice directions. Necessarily, the Court Guides are more broadly focussed than the pre-action protocols and refer to the application of ADR procedures in claims falling across the court's jurisdiction. However, litigants in person and the legal representatives of parties engaged in proceedings before those courts that have issued Court Guides are well advised to read carefully what is said about ADR, particularly if they are unfamiliar with the subject. The jurisdiction of the TCC is more specific than the other courts and the coverage of ADR procedures in that Guide is rather more detailed than that provided in the other Guides (see further "ADR in Technology and Construction Court", below). References to ADR in the Court Guides are as follows (for complete texts, see Section 1 (Court Guides) and Section 2 (Specialist Proceedings) above):

- Chancery Guide, Ch.17 (Alternative Dispute Resolution) paras 17.1 to 17.6;
- Queen's Bench Guide, Section 6 (Preliminary Case Management) para.6.6 (ADR);
- Admiralty and Commercial Courts Guide, Section G1 (Alternative Dispute Resolution), G2 (Early neutral evaluation), and App.7 Draft ADR Order. See also the Commercial Court working party report on long trials, which includes a number of provisions about ADR at *https://www.judiciary.gov.uk/publications/longtrials-working-party-report* [Accessed 15 April 2016];
- Technology and Construction Court Guide, Section 7 (Alternative Dispute Resolution and ENE) paras 7.1 to 7.5), Section 8 (Preliminary Issues) para.8.5 (Use of PI (Preliminary Issues) as an adjunct to ADR), and App.E (Draft ADR Order).

Add new paragraph at end:

The numerous publications on ADR include "The Jackson ADR Handbook" (mentioned in the section above and by the Court of Appeal in *PGF II SA v OMFS Co 1 Ltd* [2013] EWCA Civ 1288) and "A Handbook for Litigants in Person". The latter, which includes a section on mediation, has been written by the six judges who comprise the Civil Sub-committee of the Committee of the Council of Circuit Judges and is accessible at *https://www.judiciary.gov.uk/wp-content/uploads/JCO/Documents/Guidance/A_Handbook_for_Litigants_in_Person.pdf* [Accessed 14 April 2016].

D. ADR IN PARTICULAR COURTS

2. Mediation in County Courts

Delete the first paragraph.

Replace the second paragraph with:

In 2007 HMCTS introduced the Small Claims Mediation Service to all court users. **14-24**

Replace the third paragraph with:

In 2011 there were more than 11,000 mediations with an average 70 per cent settlement rate. Parties can self refer to the Mediation Service, or a judge will refer a suitable case at allocation and directions stage, when at least one party has requested this. Information about the service is provided at a website contributed by a private training organisation: *http://www.smallclaimscourtgenie.co.uk/small-claims-mediation-service/* [Accessed 15 April 2016].

Replace the fourth paragraph with:

For claims valued above the small claims limit, the Ministry of Justice provides a list of civil mediation providers who provide a service for a fixed fee. The list is accessible at *http://www.civilmediation.justice.gov.uk* [Accessed 15 April 2016].

SECTION 15   INTERIM REMEDIES

A.   INTERIM INJUNCTIONS

1. Jurisdiction

(a)   English proceedings

Add at end:

By statute, power to grant injunctions (and, in some instances, interim injunctions) is conferred **15-4** on the High Court and the county courts in particular circumstances; for example, by the Housing Act 1996 and the Policing and Crime Act 2009 (for which express procedural provision is made in the CPR in Pt 65 (Anti-Social Behaviour and Harassment)). The wide and evolving powers of the court to make injunctions in appropriate cases, and the "threshold conditions" and principles to be applied when seeking a website blocking injunction under the Senior Courts Act 1981 s.37(1) and the Electronic Commerce (EC Directive) Regulations 2002 (SI 2002/2013), were discussed in *Cartier International AG v British Sky Broadcasting Ltd* [2016] EWCA Civ 658, 6 July 2016, CA, unrep.

2.   Principles and Guidelines to be Applied (American Cyanamid Co. Case)

(c)   Interim relief pending appeal

After "(Warren J.), where", add:

15-9.1   in a supplemental judgment (given on 23 October 2015, after delivery of the main judgment on 19 October 2015)

7.   Strength of Applicant's Case in Freezing Injunction Cases

To the end of the fourth paragraph (beginning "For an explanation of the provenance"), add:

15-23   For a review of the authorities on the point, see *Metropolitan Housing Trust v Taylor* [2015] EWHC 2897 (Ch), 19 October 2015, unrep. (Warren J) paras 17 to 26.

10.   Interim Injunctions in Particular Proceedings

(a)   Restricting freedom of expression

After the first paragraph, add as a new paragraph:

15-40   In *PJS v News Group Newspapers Ltd* [2016] UKSC 26; [2016] 2 W.L.R. 1253, SC, the Supreme Court examined the distinctions between the torts of invasion of privacy (sometimes referred to as "intrusion") and breach of confidence on an interim injunction application, explaining that a threatened breach of privacy rights may attract greater protection that confidentiality rights where there has already been some disclosure (para.25). The two core components of the rights of privacy are that there should be no unwanted access to private information ("confidentiality") or unwanted access to one's personal space ("intrusion") (para.58).

After the second paragraph (beginning "In Practice Guidance: Interim Non-Disclosure Orders"), add as a new paragraph:

The principles set out in *JIH v News Group Newspapers Ltd* [2011] EWCA Civ 42; [2011] 1 W.L.R. 1645, CA, and in *McKennit v Ash* [2006] EWCA Civ 1714; [2008 Q.B. 73 CA, were approved by the Supreme Court in *PJS v News Group Newspapers Ltd* [2016] UKSC 26; [2016] 2 W.L.R. 1253, SC, at para.60 per Lord Neuberger.

(ii)   Human Rights Act 1998 s.12

In the first paragraph, replace "(for full text of s.2, see para.3D-47 above)" with:

15-42   (for full text of s.12, see para.3D-47 above)

Replace the fourth paragraph with:

An application to restrain publicity of private information involves competing ECHR rights of privacy and freedom of expression. The governing principles are: (1) to ascertain whether the applicant has a reasonable expectation of privacy, which protection may be lost if it is shown as a matter of fact and degree in each case that the information is already genuinely in the public domain; and (2) the court must conduct the "ultimate balancing test", namely (i) neither article 8 nor 10 has preference over the other; (ii) where their values are in conflict, an intense focus on the comparative importance of the specific rights being claimed in the individual case is necessary; (iii) the justifications for interfering with or restricting each right must be taken into account; and (iv) the proportionality test must be applied; see *In re S (A Child) (Identification: Restrictions on Publication)* [2004] UKHL 47, HL, at para.17, per Lord Steyn; *K v News Group Newspapers Ltd* [2011] EWCA Civ 439; [2011] 1 W.L.R. 1827, CA, at para.10 per Ward LJ.

(iii)   Claims for misuse of private information

Replace the first paragraph with:

15-43   As a practical matter, applications of the type to which s.12(3) is directed are made routinely in proceedings in which claims are made based upon alleged breaches of privacy or of obligations of confidence which may arise in contract or in tort. The values enshrined in art.8 (Right to respect for private and family life) and art.10 (Freedom of expression) are now part of the distinct causes of action for breach of privacy rights and breach of obligations of confidence.

B.   FREEZING INJUNCTIONS

5.   "Domestic" Freezing Injunctions

(a)   Relevant factors

(iv)   Risk of judgment being unsatisified

Replace the first paragraph with:

The purpose of the injunction is to ensure that the court's judgment is not rendered valueless **15-69** "by an unjustifiable disposal of assets" (*Ketchum International Plc v Group Public Relations Holdings Ltd* [1997] 1 W.L.R. 4, CA). What has to be shown is that there is, without an injunction, "a real risk that a judgment or award in favour of the claimants would go unsatisfied" (*Ninemia Maritime Corporation v Trave Schiffahrtsgesellschaft m.b.h und Co K.G.* [1983] 1 W.L.R. 1412, CA). That formulation cannot, however, be regarded as a complete statement of the law. A defendant may be likely to make perfectly normal dispositions, such as the payment of ordinary trading debts, the effect of which may be that, when any award is made, it is, in whole or in part, unsatisfied when, absent those payments, it might have been satisfied or satisfied to a greater extent (*TTMI Ltd of England v ASM Shipping Ltd of India* [2005] EWHC 2666 (Comm); [2006] 1 Lloyd's Rep. 560 (Christopher Clarke J.)). The claimant should depose to objective facts from which it may be inferred that the defendant is likely to move assets or dissipate them; unsupported statements or expressions of fear have little weight (*O'Regan v Iambic Productions* (1989) 139 N.L.J. 1378 (Sir Peter Pain).) It is a fundamental principle that a freezing order is not granted for the purpose of providing security for the claim. By procuring an order an applicant is not put in a better position than any other creditor. The mere fact that the defendant's creditworthiness is in doubt or that the actual or feared conduct would risk impairing the claimant's ability to enforce a judgment or award does not in every case mean that a freezing order should be granted. The conduct in question must be unjustifiable (*Mobil Cerro Negro Ltd v Petroleos de Venezuela SA* [2008] 1 Lloyd's Rep. 684 (Walker J) at paras 36 and 41).

Add new paragraph at end:

If the defendant's assets are held in a complex, opaque and offshore structure, that is not of itself sufficient to infer a risk of dissipation, but it is capable of being regarded as contributing to the risk if there is other material on which to infer such a risk (*Holyoake v Candy* [2016] EWHC 970 (Ch); [2016] 3 W.L.R. 357 (Nugee J) at para.27).

6.   "Worldwide" Freezing Injunctions

(f)   Permission to enforce abroad

Before the last paragraph (beginning "Where, as a quid pro quo"), add as a new paragraph:

Guidance as to the application of these guidelines from the courts has been sparse. In *Arcadia* **15-87** *Petroleum Ltd v Bosworth* [2015] EWHC 3700 (Comm), 15 December 2015, unrep. (Males J), the claimants applied for permission to enforce the order which had been continued on the return date, and some protections for the defendants were justified under Dadourian Guideline 2 as follows: (i) The order granting permission should be explicit as to what the steps the claimants were being given permission to take in each relevant overseas jurisdiction; (ii) The claimants were required to give an undertaking that the benefit of the undertakings in the inter partes WFO should ensure for the benefit of any third party notified in the overseas jurisdictions; (iii) The claimants had to undertake to undo any enforcement steps in the overseas jurisdictions if the WFO was set aside, including paying any costs reasonably incurred by the defendants in connection with such undoing; (iv) The claimants were required to undertake to be co-operative in relation to the exceptions and protections in the WFO (e.g. in relation to living expenses and legal costs). In *Ikon International (HK) Holdings Public Co Ltd v Ikon Finance Ltd* [2016] EWHC 318 (Comm), 17 February 2016, unrep. (Phillips J) the judge accepted the general proposition advanced by the claimants that a party who has been granted a freezing injunction is entitled to police that injunction and to seek further assistance from the court in so doing, regardless of the fact that there are outstanding applications to discharge, or, indeed, that a without notice WFO has not yet been considered at an inter partes hearing, but held that in the circumstances it was wrong to grant the claimants permission to enforce a freezing order out of the jurisdiction or make an order for cross examination before the return date of the freezing order which had been made on a without notice application.

D.   ANTI-SUIT INJUNCTIONS

1.   Introduction

To the end of the penultimate paragraph, add:

The longer a claim continues without any attempt to restrain it, the less likely a court is to grant **15-94** an injunction. The task for the court is not to attribute blame for separate periods of delay, but to consider whether the application was made promptly, and how far and with what consequences the foreign proceedings have progressed (*ADM Asia-Pacific Trading PTE Ltd v PT Budi Semesta Satria* [2016] EWHC 1427 (Comm), 20 June 2016, unrep. (Phillips J)).

E. INTERIM PAYMENTS

3. *Conditions to be Satisfied and Matters to be Taken into Account (CPR r.25.7)*

(a) Generally

After the second paragraph (beginning "An application for an interim payment order"), add as a new paragraph:

15-101   In *Smith v Bailey* [2014] EWHC 2569 (QB); [2015] R.T.R. 6 (Popplewell J), where a claim was made for personal injuries arising out of a road traffic accident, the defendant intimated a defence of contributory negligence, but produced no evidence in support of that defence for the hearing of the claimant's application for an interim payment. In dismissing D's appeal against a Master's award of an interim payment the judge held that, in the absence of evidence of contributory negligence, the Master was justified in treating the likely award of damages to be on the basis of full liability. In *Sellar-Elliott v Howling* [2016] EWHC 443 (QB), 3 March 2016, unrep. (Sweeney J), the hearing of the claimant's (C) application for an interim payment, in a clinical negligence claim to which the defendant (D) had pleaded a defence (putting causation in dispute), took place six weeks before the date scheduled for the exchange of the expert evidence. In advance of that hearing, C served her expert evidence. A Master granted C's application. In refusing D permission to appeal a judge (1) explained that (a) D was under no obligation to file evidence opposing C's application, and (b) as was her right, she had chosen in response only to serve limited evidence in response (not including her expert evidence), and (2) held that (a) the Master had to determine the application on the evidence before him, and (b) on that evidence he was entitled to conclude that C had proved, to the requisite standard, that the conditions in r.25.7(1)(c) were met.

(d) Judgment "for a substantial amount of money" (CPR r.25.7(1)(c))

Replace the last paragraph with:

15-108   In *Deutsche Bank AG v Unitech Global Ltd* [2014] EWHC 3117 (Comm), 3 October 2014, unrep. (Teare J.), it was predictable that the claimants' (C) claim for repayment of a loan agreement might fail at trial because the defendant's (D) defence of rescission (though opposed by C) succeeded, but on terms that D pay C a substantial sum. It was held that in those circumstances, by obtaining judgment for counter-restitution, C would not obtain judgment for "a substantial amount of money" within the meaning of r.25.7(1)(c) and an interim payment order was refused accordingly. In *Peak Hotels and Resorts Ltd v Tarek Investments Ltd* [2015] EWHC 1997 (Ch), 17 July 2015, unrep. (Barling J), the court reached the same conclusion. In that case the circumstances left open the question whether the r.25.7(1)(c) condition could be satisfied by an order for rescission that was merely conditional on counter-restitution and the court held it could not because such an order was not a judgment for a sum money within the scope of r.25.7. Subsequently, on an appeal by C from the judge's decision in the Deutsche Bank case referred to above, the Court of Appeal allowed C's appeal; see *Deutsche Bank AG v Unitech Global Ltd* [2016] EWCA Civ 119, 3 March 2016, CA, unrep. The Court held that the definition of an interim payment, given in the Senior Courts Act 1981 s.32(5) and in r.25.1(1)(k), is sufficiently wide to cover a situation in which a claimant claims to enforce a contract according to its terms and the defendant responds by saying he is entitled to rescind the contract on grounds of misrepresentation, but would only be held to be able to rescind on condition that he gives restitution of sums received from the claimant; the words "other sum" in s.32(5) and r.25.1(1)(k) were very wide, and would plainly cover a requirement in this case that C should pay a sum by way of restitution (paras 57 and 64).

INDEX

LEGAL TAXONOMY
FROM SWEET & MAXWELL

This index has been prepared using Sweet and Maxwell's Legal Taxonomy. Main index entries conform to keywords provided by the Legal Taxonomy except where references to specific documents or non-standard terms (denoted by quotation marks) have been included. These keywords provide a means of identifying similar concepts in other Sweet & Maxwell publications and online services to which keywords from the Legal Taxonomy have been applied. Readers may find some minor differences between terms used in the text and those which appear in the index. Suggestions to *sweetandmaxwell.taxonomy@thomson.com*.

(All references are to paragraph numbers)

Paragraph numbers marked "+" denote online/CD content; those within [...] refer to Volume 2

Paragraph numbers marked "+" denote online/CD content; those within [...] refer to Volume 2

Paragraph numbers marked "+" denote online/CD content; those within [...] refer to Volume 2

Paragraph numbers marked "+" denote online/CD content; those within [...] refer to Volume 2

Paragraph numbers marked "+" denote online/CD content; those within [...] refer to Volume 2

Paragraph numbers marked "+" denote online/CD content; those within [...] refer to Volume 2

Paragraph numbers marked "+" denote online/CD content; those within [...] refer to Volume 2

Paragraph numbers marked "+" denote online/CD content; those within [...] refer to Volume 2

Paragraph numbers marked "+" denote online/CD content; those within [...] refer to Volume 2

Paragraph numbers marked "+" denote online/CD content; those within [...] refer to Volume 2

NOTES